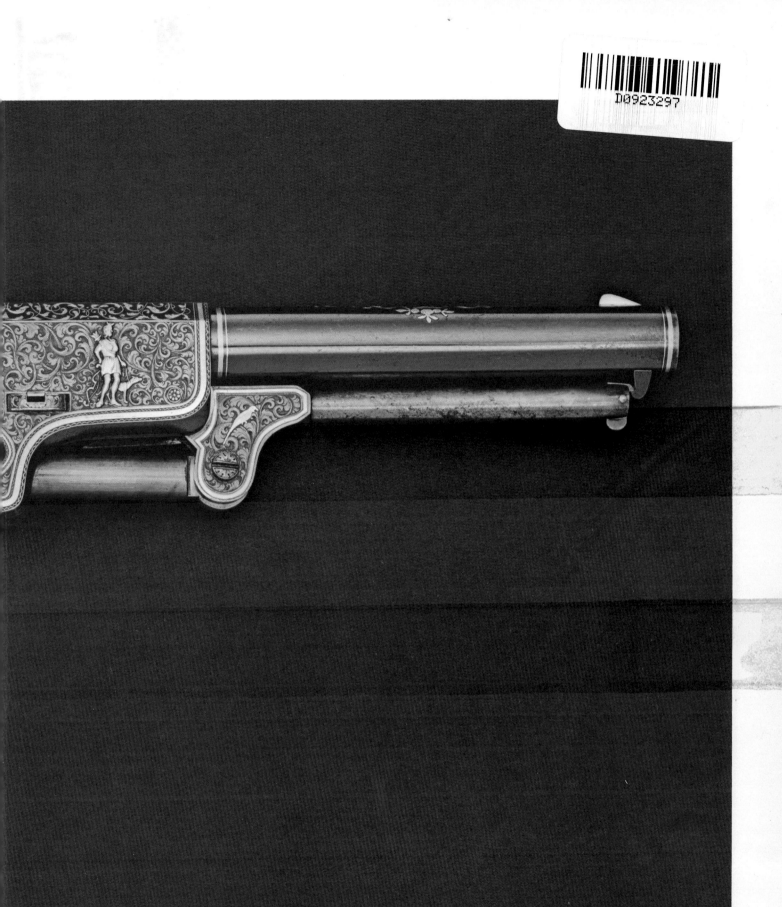

COLT
ENGRAVING

Sultan of Turkey Dragoon
(Collection of George R. Repaire)

COLT ENGRAVING

R.L.Wilson

Printed in the United States of America at Associated Lithographers.
Bound by Roswell Bookbinding.

Wilson, R. L. (Robert Lawrence), 1939—
    Colt engraving.

    Rev. ed. of: The book of Colt engraving.
    Bibliography: p.
    Includes index.
    1. Colt revolver.   2. Engraving (Metal-
work) I. Title.
NK6912.W54 1981   739.7'443   81—9954
ISBN 0-917714-30-X   AACR2
Printed in the United States of America

To
Dr. and Mrs. John M. Wilson
for tolerance, encouragement, and love
nonpareil

TABLE OF CONTENTS

FOREWORD

Since 1836, Colt Firearms has been manufacturing quality hand and long arms for countless individuals and organizations throughout the world: law enforcement, military and naval forces, sportsmen, target shooters, collectors, and the citizen gun owner. We are proud of our tradition as the oldest and most respected maker of repeating firearms. For over 140 years Colts have set the standards by which others are judged.

Samuel Colt himself established these standards of excellence, and no aspect of the manufacturing process received more loving attention from this world renowned inventor-entrepreneur than engraving.

COLT ENGRAVING presents in vivid detail, and with a profusion of illustrations, a dramatic record of Colt Firearms' unique contributions to arms embellishment. The book proves that it was the genius of Samuel Colt which launched the golden age of gun engraving in America (1850 - 1900).

With the Colt Custom Gun Shop we have returned quality engraving and inlaying to our line, in the best traditions of the nineteenth century.

Colt takes pride in its unmatchable history, and in the artistry and craftsmanship which this book so thoroughly describes and illustrates. Our congratulations to the author and publisher on publication of this important, useful, and inspiring record of the artistic and manufacturing achievements of Colt Firearms.

Gary W. French
President
Colt Firearms Division
Colt Industries

C. E. Warner
President (1975-81)
Colt Firearms Division
Colt Industries

PREFACE TO THE SECOND EDITION

When *The Book of Colt Engraving* was first published in 1974 the boom in the collecting of art and antiques had already begun. Spurred on by runaway inflation, lack of faith in politicians, bureaucrats and paper money, the deterioration of traditional investments, and by considerable media attention, the buying of collectibles continues to set new price and volume records with great rapidity. Arms and armor subjects are a key element in this rage, and no subject in the field deserves to be rated as *the* "blue chips" more than Colt firearms.

We arms collectors and enthusiasts have known all along what increasingly others are now discovering — that firearms are a more natural enthusiasm for the collector than such subjects as paintings, sculpture, furniture, silver, and porcelains. Ours is a field most men can identify with. Consider the fact that over 18,000,000 hunting licenses are sold in America annually, that millions throughout the world are familiar with arms because of sporting interest and military service, that a number of museums in America and Europe find firearms their main drawing card, that TV and movies show firearms oftimes in romantic and adventurous settings, that the Wild West is the single most attractive historical element in America's past, and that arms collecting offers a special asylum from the lunacy of modern life. Consider too that firearms offer the enthusiast a combination (unique at that) of craftsmanship, mechanics, adventure, and history and (with most of the best quality specimens) the art of the engraver, gunsmith, and stockmaker. The ranking of Colts as the *number one* make of collector firearms is obvious in the prices they command, their unique reputation, factors of design and mechanics, a history unmatched, the aura of Sam Colt the inventor-entrepreneur-manufacturer-showman, and a literature which grows and grows and grows.

Besides all the above noted appealing factors, Colts boast nearly complete factory serial number records back to 1860, and documenting correspondence and other material back to when Sam Colt was inventing the first practical revolver in the 1830s. Similar data is simply not available to document most other types of art and antiques. As a remarkably documented speciality, Colt arms present a virtual mine field for the faker. Furthermore, manufacturing a convincing fake in the Colt field is hampered by the impossibility for the craftsman to master the combination of challenging requirements - correct contours and measurements, engravings, polishes and finishes, grips, and a myriad of other matters, not the least of which is second-guessing the original ledgers. With the tremendous corpus of published material on Colt arms, and the availability of known genuine specimens in private collections, museums, and antique arms shows, the collector taken in by a fake Colt nearly always has only himself to blame.

In adding new material and illustrations to the original edition, the author has not found possible the updating of ownership credits. He also regrets that some of the pictures sent for inclusion could not be used due to limitations of space, or duplication of already published data, or (occasionally) because of the poor quality of photographs. A special effort has been made to list all the photographers whose work is represented in the Second Edition, because of the realization that taking pictures of firearms is as challenging as photographing *any* object.

After more than 30 years of research, study, and collecting of firearms, the author is just as excited, enthusiastic, and serious about the field as he was as a kid with a paper route, enduring the severities of Minnesota weather to earn a few dollars to spend on his gun collection and library. His sincere interests are by no means limited to firearms, but this is the field which he continues to find the most challenging and fascinating and appealing of any within the vast umbrella of subjects covered by the term art and antiques.

R.L. Wilson

INTRODUCTION

Quality engraving is the pinnacle of skill and art in the world of gunmaking. More than fine stocks or expertly machined metal, hand engraving well done is what elevates a firearm from the category of a fine product into the sphere of fine art.

Of course there is good engraving, and there is bad engraving, and a lot of in-between. But for the most part, what appears on the pages which follow is either good, or very good — or very, very good indeed. Taken *in toto* the caliber of work done for the famed Colt and Winchester firms has been at a very high standard. Such is particularly true of the nineteenth century (when nearly everything was better than today), but has also been the case for most of the twentieth century. It is certainly so as these words are written.

Consider all the trades which together make a fine gun. Only filing and engraving use the same basic sets of tools that have been in use for over three hundred years. An engraver of firearms from c. 1675 would feel very much at home if he returned to his workbench in modern times to cut a Colt Single Action Army revolver. His only real concern would be the hardness of the metal. Prior to the mid-twentieth century, having to fight tough steels was virtually unheard of. Today many steels are so hard that even in their so-called "soft state" they are extremely difficult to engrave.

Today, as in times past, there are some engravers who excel — who can even be termed artists — and there are those who are good or average craftsmen, able to work their tools with skill, but not of a bent to produce original designs of the creative artist's taste and beauty. Arms engraving is a field bound by tradition. Many pieces embellished today employ the same scroll designs popular with craftsmen and clients of the nineteenth century.

There is no "modern art" in gun engraving. Animals, human figures, and other motifs are expected to be realistic, not abstract. Scrollwork, though itself an abstraction, is traditionally of vine styles, leaf and floral designs, arabesques, banknote scrolls, and so forth. Gauguin, Picasso, and Pollack have had no effect on the decoration of firearms.

In American arms engraving, as exemplified by Colts and Winchesters, the dominant influence has been Germanic scrollwork. The chapters which follow will show the overwhelming influence of craftsmen with German backgrounds on the engraved decoration of these arms. Some German-born engravers are active today on American firearms, and most American born engravers use a scroll with Germanic roots as their most popular style.

Since World War II there has been a veritable explosion of interest in all fields of fine arts. Quality firearms skyrocketed in price and in popularity, and in the 1970's joined fine furniture, silver, and numismatics as among the most highly valued objects in collecting.

Engraved Colts and Winchesters bring the biggest prices and are the most actively sought after of all American antique weapons. To date no book has been written to explore in detail these two giant fields of engraving specialization.

The present volumes, one on Colts, the companion book on Winchesters, represent over thirty years of study and research. Thousands of documents were sifted through for new facts. Descendants of long deceased craftsmen were located for fragments of data, at times revealing attics bulging with records, pictures, and (sometimes) a few guns. Retired engravers and still-active craftsmen have been interviewed at length. Some having learned under now deceased masters, they were able to pass on their recollections of past associations. Several thousand photographs were assembled, mostly through the generous aid of collectors and dealers. Hundreds of trips to gun shows, museums, and private collections offered the opportunity to personally handle thousands of embellished firearms.

After the many long years of research, study, thought, and planning, the Colt-Winchester project at last found a uniquely qualified publishing house in the enthusiastic and professional firm of Wallace Beinfeld Publications. Best known as creators of the *Arms Gazette* magazine, their efficient services turned manuscripts and illustrations into finished volumes.

These volumes are not organized in the usual format of arms publications. Chapters are not divided into the strict groupings of model types by variations and evolution. This is a work dealing with firearms embellishment, and the basis for studying the field is by style of decoration. Engravers all have their preferred styles, and it is under these categories that the volumes are organized. The discontinuance of one style and the introduction of another show that a change in engravers took place; the master died, or he retired or quit and was replaced, or a new contractor was brought in (sometimes only briefly, sometimes overlapping, causing no little confusion to the student of the art many years after the fact).

Pictures in chapters which make up each volume speak for themselves in recognizing the changes which were inherent from one craftsman's dominance to another's. The text provides as much historical and technical data as known to the author, and attempts to point out details of interest which might otherwise go unnoticed.

While it is felt that a wealth of information, most of it new, is presented on the pages which follow, some matters are purposely left unexplored or unillustrated. These details are not of great moment when considered individually, but if revealed would be valuable aids to those unscrupulous few who make fake guns.

A number of presentation Colt firearms appear in the pages which follow. A separate, detailed chapter could have been devoted solely to that theme. However, on pages 570 through 573 of *THE BOOK OF COLT FIREARMS* the subject has already been covered in depth. And in an earlier book, *SAMUEL COLT PRESENTS*, the theme was principally presentation Colt revolvers from 1836 through 1873. Rather than producing a rehash of work he has already done, the author prefers to suggest these volumes as worthwhile cross references. A valuable added source for the percussion period is John G. Hamilton's detailed series, "Colt's — History and Heroes", published in *The Gun Report* magazine, April through December 1963.

It is the earnest wish of the author and the publisher that the Colt and Winchester engraving volumes will serve to dramatically accentuate the artistic aspects of antique and modern firearms. And to perhaps serve as an inspiration to the collectors of these weapons, and to the engravers who strive to make each piece "a thing of beauty" and "a joy forever".

ACKNOWLEDGEMENTS

The author and publisher gratefully acknowledge the cooperation of the many who have helped make this publication possible:

Charlotte, Heidi, Peter, Christopher, and Stephen Wilson, Richard Prosser Mellon, Walter B. Ford III, John R. Woods, Mr. and Mrs. John B. Solley III, Robert E. Hable, Jerry D. Berger, David S. Woloch, the late William M. Locke, James E. Serven, Dr. Leonid Tarassuk, P.R. Phillips, John Jarvis, Rene Delcour, Johnie Bassett, John Hovaness Hintlian, Howard L. Blackmore, Claude Blair, Merrill K. Lindsay, Arnold M. Chernoff, Buddy Hackett, Michael V. Korda, Don Wilkerson, Barry Gray, Albert and Paula Brichaux, A.T. Seymour, III, Horace Greeley, IV, R.B. Berryman, L.C. Jackson, Craddock Goins, H. Barthel, William H. Goldbach, L. Allan Caperton, Hugh E. Hayes, Norm Flayderman, John J. Malloy, Dr. Chester P. Bonoff, Dr. Robert G. Cox, Roy G. Jinks, Mrs. William D. Maver, Miss E.B. McCormick, Glenn Gierhart, Jonathan M. Peck, John S. duMont, George S. Lewis, Jr., Alvin A. White, Lynton S. McKenzie, K.C. Hunt, Karl Glahn, the late John E. Parsons, Dr. R.L. Moore, Jr., William W. Edmunds, William H. Myers, A.I. McCroskie, Thomas Haas, N. Brigham Pemberton, Joseph G. Rosa, Lewis Yearout, R.J. Smith, Eric Vaule, Arno Werner, Dr. John M. Wilson, Sr., G. Maxwell Longfield, M.D., George Taylor, Greg Martin, Chuck Williamson, Derek Palons, Ronald A. Ogan, Fred Sweeney, Stanley Shapiro, members of the staffs of the Wadsworth Atheneum, The Connecticut Historical Society, and the Museum of Connecticut History, Connecticut State Library, and the following officials of Colt Industries, Firearms Division, C.E. Warner, Gary W. French, David W. Davis, Thomas A. Thornber, William Judd, Walter F. Gleason, Jan Mladek, Al DeJohn, Robert E. Roy, Martin S. Huber, R.H. Wagner, Eric Brooker, Diane Calvo, Patt Bogush, B.J. Batignani, Judy Burnham, Edie Ocampo, and Kathy Guinan. And George A. Strichman, Chairman of the Board, Colt Industries, his secretary Virginia Macho, and John F. Campbell, Vice President, Public Relations, Peter C. Williamson, Director, Public Information, and Guy C. Shafer, Group Vice President, Colt Industries.

Photography credits to S.P. Stevens, Sid Latham, E. Irving Blomstrann, G. Allan Brown, Ed Prentiss, Harrington-Olson, Patrick L. Bowling, Randy Chandler, John Miller, Doug McLaughlin, Dale V. Monaghen, Ken Kay, H.E. Behney, Bob Sleadd, W.A. Scott, Meyers Studio Inc., Art Kiely, Tom Beiswenger, Robert E. Roy, James Parker, Dick Merfeld, Gus Johnson, Vern Eklund, Bob McNellis, Beau Pierce, Mustafa Bilal, Salem Nassiff Camera, Mark Weise, Larry D. Warrington, Terry Suttor, Brian Zakem, Jeffrey Stubbs, Phil Spangenberger, Roy Laing, Jim Kelso, Don Beardslee (Empirical Picture Co.), and Alexander S. Mikhailovich. Regretfully it has not been possible to credit each color illustration to specific photographers.

The author and publisher are also indebted to the *American Rifleman* magazine, and to the National Rifle Association, for permission to use material previously published by the Association. Portions of the introductory text to chapters III, VIII, and X appeared previously in three engraving articles by the author in the *American Rifleman* and in *The NRA Gun Collectors Guide.*

COLT
ENGRAVING

R.L. Wilson

Group of six engraved Paterson revolvers: Bottom Left, Serial number 523 Belt Model; checkered and shell carved ivory grips. Silver band inlays on recoil shield and barrel. Left Center, Belt Model serial number 537, rare ivory grips. Top Left, Serial number 833 Belt Model; silver plated frame and backstrap; the grips of walnut. Note absence of engraving on silver plated parts. Bottom Right, Serial number 882 Texas Paterson; grips mounted in silver. Silver band inlays on barrel and frame. Right Center, Texas Paterson number 519; ivory grips. Note silver band inlays on barrel. Top Right, Serial number 607 Belt Model; flared grips of varnished walnut. *(Photograph by S. P. Stevens)*

◆ ◆

Chapter I
PRE-PATERSON
and
PATERSON COLT ENGRAVING
c. 1832-1842

◆ ◆

"Rare" is a word commonly and appropriately used when discussing engraved Colt firearms. It is a particularly fitting adjective in the Paterson and pre-Paterson period of Colt manufacture.

Of the total production of Paterson handguns, (estimated at about 2850) and of longarms, (approximately 1850), only about 5 to 7% of the former and about 3 to 5% of the latter appear to have been hand engraved. Most of the approximately 26 pre-Paterson arms (1 shotgun, 9 rifles, 16 pistols) were engraved. These estimates are based on what original documents from the period exist — unfortunately a scarce few — and on years of study and tabulation of Paterson and pre-Paterson Colt arms in museum and private collections.

Out of such studies, positive identities of only the pre-Paterson engravers can be made. The major name associated with that period is one Richard B. Henshaw. Colt's own files in The Connecticut Historical Society collection document Henshaw's employment for engraving a few of the pre-Paterson arms made by John Pearson of Baltimore. These records consist of Samuel Colt's own notes, of billings, and a diary kept by Colt from early 1836 through April of 1837. One of the diary entries reads:

Joseph* Henshaw. Gunsmith & Engraver
150 William Street N. York & Corner of
Orange & Broad St. Nework, N. Jersey.
*Colt's error; correct name: Richard B.

That Colt's diary was in error on Henshaw's name is evidenced by the transcripts of *Colt vs. Massachusetts Arms Company*, the historic trial of 1851 which was a test of the validity of Colt's patented claims for basic features of his revolver. Page 255 quotes *verbatim* the testimony of one Richard B. Henshaw:

RICHARD B. HENSHAW. I am an engraver; in 1831 lived in New York; did some work for Mr. Colt then; it was on two or three pistols, I believe. I understood from him that they were his first pistols or firearms, I will not be sure which. We had some talk about it; I do

not think it possible to state exactly what he said; the substance was that they were his first pistols and he wished me to engrave them, and likewise polish and harden the stocks. I have had some conversation with him since about it; on the 2nd of May I was going from Boston to Springfield and Mr. Colt was in the cars; I forget exactly how the conversation came around, but I rather think I asked him if he did not want to buy some musket stocks; he looked at me several times and finally said he thought he knew me; I said yes; he asked me my name; I told him; he said "Henshaw, yes, you were the man who engraved my first pistols," or firearms, I cannot say which. I know the first statement was in 1835, because I lived in Green street and I took the place in 1835. I was an engraver; I did not make the pistols; I got the wood-work to them.

Ques. Were they at that time newly made or apparently old?

Ans. I rather think they were newly made; I think he brought one or two at first, I am not certain which, and then the other afterwards.

Cross-examined by Mr. Dickerson
[Colt's patent attorney]

I could not say what season of the year that was; I took the place May 1, 1835 and left next May; I cannot say whether these pistols were the ones that went to the Patent Office. I do work for the Massachusetts Arms Company, as well as for other persons. I did a little for Mr. Colt, and for the Springfield Company; I do not do all the work for the Massachusetts Arms Company; I only do it when their engraver is busy and cannot do it.

Others known to have done engraving on pre-Paterson Colt arms are C.C. O'Brien, a gunsmith-engraver on Frederic Street, Baltimore, and John Medairy, also of Baltimore. One gun was engraved in

London, in the fall of 1835, by the firm of William Parker, at 233, Holborn.

Stylistically, Henshaw's embellishment on pre-Paterson prototypes is related to the Paterson period of engraving; there are also similarities in quality. However, the same scroll style was a standard in American gunmaking of the period. The Massachusetts Arms Company trial testimony proves that R. B. Henshaw was not a factory source of engraving for the Colt Paterson firearms.

No mention of engraving has been gleaned from Colt's advertising of Paterson firearms. Judging from the high serial number ranges of most engraved pieces, the limited amounts of coverage, and the limited number of decorated guns, it seems that hand engraving was not meant to be an emphasized part of the line, and that including engraving was mainly an effort to boost sales.

The styles reviewed in the accompanying illustrations encompass all the types of Paterson engraving known to collectors. Compared to what would appear as standard styles on Colt arms of the 1850's, it was a quite modest beginning.

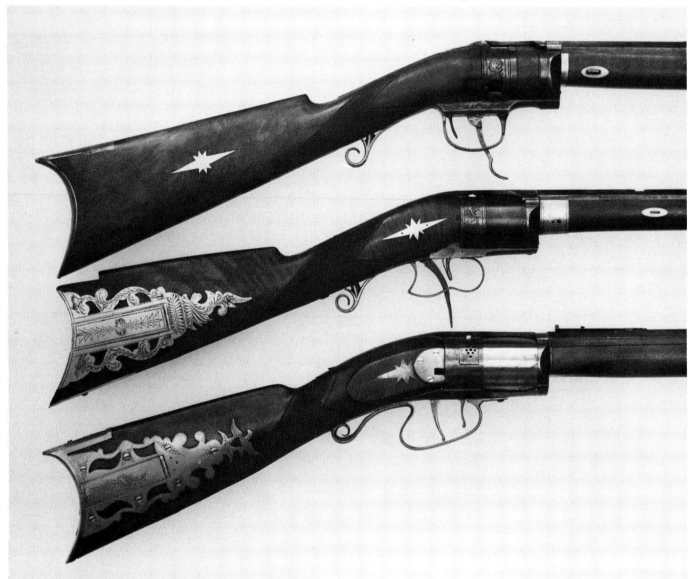

At top, a prototype experimental pre-Paterson rifle; c. 1835, made by John Pearson; .52 caliber. Possibly engraved by C.C. O'Brien or John Medairy. Decorated in scroll and vine styles which contrast to the prototype revolver. German silver stock inlay; on the cheekpiece (opposite side) an inlaid Colt horsehead motif, the earliest Colt trademark. Center, a prototype experimental pre-Paterson rifle; c. 1834, by John Pearson; .30 caliber. Believed engraved by Richard Henshaw, in the evergreen style of scrollwork as seen on the prototype revolver and most engraved pre-Paterson Colt firearms. German silver stock inlays, including patchbox and Colt horsehead motif (cheekpiece inlay). Bottom, the earliest known Colt firearm, built in 1832 by Anson Chase, Hartford, aided by W.H. Rowe. Light engraving on the patchbox. *(Samuel Colt Collection — Wadsworth Atheneum Hartford)*

CHAPTER I / PRE-PATERSON AND PATERSON COLT ENGRAVING c. 1832-1842

Only a few arms appear to have been given what could be termed custom engraving. Some of these were quite fancy long guns, profusely engraved, and inlaid and overlaid with silver. There are rumors of a Texas Model Paterson revolver engraved and inlaid with gold; however, that piece was not made available to the author for examination. Inscriptions of initials, names, or of presentations are seldom encountered. Presentations made by Colt or the factory have yet to be found inscribed.

The presentation Colt had its beginnings during the Paterson period. Most of these arms were gifts from Samuel Colt to persons of influence in Washington, D.C. The young inventor-entrepreneur purposely avoided inscriptions since he was apparently hesitant about letting such gifts become common knowledge. Bearing an inscription might prevent the recipient from showing off his Colt pistol to others. A clever device Colt used in some instances was to give a weapon for target shooting, for test firing, or some other purpose, noting 'you will please consider this pistol as your own private property and use it accordingly until called for by me.'

One naval officer actually returned his presentation revolver to Colt. Accompanying the weapon was a terse note, explaining that it would not be proper for him to accept the item. Refusals of gift guns were few and far between. Such setbacks did not deter Samuel Colt. His excesses in employing entertainments and bribes in promoting the revolver were only effectively checked by the Patent Arms Manufacturing Company's treasurer, one Dudley Selden. His remonstrances to Colt are characterized by a message sent in reply to a suggestion of bribing a high official of the U.S. Ordnance Department:

> *'I will not become a party to a negotiation with a public officer to allow him compensation for aid in securing a contract with Govet. The suggestion with respect to Col. Bomford* [Ordnance Department] *is dishonorable in every way and if you write me* [again] *I trust it will relate to other topics. . .'*

Influenced by the limitations of budgets, Colt's usual choice for a presentation piece was the Pocket Model No. 1 pistol ('Baby Paterson'). However, none of these is likely to have been inscribed; probably a few bore hand engraving. Years later, in the Hartford period, (c. 1847-1862) Colt's gifts would customarily bear both inscriptions and engraving. For presentations to naval officers or the military, the Paterson Belt and Holster ('Texas Paterson') models were more fitting; again, only rarely might these bear engraving, none is believed to have been inscribed.

Among the known recipients of presentation arms from Colt in the Paterson period were (handguns): Commodore John Nicholson, General Thomas Jessup, William S. Harney, D.E. Twiggs, the Com-

missioner of the U.S. Patent Office, the Governor General of Cuba, Czar Nicholas I of Russia, and (reputedly) President Andrew Jackson. In longarms, Colt is known to have presented a rifle to the Commissioner of the U.S. Patent Office. Information on other presentations of revolvers and longarms, which he undoubtedly made, are not presently known to the writer.

The President of the United States presented two Ring Lever rifles and two pairs of Belt and Holster Model pistols to the Imaum of Muscat, and a limited number of Paterson arms are known to have been gifts from individuals to their friends or associates. Details on the Presidential gifts appeared in the July 18, 1840 edition of the New York newspaper, the *Weekly Herald*.

> **RICH GIFT TO THE SULTAN OF MUSCAT** — Four splendid mahogany cases containing four magnificent repeating pistols and two repeating rifles, made by Colt, the celebrated manufacturer of patent firearms, and intended as a present to Seyd Seyd Bin Sultan Bin Ahmed, the Imaum of Muscat, from the President of the United States, go on board the Sultanee today.
>
> Nothing of the kind can be more splendid, or richer than these firearms, and with which an Arab, on one of his fleet steeds, could keep up a running fire pretty effectually. The pistols are the most magnificent we ever saw, and would grace the belt of any monarch. They have each five chambers on the rotary principle, and discharge balls, weighing from eighty to one hundred and twenty to the pound. Their barrels are double twisted, from eight to twelve inches in length, beautifully figured, and inlaid with silver. Their stocks are made of the mother of pearl, secured by steel, mounted and riveted by silver — the whole presenting a highly burnished appearance. The rifles have eight chambers each, discharging balls, weighing, we believe, about a hundred and twenty to a pound. Their stocks are of dark veined mahogany, also secured by steel and with a silver plate, upon which is engraved [in translation from the Arabic] 'The President of the United States to the Imaum of Muscat'.
>
> With the firearms are bullet moulds, bullet cutters, cap fitters and holders, chargers, rammers, hammers, and all the appurtances necessary, very neatly, handsomely, and compactly made, each supplied with a place in the cases, which are of mahogany, and lined with black or blue black silk velvet. On the cover of each case is also a silver plate with the above inscription [in Arabic].

The Paterson period of Colt manufacture schooled the young inventor in every facet of the arms field. In his day he became well known as a gunmaker partly due to his genius as a pioneer in the art of public relations and advertising. His use of presentation arms had only modest beginnings with the Paterson Colt. But that experience proved invaluable when production of his firearms resumed

Newly discovered unique Belt Model Paterson set, engraved, silver band inlaid, and cased in a *partitioned* and bevel lid box of mahogany. The ivory grips also a distinct rarity on Paterson revolvers. Serial number 548. 4 5/8" and 12" barrels. Unusual floral and leaf decor on the barrel lugs and recoil shield. *(Courtesy Alan S. Kelley; photo by Paul F. Korker)*

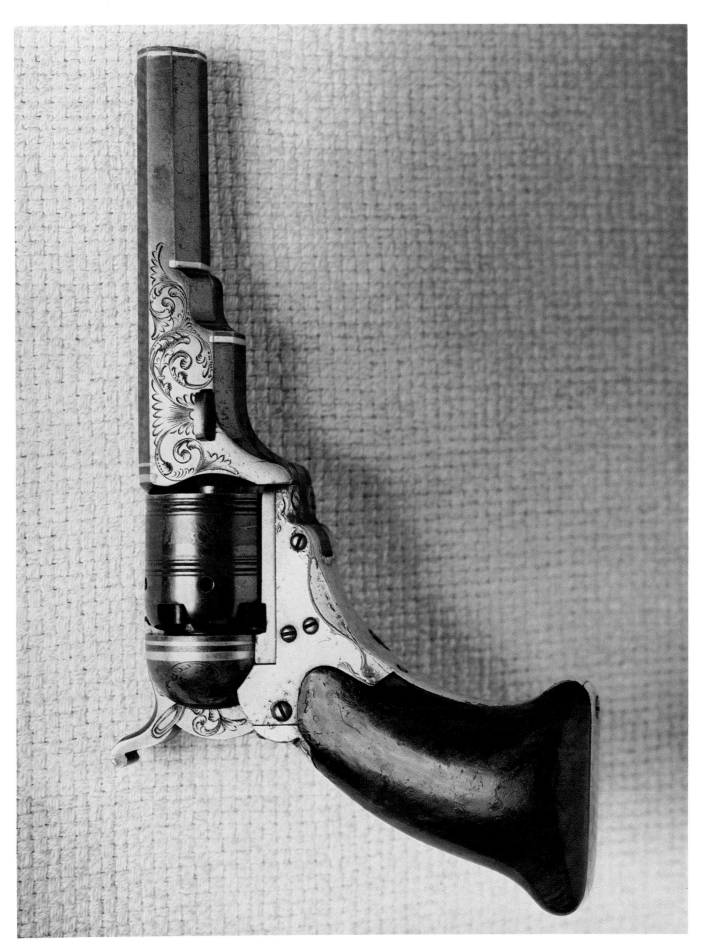

Exceptional specimen of the No. 3 Belt Model Paterson, serial number 754. German silver band inlays on the barrel and recoil shield; silver plated backstrap and frame, balance in blue. The grips of select walnut with a rich varnish finish. Engraved on the hammer, recoil shield, and barrel.

THE BOOK OF COLT ENGRAVING

again, beginning in 1847 with the Walker Model revolver.

The hand engraved firearm was a significant tool in Colt's promotional program, as a review of the pre-Paterson and Paterson decade has shown. Engraving as a boost to sales did not help keep the Patent Arms Manufacturing Company from bankruptcy, but its use on Colt firearms from 1832 to 1842 has provided the arms enthusiast with a challenging area in collecting. Few categories in the Colt field can compare in rarity to engraved arms from this important pioneer period.

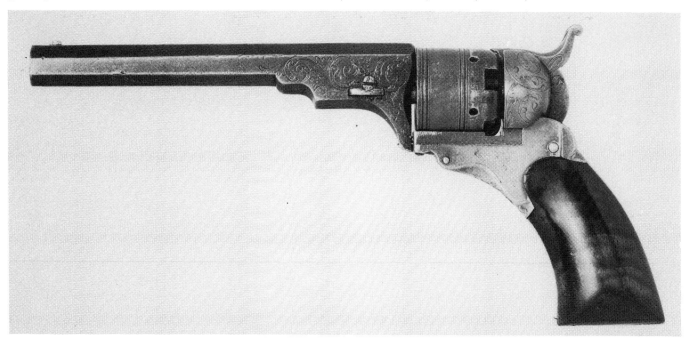

Belt Model Paterson pistol; serial number 523. Due to the silver plated finish on the frame and backstrap, there is no engraving present on these parts. The author has yet to see silver plating over the engraving on a Paterson arm. Coverage on number 523 is on the recoil shield, barrel, and hammer, in the standard vine style scroll. Straight type grip of select grain walnut. *(Dr. Chester P. Bonoff Collection)*

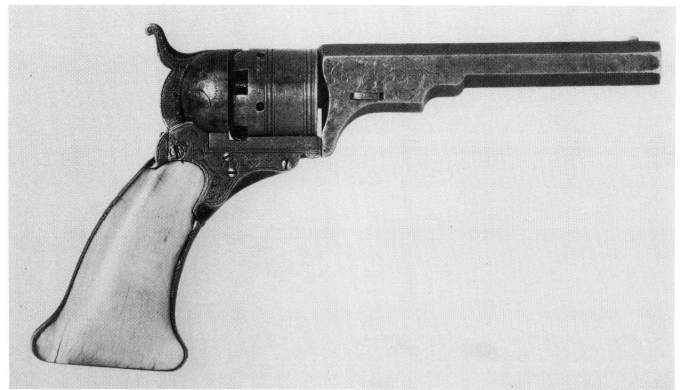

Belt Model Paterson pistol; serial number 537. Coverage in a vine style (the standard Paterson scroll) on the frame, backstrap, recoil shield, hammer, and barrel. No silver band inlays. Flared grips of ivory. *(Dr. Chester P. Bonoff Collection)*

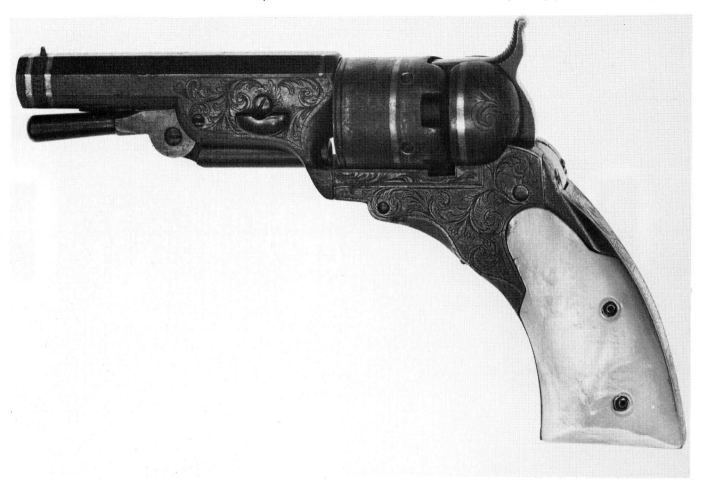

Serial number 265, the only specimen known to the writer of an engraved Fourth Model Ehlers Paterson Colt. 2 15/16″ barrel. Scroll coverage is on the frame, backstrap, barrel, frameplate, and recoil shield. Silver band inlays are on the recoil shield, cylinder, and barrel. A rectangular escutcheon inlay on the backstrap is engraved and inscribed (in script): *Fanny/to/Fielding.* The grips are one piece style pearl. Engraving is different from other Paterson styles observed to date, and may have been done by a different craftsman from those who executed the few other embellished Patersons presently known. Loading lever was missing at the time of discovery, so it is unknown whether that part may have been engraved. Extremely rare not only as an engraved Paterson, but as an engraved *Ehlers* Paterson, and as a presentation inscribed pistol — the only such arm known to the writer. *(Alan S. Kelley-R. B. Berryman Collection, Ed Prentiss Photograph)*

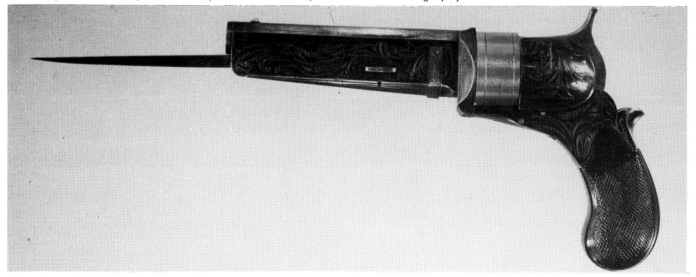

Serial number 1 of the Colt revolver; made c. 1834-35 by John Pearson, under personal supervision of Samuel Colt. Pistol served as a sample piece, in putting together financing for the first Colt manufacturing facility, Paterson. Engraving attributed to Richard Henshaw. A firearm of major significance, since from this serial number 1 evolved the entire production of the Colt firm. It is fitting that number 1 should itself feature engraved decoration since Samuel Colt held the decoration of his products in such a high regard. *(Museum of Connecticut History, Connecticut State Library)*

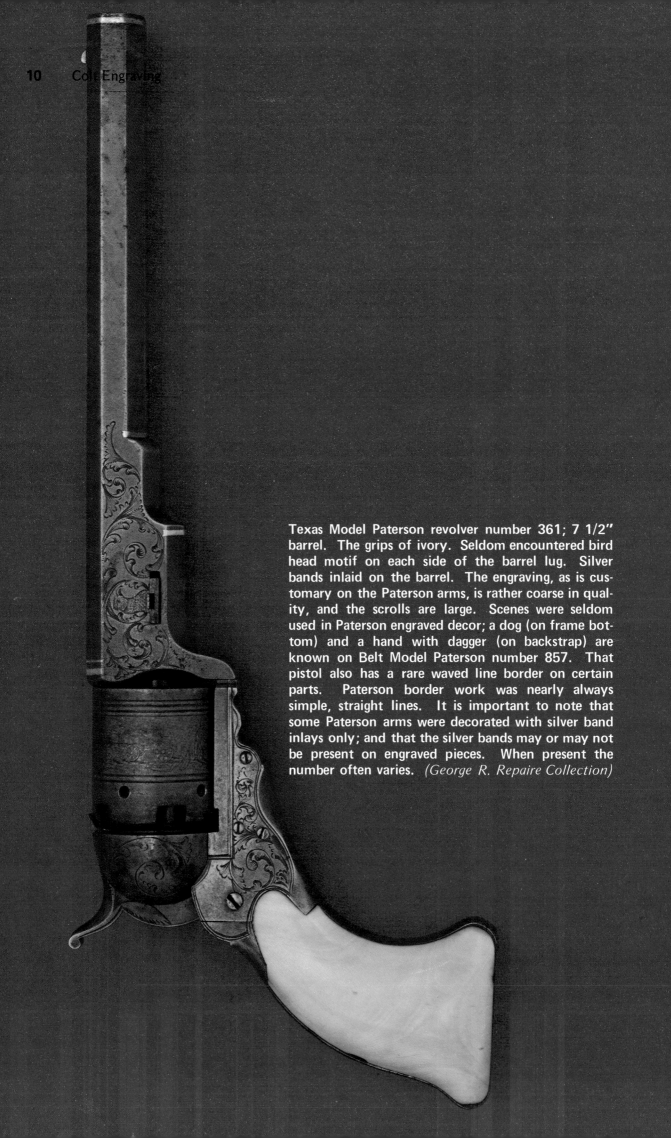

Texas Model Paterson revolver number 361; 7 1/2" barrel. The grips of ivory. Seldom encountered bird head motif on each side of the barrel lug. Silver bands inlaid on the barrel. The engraving, as is customary on the Paterson arms, is rather coarse in quality, and the scrolls are large. Scenes were seldom used in Paterson engraved decor; a dog (on frame bottom) and a hand with dagger (on backstrap) are known on Belt Model Paterson number 857. That pistol also has a rare waved line border on certain parts. Paterson border work was nearly always simple, straight lines. It is important to note that some Paterson arms were decorated with silver band inlays only; and that the silver bands may or may not be present on engraved pieces. When present the number often varies. *(George R. Repaire Collection)*

Belt Model Paterson serial number 607, engraved in the vine style scroll coverage usually found on those arms of the Colt Paterson period which were factory engraved. Coverage on the barrel, frame, recoil shield, hammer, and backstrap. Compare with Belt Models numbers 537, 523, and 857, shown elsewhere in the present chapter. *(John Castro Collection)*

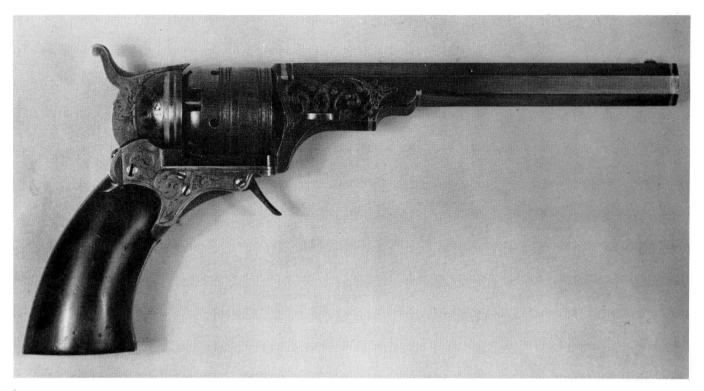

No. 2 Belt Paterson serial 566, engraved on the hammer, backstrap, frame, recoil shield, and barrel. German silver inlaid bands on the barrel and recoil shield. The backstrap inlaid with a German silver escalloped escutcheon. Bottom of the frame features a bird within scrollwork. Revolver is from a cased set, recognized as among the supreme examples of Paterson Colt production. *(William S. Serri Collection)*

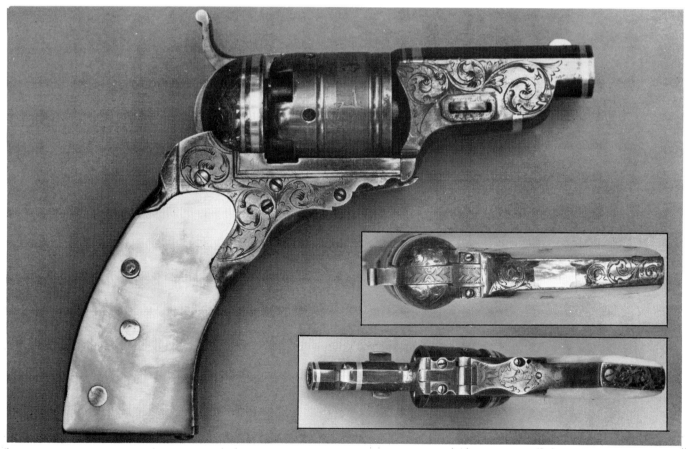

Serial number 98 No. 1 or Baby Paterson is the earliest known factory engraved production model Paterson revolver, and therefore (at this writing) is the *earliest known factory engraved Colt handgun*. Vine style scroll, without background motif. 1 3/4″ barrel (shortest length known on any Paterson). Four German silver band inlays are on the barrel, and two on the recoil shield. An escutcheon is inlaid on the backstrap. Rare mother of pearl grips. Blued finish, with case hardened frame and hammer. *(Private Collection)*

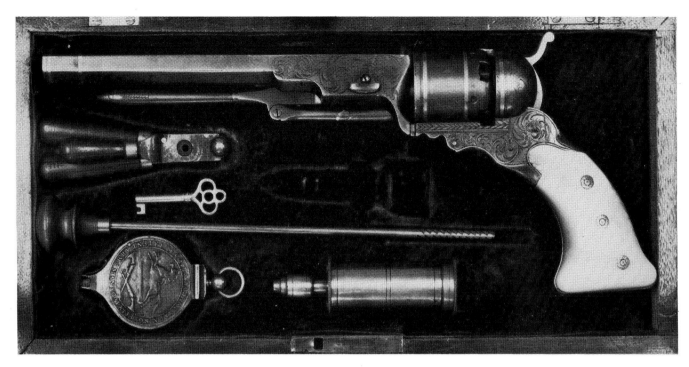

Holster Model revolver; serial number 755.   Inlaid with six silver bands. The engraving is of the basic Paterson vine scroll style, but is executed with lined backgrounds, except on the recoil shield, the bottom of the frame, and the backstrap.   The lined background gives the scrollwork an appearance of greater coverage. Note the feather style of finial on the factory-installed loading lever. Wheat chaff style border on the frame plate (beneath the cylinder). Rare casing, lacking only the special screwdriver tool. Equally rare mother-of-pearl grips, secured with German silver studs decorated in a rosette pattern. *(Anonymous Collection)*

Holster Model Paterson; serial number 603. A classic and complete specimen in a deluxe Paterson handgun. The case, lined in brown velvet, is of mahogany with all accessories. Ten silver band inlays are on the pistol, and six are on the extra 12″ barrel. Scrollwork of the vine style. Rare motifs are an eagle head in profile on the left and right sides of the hammer, and a dog on the frame bottom, picking over the body of a prone bird. Grips of varnished select walnut. The backstrap is inlaid with a silver rectangular escutcheon, on which is engraved in script: *W.A. Williams.* A silver plate inlaid on the case lid is identically inscribed. Inscriptions are extremely rare on Paterson Colt firearms. *(Herbert E. Green Collection)*

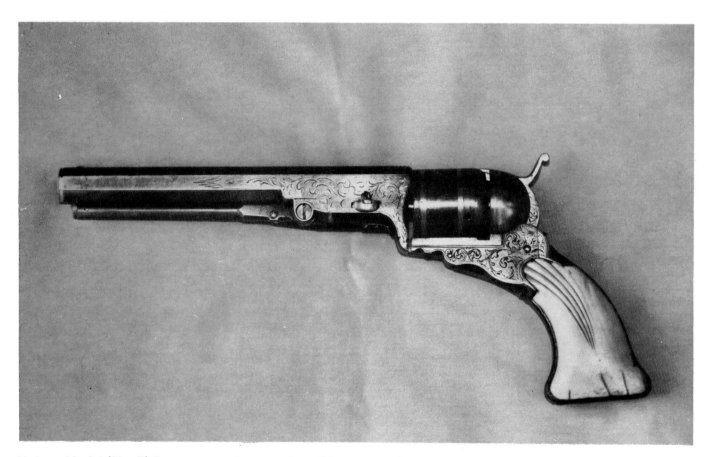

Holster Model (No. 5) Paterson revolver, number 530. An experimental, which also featured engraved decoration and shell type ivory grips. Rare loading lever device; revolver pictured and described in detail in *Paterson Colt Pistol Variations.* Note presence of German silver band inlays on the barrel, cylinder, and recoil shield. *(John Castro Collection)*

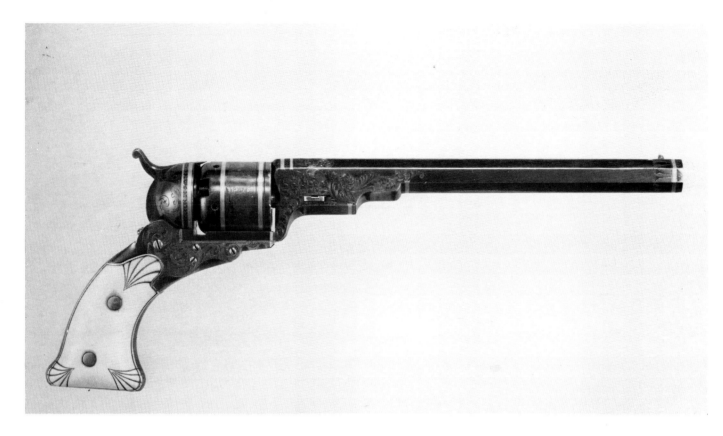

Considered by many Colt enthusiasts as the finest Paterson Holster Model revolver known, this specimen from Samuel Colt's own collection bears serial number 984. Inlaid with ten silver bands. The vine style scrollwork has horizontal lining on the barrel and frame; no lining is present on the recoil shield scrolls. An eagle head in profile appears on each side of the hammer. On the backstrap is a silver rectangular escutcheon inlay. The grips are carved in the rare shell pattern, and are mounted onto brass plates by German silver studs. *(Samuel Colt Collection — Wadsworth Atheneum Hartford)*

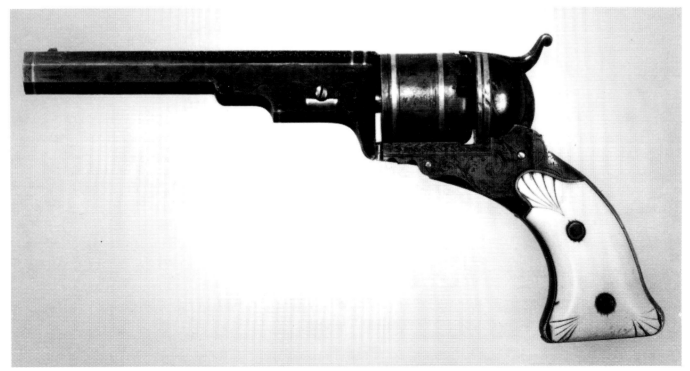

The consecutive serial number to Samuel Colt's Holster Model pistol; serial number 985. Identical grips and silver band and escutcheon inlays. However, number 985 was engraved in the Paterson vine style without the horizontal lined background. *(Walter B. Ford III Collection)*

CHAPTER I / PRE-PATERSON AND PATERSON COLT ENGRAVING c. 1832 — 1842

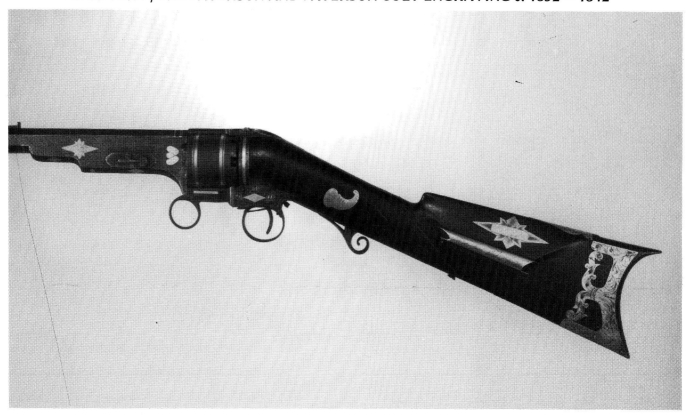

No. 1 Model Ring Lever rifle; serial number 41. Vine style scroll engraving; with the inlaid silver motifs also engraved, excepting the silver bands. Profusely inlaid in silver with bands on the barrel, cylinder, recoil shield, and frame; diamond and dot motifs on the barrel and frame; an eight-pointed star and intertwined heart on the left side of the barrel lug; rectangular escutcheon plate on the backstrap; and an arrow on top of the barrel pointed in the direction of the muzzle. Silver inlays on the checkered, deluxe walnut stock as follows: Cornucopia, eight-pointed star, long sheathing on the cheekpiece, running deer and hunter on horseback. The butt decorated with pierced silver inlays; toe plate of silver; and a silver cap inlaid forward of the buttplate top. The pierced and engraved silver plates on the stock are engraved to match the balance of the gun. The forward portion of the loading lever was silver plated; an unusual detail also noted on serial number 940 engraved Holster Model revolver (pictured in *Samuel Colt Presents,* page 18). Serial number 143 of the No. 1 Model Ring Lever rifle is decorated similarly to number 41; illustrated in *The Book of Colt Firearms,* **page 44.** *(Anonymous Collection)*

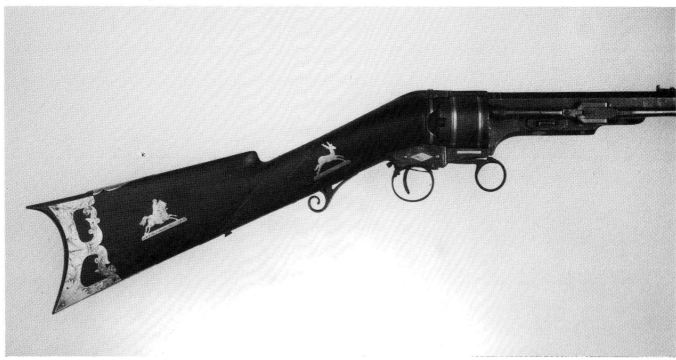

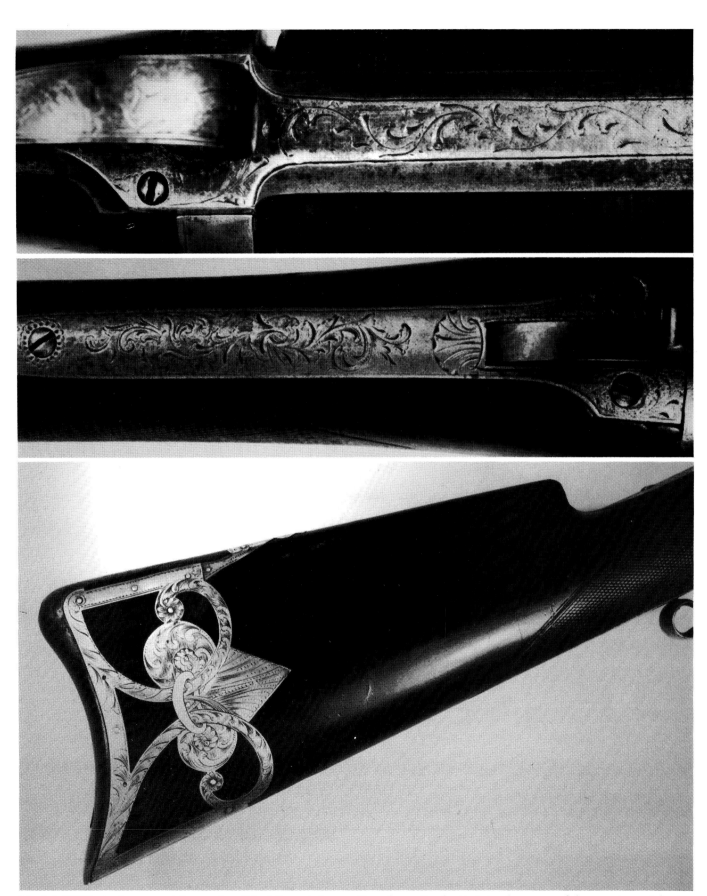

Model 1839 shotgun; serial number 14. Vine style scrollwork on the buttplate, frame, and frame strap, trigger-guard, and backstrap. Checkered deluxe walnut stock, with pierced silver inlays, the engraving on which is stylistically quite similar to that on the steel parts. The triggerguard motif is a dog, a bird, and foliage. The name [?] A. CUTLER is stamped on the wood on both sides of the butt. Paterson longarms decorated in the fashion of rifles number 41 and number 143, and shotgun number 14 are *extremely* rare. *(Frank Russell Collection)*

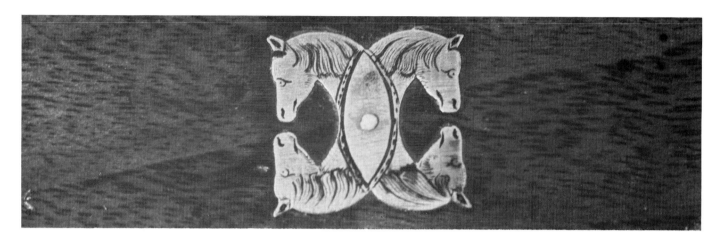

The hand engraved four horses head cheekpiece inlay, standard on the First Model Ring Lever Paterson rifles. As on serial number 187. *(Ray E. Limbrecht Collection)*

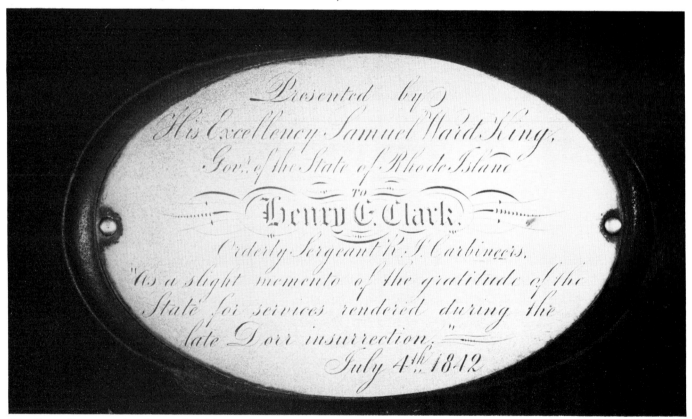

Sterling silver stock plaque inlaid on the buttstock of a Model 1839 Carbine. For further information on the background of the presentation, see page 114 of *Paterson Colt Pistol Variations*. Carbine was for many years in the William G. Renwick collection. *(Richard P. Mellon Collection)*

Number 524 Model 1839 Paterson Carbine has coverage on the barrel (opposite page, bottom), frame, upper tang, recoil shield, lower tang, triggerguard, upper buttplate, frame strap beneath the cylinder, and the upper and lower tang screws. Note also the German silver trim behind the recoil shield and the engraved silver inlay on the right side of the deluxe walnut stock. A rare specimen of Paterson firearm. *(Ray E. Limbrecht Collection)*

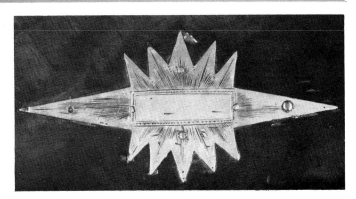

Chapter II
COLT'S HARTFORD ENGRAVING
c. 1847 — c. 1852

When Samuel Colt returned to gunmaking in 1847, after a hiatus of five years since the failure of the Paterson enterprise, his approach to engraving picked up where his previous experience had left off. In the years 1847 through 1852 his use of engraving gradually became more frequent, evolving into a popular facet of the Colt firearms line.

The first style, a vine type reminiscent of the Paterson, remained the standard from c. late 1847 or early 1848 through into the year 1851. The earliest coverage was a simple scroll and border design on the frame, backstrap, and triggerguard, as noted on a few of the First Model Dragoon and Model 1848 Pocket revolvers. In regard to the Walker Model — no factory hand-engraved Walkers are known; the possibility exists that some were produced, but original records do not indicate that any such work was done on that model. A few may have been inscribed for the factory, possibly for special presentations (several of the Civilian series Walkers were presented by Colt to military officers and other dignitaries).

The only known decorated Colts of the 1847 period are a handful of Whitneyville-Hartford Dragoon revolvers. The first of these, serial numbers unknown, was noted in *The Connecticut Courant*, November 6, 1847, which revealed that the Colt factory was preparing a pair of presentation revolvers as a gift from President Polk to his brother Major Polk. The decoration was not revealed, but at the least would have been backstrap inscriptions.

The second of the known Whitneyville-Hartford engraved pieces, serial number 1337, was inscribed on the backstrap from Colt to Major Ben McCulloch, January 1, 1848. At the top flat of the backstrap was a running horse motif, with FREE inscribed above and a cactus engraved beneath. McCulloch was a friend of Colt, active in endorsing the inventor's products.

A matched pair of the same model of revolver, serial numbers 1118 and 1123, were fitted with sterling silver grips, which were later profusely inscribed by New York dealers Moore and Baker,

for presentation to Colonel George Washington Morgan. These exquisite and unique arms are pictured in the section on Tiffany grips.

The last known factory embellished Whitneyville-Hartford Dragoon is number 1331, a plain factory model, but with a special backstrap inscription (in italics); *Hon. Ed. A. Hannegan from his friend Jno. A. Addison.* Hannegan was a nationally prominent political figure (a Congressman and U.S. Senator from Indiana) and was an acquaintance of Samuel Colt. It is likely that Addison presented the gun to Hannegan as a favor to Samuel Colt, then (as witness the McCulloch gift) doing his best to increase gun sales to the U.S. government. The revolver is now in the collection of Walter B. Ford III.

Soon complementing the use of limited coverage on the frame and gripstraps — as observed on a few First Model Dragoon and Model 1848 Pocket revolvers — the vine style of scroll was added to the hammer, wedge, barrel, and loading lever. Through the end of the percussion period, coverage in all styles of engraving continued to be found concentrated on these major parts.

The vine style marks the first use of the dot stamping accompanying the serial numbers on the barrel lug, frame, triggerguard strap, and buttstrap. During the years c. 1849 to c. 1861 the dot or "center punchmark" was the standard means of denoting deluxe engraving, grips, and finish on Colt arms in the manufacturing process. Variations appear in such markings, and these will be noted as they appear in the sequence of evolution. Presence of the dot is indicated by the /. suffix in appropriate picture captions or other textual matter.

Standard on all the early styles of engraving was the finish of case hardened frame, hammer and lever, with the balance blued — excepting the brass gripstraps which were silver plated. Any exceptions to this combination are recognized today as great rarities. Records do reveal a few requests for specials, in finishes and in other means of decoration.

Serial number 8092 of the Baby Dragoon, Model 1848, revolver exhibits the scarce and desirable early coverage in the vine style of scroll engraving. Note the lack of coverage on the barrel or hammer. Only the frame, backstrap and triggerguard were engraved, and that in a simple scroll motif. Representing Colt's beginnings of hand decoration in his Hartford period, revolvers like number 8092 are highly prized collector's pieces despite the relatively simple decor. Their almost primitive quality is comparable to the style and quality which dominated the Colt Paterson work. As Colt became increasingly successful, the improved fit, quality, and decoration of his products were an expression of the company's progress and accomplishments. Engraving began in a plain and simple style, and by 1851 had reached a rather elaborate state (the donut scroll); in 1852 the Gustave Young scroll was one indicator that Samuel Colt and his guns had "arrived". *(Buddy Hackett Collection)*

Some examples follow:

We saw a beautiful Repeating Pistol, made by Mr. Colt of this city, the present week, intended as a present from Col. T.H. Seymour to Mr. Bellange, proprietor of the mint in Mexico. . . . Col. S. as a token of regard, had a Repeating Pistol made by Mr. Colt, beautifully trimmed, and the following inscription engraved upon it — 'A mi amigo Bellange,' — (to my friend Bellange.). . . .

The Daily Times, *Hartford, October 25, 1848*

An order to Colt from dealers Francis Tomes & Sons, New York, dated October 21, 1850, requested: *"1 pair of 3 inch Revolvers to be gold mounted".* A later letter from Tomes indicated they changed the order to: *"one with mtgs. of German Silver but gilt or galvanised with gold — but of a clean good finish & have the mountings burnished or polished to look like bright gold. . . ."* The guns involved were the Model 1848 or Model 1849 Pocket revolvers.

Another letter from Tomes (November 15, 1850) asked about having a Model 1849 revolver made with sterling silver gripstraps, and also asked of progress on *"the pair of Gold mounted pistols. . . ."*

Original correspondence in Colt Collection—
Connecticut State Library

Despite extensive research, the craftsmen who engraved Colt weapons of the period c. 1847-1852 remain unidentified. Names of engravers who were active in Hartford c. 1850-52 are known, but as yet no evidence shows they worked for Colt or even on firearms. These individuals are: James and Asaph Willard, Richard Armstrong, and John Fuller. A.J.G. Kellogg is also known, but he was in the printing business, as a lithographer.

Not once has a factory engraved Colt percussion firearm been found which bears the signature of the engraver.* The scarcity of early records makes identification of the artisans problematic. Thus at least for work of the period 1847-52, the best one can do is to delineate each style and establish periods of use and weapons on which the work appears.

"EXHIBITION GRADE"

The second of three styles of early Hartford Colt engraving is the "exhibition grade", so named because specimens so decorated were featured by Colt in exhibits of his pioneer revolving firearms in

*Excepting the modern series of percussion Colt arms, introduced in 1971.

America and Europe, c. 1849-51. The most distinguished examples of the exhibition grade are a Second Model Dragoon, a Model 1851 Navy, and a Model 1848 Baby Dragoon presented by Colt to British royalty. An interesting specimen of the Model 1848 Baby Dragoon, number 12329, was reproduced by Colt in an early advertising brochure. Artist's license distorted the engraving style on the frame, but the pattern was more accurately depicted on the barrel.

From Vienna, Austria, on July 18, 1849, Samuel Colt wrote to his brother Elisha, ordering a total of fifty revolvers of this style. The letter, quoted in full in *Samuel Colt Presents* (page 236) reveals that a total of fifteen "Large size pistols" and 35 "Small size pistols" was required. Large size arms were the Second Model Dragoon and the soon to be produced Model 1851 Navy. The small size referred to the Pocket Model 1848. ". . . . I want to have specimens of our arms prepared. . . & exibated in their *[special Austrian-made "Buhl"]* boxes at the anual fairs of the American Institute & the Mecanicks institutes of N. York, also the fares to be hild this fall in Boston & Philedelphia & any other places where they award gold medols in premeum for the best inventions. Theis medles we must get & I must have them with me in Europe to help make up the reputation of my arms as soon as I begin to make a noyes about them. . . ."

Judging from Colt's letter it appears that not more than fifty of the "exhibition grade" revolvers were produced, making this pattern one of the rarest in engraved Colt firearms.

THE "DONUT SCROLL"

Number three of the early styles of Colt Hartford engraving is known as the "donut scroll". This is a dramatic departure from the vine style, and contrasts strongly with the "exhibition grade" and the new style which would be introduced by Gustave Young in 1852. No records identify the craftsman responsible for introducing the donut scroll, but judging from the study of revolvers bearing the style, its life was brief, c. 1851-52.

A few details of manufacture accompany the donut style. In the Model 1849 Pocket revolver, most specimens have the hand engraved barrel marking "Saml Colt" in old English letters or italics; other models, of which there are the Second and Third Dragoons and the 1851 Navy, retained the standard stamped markings. Another standard feature is the presence of varnished selected walnut grips; replacing the varnished plain walnut standard to previous Hartford engraved revolvers.

The number of illustrations available for this pattern, despite its brief period of use, testifies to the increased numbers of engraved arms which were coming out of the Colt factory c. 1851-52.

Whitneyville-Hartford Dragoon number 1331, one of the earliest of factory inscribed Colt revolvers from the Hartford period. *(Photograph courtesy of Herbert G. Glass)*

Whitneyville-Hartford Dragoon, serial number 1337. The backstrap reads: *Presented by Sam. Colt/to. Maj. Ben McCulloch/Jan. 1. 1848.* **The backstrap marking is the earliest known presentation inscription from Samuel Colt. A specimen of the modest Hartford beginning to a major aspect of Samuel Colt's method of operation.** *(Joe W. Bates Collection)*

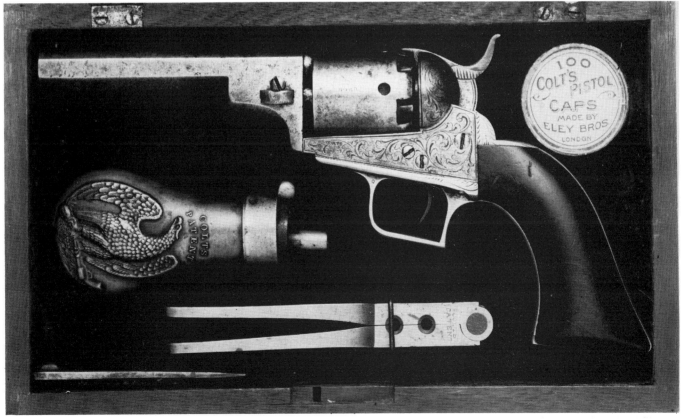

Number 8069/. Baby Dragoon is a specimen of the sought-after early coverage in the vine style scroll; note lack of engraving on the barrel. Noted on a few early Dragoon and Baby Dragoon revolvers; an even earlier type lacked coverage on the hammer. The casing of the equally rare bevelled lid style, slightly recessed inside for the revolver, can of caps, early eagle flask, brass bullet mold, and L-shaped screwdriver nipple wrench. *(William H. Myers Collection)*

The serial number 8478 Second Model Dragoon; engraving in the early vine style of scrollwork. *(Jerry D. Berger Collection/Photograph, Doug McLaughlin)*

Third Model Dragoon with "donut scroll", number 12389, came from the nephew of Maharajah MahIndra Bhati, M.H.A., of India, and was imported by Jackson Arms. The sensational Goddess of Liberty ivory grips (left side a relief American eagle and shield) were formerly in the Larry Sheerin collection, and rank among the most rare of all grip types as found on Dragoon Colts. *(George R. Repaire Collection)*

Second Model Dragoon, serial number 9625. Characteristic vine style scroll cut on the hammer, gripstraps, frame, barrel lug, and loading lever. Rosette motifs on the screw heads and on the finials of the frame and barrel lug screws. Fine leaf borders on the frame and barrel lug. The grips of varnished select walnut; the customary type stock wood for engraved percussion Colt arms — excepting several of the pieces predating c. 1851. *(The Armouries, H.M. Tower of London)*

Serial number 8478 Second Model Dragoon. The same basic scroll style as on the Tower Armouries pistol, but less in coverage, and with a less detailed border. Select walnut grips; cased in a varnished mahogany box with velvet lined American style interior and full accessories. *(Jerry D. Berger Collection)*

Baby Dragoon Model 1848 revolver; number 7623. Basic vine style scroll. Note the lack of borders on the frame, and the absence of engraving on the sides of the backstrap and triggerguard strap. Standard varnished walnut grips. *(L. Allan Caperton Collection)*

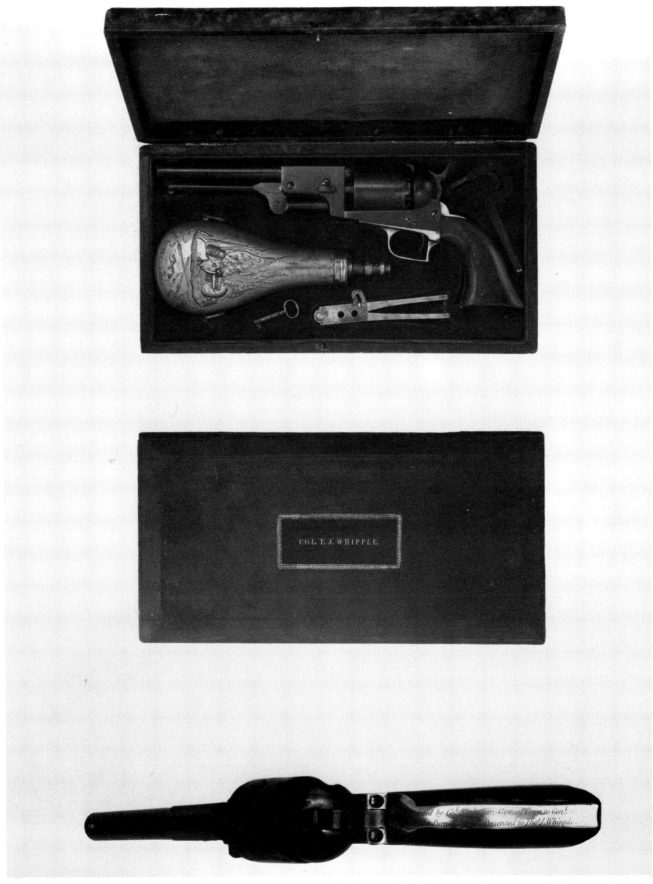

Number 3969 First Model Dragoon was a gift of Colonel Thomas H. Seymour, Governor of Connecticut, to General Franklin Pierce (later U.S. President). Pierce in turn gave the revolver to Thomas J. Whipple. All of this is documented by the revolver's backstrap inscription. The contemporary casing of leather is lined in velvet and is recessed for the flask, mold, and question mark shaped combination tool. A historic and rare outfit, formerly in the W.M. Locke collection. *(Charles Schreiner III Collection)*

Model 1851 Navy, with squareback triggerguard; serial number 344. Vine style scroll of the earliest type known for the Navy Model. Serial number 2, identically engraved, appears in *Samuel Colt Presents,* page 105. The scroll extending the entire length of the barrel has been noted also on a few Model 1848 Baby Dragoon revolvers (e. g., number 8155/.). Wavy line borders on the frame, recoil shield and barrel lug. Crowned muzzle decorative pattern. Varnished walnut grips. *(Dr. Robert J. Nelson Collection)*

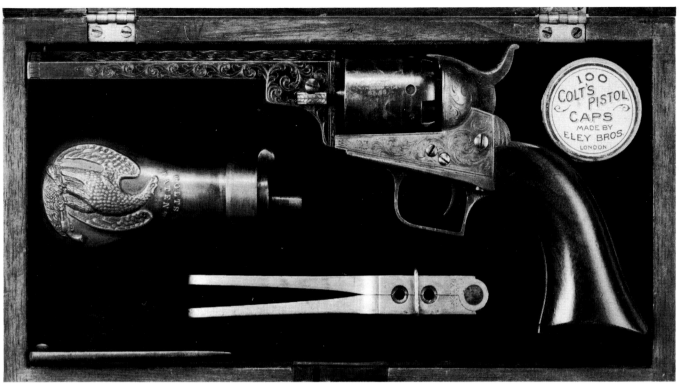

Model 1848 revolver, serial number 8155/. More profuse coverage of the vine style scroll, with comparatively extensive border work, but the frame scroll design is nearly identical to that on serial number 7623. The casing is of Paterson type (having the bevelled lid), and is slightly recessed for the pistol and all accessories. Case wood of mahogany; the lining of green velvet. *(Formerly in the William M. Locke Collection)*

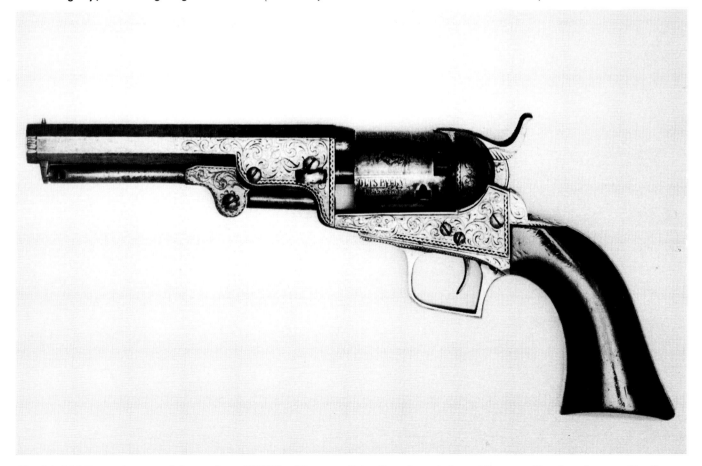

Model 1848 revolver; serial number 12330. The scroll in the vine style, with wavy line borders on the frame, recoil shield, barrel lug, triggerguard strap, and loading lever. Crowned muzzle decorative motif is a standard detail of the vine style series. *(George R. Repaire Collection)*

Second Model Dragoon revolvers; serial numbers 8154 and 8913. A unique cased set, custom made for James Janeway Van Syckel, a wealthy Philadelphia wine merchant. All pistol parts except the gripstraps, grips, and triggers are of Colt manufacture. The engraving is not a Colt style; judging from the style of scrollwork, the unusual combination of finishes (browned barrels, blued loading levers and gripstraps; the remaining parts case hardened), and the presence of the unusual bullet mold and loading-cleaning apparatus, the outfit should be attributed to Belgian manufacture. However, the silver bag style flask was made by Philadelphia silversmiths J. & W. Wilson and Company, and the casing is attributable to the Philadelphia firm of J.C. Grubb & Company. There are no Belgian proofmarks on the revolvers, and no Colt markings appear on the barrels. It appears that the set was put together in Philadelphia, and the work was done through a dealer in that city. Engraving and finishing may have been executed there by Belgian trained gunsmiths. Readers should compare the outfit with the cased pair of Mullin deringer pistols appearing on the cover of the July 1969 *The Texas Gun Collector* **magazine.** *(Museum of Connecticut History, Connecticut State Library)*

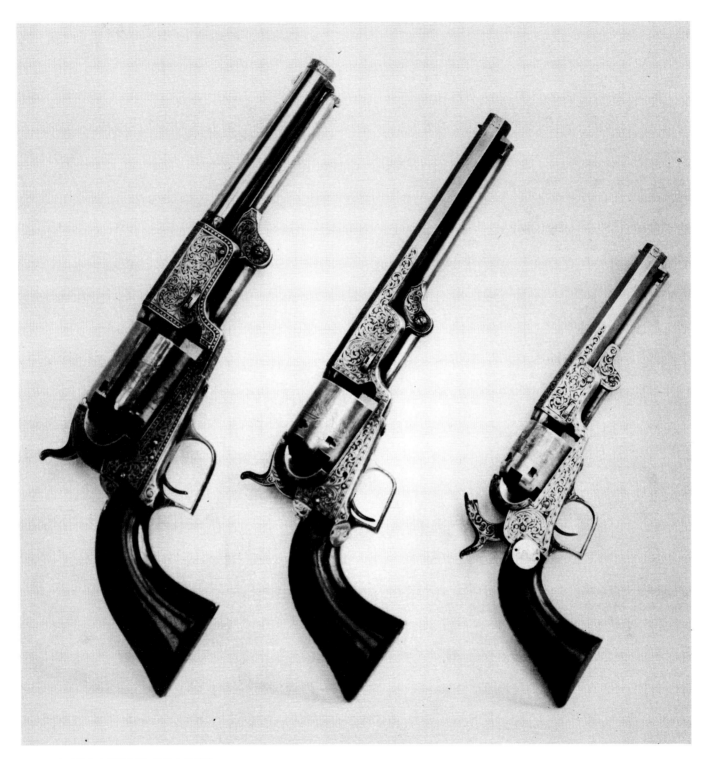

THE "EXHIBITION GRADE"

Left: Second Model Dragoon; serial number 9623. Varnished select walnut grips. Believed presented to Albert, Prince Consort of England (1819-61) by Samuel Colt. No inscriptions appear on this pistol or its accompanying Navy and Baby Dragoon models. **Center:** Model 1851 Squareback Navy; number 843. Varnished select walnut grips. Believed presented, with Dragoon number 9623, by Samuel Colt to Prince Albert. The Navy and Dragoon are cased together in an elaborate inlaid rosewood case. **Right:** Model 1848 Baby Dragoon; number 12571. Varnished select walnut grips. Believed a gift from Colt to Edward, Prince of Wales. Cased in a deluxe rosewood box, decorated in the same exquisite style as the Dragoon and Navy revolvers. **NOTE:** The dot serial number stamping has not been observed in "exhibition grade" pistols. *(Reproduced through gracious permission of H.M. Queen Elizabeth II. Windsor Castle Armoury Collection)*

Model 1848 revolver; serial number 12570. Specimen of the "exhibition grade" coverage of c. 1849-50, believed used on a total of only about 50 revolvers. For comparison, see *The Book of Colt Firearms,* page 106A; the illustrated revolver, number 12329, appears with a Colt advertising woodcut of the period, also marked with the number 12329. *(Saunders Memorial Museum Collection)*

Exhibition style scroll on Baby Dragoon number 12322. *(Woolaroc Museum, Bartlesville, Oklahoma; P.R. Phillips Collection)*

THE "DONUT SCROLL"

Second Model Dragoon revolver; number 10333. The donut scroll is seldom found on the Second Model Dragoon; more often appearing on early specimens of the Third Model, and the Model 1849 Pocket and Model 1851 Navy. On number 10333 the barrel lug exhibits the rarity of a soldier on horseback shooting a buffalo with a revolver. Coverage on the barrel, loading lever, wedge, hammer, frame, gripstraps, and the frame and barrel screws. The hunting scene likely had a George Catlin print, or similar picture, as its source. Revolver's backstrap is inscribed: *Charles Nephew & Co. Calcutta.* Sanskrit inscription on left side of the barrel. *(Dr. Chester P. Bonoff Collection)*

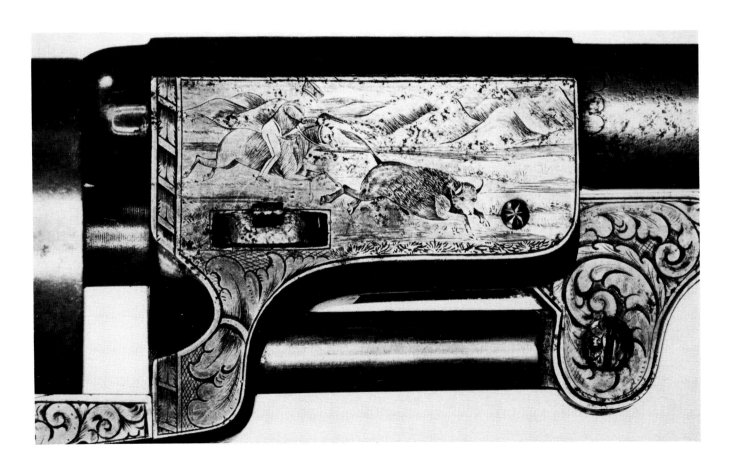

Third Model Dragoon; number 12396/. Detail shows clearly the distinctive donut scroll. The hammer decor is a stylized wolf or lion head. *(L. Allan Caperton Collection)*

Detail from the barrel lug of Third Model Dragoon number 12389. Such scenes are quite rare; the stylized nature of the motif is apparent. *(George R. Repaire Collection)*

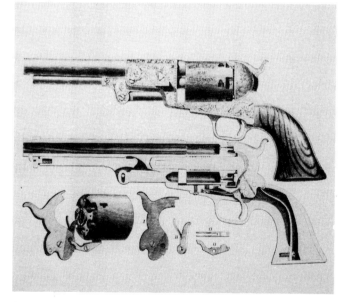

Serial number 12397 Third Model Dragoon; with the donut scroll, and a panel scene on the left side of the barrel lug. The artist made his drawing directly from revolver number 12397, and the whereabouts of the gun today is unknown to collectors. Serial number 12398 Third Dragoon was discovered in India, 1973, and had belonged to His Highness of Jaisalmer; engraving on the gun is nearly identical to number 12397, but even more profuse. Illustration is from the book *Armsmear,* published in 1866.

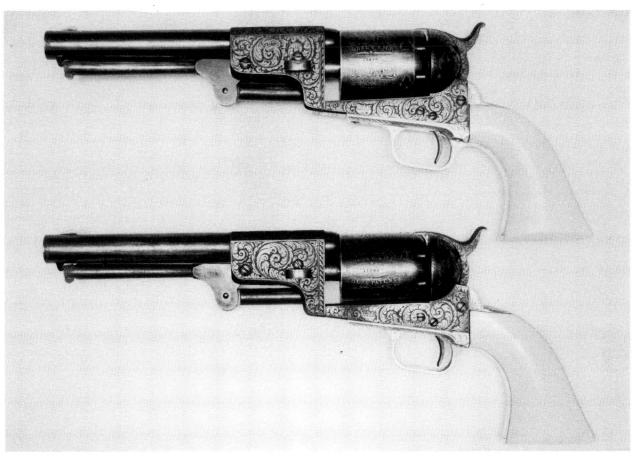

Deluxe pair of Third Model Dragoon revolvers; serial numbers 11790 and 11850.   Returned to the United States from Central America, c. 1972, this important pair has blued frames, and no engraving on the screws, wedges, or loading levers.   U.S. stampings are on the left side of each frame.   Scarce one piece ivory grips. Engraved pairs of dragoon revolvers are among the extreme rarities in Colt collecting.   Ivory grips are rare on Colt percussion arms predating c. 1852, and are by no means common thereafter. *(Johnie Bassett Collection)*

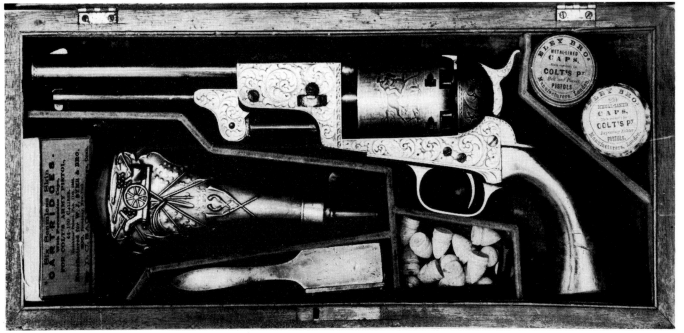

Third Model Dragoon; number 12379/.   A series of Third Model Dragoon revolvers in the serial range approximately 12365 through 12410 was specially engraved.   Nearly a dozen pieces within this serial range are known, and most are of the donut scroll of number 12379.   Variations do exist, but they are relatively minor.   Coverage is the same as on the Second Model Dragoon number 10333.   The dot serial stamping is standard; as is the varnished select walnut grip.   Standard factory casing of varnished mahogany, lined in velvet and partitioned in the American style. *(George R. Repaire Collection)*

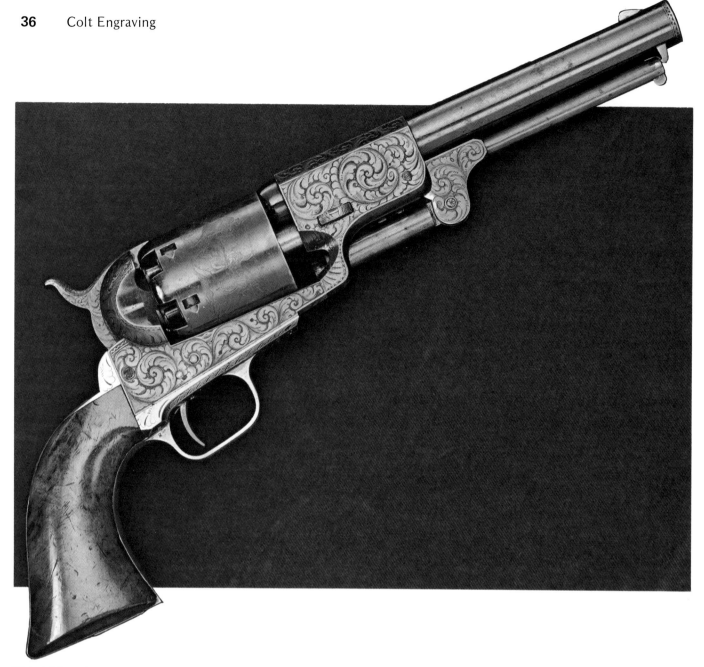

Third Model Dragoon; number 12405/. A presentation from Samuel Colt to Eli Whitney, Jr. Comparison with some dragoon specimens in the range from number 12365 to 12410 reveals differences in scroll placements, but an identical scroll style. This historic weapon was in the possession of the Whitney family until 1971. The two chapters which follow illustrate consecutively numbered revolvers embellished by Gustave Young.

A few specimens in the donut style scroll have panel scenes on the barrel lug, comparable to the Second Model Dragoon number 10333 and to Third Model Dragoons numbers 12384, 12397, and 12398. *(George R. Repaire Collection)*

Third Model Dragoon; number 12405/.
A presentation from Samuel Colt to Eli
Whitney, Jr. The consecutive serial
number to the Sultan of Turkey Third
Model Dragoon. *(George R. Repaire*
Collection)

Model 1849 Pocket revolver; number 19053/. Six inch barrel. The standard coverage and treatment of the Model 1849 revolver in the donut scroll pattern. Coverage on the barrel, wedge, loading lever, frame, hammer, straps, and frame and barrel screws. An early wolf head motif is on the hammer. An uninscribed but documented presentation from Samuel Colt to Joseph Trumbull (Governor of Connecticut, 1849-50). *(Anonymous Collection)*

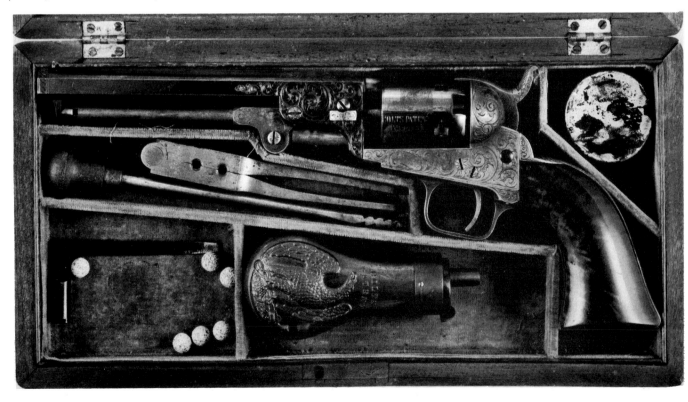

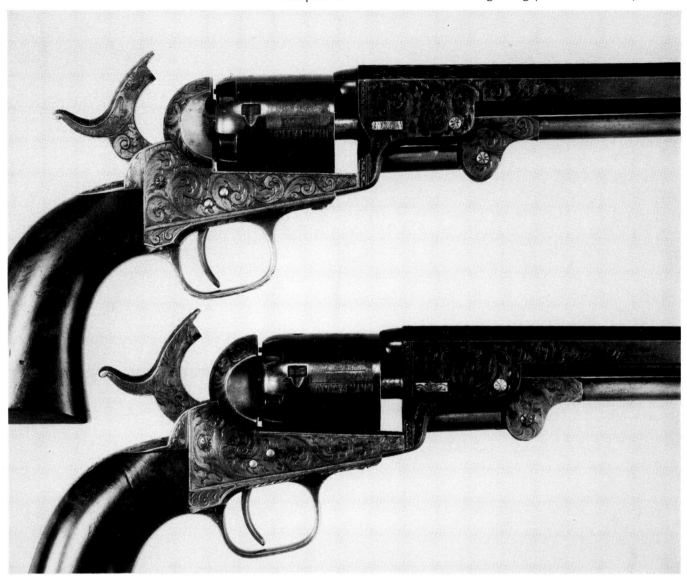

Model 1849 Pocket revolvers; serial numbers 33612/. (top) and 33633/. Six inch barrels; a cased pair. The lower specimen was executed by a superior hand to the upper piece. Apparently in an attempt to satisfy the growing demand for engraving, at least one untalented craftsman (perhaps an apprentice) was allowed to try his skill. The unsatisfactory results have been observed on a handful of other pieces of the period. Most clear on examination of gun number 33612/. are the clumsy scrolls, roughly cut and lacking symmetry (known as "potatoes" in the trade today). Wolf head or dolphin motifs appear on the hammers. Coverage on these revolvers is the same as on number 19053/., but the scroll patterns show variations. *(Formerly in the William M. Locke Collection)*

The highest serial number known in the donut scroll style on the Model 1849 Pocket series, 70745/. is believed to date well into 1853! *(J.D. Breslin Collection)*

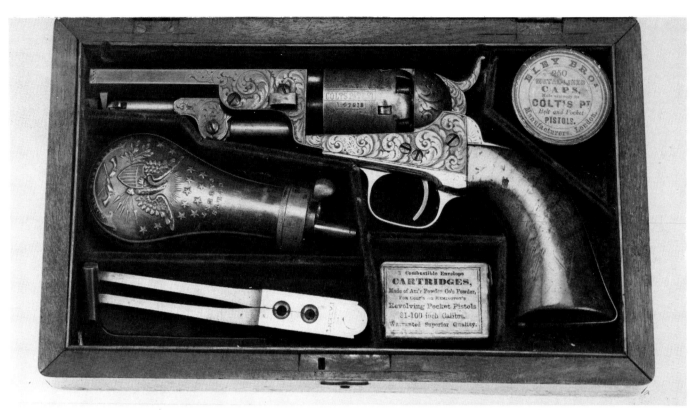

Model 1849 Pocket number 47815 exhibits the donut scroll, and includes the COLTS/PATENT frame marking hand lettered. The casing is inlaid on the lid with presentation plaque shown *(William H. Myers Collection)*

Model 1849 Pocket revolver; serial number 38169/. Five inch barrel. A standard specimen of the donut style, but with rare panel scenes; a jumping deer on the left side of the barrel, and a spread eagle on the right side. Panel scenes on the pocket model Colt percussion revolvers of the "donut" period appear with much less frequency than on the Dragoon or Navy sizes. Saml Colt marking, hand engraved, on top of the barrel. *(Dr. Chester P. Bonoff Collection)*

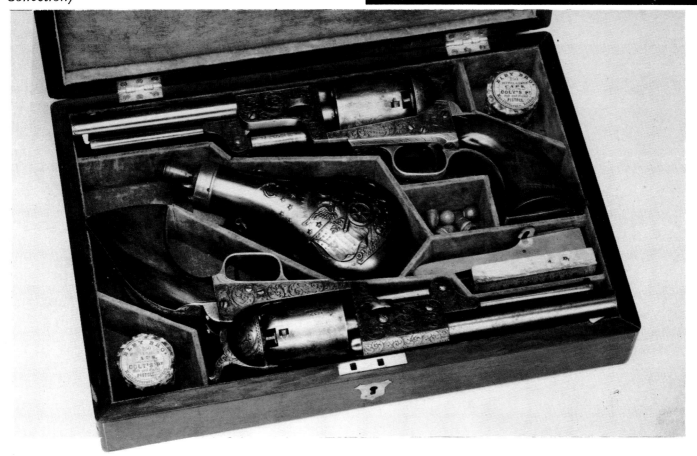

Third Model Dragoons **12346** and **12396** feature the "donut scroll," and are in a rosewood casing; the lid plaque of which is illustrated (right). Cased pairs of Dragoons rank among the ultimate in Colt rarities. Formerly in the John B. Solley III collection. *(Private Collection)*

Rare barrel lug portrait from Model 1849 revolver, serial number 38382/. Compare with number 38385/., which follows. *(Ray Hellier Collection)*

An extra-deluxe Model 1849 Pocket revolver; serial number 38385/. Six inch barrel. About twice the effort went into the decoration of this pistol, as compared to number 19053/. or numbers 33612/. and 33633/. In the panel on the right side of the barrel is a running deer motif. The identity of the portrait bust on the left side of the barrel is unknown; though probably it is of Colonel Samuel Colt. Identically placed on Pocket Model number 38382/. is a portrait of a bearded gentleman, perhaps also of Samuel Colt. No valid reason has been advanced for the departure from the standard donut scroll pattern on pistol number 38385/., nor for the presence of the portrait bust. This is the most deluxe specimen known of the donut scroll pattern in the Model **1849** revolver. *(William H. Myers Collection)*

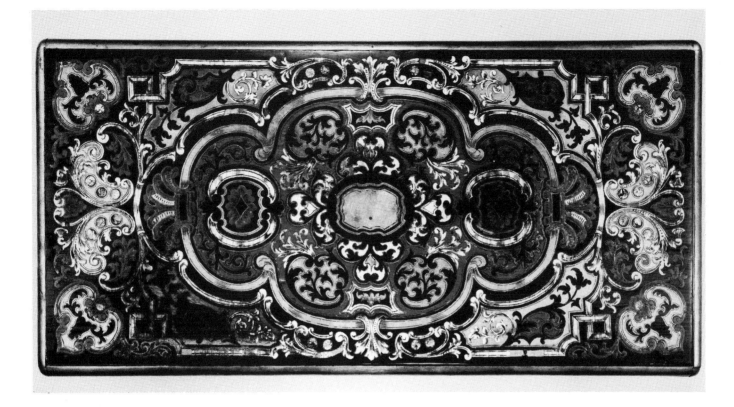

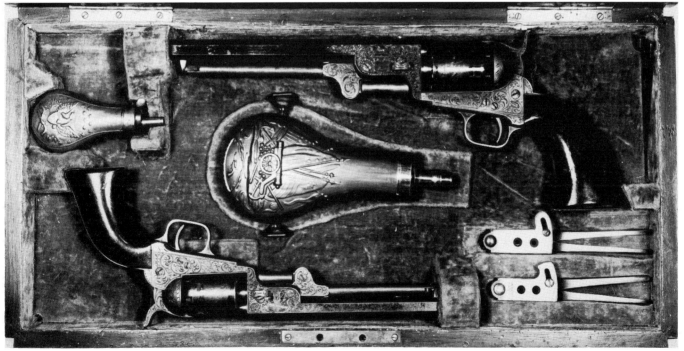

From Colonel Samuel Colt to his chief patent attorney, Edward N. Dickerson. The Model 1851 Navy bears serial number 3769; the Model 1849 Pocket number 19395. Both exhibit the donut scroll style, but both also exhibit important departures from the norm. On the Navy's barrel lug (see details) are a portrait bust of Samuel Colt within an oval and with a stand of flags backdrop, and the Colt family coat of arms. The barrel lug of the Pocket pistol has a figure of Justice with scales on one side, and an American eagle motif on the other. The backstraps are inscribed to Edward N. Dickerson from Colt, in a rare combination of script and italic lettering. On the upper flats of the barrels are quite odd reverse scroll designs, visible in the detail photographs from the Navy. The pistol case is a most unusual style; the same as used in the Colt gifts to Edward, Prince of Wales, and to Prince Albert. The case is of rosewood, brassbound, and inlaid with ivory, silver, brass, and pearl. The lining of reddish velvet. These boxes were made in Austria, in 1849, and were ordered personally by Samuel Colt. Mrs. Colt, at a later date, had jewelry cases made (by Tiffany & Company, New York) from pistol cases of this style. These are now in the Colt collection, Wadsworth Atheneum Hartford. *(Anonymous Collection)*

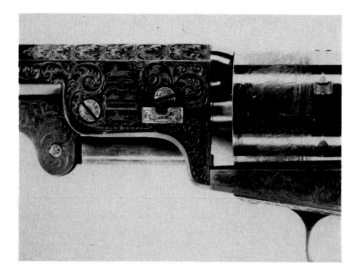
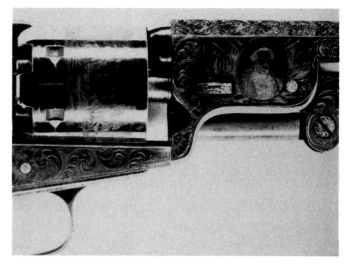

Number 33598/. Model 1849 Pocket revolver; 5" barrel. The backstrap inscribed: Anson Chase [in old English]/*From the Inventor* [in script]. Chase was the first gunsmith to work with Samuel Colt in manufacturing prototypes of his revolver, c. 1831-33. Gun number 33598/. was presented to Chase soon after he appeared as a witness on behalf of Colt in the Massachusetts Arms Company trial of 1851. The author regards this gun as one of the most historic and interesting of presentations made by Samuel Colt; it honors the man who made the first of the Colt revolvers, and was a gift from the inventor himself. Without the aid of master gunsmiths like Chase and John Pearson, Colt might never have achieved such considerable success as a gunmaker. Mahogany casing; lined in blue velvet. A gunmaker's pull on the interior of the lid was taken from a Colt revolver's barrel lug, and is a portrait of Samuel Colt. *(Alan S. Kelley Collection)*

A presentation from Samuel Colt to his friend Colonel Thomas Lally. Model 1851 Navy; serial number 5604/. Lally's pistol represents the standard style and coverage of the donut scroll on the Model 1851 Navy. Presentation inscribed on the backstrap. Serial number 5270/., similarly engraved, was inscribed from Colonel Colt to General Franklin Pierce, later to be President of the United States. Navy number 6471/. was inscribed from Colt to his friend Ben McCulloch. The McCulloch pistol is decorated in the same style, but has a portrait bust on the barrel lug (left side) and a Texas star, shield, and stand of flags motif on the right. The Pierce and McCulloch revolvers are illustrated in *Samuel Colt Presents*, pages 111 and 112. *(Arnold M. Chernoff Collection)*

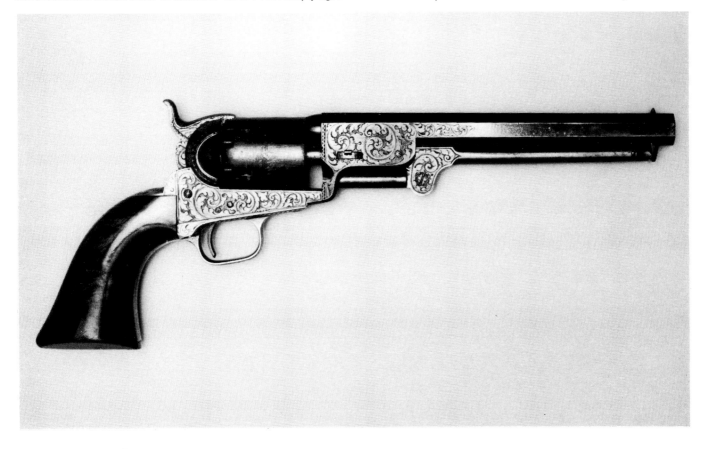

Documented Model 1851 Navy, serial number 6354/. The backstrap inscribed: *W.H. Morris U.S.A.* **W.A. Thornton, U.S. Ordnance, ordered the revolver, cased with accessories, on June 21, 1852. Writing directly to Colonel Colt, Thornton explained that Morris was soon headed West as a young Army officer, and wanted a cased Navy, the backstrap to be inscribed with his name and "U.S.A." The revolver demonstrates Colt's willingness to have special inscriptions engraved gratis whenever a military or naval officer might request it. Such an inscription was part of Colt's public relations program, best known to collectors through his policy of making presentations of firearms. The bust on the left side of the barrel lug is Samuel Colt. Revolver is cased with accessories.** *(H. Barthel Collection)*

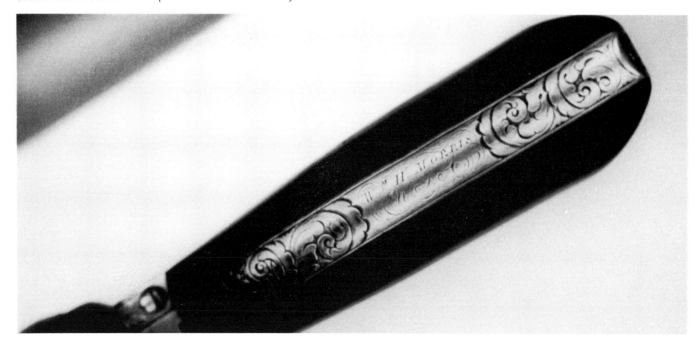

Right side of the *W.H. Morris U.S.A.* **Model 1851 Navy revolver, pictured on previous page. Rare dog motif on barrel lug. Revolver cased with accessories, and had been located by the author in Virginia c. 1967.** *(H. Barthel Collection)*

Model 1851 Navy 5605/. is a mint example of the donut scroll on a Model 1851 Navy. The revolver is also cased (mahogany box, velvet lined, with accessories). Grips are of select walnut; backstrap and trigger guard strap are *gold* plated. *(Harry W. Durand Collection)*

Historic presentation, inscribed on the backstrap: To GENL FRANK PIERCE/from COL. COLT. Pierce became U.S. President not long after the presentation of this revolver, in 1852. Serial #5270/. Pictured in color in *The Book of Colt Firearms,* and appearing as item 65 in *Samuel Colt Presents.* Both books show the revolver in its original mahogany case with complete accessories. Neither illustrated the right side, which is depicted here. Note the scene of a sailing ship on the barrel lug. Lug scenes and motifs are most prevailant in the donut scroll revolvers than in any other style of percussion Colt factory engraving. *(Johnie Bassett Collection)*

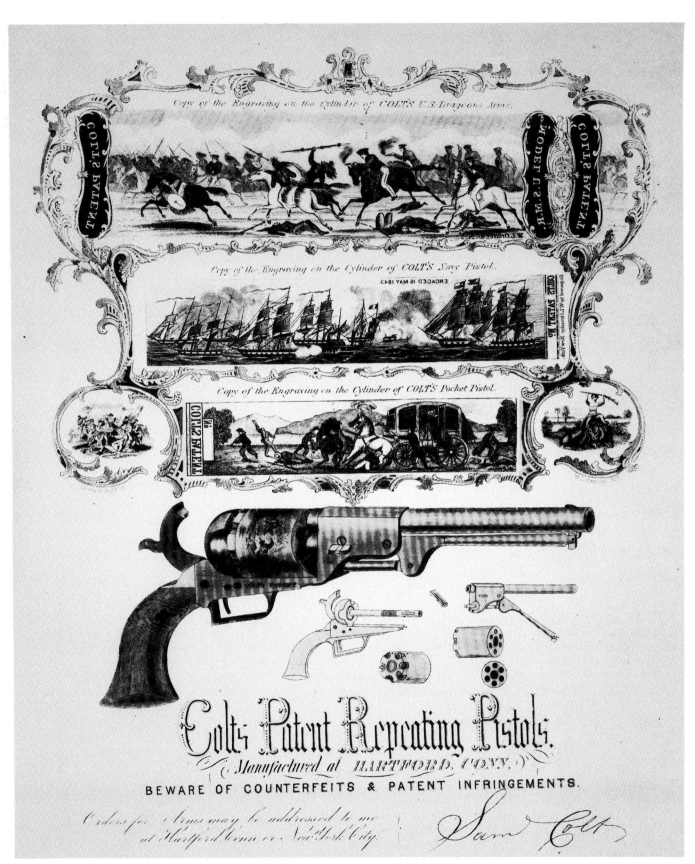

A classic document from Colt collecting, the famed cylinder scene broadside, designed and engraved for Colt by W. L. Ormsby, c. 1850. At top, the Dragoon roll engraved scene, at center, roll for the Navy and Army models, and at bottom, for the Pocket and Police revolvers. In the ovals at left and right are scenes from the cylinder roll die for the Model 1839 Paterson carbine. Source of the battle motif (at left) was the John Trumbull painting of the Battle of Bunker's Hill. Ormsby was primarily a banknote engraver, who occasionally did some special work for Colt, notably the roll designs for percussion revolver cylinders. *(John Hintlian Collection)*

One of the finest known Third Model Dragoons, number 16477, was engraved by Gustave Young, and includes the backstrap inscription: *Col. P.M. Milliken.* Note rarity of finely detailed scrolls, coverage on the cylinder and bordering the MODEL U.S.M.R. and COLT'S PATENT cylinder inscription, the ivory grips, and the remarkable condition. Among revolvers serial numbered near this revolver are the matched pair 16474 and 16476, the stocked presentations to Czar Alexander II of Russia and two of his brothers, 16480, 16481, and 16482, the Root revolver given to E.K.Root by Colonel Colt, 16461, and the John B. Floyd stocked Dragoon number 16467. The gripstraps on the Millikin revolver (Millikin is correct spelling, despite the backstrap inscription) are believed to be of sterling silver. *(George R. Repaire Collection)*

Chapter III
THE GUSTAVE YOUNG SCROLL
c. 1852 — 1869

Born in Berlin, Germany, in 1827, Gustave Young (formerly Jung) began his six year apprenticeship in engraving and die-cutting at the age of eight and settled down to his life's work at 14. Before emigrating to the United States at 19, Young engraved locks, breeches, triggerguards and buttplates of German-made long arms in his native land. He was also a brilliant die cutter, often called upon to cut royal crests on signet rings and punches.

The youthful engraver arrived in New York City in 1846 and is believed to have worked in that area for several years. But the first significant chapter of his career opened when, lured by New England's thriving arms industry, he moved to Hartford in 1852 and joined Colt's engraving staff. It is significant that, almost immediately upon Young's arrival, Colt adopted the forceful German designs which were Young's specialty.

By 1854, barely two years after joining the Hartford gunmaker, Young was Colt's engraving contractor. In this capacity he is believed to have handled most of Colt's engraving work through into the mid or late 1860's. During part of this period he maintained a shop at 8 State Street, Hartford, which, in an 1865 photograph, carries a sign imprinted: G. YOUNG GUN ENGRAVER. He is also known to have worked for some years at the Colt factory's own engraving shop.

The years with Colt were productive ones for Young. A published list of the serial numbers of 108 Colt Pocket and Navy revolvers, dated September 23, 1854, bears Young's name. The list specifies delivery following four weeks of work. The size of the order indicates that Young must have had at least seven engravers working under him, but the pistols on the list also enable the identification of the engraving style Young developed for Colt.

From this group of pistols and from other evidence, it has been established that Young was responsible personally for the superb engraving and gold inlay on the Colt Model 1860 Army revolvers which Abraham Lincoln presented in 1863 to the Kings of Denmark, and of Sweden and Norway (covered in the chapter on gold inlaid revolvers).

Presentation sets of pistols and rifles given to Secretary of War John B. Floyd by the Colt factory workmen in 1857 were engraved at Young's shop, as was a similar set presented by Samuel Colt to his chief engineer E.K. Root in the same year. A few very exquisite gold inlaid Colts were done by Young, and these included three revolvers presented by Samuel Colt to the Czar of Russia in 1854. The two pairs of Abraham Lincoln Model 1860 Army revolvers were done by Young in 1862-63, and interestingly enough, each pistol was billed to Colt for the rather reasonable sum of $225! In March of 1867 "3 Pistols for the Fair in Paris" were billed by Young to Colt. The engraving was listed as "fine", which is interpreted as meaning extra work beyond standard patterns.

Young is also known to have done die cutting work for the Colt company. Impressions in his pattern book include barrel markings for Model 1849 London and Hartford Pocket revolvers, Model 1851 Navies, Model 1855 Sidehammer rifles and pistols, and 1st and 2nd Model deringers. In addition, dies were cut for the Russian barrel markings on Colt Berdan rifles.

Records in Young's account book also show that in April-July 1868 he cut one full alphabet and a total of 173 letters and numbers for the Colt firm. Judging from surviving records, it is probable that work as a die cutter paid better than gun engraving and that gradually Young devoted greater effort to the die cutting aspects of his business.

Despite the demands of contract work for Colt, Young's shop was still capable of handling additional work, and account records show that other clients, at least in the 1860's, included the Sharps Rifle Company (Hartford), Smith & Wesson, Charles Parker (Meriden, Connecticut), the Connecticut Arms and Manufacturing Company (Naubuc, Connecticut), the Wesson Arms Company (Springfield, Massachusetts), and the Meriden Arms Company (Meriden, Connecticut). He is also known to have handled a small amount of work for Winchester, in the 1860's and 1870's.

In 1869 Young, his wife Marie, and their

three sons — Eugene (born 1863), Oscar, and Alfred (both born in the 1860's), moved to Springfield, Massachusetts. There they lived at 39 and 41 Broad Street, and Gustave had his shop at the same address. A rare photograph shows him in the window of the second story room where he had his engraving shop.

By this time Young had a reputation throughout New England as a master engraver and die cutter of exceptional ability. His account book for the period 1869-1883 includes a great many guns and dies done for Smith & Wesson and others. Among these, selected at random, (the spelling errors are Young's):

"Gun for Frank Wesson" [January 1875]
"Fine Pistol Nᵒ 3 with Gold inlaid $200.00" [July 1875]
"Roll cut for No. 1. Pistol verry smal" [June 1877]
"two Deis for Nᵒ 3 Pistol stocks" [September 1878]
"on a Pearl Stock monogram F.C." [August 1881]
"Dogs coller D.B. Wesson. . . ." [December 1882]

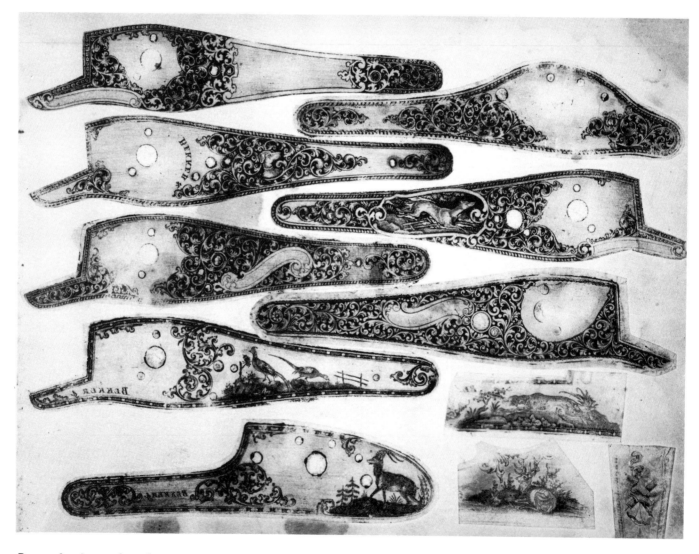

Page of prints taken from gun parts engraved by Gustave Young while still in Europe, c. 1840-45. Germanic scrolls like these were the origin of the dominant engraving style used in America since the mid 1850's. The original pattern book of Young contains several pages of prints similar to that illustrated, plus impressions from a variety of roll dies and stamps cut by Young for Colt's factory in the 1850's, 1860's, and 1870's. *(Johnie Bassett Collection)*

According to family tradition, Gustave Young, like many artist-engravers, was very temperamental, as when he is said to have told talkative D.B. Wesson of Smith & Wesson to "get out of my shop, you talk so much I can't work!" Certainly had Young not been so skilled an artisan, an individual of Daniel Wesson's status would not have permitted such a reprimand.

Other work during the 1869-1883 period include die cutting for the Sharps Rifle Company, Pratt & Whitney Company (Hartford), Parker Brothers (Meriden), Hartford Alarm Register Company, American Arms Company (Boston), and Hoopes & Townsend (Philadelphia). The great bulk of gun work was done for Smith & Wesson, though a few pieces were done for private clientele, and some are believed to have been done for the Colt factory. A large volume of jewelry engraving was also done during Young's years in Springfield, and a noteworthy amount of such work is known to have been done by him previously during the 1860's in Hartford. It is the author's opinion that following the death of Colonel Colt in January 1862, the demand by Colt's factory for lavishly engraved and inscribed arms was noticeably curtailed.

May 6, 1891 marked the 50th Anniversary of Gustave Young's career as an engraver and die cutter. On this occasion he was presented with a gold mounted cane, suitably inscribed, and was feted at a special dinner celebration. Still active, Young was assigned by Smith & Wesson to prepare special guns for the Chicago World's Fair, 1892-93. Illustrated in the gold inlay chapter is a masterpiece created for the S & W display. It is of interest to note that this gun is the only signed piece known to have been done by Gustave. Signatures on their more involved creations were common with certain nineteenth century engravers, such as L. D. Nimschke and John Ulrich, but for some unknown reason Gustave Young rarely marked his work. Old age did not affect Young until about 1894, and his penmanship at that time reveals a very unsteady hand. Probably he did very little engraving between then and his death, January 2, 1895.

Further information on Young appears in the gold inlay chapter and in some later chapters. Data on his sons will be found in the chapter on Cuno A. Helfricht.

Contemporary with Gustave Young's years in Hartford, 1852-69, a few other craftsmen known to have engraved for Colt have been identified. One of these was Thomas Barlow, listed in Hartford city directories from 1854-60, though he began working for Colt c. 1852. A letter in the Colt Collection of Firearms, Connecticut State Library, is the source of some background on Barlow; spelling and grammatical errors are in the original:

New York   May 19, 1852
Mr. Saml Colt
Dr Sir
Your letter Invoice & Two Cases pistols all came duly to hand am obliged by your promptness. in regard to Mr Barlow the Engraver we think he will Suit you both as to skill in his profession and as to Character. he seems to be a very respectable man tho' we have no means of ascertaining further about him. but think it would be worth you while to give him a trial
Yours Truly
Moore & Baker
Mr. Barlow has just finished his Engagement with Blunt & Syms where he has been for Two Years, & who wish to retain for a longer period. have seen specimens of his work. they are good.

Barlow was given a trial at the factory and was added to the engraving staff.

Another document in the Colt Collection of the Connecticut State Library reads as follows:

Gustav Young's Acc^t
14 Navy = N° 2
18 "   = N° 1
18 Small = N° 1
31 "   = N° 2

Augustus Groundweld [Grunwald] *Acc^t*
9 Navy
7 Small

Ending the 11th February 1854
Correct
R.L. P.
[Colt executive R.L. Peard]

The references to No. 1 and No. 2 are to degrees of coverage in engraving. The No. 1 would appear to have referred to less coverage than 2, but it is difficult to determine precisely, mainly due to the limited documentary material available on that aspect of percussion Colt engraving. The No. 2 coverage is pointed out by many examples in the illustrations of the present chapter.

The separate listing for Augustus Grunwald shows that he was also an engraving contractor to Colt at this period. He is listed in Hartford city directories c. 1856-60, but obviously began to serve Colt as early as February of 1854. Grunwald's output for the time span ending February 11 (presumably a month's work) was only 16 guns, while Young's shop turned out 81.

Another source in the Colt Collection of the Connecticut State Library identifies a Herman Bodenstein as an engraving contractor. The information appears in a notebook dated February 15, 1860, which lists contractors and their employees; beside each name is their "Assumed Price per day" and pencilled notations identify the individual's political inclinations. Colt's was a Democratic shop, and the management expected the employees to vote for Democrats!

Contractors & their men			Assumed Price per day	
Hermann Bodenstein (Contractor)				
	R[epublican]	*2.00*	*Engraver*	
Max Gerin	*D*[emocrat]	*1.80*	*Works for H. Bodenstein*	
Augustus Timme	*R*	*1.75*	*[Works for H. Bodenstein]*	
C.F. Ulrich	*dont vote*	*1.25*	*do*	*do*
Daniel Regan	*dont vote*	*1.00*	*do*	*do*

Bodenstein appears in Hartford city directories c. 1858-65, Gerin from 1859-60, and Timme (correct first name was Ernest) from 1860-62. Ulrich is Conrad F. Ulrich of the famous family better known as engravers for Winchester and Marlin.

Since Young's style was the norm for the Colt factory c. 1852 — c. 1865, it is correct to so identify the period even though for a few year's time, at least two other contractors were active. To further confuse the picture, a set of Colt ledger books in the John Hintlian collection identifies the following engravers who billed for work directly to the company; the amounts involved were small in every case except that of Gustave Young: W.B. Johnson, William Richardson, Ulrich, Henry C. Curtis, and Gustave Young.

Price lists published by Colt in the 1850's and 1860's offer some useful insight into the company's engraving operation. A list dated May 1, 1855 stated that engraved Navy pistols were priced at $6 above the cost of the standard, unembellished revolver. The price of engraved 4", 5" and 6" Model 1849 Pocket revolvers was $5 additional.

OLD PHOTOGRAPH OF EXCHANGE CORNER, HARTFORD, IN 1865

The Hartford shop of engraver Gustave Young. This rare photograph, reproduced in an early book on Hartford, shows Young's shop on State Street, 1865. A large sign over two second story windows bears the fancy lettering: G. YOUNG GUN ENGRAVER. NOTE: The word GUN is difficult to read, and the possibility exists that the word was GENL., an abbreviation for general. *(Connecticut Historical Society Collection)*

Young family portrait, c. 1890. At center, Gustave, with his wife Marie. From left, Alfred and his wife Julia, Oscar, and at right, Eugene and his wife Emma. The sturdy build of Gustave contributed to the excellence of his engraving. Great strength in the hands, arms, and shoulders is necessary for any engraver who cuts in steel particularly if they do much of it with hand gravers, instead of relying primarily on the hammer and chisel. *(Johnie Bassett Collection)*

A list published by A.W. Spies & Company, New York (one of the Colt allies), c. 1859, quotes prices for guns engraved and for guns engraved with ivory grips. The models so available were the 1849 Pocket (4", 5", and 6" barrels), the 1851 Navy, and the 1855 Sidehammer Pocket.

A Colt factory broadside of 1859 listed "Ornamental Engraving on Pocket Pistols extra. . . . $4" and the same for the Model 1851 Navy and Dragoon revolvers, at $5 extra. Ivory grips for the same models were quoted at $5 extra for the Pocket pistols and $6 extra for the Navy and Dragoon.

In 1860, Colt's price list for engraving and ivory grips was the same as that of 1859, but had the added item: "[Ornamental Engraving for] Attachable Carbine Breech, extra. . . . $3".

The 1865 and the 1867 Colt listings were the same in prices and available items as that of 1860, though the Model 1860 Army, the Model 1861 Navy, and the Model 1862 Pocket Navy (and presumably the Police) revolvers were included in the line of availability in engraving and ivory grips. Pricing remained unchanged.

Note that these listings did not quote prices for engraving on the Model 1855 Sidehammer long-arms; and judging from factory serial ledgers and surviving specimens, only a handful were engraved, most on special order. A few were engraved as display pieces or on speculation for possible sales.

There was no indication that more than one standard degree of coverage was available. Thus, it is assumed that the No. 2 style was the regular pattern and amount of engraving from the period c. 1852-53 through into the 1860's. Beginning in the early 1860's there were some basic changes in style and content, but the coverage remained about the same as in previous years. Apparently the No. 1 style noted in the document of February 11, 1854, was a short-lived experiment. Variations from the standard style quoted in the company's price listings would generally be special order guns.

Note also that to have ivory grips on a specific model cost more than buying the same model engraved. At the time the price of elephant ivory was about $1.75 to $2 per pound. As a matter of interest, the price of ivory c. 1970 was only $6 per pound!* Colt's major ivory source during the 1850's and 1860's was the firm of F. Grote, 78 Fulton Street, New York City; another known supplier was Rogers & Brothers, address unknown. The amounts of ivory used by Colt for pistol grips were substantial. In August of 1865, Grote sold the company $1552 worth, and a few months later, Colt bought another shipment in the amount of $2606.

*At this writing, ivory value has soared.

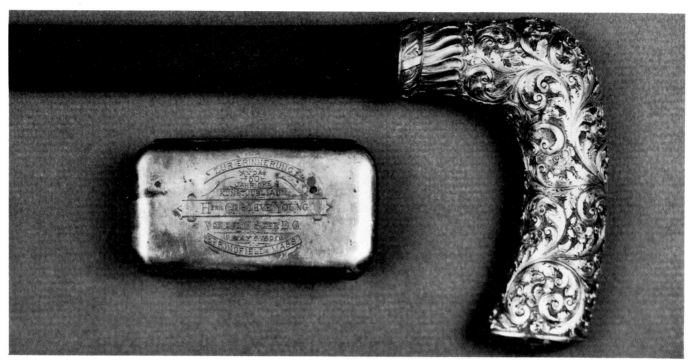

Gold mounted cane and sterling silver snuffbox, both inscribed and presented to Young on the 50th anniversary of his career as an artist-engraver, May 6, 1891. The other side of the cane is finely inscribed. Another present on the occasion was an original biographical poem, in German, hand-lettered, and decorated with painted scrolls and engraving scenes. *(Johnie Bassett Collection)*

A fascinating powder keg for the Colt collector, since the label is signed by Samuel Colt's friend and associate, W.L. Ormsby (close-up left), New York, and the manufacturer of the powder was another Colt friend, Colonel Hazard. *(John F. Besciak Collection)*

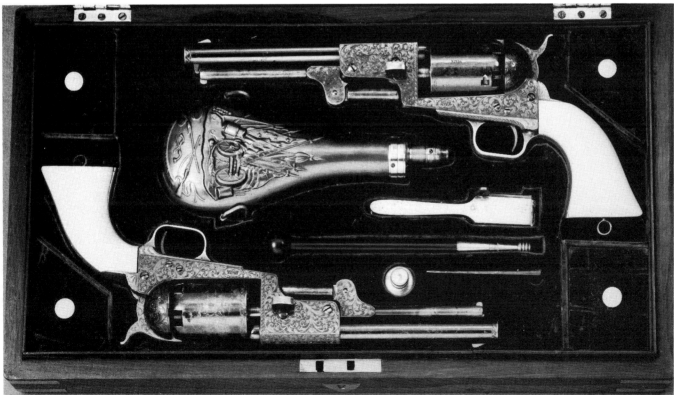

A cased pair of Third Model Dragoon revolvers, serial numbers 13128 and 13551. Though decorated in the Gustave Young style of scroll, significant variants from known patterns indicate that another craftsman was responsible for these arms; probably an engraver in Young's employ. The scroll border on the front of the cylinder, the eagle and the bird head motif are all rare details. c. 1853. Deluxe brassbound rosewood casing, lined in velvet. One of the finest Dragoon sets known. *(R. E. Hable Collection)*

Presented to E.K. Root by Col. Saml. Colt Prest. Colt's Pat. F.A. Mfg. Co. May 16th 1857, **is inscribed on the lid plaque of this finely decorated and cased Third Model Dragoon; serial number 16461. All engraving was done by Gustave Young himself, and the coverage is extremely fine and rich, nearly on a par with the ultra-refined scrollwork usually cut only on the gold inlaid percussion Colt revolvers. As a means of emphasizing the importance of the gun, an interior glass lid was provided, fitting flush with the upper level of the case proper. The rosewood case was lined in an elegant soft cloth, with engraved and silver plated brass mountings. Silver plated flask is of Navy type, but was with the revolver when discovered in the hands of Root descendants, c. 1961. See also Model 1851 Navy number 80108 (with shoulder stock) and Sidehammer rifle number 140, pictured in** *Samuel Colt Presents,* **pages 249-253.** *(Richard P. Mellon Collection)*

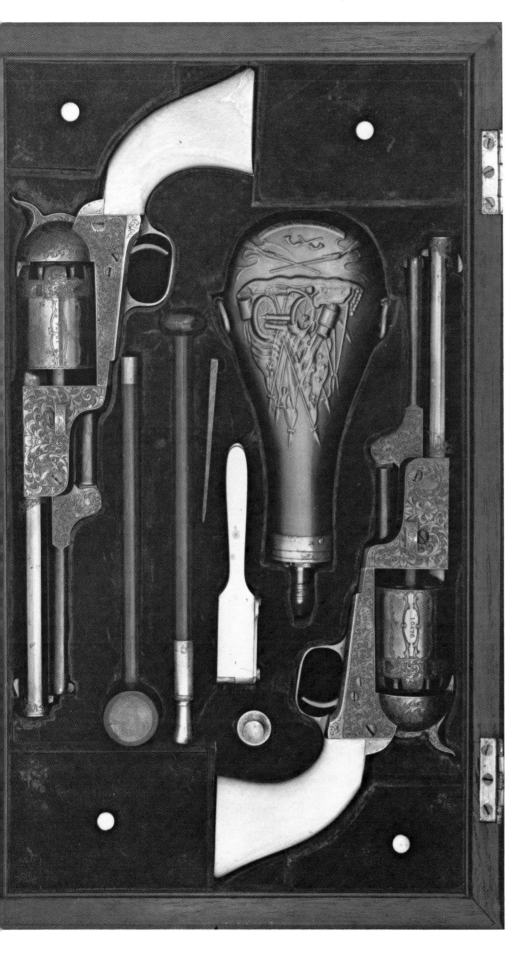

Deluxe pair of Third Model Dragoons engraved personally by Gustave Young; serial numbers 16474 and 16476. Coverage includes the rarity of scroll and border decor on the cylinder, and extra scrolls on the barrels. Dog heads are within the scrolls on the frames and barrel lugs; and an eagle head is on the right side of the barrel lug of revolver number 16476. The rosewood casing features brass-bound corners, green velvet-lining, and full accessories. Colt ledgers document these revolvers as follows: "O.M. Army Ivory Engd 16476 474 . . . P.H. Huntington April 30th 84". *(Jerry D. Berger Collection)*

SPECIAL FACTORY MARKINGS FOR ENGRAVED ARMS

As a means of indicating special handling, polish, and finish in the manufacturing process, Colt's employed a system of symbols during much of the Hartford percussion and early cartridge period of manufacture. The markings are categorized as follows.

THE DOT (·) The dot or center punch mark was in use c. 1849 to c. late 1861. During that period it was the standard means of denoting special finish and handling. Not every engraved piece from that period was so marked, but most were. Location: Beneath or above the number markings visible when looking at the bottom of a revolver — barrel lug, frame, triggerguard strap, and buttstrap. The dot will sometimes also be found on the cylinder.

A minutely sized "o" was a symbol similarly employed and located, but its use was brief, at the very early period of the dot.

THE APOSTROPHE (') In use at the same locations and for the same purposes as the dot; except that its period was c. 1854 to c. late 1861, and its presence denoted ivory grips *and* engraving.

Exceptions have been noted in the use of the dot and apostrophe: Some arms have been observed so marked after the end of 1861, primarily model 1851 Navy revolvers with high serial number ranges. The dot and apostrophe were Colt in-house symbols. Thus they are not expected to appear on guns by Nimschke or other non-factory craftsmen. Exceptions do occur however, since the special handling and polish would also be necessary for a piece ordered for outside engraving. Another factor: Due to a sudden push for plain arms for war sales, sometimes pieces bearing dot and apostrophe stampings were run through the production process without including engraving or special grips. Note: From c. 1851 engraved percussion Colt arms automatically included select walnut grips; less often used on these deluxe revolvers was ivory; *rare* was pearl, relief carved wood, rosewood, ebony, or metal.

The dot marking was dropped c. 1861 due to its use by U.S. Ordnance inspectors to indicate weapons which were rejected. The Ordnance Department represented a major client of Colt's at the time — the United States Government.

"E" Though first observed in use in mid 1861, the E stamping was standard from late 1861 into the early 1870's; it succeeded the dot as an indicator that engraving was to be used on a specific handgun, and was similarly marked as the dot (though sometimes next to the serial number, rather than above or below it).

"I" In use during the same period as the E, the I marking was similarly located, and denoted ivory grips.

"P" Contemporary with the E and I markings, the P is believed to indicate plating, although the possibility exists that P meant special polish. An extra fine polish was required for any type of extra-quality finish then in use by the factory. Plated finishes were usually full silver, silver and gold or nickel and gold combinations, full nickel, and full gold. All were scarce, and nickel and gold and full gold are extreme rarities.

Not every weapon marked E, I, and/or P will have present the features these abbreviations represent. By error the detail was at times omitted, and sudden needs for plain guns would usually override requirements for engraving, ivory, or special finishes.

Varying uses, and combinations, of the E, I, and P markings will be observed in caption material for many pieces in the 1861-1874 period.

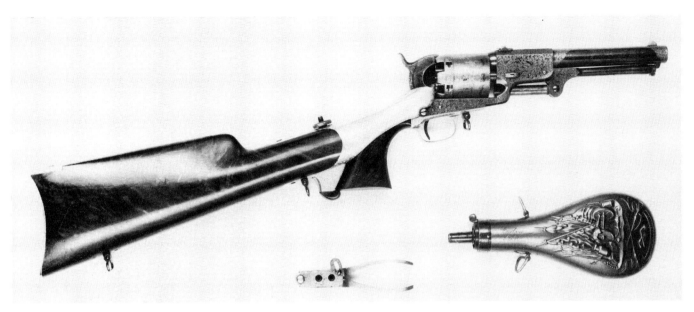

Consecutively numbered Third Model Dragoons presented by Colonel Colt to Czar Alexander II of Russia, and to two of his brothers, Grand Dukes Michael and Constantine. The guns are part of a set of fourteen presentation Colts of various models, given to the three brothers during a trip Colt made to Russia in 1858. Three Model 1851 Navies, six Model 1855 Sidehammer rifles, two Model 1855 Sidehammer revolvers, and possibly still other guns were presented on the occasion. All were inscribed, and most were deluxe engraved. See *The Book of Colt Firearms,* pages 570-571, for color illustrations of most of the Russian presentations, and for further textual data. (Above) Dragoon number 16480 is inscribed in script on the stock yoke: *To His Majesty Alexander 2d/Emperor of all the Russias./From the Inventor Col. Colt.* Mountings to the shoulder stock and the grips are gold plated *(rare)*. Engraving is nearly as profuse as that on the E.K. Root Dragoon, number 16461. Note the accompanying flask, the body of which is inscribed *Carbine/Pistol* so it would remain matched with the shoulder-stocked Dragoons. (Below) At top, the stocked Dragoon presented to the Grand Duke Constantine (number 16481). At bottom, the Dragoon given to Grand Duke Michael (number 16482). Both stock yokes are inscribed, in script, from Colonel Colt. Note the cheekpiece on Constantine's shoulder stock — a detail of the utmost rarity, probably unique. *(The State Hermitage Museum, Leningrad, U.S.S.R.)*

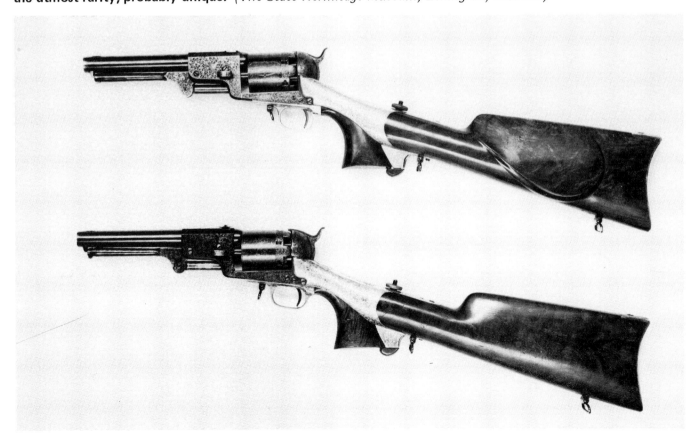

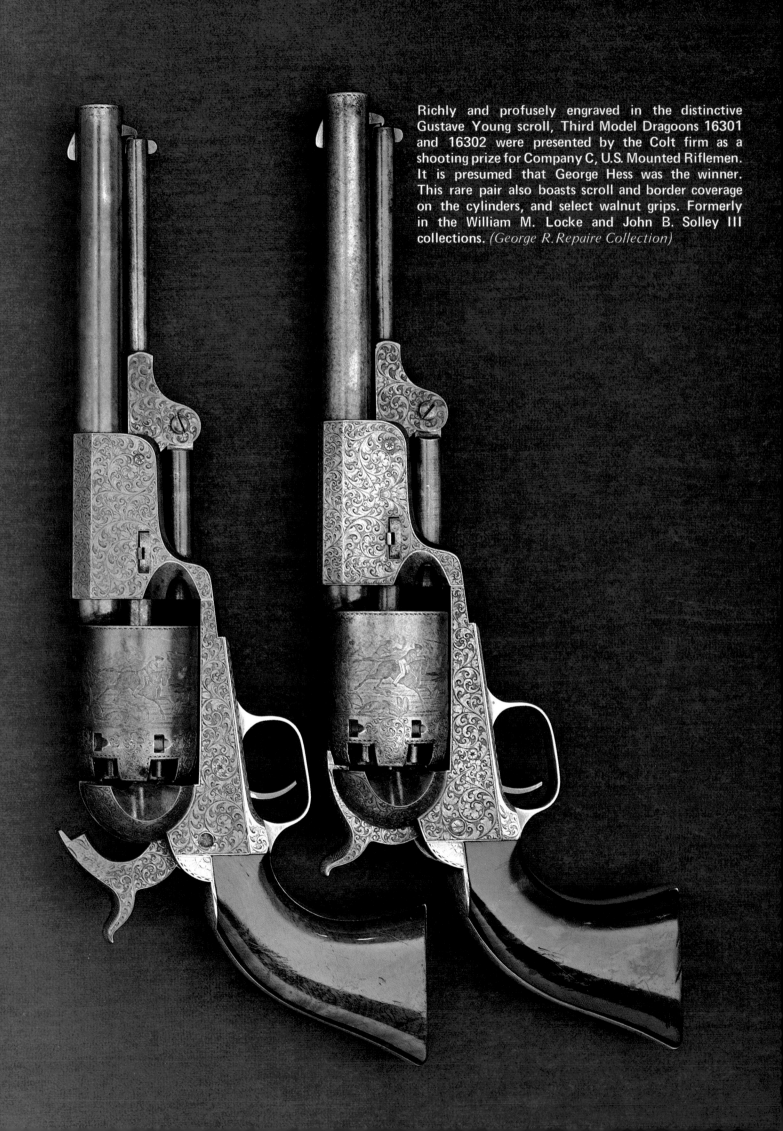

Richly and profusely engraved in the distinctive Gustave Young scroll, Third Model Dragoons 16301 and 16302 were presented by the Colt firm as a shooting prize for Company C, U.S. Mounted Riflemen. It is presumed that George Hess was the winner. This rare pair also boasts scroll and border coverage on the cylinders, and select walnut grips. Formerly in the William M. Locke and John B. Solley III collections. *(George R. Repaire Collection)*

Inscribed twice from Samuel Colt to the Marshfield (Massachusetts) Fair, Model 1849 Pocket number 91967/. was cased in a rosewood box, with full accessories. Among the desirable features of the outfit is the heavily silver plated finish on the handles of the brass bullet mold, the silver plated top and spout to the powder flask, and the highly polished finish to the wrench end of the screwdriver-nipple wrench. Presentations for fairs or expositions or institutions are extreme rarities in a category of Colts already ranked among the ultimate for desirability — presentation arms. *(Norm Flayderman Collection)*

Listed on the Gustave Young billing of September 23, 1854, 5" barrel Model 1849 number 97286/ˈ is an excellent example of the No. 2 pattern engraving. Blue and case hardened finish, with silver plated gripstraps. Dogs head device on the left recoil shield, and an eagle head on the left side of the barrel lug. *J. Wade* inscribed in script on the backstrap; on top of the barrel, the old English *Sam\ Colt*. Ivory grips, as denoted by the ˈ marking. *(Robert E. Bright Collection)*

Serial number 58879/. of the Model 1849 Pocket revolver. The scroll is from the shop of Gustave Young, though not done by the master himself. *(L. Allan Caperton Collection)*

Highly rare presentation percussion revolver from the Colt factory. The D.L. Stone Model 1849 Pocket bears serial number 109089, and was formerly in the Stagecoach Museum collection of Osborne Klavestad, Shakopee, Minnesota. Inscription in the style of Gustave Young, as is the engraved decoration of the revolver. Grips of relief carved helmeted soldier motif. Engraved decoration on the Stone Model 1849 virtually the same as on number 91459/., barrel length also 6". *(Stanley I. Kellert Collection)*

Extremely rare oval lid plaque, in sterling silver, inscribed in script. The casing of mahogany, lined in blue velvet; for a 4" Model 1849 Pocket revolver. *(William H. Myers Collection)*

Inscribed to *Captn Bragg/From the Inventor*, **Model 1849 Pocket** number 103938/. has a 4″ barrel, the Sam[1] Colt barrel address, select walnut grips, and is cased in a rosewood box, lined in burgundy velvet, trimmed in green. *(William H. Myers Collection)*

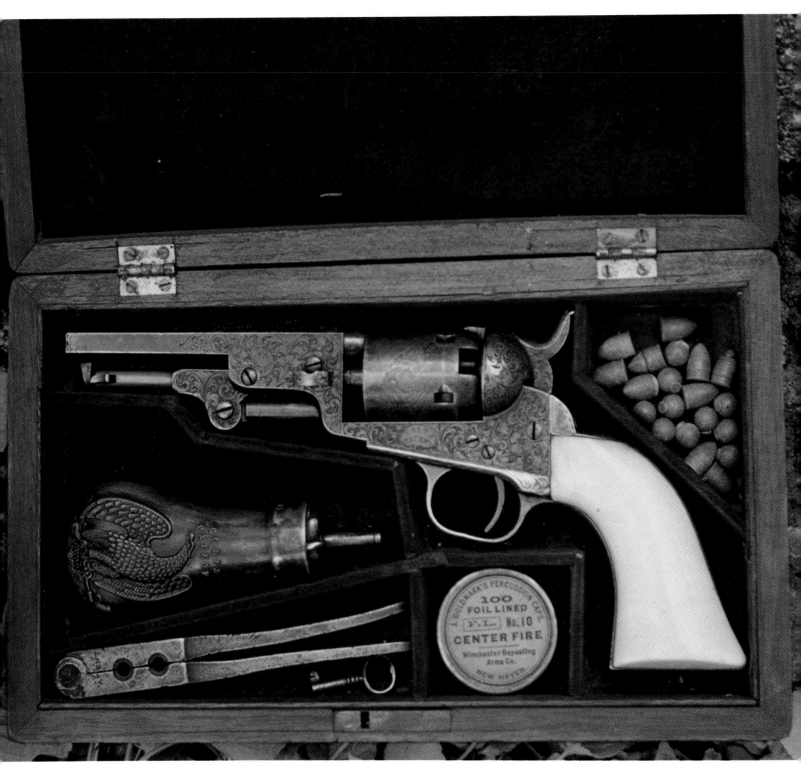

Engraved by the Gustave Young shop, and documented by Young's invoice of "4 Weeks ending the 23rd Septr 1854", serial number 97325/'1849 Pocket revolver appears under "4 inches [barrels]", of which 21 appear out of a total of 81 Pockets and 27 Navies. The actual invoice reproduced in Chapter III. Only a handful of specimens from the September 23 and June 3, 1854 invoices have been located. *(Howard Trivelpiece Collection)*

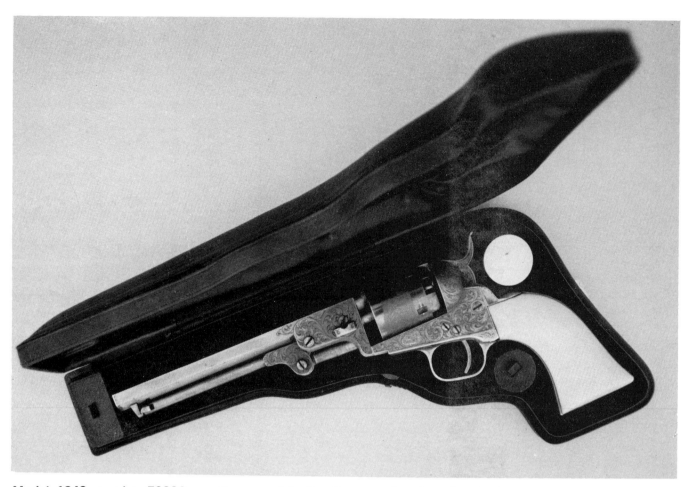

Model 1849, number 59826; scroll engraved in the Young style referred to in their records as "No. 2". The leather covered "pipe style" casing is lined in velvet and satin, with compartments for caps and cartridges. The box at upper right is ivory. Casings in this style for Colt revolvers are the utmost in rarity. *(Jerry D. Berger Collection)*

Rare extra-deluxe Model 1849 revolver; exhibiting a more profuse scroll treatment, with the considerable rarity of a checkered rammer lever. Added scroll present on the muzzle, and the frame and barrel lug scrolls are of a finer and more involved nature than the standard No. 2 style. Serial number 157295/. *(Dr. Chester P. Bonoff Collection)*

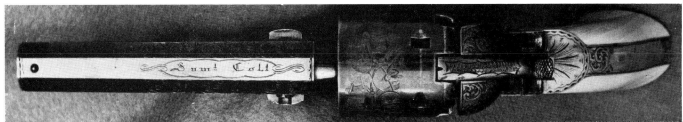

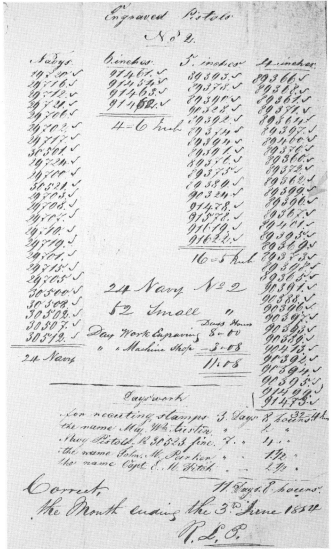

(Above and above right) **Photographs of Model 1849 number 97335 show clearly the rich scroll coverage developed by Gustave Young for these pocket revolvers. Unusual details are the leaf-like device above the loading lever screw on the left side of the barrel lug, and the central area of the right side of the barrel lug. The eagle head detail on the left side of the frame is also an extra touch not normally observed. The top view shows the** *Sam¹ Colt* **hand inscribed old English marking. 4" barrel; blue and case hardened finish; this pistol also cased, in a mahogany box, partitioned in the American style, and lined in burgundy velvet.** *(Hale E. Andrews Collection)*

Serial number 89396/. from the list of "Engraved Pistols/No 2." dated June 3, 1854. Only a few revolvers from the two lists published herein have thus far been located. *A.A. Armington* **inscribed on the backstrap. Sam¹ Colt, in Old English letters, on top of the barrel.** *(William H. Myers Collection)*

Work list covering a month's Colt engraving from the Young shop, ending June 3, 1854. Identified by serial number in style No. 2 are 24 Model 1851 Navy and 52 Model 1849 Pocket revolvers. Also recorded were die cutting, inscriptions, and Navy number 30523, which was probably inlaid with gold. *(Colt Collection of Firearms, Connecticut State Library)*

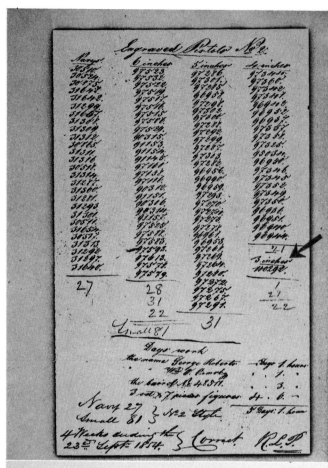

A second list of engraved Colt revolvers, done by the Young shop, delivered covering the month ending September 23, 1854. These also were in style No. 2. By totaling up the estimated number of work days involved in these two listings (48 days) and estimating the number of days (at 10 hours per day) required to do the total of work given in the lists, it is possible to estimate the work force Young had at his disposal. The figure comes to a staff of about 8, including Young himself. *(R. Q. Sutherland Collection)*

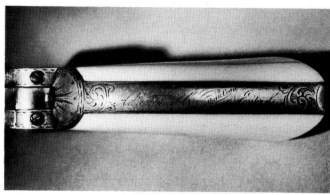

Rare factory inscription on the backstrap of Model 1849 revolver number 97281, also from Young's shop, and assumed to have appeared on a future serial number listing to the factory. *(James T. Brown D.V.M. Collection)*

A key to the identification of the Gustave Young style of scroll engraving. This Model 1849 revolver, "Wells Fargo" type, serial number 100292/1, is recorded on the Young billing to Colt, dated September 23, 1854. The engraving is of the "No 2 Style". Hammer is the wolf head type; the most common of the various animal motifs appearing on engraved Colt arms. Young and his workshop number among the many engravers who employed it. *(William H. Myers Collection)*

Model 1849 Pocket, serial 104007/., 6'' barrel; exhibiting the No. 2 pattern Gustave Young shop coverage. *(Jack H. Meyers photographs; John R. Woods Collection)*

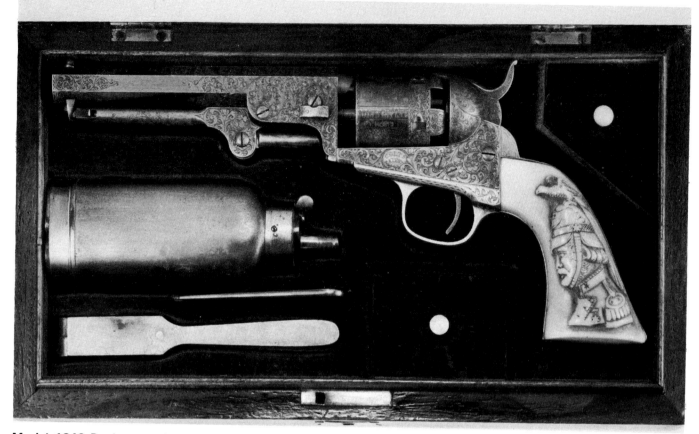

Model 1849 Pocket number 140372, with extra deluxe coverage on the barrel, loading lever, frame, and cylinder. Any hand engraving on Pocket Model cylinders is extremely *rare.* Among other specimens known with engraved scrollwork on the cylinders are number 67777/. (has scrolls in place of the customary roll engraved scene), and number 113858/. (similarly engraved overall to number 140372; and a presentation to Secretary of War John B. Floyd from the Workmen of Colt's Armory). *(Collection of the late Jack Dutton)*

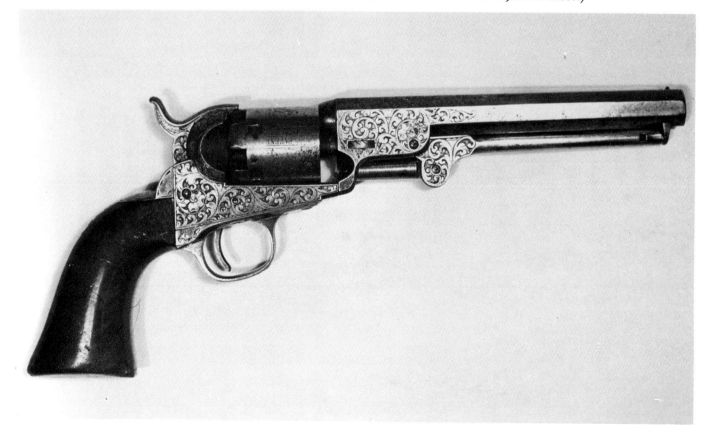

Model 1849 Pocket number 146664 is of the No. 2 style. 6" barrel; select walnut grips. *Saml Colt* barrel address, engraved in old English. The backstrap bears the inscription, "Howard Woodrow-Guthrie Regt." *(John G. Hamilton Collection)*

In the period c. 1860, the Young style usually took on a somewhat coarse look, generally lacking the overall finesse and exquisite style characteristic of the period c. 1852-59. There were some exceptions to this, as will be seen later in this chapter. A major feature bringing about this change was widening the basic line of the scroll, thus creating a thicker look. The small scrolls which curl off the main scroll are usually less in number — a detail also affecting the overall appearance. The customary scroll coverage on the loading lever lug is absent on this specimen; number 180716. Another noteworthy feature: Instead of the hand engraved Saml Colt barrel address, a roll marked address was present, identical to those on the standard Model 1849 revolvers without engraving. *(William H. Myers Collection)*

A presentation and so inscribed on the ivory grips, backstrap, and lid plaque, Model 1849 Pocket number 176150/', has *Saml Colt* in old English on the top of the barrel and is cased in a rosewood box, lined in maroon velvet (partitioning in the American style). The left side of the grip is inscribed *to/Samuel J. Hewitt*, the backstrap *Henry R. Benkard.*, and the right grip and lid plaque as illustrated. *(William H. Myers Collection)*

Comparison of Model 1851 Navy 79281 (top) with Model 1849 Pocket 180728/. The former dates from c. 1857, the latter from c. 1860. Both have select walnut grips. Scroll style obviously under the influence of the same master, Gustave Young. The Navy is also from a cased set (not pictured); the casing of mahogany, lined in burgundy velvet. On case bottom the inscription: "Was used by the bank for protective purposes for forty feats - + loaded for the length of time — but never used until 1912 and then shot for the first time. Property of Philip W. Braun given by the Peoples National Bank Lawrenceburg Indiana". *(William H. Myers Collection)*

Model 1849 number 180728/. features a more open style Young scroll than on 86092/. and 103938/., and the engraving on screws has been dropped. Instead of the *Saml Colt* barrel address hand engraved in old English, the address is roll marked: ADDRESS SAM^L COLT/HARTFORD CT. 4″ barrel; select walnut grips. Casing of mahogany, lined in maroon velvet. *(William H. Myers Collection)*

Backstrap detail from Model 1851 Navy number 19467, inscribed by the Inventor to Judge Wayne. Wayne served as mayor of Savannah, Georgia, and held other high political offices. Engraving pattern similar to revolver number 19471 (this chapter), and to revolver number 19474, pictures of which were supplied to the writer by Theodore M. Hutcheson. All three revolvers are among the earliest Navy Colts exhibiting the Gustave Young scroll style, and date c. 1852. *(Derek Palons Collection)*

(left) Barrel detail from Navy number 27054, showing the neatly cut scrolls and finely punched background characteristic of the Gustave Young shop. Revolver finished in blue and case hardening, with silver plated grip straps. *(Doris and David Knollhoff Collection)*

A target shooting prize, presented by Colonel Colt to the Hartford Light Guard. Documentation of this Model 1851 Navy, number 19471, appeared in the *Hartford Daily Courant* of September 15, 1852: *The Hartford Light Guard, Capt. Brace, appeared in full uniform today. In the morning they marched out, and fired at a target, which was 'bored' unmercifully. Three shots pierced the bull's eye, and the rest of the board looked like a cullender, so far as the holes are concerned. In neat appearance, few companies show to better advantage than the Hartford Light Guard. The first prize, a Colt's Revolver, was won by private B.R. Stone . . . .* Inscribed on the triggerguard strap, the date of the shooting match, *September 14th, 1853.* Private B. R. Stone was a machinist who resided in Hartford; he died in 1884, aged 51. Arms contributed by Colt as shooting prizes are rare and desirable collector's items. Only a handful were given during the percussion period, and four are pictured in the present study (the others a Model 1855 Sidehammer sporting rifle, serial number 493, Model 1855 Sidehammer revolver, number 4458, and a Dragoon, number 16302). *(George L. Taylor Collection)*

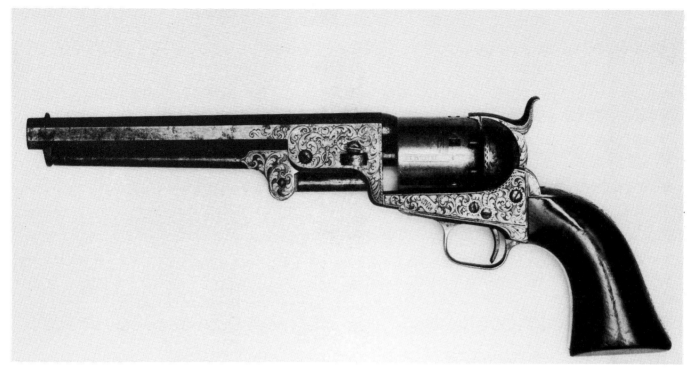

Model 1851 Navy; number 13726. One of the earliest examples of engraving by Gustave Young for the Colt factory. The style is in a transition from the large donut scrolls of c. 1850-51, and has yet to take on the distinct pattern most frequently employed by Gustave Young and his shop. The barrel lug scrolls approach the new Young pattern; whereas the frame decoration is partly the donut style, and partly the new pattern. Compare with guns number 37697/. and 37716/. which follow. *(Jack Cureton Collection)*

A quite fancy Young scroll on Navy number 23628/.; presentation inscribed on the backstrap, in script: *Col. Tho*S*. H. Seymour/From the Inventor.* The background is hatched, rather than the customary punched granular scroll ground. An early specimen of Young's scroll cut smaller and more intricately than what evolved as the "No. 2 Style". *(Colt Collection of Firearms, Connecticut State Library)*

Model 1851 Navy number 29705 appears on the Gustave Young billing of June 3, 1854, engraved in style No. 2. An important example for reference comparison, since the revolver conforms to the standards of quality, style, and coverage which the billing form documents. A dot appears on the barrel lug (above the number), frame, triggerguard, and buttstrap (below the number). Select walnut grips. Velvet lined casing of mahogany. *(Harry Sayre Collection)*

From Colonel Colt to E.M. Reed, Esq. Model **1851 Navy 40863/.** An excellent example of presentation Colt revolver, in the Colonel's own favorite model, the Navy. Compare with Navy **40847/.**, elsewhere, this chapter. *(Greg Martin Collection)*

From Colonel Colt to The Connecticut Historical Society; December 1855. Model 1851 Navy number 37697/., engraved in Young's No. 2 style. Presentation inscriptions (in script) are on the backstrap and the lid plaque (see upper right corner of picture). The complete factory casing is of rosewood, with a now faded maroon velvet lining. The consecutive serial number to this revolver (37698/.) belonged to General Robert E. Lee, and was used by him during the Civil War. Coverage identical on both revolvers; *viz.*, on the barrel, loading lever, frame, hammer, gripstraps, wedge, and screws. Varnished select walnut grips. *(The Connecticut Historical Society)*

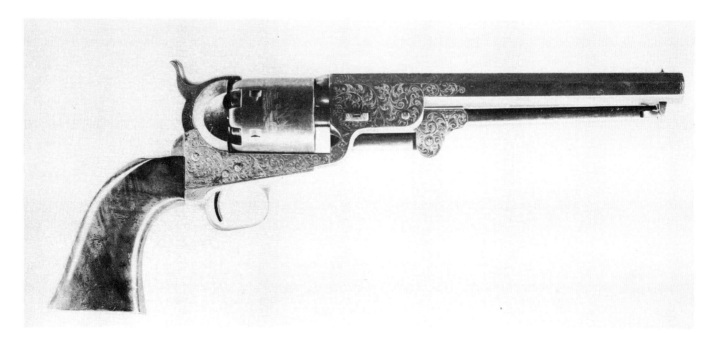

Col. J.W. Ripley/From the Inventor is inscribed in script on the backstrap of this Navy revolver; serial number **37716/.** At the time of presentation (c. 1854) Ripley was superintendent of the Springfield Armory. Note the close proximity with the serials of the Connecticut Historical Society and Robert E. Lee revolvers. *(Anonymous Collection)*

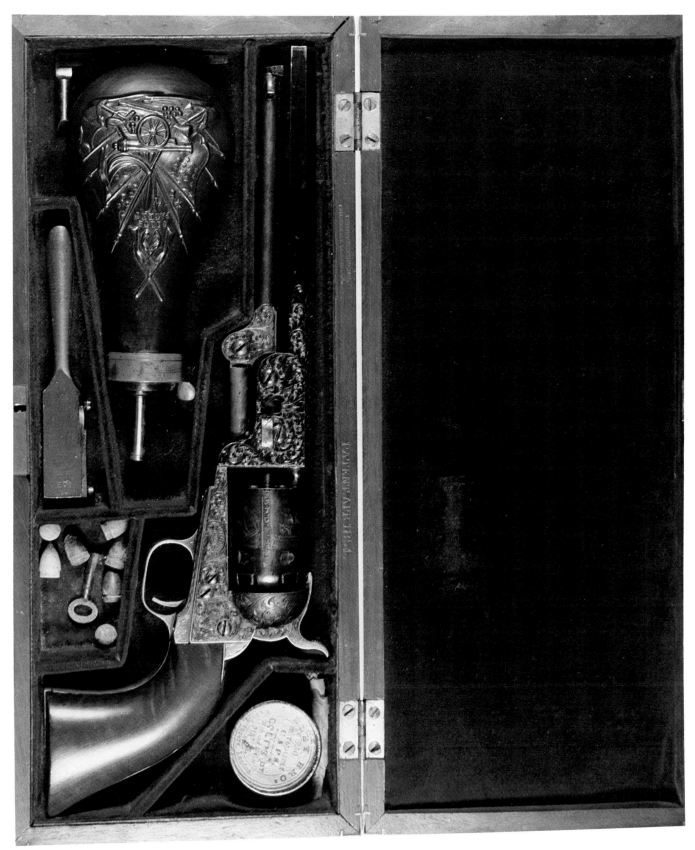

Small triggerguard Model 1851 Navy embellished by the Young shop, and cased in a Kidder box (note PATENT APR 1854. stamping). Serial number 58064. This revolver, in remarkable, unfired, condition, is plate XIX, item 62, in John E. Parsons' PERCUSSION COLT REVOLVERS book, published by The Metropolitan Museum of Art, 1942. Formerly in the Albert Foster Jr., John E. Parsons, and Dr. Chester P. Bonoff collections. *(Dr. Ronald Slovick Collection)*

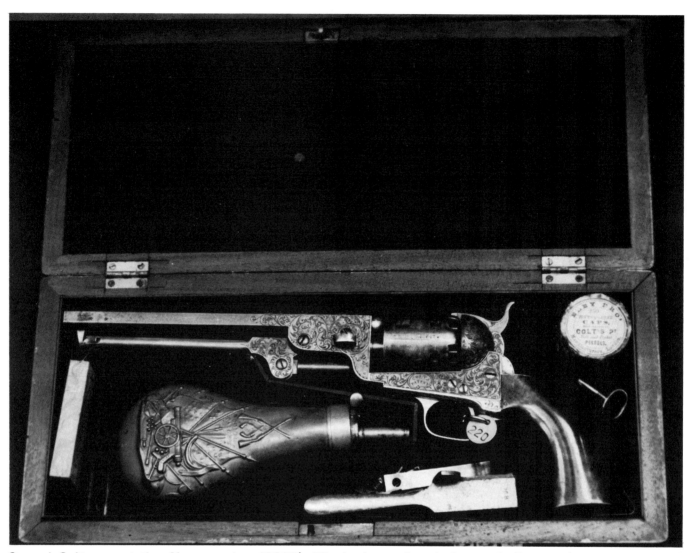

Samuel Colt presentation Navy number 40847/. The backstrap inscription reads (in script): *R.D. Hubbard/ From the Inventor.* Engraved in No. 2 style. Hubbard was a prominent political figure in Connecticut, and is known to have served Colt as an attorney. Select walnut grips; factory casing of mahogany. *(Glenn Gierhart Collection)*

Backstrap of the Model 1851 Navy (serial number 63838/.) from the set of arms presented by Colt's factory workmen to Secretary of War John B. Floyd. The script by Gustave Young himself. The gift consisted of a Dragoon with matching shoulder stock, a Model 1849 Pocket revolver, the Model 1851 Navy above, and a Sidehammer revolving rifle. Possibly more pieces were involved in the set than these five; records are sketchy. All items in the set were engraved and inscribed. Colt cleverly used his workmen as a front in making this quite important presentation. Subterfuge of this nature was unusual for the normally quite open and direct Colonel. Of historical interest, Young was one of the factory workmen who journeyed to Washington, D.C. for personal presentation of the set to Floyd. *(Dr. Robert J. Nelson Collection)*

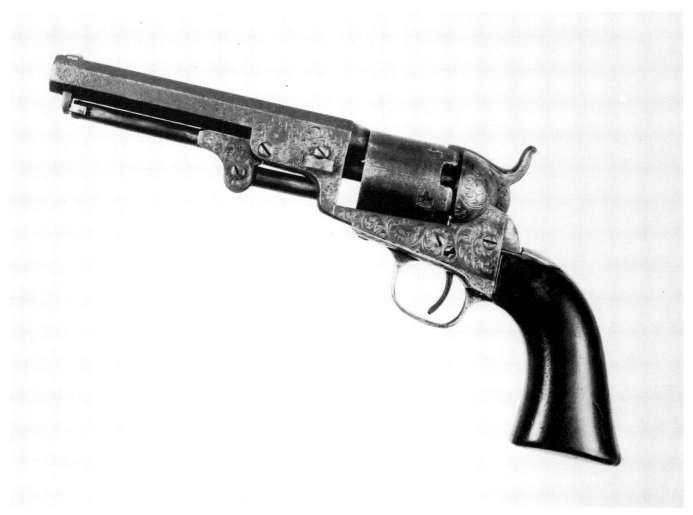

The Model 1849 Pocket revolver from the Colt Workmen presentation garniture of arms to John B. Floyd. Serial number 113858/. Saml Colt, in old English letters, was the hand engraved barrel marking. Scroll coverage includes the breech end of the cylinder, a detail rarely seen on the Model 1849 Pocket. *(Formerly in the John S. duMont Collection)*

Extra-deluxe shoulder-stocked Model 1851 Navy revolver, with its matching canteen stock; serial number 80108. Part of a presentation made by Samuel Colt to his factory superintendent Elisha King Root, May 16, 1857. The Board of Directors of Colt had elected to present Root, then resigning, "a complete set of all the different Kind of arms manufactured by the Company made and finished in the best style. . . as a special mark of regard from the members of the Board." Also known to have been given are a cased Third Model Dragoon (illustrated earlier in this chapter), a cased Model 1851 Navy, and a Sidehammer rifle. Now missing but considered to have been presented are a Sidehammer revolver and a Model 1849 Pocket revolver. The fancy glass fronted mahogany case held the Navy with stock and the rifle. The presentation legend on the front is in gilt letters and numerals. A maiden on the right side of the barrel lug and a leopard motif on the right side of the shoulder stock yoke were both copied from an engraver's pattern book published c. 1840 by G. Ernst of Zella, Germany. Colt's presentation inscriptions appear on the yoke of the revolver's shoulder stock and on the backstrap of the rifle. Engraving coverage includes the cylinders, and checkering on the Navy's loading lever. The Colt-E.K. Root presentations represent some of the most inspired work in Gustave Young's long and distinguished career. Other engraved and stocked Navies known, but done in less profuse coverage, include numbers 68203/. and 68217/. *(Colt Collection of Firearms, Connecticut State Library)*

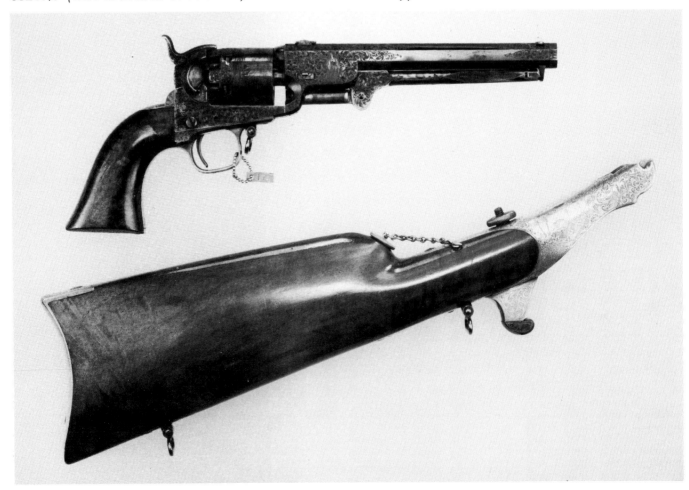

Formerly in the W.M. Locke collection, Navy number 92286 was accompanied by papers documenting its presentation to William H. Vanderbilt, from the Colt factory (papers have since been lost). Rare carved helmeted soldier grip motif in richly patinaed ivory. Gustave Young shop scroll engraving; casing of mahogany. Hartford barrel address. *(Dr. Jon Parker Collection)*

An elaborate presentation from Colonel Colt to H.A.G. Pomeroy; inscribed in script on the shoulder stock yoke, and on both backstraps. The Navy and stock bear serial number 69640; the Sidehammer revolver is number 4473. The scroll coverage on the Navy is greater in the amount than the standard No. 2 style, with scrolls and borders on the cylinder, scroll on the bottom of the loading lever, and extra-involved and profuse scrolls on the frame, gripstraps, barrel, and hammer. Several wolf head motifs are present, and one eagle head. Full presentation casing in brassbound rosewood, lined in maroon velvet. *(Johnie Bassett Collection)*

One of the three Model 1851 Navy revolvers presented by Colt as part of the multi-gun sets for Russian royalty, 1858. The Navies were serial numbers 70155 (Grand Duke Michael), 70156 (Grand Duke Constantine), and 70157 (Czar Alexander II). The Czar's revolver is illustrated. Backstraps of all three revolvers were fully inscribed in script from Colonel Colt. Number 70157 is inscribed: *To His Majesty Alexander 2d/Emperor of all the Russias./From the Inventor Col. Colt.* Gripstraps of the Czar's pistol were gold plated. Note scroll and border coverage on the cylinder; not present on the Navies of Michael and Constantine. *(State Hermitage Museum, Leningrad, U.S.S.R.)*

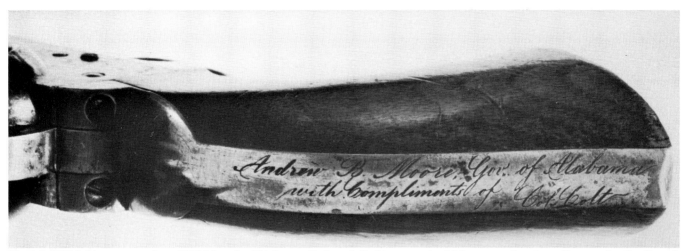

Model 1851 Navy; number 95844. A gift from Colonel Colt, as part of his campaign to sell arms in the South before the outbreak of the Civil War. The gift was made in December of 1860, and was sent via express through Colonel J. R. Powell. Powell had visited Colt's Hartford factory as Governor Moore's agent. The number of similar presentations made to Southerners in this period is unknown. Suffice to say, Colt's approach, in his own words, was: "Make hay while the sun shines". *(R. Q. Sutherland Collection)*

Detail of scroll engraving on the barrel lug of a Model 1851 Navy of post-1860. The Indian head motif is a rarity; the scroll is typical of the period. Punched dot background. *(S. P. Stevens Collection)*

The modified Gustave Young scroll style, as used on Model 1851 Navy number 132969/E. (c. 1863). Style No. 2 engraving. *(George R. Repaire Collection)*

Model 1851 Navy 93223 features a distinctive variant from the scroll pattern to be expected on the barrel lug of a Young engraved pistol of this model. Barrel address is the Hartford rollmark; grips of ivory; finish blue and case hardening, with silver plated gripstraps. *(John G. Hamilton Collection)*

Richly cased and stocked Navy; number 90140; made for sale in England. The scroll is style No. 2, and a cartouche was engraved at the top of the yoke, to allow for a special inscription. Note case decoration in embossed gold leaf; the case of brassbound mahogany, made in England. An identically engraved Navy, number 90137/., is also known; fitted in an English style oak casing. A rare triple casing of Navy stock and Model 1849 Pocket (all engraved) is pictured in *Samuel Colt Presents*, page 130; the Navy is number 94449/. the stock number 90138. Closeness of numbers (90137, 90138, and 90140) shows that the usual practice was to take groups of serials from production for engraving. Awareness of that fact is often helpful in assessing the engraved decoration on percussion and cartridge Colt firearms of the 19th century. *(Johnie Bassett Collection)*

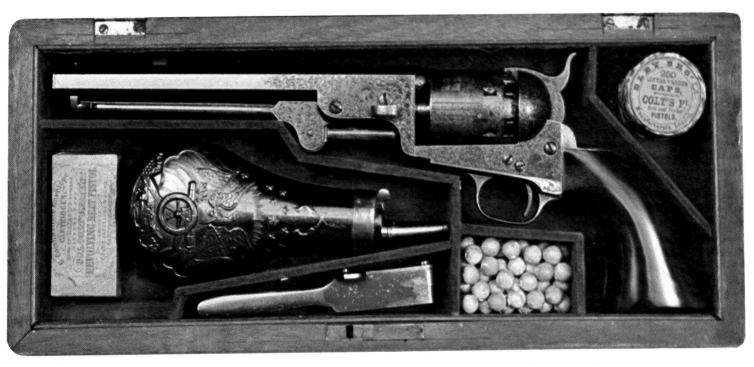

Number 30520 Model 1851 Navy was engraved personally by Gustave Young. A paddle wheel steamer motif on the right side of the barrel lug is believed unique. Imaginative animal motifs on the left side of the recoil shield, frame, and barrel lug have also been observed gold inlaid on some percussion Colt revolvers by Young. The serial number is in the same sequence as the Navies in No. 2 style from the Young lists of June 3, and September 23, 1854. However, coverage on revolver 30520 is of the "fine" grade of work, and would be in the same decorative category as revolver 30523 near the bottom of the June 3 listing. The notation "fine" indicated coverage and detail beyond the standard No. 2 type. Note presence of scrolls on the cylinder and on the breech end of the barrel (bolster adjacent to the cylinder). Also rare is the presence of engraving on the major screws. An important and rare Young-engraved Colt revolver. *(George S. Lewis, Jr. Collection/ Photograph, Dale V. Monaghen)*

Charter Oak gripped Model 1855 Sidehammer, number 4458, presented by the Colt factory to Charles E. Billings, as third prize in the shooting competition of June 17, 1858, of the Colt Armory Guards (see *The Book of Colt Firearms*, page 565). Mahogany case, velvet lined. From the estate of Billings, a Colt factory employee, who was an inventor in his own right. Patent 82279, September 22nd 1868, was granted to C.E. Billings for an "improvement in combined pistol and sword". A specimen of the knife-pistol came to the present owner from the Billings family, along with Sidehammer number 4458, and Model 1862 Police number 8633. The latter revolver was factory cased, has a 4-1/2" barrel, and bears the backstrap inscription: *C.E. Billings/From fellow workmen in Colts Armory*. Photograph shows the backstrap detail; revolver itself does not bear scroll engraving. For a photograph of Billings, in the uniform of a Colt bandsman, see page **74** of *The Colt Heritage*. *(Norm Flayderman Collection)*

Two early Sidehammer revolvers, numbers 5886 (bottom) and 5887, part of a group of presentations made by Colonel Colt to his allies in 1856. The engraved style and coverage was characteristic for the Sidehammer pistols with octagon barrels. Unusual features are the grips of Charter Oak and the backstrap inscriptions; all of the presentation group were cased. The inset shows the backstrap from pistol number 5886. Complete details appear in the article "The Charter Oak Colts", by Arnold M. Chernoff, in the *Antique Arms Annual,* 1971, pages 201-205. A series of engraved Sidehammer revolvers appears in *Samuel Colt Presents,* pages 145-159. Additions to that group are pictured in the pages which follow. A recently discovered specimen not illustrated is number 8496; cased, engraved, and inscribed on the backstrap, in script: *Dr E.C. Robinson/From the Inventor/ Col. Colt.* The pistol is in the collection of R.S. Dodson. *(Number 5886: Richard P. Mellon Collection/ Number 5887: Fred Sweeney Collection)*

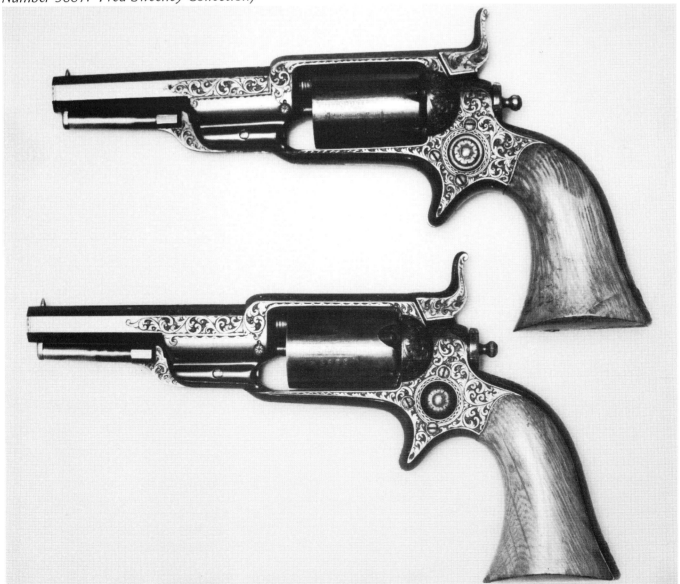

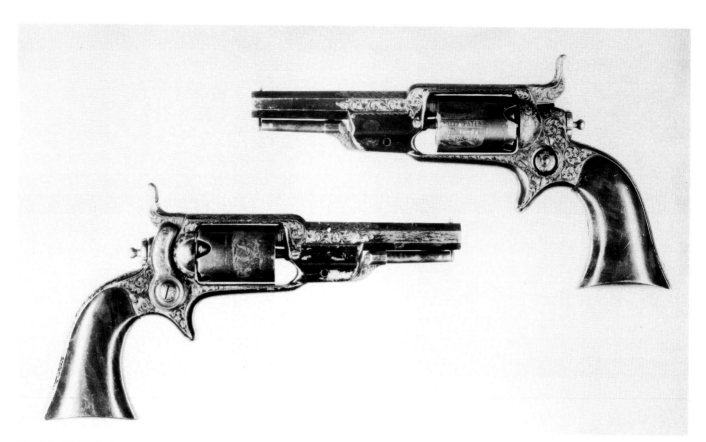

Model 1855 Sidehammer revolvers numbers 10234 (top) and 9126. Two more pieces from the group presentation by Colt to Czar Alexander and his brothers Michael and Constantine. Number 10234 was given to Michael; Number 9126 to Constantine. Both guns were inscribed in script on the backstrap; e.g., *To His Imperial Highness/The Grand Duke Constantine/From the Inventor Col. Colt.* The Sidehammer revolver of Czar Alexander II has not as yet been located. Engraving of the standard Young scroll of the period; probably the Sidehammer version of the style known in Young's shop as "No. 2". *(State Hermitage Museum, Leningrad, U.S.S.R.)*

Deluxe Sidehammer revolver; number 14330 (c. 1856); the grips of Charter Oak. Coverage beyond the standard style (see numbers 5886 and 5887), as seen in the checkered rammer lever, the scroll and border coverage on the cylinder, and the added scrolls on the muzzle and on the gripstrap. Sidehammer pistol number 499 (octagon barrel; see *Samuel Colt Presents,* pages 146-147) has the possibly unique treatment of a portrait bust and coat of arms motif plus profuse scroll and border work on the cylinder; its overall scroll treatment is more deluxe and profuse than the standard, and its backstrap is inscribed to a publisher and politician (W.J. Hamersley) from the Inventor. The extra-fancy revolver in the Sidehammer series is a rarity (i.e., with coverage above the grade of No. 2 Style); others known include numbers 14705 and 21056. *(Dr. Chester P. Bonoff Collection)*

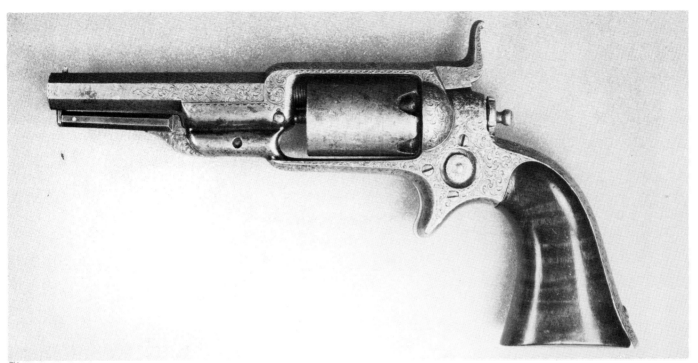

Model 1855 Sidehammer revolver, number 306. Backstrap inscribed *C.F. Pond/From/Col. Colt.* Pond was president of the Hartford and New Haven Railroad Co. Scarce early variation (note full octagonal loading lever) with profuse scroll coverage. Not illustrated is Model 1855 number 2462, inscribed on the backstrap: *Willis Thrall Esquire/from Col. Colt.* Thrall was a prominent Hartford businessman and hardware merchant, known to have had business connections with Samuel Colt and the Colt's Pt. F.A. Mfg. Co. The Thrall revolver is engraved, cased, and has select walnut grips. Both Pond and Thrall revolvers exhibit the fine Gustave Young scroll, and judging from their script backstrap inscriptions, could well have been inscribed by Young's own hand. *(Norm Flayderman Collection; Thrall Revolver from a Private Collection)*

An important presentation from Colonel Colt; Sidehammer pistol number 21866 (c. 1859). Major George D. Ramsay was a high ranking officer in the U.S. Army, and during the Civil War was Chief of Ordnance. His pistol is cased in a standard factory style mahogany box, with accessories. The lining (American style of partitioning) is of green velvet. *(Collection of the late Harry C. Knode)*

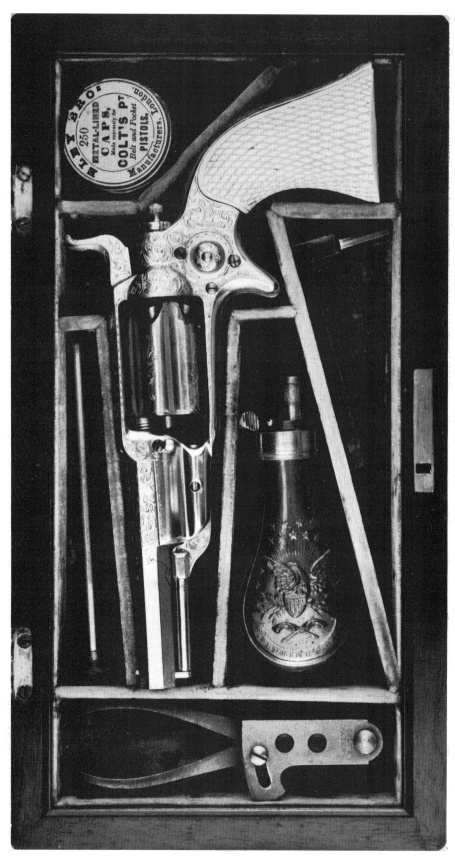

To the Reverend D.W. Cahill from employees of Colt's factory, June 1, 1861. Sidehammer revolver number 25318. Among the features of this set which are seldom observed are: Two inscriptions (one on the backstrap and the other on the case lid escutcheon; both in script), gold and nickel plating, checkered ivory grips, and the scarce casing of rosewood (the lid opening to the vertical position). Presentations to a man of the cloth are of the utmost rarity in Colt firearms, whatever the period. *(Chris deGuigne and Greg Martin Collection)*

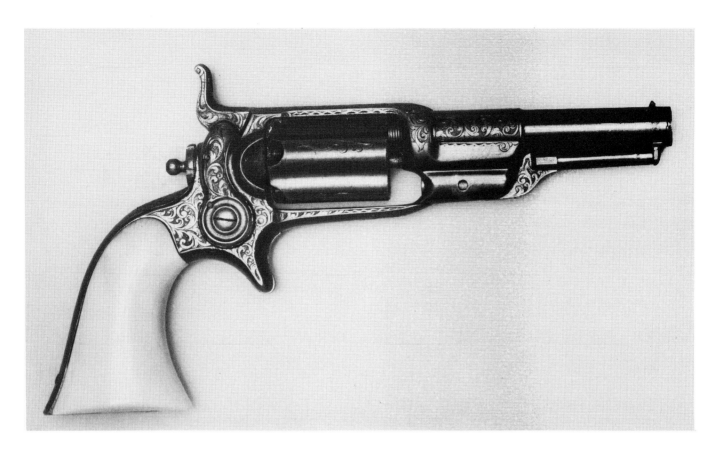

To the Metropolitan Fair, New York, from the Colt company; the backstrap bears the presentation inscription (in script). Serial number 7891; c. 1864. Standard scroll as usually found on the engraved round barrel Side-hammer pistols; the fluted cylinder with small cuts over the chambers. French style casing; rare in the Side-hammer series. *(Dr. Chester P. Bonoff Collection)*

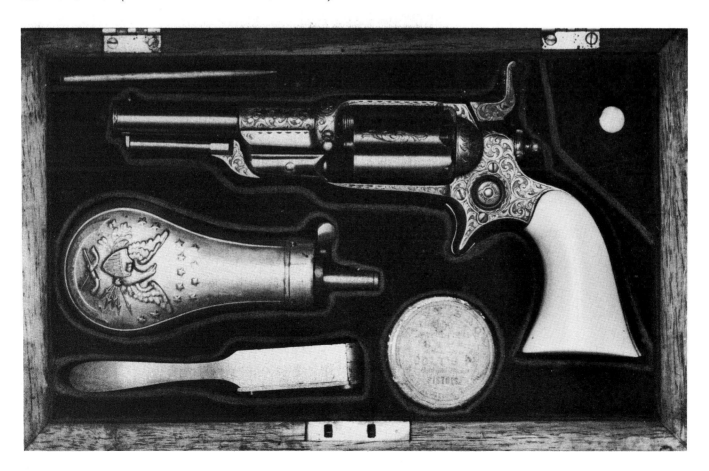

Overall view, Sidehammer long arm serial number 29.

Presentation Model 1855 Sidehammer, serial 7466P, the backstrap inscribed: *H.B. Hayes/with compliments of Col. Hazard.* Revolver documented in the Colt ledgers as in inventory, engraved, May 5th 1863, the records further noting its barrel length as 3-1/2″ and the caliber as .31. Blue, with case hardened lever and hammer. Scarce engraved in this type Model 1855, having fluted cylinder. Colonel Hazard was supplier of powder to the Colt firm for many years, and a personal friend of Samuel Colt. H.B. Hayes also received a book cased and inscribed Model 1862 Police from Hazard, pictured elsewhere in the present book. *(Private Collection)*

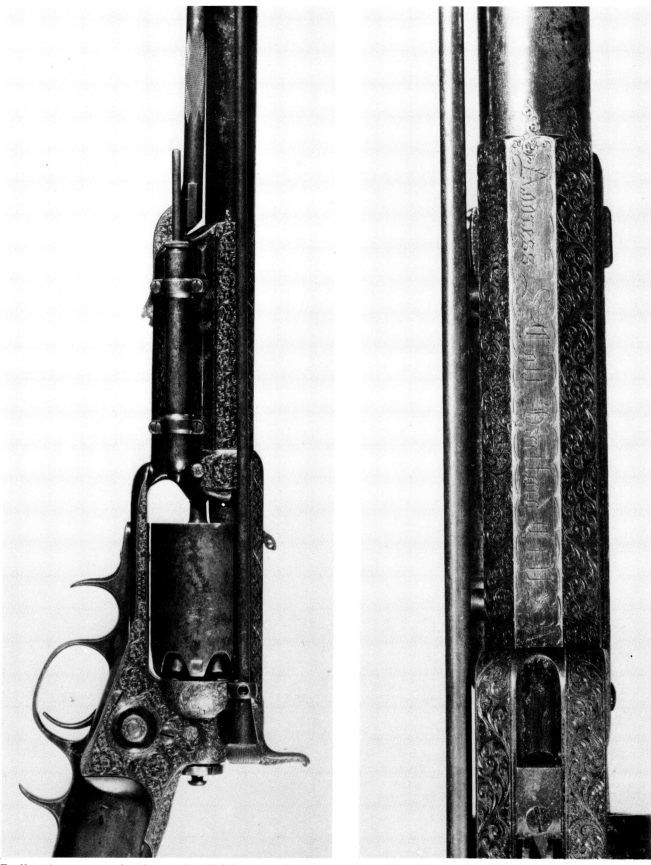

Earliest known production series Sidehammer longarm engraved, serial number 29, of the First Model Sporting Rifle. Profusely embellished by Gustave Young. 21" barrel, blue and case hardened finish. Note rare COLTS/ PATENT inscription on left side of the frame. Top of barrel inscribed in old English; note rare checkered rammer lever; checkered buttstock of select walnut. Apparantly this arm was intended as a display piece. It eventually found its way to India, and came out of the private armory of the Nizam of Hyderabad. David Winks of Holland & Holland, London, spotted the rarity and desirability of this rifle, and brought it to the attention of the author. *(Photographs courtesy of Holland & Holland, Ltd., London)*

Half Stock Sporting rifle; number 493. Exquisite and profuse scroll engraving by Gustave Young. Inscribed on the barrel (in script except as noted):

Presented by Colts Armory Guard
To George Best. [old English letters]
who at the Target Shoot at Middletown June 16
1858 won the First Prize which by mistake of the
Judges was unjustly awarded
Hartford. Aug. 7. 1858.

The buttstock of varnished select walnut; the forend of varnished rosewood. One of the finest and most desirable Colt longarms known to collectors. Engraved Sidehammer longarms are extremely rare; only a handful are known to have been produced. See also *Samuel Colt Presents,* pages 228-231 for additional specimens. *(Colt Collection of Firearms, Connecticut State Library)*

An elaborate presentation from Colt's workmen to Secretary of War John B. Floyd. Serial number 1935. As with the Best rifle, the inscription was placed on the barrel, and shows the unmistakable skill of Gustave Young himself. Varnished select walnut buttstock; varnished walnut forend. Dragoon shoulder stock number 16467, Model 1849 Pocket 113858/., and Model 1851 Navy 63838/., also given to Floyd, are pictured elsewhere in this chapter. *(John J. Malloy Collection)*

Three of the six Model 1855 Sidehammer rifles presented by Colt to Russian royalty in 1858. (Above) Serial number 9 of the Military full stock rifle was profusely engraved in an extremely fine scroll; the tang inscription reads (in script): *To His Majesty Alexander 2ᵈ,/Emperor of all the Russias./From the Inventor Col. Colt.* **Note** the rare triggerguard attachment, presumed as a preventive measure to avoid hand burns when shooting. (Below) At top, serial number 442 Military full stock rifle; presentation engraved and inscribed (on the tang), to Czar Alexander II. At bottom, serial number 443; identically engraved; the tang inscription to the Grand Duke Constantine. Note the rare plunger style flasks, each inscribed *44 Cal. Rifle/or Carbine.* Also known to have been presented in longarms were serial number 39 of the 1st Model Sporting rifle, and serial numbers 10 and 11 of the full stock Military rifle. An inscription is not present on number 39; number 10 was inscribed on the tang to Grand Duke Michael, and number 11 to Grand Duke Constantine. None of the three was scroll engraved. *(State Hermitage Museum, Leningrad, U.S.S.R.)*

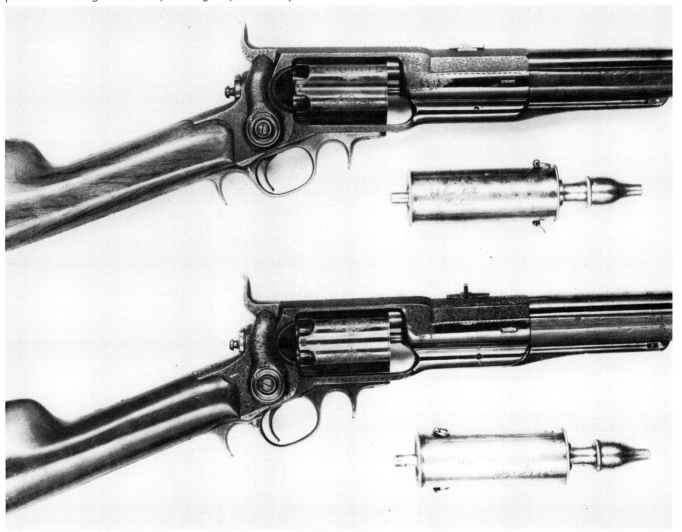

One of the very ultimate rarities in the collecting of Colt firearms — a triple casing, engraved, and presentation inscribed from Samuel Colt. The recipient, Hugh Rose, was not only a personal friend of the Colonel, but a witness to Colt's will. For documentation and further information see *Samuel Colt Presents*, page 121. A letter from Samuel Colt to a key aid, Milton Joslin, in the Connecticut Historical Society Colt collection, documents the specific inscription on the Navy revolver. Casing of rosewood, lined in velvet; case lid inscribed in script. Inscriptions by Gustave Young. The only other known triple set at this writing is pictured page 52, *The Colt Heritage*, and was presented at the same time to Lt. Silas Bent, also a personal friend of Colonel Colt. *(Buddy Hackett Collection)*

Opposite:Colonel Colt to General Irvin McDowell. The Model 1860 Army revolvers are serial numbers 11706/. and 11707/. The Model 1861 Navy is number 1810/.; the Model 1862 Police number 6495/. Backstraps inscribed in script: *Genl Irvin McDowell/with Compliments of Col. Colt. (Jerry D. Berger Collection)* NOTE: Approximately 60 Colt revolvers were presented by Colonel Colt on or about November 1, 1861. The sets appear to have been the same makeup as McDowell's presentation, all suitably inscribed on the backstraps, and elaborately cased. Known recipients include Generals J.K.F. Mansfield, R.B. Marcy, T.W. Sherman, Andrew Porter, Irvin McDowell, George B. McClellan, N.P. Banks, and J.W. Ripley. Government officials Simon Cameron and E.S. Sanford also received presentation arms from the series. For further details, see *Samuel Colt Presents*, pages 176-185, and *The American Rifleman*, July 1969, pages 26-28. Serial ranges of known specimens are: Model 1860 Army — 11672. to 11719/.; Model 1861 Navy — 1803/. to 1825/.; Model 1862 Police — 6494/. to 6511/.

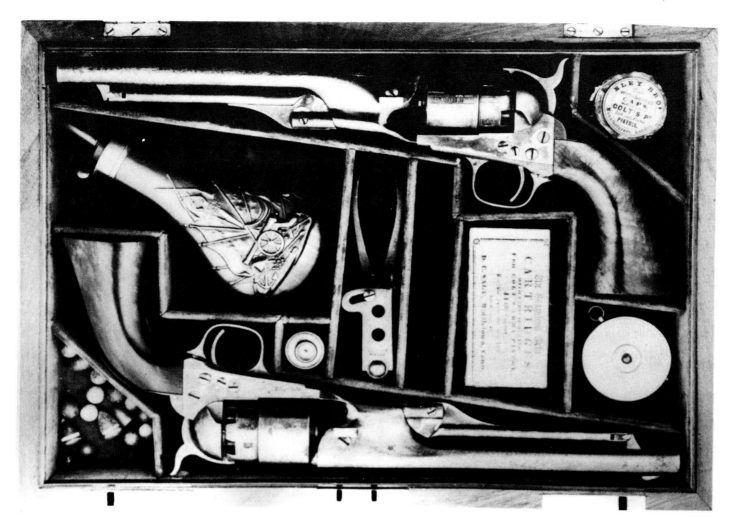

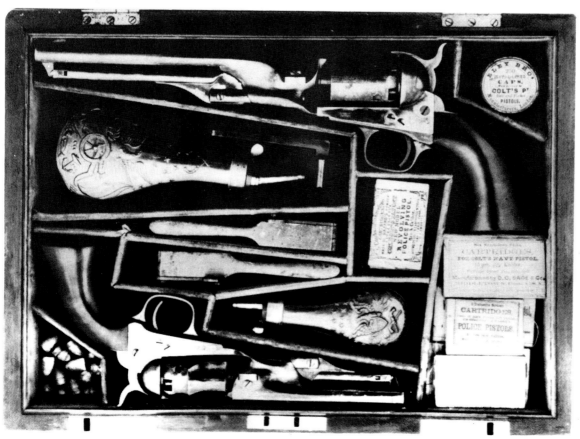

Cased pair of Model 1860 Army revolvers, inscribed in script on the backstraps *Maj Genl. B.F. Butler/with Compliments of Col. Colt.* These pistols were part of Samuel Colt's ambitious November 1st 1861 presentation group, detailed on pages 101-102. *(United States National Museum, Smithsonian Institution)*

First Model Revolving Sidehammer Rifle presented by Colonel Colt to his friend and booster General William S. Harney, U.S.A. The upper tang inscribed by Gustave Young or a member of his shop in the distinctive script employed in the Young period. *(United States National Museum, Smithsonian Institution)*

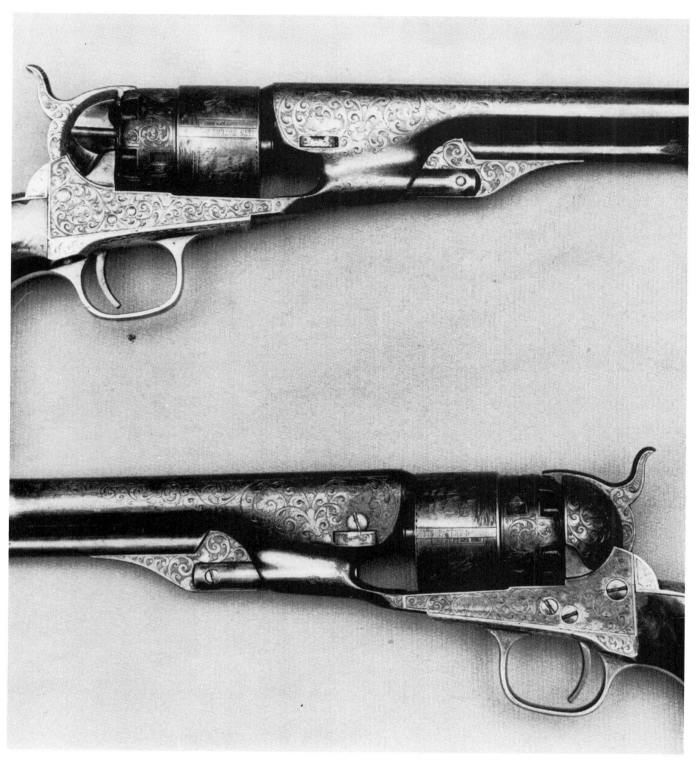

The backstraps of these extra-deluxe Model 1860 Army revolvers are inscribed: *Col. L.B. Parsons/From his brother P. Parsons.* Serial numbers 76608 and 76609. Extra-fancy Gustave Young scroll coverage on the barrels, cylinders (including hand engraved scenes), frames, loading levers, and gripstraps. Animal and bird head motifs are within the scrolls on the frames and barrels. Note the checkered rammer levers, and the rich select walnut grips. Top and charger of the flask are silver plated; a rare detail. Spare parts present, along with full accessories for the set. The casing of brassbound rosewood, lined in velvet. Parsons was a prominent businessman and an officer in the Union Army during the Civil War. He was active in the founding of Parsons College, Fairfield, Iowa. Revolvers listed in a Colt inventory of November 13, 1862. The entry documents they were in stock at that time, as an engraved pair. *(George S. Lewis, Jr. Collection)*

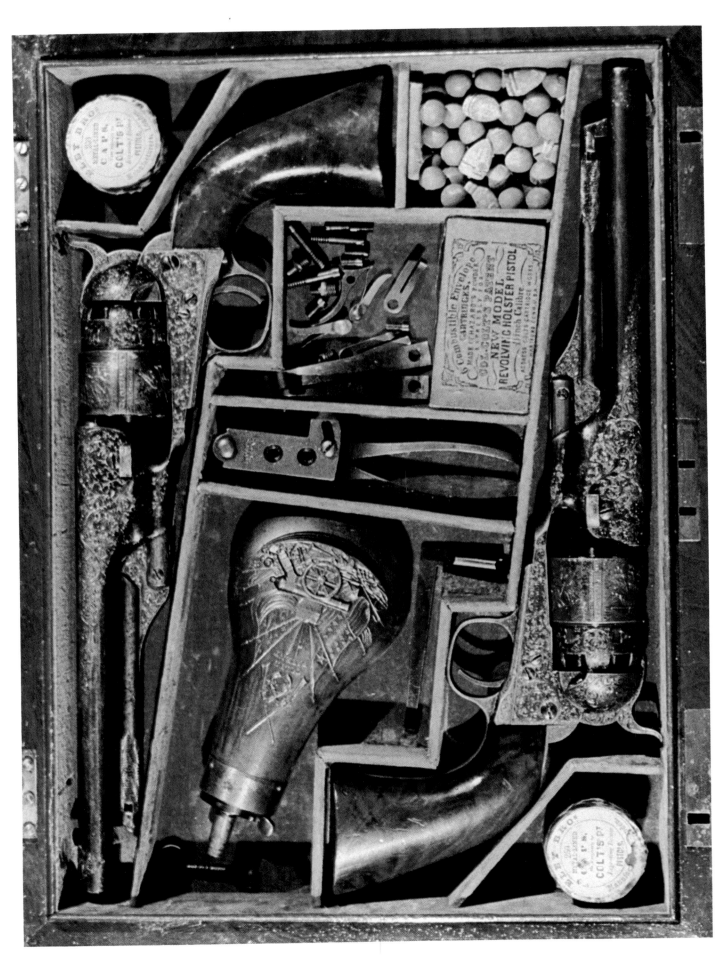

The Colonel L. B. Parsons presentation Model 1860 Army revolvers, 76608 and 76609, in their deluxe case with full accessories. *(George S. Lewis, Jr. Collection/Photograph, Dale V. Monaghen)*

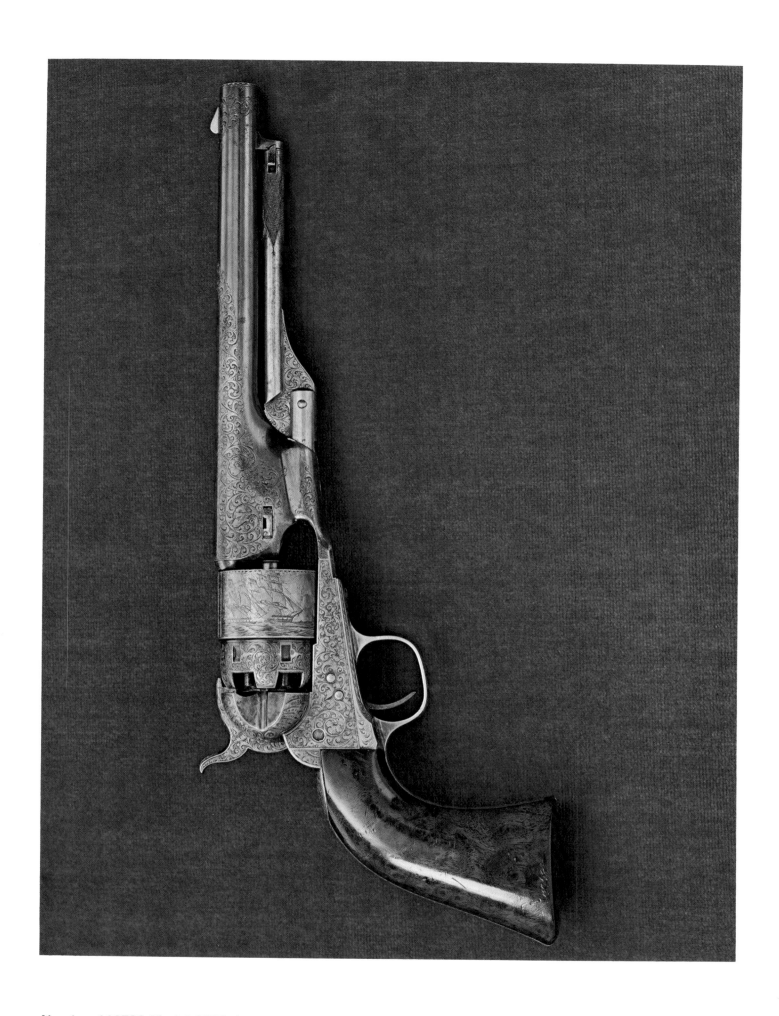

Number 111592 Model 1860 Army, presented to Major General W. S. Rosecrans by Colt's firearms company.
(George S. Repaire Collection)

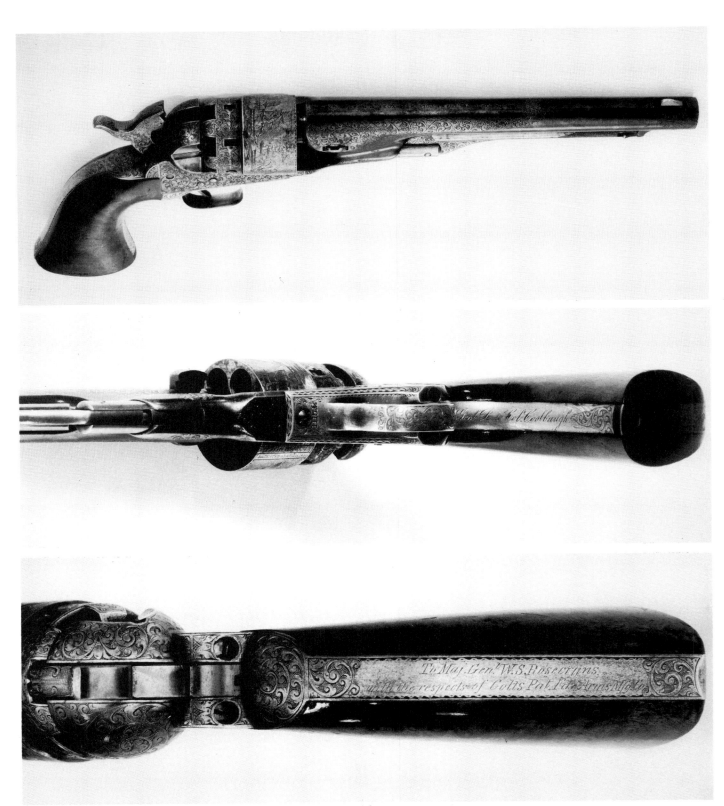

After Colt's death the company continued to make presentations, some quite lavish, but comparatively limited in number. Model 1860 Army number 111592 was inscribed on the backstrap from the factory to General W.S. Rosecrans. The engraving is in a profuse style bearing several similarities to the Baker Army number 7569 and to the Parsons pair, numbers 76608 and 76609. Details show the hand engraved cylinder scene and the scroll and border trim, the wolf head hammer, the cross-hatched and scroll engraved loading lever, and the backstrap inscription (in italics). Similarly engraved Army pistols numbers 100359/E and 100362/E were presented by Colt to General George B. McClellan, in a double case. It is probable that the Rosecrans presentation was also a matched pair, cased. Number 111592 was later presented by the General to a Colonel Coolbaugh, and is so inscribed on the triggerguard strap. *(George R. Repaire Collection)*

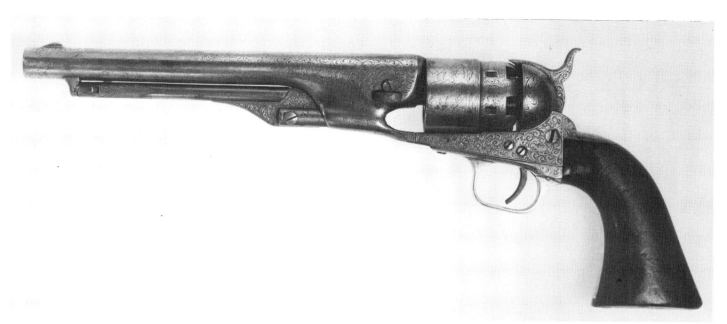

Model 1860 Army 111594 is the mate to the Rosecrans Army pictured on pages 105-106 (number 111592). Extra deluxe engraving throughout; select walnut grips. Backstrap inscriptions identical on both revolvers, as are the inscriptions on the triggerguard strap. Colonel Coolbaugh served under Generals Rosecrans, U.S. Grant, W.T. Sherman, James B. McPherson, N.P. Banks, Osterhaus, J.A. Rawlings, and Halleck. The Colonel was Superintendent of Military Railroads and an emissary between Union and Confederate troops prior to surrender. *Rare* matched pair, and of considerable historic importance. *(Robin O. Cotten Collection)*

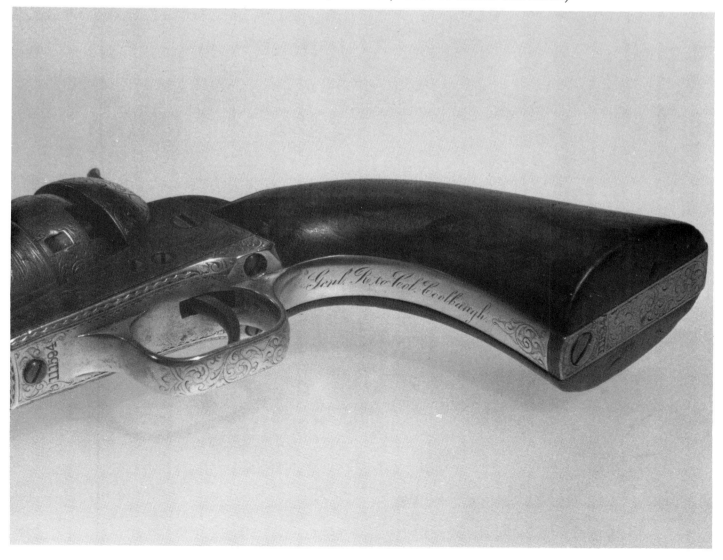

Presentation set of Model 1861 Navy revolvers, to Major General McPherson, *From his Friends/O.N. Cutler, W.C. Wagley.* **Serial numbers 11756/I and 11757/I; mahogany casing.** *En suite* **with the cased Model 1862 Police revolvers, numbers 15591 and 15601, which follow. The Navies are pictured, with detailed descriptions, later in the present chapter.** *(Johnie Bassett Collection/Photograph, S. P. Stevens)*

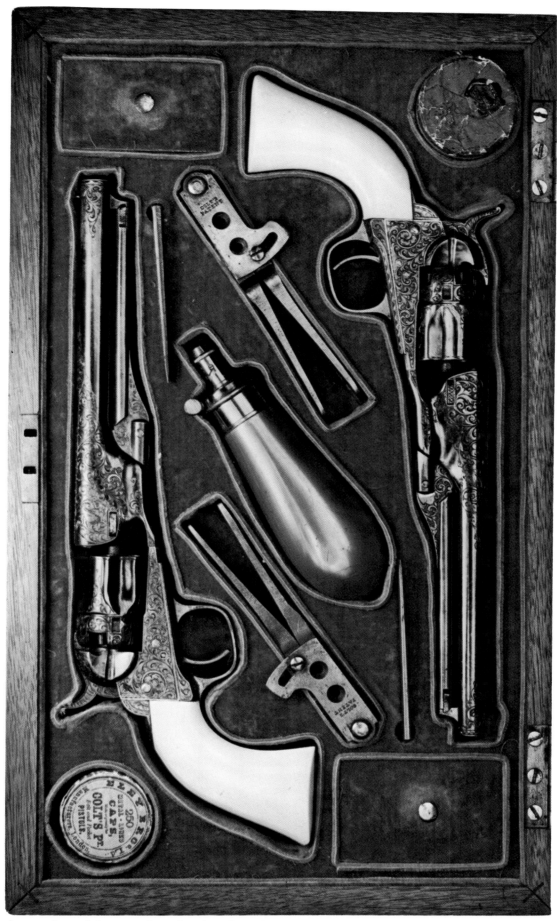

Deluxe engraved, cased, and ivory gripped pair of Model 1862 Police revolvers, serial numbers 15859/I and 15860/I. The profuse Young style coverage includes scrolls on the cylinders, and human, eagle, and wolf head details. Though not inscribed, these arms are considered to have been *en suite* with the presentation pair of General McPherson Model 1861 Navy revolvers, numbers 11756/I and 11757/I. Both sets formerly in the William M. Locke Collection. *(Johnie Bassett Collection/Photograph, S.P. Stevens)*

One of Gustave Young's most inspired masterpieces; Thuer conversion Model 1860 Army number 185326/I.E.; c. 1870.   Relief carved ivory grips of Colt manufacture.   Silver plated, with cylinders, hammers, and loading lever plunger plated in gold.   The casing (with an unusual, perhaps unique, interior layout) is of rosewood, bound in silver plated brass and lined in reddish velvet.   In the finely executed and ingeniously intertwined scrollwork, Young outdid himself.   The resulting decor proved to be a dramatic departure from all other styles attributed to him.   NOTE: The extra percussion cylinder was not done by Young, but can be attributed to an assistant. *(Anonymous Collection)*

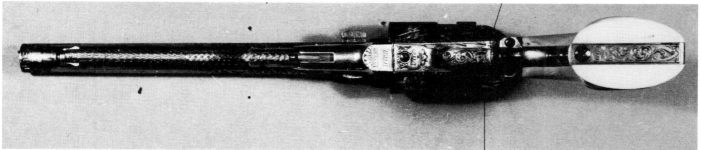

Details of a richly engraved pair of Thuer conversion Model 1860 Army revolvers, reproduced here for comparison with the Thuer Army number 185326/I.E. Serial numbers 176448/E and 177727/E. For further details, see page 146. *(Anonymous Collection)*

Thuer Conversion Model 1860 Army number 185326/I.E. *(Anonymous Collection/Photograph, S. P. Stevens)*

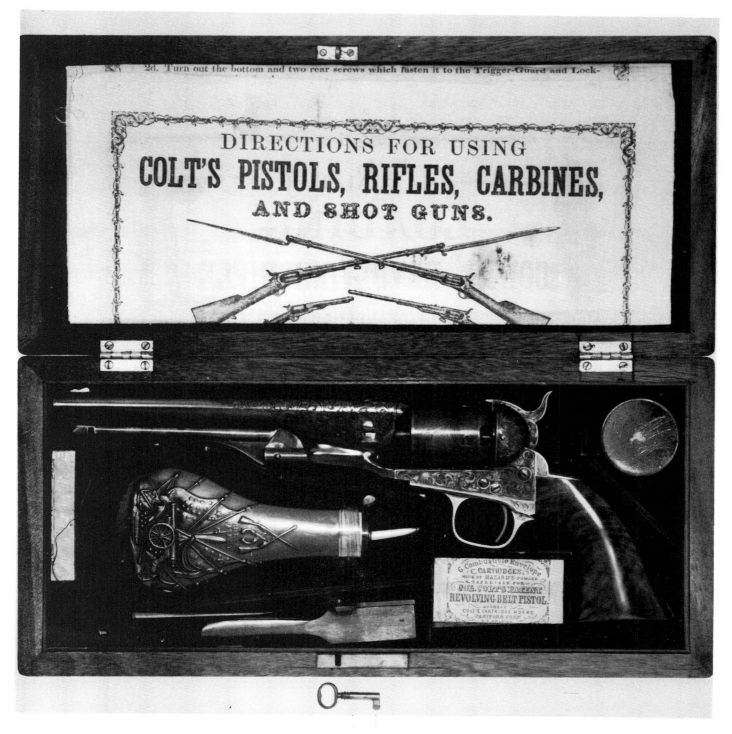

Model 1861 Navy revolver serial number 5726/. is generally regarded as the final presentation from Colonel Colt, prior to his death on January 10th, 1862. On the backstrap the inscription, in script: *Wm Faxon/with Compliments of Col. Colt.* Faxon was Chief Clerk of the Navy Department during the Civil War. Scroll coverage, of the late Young style, on the barrel, wedge, frame, hammer (wolf head), backstrap, and triggerguard. A complete cased set, the box of factory style (varnished mahogany), with the very rare "Directions" cleaning cloth. *(Wadsworth Atheneum Hartford)*

Serial number 13520; Model 1861 Navy revolver. The backstrap inscribed in script: *Presented to E.H. Johnson by/the Workmen in his Employ/June 13th 1863.* **Note hand engraved cylinder scene, with rare detail of the extra scroll coverage and the wavy line and dot border at the muzzle end.** *(Dr. Chester P. Bonoff Collection; formerly Jonathan M. Peck Collection)*

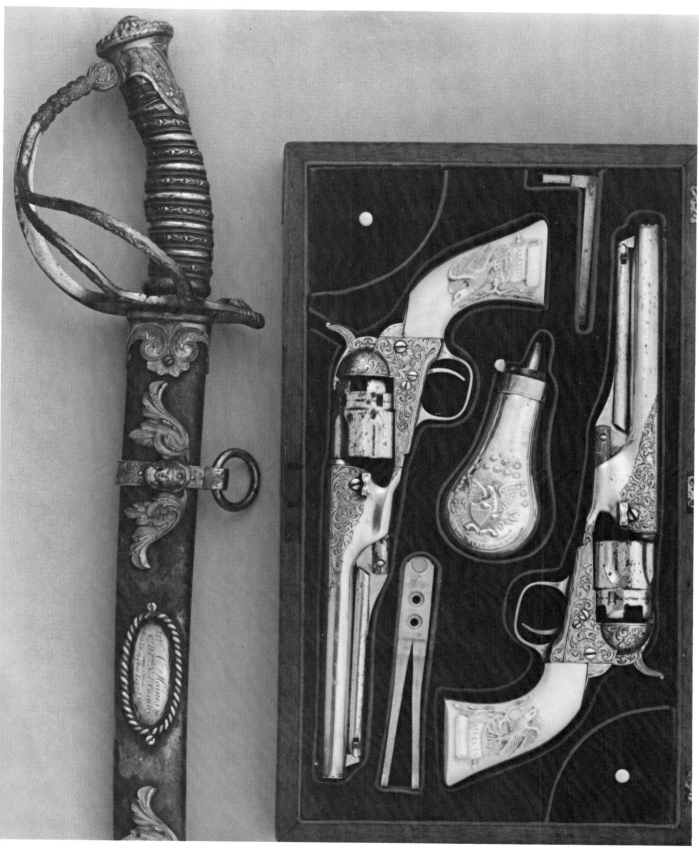

Matched set of Model 1862 revolvers, inscribed on each backstrap to Lieutenant A. Haines, 1863. Gustave Young No. 2 style of scroll coverage; nickel plated finish; serial numbers 23798 and 23800. The ivory grips were carved at Colt's factory, and the backstrap inscriptions were also done "in house". However, the French-style, velvet-lined mahogany casing was supplied by Joseph C. Grubb and Company of Philadelphia. Compare with the Sheridan Model 1861 Navy pistols, also pictured in the present chapter. Grubb label on the bottoms of the Haines and Sheridan cases proves this type box originated from that firm. The sword, suitably inscribed, was part of the Haines presentation set. *(Jerry D. Berger Collection)*

An extra-deluxe Model 1861 Navy, serial number 14369 features hand engraved cylinder scene and scroll and border cylinder trim, one piece ivory grips with bell-shaped checkering pattern and checkered butt panels, special treatment to the loading lever (including cross-hatching at the muzzle end), scrollwork on the barrel bolster adjacent to the muzzle end of the cylinder, and extra-fancy, fine, and intricate scrollwork throughout. The casing is of rare rosewood, brassbound, and lined in velvet. Revolver finished in blue and case hardening, with silver plated brass gripstraps. *(George S. Lewis, Jr. Collection)*

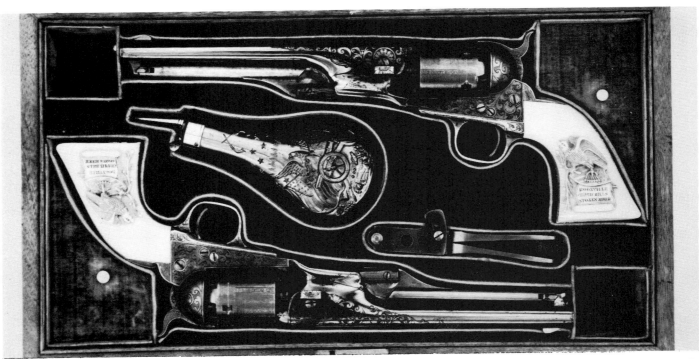

Although these Model 1861 Navies were engraved at the Colt factory, their case was supplied by Joseph C. Grubb and Company of Philadelphia. A portion of the Grubb label still remains on the case bottom. The unique motif on the ivory grips was done to order by stockmakers (or engravers) at Colt. Engraving on the barrel, wedge, frame, hammer (wolf head), and gripstraps; the style is the late type of Young scrollwork. The backstraps are inscribed in italics: *Presented to Maj. Genl P.H. Sheridan/by the Officers of the 3^d Division 20th Army Corps/Department of the Cumberland.* Serial numbers **11787/E and 11791/E.** *(United States National Museum, Smithsonian Institution)*

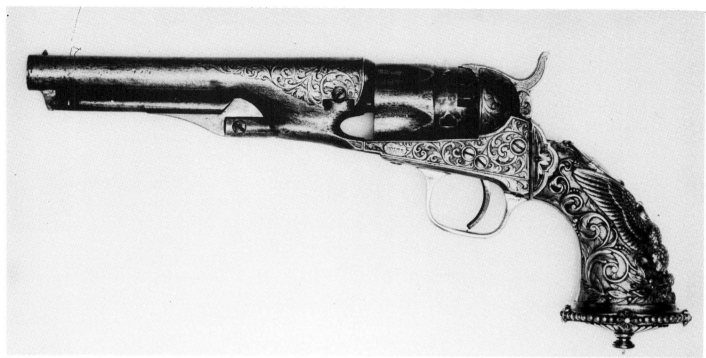

The Gustave Young style of scroll on a "Tiffany" gripped Model 1862 Police revolver, serial number **12953** (c. 1862). Silver plated, with the cylinder, hammer, lever, and grip finished in gold. A standard "No. 2" Style engraving; note the customary lack of coverage on the lever, screws or cylinder. Information on "Tiffany" grips appears in a later chapter. *(Richard P. Mellon Collection)*

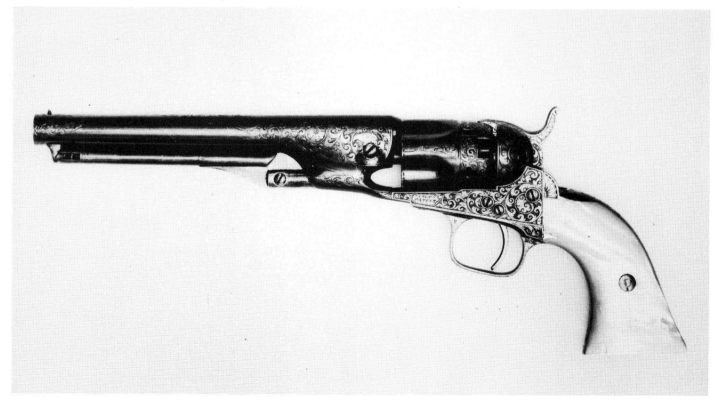

The backstrap of this profusely decorated Model 1862 Police revolver is inscribed: *Prof. J.D. Butler/From Colts P.F.A.M.C⁰.* Butler was instrumental in the publication of the book *Armsmear*, the first biography of Samuel Colt (1866); he is credited with authoring the section on the company's guns and their manufacture. The pearl grip is an extreme rarity, as are the scroll and border coverage on the cylinder, the early style of Young scroll in overall profusion, and the scrolls on the barrel at the muzzle. Serial number 14303. *(George R. Repaire Collection)*

Model 1860 Army revolver; number 7569/. One of the last presentations made by Colonel Colt prior to his death in January, 1862. The backstrap inscribed in script: *Major Charles T. Baker/From Col. Colt.* The engraving both exquisite and profuse; noticeably beyond what would be regarded as a "standard" treatment. Coverage is on the barrel, wedge, cylinder (hand engraved scene plus scroll and border trim), hammer, backstrap and triggerguard strap (note lack of coverage on the lever and screws). The grips of varnished select walnut. Complete factory casing; mahogany, lined in reddish velvet. *(Jerry D. Berger Collection)*

Featured as Lot 100 in the "Colt/Christie's Auction of Rare and Historic Firearms", held in New York City at Christie's Park Avenue Galleries, October 7, 1981, Navy 51808/' was described in the lavishly illustrated catalogue as: "A fine deluxe Model 1851 Navy revolver, No. 51808/', decorated with the 'No. 2 style' scroll of the Gustave Young shop as designed for the Navy model. Coverage is on the barrel, lever, frame, hammer, back-strap, triggerguard, wedge, and screws. On the left side of the barrel lug a wolf head motif, hand engraved 'Colt's/Patent' marking on the frame, New-York address on barrel....Casing of varnished mahogany lined in burgundy velvet, partitioned in the American style, with accessories including stand of arms flask." *(Horace Greeley IV Collection; G. Allan Brown photograph)*

Book cased percussion Colts are both intriguing and rare. The leather covered cases were made up for Colt by bookbinders, and the first such sets were produced in the Paterson period, with clever titles such as LAW FOR SELF DEFENSE and COMMON LAW OF TEXAS.

Colt appears to have revived the book casing concept in about 1849. Three specimens of the Hartford period appear in *Samuel Colt Presents,* in two basic designs of exterior leather covers. The favored title of the Hartford book casings was shown with the Floyd presentation. Cases with the George Washington cover motif are known having the author dedication imprint and the marking JAN^Y 1st 1861 on the base of the spine. A less elaborate cover design, featuring an urn and scroll and border decorations, usually has the same title, but lacks the date or the author's dedication imprint. A book casing of c. 1849 is pictured on page 112 of James E. Serven's *Colt Firearms From 1836.* **The volume is entitled** *Colt's Pocket Companion,* **and is inscribed on the spine:** *FROM/ THE AUTHOR/TO/GEN^L W^M. GIBBS M^CNIELL.* **The front and back cover imprint (in gold leaf) is a combina-**tion of scroll borders and, an intertwined scroll, vine and arabesque motif at the center.

Model 1861 Navy; number 13620. Mahogany casing; lined in velvet. Relief carved and checkered American eagle and shield grips. Compare with similarly engraved Navy number 12240 presented by Colt's factory to Horace Greeley (see *Samuel Colt Presents*, **page 204**). *(George R. Repaire Collection)*

Presentation from Colonel Colt to the wife of the recently retired Secretary of War, John B. Floyd. Serial number 781; the backstrap and spine of the book casing fully inscribed. Profuse scroll engraving in an extra fancy

Gustave Young style; including coverage on the cylinder, Saml Colt hand-engraved barrel address, and human head motifs in profile on each side of the barrel lug. Checkered one piece ivory grips.

Three of the finest and most historic firearms made in the Colt company's long and colorful history. Colonel Colt himself presented these revolvers to the Russian Czar Nicholas I, in 1854. Prior to presentation the pieces were featured in Colt displays in England and on the Continent. Engraving and gold inlaying was by Gustave Young, the most skilled of all arms engravers active in America in the nineteenth century. At top, Third Model Dragoon number 12407, the mate to presentation Dragoon 12406, believed presented to the Turkish Sultan, by Colt, also in 1854. At center, Model 1851 Navy number 20131; the mate to number 20133/. in a private collection in England. At bottom, Model 1849 Pocket revolver 63305, the most deluxe Pocket Model Colt handgun produced out of the entire production run of over 300,000. *(The State Hermitage Museum, Leningrad, U.S.S.R./Photograph by Dr. Leonid Tarassuk)*

Chapter IV
GOLD INLAID
PERCUSSION COLT REVOLVERS

Of all the American gunmakers, Colonel Samuel Colt was the acknowledged master salesman and entrepreneur. His almost instant success in the years 1847-48, when the Colt-Hartford operations began, propelled him into national, and indeed international, renown. Keenly aware of potential firearms markets the world over, Colt eyed European sales and profits with a special interest and enthusiasm.

As a young seaman (c. 1831-32), Colt had visited London, touring the Tower Armouries, and delighting in the products of British gunmakers. A genuine love for Britain and things British was one of several factors influencing the Hartford Colonel's decision to not only aggressively pursue sales in Britain and the continental countries, but in fact to open a factory on the Thames (near Vauxhall Bridge), where Dragoon, Navy, and Pocket model pistols were manufactured under Colt's patents through 1857.

Two of Samuel Colt's prime promotional techniques — exploited by him on as grand a scale in Europe as in America — were (1) displays at fairs and expositions and (2) special presentations to monarchy, military brass, and selected politicians. At the Great Exhibition of 1851 in London, Colt's stand was rated among the most popular of the American exhibits. Among other widely heralded showings of Colt arms were the Paris Exposition of 1855, and the New York City Crystal Palace of 1853. Always there were engraved specimens forming part of Colt's displays. A great many notes in contemporary reports commented on these elaborate firearms in 'assorted sizes, engraved and highly finished. . . .' The finest of deluxe Colt firearms were in fact the specific commissions of Colonel Colt as special display pieces or as special orders for presentation arms.

In 1846, unacceptable working conditions in Germany forced the youthful but brilliantly talented engraver Gustave Young to emigrate to America. Working first for some six years in New York City, he moved to Hartford, Connecticut, in

1852 to join the Colt firearms company. No engraver in America, before or since, could match Young in his complete mastery of the Germanic style. In Gustave Young, Samuel Colt hired the services of a man trained in engraving and fully experienced in over fifteen years of professional pursuit of the craft. For the creation of lavish presentation and display arms, Gustave Young was the perfect candidate, and the perceptive Colt was destined to make full use of the special abilities of his new engraver.

Young's first important commissions are believed to have been six gold inlaid pistols for displays in Europe: Two Third Model Dragoons (numbers 12406 and 12407), two Model 1851 Navy's (numbers 20131 and 20133), and two Model 1849 Pocket pistols (numbers 63271 and 63305). All six were superbly engraved and mounted in flush and relief gold. Each was fitted with deluxe walnut grips, and bore the barrel marking, Saml Colt, in old English letters. These pistols accompanied Colonel Colt on an important promotional trip he made to England and the Continent in 1854. Among the calls made by the pitchman-gunmaker was one to Russia, another to Turkey, and a third to England. The Crimean War (1854-56) pitted Great Britain, France and Turkey against Russia; but it was Samuel Colt's business approach to 'make hay while the sun shines' — selling to all sides in the process.

Original records of the armory of Czar Nicholas I show that the gold mounted Dragoon revolver number 12407, the Navy number 20131 and the Pocket pistol number 63305 were personally presented by Colonel Colt, at Cratchina, in 1854. To quote an extract from these archives (translated from the original French):

These three revolvers of different caliber have been presented to his Majesty in the autumn of 1854 (at Cratchina), by Colonel Colt, inventor of the arm. Each one of them in its case, with accoutrements necessary for its use.

The Dragoon number 12406 (mate to the pistol given Czar Nicholas) is believed to have been presented by Colt to the Sultan of Turkey. It was discovered in Istanbul c. 1967 by a British arms collector, and eventually acquired by Colt dealer Herb Glass. It is now in the collection of George R. Repaire. The Navy number 20133 apparently was left in England as a display piece, and it remains there to this day, in private hands. The final gold-mounted pistol, Pocket model number 63271, was discovered behind the "Iron Curtain" in 1961, and is now in a private American collection.

Ironically none of the pistols so presented to the Czar or the Sultan was presentation inscribed. Certainly the reason for this was that Colt had intended to use the fancy pistols for special displays, perhaps hoping that the monarchs would be so taken by them that Colt would have no choice but to leave specimens as special gifts.

Matching the Czar's pistols in magnificence, and surpassing them in historical importance, are two pairs of gold and silver mounted and engraved Army Model 1860 pistols commissioned from the Colt factory by President Abraham Lincoln. These were presented in 1863 as gifts of state from Lincoln to King Charles XV of Sweden and Norway and to King Frederick VII of Denmark. Every detail of these arms is of perfection, and their designs are characteristic of the ultra-richness of Victorian America, with Germanic influences richer still.

Both pairs have buttcaps and gripstraps of sterling silver, the butts finely engraved with the seal of the President of the United States. Silver grip plaque inlays are engraved with the simple yet rather awesome inscription: "The President/of the United States of America/to his Majesty/The King of. . . ."

In addition to the above, only nine other gold inlaid percussion Colt revolvers are known to collectors today, and the estimated total original production is some 25 to 30 (from the total of Colt percussion arms which is in excess of 1,000,000). In workmanship, rarity, and historical interest, gold inlaid percussion revolvers represent the most important and desirable single group of arms in Colt collecting.

Material recently discovered offers new data on the gifted craftsman Gustave Young. After the celebrated Colt factory fire of February 4, 1864, Young drafted in his own hand an advertisement for publication in Hartford's newspapers. The original manuscript reveals something of the man, his assignments under Colonel Colt, and his general abilities.

GOLD & SILVER, STEEL & GENERAL ENGRAVER

The Advertiser having been deprived of employment by the late destructive fire at Colt's Armory, respectfully offers his services to the public, as an Engraver on Gold and Silver plate, rings, and every kind of ornamental jewelry, Steel and all other metals. He has been engaged in Colonel Colt's Establishment for the past twelve years in the highest walks of the art; and abundant proofs of his Skill are extant in this country, and in Europe, in the splendid presents that have been made to Crowned Heads, and illustrious personages in different countries. Specimens of his work have been exhibited at the different World's Fairs and elicited the highest praise. In soliciting public patronage, the subscriber is confident, that he cannot be outdone, if equalled, in his line of art; and he is willing to hazard his professional reputation on any work with which he may be entrusted. He can be found at his Office, No.   Main Street, up Stairs.

Young did not give the street number, an indication that he was setting up his new shop at the time.

A unique ink impression pulled from the frame of an elaborately embellished Colt Dragoon was also recently discovered, in the papers of the Young family. It reveals perfectly the rich German-American style which he used in engraving the pistols of the Czar and the Sultan, and shows in addition the imaginative animal motifs, which along with American patriotic scenes, were a speciality of this master craftsman.

Collectors of Smith & Wesson arms will note an occasional magnificent pistol by that maker engraved or gold inlaid in a similar style. After the Colt fire of 1864, Gustave Young is known to have accepted commissions from S & W (whose factory in Springfield, Massachusetts, was but 25 miles from Hartford), and the year 1869 saw Young and his family move from Hartford to Springfield where he became the chief engraver for the Smith & Wesson firm. Among the fancy pistols done by Young for his new employer were gold inlaid presentations for President U.S. Grant and for the Russian Grand Duke Alexis, plus miscellaneous display arms for the Philadelphia Centennial Exposition of 1876 and the Columbian

Exposition of 1892-93, in Chicago. One of the latter pistols, a single action .44 caliber New Model No. 3, is the only known signed engraved firearm by Young — something of a contrast to the well known L. D. Nimschke and certain members of the Ulrich family, who left a great many examples of signed work, particularly on Winchester firearms.

The obituary of Gustave Young, published in the *Springfield Daily Republican*, January 3, 1895, adds further detail on the background of this remarkably talented craftsman:

> *Gustave Young, the well known engraver . . . died at his home on Broad street yesterday from tumor on the brain. Mr. Young was trained abroad and did some superior work, engraving the most costly pistols for the Colts while at Hartford and for Smith & Wesson in this city. In 1893 he finished the pistols sent to the Chicago fair by Mr. Wesson, including a revolver [the New Model No. 3 noted above] that cost $1,500, probably the most expensive ever made. While in Hartford he engraved a revolver sent to Gen. Grant, which had military emblems in gold on the handle. Mr. Young was born in Thuringia, Ger., May 6, 1827, and worked for a time in Berlin for the imperial engraver. While following his trade in Warsaw he furnished two fowling pieces for the czar of Russia. He moved to this country 43 years ago, and after working a short time in New York, settled in Hartford. . . . He was employed at Colt's for many years, and in 1869 came to Springfield as engraver for Smith & Wesson. . . . Mr. Young leaves a widow and three sons, Oscar and ex-Councilman Eugene Young (both master engravers in their own right), and Alfred O. Young, a machinist. . . .*

For collector reference, some of the salient features of Gustave Young's engraving and gold work on Colt arms are as follows (compare with illustrations):

Serial numbers are usually gold inlaid; some are hand engraved; a few are stamped.

Barrel markings are usually gold inlaid, Saml Colt, in old English style lettering.

Gold inlays are usually flush, but often relief figures were used for special motifs. Among the flush and relief scenes are the American eagle, goddess of liberty, the Capitol of the United States, a bust of George Washington, cavalry, infantry, and Indian figures, birds, leopards, lions, bears, wolves, dogs, serpents, horses, and imaginative dragon motifs. The cylinders of the Lincoln pistols have superb flush gold panels of naval, industrial, and agricultural themes.

Scroll border inlays are generally flush, and are usually single or double lines.

Cylinders are sometimes hand engraved, sometimes machine roll-engraved (both in the standard patterns). A few are fully engraved and inlaid in special designs contrasting noticeably with the standard stagecoach, naval engagement or Texas Ranger and Indian fight scenes.

Backstraps and triggerguards are usually plated or partially overlaid with gold.

Grips are most often deluxe grain varnished walnut; though some are relief carved black walnut, and one pistol is known having the Tiffany style cast grip.

To date only three Third Model Dragoons, five Model 1860 Army's, four Model 1851 Navy's, two Model 1861 Navy's, four Model 1849 Pocket pistols, and one Model 1862 Police pistol are known in percussion Colts having original engraving and inlay by Gustave Young. Interestingly, original factory and Young family records indicate that other gold-mounted Colt arms are yet to be found. Among these is a pair of Model 1861 Navy pistols and a Model 1862 Police inlaid and engraved for display at the Paris Exposition of 1867. Another pair, the Army Model of 1860, was prepared for presentation to General Ulysses S. Grant, in 1864. A gold inlaid Model 1862 Police pistol was made on order of James T. Ames of the Ames Manufacturing Company (swordmakers), of Chicopee Falls, Massachusetts. And certainly a few additional gold-mounted and engraved pistols were presented by Colonel Colt to dignitaries in America and Europe. These are all treasures awaiting discovery by arms collectors.

From all indications, Samuel Colt anticipated his opportunities for business in Europe to have been every bit as promising as his sales in America. In this relentless push for sales, the artistry of Gustave Young played a distinctly significant role. And certainly in Samuel Colt, the Czar of Russia, the Sultan of Turkey, the King of Denmark, the King of Sweden and Norway, and in the gun collector of today, Young has enjoyed the enthusiastic recognition which in the final measure is the reward most artists and craftsmen strive for throughout their creative lives.

An ink impression ("gunmaker's pull") taken by Gustave Young from the frame on one of his elaborately engraved Colt Dragoon revolvers. The style and workmanship match perfectly with the gold inlaid and engraved Colt percussion firearms known to collectors (excepting variant style Model 1862 Police number 38549). This tiny piece of paper of c. 1855 served as a key piece of evidence in identifying Young as the craftsman responsible for the finest grade of engraved and gold inlaid Colt firearms of the period c. 1852-69. From the Young family collection of documents and memorabilia, discovered by the author in an attic, 1967. Engravers' records of their work are usually of far greater rarity than the firearms they decorated. *(Johnie Bassett Collection)*

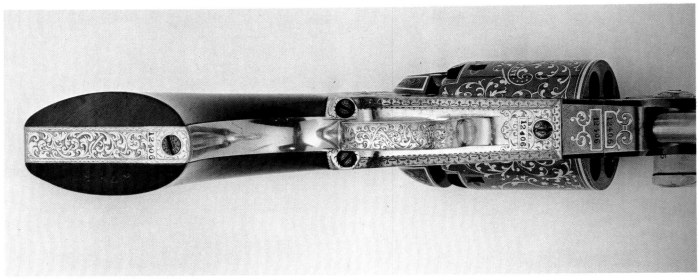

Exquisite gift believed presented by Colonel Colt, c. 1854, to the Sultan of Turkey. Third Model Dragoon number 12406. One side of the cylinder was flush gold inlaid with a portrait of George Washington. As on the three presentations to Czar Nicholas I, the gripstraps are heavily plated or overlaid with gold. In the top view the characteristic Sam¹ Colt gold inlaid barrel marking is visible. See also frontispiece, dust jacket, and the pages which follow. *(George R. Repaire Collection/Photographs, S. P. Stevens)*

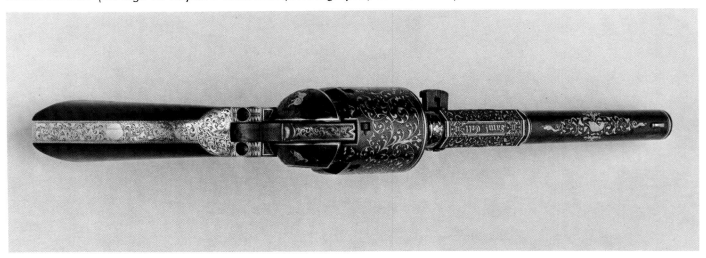

Sultan of Turkey Dragoon, in its case. See previous page, *(George R. Repaire Collection)*

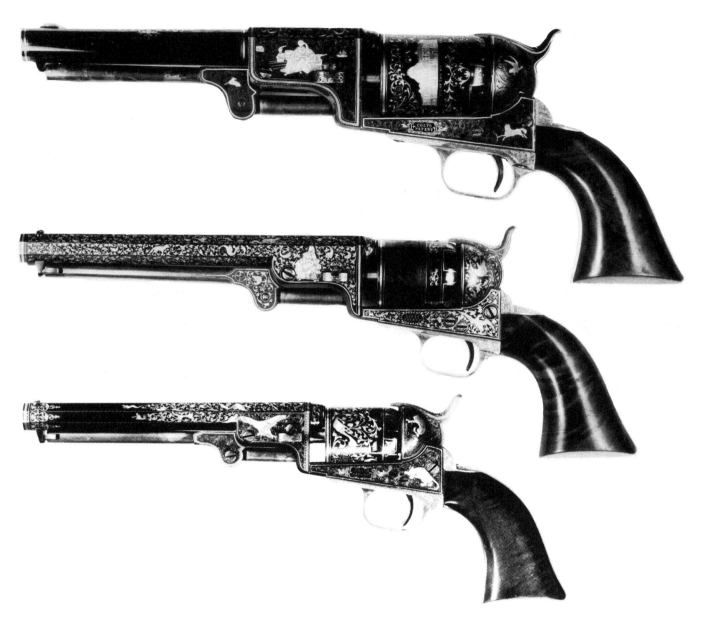

Three deluxe presentations from Colonel Colt to the Russian Czar Nicholas I. Though given to the Czar in **1854,** the date of manufacture is c. **1853.** After having used the weapons for displays in continental Europe and in England, Colt elected to present these extraordinary pistols to the Czar for his arms collection. All three pieces are pictured (in their original London Colt cases) on page **570** of *The Book of Colt Firearms,* and are now in The State Hermitage Museum, Leningrad, U.S.S.R. (Top) The Czar's Third Model Dragoon, serial number **12407,** was the mate to the Turkish presentation (number **12406**) made by Colt in the same year. Saml Colt, in old English letters, is gold inlaid on top of the barrel. Relief gold inlaid on the left side of the barrel lug is a motif representing American industry. Flush gold inlaid on the cylinder is the Capitol of the United States and intricately intertwined scrollwork. Animal motifs and foliate scroll gold inlay and engraving are profuse. (Center) The Model 1851 Navy pistol, number **20131,** represents one of the finest Colt firearms ever made. The gold inlay and engraving are extremely fine and profuse. Themes are of American origin, e.g., eagles and wolves. The barrel lug features the goddess of liberty, American eagle and shield motifs, and a crouching lion — all richly executed in high relief. Mate to this revolver is pictured on pages **264** and **266** of *Samuel Colt Presents;* serial number **20133/.** The Saml Colt barrel marking matches the Czar's Dragoon and Pocket model revolvers. (Bottom) Patriotic and animal motifs also formed the theme for Colt's gift of the Model 1849 Pocket revolver, serial number **63305.** An eagle in high relief gold inlay appears on the barrel lug; grotesques, animals, scrolls, and borders — engraved and/or gold inlaid — abound. The barrel marking of Saml Colt, gold inlaid, matches that on the Dragoon and Navy.

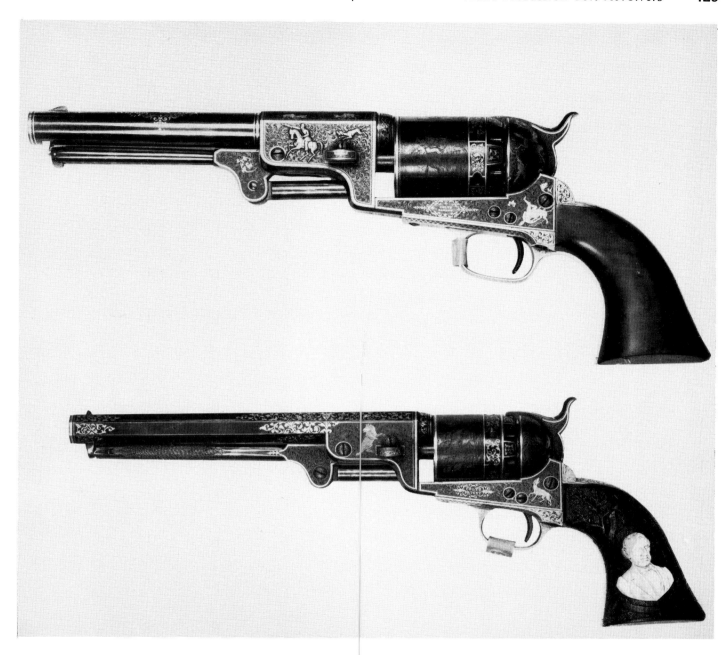

Two display pieces made for Colonel Colt's use by Gustave Young, c. 1854 (bottom) and c. 1856 (top). The Third Model Dragoon, number 15821/., has gold inlaid barrel (Saml Colt, in old English) and cylinder markings, and a hand engraved Ranger and Indian fight cylinder scene. Among the engraved details are a wolf head on the hammer (the teeth and eyes in gold), and various wolf, eagle, and deer motifs. Gold inlaid details, flush unless noted otherwise, are a man in a stove pipe hat shooting a revolver, wolf, various serpent, eagle and horse figures, a spotted cat mauling an Indian, a mounted figure whose horse is rearing above a dragon, a charging soldier with musket and bayonet, an Indian on horseback, and in high relief: a mounted, bearded man firing a revolver, a running dog (left side of the barrel lug), and a thief being pursued by a mounted figure aiming a revolver. The Model 1851 Navy, number 38843/., features engraved wolf, eagle, and serpent, and gold inlaid bear, lion, lioness, dog, vulture, wolf, and eagle motifs. Unlike the Dragoon, all of the gold inlays are flush. The bear design was copied from the G. Ernst, Zella, engravers' pattern book. The carved, pearl mounted grips were added c. 1865, after the death of Abraham Lincoln. *(Colt Collection of Firearms, Connecticut State Library)*

NOTE: See also *The 'Russian' Colts* monograph, published in 1979 in conjunction with the loan exhibitions of the gold inlaid Czar Nicholas I revolvers at The Metropolitan Museum of Art and the Museum of Connecticut History, Connecticut State Library. Detailed references to gold inlaid percussion Colts are presented, and much new data on the presentations from Colonel Colt to Czars Nicholas I and Alexander II.

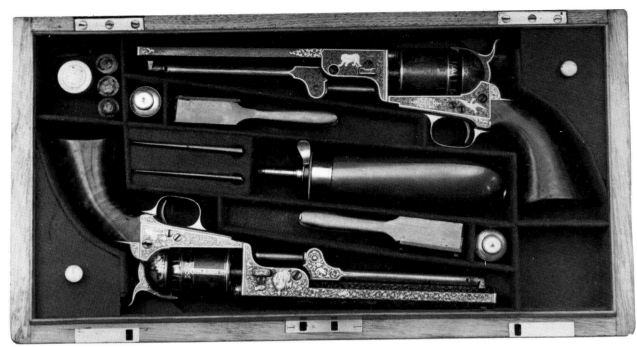

Two show guns, taken by Colt or an associate to Europe, and eventually coming into possession of a private collector. The lower revolver, number 20133, is mate to the Czar Nicholas I Navy 20131. The upper pistol, number 23477 is less profusely embellished, but does feature gold bird and animal motifs, flush gold borders and scrollwork, and deluxe walnut grips. Its barrel marking, in flush gold, is quite unusual; instead of the standard Saml Colt in old English, the legend reads: ADDRESS SAM^L COLT NEW YORK CITY, in flush gold serif block letters. The casing is a standard English oak type, and likely was used as a convenient receptacle. For further information on the gold inlaid Colt revolver production by Gustave Young, see *The 'Russian' Colts*, co-authored by the present writer and Dr. L. Tarassuk, 1979. *(Private Collection)*

View of the display of the gold inlaid Russian Colt revolvers, held at The Metropolitan Museum of Art, New York, from May of 1979 through January 1980. A loan from the Hermitage Museum, Leningrad, arranged through the offices of Colt Industries, New York. The revolvers were also displayed at the Museum of Connecticut History, Connecticut State Library, Hartford, during the summer of 1979. *(Photograph, The Metropolitan Museum of Art)*

Cased Model 1849 number 63303 is quite unusual in scroll and gold inlay styling, and is believed to have been done as one of the first deluxe projects by Gustave Young for Colonel Colt. The inlaying is limited primarily to barrel, frame, and cylinder inscriptions, and to borders. Casing of rosewood, extra-deluxe, and lined in velvet. *(R.E. Hable Collection)*

Serial number 63271 Model 1849 Pocket is one of the earliest known gold inlaid Gustave Young revolvers. It was discovered c. 1960 in Czechoslovakia, by an Italian museum official, and was exhibited in the *Samuel Colt Presents* exhibition at the Wadsworth Atheneum, Hartford, in 1961. Coverage is quite profuse, and distinctively Gustave Young. Revolver undoubtedly served as a show piece for the Colt firm. *(Stanley Diefenthal Collection)*

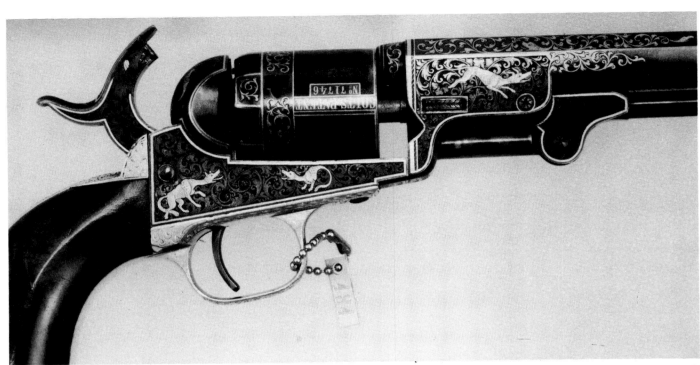

Model 1849 Pocket revolver; number 71746/. A show piece made by Gustave Young in a more deluxe style than number 67498/. All gold inlays are flush; wolf, dog, and eagle figures are used, with gold scrolls, borders, and markings. Hand engraved cylinder scene. Gold overlaid or plated gripstraps; Saml Colt barrel marking (old English letters); and the characteristic Young style of borders, and engraved and gold inlaid wolf head hammer. *(Colt Collection of Firearms, Connecticut State Library)*

Serial number 67498/.; Model 1849 Pocket revolver. Flush gold inlays on the barrel, loading lever, wedge, cylinder (which also has the hand engraved cylinder scene), frame and hammer (the wolf head pattern). Leopard, wolf, fox, lion, dragon, and wolf head motifs are in flush gold inlay. The eyes, teeth, and tongue of the wolf head hammer are also in gold. The gold tulip between each chamber on the cylinder is a characteristic Gustave Young design. Borderwork of single and double lines is also a mark of Young's style. Gold overlaid or plated gripstraps; customary varnished select walnut grips. c. 1853. *(William M. Locke Collection)*

Title page and plate 12 from W.L. Ormsby's book on bank note engraving and on counterfeiting. Compare scenes 1 and 8 (upper right corner; and second row in from right, second figure down from top) with cylinder details from the pair of revolvers presented by Lincoln to King Charles XV. Pictures such as published by Ormsby, postage stamps, picture books, coins and money, all number among the sources useful to the gun engraver. Some details on Ormsby's book: 101 pages in length; published as a system of bank note engraving designed to prevent counterfeiting; the book was dedicated "To the Presidents and Directors of the Banking Institutions of the United States". Second half of the book was illustrated with twelve plates of various bank note motifs. The copy illustrated was personally inscribed by Ormsby to Samuel Colt. Published in 1852. *(William H. Myers Collection, Photograph Courtesy Mike Clark)*

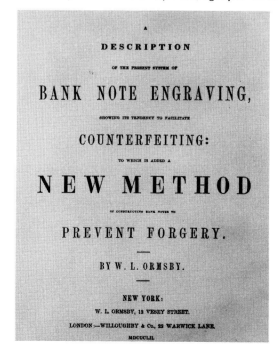

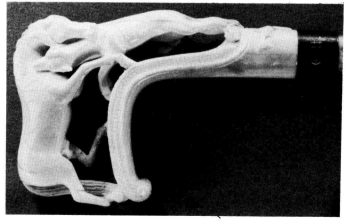

Colonel Colt's ivory handled cane, the steel furrule gold inlaid by Gustave Young (in old English letters): Saml Colt. Young may also have done the ivory carving, an art in which he is known to have excelled. The intricately carved scene depicts a horse (or "colt") battling a wolf. Just below the hind legs of the wolf is a relief carved crossed revolvers design. c. 1855. *(James E. Serven Collection)*

Collectors generally regard these Abraham Lincoln presentation Model 1860 Army revolvers as the finest and most historic percussion arms made by Colt. One pair was prepared as a state gift to Charles XV, King of Sweden and Norway (detail photos; serial numbers 31906 and 31907). The other pair was from the President to Frederick VII, the King of Denmark (numbers 31904 and 31905; photo of pair). Both sets were nearly identically engraved and gold inlaid. The deluxe walnut grips were relief carved and checkered, with mountings and gripstraps in sterling silver; on the buttcaps the great seal of the President of the United States. Other than the grip mounts, nearly all decorations are of engraved gold inlays. Serial numbers and barrel markings were also gold inlaid. Rather than the customary Saml Colt as used on nearly all other gold inlaid percussion Colt arms, the Lincoln pistols used the legend: ADDRESS COL. SAML COLT NEW-YORK U.S. AMERICA. Numerous dog, wolf, and eagle head motifs appear on both pairs. The foliate gold scrolls are of the most intricate and deluxe design and execution. Despite the fact that the Lincoln presentations represent the ultimate in artistry by Gustave Young, none of the arms appears to have been signed by him in any way. The casings were of silver bound rosewood, with reddish velvet linings; and complete accessories. Casemaker was William Milton, 13 Albany Avenue, Hartford. *(Charles XV pistols: The Royal Armoury, Stockholm/ Frederick VII pistols: Frederick VII Foundation, Jaegerpris, Denmark)*

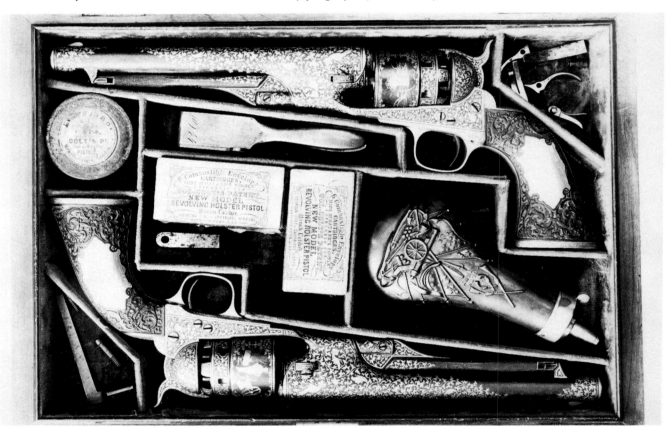

Cased set, top and bottom views of the Frederick VII pistols. Note script engraving of "44 Cal" on the bullet mold, variations in decor from the Charles XV pistols, and the butt and serial number details visible in the bottom view.

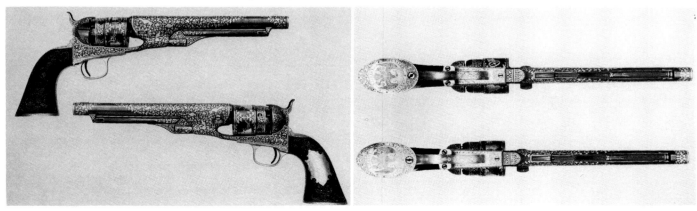

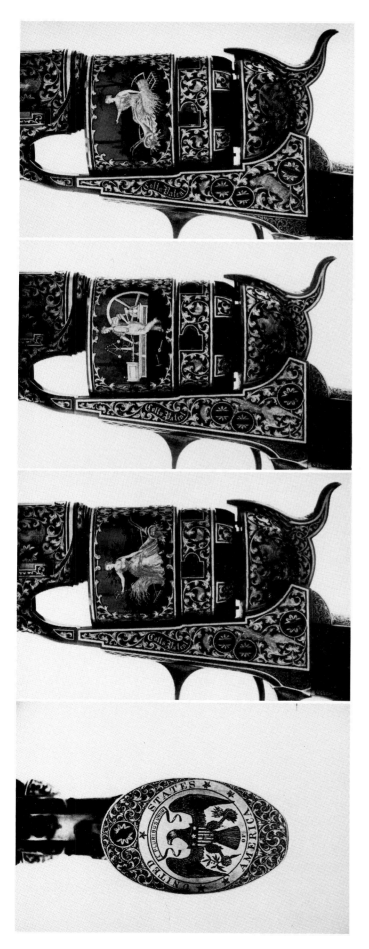

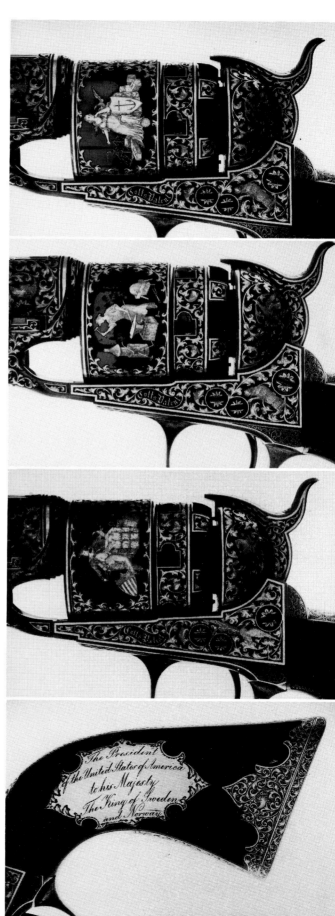

Detail from a gold inlaid and engraved matched pair of Model 1861 Navy revolvers presented by E.K. Root to a Lewis Lippold, c. 1864. The backstraps inscribed in script: *From/E.K. Root Pres^t Colts P^t F.A. Mfg. C^o/to/ Lewis Lippold.* Serial numbers 17239 and 17240. The decoration is made up primarily of engraving in the most deluxe Young style; with borders gold inlaid. Wolf head hammers, with the eyes gold inlaid. Engraved motifs are soldier figures on both sides of the barrel lugs; all markings and the cylinder scenes cut by hand. Loading levers are cross hatched. Note the lack of any decoration on the screws. This photograph depicts the perfection of detail found in scrollwork by Gustave Young. See *Samuel Colt Presents* for overall views of the pair of revolvers; pages 275-276. *(William M. Locke Collection)*

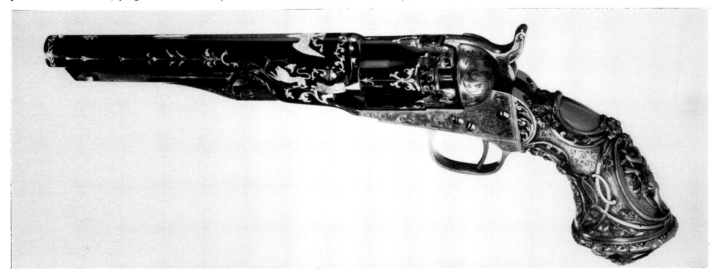

The style of decoration on Model 1862 Police number 38549 (c. 1866) is a distinct contrast to the other gold inlaid percussion Colt revolvers. However, details of the animals and scroll coverage strongly point to Young as the engraver. COLT'S PATENT (flush gold inlaid) is the marking on top of the barrel. Gold inlay appears only on the cylinder and barrel, which are blued in a bright, lustrous finish. The hammer, frame, wedge, and loading lever are engraved and case hardened. The lack of a punched or engraved background makes this pistol relatively plain in appearance, except for the elaborate cast grip. Arrows are gold inlaid on the chambers and on the top of the barrel. On top of the barrel at breech is a flush gold inlaid American eagle. None of the gold work is in relief. Note that the screws are not engraved. Similar engraving appears on a pair of Model 1862 Police revolvers (numbers 25513/E and 25514/E) presented by President Abraham Lincoln to Kibrisili Pasha, Governor of Adrianople, in 1864. The Pasha pistols have nearly identical arrow and scroll motifs on the chambers, have no barrel markings, share the same scroll style on the barrels and frames, and have identical cross hatching on the loading levers. Furthermore, all three pistols have the same type of "Tiffany" grip. Barrel lengths (5½") also are the same. A somewhat similar eagle motif appears on the top of the Pasha pistols' barrels, in the identical location as on number 38549. It is possible that any gold overlay on the Pasha pair has long since been lost; in any event, the style of decoration (even if gold was not used) is the same. The Pasha pistols, a cased set, are now in the Franklin D. Roosevelt Collection, Hyde Park, New York (see *Samuel Colt Presents*, pages 216-219). *(William M. Locke Collection)*

Right side detail from Model 1862 revolver number 38549. *(William M. Locke Collection)*

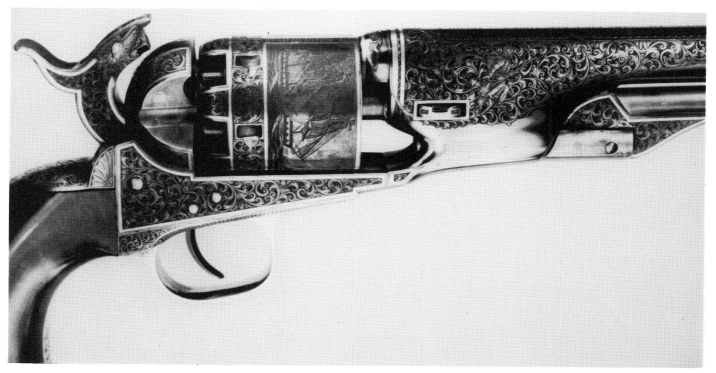

Detail from the right side of Model 1861 Navy number 17239. *(William M. Locke Collection)*

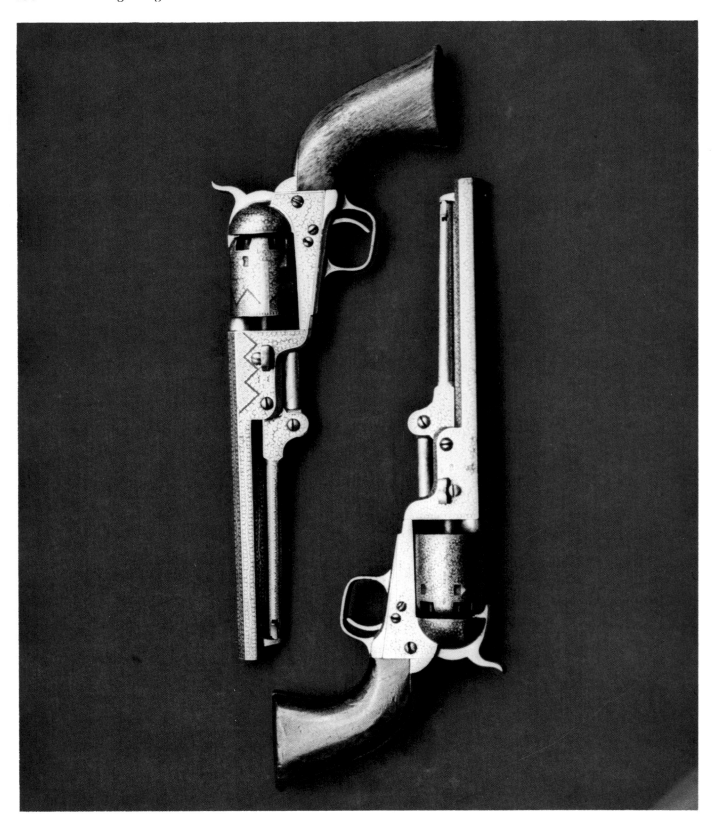

Gold overlaid (damascene) pair of Model 1851 London revolvers, serial numbers 26115 and 26347. A quite rare form of gold decoration on Colt firearms, and observed to date on the following (a few specimens only): Model 1849 and Model 1851 London revolvers, Third Model London Dragoon, and Third Model 41 caliber deringer. A few of these arms are known inscribed, presumably with names of the engravers. Not a true inlay, as used by Helfricht, Young, White, and most engravers post 1850, the gold is a surface decor. The steel is finely hatched, and the soft metal is then hammered into position, using gold wire. This process is still in use today by Indian artisans. It is believed that most of the work found on Colt, Adams, and certain other arms dating from the mid and late nineteenth century was done by Indians either in India or residing in England. *(Glenn Gierhart Collection)*

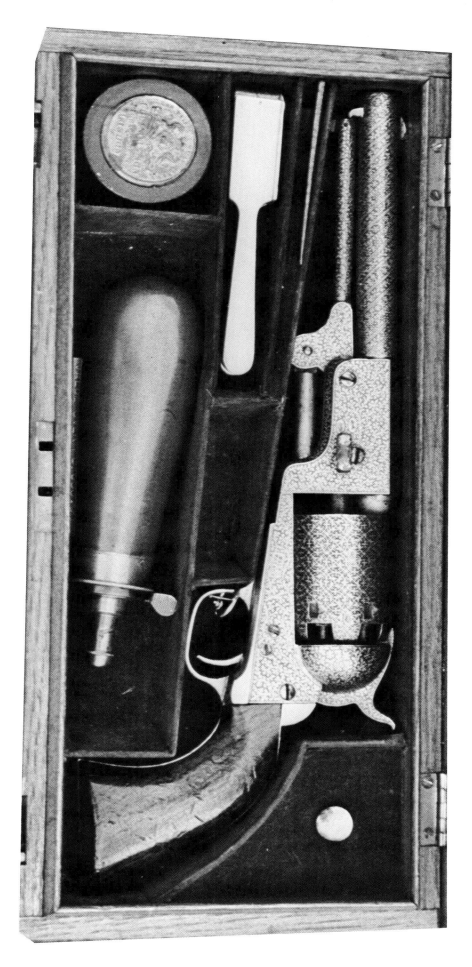

Number 529 London Colt Dragoon represents the finest known example of gold damascene decoration on a percussion Colt revolver. British proofmarks are within the design on the barrel lug and cylinder. Oak casing of London manufacture. *Note:* Damascene embellishments based on original designs are known to have been faked on antique Colt arms in England, beginning in the late 1950's — early 1960's. *Caveat emptor!* *(Glenn Gierhart Collection)*

London Colt Navy number **17048** is profusely damascened, with gripstraps silver plated. Backstrap inscribed: "Capt. I.G.H. Rich 7 Hq. Lt. Inf." An old formula for damascening via electrolysis was brought to the writer's attention by A.A. White: "Prepare acid resisting coating on object. Apply designs and suspend object into a bath of copper sulphate — connecting it to the positive (+) pole of the battery. The negative (–) pole being connected to a copper plate also suspended in the bath. After the object has been sufficiently etched, wash in weak hydrochloric acid solution. Place object in silver or nickel solution and connect this time to the negative (–) pole. The positive (+) pole being connected to a leaf of platinum. The silver or nickel will fill the etched places until flush with rest of object (the result is similar to hand damascening)." *(Ronald N. Swanson Collection)*

Invoice to the Colt Fire Arms firm for gold wire, from the J.M. Ney Company. The Ney firm is still in business, and has been since 1812. Paul A. Lemire, Educational Director, Dental Sales Division, advised the author that this 1866 billing is the earliest recorded invoice by Ney, and Colt's purchase was indeed for the inlaying of deluxe firearms. *(The J.M. Ney Company Collection)*

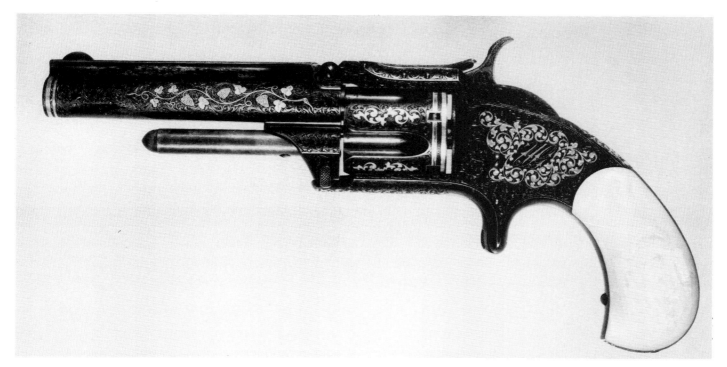

From Smith & Wesson to President Ulysses S. Grant; presented in August, 1870. Superbly gold inlaid and engraved by Gustave Young. A similar decorative style was used by Young on most of the Colt arms with gold inlaid and engraved combinations. On the left side of the frame, a flush gold USG monogram. Note the grapevine treatment on the barrel. Carving of the mother-of-pearl grips may also have been the work of Young. Model 1½; .32 rimfire caliber. Serial number 41993. *(John G. Griffiths Collection/Photograph courtesy of the National Rifle Association)*

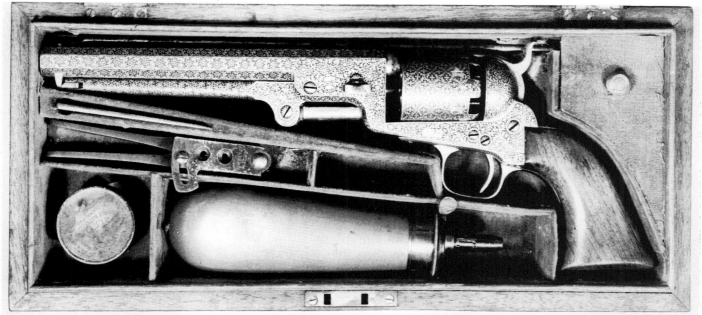

Gold overlay of Indian origin; though rare, this decor has been observed on a few London Model 1849 and Model 1851 revolvers. Some few Third Model London Dragoon and Third Model .41 caliber deringer pistols are also known with the Indian damascene gold work. The illustrated specimen, number 35232, is a London Model 1851 Navy, c. 1855. Coverage of the damascening is profuse, on all steel parts including the screws. A few of these arms are known bearing inscriptions which are presumably the names of engravers. The gold is only a surface treatment, and the steel is not cut and inset to depth as standard with gold inlaid arms by such craftsmen as Gustave Young and his successor at Colt, Cuno Helfricht. It should be noted that damascening is still being done by Indian artisans. Presumably most of the work found on Colt, Adams, and certain other makes of arms in the mid and late nineteenth century was done by Indians either in England or in India. *(Frank Russell Collection)*

Two specimens of the rarest form of decoration on the Third Model Deringer pistols — gold damascening. Serial number 28783 has full coverage, even including the hammer and trigger. Its frame may be unique — instead of the standard brass it is of iron. In contrast serial number 10135 was damascened on the barrel and the hammer; the brass frame was left silver plated. This pistol belonged to the Countess Constance Markievicz, leader in the Irish Rebellion, early in the twentieth century. Both pistols were shipped by the Colt factory to their London Agency, who may have arranged for the unusual decor. *(Glenn Gierhart Collection)*

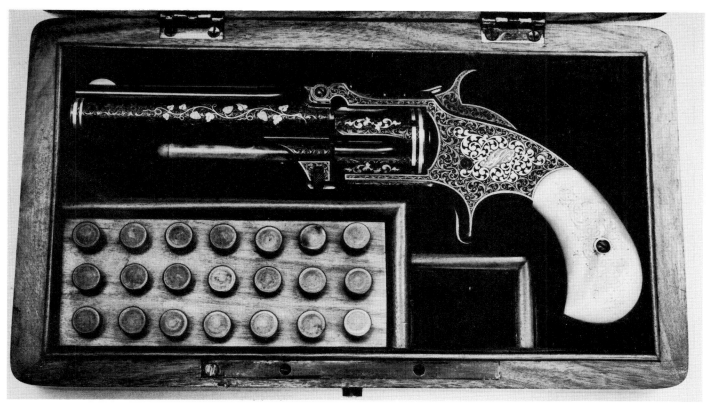

Model 1½ Second Issue Smith & Wesson revolver is an artistic rival to the Model 1½ of President Grant. Decor on both pieces was done in the finest style of gold inlay and engraving by Gustave Young. Serial number 30451. Unique silver mounted and velvet lined case, with dummy cartridges set into the cartridge block. The gun has been identified by S & W Historian Roy G. Jinks as specially produced for shows and expositions. *(R. G. Jinks Collection)*

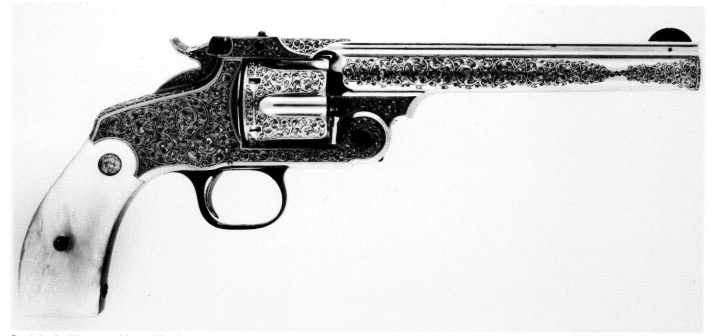

Smith & Wesson New Model No. 3; engraved and partially gold overlaid by Gustave Young for display at the Columbian Exposition, Chicago, 1892-93. The top flat of the topstrap (above the cylinder) is signed: G. YOUNG/ENGRAVER. The background in the scrollwork has been cut away, and a gold finish applied to provide a striking contrast to the bright steel overall finish. A masterpiece of Young's artistry, and the only firearm known to bear his signature. Serial number 27940; pearl grips. Despite the unusual placement of gold overlay on this revolver, the exquisite scroll style is quite similar to the deluxe scrollwork normally used by Young on his gold inlaid Colt percussion revolvers. *(Smith & Wesson Factory Collection)*

Published by New York bank note engravers Rawdon, Wright, Hatch & Edson, this poster sized advertisement offered the gun engraver a great many images ideal for adapting to firearms. Some of these devices will be observed on extra-deluxe Colt arms, since the original was in the Colt factory for many years, and was published c. 1860. *(Colt Collection of Firearms, Connecticut State Library)*

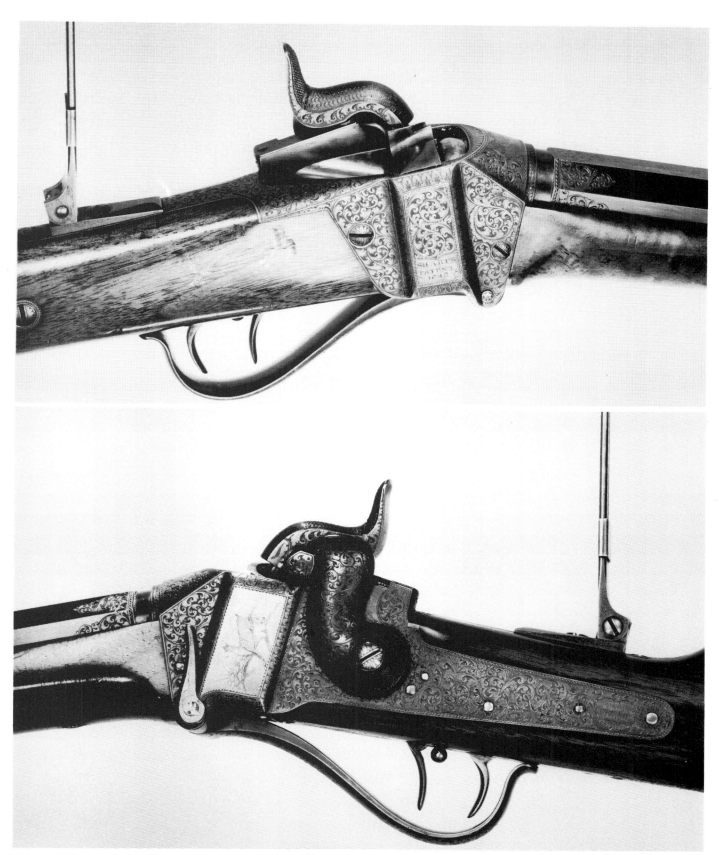

Unique left handed Sharps rifle, exquisitely engraved by Gustave Young as a factory exhibition piece. Manufacture of the gun was in Hartford, c. 1856; serial number 214. Young and his shop are known to have engraved a quantity of the Hartford made Sharps rifles. Rifle number 214 is of the ultra-deluxe grade scroll found on the finest Colt presentations by Young, including some of the gold inlaid pieces. *Note:* **214 is visible on the rifle but is not considered to be the full serial number.** *(Alan S. Kelley Collection)*

Serial number 186 of the London Dragoon series is engraved on top of the barrel: COL. COLT LONDON. The backstrap inscribed: Col. T. D. Lawrence. Lawrence is believed to have been presented the gun for his participation in the Great Exhibition of 1851 in London. He served as a member of the Exhibition's Board of Directors. His father was a U.S. Minister to England. Engraving is in the British style used on most of those London Colt arms which were engraved. The gun is cased with complete accessories; formerly in the William M. Locke Collection. *Note:* See a list of presentations planned by Colt in London, published in an appendix of the present book. *(Buddy Hackett Collection)*

Chapter V
COLT'S LONDON ENGRAVING
c. 1853-57

Colonel Colt's London factory was in operation from c. 1853 through 1857, turning out some 11,000 Model 1849 Pocket revolvers and some 42,000 Model 1851 Navies. An additional 700 Dragoons were made, but their basic manufacture was done in Hartford, the final finish — with engraving on several — being applied at the London factory.

The London Colts are quickly discernable from their Hartford brothers, and this is particularly true when hand engraving is present. All decorated London pieces were engraved by British craftsmen, and thus the styles are invariably the same as those common to the London gun trade of the period. No doubt the use of native engravers contributed to a degree of acceptance for London Colt firearms in the Empire. Even the barrel address markings (sometimes hand inscribed on early guns) nearly always included LONDON in their text.*

No data has been gleaned which would identify the engraving staff of the London armory. However, the number of known London Colts with hand cut decor enables a reasonably complete identification of style and coverage in this unique chapter from the Colt engraving story.

*With the notable exception of the Hartford-London Dragoons, normally marked with the New York City address.

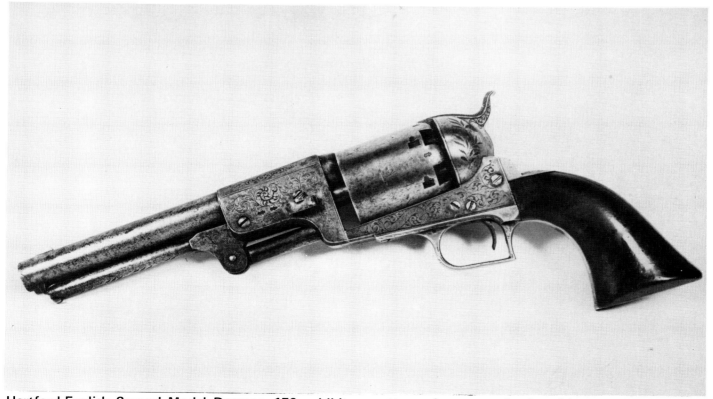

Hartford-English Second Model Dragoon 159 exhibits a pattern of coverage developed by engravers from the London gun trade for Colonel Colt. The Second Model engraved is an extreme rarity. *(Lewis E. Yearout Collection)*

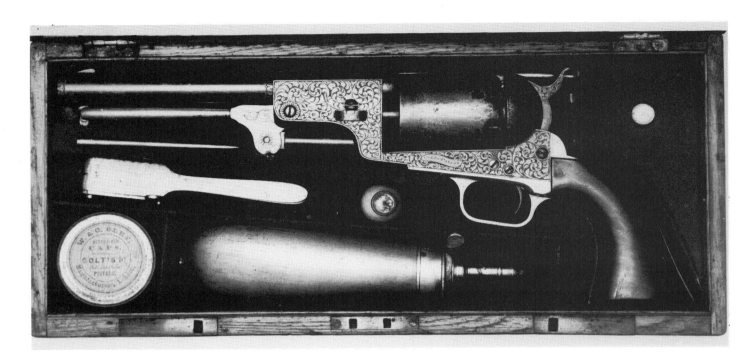

Probably one quarter of the estimated total London Colt Dragoon production of 700 was engraved. As also found on London Navy and Pocket Models, the decorative styles were English, and the engravers were drawn from the London gun trade. Three basic styles of engraving appear on Colt arms of the London series. Third Model Dragoon number 18, with a hand engraved London barrel address, exhibits a profuse style of scroll, with a lined background on the barrel lug and frame. A floral design appears on the bottom of the loading lever, and the recoil shield (both sides); no coverage was used on the sides of the backstrap and triggerguard. As was customary, the government proofmarks on the barrel are enclosed within an engraved oval cartouche. Coverage on the barrel, loading lever, wedge, frame, hammer, and gripstraps; the screws not engraved. NOTE: Some pistols in this style include scrolls on the sides of the gripstraps. Specimen number 208/., so observed, also has scroll coverage instead of the floral designs on the recoil shield and on the bottom of the lever; plus greater scroll coverage on the barrel, lever, and gripstraps. The cylinder cartouche on number 208/. was also hand engraved. *(Arnold M. Chernoff Collection)*

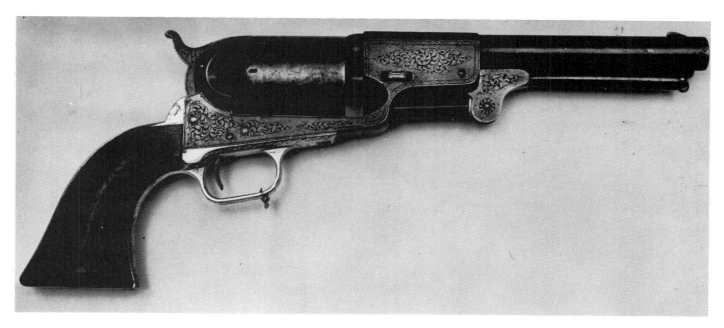

Although the scroll on Dragoon number 129 is similar to Dragoons number 18 and number 25, the coverage is noticeably less, and a roped border appears on the barrel lug flats. Leaves from the vine decor on the bottom of the loading lever are visible in the photograph. Floral motifs also in use on the recoil shield. Hand engraved London barrel address. Second Model London Dragoon number 159 (Lewis Yearout Collection) has a similar scroll and vine style, but somewhat less profuse. *(Courtesy Jackson Arms)*

Examples of the most sparse engraving on the London Dragoons; serial numbers 135 and 136. No lined backgrounds appear on the barrel lugs or frames. This scroll is often seen on English sporting guns of the mid-nineteenth century. Floral motifs similar to the other illustrated Dragoons appear on the recoil shields and on the bottom of the loading levers. New York City Colt barrel address, roll-marked. A similar style of scroll coverage has been noted having a fancy border on the frame, and double line borders of the barrel lug (serial number 186, in the collection of the late William M. Locke). *(R. Q. Sutherland Collection)*

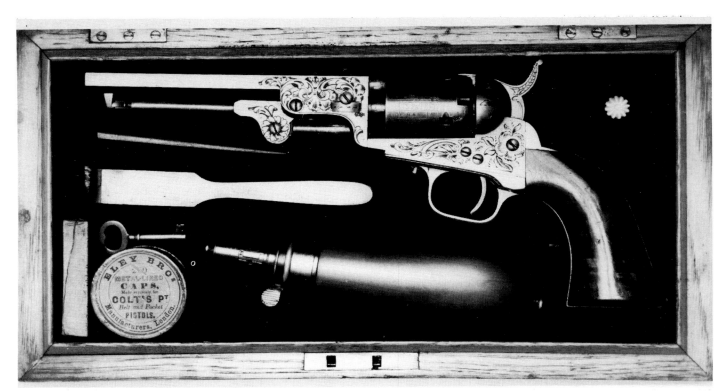

Serial number 26 of the London Model 1849 Pocket revolver. The floral and scroll design is quite unusual, and rarely observed. Three basic types of engraving are standard in the Model 1849, and pistol number 26 exhibits the rarest of these. Hand engraved London barrel address, present due to the low serial number. The casing of typical London design and manufacture (of oak). *(Arnold M. Chernoff Collection)*

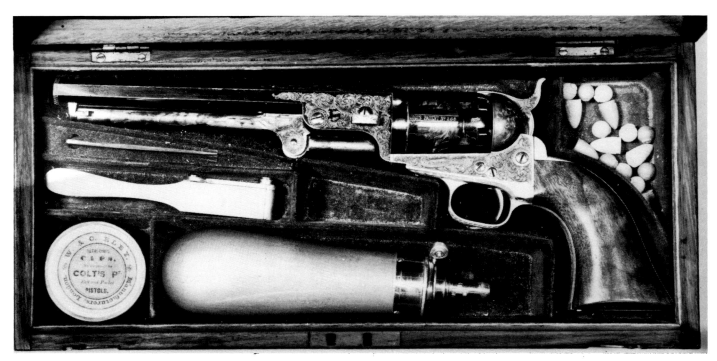

Inscribed on the backstrap and on a plaque inlaid on the case lid: *Lieut. Col. Gustavus Schindler Imp. Royal Engineers — Vienna from the Inventor.* Model 1851 Navy; serial number 153. The scroll style is comparable to the Dragoons numbers 18, 25, and 129. A lined background was used on the frame, barrel lug, and hammer. Coverage on the barrel, wedge, lever, frame, hammer, and gripstraps. Vine motif on the wedge and on the bottom of the lever. No engraving on the sides of the gripstraps, or on the screws. New York barrel address marking. Standard London casing, of oak, the lining of velvet (felt was more commonly employed). Compare with Navy 1129. *(Harold L. Bailey Collection)*

Cased pair of London Model 1849 Pocket revolvers; numbers 609/. and 614/. 6" barrels. Engraved similarly to numbers 4139/. and 4140/. which follow, but variants are noticeable. Double oak casing, with brassbound corners and carrying ring mount; of London make. An estimated 1,000+ Model 1849 Pocket revolvers were engraved (usually in the style pictured here), and at least 3,000 are believed to have been cased, most in the single type oak box as pictured with revolver number 26. London Pocket Model coverage was usually on the barrel, loading lever, wedge, frame, hammer, backstrap, and triggerguard strap. *(William H. Myers Collection)*

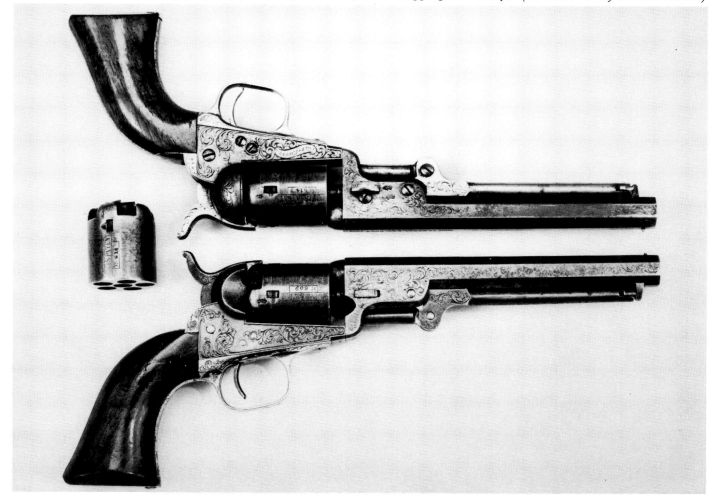

Pocket Model number 141 was built using parts imported from the U.S. Note hand cut barrel address, and the London gun trade scroll and border work. The backstrap of this revolver is presentation inscribed from Samuel Colt. *(Woolaroc Museum, P.R. Phillips Collection)*

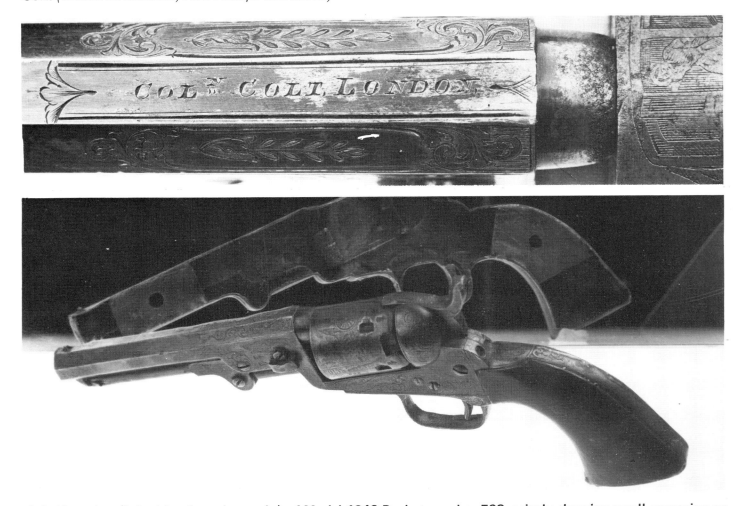

A half casting (left side of revolver only) of Model 1849 Pocket number 593, crisply showing scroll engraving on the barrel, loading lever, frame, and hammer; the roll engraved cylinder scene is also visible. Coloration indicates finish of bluing on all parts, except for silver plating on the gripstraps, and wood-colored grips. Speculation suggests that this casting was used in some way to promote Colt's London revolver sales. *(William H. Myers Collection)*

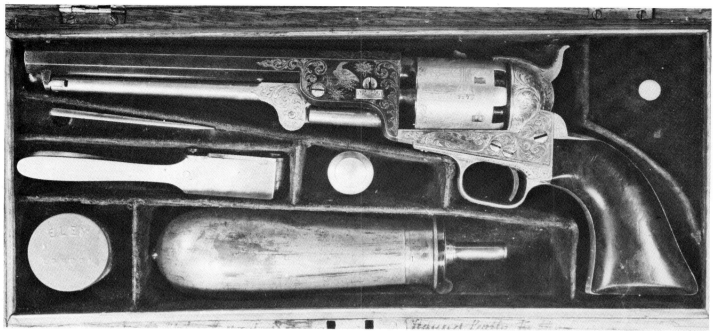

Number 7970 Model 1851 Navy is richly engraved and features the quite rare barrel lug panel scenes of an eagle on the left side and a lion on the right. HC initials inscribed on the backstrap. Scroll style on the frame and barrel is not typical of the estimated total of less than 1000 London Navys which were engraved. Styles of scroll were basically the same as found on the London Dragoons, and on the majority of London Pocket models. Standard coverage on the barrel, loading lever, wedge, frame, hammer, backstrap, and triggerguard. Oak casing, velvet lined. *(Peter J. Van Zyl Collection)*

Detail of London Navy number 208, with scroll and decorative border coverage on the triggerguard. Revolver is from the early production, utilizing Hartford made parts, and thus has the small silver plated brass triggerguard. *(W.F. McLaughlin Collection)*

Inscribed London Colt revolvers are extreme rarities, and serial number 204 Navy has the added feature of U.S. historical importance. Vanderbilt had visited the Colt London armory in 1853, as discovered by researcher-author Joseph G. Rosa in correspondence from Colt employee Jabez Alvord (then at the London factory) to his brother Charles, June 13, 1853: "The 'Vanderbilt excursion party' have arrived in London and they are to make a visit to the Armory sometime this week. They cause considerable excitement here, the papers are full of comments upon them ...."

Vanderbilt and party had sailed to London on his steam yacht the *North Star*. Misspelling of Commodore testifies to the questionable facility of Sam Colt (and apparently some of his employees) at spelling. *(Steve Englert)*

Model 1849 London cased pair, serial numbers 2073/. and 2108/. Brass-bound rosewood casing, with carrying ring inlaid handle. Each of the silver plated steel backstraps is inscribed: LIBORIO RAMON FREIRE. Freire was Minister of War for Chile in 1856, and became President in 1858. Illustrating the basic pattern of scroll engraving found on the Model 1849 London revolvers. *(Dr. Chester P. Bonoff Collection)*

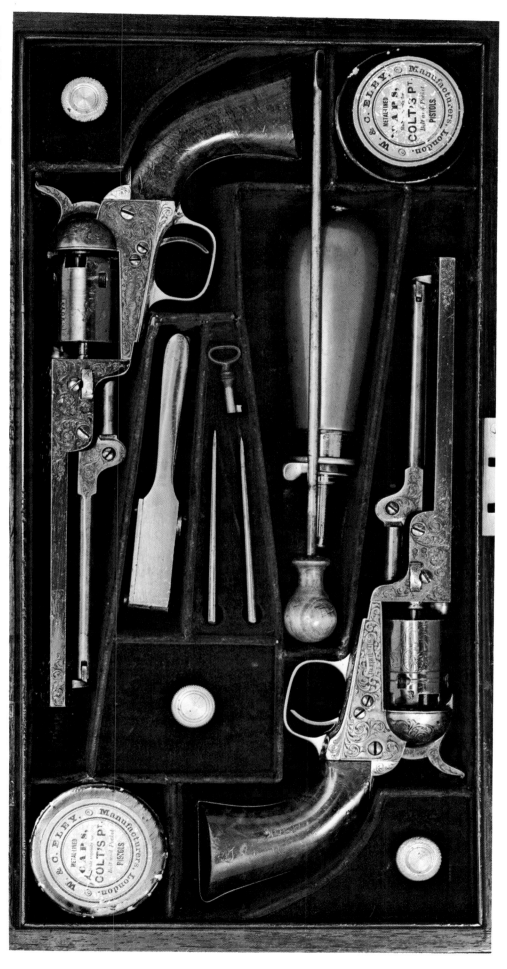

London Navies believed presented to Napoleon III of France. The ebony grips bear gold inlaid Napoleonic motifs. Engraving is the most deluxe style of coverage and scroll to be found on the London Navy revolvers. Casing of brassbound mahogany with green felt lining. Inlaid on the lid a brass disc with the Napoleonic N within a wreath. The interior exhibits the standard London approach to casing. Serial numbers 21900/. and 21904/. Ivory grips did not figure in the decorative scheme of things for London Colt revolvers, in marked contrast to the demand for ivory in the American gun market. NOTE: Serial number 1 of the London Navy was similarly engraved to the pistols of Napoleon III; with the added rarity of an American eagle motif on the left side of the barrel lug and a British lion on the right. *(Formerly in the collection of the late Hugh J. Fitzgerald)*

RIFLES AND VOLUNTEER RIFLE CORPS.

56

the Baltic, in the Crimea, in China, and in India, with the utmost effect.

The shooting with Colt's arms is highly satisfactory; and although we have a decided predilection for an arm which revolves with the trigger, we cannot but say that we have heard some very cogent arguments in favour of Colt's principle over them. With Colt's Revolver we have made first-rate shooting, and have been perfectly satisfied with its action. As a proof that it is not liable to get out of repair, we need only state that the American Board of Ordnance had a holster pistol fired 1,200 times, and a belt pistol 1,500 times, without the slightest derangement. The penetration of the first named was through seven inches of board, and of the second, through six inches.

The form of the pistol will be best understood by the following engraving, in which B, of course, is the barrel; C, the cylinder; G, the hollow groove for capping; H, the hammer; T, the trigger; R, the ramrod, and L, the lever by which it is worked. The mechanism of the pistol is extremely good, strong, and simple, and is not easily deranged. In actual use the arm is set at half cock, as in the case of other revolvers, and thus the cylinder is set at liberty. The powder is then poured into each chamber in succession (or the cartridge inserted whole), and the balls placed in their position without patch or wad; they are then driven home by the lever ramrod. The chamber not being rifled, of course there is no difficulty in ramming the balls down—the only care requisite being that the bullet is fairly down on the powder, and its point beneath the end of the cylinder. In capping, the caps are placed on the nipple in succession, as they pass under the hollowed side of the boss; the hammer is let down gently, and

London Pocket Model number 9251 is pictured on page 56 of RIFLES AND VOLUNTEER CORPS, published in London, c. 1860. The woodcut artist made a reasonably faithful interpretation of what was clearly a London engraved specimen from the tail end of production. Hans Busk's THE RIFLE (London, 1862; p. 47) pictured a somewhat sketchy illustration of an engraved London Pocket Model. *(William H. Myers Collection)*

London cased Model 1849 Pocket revolver with the customary scroll coverage and style. No engraving on the screws or on the sides of the gripstraps. Part of the scroll has a lined background (e.g., on the front of the frame) but most appears in an open style. The bottom view of this pistol (number 4139/.) appears with that of number 4140/., exhibiting identical embellishments. Note instruction label in lid, a feature commonly found on London casings of the London factory period. The third style of London Model 1849 Pocket revolver engraving was the same as on the Napoleon III Navies and Navy number 69368, which follow. *(Ron Dean Collection)*

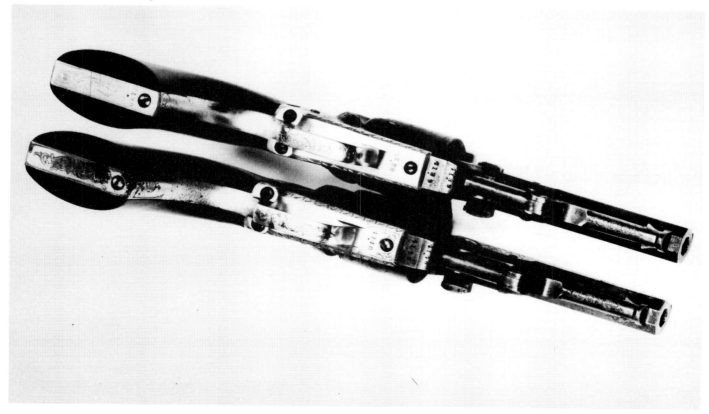

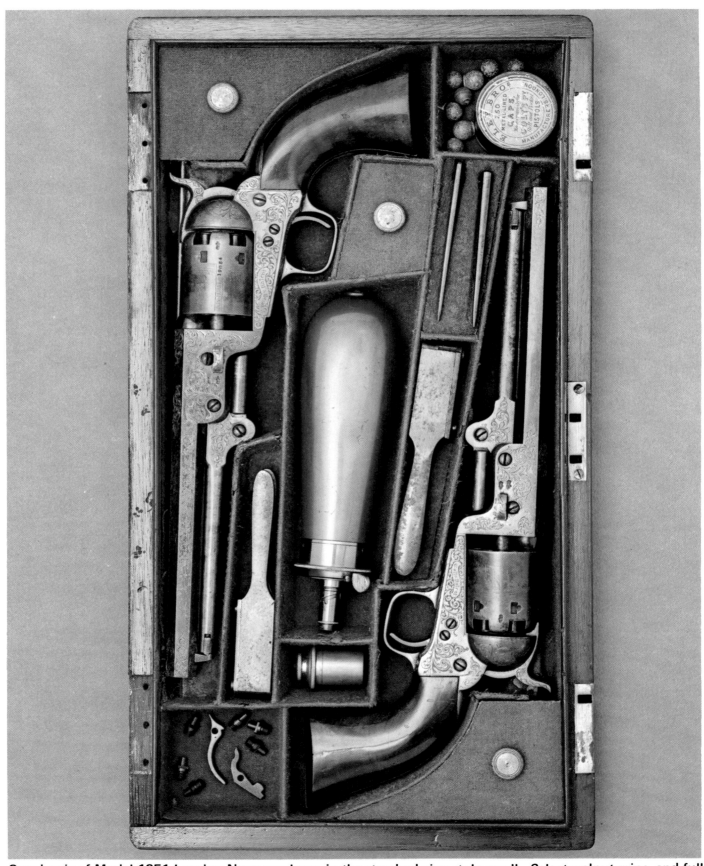

Cased pair of Model 1851 London Navy revolvers, in the standard vine style scroll. Select walnut grips, and full oak casing of London manufacture. Serial numbers 19084/. and 23614/. Compare with the presentation pair of Navies inscribed from Colonel Colt to the Earl of Cardigan; serials of that set are within a few numbers of pistol 19084/. These color photographs show clearly the basic differences between the British style scroll engraving, and the Germanic influence dominating the decoration of contemporary Hartford made Colt firearms. *(Buddy Hackett Collection)*

London Navy number 69368, cut in fine scrolls with hatched background; representing the most profuse scroll pattern on the London Colt revolvers. Rare inscription of *"Colts Patent"* on the *right* side of the frame. Unusual high serial number, well above the accepted terminal range for the London Navy series. *(The Armouries, H.M. Tower of London)*

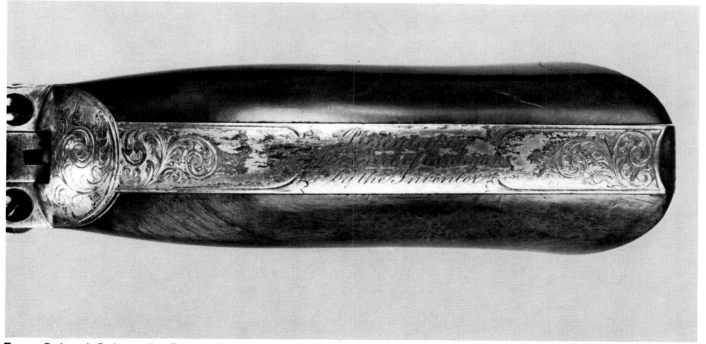

From Colonel Colt to the Earl of Cardigan; cased pair of London Model 1851 Navy revolvers, numbers 19089/. and 19092/. Cardigan had the distinction of leading the charge of the Light Brigade in the Battle of Balaclava (October 25, 1854). The pistols were presented in a double casing of oak, lined in green felt, complete with accessories. On the customary lid inlay of a brass disc, Cardigan's crest was engraved. A standard vine style of scroll, comparable to the pair of Dragoons numbers 135 and 136. The backstraps bore the simple inscription, cut in script letters. Other known recipients of presentation London Colt revolvers were Marshal Jean Jacques Pelisier and Napoleon III of France, and Albert, Prince Consort of England. A "pair of. . . highly finished ornamented [Navy] Weapons, in Mahogany case complete" were sold to Prince Albert's private secretary in January of 1854 (quoting from correspondence in Windsor Castle Archives). *(Charles L. Bricker Collection)*

Liege (Belgium) copy of the Third Model Colt Dragoon, its embellishments acid etched, except for the engraved hammer and gripstraps. *(Musee d'Armes, Liege, Belgium)*

(opposite page) First page of a draft of proposed recipients of presentation arms from Samuel Colt, signed and dated October 28, 1851. Colt had been allowed by the British government to sell several guns from his display at the Great Exhibition of 1851, in London. In one of his most ambitious giveaways, he felt it would be advantageous to present several of the remaining show guns to dignitaries, publications, and institutions. A very few of the gifts themselves are now known to collectors, but it is apparent that only a limited number bore inscriptions. In pencil by most of the listed recipients were notations regarding what should be given, e.g., N.E. meant Navy engraved. Colonel Lawrence was to receive engraved Navy and Pocket revolvers. A London Dragoon with his name on the backstrap was made after Colt began his factory at Vauxhall Bridge, a project which received dramatic encouragement during the Great Exhibition of 1851. (See page 146.) "The African Traveller Gordon Cumming" was also on the list, as were Prince Albert and The Prince of Wales (see Chapter II, "Exhibition Grade" scroll). Most of the list was written by a secretary or associate, but the notations on the right columns, some of the names, and the statement on the third page were in Samuel Colt's own hand.

It is believed this detailed listing was the most ambitious presentation by Colt up to that time. He reached a total of 86 pistols, and had estimated the value of the presents at about four pounds each. The Great Exhibition presentation list is one of the most interesting documents in the study of Colt Firearms. *(Harold L. Bailey Jr. Collection)*

2. His Royal Highness Prince Albert A.E

1. His Royal Highness Prince of Wales.

2. Duke of Wellington ———— army ingrav

2. Marquis of Anglesea ———— army ingrav

1. Admiral Deans Dundas — Navy ingrav

1. Rt Hon Sir Fran*s* *T.* Baring Bt.

1. Rt Hon Fox Maule.

1. Lord John Russell

1. Rt Hon Sir Charles Wood
   General W*m* Febbs M*c* Neil

1. Viscount Palmerston

2. Maj. Gen*l* C. R. Fox &c.&.
   Gordon

2. Col. Chalmers, Ordenance Dep*t*
2. Le Grand Smith, Woolwich &c.
1. Geo. Lovell

2. M*r* Newton P*t* agent

1. United Service Club museum.

1. Army & Navy Club
2. Institution of Civil Engineers.
   Do. Sec*y* of M*r* Manby.
1. J. Mac Dougall Smith Esq

1. The African Traveller Gordon Cumming
1. Robert J Walker
1. British Museum
1. M*r* Colburn the Indian New service corr
5. Cullen American corr Winchester
   American

1. Col Lawrence
   Davis Sec*y* Legation
   Col Cullender, Liverpool
   M*r* van Wicte, Birmingham
   wright Liverpool

Model 1860 Army revolver number 173629 was plated in gold and silver, and fitted with relief carved ivory grips of the eagle and shield type. The border trim on the cylinder is rare. Note that the S curve with berry fill-in motif on the barrel lug appears also on some Winchester Model 1866 rifles of the late 1860's. Three Ulrich brothers (Conrad F., Herman L., and John) took that and other decorative devices and styles with them when they left Colt to join the Winchester firm, 1869. *(Buddy Hackett Collection)*

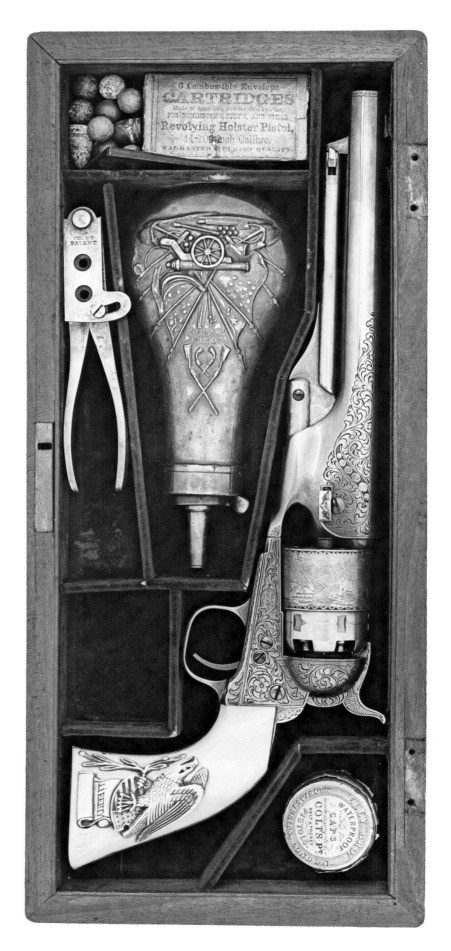

Chapter VI
LATE PERCUSSION
VINE STYLE SCROLL
c. 1861 — c. 1870
THE HEAVY LEAF SCROLL
c. 1870

Colt continued to use the Gustave Young Germanic scroll with punched dot background until as late as c. 1870. But for all practical purposes the Young scroll had been joined by another style c. 1861, and had been nearly discontinued by c. 1864 — the year of the factory fire. That disaster is known to have taken the Colt in-house engraving shop up in smoke.

The new scroll appearing c. 1861 is known as the late percussion vine style. Its coverage was the same as the previous scroll, but its distinguishing detail was the lack of a punched dot background. By eliminating the punched dot, the pattern could be cut with a savings of about one quarter from the time required when the dots were used. The new

style offered a quite graceful and elegant look, and judging from the extra fine quality of some known revolvers, Young himself sometimes employed it.

Details of coverage, patterns, and variations from the standard are pointed out in the picture captions. As with the Young scroll, only one basic degree of coverage was advertised, and variations were special-order pieces.

The late percussion vine scroll was the predominant type of engraving used on Colt revolvers from c. 1861 through c. 1870. Its successor was the scroll of Cuno A. Helfricht, who became Colt factory engraving contractor c. 1871, but whose career with the company began in the 1860's, under his father's tutelage.

Model 1849 Pocket revolver; engraved in a vine style of scroll on the barrel, loading lever, frame, hammer, and gripstraps. The wedge was cut with border designs and the screws were not engraved. *(H.A. Redfield Collection)*

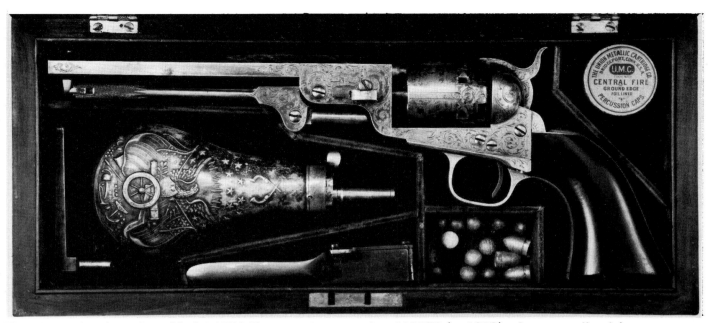

The vine style of scroll on Model 1851 Navy revolver, number 163853 (c. 1863). An unusually elaborate coverage, with the rare checkered lever, and scroll and border work on the cylinder. The most striking feature however is the presence of special motifs on the barrel lug — on the left side the ironclad warship *Merrimac*, and on the right side the *Monitor*. Customary lack of engraving on the screw heads. Rare ebony grips. American style casing, lined in velvet; complete accessories; the percussion cap tin dating from the metallic cartridge period. *(Formerly in the William M. Locke Collection)*

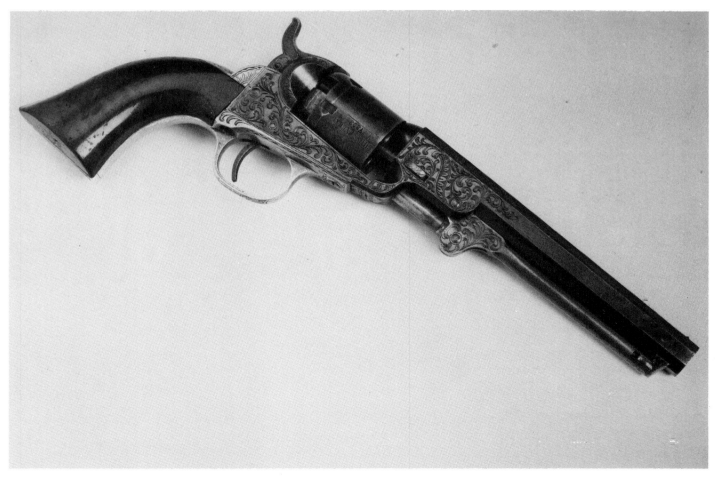

Model 1849 Pocket number 317503/E is an excellent example of the late vine style scroll. 6" barrel, select walnut grips. The revolver is cased in a patented (April 1854) box of brass bound mahogany by W. Kidder. *(William H. Myers Collection)*

An extraordinary cased pair of Sidehammer pistols, the backstraps inscribed: *His Highness Prince Louis of Bentheim With the Highest Esteem, Presented by Alexander Thuer.* Scroll engraved in the vine pattern, with relief carved and checkered ivory grips. Levers finely cross-hatched as are the hammer spurs. Serial numbers 6662 and 6663; engraved c. 1863. Special casing of varnished walnut with partitions for six packets of Colt combustible cartridges; note supply of extra parts. The Prince's royal coat of arms is relief carved on one grip, and a relief carved portrait bust of the Prince appears on the other. The bottoms of each grip neatly checkered. A shield-shaped plaque was inlaid on the case lid, engraved with a crown, beneath which is the elaborate two letter monogram L.B. (old English letters). A similar deluxe cased pair of Sidehammer revolvers is known, engraved in the Gustave Young style scroll; these pistols have ivory grips relief carved with portrait busts of Colonel Colt. *(Formerly in the William M. Locke Collection)*

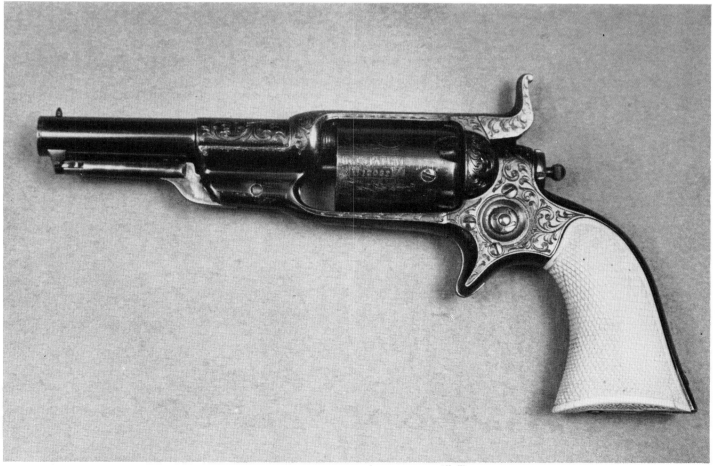

Model 1855 Sidehammer number 12083 should be compared with number 11224/IE, on page 166. Note screw in cylinder, and the checkered ivory grips (even a panel on the butt). Blue and case hardened finish. *(George S. Lewis, Jr. Collection)*

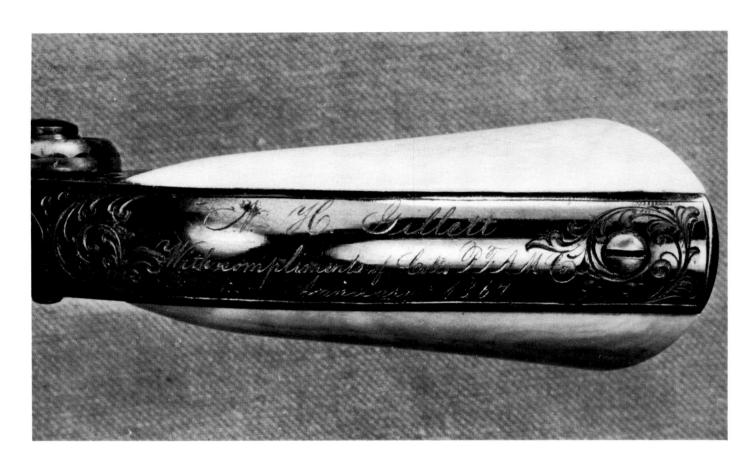

The scarce ''screw-in-cylinder'' model of the Sidehammer series; serial number 11224/IE. Backstrap inscription in script, with the seldom seen feature of a date. Vine style scrollwork on the barrel, frame, hammer, sideplate, and gripstrap. Complete factory casing in varnished mahogany, lined in reddish velvet. *(H. A. Redfield Collection)*

Serial number 163902/. Model 1851 Navy, engraved in the late vine style scroll, and featuring the extremely rare detail of relief carved and checkered ebony grips. Stocks of this type are as rare as Charter Oak in percussion Colt revolver production. *(Buddy Hackett Collection/Photograph, S. P. Stevens)*

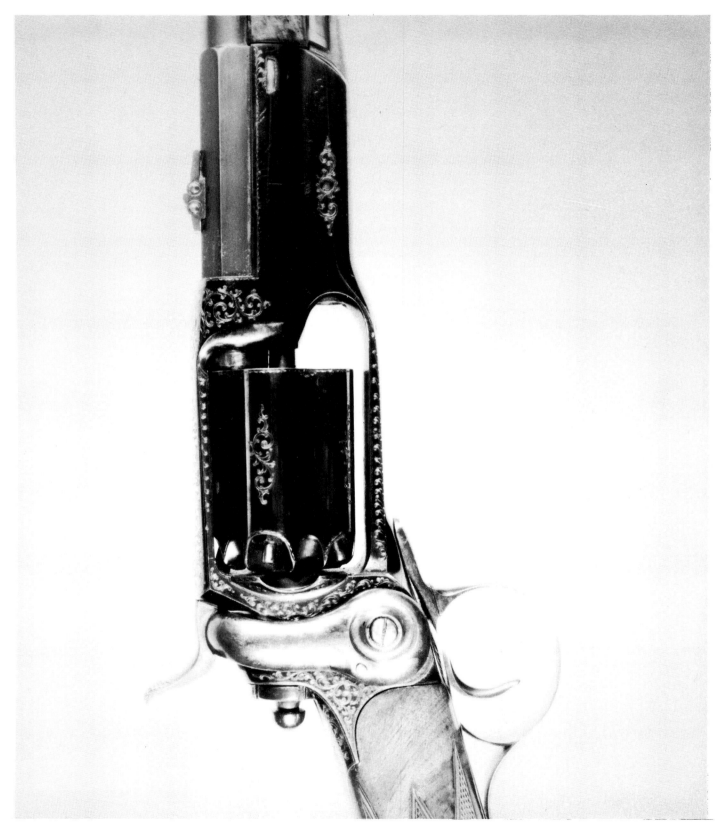

NOTE: On the matter of plated finishes, the student should consult an article by Paul S. Lederer in Volume XXXI, No. 1 of the *Military Collector & Historian* (Spring 1979), published by the Company of Military Historians: "A Brief Account of Nickel Plating". Among the writer's conclusions, certainly born out by *The Book of Colt Engraving:* "It appears . . . that nickel-plating for guns became popular between 1867 and 1871." Another article of interest to the student is by John F. Dussling, and appeared in the November 1976 "Monthly Bugle", published by the Pennsylvania Antique Gun Collectors Association, Inc. The latter story includes comments on serial numbering of the Model 1862 Police and Pocket Navy revolvers, and suggests they may have been produced in separate serial ranges. The matter of their respective engraving styles is also discussed.

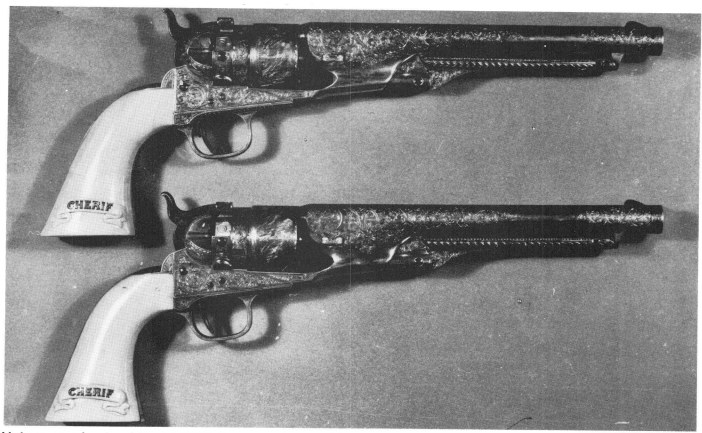

Unique cased pair of Model 1860 Army revolvers, with extra set of Thuer conversion cylinders. Serial numbers 176448/E and 177727/E (c. 1869). The left side of each grip is relief carved with a star and crescent motif; CHERIF inlaid in gold letters on the right grips. Hand engraved cylinder scenes. Profuse vine style scroll coverage, with variations especially evident on the barrel to give an Egyptian feeling to the decoration. Crescent and star motifs are part of the design on both sides of each barrel. Complete coverage on the levers, including rope and wheat chaf motifs. Rare maize border motif on the muzzles. Full plated finish, with blued screws. French style double casing, with silver plated accessories. Colt ledgers show number 176448 in inventory, October 10, 1868: "Soft State/Stock". *(Anonymous Collection)*

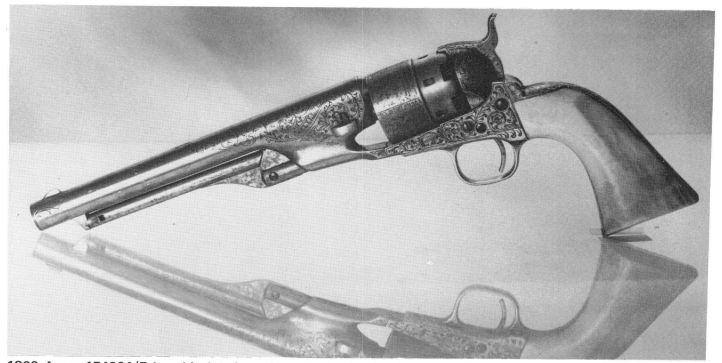

1860 Army 154301/E is gold plated on the cylinder, loading lever, and hammer; the balance finished in silver. Grips of ivory. *(Corydon B. Rich Collection)*

Presentation cased 1860 Army to H. D. Norton, with the compliments of the Colt Company, October 1865, and so inscribed. Serial number 154768. *(Jonathan M. Peck Collection/ Photograph, Ken Kay, made for Time-Life Books)*

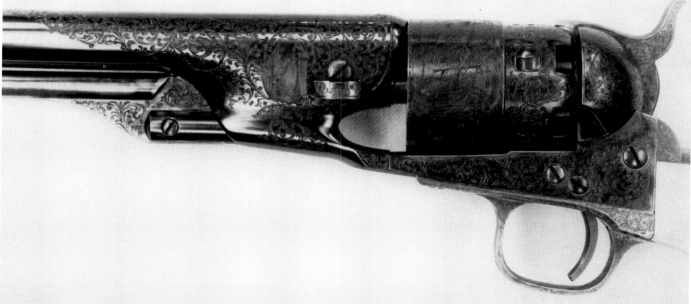

Presented to H.D. Norton, with the compliments of the Colt company, October 1865. Norton was a prominent San Antonio businessman, and his firm, H.D. Norton & Brother, was the only Texas company to become one of the Colt allies in the period 1850-70. Among others in this elite group of Colt jobbers were Schuyler, Hartley and Graham, Joseph C. Grubb & Co., Kittredge and Folson (New Orleans), and W. Read & Son (Boston). The pistol, a Model 1860 Army, is engraved in an extra-profuse vine scroll style. On the backstrap is the presentation inscription, and on the case lid Norton's name and an October 1865 date. Note the rare checkered rammer lever, the checkered ivory grips (with the curved border), and the hand engraved cylinder scene. Coverage on the barrel and frame are beyond any standard treatment. The goddess of liberty is encircled by elaborate and exquisite scrolls on the left side of the barrel lug; an American eagle similarly encircled on the right. Rare scroll and border motifs add to the embellishment of the cylinder (which lacks a serial number marking). Minute animal and floral motifs abound in the finely detailed scrollwork. Extremely rare brassbound walnut casing, of extra large size. Lined in blue velvet; and fitted with complete accessories. High luster blue on the barrel, cylinder, bullet mold, and screwdriver-nipple wrench. Eight extra packages of Colt combustible cartridges. Silver plated flask mounts.

(Jonathan M. Peck Collection)

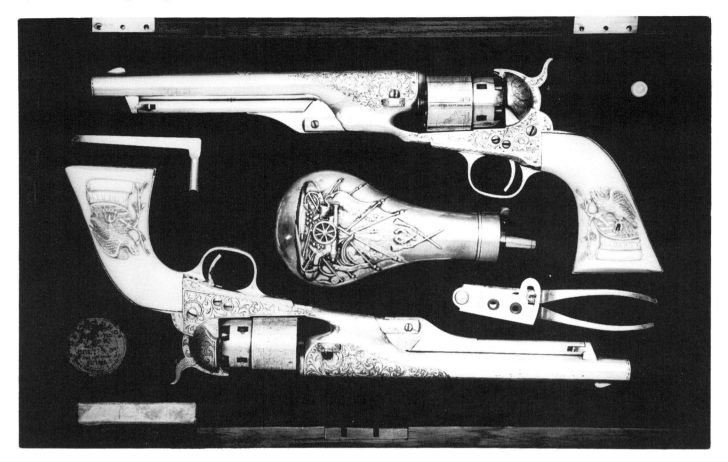

A unique cased pair of Model 1860 Army revolvers. The upper pistol, number 150163/E (c. 1864) illustrates the vine style of scrollwork, contrasting to the Gustave Young pattern on the lower gun. Plated finish, including accessories; French style contour casing. *(Pennsylvania Historical and Museum Commission)*

The standard vine scroll pattern as used on the Model 1860 Army. Serial number **169559** (c. 1867). The heavy dash and fine dot border will sometimes be found on the cylinders. *(Hugh E. Hayes Collection)*

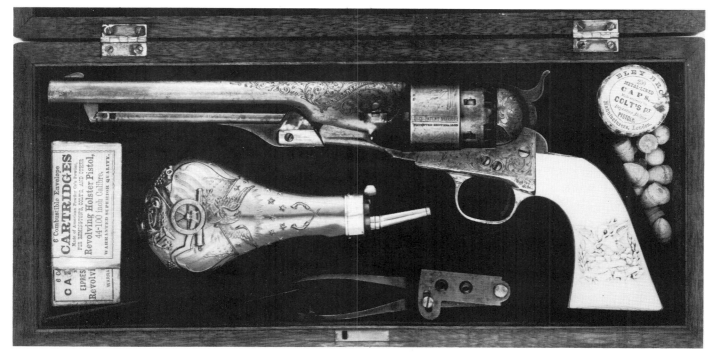

Model 1860 Army number 181684 (c. 1869). Standard vine scroll, with rare relief carved Mexican eagle and snake ivory grips. *(George R. Repaire Collection)*

Presented by the Colt Company to a New York banker, William H. Cox. Model 1861 Navy number 23371IP.
(Jerry D. Berger Collection/Photograph, S. P. Stevens)

Presented by the Colt company to a New York banker, William H. Cox. Cox's pistol, Model 1861 Navy number 23371IP, is one of the finest engraved Colt arms of the 1860's. On the left side of the barrel lug a sailor firing a revolver; on the right side a bare breasted maiden. Finely checkered loading lever; extra scroll coverage on the barrel at the muzzle and on the lug. Hand engraved cylinder scene, with the vine pattern of trim. Note the lack of engraving on the screws. The ivory grips, with the curved border to the checkering, are of a design rarely seen. Brassbound walnut casing, lined in purple velvet, with purple silk hinge covers. High gloss blued steel bullet mold. *(Jerry D. Berger Collection)*

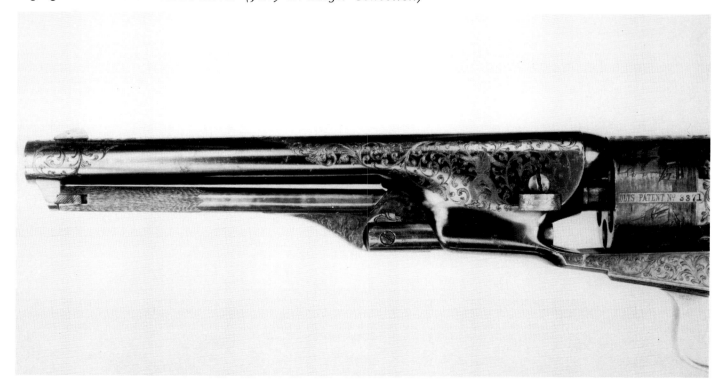

Vine style scroll on Model 1849 Pocket 309559; revolver finished in blue and case-hardening, with silver plated gripstraps.   One line New York address barrel roll marking; 6″ barrel. Casing of brass bound rosewood, lined in velvet, and fitted in the French style. *(George S. Lewis, Jr. Collection)*

Model 1862 Police conversion number 37939 is finished in blue and case-hardening; grips of walnut, the gripstraps silver plated. A zig-zag line device decorates the conversion plate. *(George S. Lewis, Jr. Collection)*

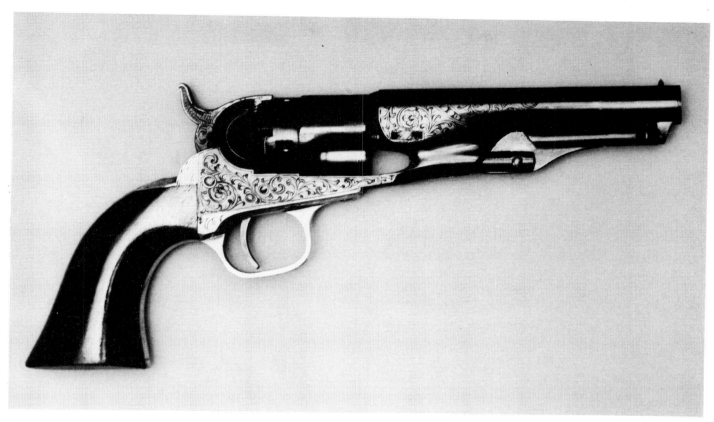

Model 1862 Police and Model 1862 Pocket Navy (formerly known as the Model 1853) revolvers were manu-factured in the same serial range. They also share similar engraving styles and coverage of their period of manufacture (c. 1861-73), as shown here in comparison of the Model 1862 Police number 30073 with Pocket Navy number 2378/E. 30073 bears the backstrap inscription: *To Henry Kellogg with compliments of Colts Pt. FA Mfg. Co., Hartford, Conn.* The revolver is pictured cased on page 182. *(Dr. Chester P. Bonoff Collection)*

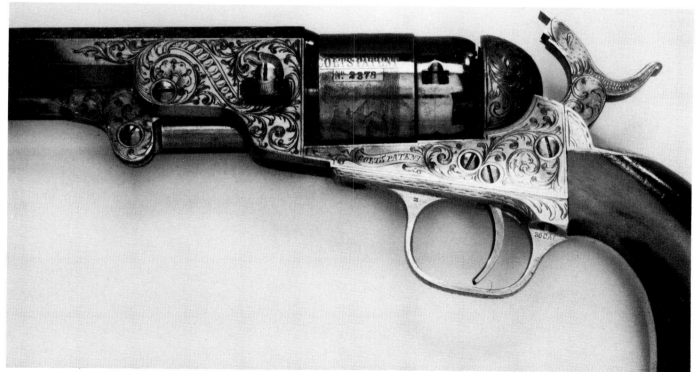

Serial number 2378/E of the Model 1862 Pocket Navy. Note hand engraved COLT'S PATENT frame marking; coverage on the barrel, rammer lever, wedge, frame, hammer (wolf head), backstrap, and triggerguard. Screws not engraved. c. 1861. *(Jerry D. Berger Collection)*

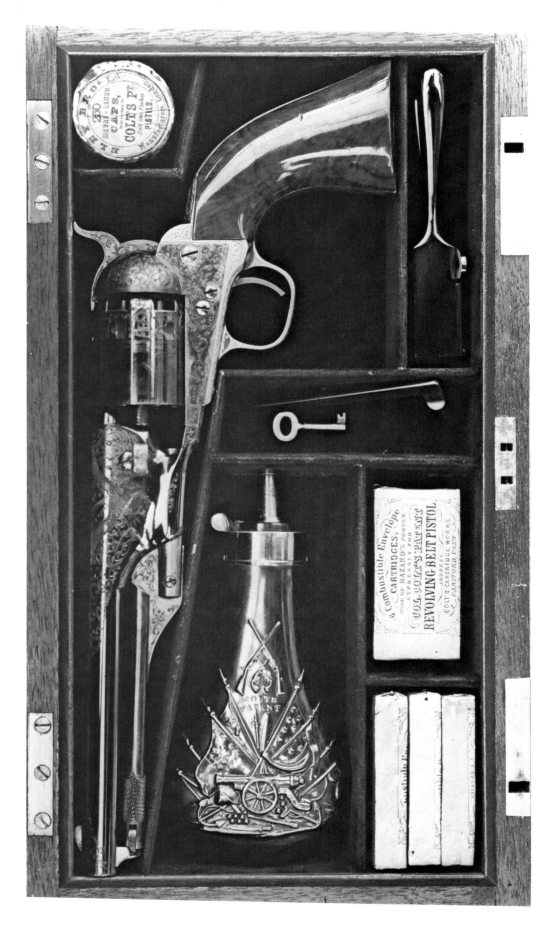

Model 1861 Navy revolver; serial number 19928/E. Inscribed in script on the backstrap from the Colt company to E.W. Parsons; presented in December of 1865. A superb specimen of the vine style scroll, in an extra-deluxe treatment. On the left side of the barrel, an American eagle and shield motif. Finely checkered loading lever; scroll trim and wavy line border on the cylinder (which lacks a serial number). Varnished select walnut grips. On the barrel and cylinder a rich high gloss blue finish; the same finish appears on the bullet mold and the screwdriver-nipple wrench. The brassbound walnut casing, lined in blue velvet, is of a rare extra-large type. Complete accessories, including packages of combustible cartridges. *(Richard P. Mellon Collection)*

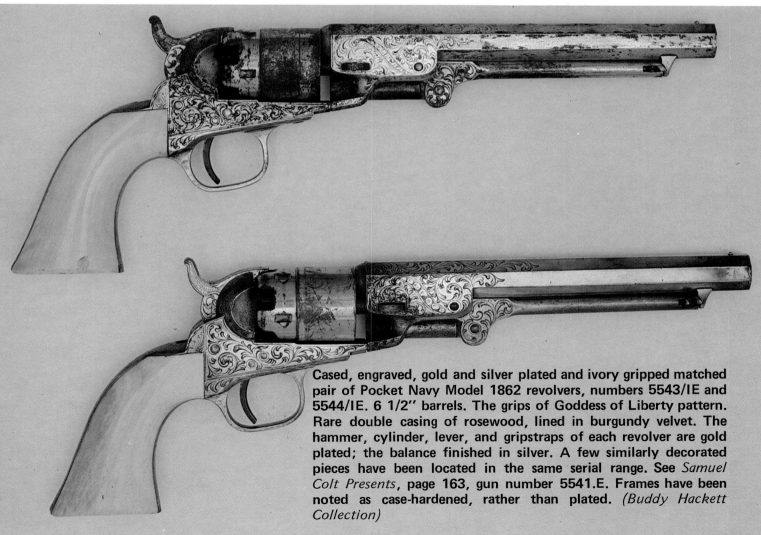

Cased, engraved, gold and silver plated and ivory gripped matched pair of Pocket Navy Model 1862 revolvers, numbers 5543/IE and 5544/IE. 6 1/2" barrels. The grips of Goddess of Liberty pattern. Rare double casing of rosewood, lined in burgundy velvet. The hammer, cylinder, lever, and gripstraps of each revolver are gold plated; the balance finished in silver. A few similarly decorated pieces have been located in the same serial range. See *Samuel Colt Presents*, page 163, gun number 5541.E. Frames have been noted as case-hardened, rather than plated. *(Buddy Hackett Collection)*

Model 1862 Pocket Navy, factory conversion from percussion to .38 c.f. Serial number 17613/E. Finished in nickel plating. 4½" barrel. *(William H. Myers Collection)*

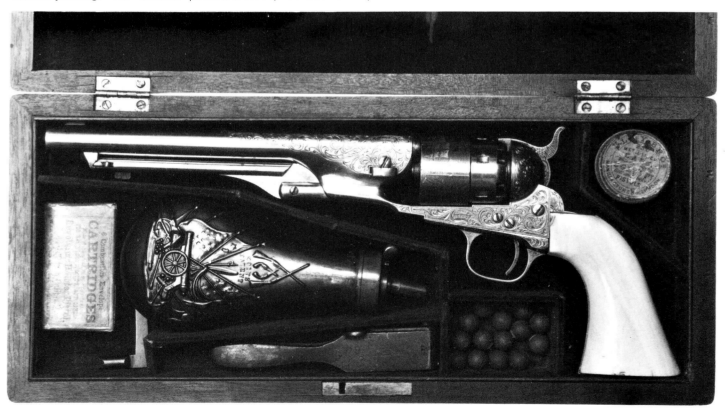

Nickel plated and ivory gripped Model 1860 Army number 159800. Late vine scroll sharing several features with the Pocket Navy above. Formerly John B. Solley III collection. *(Ronald A. Ogan Collection)*

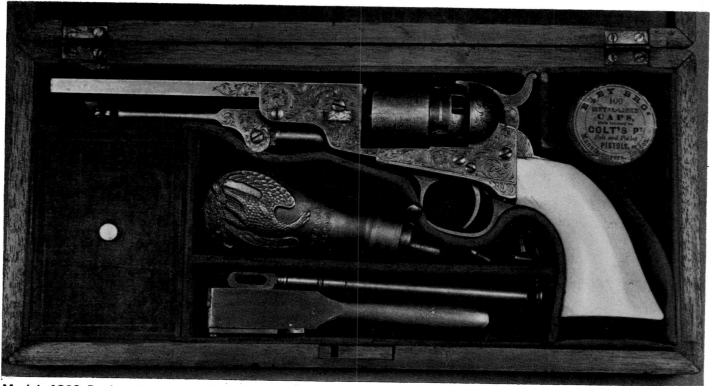

Model 1862 Pocket Navy 6404/E includes the quite unusual feature of the left side of the frame engraved COLTS (in an arc), rather than the customary COLTS/PATENT. Finish of blue and case-hardening, with silver plated gripstraps. Grips of ivory. Note quite rare casing for this model revolver. 5½" barrel. *(George S. Lewis, Jr. Collection)*

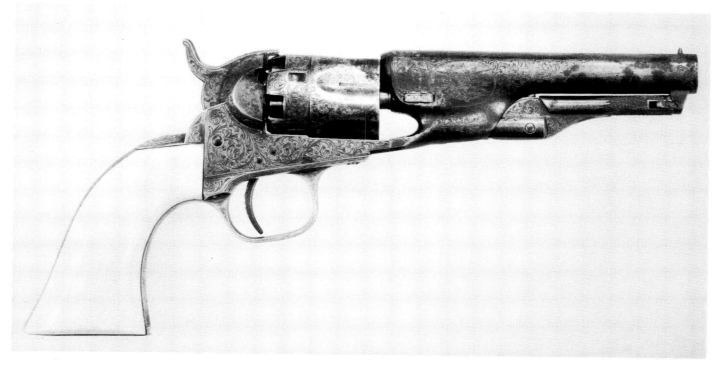

The vine style in an extra degree of coverage; Model 1862 Police revolver, serial number 29085; c. 1865. Scrollwork on the cylinder; finely checkered loading lever; extra scroll coverage on the barrel lug and at the muzzle, and on the frame. On the barrel lug the extreme rarity of a figure of Justice on the left side, and an American eagle with outstretched wings on the right; both within oval borders. On the backstrap the inscription: W. W. W. Wood./June 25th 1865, U.S. Navy (in old English letters). Wood, one of the pioneers of the American steam navy, owned a double cased set; the other pistol was a Model 1861 Navy, number 17520. The weapon was similarly engraved and inscribed; the casing of brassbound mahogany. Wood's Navy revolver and the casing are now in the U.S. Naval Academy Museum, Annapolis. *(Norm Flayderman Collection)*

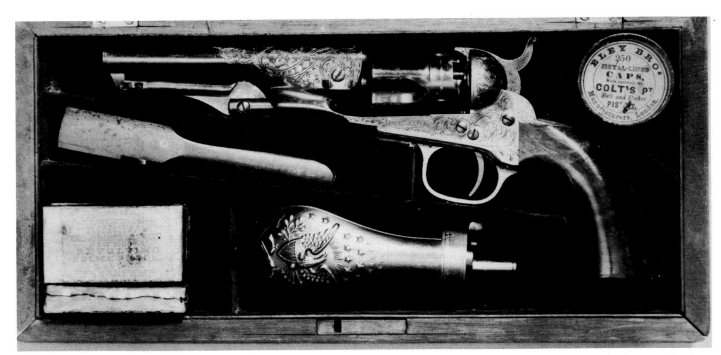

The standard pattern of vine style scroll as cut on the Model 1862 Police revolver. Number 30073; inscribed on the backstrap, in script: *To Henry Kellogg with compliments of Colts Pt. F A Mfg. Co., Hartford, Conn.* Mahogany case; lined in velvet; with complete accessories. *(Dr. Chester P. Bonoff Collection)*

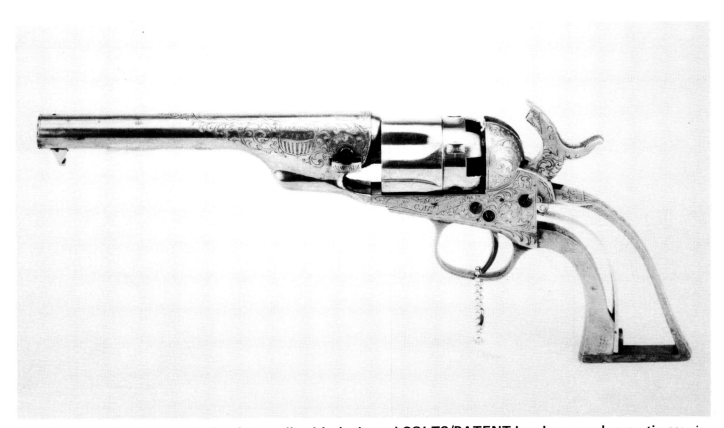

A unique sample piece cut in the vine scroll, with the legend COLTS/PATENT hand engraved seven times; *viz.,* on the left and right sides of the barrel lug and frame, the bottom of the triggerguard, the top of the hammer, and the top flat of the backstrap. Wolf head hammer; rare shield motifs, and equally rare eagle head (on the recoil shield). Believed made as a promotional pistol, and for some reason never completed. Serial number 30729/E (c. 1867). *(Colt Collection of Firearms, Connecticut State Library)*

The heavy leaf scroll style of c. 1870 is one of the least observed of all types of Colt engraving. From known examples, it is possible to pinpoint the style at about 1870. The identity of the engraver (or engravers) is unknown. The scroll is so distinctive and so specific in period of use that the source likely worked for Colt for only a matter of several months.

Post-dating the work of Gustave Young and Herman Bodenstein, and pre-dating the Helfricht period, the heavy leaf scroll represents an interesting and difficult to possess interlude for collectors.

Illustrated with these specimens is a revolver of a slightly later period, done in a distinctive style which is also documented by Colt company records.

Nickel plated conversion of the Model 1862 Pocket Navy revolver; serial number 20127/E. Leaf style scroll engraving on the barrel, frame, hammer, gripstraps, and cylinder (line and dot border only). Full nickel plating. *(Glenn Gierhart Collection)*

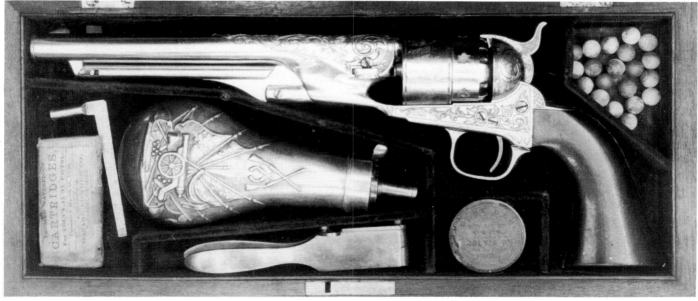

The heavy leaf scroll in a contrasting layout to Model 1860 Army number 187265. Serial number on illustrated revolver is number 187300/E; shipped on April 10, 1877, to Schuyler, Hartley and Graham; part of the same shipment of 70 as number 187265. Full nickel plated finish. Mahogany Colt casing with full accessories. *(Jerry D. Berger Collection)*

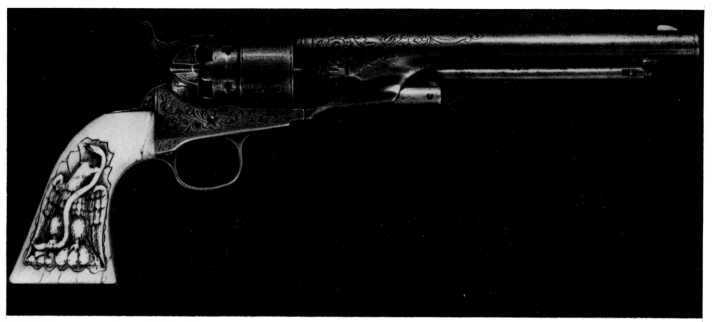

1860 Army number 185335/E was shipped to Schuyler, Hartley & Graham on March 21, 1878. No mention of the ivory grips in the factory letter, but that is a detail known to have been provided by SH & G. Note the coverage includes a line and dot border on the cylinder. *(Robert G. Smith Collection)*

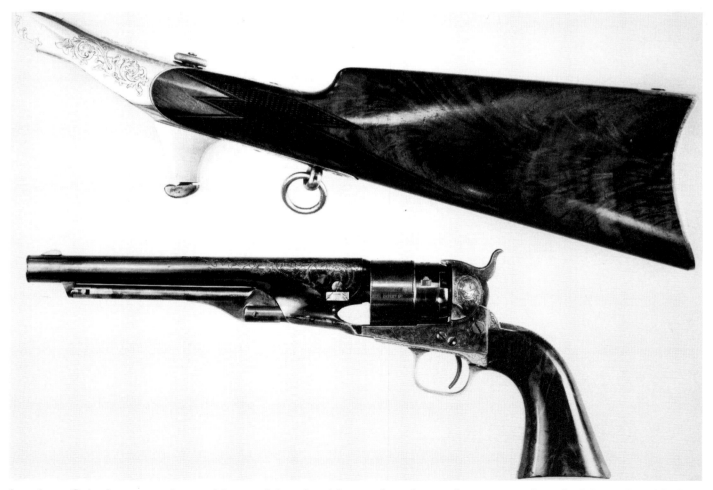

A unique Colt Army revolver, with matching shoulder stock and complete accessories. Serial number 183226; c. 1870. Engraved in the heavy leaf scroll pattern on the barrel, wedge, cylinder (border motif only), frame, hammer, and gripstraps, and on the stock yoke and buttplate. The checkered select walnut buttstock is of exceptional rarity. NOTE: No serial number present on the cylinder. Revolver and stock are cased, see overleaf. *(Johnie Bassett Collection)*

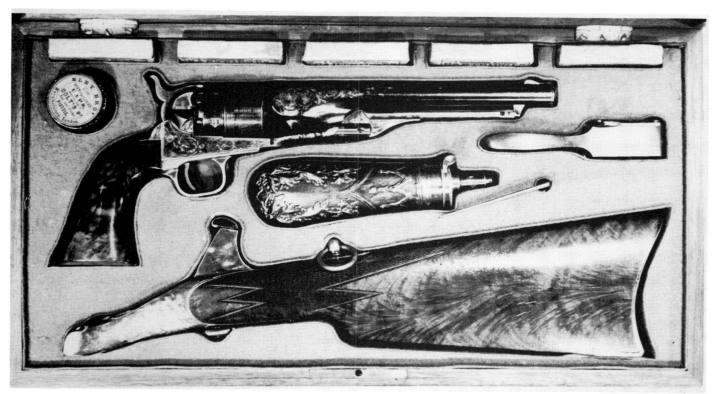

The serial number 183226 Model 1860 Army, in its original case with full accessories. *(Johnie Bassett Collection)*

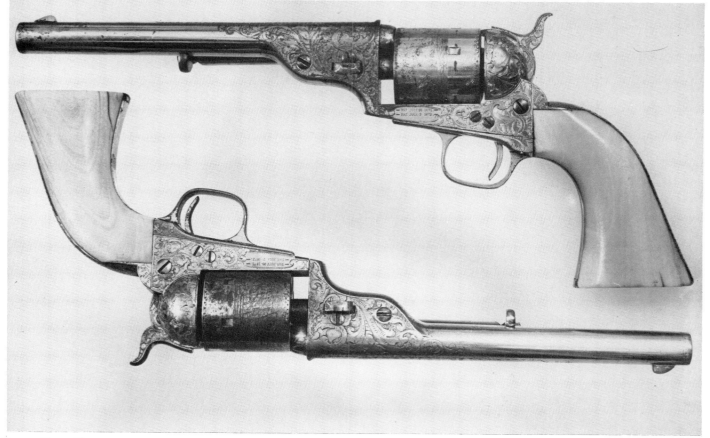

Open Top Frontier .44s numbers 1970 and 2003, shipped by Colt's to J.P. Moores Sons, New York, in July 1876; and recorded in the ledgers as engraved, nickel plated, and .44 rimfire caliber. Part of a total of eight revolvers of like configuration, the balance bearing numbers 1932, 1983, 1992, 1993, 2004, and 1982; likely date of work c. 1872-74. Engraving of a rather unusual scroll, with large leaf motifs; cut and punched borders on the cylinders. Probably attributable to one of the novice factory craftsmen. Engraved Open Top revolvers are quite *rare. (Paul Sorrell Collection)*

These superb pictures of Model 1860 Army number 187277/E graphically reveal the features of a scroll directly related to the Heavy Leaf style. Engraver likely is the same person responsible for the Heavy Leaf pattern, as revealed in comparison of such details as the overall heavy effect of the scroll, the depth, liner, and punched background. No other identically engraved Model 1860 Army revolver has come to the attention of the writer, but the relation of 187277/E to Heavy Leaf Colts is apparent. Like numbers 187300 and 187265, this Army was one of 70 shipped from the factory on April 10th 1877 to Schuyler, Hartley and Graham. Reportedly around 1902 it was found with Apache remains and artifacts in the "Cochise Stronghold" near Tombstone, Arizona. *(Private Collection; Photographs by and courtesy of Dr. R. L. Woolery)*

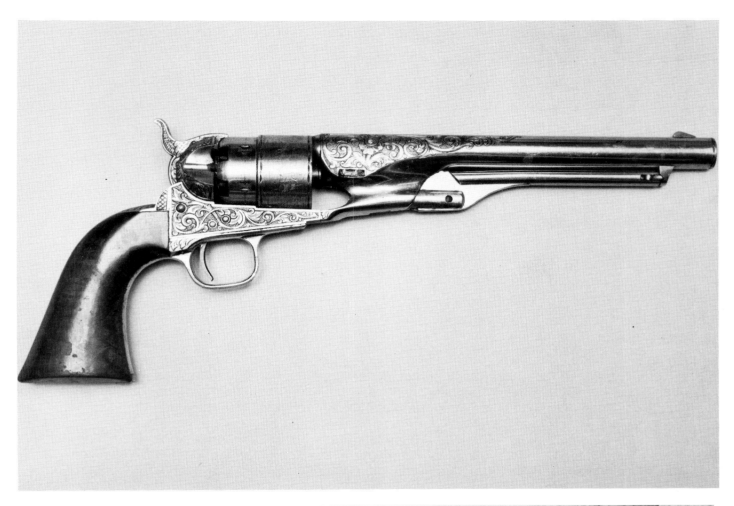

An example of the heavy leaf scroll coverage. Large floral patterns, with punched dot backgrounds. Coverage on the same parts as Army number 183226. The cylinder border is of the dot and dash type. Full nickel plating; blued screws. Serial number 187265. Mahogany Colt casing; lined in velvet; complete accessories. Colt factory serial records show this piece to have been shipped April 10, 1877 to Schuyler, Hartley and Graham, New York, as part of a group of 70 engraved Model 1860 Army revolvers. Manufacture and engraving was done c. 1870, and for some unknown reason the guns did not leave the factory for another seven years. Sales of percussion Colt firearms were quite slow during the period of the late 1860's and 1870's. *(Dr. Chester P. Bonoff Collection)*

◆ ◆

Chapter VII
"TIFFANY" GRIPS

◆ ◆

Metal grips and stocks have centuries of precedent in European, Oriental, and American gunmaking. Specimens are known of German and Austrian wheellock pistols of the sixteenth century, of flintlock Flemish, Austrian, and German pistols of the seventeenth century, of Scottish snaphaunce and flintlock pistols (all-metal stocks were standard on these), and Belgian flintlock and percussion pistols. Of American makes, the Massachusetts arms revolver and the Henry Deringer pistol, the Colt and Smith & Wesson revolvers, Winchester rifles, and (standard) the Reid Knuckledusters represent nineteenth century pieces known with all-metal or metal-covered stocks.

The rare cast grips on Colt revolvers of the period c. 1861 through c. 1875 have long been an enigma to collectors. Although the various types have been classified no exact provenance has been ascribed as to original manufacturers. Furthermore, limited data has been published on the cast grips found on some New Line Colt pistols and similar pocket type handguns. These stocks, which invariably bear an 1874 patent date, are akin to the cast Colt grips of the earlier period. Still a third distinct group of metal grips exists in nineteenth century arms Americana. These are the silver stocks made by Tiffany & Company for certain Smith & Wesson and Colt revolvers of the 1890's and early 1900's, and for at least one Winchester rifle.

The earliest known Colt all-metal grips date from 1847 and were made in the Hartford factory, of sterling silver. These were not cast but were formed into a contour consistent with the standard wooden grip on each pistol. A hero of the Mexican War was the fortunate recipient of the pistols, a presentation matched pair of Dragoons whose unique grips were later fully inscribed. The order had come to Colt from New York dealer Moore & Baker. These silver stocks were by no means a production item, and none in addition to the initial set is known to have been available from Colt commercially thereafter. A pewter canteen attachable shoulder stock and a copper grip for a Model 1855 Sidehammer pistol

are known. But these were experimental only, and were not available to the trade, nor were they made for purposes of embellishment.

Elaborate all-metal sword hilts were presentation items which received a decided boost in popularity as a result of the Mexican War (1846-48). Several luminaries from that conflict received presentation items from a grateful citizenry, and the sword was the customary gift. The list of recipients is long, and includes General Schuyler Hamilton, General Persifer Smith, Brigadier General James Shields, Colonel George Washington Morgan, and Major Braxton Bragg.

At the time of the Civil War the presentation sword truly came into its own. The designs of the most profusely decorated were often bedazzling and are representative of the high period of Victorian decoration. Inspirations came primarily from mythology and from patriotic subjects, with frequent scroll and floral embellishments. The War created an emotional atmosphere where many persons felt — and often directly were — obligated to individuals for their services either on the battlefield or the home front. Thus there was a rash of presentation objects — from swords to guns, to books to lockets, *ad infinitum*. It was the presentation deluxe hilted sword which was the forerunner of the metal-gripped Colt revolver, and it was during this peak period that the cast grip was first manufactured in any quantity for these arms.

There are three basic designs of Colt percussion cast metal grips of the period c. 1861 — c. 1875; the American and Mexican eagle, the Civil War battle scene, and the so-called missionary and child. All are rare, and the latter is the rarest. All three types share the design feature of a presentation escutcheon just below the hammer, and are nearly always cast

Based on the article " 'Tiffany' Stocked Firearms", *Antique Arms Annual*, 1971, co-authored by Roy G. Jinks and R. L. Wilson; only portions of the Colt material from that article are used here.

Specimen of Smith & Wesson revolver mounted by Tiffany & Company, with etched sterling silver grips and etched barrel. Model 1896 Hand Ejector; number 15310; c. 1898. Silver plated barrel, frame, and cylinder.
(Smith & Wesson Factory Collection)

in bronze and subsequently plated in gold or silver. Details of design, construction, and manufacture are given in Jay P. Altmayer's article in the December 1955 issue of *The Texas Gun Collector* magazine. A chapter on "Tiffany" grips also appears in *The Book of Colt Firearms* and in the *Antique Arms Annual*, 1971.

Generally Colt revolvers with cast metal grips of the above three types are found to have been engraved outside the factory, and the majority have the style and flavor of the famed Louis D. Nimschke. Nimschke was active in the New York City area, and is associated primarily with the firm of Schuyler, Hartley & Graham. SH & G advertised the cast metal grips in their 1864 catalogue; they were the source of the majority of cast grip percussion and early cartridge Colt revolvers. To them must be ascribed the Civil War battle scene and the American and Mexican eagle patterns. The rarer "missionary and child" (actually a figure of justice and American eagle pattern) is attributable to the sculptor John

Quincy Adams Ward, who designed it on commission of the United States Government. The maker of the grips for SH & G and for Ward is problematic.

From as early as the 1860's, John Quincy Adams Ward (1830-1910) was employed by the Ames Sword Company in the design of sword hilts and other objects. Ward was a prominent American sculptor known for his work in bronze; portrait busts were a specialty. He was a member of the National Academy of Design, and in 1874 was elected its President. Ward also was the first President of the National Sculpture Society, a Trustee of the Metropolitan Museum of Art, and an enthusiastic outdoorsman. Socially he was of considerable prominence. According to the Metropolitan Museum of Art's *American Sculpture (1965)*, Ward had "a prestige and power matched by no other American artist of his generation."

Government records prove that Ward designed the grips and the engraved decorations for a pair of Colt Model 1862 Police pistols presented by

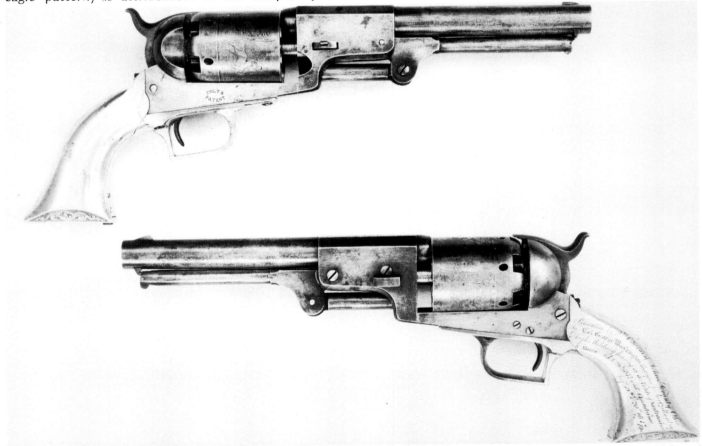

Ironically the earliest recorded metal Colt grips were supplied by the factory itself. Serial numbers 1118 and 1123 (c. 1847) of the Whitneyville-Hartford Dragoon revolvers were prepared on order of New York arms dealers Moore & Baker. The firm had requested: *". . . the Stocks* [be] *covered entirely over with Silver & finished plain, for a long Inscription to be Engraved upon them, they are for a present to be made to Col[1] Morgan Ohio. . . ."* **Besides the inscription (on the left side of each grip), the backstraps bore the patriotic motto: HONOR TO THE BRAVE. Scroll trim on the curved portions of the butts was in a pattern in use by mid nineteenth century American jewelry engravers. The grips are of sheet silver, formed to attach to the triggerguard straps by the customary butt screw, and to the top of the back of the frames by the customary backstrap screws. No other all-metal Colt grips are known to have been made until the early 1860's.** *(United States National Museum, Smithsonian Institution)*

American eagle "Tiffany" grips on Model 1862 Police revolver number 9174. The elaborate velvet lined rosewood casing includes full accessories for the Thuer conversion, and in exchange percussion cylinder. Silver and gold plated finish. In the case lid a leather Schuyler, Hartley and Graham label. Inscribed within the escutcheon oval between the eagle's wings (on the back area of the grip): *Benito/Valdeavellano.* Case lid escutcheon inlay is also inscribed with that name. One of the classic cased sets in Colt collecting. *(Johnie Bassett Collection/ Photograph, S. P. Stevens)*

Abraham Lincoln to Kibrisili Pacha, Governor of Adrianople, in 1864 (serial numbers 25513/E and 25514/E). The work was executed under Ward's personal supervision. The grips on Model 1862 Police revolver number 38549 are identical to those on the Lincoln-Pacha pair, and unquestionably were cast from the same mold. Interestingly Colt factory ledgers note a gold mounted and engraved Model 1862 Police pistol as being made for James T. Ames of the Ames Manufacturing Company. The date was October of 1866, and the barrel length 5½" — exactly that of pistol number 38549. Of further interest, no reference is made to a deluxe grip, which indicates that Ames may have supplied this himself.*

There is no evidence that Colt themselves manufactured these metal grips. Their records are extensive enough from the period of the 1860's so that if they had made them, proof would exist. Miscellaneous bronze castings from the Ames estate, now in private collections, show the diversity and excellence of the Ames casting operation. Details of design in these fragments suggest that attributing most of the so-called "Tiffany" Colt grips to the Ames company is valid.

Schuyler, Hartley and Graham are best known to collectors as retailers of Colt and of several other makes of firearms, in the second half of the nineteenth century. The SH & G catalogue of 1864 illustrates a Model 1862 Police with the Mexican eagle grip and a Model 1851 Navy with the Head of Zeus or of Medusa grip (an unusual pattern not yet observed by collectors). An adjacent page illustrates a Model 1851 with the Civil War battle scene pattern. It is well known that SH & G farmed out their engraving to such craftsmen as Louis D. Nimschke. The casting of metal grips was as specialized — if not more so — as arms engraving, so it follows that these were likewise done elsewhere. Ames was renowned for their cast sword fixtures, and several swords with these embellishments appeared in the Schuyler, Hartley and Graham 1864 catalogue.

Although it appears probable that Tiffany & Company cast some of the deluxe metal grips used on a limited number of Colt revolvers of the period c. 1861 — c. 1875, the author is of the opinion that the major share of this work was done by the Ames Manufacturing Company. Further research should make more precise attributions possible. Intriguing evidence that Tiffany also produced all-metal grips was published in the *Hartford Evening Press*, February 6, 1864; the item appeared in an article covering the disastrous Colt factory fire of February 4: "The

The Book of Colt Firearms estimates the 38,000 serial range at c. 1868. However, that estimate was supposition — not based on known shipments from company ledgers. It is quite likely that production had reached 38,549 by October 1866.

splendid pistols made for presentation to Gen. Grant, were not destroyed, having been sent a few days ago, to Tiffany & Co., New York, to receive their gold mountings." The newspaper's reference to "gold mountings" could only mean metal grips, not plating, or inlay, or even overlay. Being a distinguished retail and manufacturing firm, it is logical that Tiffany would have signed such work, especially a pair of guns for one of the most important officers in the Union Army.

DE GRESS ALL-METAL GRIPS

The cast all-metal grips sometimes found on New Line Colt revolvers and on similar pocket type handguns (c. 1874 — c. 1885) were the subject of United States patent number 150229, April 28, 1874, issued to Francis De Gress. The inventor was part of the export firm of Wexell & De Gress, whose offices were in New York City, Mexico, and elsewhere. Specifications in the patent included the reference:

> My improvement relates to a new article of manufacture, consisting of an electrotype shell filled with type-metal, or similar alloy, and concaved in the inner surfaces, and provided with the holes for attaching pins or screws, and colored by the action of acid to imitate bronze. These handle-pieces are accurate in size and shape, and the designs upon the surface can be of the most elaborate and beautiful character without increasing the cost after the first one has been produced.

Sets of grips made under the De Gress patent are illustrated; note the inclusion of the patent date in the upper sections of the left handles.

Production of the De Gress grips may have been done in Mexico. The sizes generally seen by collectors were made to fit the New Line Colt pistols, and similar pocket arms. These also carry the April 28, 1874 patent marking. At this writing the amount of detail available is limited; collector Robert G. Cox M.D. is studying the Wexell & De Gress firm and has in preparation an article on the patented cast grips.

TIFFANY GRIPS AND COLT'S PATENT FIRE ARMS MANUFACTURING CO.

From 1890 to 1909 the Tiffany Blue Book catalogue advertised under the heading "Pistols": "Revolvers of the most improved types, mounted in silver, carved ivory, gold, etc. with rich and elaborate decorations, $50.00 to $300.00. Cases, boxes, belts and holsters made in appropriate styles for presentations". From studying surviving specimens so decorated, it is clear that the firm of Smith & Wesson benefited most from these Tiffany creations.   Several revolvers from the 1890's are in the factory museum collection, and additional pieces are known in private collections. Interestingly enough most of the designs are unduplicated, and it would appear that most of the work performed was on an individual basis.   Much rarer than the S & W specimens are Winchester rifles mounted in silver by Tiffany.   The author is aware of only one such arm, and it is profusely decorated in the most Victorian art-nouveau manner. The silver on the frame is clearly marked with Tiffany & Company stampings.   Only one specimen of a Tiffany-marked Colt revolver is known, and this unusual piece unfortunately has been refinished; the engraving on the steel parts appears to be contemporary with the grip. The Model is the New Army and Navy, and dates from the mid 1890's.

NOTE: The student and collector should refer to *Tiffany Silver,* **by Charles H. Carpenter, Jr. and Mary Grace Carpenter, published 1978 by Dodd, Mead & Company, New York.   Chapter 8 is entitled "Presentation Swords and Guns", and includes the important reference to Tiffany plant journal No. 1 (c. 1851-70), which lists "in entry No. 1304, dated January 6, 1863, a 'Pistol Mounted Colts Navy size A.W. Spies.'   It lists a plant cost of $7.00 each." The Carpenter's swords and guns chapter is 14 pages in length, and quite important and informative. The plant journal No. 1 reference proves positively that Tiffany did indeed do at least some of the socalled "Tiffany grips".**

The firearms pieces created by Tiffany & Company in the late nineteenth and early twentieth centuries have always been found marked with the firm's name.   The signature usually reads: TIFFANY & CO. MAKERS STERLING, stamped in small letters on the silver in a relatively obscure place.   In one example known the signature was positioned on a separate plate which was soldered to the front of the grip strap, directly behind the triggerguard.   Tiffany was allowed to mark the pieces made on order by Smith & Wesson, and they marked all the grips made directly for private customers.   Due to the rarity of Colt revolvers of the turn of the century having Tiffany grips, some of the information presented in these two paragraphs is based on examination of a number of Smith & Wesson revolvers with Tiffany marked silver grips.

As an added note, the reader should consult Chapter XVI, which illustrates Colt's Tiffany Grip Special, Single Action Army SAA1, with an 18k gold and sterling silver Tiffany style grip, fully deluxe gold and silver decorations on the revolver, and a casing custom built for Colt by Tiffany & Co., in sterling silver and vermeil.   Actually even more elaborate and spectacular than anything done by Colt or Tiffany on a firearm previously, the Tiffany Grip Special outfit revived the historic link between the venerable firms of Colt and Tiffany.

Original photograph of the Civil War period, showing a cased presentation sword made either by Tiffany & Company or by the Ames Manufacturing Company.   The hilt and cross guards of heavy castings, in similar style to the revolver stocks known to collectors as "Tiffany" grips. *(National Archives Photograph)*

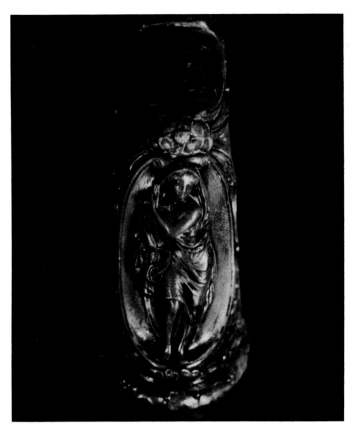

Grip details from the pair of Model 1862 revolvers (numbers 25513/E and 25514/E) commissioned by the United States government as gifts of state, 1863, and presented in 1864. State Department records, Instruction No. 68 of January 11, 1864, noted the following: *"The designs for the handles, which are of solid silver (oxidized) and those on the barrels were made by Mr. Ward, a young and promising sculptor of New York, who also superintended the workmanship, which as you will perceive, is of the finest description."* The figure on back of the grip is Justice with scales; above her head an oval cartouche bearing the presentation inscription. On the butt the American eagle. This is the type grip known to collectors as the "missionary and child". Properly it should be termed the Ward type (in recognition of the designer, John Quincy Adams Ward) and the eagle and Justice (in reference to the two major decorative motifs). *(Franklin Delano Roosevelt Library Museum)*

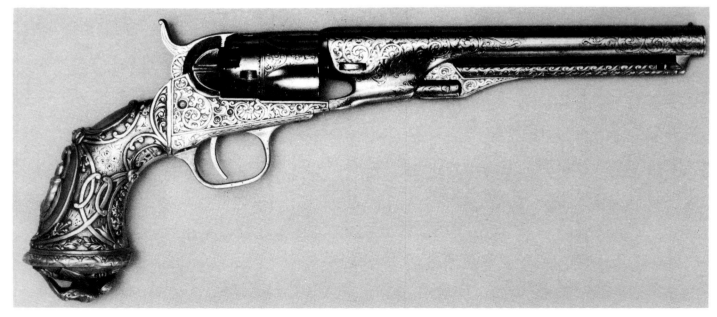

Ward eagle and Justice "Tiffany" grip on a Nimschke engraved Model 1862 Police revolver, number 27931 (c. 1864). Bronze grip, plated in gold. The revolver finished in silver, with gold plated hammer, cylinder, trigger, and rammer assembly. *(Arnold M. Chernoff Collection)*

Serial number 38549 Model 1862 Police revolver; gold inlaid, with cast grip of the Ward eagle and Justice pattern. The revolver is believed to have been the one recorded in Colt ledgers as shipped in October 1866 to James T. Ames of the Ames Manufacturing Company. Richly cast and chased; the gun and grip in excellent condition. Note the bearded head positioned on each side of the gripstrap behind the triggerguard. *(William M. Locke Collection)*

Model 1851 Navy, number 163826/. (c. 1863), with the Civil War battle scene type grip. The factory running vine scrolls on the revolver appear to have been augmented by Nimschke style scrollwork on the cylinder. The arrow and crossed bands motif (both sides of the barrel) and the twirl pattern lever design are other distinctive LDN motifs. Finished in gold and silver plating; the grip of plated bronze. *(Dr. Chester P. Bonoff Collection)*

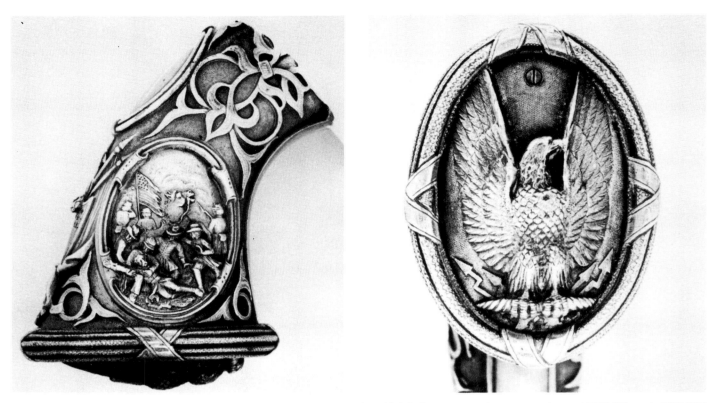

Eagle buttcap and Civil War battle scene panel on Model 1860 Army revolvers numbers 156567 and 156633 (c. 1866). See L. D. Nimschke chapter for details on this deluxe pair of gold and silver plated revolvers. Grips of silver plated bronze. Though the American eagle was the standard buttcap motif, a few Civil War battle scene grips were capped in the head of Zeus or Medusa. *(United States National Museum Collection, Smithsonian Institution)*

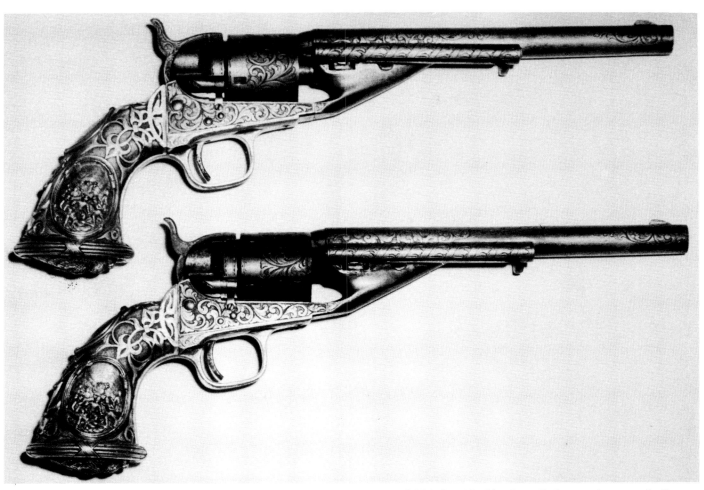

Conversions of the Model 1861 Navy, serial numbers 8875 and 9200 (c. 1872). Detail shows the stand of arms and shield motif and the escutcheon, on back of each grip. The majority of "Tiffany" grips appear on Colt conversion revolvers. *(Charles Schreiner III Collection)*

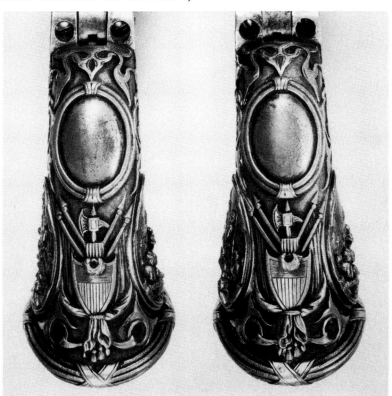

Civil War battle scene grip on a deluxe Open Top revolver (c. 1872). Plated finish. One of a pair. *(Larry Sheerin Collection)*

TIFFANY & CO.

Importers and Manufacturers of

FINE MILITARY EQUIPMENTS,

Nos. 550 & 552 Broadway, New York,

—AND—

RUE RICHELIEU, No. 79, PARIS.

RICH PRESENTATION SWORDS, FLAGS, ETC., ON HAND AND MADE TO ORDER.
FINE GUNS, PISTOLS, SWORDS, EPAULETTES, SASHES, BELTS, ETC., ETC.

New York, *Nov 13* 186*1*

Sold to *Col S Colt*

TERMS CASH.

Mounting Brooch $28

That Samuel Colt was a client of Tiffany & Co. is evidenced by this November 13, 1861 billing, for "Mounting Brooch". Note the sub-heading "Rich Presentation Swords, Flags, etc., on hand and Made to Order. Fine Guns, Pistols, Swords, Epaulettes, Sashes, Belts, etc., etc." The firm at this time was known as "Importers and Manufacturers of Fine Military Equipments" — not as a jewelry firm. Tiffany & Co. ranked among about 30 jobbers and dealers of Colt arms in the Civil War period, and were thus allowed to acquire Colt products in case or quantity lots. Several thousands of Colt arms are detailed in the Colt Civil War shipping ledgers, as having been sent to Tiffany & Co. See also page 43, Chapter II. *(Colt Collection, The Connecticut Historical Society)*

The American eagle type grip on Model 1862 Police number 12953. Gold and silver plated finish; the grip of gold plated bronze. Note characteristic buttcap device standard on the Mexican and American eagle pattern. Gustave Young style scrollwork. The revolver dates c. 1862. *(Richard P. Mellon Collection)*

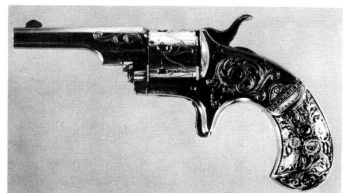

De Gress cast grips in a floral pattern on Open Top .22 revolver serial number 64904. Nickel plated finish; Colt factory engraving. The April 28, 1874 patent date is marked on the left grip, at top border, c. 1874. *(R. Q. Sutherland Collection)*

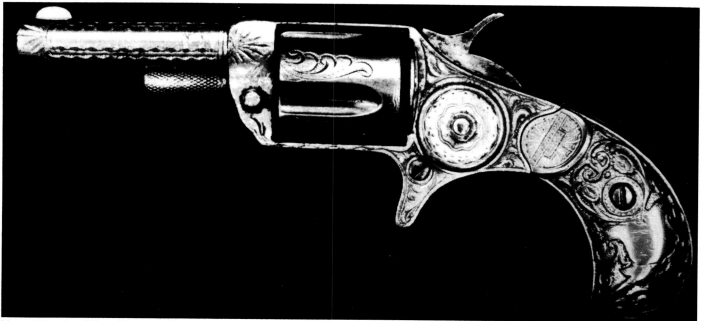

New Line in .30 caliber with De Gress grips; the 1874 patent date on the upper section of the left side; the right side in the horsehead pattern. *(Dr. Robert G. Cox Collection)*

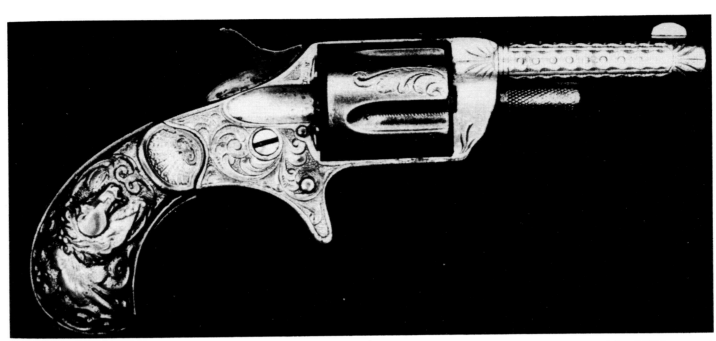

.30 caliber New Line revolver with Colt factory engraving. Horsehead pattern on the right side; 1874 patent marking on the left grip. A Mexican eagle theme is known on a De Gress stock for Smith & Wesson revolvers. *(Dr. Robert G. Cox Collection)*

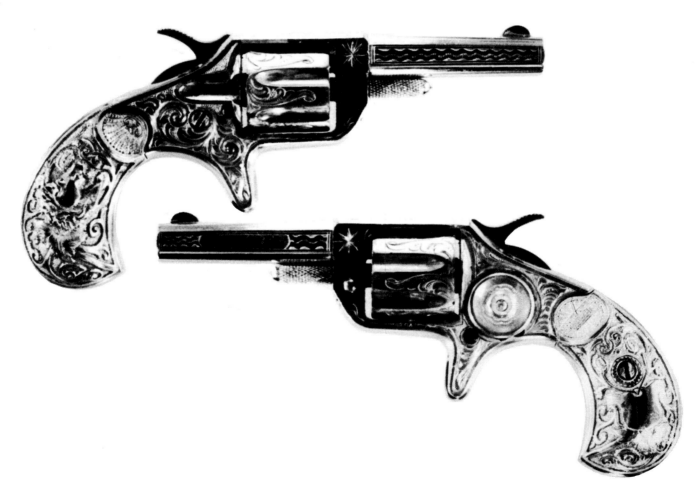

New Line .22 number 20429 (c. 1876) with horsehead pattern De Gress grips. Again, the patent dates are present marked on the left handle; note also the escutcheon for inscription or a monogram. Plated finish on the revolver. *(R. Q. Sutherland Collection)*

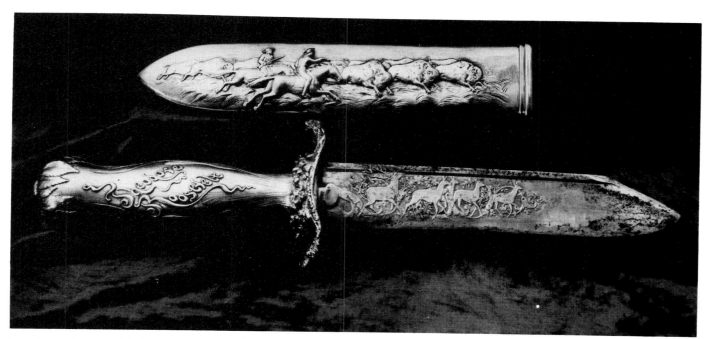

Theodore Roosevelt's Bowie-type knife; mounted in cast and chased silver by Tiffany & Company. c. 1884. Blade relief engraved with game scenes and floral scrolls. 7½" blade; 6" length to the hilt and crossguard. Scabbard marked: Tiffany & Co. M Sterling. *(Ethel Roosevelt Derby Collection)*

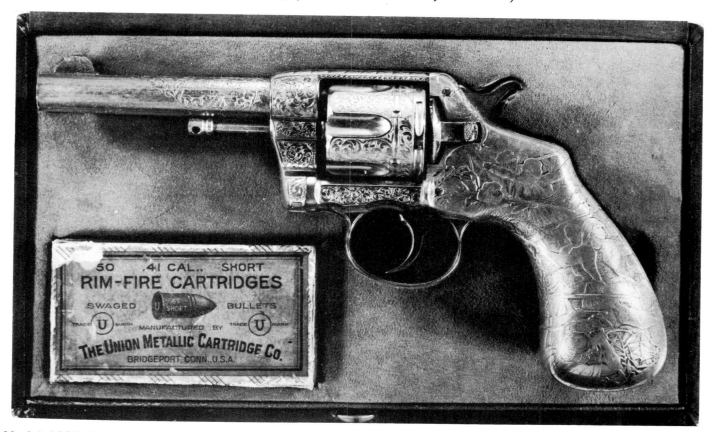

Model 1895 double action revolver with Tiffany & Company grips, of the type described in the firm's Blue Book from 1890 to 1909. Grip etched with a French Foreign Legion battle scene. TIFFANY & CO/ STERLING MAKER marked on bottom of the grip behind the triggerguard. Silver is secured to the frame by four screws. Contemporary engraving on revolver may have been the work of Tiffany; gun has old refinish making further speculation difficult. Rare casing by Tiffany; dark red leather over wooden frame; the lining in chamois, recessed for revolver and box of cartridges. Most Tiffany mounted guns of the c. 1890 — c. 1909 period were of Smith & Wesson manufacture. Contemporary Colt arms by Tiffany are *rare.* *(R. Q. Sutherland Collection)*

Formerly in the Charles D. Cook collection, and pictured on the cover of James Serven's catalogue (item C-14), number 17243 is attributed to L.D. Nimschke. Among its rare features are the decoration on the cylinder and being cut for shoulder stock attachment. The revolver was later a featured item among the dragoons in the W.M. Locke collection. *(George R. Repaire Collection)*

Chapter VIII
COLT FIREARMS
BY L. D. NIMSCHKE
c. 1850 — c. 1900

The nineteenth century marked a significant period in the decoration of firearms. The first fifty years continued the tradition that any gun not constructed for military purposes was likely to be engraved. At that time the assembly-line production of arms was still in an infant state. In the second fifty years, gun engraving was at its peak in popularity. At the same time, the mass production of firearms became a general practice. Nevertheless, most manufacturers had engraved weapons available as stock items. This fifty year period may be regarded as gun engraving's golden era in America. Louis Daniel Nimschke was one of America's leading firearms engravers during this time.

The personal work record of L.D. Nimschke was discovered c. 1960, after laying neglected in an attic for over fifty years. It is in scrapbook form, totalling 100 pages. Compiled by Nimschke from about 1850 to about 1900, it features impressions taken from the actual engraved surfaces. Over 100 different makers and manufacturers of firearms are represented in the scrapbook, as well as all of the contemporary engraving styles. Colt firearms are present in significant numbers, and an estimate of arms of Colt manufacture engraved by Nimschke would be in the several hundreds. This unique record book is an archive of gun engraving during the period it covers.

L.D. Nimschke was born in Germany in 1832 and came to the United States about 1850. He died on April 9, 1904. Little is known of him personally, but it is obvious from his engraving record that he was a dedicated, serious craftsman with an active imagination. Judging from the tremendous number of guns he engraved (estimated at approximately 5,000) he was extremely industrious. Research has also shown that he had the services, for at least part of his career in America, of an assistant. Such an assistant was expected to work in the same styles of scroll as the master.

New York and Brooklyn city directories record Nimschke's years of activity there as follows:

1860-1870	35 Essex Street, New York City
1870-1891	1 Essex Street, New York City
1892-1904	180 Baltic Street, Brooklyn

Number 16783 Third Model Dragoon should be compared with revolver number 16592 pictured elsewhere. Scrollwork on 16783 includes the cylinder; note also the Mexican Eagle ivory grips (the right grip is carved with a liberty cap and the motto: LIBERTAD). Silver plated, with gold plated hammer, cylinder, folding leaf sight, and the loading lever. *(Woolaroc Museum, P.R. Phillips Collection)*

His address from about 1850 to 1860 is unknown, but he was probably in the New York City area. In Nimschke's day, New York City was a preferred place of business for many individuals in the firearms trade.

There are several indications of the high regard in which Nimschke was held by his contemporaries. One is the substantial number of customers, and another, the stature of many of these. A third is the nature of work which he did for the many factories who already had engravers in their employ. For tasks requiring the finest quality, they often turned to Nimschke.

As a custom engraver, Nimschke worked on individual order, executing virtually anything the customer wanted; thus the high proportion of added touches to his work — monograms, inscriptions, coats of arms, and other personal motifs. The weapons to be engraved were brought to him, generally in the white. Bluing, case-hardening, or plating was done after completion of the engraving. This remains standard practice today.

Nimschke engraved guns for more than 100 leading makers and manufacturers, most of the work being done directly for them but some for dealers or for individual owners. Nimschke's customers also included gunsmiths, shooting clubs, and various persons and firms outside the sphere of firearms. The locale was almost 100% in and around New York City with, however, such notable exceptions as Nashville, Tennessee (Bitterlich & Legler), Kansas City, Missouri (E. Masuch), and Houston, Texas (E. Schmidt & Company). These cities all had capable gun engravers, but in these instances the work was sent to Nimschke.

In his international clientele, Nimschke could boast Maria Cristina of Austria, who, as widow of King Alphonso, controlled the Spanish monarchy for many years after her husband's death. A Frank Wesson rifle engraved for her is recorded in the book. The fanciest Winchester in the record book was done for a customer in Peru. In Nimschke's words, the frame for this gun was "solid silver". A quick survey of the many owners noted in the record book shows better than 20% to be of Mexican, South American, or Spanish blood. Engraved, plated, and pearl- or ivory-gripped guns were highly prized by the Spanish-speaking people. The decoration of this type of gun was a Nimschke specialty.

Nimschke was skilled in many forms of engraving. His two mainstays were the American (derived from the Germanic) and English styles. The principal differentiation between them was the treatment of scrollwork. It was in scrollwork, particularly, that Nimschke excelled. He could execute the rich, bold scrolls of the American style and, with equal skill, the fine and delicate English scrolls. Nearly all engraving done in the United States in Nimschke's era was in the American style.

The prints in Nimschke's record book also encompass silverware, watch cases, jewelry, stamps, seals, nameplates, and even dog collars. Though the major share of his work was on firearms, he obviously did not limit himself to them for his livelihood.

No less than 35% of the arms in Nimschke's record book bear some form of his signature. The usual form was initialing, particularly N, LN, or LDN. As a rule, the larger the signature the more important and fancy the gun. Approximately 85% of his signatures are on longarms. Nimschke rarely signed a handgun. When he did, it was rarely more than initials only.

It was not common practice for an engraver to sign a firearm. During the 1850 to 1900 period in the United States, only Nimschke and the Ulrichs are known to have done so to any noticeable extent.

Nimschke, in common with many of his contemporaries, made use of pattern books. There were, in fact, four books of gun engraving patterns found with his records. Their value is clear on comparison with his work. A careful tabulation indicates that several motifs in Nimschke's record were copied directly from these sources.

The four books are all of German origin, and two are the work of a G. Ernst of Zella. Although none is actually dated, they are from around 1840. Lockplates, hammers, triggerguards, buttplates, and various other gun mountings total most of the designs. None of the four books exhibits scrollwork in the American style.

These pattern books were Nimschke's main source of animal figures, but he found inspiration and ideas from a variety of supplementary sources, including the 1864 Schuyler, Hartley and Graham military goods catalogue (for state seals and coats of arms), newspaper cuts, American coins, currency, stamps, and a Spencer gun catalogue of 1866.

Most of Nimschke's scroll motifs were bold and rich, with lining and shading in strength. Nearly all scrolls were intertwining and, space permitting, often had small hair-line frills. His backgrounds were mostly punched dot matting; second to this was fine hatching. Sometimes, little or no background was present.

The accompanying illustrations show characteristic L. D. Nimschke engraving motifs; although the mere presence of some of these on a firearm does not necessarily identify the arm as having been engraved by Nimschke. For such an identification, the quality, skill, design, and "feeling" must be considered, because many of these motifs were also employed by other arms engravers.

The use of animals and animal heads in American gun engraving of the 1850-1900 period was not uncommon. The best example, and one often seen, is the wolf head on the hammers of Colt percussion revolvers. In Nimschke's work, the use of animal motifs was strongly in evidence, more so than in the work of most of his contemporaries.

In discussing L. D. Nimschke's work, reference has been made to the American style of gun engraving. This engraving style was an outgrowth of German techniques of the mid-nineteenth century, and nearly all engravers who developed it were emigrants from Germany. In use from about 1850 to the present, it was especially prevalent up to about 1900. Peculiar to this country, it featured smoothly flowing foliate scrollwork, with occasional animal motifs, of which the wolf head is best known. The background was commonly punched dot matte, or sometimes hatching.*

Coverage varied according to the amount of engraving desired by the client as well as the shapes and sizes of surfaces. Handguns often had little non-engraved surface remaining.

Major variations in the distinctive American engraving style are: (a) tight, close, fine scrolls; (b) heavy, bold scrolls; (c) intermediate scrolls.

In addition to American style engraving, Nimschke's record illustrated two other distinctive engraving styles. The English or "shotgun scroll" featuring close, delicate scrolls with fine hatching and plenty of blank metal, and the arabesque style consisting of geometric scrolls with plain or finely hatched background, were used.

For further data on L. D. Nimschke, see the book, *L. D. Nimschke Firearms Engraver,* a complete reproduction of the original record volume. The engravings are complemented by a detailed text and photographs of known firearms by Nimschke.

*Note: *Several examples of American scrolls derived from German origins have already appeared in Chapters III, IV, VI, and VII.*

One of the most significant of all Nimschke revolvers, this Manhattan Navy appears on pages 3 and 37 of L.D. *Nimschke Firearms Engraver,* and was a presentation for Napoleon III of France. The Emperor's portrait is gold inlaid on the left side of the barrel lug. Among the design features are crossed flags engraved on the cylinder, wolfhead hammer, gold inlaid border work on the hammer, frame, cylinder, and barrel, and relief carved Goddess of Liberty ivory grips. The casing is of rosewood, velvet lined. *(Ron Romanella Collection)*

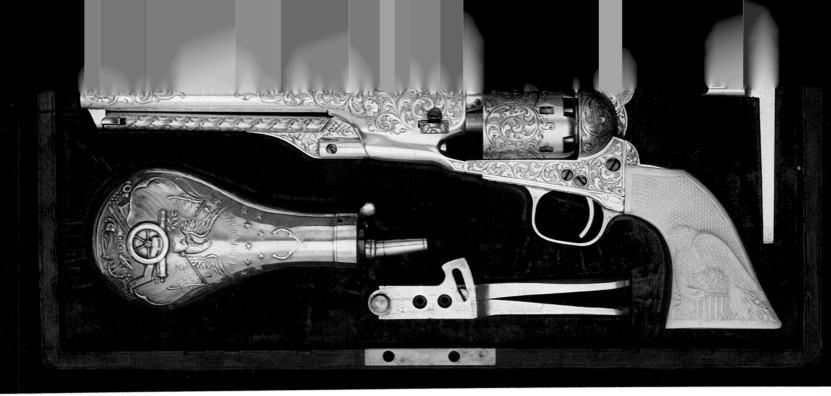

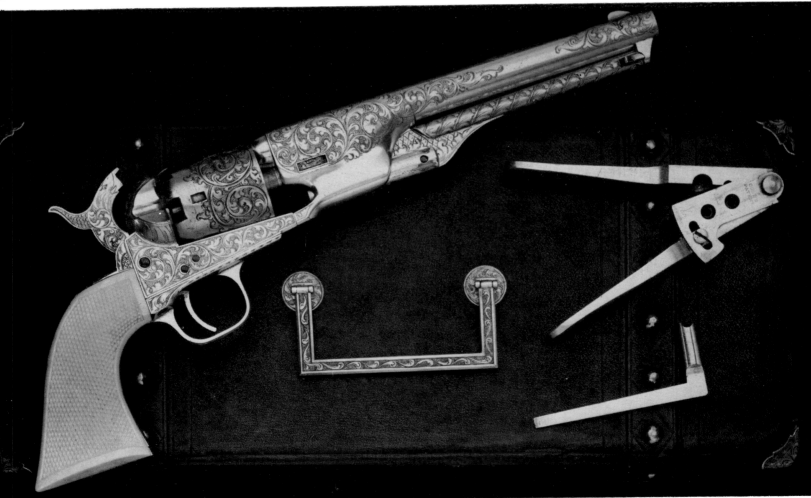

In a remarkable state of preservation, 1861 Navy 21838 bears a German inscription on the triggerguard: *ALOYS SEINEM JOSEPH.* The set was discovered in the 1950s in a museum in Mexico. Due to the inscription, the New York source of engraving and deluxe gold and silver plating, carved and checkered ivory grips, and leather casing (silver mounted), and the outfit's Mexican pedigree, there is a strong possibility of original ownership by an aid to the Emperor Maximilian. For many years the set was displayed at the Buffalo Bill Historical Center, Cody, Wyoming, as part of the loan of the Larry Sheerin Collection. *(George R. Repaire Collection)*

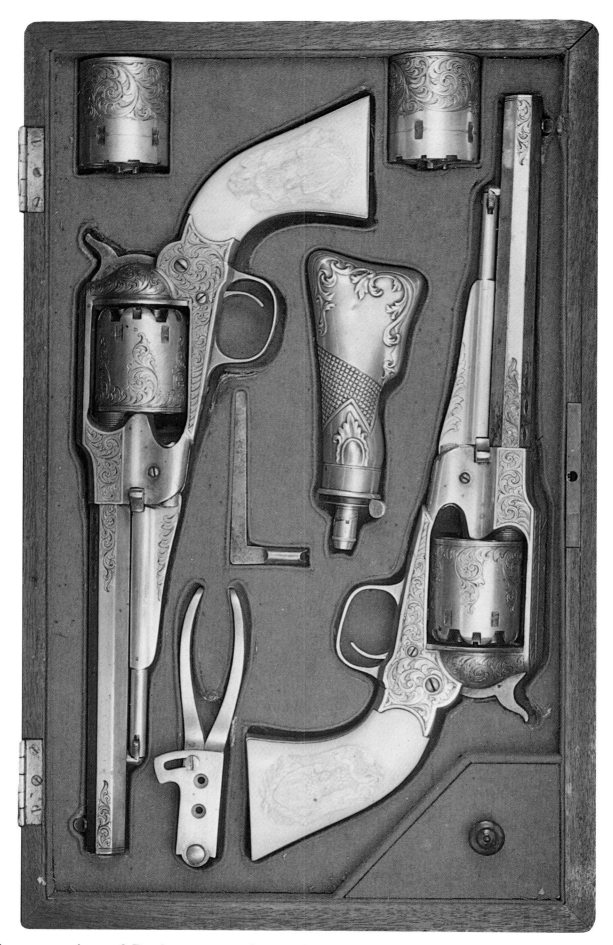

Finest known cased set of Remington percussion revolvers, New Model Army's numbers **115896** and **123329** feature scroll engraving either by or in the style of L.D. Nimschke. They have been factory converted to .44 rimfire, are plated in gold and silver, are cased in a mahogany box with contour lining of felt, and the grips are high relief carved elephant ivory. Note extra cylinders, and Colt bullet mold. Conversions were authorized by Rollin White license, and the cartridge cylinders bear important marking: PATENTED APRIL 3D 1855. Formerly in the William M. Locke and John B. Solley III collections. *(Joseph T. Hajec Collection, Sid Latham Photograph)*

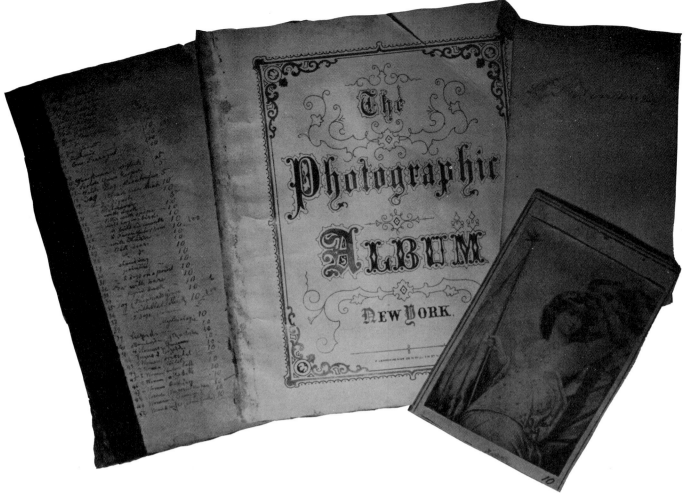

Photograph album of L.D. Nimschke, from which he drew motifs for embellishing various firearms and other objects. Photos are of stock types, available from photographic studios or individual photographers. Among the subjects are portraits (e.g., Generals Grant and Sherman), hunting, sporting, and animal scenes, patriotic themes, and even some erotically posed nude women. Total number of pictures (*carte-de-visite* size and type) is about 39, and each bears Nimschke's autographed signature on the back. The album was used by Nimschke as a key source for engraving firearms and other objects. The list at left identifies each of the pictures, and the number opposite (at right) appears to be a cost figure for engraving each, or an estimate of the time required in hours. *(Norm Flayderman Collection)*

Two of the *carte de visite* photographs from Nimschke's photo album. For comparison with the dog motif as engraved by Nimschke on firearms, see *L.D. Nimschke Firearms Engraver*, pages 74, 85 and 93. For the elk, see pages 72, 143, 145, 146, 147, 148, 149 and 151 of *The Book of Winchester Engraving* (but as employed by other engravers). *(Norm Flayderman Collection)*

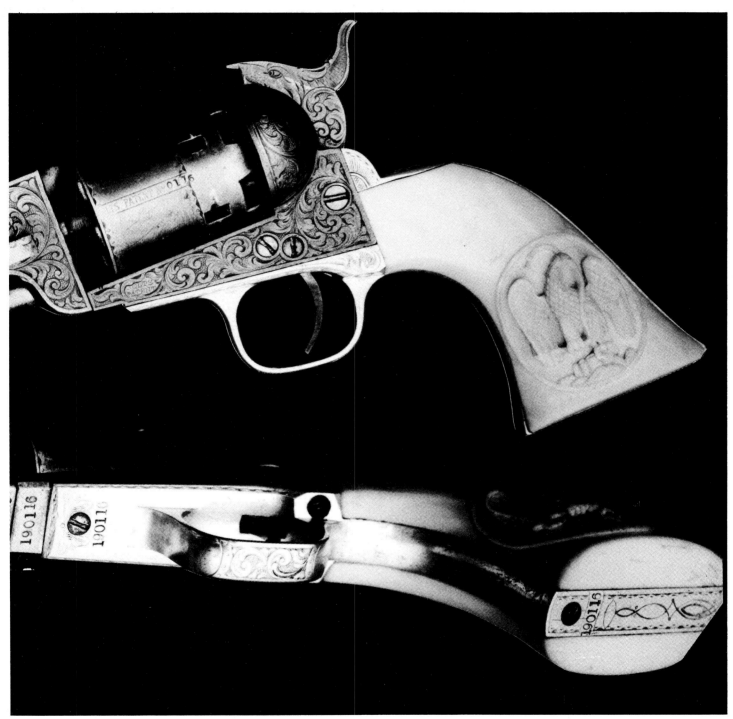

Details point out some of the characteristics which serve to identify a Nimschke engraved Colt revolver. First, the distinctive scroll; second, the intertwined border motif on the barrel and butt; third, the wavy line and punched dot border on the cylinder; fourth, the cross-hatched motif on center area of the barrel lug; and fifth, the scalloped "bat wing" decor on the rammer lever lug. Model 1851 Navy; serial number 190116 (c. 1866). *(Anonymous Collection)*

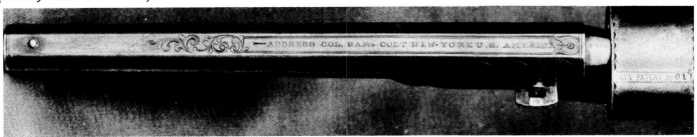

A Nimschke Third Model Dragoon, cut for shoulder stock, number 16592 also features scroll coverage on the cylinder and the richly mellowed Mexican Eagle relief carved ivory grips. Compare with number 16783 Dragoon, as displayed at the Woolaroc Museum. *(George R. Repaire Collection)*

Nimschke engraving on a Sidehammer Pocket revolver; serial number 8678. Note the use of silver plating, and relief carved ivory grips (rare dragoon motif). Complete cased set; the percussion caps dating from the early twentieth century. The case of mahogany, lined in velvet. The right side of the grip (not visible) bears a long presentation inscription to a Henry G. Brant, from seven of his friends. *(Formerly in the William M. Locke Collection)*

Serial number 67899 Model 1860 Army; with the full scroll treatment by LDN. The cylinder scroll includes the three line tentacles and wavy line and dot borders. Checkered ivory grips, and an exchange cylinder for Thuer cartridges. Finished in gold and silver plating. *(H. L. Visser Collection)*

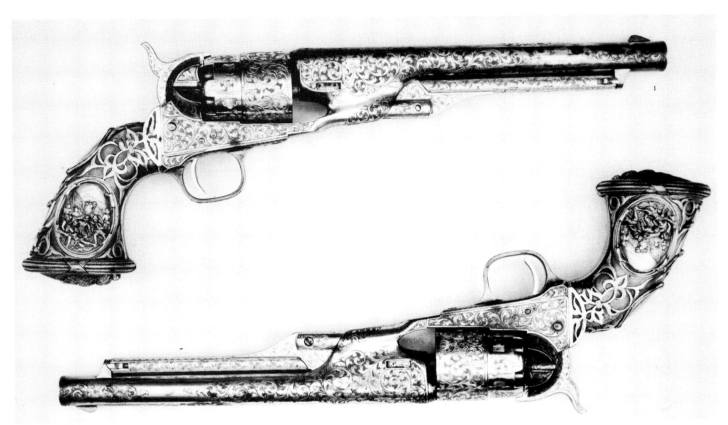

Two of Nimschke's most inspired creations in Colt firearms; serial numbers 156567 and 156653. On these arms, contrary to his usual approach, a matted (not punched dot) background was used. Profuse scroll coverage. American eagle motifs formed scenes on the cylinders (the Nimschke record shows prints from Colt Army cylinders engraved with busts of two Civil War generals). Gold plated, with silver plated frames, barrels, and Civil War battle scene "Tiffany" grips. The case and accessories are pictured in *Samuel Colt Presents*, page 191. *(United States National Museum, Smithsonian Institution)*

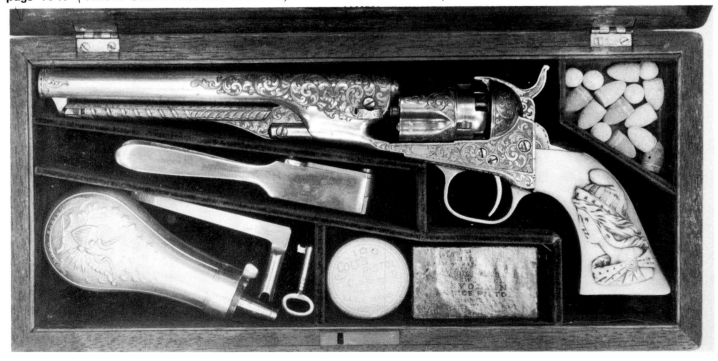

Embellishment of a Model 1862 Police, in the typical Nimschke style of scroll engraving. Plated in gold on the lever, cylinder, and hammer; the balance plated in silver. Ivory grips relief carved in the scarce liberty head pattern. Serial number 28899. *(Jerry D. Berger Collection)*

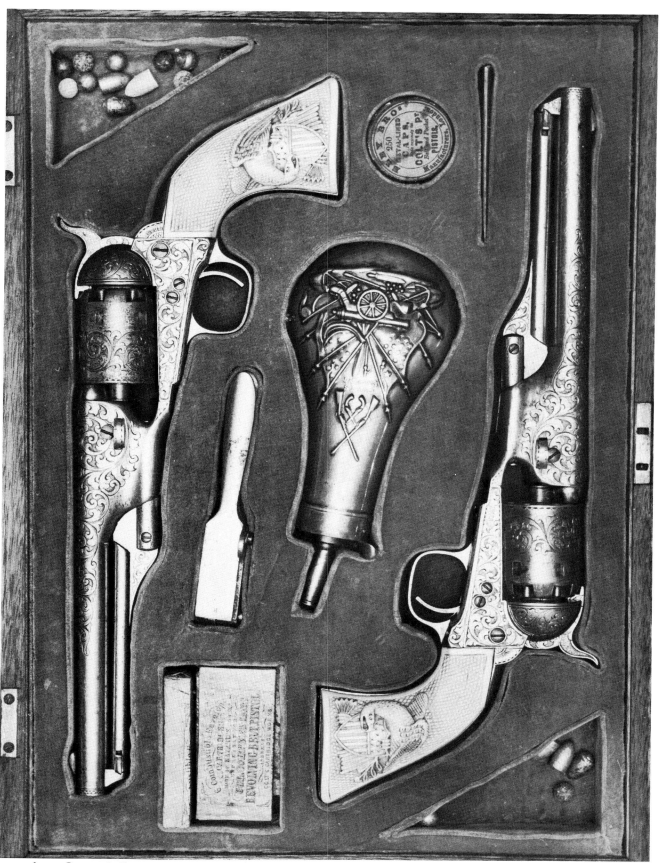

Presented to General George A. Custer, Model 1861 Navy revolvers, c. 1863 (numbers 13511 and 13514).
Gold plaques bearing the presentation inscriptions were fastened to the ivory grips, and have long since vanished.
Again the finish was a combination of gold and silver plating; with relief carved and checkered grips of ivory,
the American eagle and shield motif in prominence. Rare mahogany double casing, lined in the French (contour)
style with brown velvet lining. *(Arnold M. Chernoff Collection)*

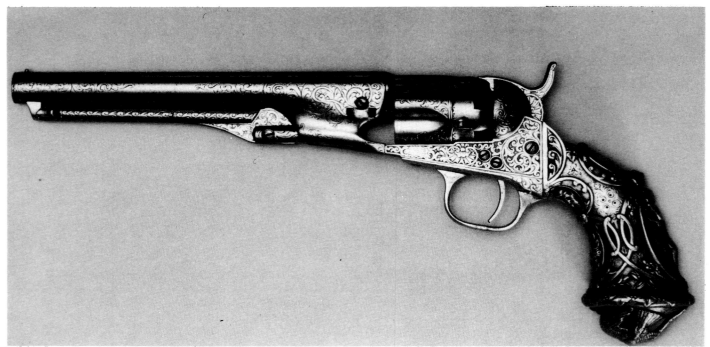

An extremely unusual arabesque and scroll approach was used on Model 1862 Police revolver number 27931. Silver plated, with the cylinder, hammer, trigger, and lever plated in gold. Prints from this revolver appear on page 33 of Nimschke's own record book. The gold plated "Tiffany" grip was cast in the Missionary and Child or Ward eagle and Justice style. *(Arnold M. Chernoff Collection)*

A Nimschke Model 1860 Army, number 152191 is fully silver plated and has ivory grips. Border of wavy line and dot pattern on the cylinder, the hammer of wolfhead type. The three line tentacles come off some of the barrel scrolls, and note how the finial at left lacks punched dot background. *(Derek Palons Collection)*

American eagle style Tiffany grips grace the *top* two Model 1862 Police conversions, numbers 40400 and 26482. Silver plated barrels, frames, ejector rod heads and grips; the cylinders and hammers gold plated. Note coverage on the cylinders, and profuse nature of scroll and border work on frames, frameplates, barrels, triggerguards and ejector rod tubes. Gustave Young style factory engraving. *Third from top,* Nimschke engraved Model 1862 Police, number 28940; gold plated cylinder and loading lever; silver plated barrel, frame, hammer, and triggerguard. Grips of checkered ivory. Still another Nimschke piece, Model 1860 Army 174331 *(bottom)* was finished in silver plating on the barrel and frame, and gold plating on cylinder, loading lever, hammer, and triggerguard. Ivory grips, checkered. *(Joseph T. Hajec Collection)*

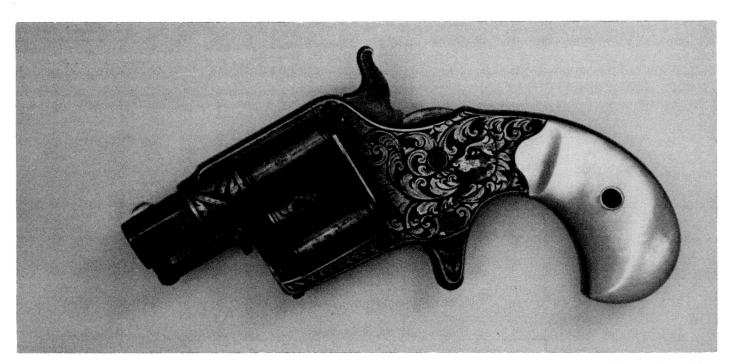

A cloverleaf of the rare short barrel configuration, serial number **1776** is richly embellished and finished, and has pearl grips. Note how the doghead device is worked into the cascading scrollwork. *(Eric Vaule Collection)*

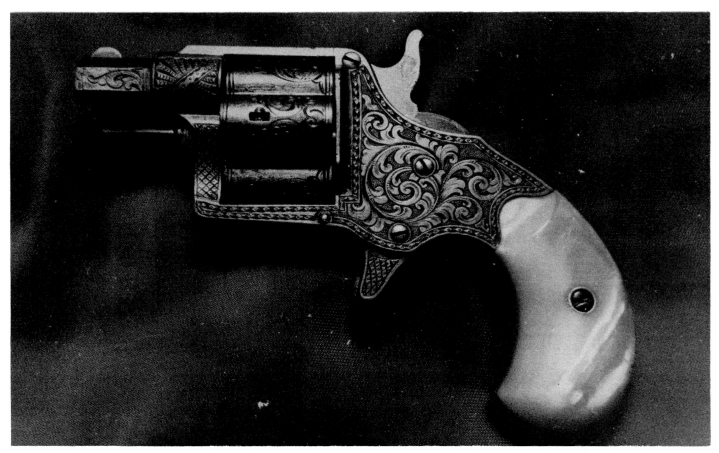

Another of those very few known Cloverleafs by Nimschke, serial number 1456 is silver plated, with gold cylinder and hammer, the grips of pearl. It is of interest to compare the variations in scrolls and borders between this revolver and Cloverleaf number 1776. *(George Taylor Collection)*

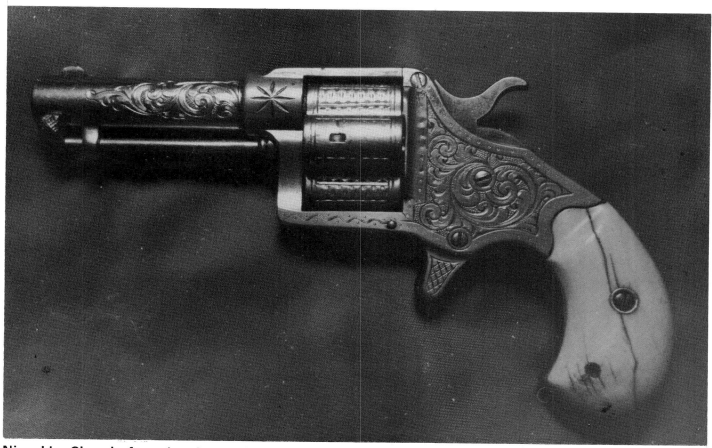

Nimschke Cloverleaf number 6596 is finished in nickel and silver, the grips of ivory. A folded paper inside the grips bears the name E. Ward. *(George Taylor Collection)*

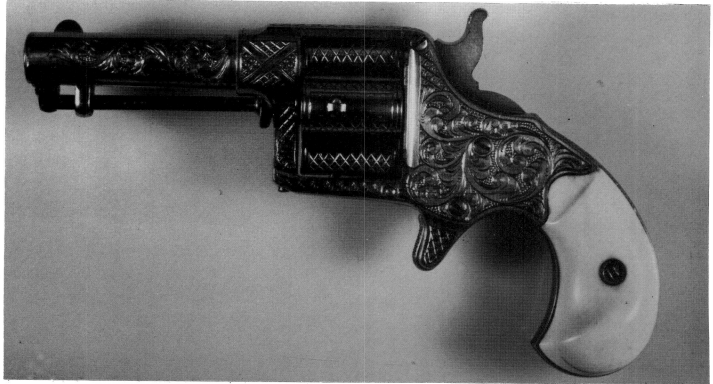

Cloverleaf attributed to L.D. Nimschke; serial number 2320; 3″ barrel; nickel plated, with ivory grips. Note geometric patterns on the cylinder and frame, and distinctive scrollwork. What was perhaps Nimschke's most deluxe Cloverleaf pistol appears on page 44 of his record book; on it the rampant colt trademark was cut on the right side of the frame and a serpent and bird motif on the left, plus profuse scrollwork. *(Fred Sweeney Collection)*

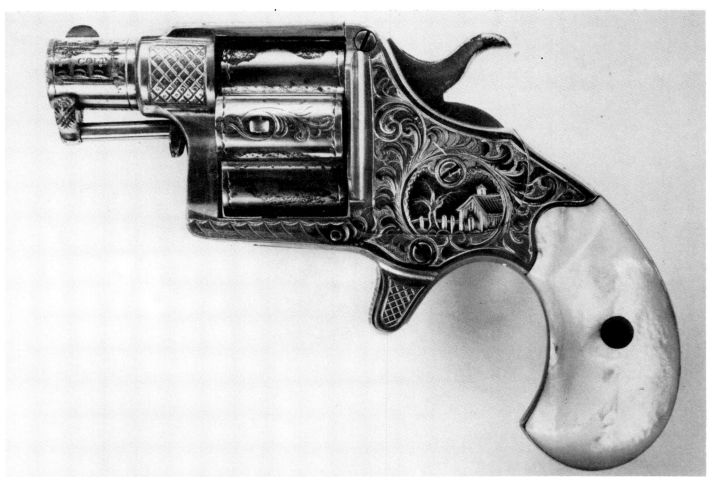

Nickel plated Cloverleaf 6940 includes a rare panel scene on the frame, and the cylinder scrolls have the small three line tentacle clusters. Grips of pearl; note short, round barrel, with COLT marking on the left side. *(Woolaroc Museum; P.R. Phillips Collection)*

.44 Rimfire Single Action number 479 was shipped to Hartley & Graham in May of 1878; finish and stocks not listed. Attribution is to the shop of Nimschke, or another New York engraving source. Nickel plated; 7-1/2" barrel; grips of ivory. Another Nimschke engraved rimfire is number 1891, shipped to H&G in March of 1880. *(William L. Rogoski Collection)*

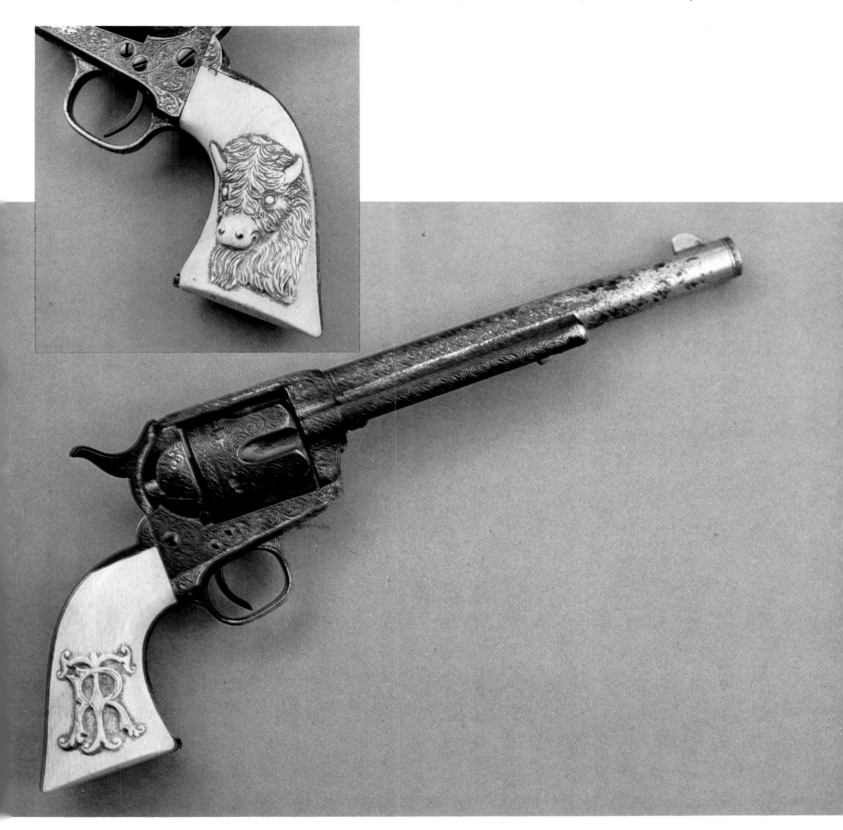

Theodore Roosevelt's favorite Colt six-shooter. Easily the most historic Colt revolver engraved by Nimschke, and one of the most profusely decorated. Shipped soft to Hartley and Graham in May of 1883. Subsequently custom engraved and fitted with relief carved ivory grips. On the right grip a TR monogram; on the left a buffalo head, representing TR's first trophy of big game in the American West. All major parts richly engraved in scroll and geometric motifs; on the recoil shield a TR monogram chiselled in relief. Plated in silver and gold. Serial number 92248. A deluxe Winchester engraved for TR by Nimschke is pictured in *The Book of Winchester Engraving. (Richard P. Mellon Collection/Photograph, Bruce Pendleton; courtesy Merrill K. Lindsay)*

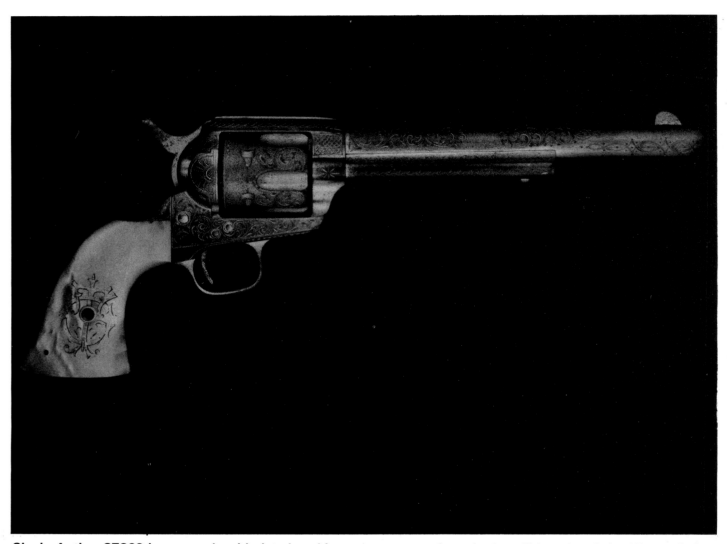

Single Action 27269 is engraved, gold plated, and has monogrammed pearl grips. Shipped to Spies Kissam & Co., New York, in October 1876. Attributed to L.D. Nimschke. Fully gold plated Single Actions are extreme rarities. *(Ridge Todd Collection)*

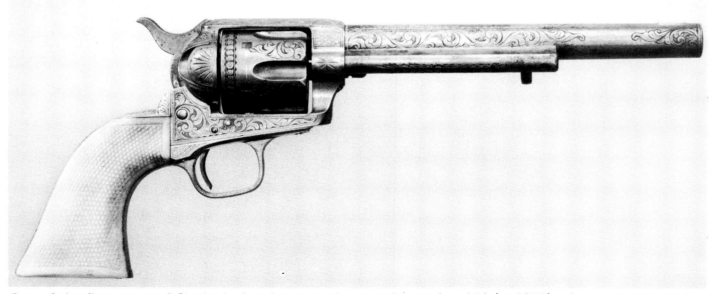

One of the first engraved Single Action Army revolvers; serial number 114 (c. 1873). Coverage in characteristic LDN scroll and border motifs on the barrel, ejector rod housing, frame, loading gate, cylinder, and grip-straps. As was customary, no engraving was given the screws. The embellishment on this pistol appears to be a standard LDN approach to the Colt Single Action Army. Finished in gold and silver plating; the grips of checkered one piece ivory. *(R. E. Hable Collection)*

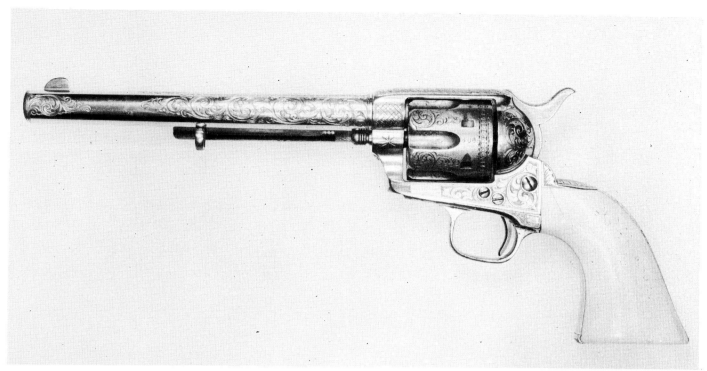

Single Action Army number 26006 has the identical scroll treatment as found on number 114. The major difference is in the plain ivory grips, without checkering. Finished in nickel plating, with the cylinder, hammer, and ejector rod housing plated in gold. It should be noted that at times there is a considerable closeness in coverage, design, and quality of execution in scroll engraving between Colt factory work and the Nimschke school, particularly in the period c. 1870-1900. There are also similarities at times between Nimschke school decoration and some of the engraved guns produced by Remington, Winchester, and certain other gunmakers of the same period. This situation can be explained by the fact that most of the American arms engraved in the second half of the nineteenth century were done by craftsmen from Germany; thus the use of closely similar scroll styles. Due to the high standards of the period, the quality of engraving was also very much alike.   *(Dr. R. L. Moore, Jr. Collection)*

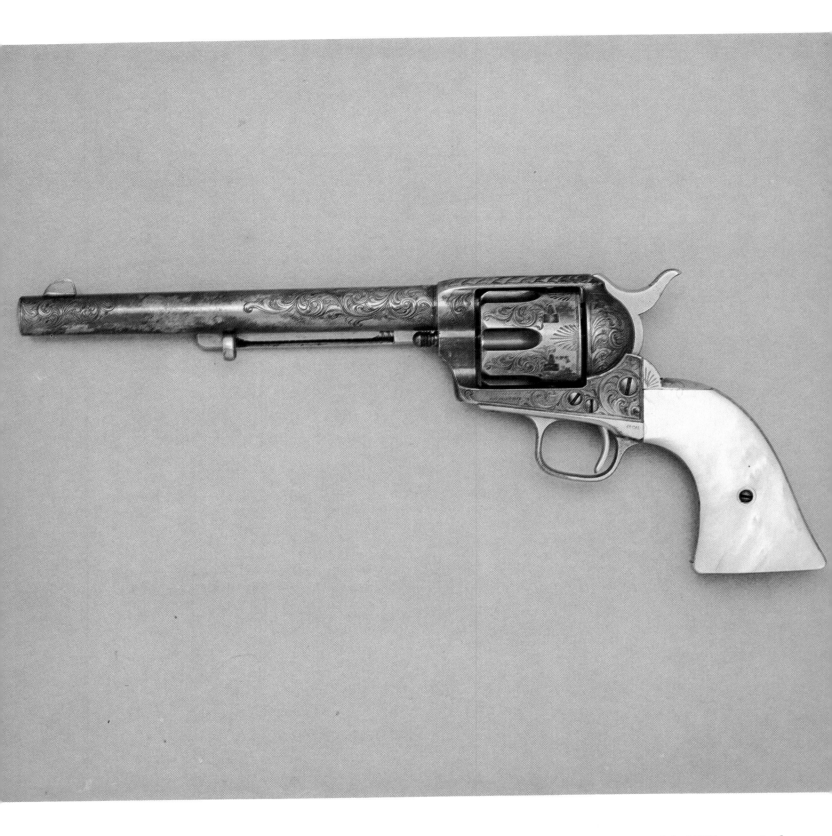

Serial number 22070 Single Action Army was shipped from Colt's factory on December 31, 1875, as part of a group of 67 revolvers of that model ordered by Schuyler, Hartley & Graham, of New York City. The factory ledgers listed .45 caliber and blued finish; no stocks or barrel length indicated. Number 22070 is an intriguing specimen of the closeness in coverage, design, and quality of execution sometimes evident between Colt factory engraving and Nimschke-school engraving in the period c. 1870-1900. The gun was either engraved and then gold and nickel plated by Nimschke's shop (on order from Schuyler, Hartley and Graham), or it may have been returned to Colt in Hartford, where the engraving and plating was done under the big blue dome. Because of the incomplete survival of Colt factory records, the latter event — if that is what occurred — is now a matter of speculation. It should be noted as a matter of interest that other similar instances of such closeness have been observed between Nimschke-school decoration and some engraved arms by Remington, Winchester, and certain other armsmakers of the period. *(Buddy Hackett Collection)*

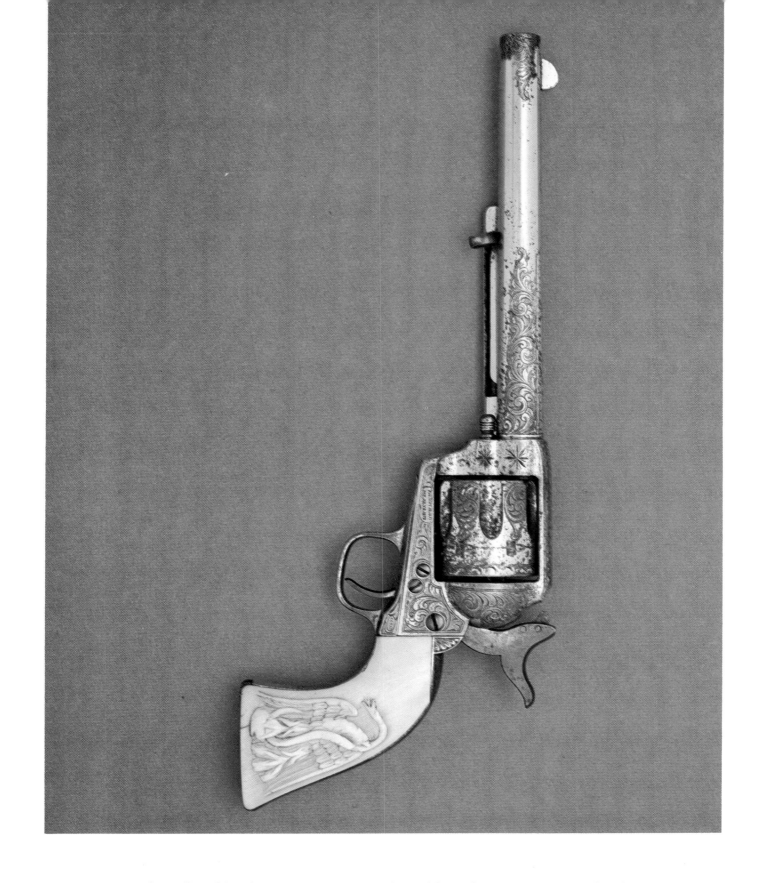

Classic example of scroll and border engraving by L. D. Nimschke. The revolver is also of collector interest because it is from the limited issue of Single Action Armies in the .44 rimfire series. Serial number 687. Apparently intended for the Mexican market, that country's distinctive eagle and snake motif is relief carved on the left side of the one piece ivory grips. Besides the characteristic scrolls, Nimschke-design details are in evidence in the star (bottom of triggerguard, on each side of the frame at its juncture with barrel and ejector tube, and, as partial motifs, terminating main theme on the ejector rod tube), the wavy line and dot border (topstrap, top of barrel, and on ejector rod tube), entwining lines (top of barrel, buttstrap, and on lower section of backstrap), cross hatching with dots (ejector rod tube and bottom of frame above serial number), fish fin (on top flat and on each side of screw bolster at top of backstrap), and wavy line border (on backstrap). Engraved .44 rimfire revolvers, whether by Nimschke or by the factory, are highly prized rarities in Colt collecting. *(Buddy Hackett Collection)*

Featuring a rather profuse and richly modelled scroll, number 89332 Single Action Army was shipped soft, March 19, 1883, to Hartley & Graham of New York, in .44-40 caliber, with 5 1/2″ barrel. The finish is nickel plating, and the grips are of pearl. *(Jonathan M. Peck Collection)*

Sheriff's Model Single Action, number 80118. Shipped in the soft state to New York City dealers Schoverling, Daly & Gales, and then engraved by Nimschke. Rich scrollwork (with the three line tentacle clusters), entwining lines, zig-zag borders, and other favorite LDN motifs are much in evidence. Full nickel plating; ivory grips. *(N. Brigham Pemberton Collection)*

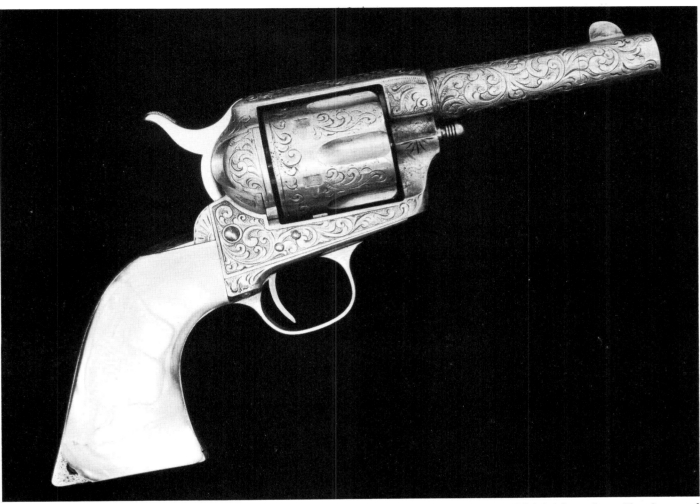

Sheriff's Model Single Action from the Nimschke shop.   Serial number **132084**; shipped to Hartley and Graham, soft finish, in May of **1890**. Steerhead (right side) and goddess (left side) relief carved pearl grips. The unusual triggerguard inscription is a sample of lettering by **LDN.** *(David S. Woloch Collection)*

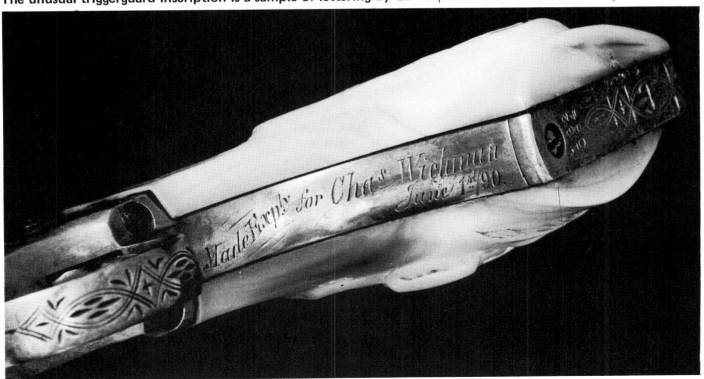

Matched pair of Nimschke engraved Single Action Army revolvers, Nos. 25499 and 26094, displayed for many years at the Texas Ranger Museum, Waco. Rare checkered rosewood grips and combination gold and nickel plating. *(Formerly Edward L. Benson and Stanley Shapiro collections, presently Ken Karnak Collection.)*

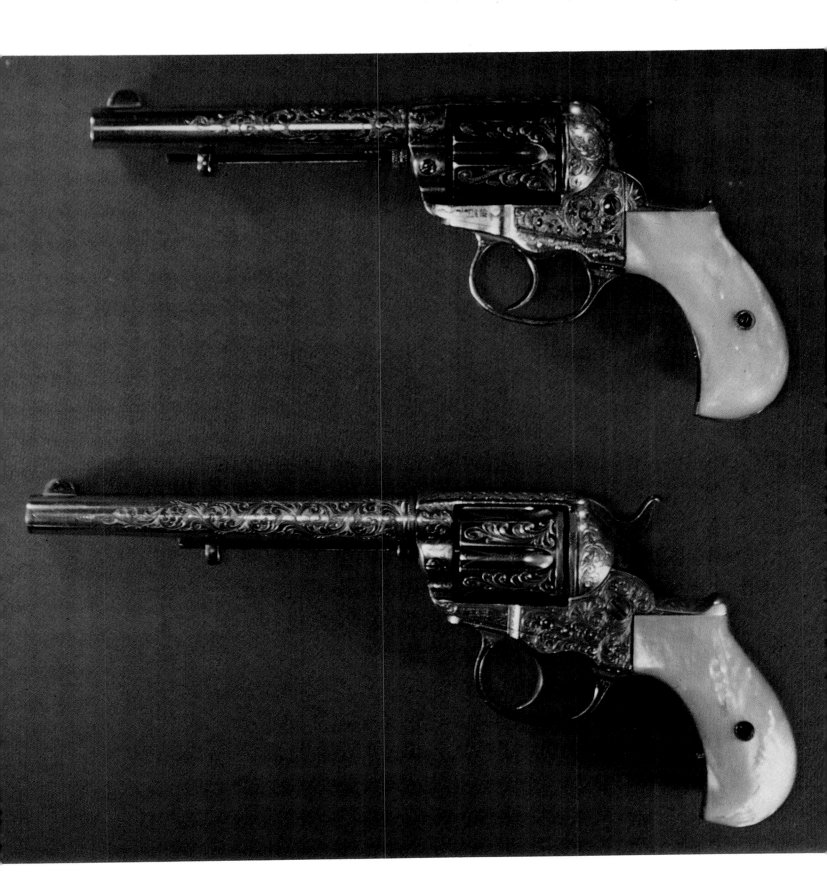

Two Colt Lightning Model 1877 revolvers, attributed to L.D. Nimschke. Top, number 59411, .38 caliber, 5" barrel, with pearl grips; shipped in March 1887 to Hartley & Graham, in the "soft" state. At bottom, 39537, in .41 caliber, 6" barrel; shipped in October 1882 to Hartley & Graham, also "soft". An unusual opportunity to compare two revolvers of the same model from the hand of L.D.N. *(Dr. Richard C. Marohn Collection)*

Early Lightning engraved; .41 caliber, 4 1/2" barrel; shipped to Spies, Kissam & Co., July 1878, no reference to engraved in ledgers. Scroll and border coverage attributed to Nimschke or to another New York craftsman. Punched star and wriggle line motif in cylinder flutes. *(James E. Kattner Collection)*

Shipped "soft" to Hartley & Graham, June 1889, number 68662 Lightning is attributed to Nimschke or another New York engraver. Compare with Lightning 100981, embellished with a nearly identical pattern, but at the Colt factory. Collector James Kattner has suggested this duplication is a result of engravers "job hopping", or that perhaps when Hartley & Graham's work load would peak, some of their jobs would be done at Colt's in H & G patterns. *(James E. Kattner Collection)*

The exact medium frame Lightning rifle pictured on page 52 of the L.D. Nimschke scrapbook. Scarce few Colt arms represented in the Nimschke book have been located by collectors. *(Jackson Arms Collection)*

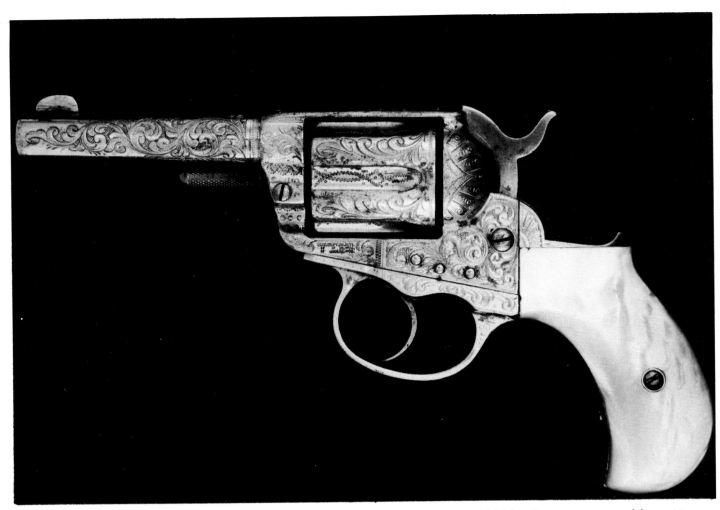

Still another Colt revolver from the Nimschke workshop; serial number 33462. As customary, shipment was from Colt to New York dealers Hartley and Graham, December 1881. The finish in this instance was blue, which was removed prior to engraving. After engraving the full nickel finish was applied by Hartley and Graham. Pearl grips were also added by Nimschke. Gun was once a personal sidearm of circus trick shot artist Prairie Rose. For a similarly engraved Colt Lightning see page 6 of the Nimschke record book. *(David S. Woloch Collection)*

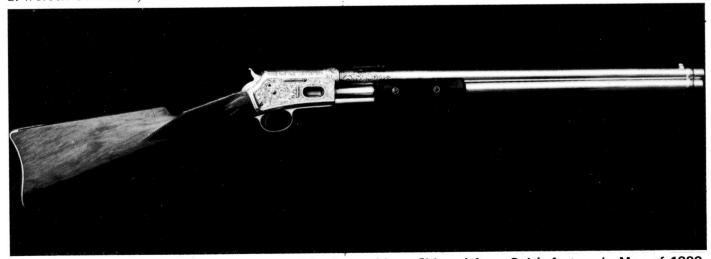

Serial number 27981 medium frame Baby Lightning carbine. Shipped from Colt's factory in May of 1888, to Hartley and Graham, New York; ledgers list the finish as "soft", with "fancy" stock. The special wood and checkering were done at Colt's factory. Following Nimschke's scroll engraving, the metal was finished in silver plating, with gold plated frame, hammer, and barrel bands. Engraved Baby carbines are extreme rarities. *(David S. Woloch Collection)*

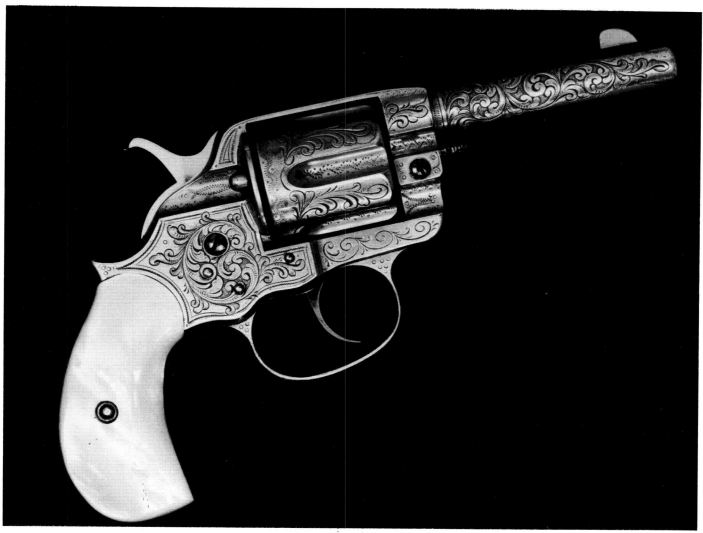

Sheriff's Model of the Frontier Double Action revolver. Pearl grips; plated finish; and characteristic Nimschke scroll engraving. Serial number 8498. Shipped by Colt to Hartley and Graham, May 23, 1882; blued finish, stocks not listed. Hartley and Graham had Nimschke embellish the revolver, and then had it refinished. *(David S. Woloch Collection)*

Medium frame Lightning slide action carbine; serial number 29282 (c. 1888), with coverage on the bolt, frame, triggerguard, barrel, and buttplate. Plated finish. For similarly engraved Lightnings, see pages 49, 52, and 56 of Nimschke's own record book. *(A. I. McCroskie Collection)*

The diminutive Model 1849 Pocket revolver proved a popular item for individual inscription or presentation, particularly during the Civil War. Richard Gray, Jr., Assistant Surgeon of the 21st Ohio Volunteer Infantry, had his Model 1849 pistol (number 199139; c. 1862) inscribed in script and italic letters on the backstrap. The Pocket pistol of Captain E. W. Stone, Jr. of Roxbury, Massachusetts, was inscribed in script. Its serial, number 263289, also dates the gun at c. 1862. Photographs from the Civil War show the pocket type Colts as popular sidearms for infantrymen. *(John G. Hamilton Collection)*

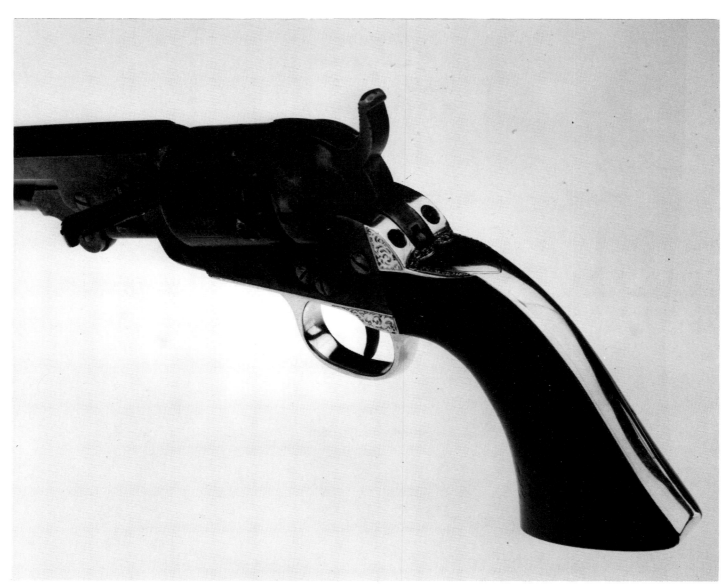

Comparison of Model 1849 Pocket number 145387 should be made with revolver 93102 pictured on previous page. 145387 has one piece ebony grips, and the backstrap and triggerguard are overlaid with a thick layer of gold. The wedge is also overlaid, at each end, with gold. Pocket Model number 145271 is pictured on page 92 of *Samuel Colt Presents*, and is similarly embellished on its gripstraps. *(William H. Myers Collection)*

Chapter IX
NON FACTORY ENGRAVED COLTS
Percussion Period
NON FACTORY ENGRAVED COLTS
c. 1873 — 1900
SPECIAL SCROLL
c. 1873-79

In the percussion period, those relatively few Colt firearms engraved outside of the factory usually offered only gripstrap inscriptions. Since the straps were generally brass, the work could be done by any jewelry engraver. Crude inscriptions were sometimes done by anyone with a knife point, nail, or other basic tool.

L.D. Nimschke was the major non-factory engraver of Colt firearms in the nineteenth century. His output is so significant that it is covered in a separate chapter. Other non-factory engravers who did Colt percussion arms are represented only by occasional pieces. A selected few are shown in the present chapter as an indication of what the collector may encounter.

Since Colt ledgers do not reflect what was done to a gun after it was shipped, the only way to be satisfied of a specimen's authenticity is by a careful examination, which sometimes can be aided by an ironclad pedigree. Available information on specific non-factory engravers of percussion Colts is quite limited, with the notable exception of Nimschke.

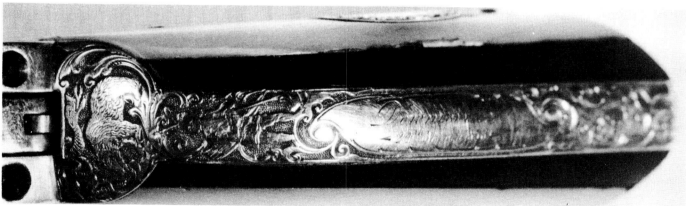

Model 1849 Pocket revolver, serial number 93102. "The Express Boys Tribute to John E. Ager"; a unique special presentation, with the gold and pearl grip work done by jeweler J. W. Tucker of San Francisco (and so signed under the triggerguard). On the butt an oval piece of polished gold quartz. Inscriptions on the gold backstrap and the right grip plaque (also of gold) are pictured. On the left grip plaque a mounted express rider. On the gripstraps are scroll engraving, a bear and serpent motif, a miner swinging a pick, and an Indian warrior. The wooden grips have pearl sideplates. A comparable gold mounted Model 1849 pistol (number 145271) was presented to Captain John S. Ellis of the First California Guard in August of 1860 (see *Samuel Colt Presents,* page 92). The Ellis pistol has ebony grips and custom made gold gripstraps, inscribed and engraved. *(Hugh E. Hayes Collection)*

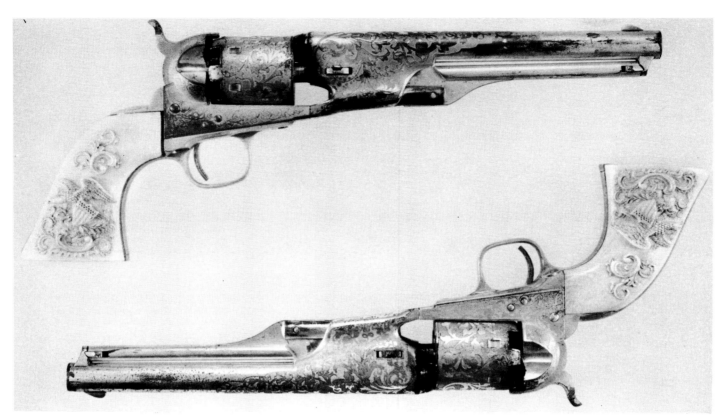

Model 1861 Navy revolvers numbers **14143** and **14239**, whose decor is a unique combination of *acid etching* (on the barrels, cylinders, and frames), engraving (*Wm Mathewson* on the buttstraps, powder flask, and a presentation inscription on the case lid plaque), silver plating (with the ground on the etched parts gilt), and relief carved ivory grips (on the right, eagle and shield and scroll motifs; on the left, standing figure of liberty with scrolls). These revolvers are fitted in a French style (contour) double case; mahogany, lined in blue velvet. Accessories silver plated to match. The possibility exists that the decorative work was done by the Colt factory; but the unique embellishments suggest an as yet unidentified outside source. Mathewson was a colorful pioneer figure in the American West. These revolvers, cased, are pictured in *Samuel Colt Presents*, page 206, showing the opposite sides. *(Anonymous Collection)*

Manhattan Navy revolver, serial number **43** (special number), engraved in a standard scroll pattern quite similar to that found on Colt arms of the 1860's. Relief carved on the left ivory grip was a scene commemorating the signing of the Declaration of Independence, and the finely lettered motto: United we stand, divided we fall. Inscribed in script on the butt: *Presented to/Gen. U.S. Grant by/Co. B. 91st Reg. Ill. Vol.* The similarity to scrollwork on a contemporary Colt shows the widespread influence of the Germanic engravers in the decoration of American firearms beginning in the mid nineteenth century. *(Formerly in the William M. Locke Collection)*

New Line .32 caliber revolver; number 4950. Nickel plated with case hardened hammer; rosewood grips; oak casing lined in velvet. Special style scroll coverage on frame, cylinder, and barrel. c. 1874. *(David S. Woloch Collection)*

New Line revolvers inscribed to Joseph Gales from Colt's factory. Gold and nickel plated finish; pearl grips. Extra profuse and deluxe scrolls, finely overlapped and intertwined. At top, .41 caliber; bottom, .32 caliber. Velvet lined oak casing. A similar pair is known presented to George I. Moore, from Colt, on January 1, 1874. Moore and Gales were among the Colt allies who received presentation sets of New Line pistols on January 1, 1874, apparently as part of a promotion of this model. *(Formerly in the William M. Locke Collection)*

Within the years c. 1873 — c. 1879, a limited number of handguns (estimated at a few hundred) were embellished in a quite stylish scroll, done in a fine hand, and in a contrasting fashion to the scroll-work associated with Cuno Helfricht. Elements of the style suggest Gustave Young as the originator.

This conclusion rests on the fine quality of most observed specimens (a few arms are known which were obviously done by members of the craftsman's shop and not by the master), the elegant scroll style of intertwined and overlapping floral and vine details (compare with illustrations in Gustave Young and gold inlaid percussion chapters), and the style of panel scene figures when present. It is known that Young continued to do some work for Colt after leaving Hartford in 1869.

All pieces of this special scroll style which have been observed to date were finished in plating (usually nickel), most often the grips are of ivory or pearl. A close examination of Colt's Centennial Exposition display at Philadelphia shows this elegant scroll to have been present on several of the show guns, most of them having plated finishes and ivory or pearl grips.

Though attributed to Young, it is possible that Helfricht and his shop may have done these stylish arms, or at least some of them. However, based on the evidence noted above, the best opinion at present points to Gustave Young as the initial source, and to him as the engraver of the best quality specimens.

.32 caliber New Line; 2¼" barrel; full plated finish; pearl grips. Relatively profuse scroll coverage; the barrel marking, COLT NEW 32, cut in relief *(rare)*. Several overlapping curves appear in the scrolls. *(L. Allan Caperton Collection)*

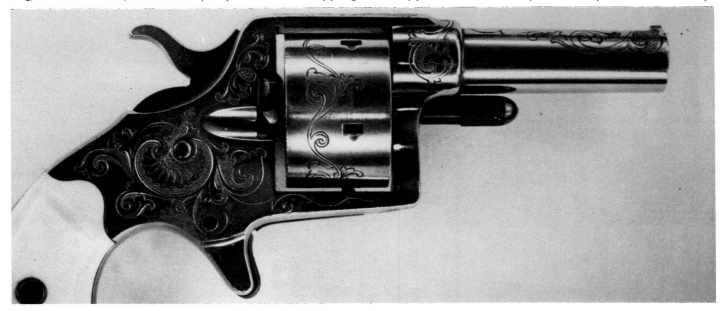

House Pistol number 9864 exhibits the special scroll influenced by Gustave Young on the frame, cylinder, and barrel. Grips of ivory; plated finish. *(Woolaroc Museum; P.R. Phillips Collection)*

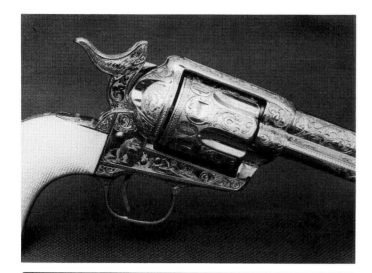

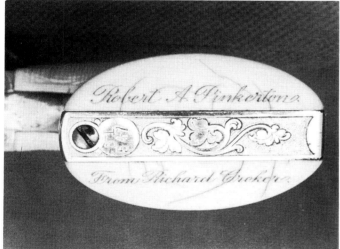

Number 51547 Single Action Army, in the same style as number 50932. Identical finish, grips, barrel length, and caliber. Although the two revolvers are from the same hand and are in the same style, the scrolls are quite different in layout. Panel scenes are of differing motifs (excepting left side of frame), though each scene is located in identical areas of the frame and the backstrap. Hammer designs also similar, but not identical. Colt ledgers record shipment of number 51547 in April of 1879. Rare inscription on the butt; Pinkerton was a member of the famous detective agency family. *(Raymond H. Vanyek Collection)*

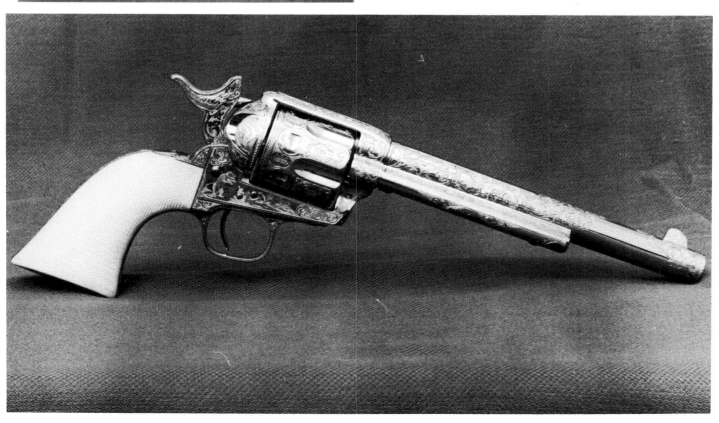

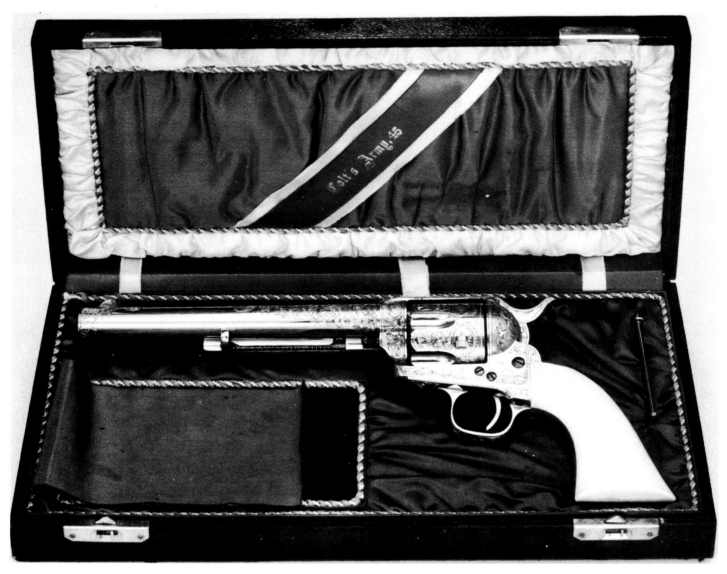

One of the finest of engraved pre-World War II Single Action Army revolvers; number 50932. Nickel plated, with blued screws and cylinder pin; checkered ivory grips; 7½'' barrel, .45 caliber. Factory casing: Leather covered box, lined in white and blue silk and including wooden cartridge block and nickel plated L-shaped screwdriver. Besides the distinctive and profuse scroll-work, note the delicate and *rare* panel scenes, seldom found on any pre-WWII engraved Colt firearms. *(R.E. Hable Collection)*

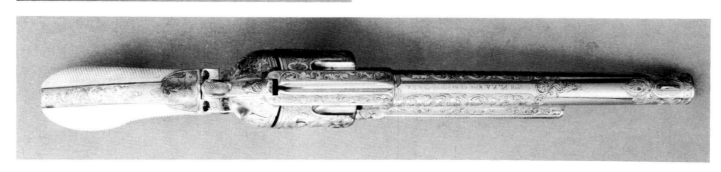

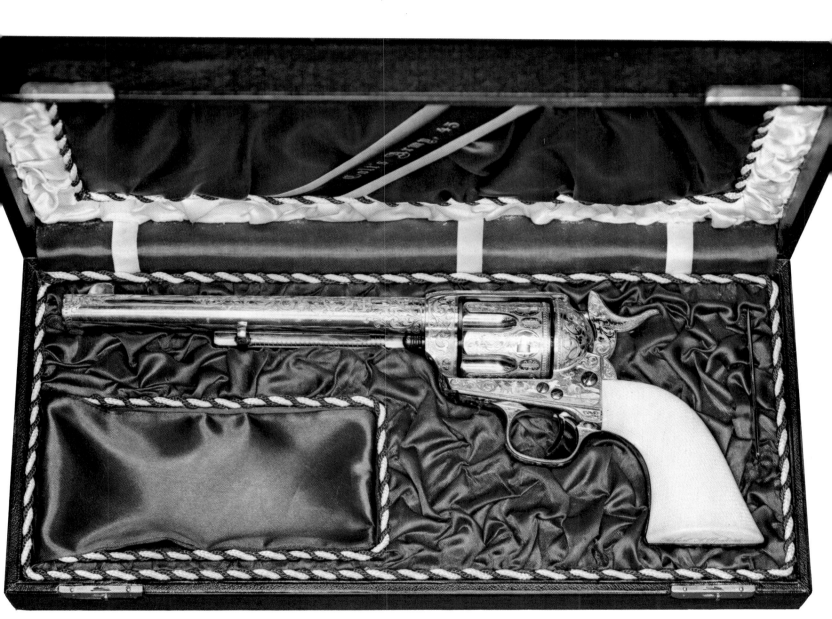

Number 51547 Single Action Army. Inscribed on the butt to Robert A. Pinkerton. *Note:* **The casing a modern reproduction based on a Colt original.** *(Raymond H. Vanyek Collection; courtesy of* A Study of the Colt Single Action Army, *Photograph, Ed Prentiss)*

Gold and silver or nickel plated Single Actions, numbers **11088** (top) and **11089**. Grips of ivory. From the Colt display at the Philadelphia Centennial Exhibition of 1876. Number 11088 served as a company sample gun from its production in 1874 until c. 1894. In style and quality these pistols rank among the most artistically appealling of all Single Actions made by Colt from 1873 to date. *(David S. Woloch Collection)*

Non-Factory
Engraved Colts

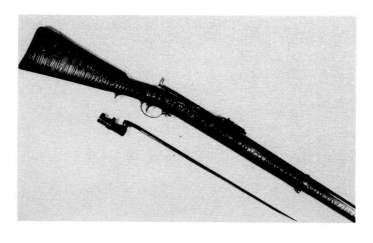

Unique Colt Berdan military rifle; a standard model made for the Czar's Army, but decorated by a Russian silversmith. The relief cast and chased inscription on the right side of the stock is of solid sterling silver. Text, in Russian, translates as follows: "Exalted Chief of the [Enlisted] Soldiers of the Life Guards, Finnish Shooters' Battalion". Serial number 745; c. 1868. Though pre-dating 1873, the rifle is shown here since it is chambered for the metallic cartridge. *(The State Hermitage Museum, Leningrad, U.S.S.R.)*

Judging from surviving Colt firearms of the period 1873-1900, only a limited number were decorated by non-factory engravers. The major craftsman in this area again was Nimschke. Jewelry engravers could no longer embellish most Colt pieces, since the use of brass was eliminated from grip-straps, and only some of the deringers and small pocket revolvers offered brass frames.

Excepting Nimschke, very little information is known on non-factory engravers, 1873-1900. The selected specimens illustrated suggest some of the variations one encounters from varied geographical areas.

Again, since Colt ledgers do not include data on guns after their shipment from the factory, the collector should exercise caution in considering a piece of non-factory origin. A number of pre-1900 pieces, particularly Single Actions, have been engraved post 1950!

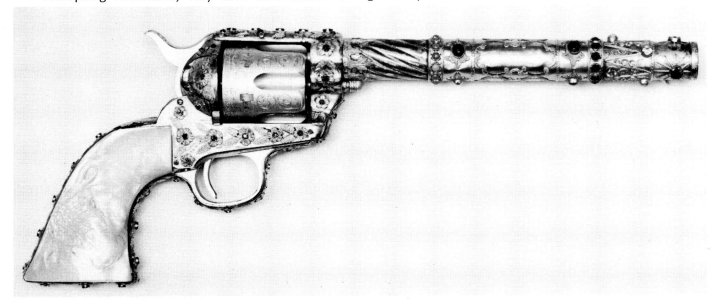

Unique baton used by Jack Sinclair, the bandmaster in the Dodge City Cowboy Band. The Single Action Army Colt is plated, encrusted with engraved and chased soft metals, and mounted with an assortment of paste stones. The pearl grips have a relief carved steer head on the right side, and the bandmaster's first name encrusted on the left. One of the most unusual and interesting revolvers encountered during the course of this study. *(Photograph courtesy of Arnold M. Chernoff)*

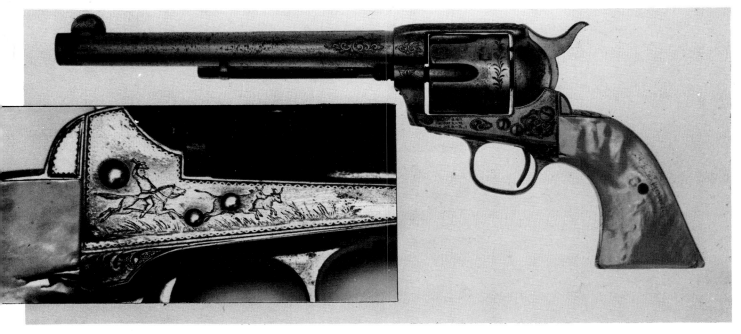

Rare example of Single Action embellishment on the Western Frontier, serial 75282 was engraved, nickel plated, and fitted with inscribed pearl grips and an 1882 dime front sight. On the left grip, *T.F. Gryson,* in old English letters. Note rare panel scene on the right side of the frame. The revolver represents the work of Freund's Armory. *(Jonathan M. Peck Collection)*

Freund's Armory, Cheyenne, Wyoming, customized this unique Single Action Army revolver, serial number 83639. Finished in gold and silver plating, the gun features a faceted and engraved hammer, engraving in the style of the Freund customized Sharps rifles, coin front sight blade, engraved pearl grips, and the inscription FREUNDS ARMORY/CHEYENNE WYO. on the topstrap. *(David S. Woloch Collection/Photograph, Thomas Beiswenger)*

Two Lightning 1877 revolvers, with documented and intriguing histories. *At top*, number 73728, shipped December 30th 1889 to Ketelsen and Degetau, El Paso, Texas, and sold to John Wesley Hardin in April of 1895. Research has substantiated that this revolver was used by Hardin in the holdup of a dice game at the Gem Saloon, El Paso, on May 1st 1895. Hardin ranks among the top gunfighters of the American West. *At bottom*, number 138671, .41 caliber, 4 1/2" barrel, shipped in the soft state to M. Hartley and Co., New York, on October 29th, 1902. Revolver was subsequently engraved, fitted with sterling silver grips, and gold plated. The backstrap is inscribed: Pat F. Garrett from his El Paso Friends. On the left grip: *Lincoln, Dona Ana, El Paso* (localities of Garrett service), and on the right grip: *Customs Collector*. Presented to Garrett, best known as killer of Billy the Kid (W.F. Bonney), in commemoration of his appointment by President Theodore Roosevelt as Customs Collector for the El Paso district, a position he held from 1902 to 1906. *(Dr. Richard C. Marohn Collection)*

Cased .30 caliber New Line number 7968 has pearl grips, nickel plated barrel and frame, the balance gold plated (screws blued), rare casing of leather-covered wood, lined in velvet. Scrollwork cleanly executed in the Young style. 2¼" barrel. *(Fred Sweeney Collection)*

New Line .32 cased set finished in nickel with gold plated cylinder, cylinder pin and hammer. Leather and velvet casing, with wooden cartridge block. Factory ledgers note that the pistol was a presentation from a Mr. Hopkins to E. Ryder, Superintendent of Minneapolis and St. Louis Railway; December 1881 shipping date. *(George Taylor Collection)*

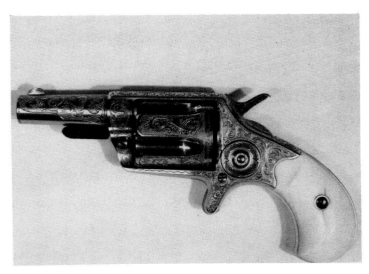

.38 rimfire New Line number 3768E is nickel plated and has ivory grips. Note overlapping and intertwining of scrolls and the rather profuse coverage. *(R.M. Scott Paul Collection)*

Number 1306 New Line .41; richly embellished, and finished in blue and case hardening; grips of pearl. Leather casing lined in velvet, with wooden cartridge block; note cleaning rod-screw driver. Formerly in the R.E. Hable collection. *(David S. Woloch Collection)*

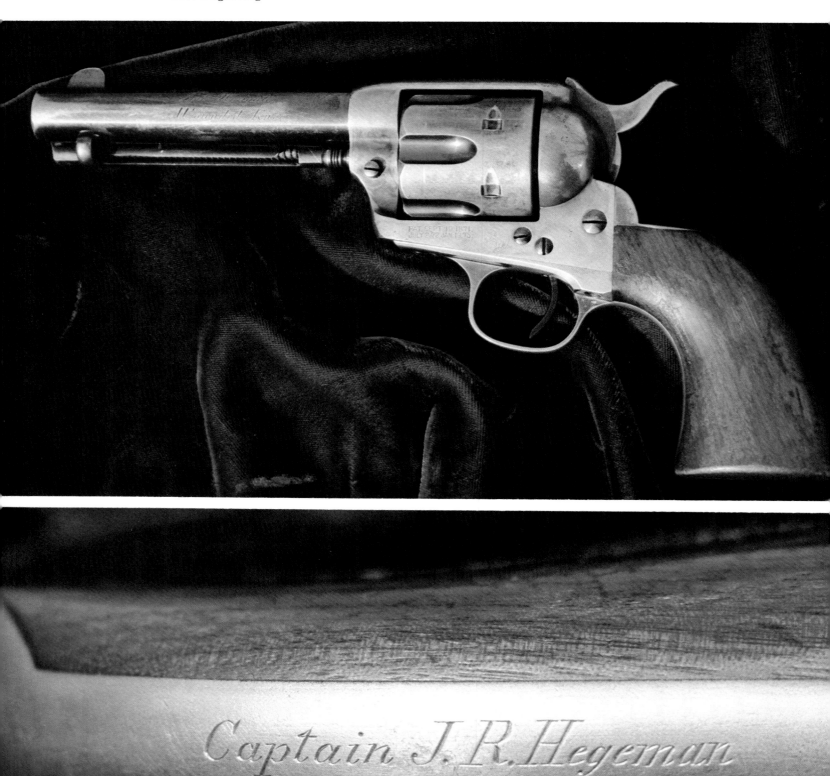

Fully documented in Colt ledgers, Single Action Army 168554 was customized for renowned pioneer Colt collector John R. Hegeman, son of the first president of the Metropolitan Life Insurance Co. Ledger "Sales Book" of the late 1890s noted such specific information as: "1 5 1/2" 45/c S.A. Army Pistol Ivory Blue #168554 with extra 4 3/4" barrel Fitting extra barrel & Engraving on barrel SECRET SERVICE 1898 FORT WINGATE WOUNDED KNEE Engraving on backstrap CAPTAIN J.R. HEGEMAN. 1 Pkg Ad Ex [one package Adams Express]." The ledgers also noted no charge for the revolver or extra barrel, but what appears to have been $1.75 for the inscriptions! Factory ledgers also list number 168554 as shipped on December 8, 1896, to Hegeman. For further information on the remarkable John R. Hegeman see the November/December 1979 issue of *Man at Arms* magazine. *(Clark V. Cail Collection)*

Handsome and unusual embellishments are on Single Action 30259, fully documented in the Colt ledgers as of .45 caliber, nickel plated, ivory grips, engraved, and part of a shipment of five to Simmons Hardware Co., St. Louis, in January of 1880. Note coverage on the hammer, and the quite light and graceful scroll. *(Richard R. Atkinson Collection)*

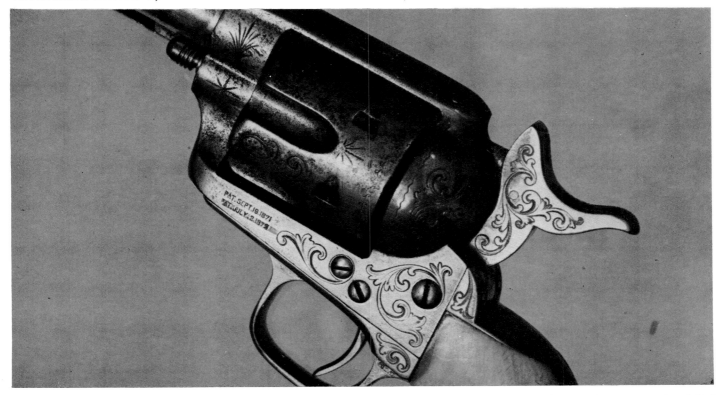

Single Action number 30259 was shipped in January 1880 to Simmons Hardware, St. Louis; engraved, nickel plated, .45 caliber, and with ivory grips. The scrollwork not profuse, but including the quite scarce coverage on the hammer. *(Richard R. Atkinson Collection)*

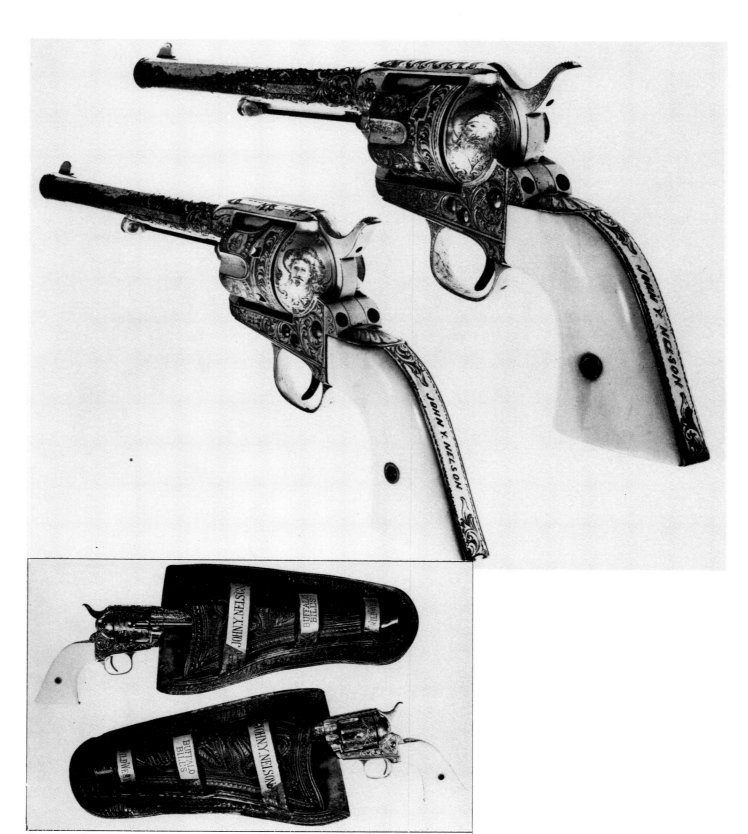

Custom Single Action revolvers made for John Y. Nelson, a featured member of the Buffalo Bill Cody Wild West troupe. Serial numbers 98489 and 99615. Shipped from Colt in September, 1883, and believed to have been engraved through the recipient dealer, Hartley and Graham, New York. The scroll was done similarly to Colt factory work, but lacks any coverage on the butts or the bottoms of the triggerguard straps. Nickel plated, with ivory grips. Gun number 99615 was engraved on the recoil shield with a portrait bust of Nelson; gun number 98489 with a portrait bust of his patron and friend, Buffalo Bill. The Buffalo Bill pistol has animal figures cut within cartouches on the cylinder. The custom holsters have German silver plaques, identifying the original owner. A photograph of the Wild West troupe in London, 1887, clearly pictures Nelson wearing these pistols and holsters. *(W.C. Ford Collection)*

Hand cut barrel marking (left side) and nickel and gold finish are among the exotic details of Lightning number 16882, shipped in 1879 to E.C. Meacham. Records document the engraving, the finish, pearl grips, and above noted shipment. *(Ron Peterson Collection)*

Four handguns from the shop of Cuno A. Helfricht, and a longarm from that of L. D. Nimschke. At top, serial number 286256 Officers Model Target revolver, shipped to C. C. Crossman October 19, 1907.

Second from top, a 4″ barrel New Line revolver, shipped in 1879.

At center, the L. D. Nimschke Baby Lightning carbine, serial number 27981. Listed in Colt ledgers as .44-40, 20″ barrel, soft finish, fancy stock; shipped May 9, 1888 to Hartley and Graham, New York.

Below the carbine is serial number 36854 Model 1878 double action revolver, shipped from the factory January 30, 1897.

At bottom, New Pocket revolver number 10384, with CHP monogram inlaid in gold on the side of the frame. This revolver went to F. E. Belden, a Colt official, on October 5, 1897. *(David S. Woloch Collection/Photograph, Thomas Beiswenger)*

Chapter X
CUNO A. HELFRICHT AND HIS SHOP
c. 1871 — 1921

A presentation engraved and silver inlaid rifle for Buffalo Bill Cody, a fancy Peacemaker revolver for Bat Masterson, a pair of engraved and pearl handled pocket pistols for the president of Guatemala — these guns and many thousands more like them were ornamented by Colt engraver Cuno A. Helfricht and his team of assistants. As engraving contractor to Colt c. 1871-1921, Helfricht's career encompassed an era as exciting and colorful as any in our nation's history, and the profusion of guns he and his staff engraved were enthusiastically admired throughout the world. Their quality helped advance the image of Colt arms as among the finest made anywhere.

Cuno A. Helfricht and his father, Charles J., are part of the tradition common to German families emigrating to nineteenth century America, in which trades passed from father to son. Both were master engravers and stockmakers, and they had much in common with the Youngs of Hartford and Springfield, the Ulrichs of New Haven and Hartford, and the Glahns of Connecticut and New York. All were family "dynasties" prominently active in American arms engraving during the period 1850-1920. Certainly at least the working members of these four families were known to one another, and geographically their working areas in Connecticut, Massachusetts, and New York were conveniently reached even with the relatively slow travel times of that period. Between them, the Helfrichts, the Youngs, the Ulrichs, and the Glahns boasted a total of better than 16 engravers, all master craftsmen.

Cuno Helfricht was born January 26, 1851, in Thuringen, Germany, and resided in Hartford from 1860. His father Charles was a German-trained master gunsmith, capable of fancy stockwork, gold inlay and engraving, or any other gunmaking skill. As contractor to Colt for hand and long gun stocks, Charles and his workmen played an important role in filling badly needed government and commercial needs during the turbulent period of the Civil and Indian Wars. It is believed that young Cuno was trained as an arms engraver while apprenticed to his father from c. 1860 through 1869.

Cuno Helfricht's only employer throughout his career was the Colt firm. For almost the entire

50 years of his employment with them he was a contractor, as was his father from about 1860 through 1900. Long terms of employee service were traditional with the Colt firm.

As previously noted, Gustave Young, who had been Colt's chief engraver during much of the period from c. 1852, decided in 1869 to move his shop to Springfield, Massachusetts. Any satisfactory successor to a man of Young's caliber had to be not only thoroughly experienced but academically trained. Realizing this, Charles Helfricht sent Cuno to Berlin, Germany to study engraving there. In 1871 young Helfricht now 20 years old returned to America to Colt's engraving and stockmaking departments. Within a few years he would be Colt's chief engraver, a position he was destined to hold until retiring in 1921. Young's skill, incidentally, was still available to Colt when needed, until his death in 1895.

From 1871 through 1921 Colt's production included the last of the percussion revolvers and long arms, and the beginnings of their single action cartridge arms (1871), the double action revolvers (1889), the automatic pistols (1900), plus their shotgun lines (1878 through 1900), and the Lightning rifles (1885 — c. 1910). Until the turn of the century, engraving on Colt firearms was in such demand that an engraved supply of the more popular models was kept in stock. The rapidly developing market created by the settlement of the Western United States accounted for a large share of the demand for engraved arms. Cattlemen and lawmen were enthusiastic admirers of fancy Colt handguns; particularly the classic Single Action Army, and hunters held the Colt shotguns in high regard. The Lightning and Frontier double action revolvers, the New Line single actions, and the deringers were other popular engraved Colt firearms during this period. In long arms, the shotguns were the only models engraved in any noteworthy quantity. Any other rifle, carbine, shotgun, or musket made by Colt from 1836 to the present is a rarity hand engraved. Only three of the Burgess model lever action rifles were engraved out of the total production of 6,403.

The decline in demand for engraving on Colt and other makes of firearms was not evident until the early 1900's.   At that time Cuno Helfricht reduced his engraving staff from as many as six regulars (c. 1875-85) to as few as two.   By c. 1910 Colt firearms were usually engraved only on special order.   The table gives a clear picture of the change in tastes from 1875 through 1925.   These figures are for handguns only, and are based on original factory records.   It should be noted that the vast majority of this work was done on a production basis, and therefore very few custom designs were executed.   In mass producing predetermined patterns, production was much greater, and the factory could realize a better profit and at the same time better satisfy the demands of the public for fancy firearms.

Single Action Army Revolvers		Other Handguns
1875	50 (estimated)	250 (estimated) *
1885	102	100 *
1895	66	65 *
1905	45	30 *
1915	31	60 * †
1925	33	15 *

†Production large due to World War I
*These figures do not include .22 caliber revolvers or .41 caliber deringers, none of which is scarce in engraved condition.   In addition to the above, some models of pistols and long arms were engraved by individual Colt dealers.   This practice was known as early as 1850, and was occasionally done as late as 1900.   Hartley and Graham of New York City was responsible for much of this work.   Their regular engraving supplier was the renowned L. D. Nimschke (active 1850 — c. 1900).

The demand for decorated Colt arms meant a continued need for engraving talent and some significant information is available on the force employed by Cuno Helfricht as Colt's engraving contractor.

Helfricht's records from August 1875 through August 31, 1886, provide a clear picture of Colt engraving during this period.   These account books list the following engravers, all of whom worked under the supervision of Helfricht.   Those considered as "regulars" are marked with an asterisk:

*William Aubray (April 1884 — June 1885; May — August 1886; known to have worked as late as 1892 as a Colt engraver);

William Avery (July — August 1886; known to have worked as late as 1888 at Colt's);

*Elliott L. Green (Sept. 1879 — Feb. 1880; Jan. 1881 — April 1884);

*William Hahn (Jan. 1880 — April 1886);

*Cuno Helfricht (1871 — 1921);

Charles Kummer (Nov. 1877; April 1885);

Fred M. Martin (Feb. — April 1881);

*Hans Morba (June 1878 — July 31, 1881; died July 31, 1881);

Louis Muller (Aug. 1886.   May have worked longer);

*Hugo Reuss (Jan. 30, 1883 — August 1886; formed own business in 1887, continuing in Hartford);

Harry Schonhaar (Feb. — June 1880; April — May 1884);

M. Southeimer (Nov. 1879 — Sept. 1881);

Eugene Young (August 1879 — Oct. 1880; Feb. — April 14, 1881);

*Oscar Young (Feb. — May 1877, Oct. 1877 — Jan. 1884);

The following are considered to have been apprentices:

W. A. Allen (Sept. — Nov. 1879);

Thomas Appleyard (July 1884 — April 1885);

George Davis (Dec. 1879 — June 1880);

Thomas Flynn (Oct. 1884 — Jan. 1885);

James McFarlane (Oct. 27, through end of month, 1885);

Julius Meffert (August — Nov. 1879);

Ed Molraine (Nov. 1879).

With these several engravers having worked on Colt arms, how can one possibly hope to identify which artisan engraved a specific gun?   For the years 1871 through 1900 this is often difficult.   Some pieces can be identified by their degree of excellence and by strong stylistic features.   However, working from predetermined patterns restricted the craftsman's individuality.   Without these patterns (even though the engravers were not required to copy them precisely), it would be relatively easy as the identity of a workman's engraving can be likened to the uniqueness of fingerprints.   In a few cases identities can be determined by engraver's records.   A notebook kept by Eugene Young, from August 1879 through October 1880, and from February through April 1881 lists a total of 300 serial numbers of Colt shotguns engraved by him.   All are the Model 1878 Hammer type; and the serial numbers range from 902 through 10553.

No Colt firearms engraved by the factory contractors are known with engraver's signatures until the twentieth century.   Even the fancy presentation pistols went unsigned.   The practice of engraver's signatures did not become popular until after World War II.   With the surge of interest for collector's firearms, clients began to encourage artisans to sign their work.   In Europe the old custom of usually not signing work continues to this day, but in America most engravers sign their firearms no matter how limited the decoration might be.

In December 1879; a total of 1,261 hours was devoted to engraving by Cuno Helfricht and his staff; the workhorse of December was one Hans Morba, who put in 255½ hours, better than 60 per week.   Ten and sometimes twelve hour days, six days a week, were not unusual for the stockmakers, machinists, and engravers of the New England gunmakers during the nineteenth century.   In January 1885 a total of 1,142 hours of engraving was done by Helfricht's six man work force. Production was so active that the contractor used a delivery form which listed standard work, and left blank spaces for tabulations for completed arms.

In Helfricht's records of 1885-1889, nearly complete notes were kept on the types and quantities of Colt work he and his staff engraved. Most of the engraving shown on these records was on the Model 1878 and Model 1883 double barrel shotguns, plus various models of pistols. Handguns engraved during this period are not plentiful. These figures, however, are not believed to have encompassed the deringers and the .22 caliber pocket revolvers. Engraving on these was usually done so quickly that Helfricht's records do not seem to have included them. Engraving on the Lightning magazine rifle has always been considered a rarity — these records confirm that assumption.

The items listed in "miscellaneous" are of interest because they show the versatility of Helfricht's craftsmen. Their skills included die and stamp cutting, pearl and ivory carving, barrel and rib matting, and trigger checkering. Colt, manufacturing the Gatling gun, commissioned hand engraved mark-

ings for some, plus special engraving or marking on some railway ticket punches (a Colt product hardly known to collectors), and the engraving of a marking plate for one of the Colt Armory printing presses, another unusual Colt product.

As with his predecessors (Gustave Young and his shop and Herman Bodenstein and his shop), Cuno Helfricht determined standard patterns for engravings, and drew up many of these himself. As a graphic example, his role in developing styles for Colt double barrel shotguns is documented by a set of pencil sketches showing different degrees of engraving coverage. These testify to Helfricht's artistic skill, and to an expert knowledge of the English style of scrollwork which, with rich Germanic influences, was standard on Colt doubles.

Basic engraving styles changed with changes in personnel. Young's and Bodenstein's staffs had engraved according to patterns meeting with their chiefs' approval and presumably of their own design. Helfricht's patterns included some which were strongly Germanic, but already in the early 1870's definite style changes are obvious. The various patterns and their periods are shown in the dozens of illustrations in the present chapter.

NOTE: Hartford city directories list Herman L. Ulrich as an engraver, from c. 1867-70 and from c. 1890 through c. 1900 as an engraver at Colt's; he was not listed in the Helfricht account books.

Cuno A. Helfricht, at left; at right his mother and father. Charles J. Helfricht served Colt for many years as a stockmaker, and engraver. Cuno died August 22, 1927 and Charles died February 2, 1909. *(Helfricht Family Collection)*

Rifles show little regularity, since so few were engraved (estimated at an average of about five or less per year, from 1885 through c. 1910), and few were ever done as stock items. Patterns vary, as confirmed by personal examination of factory authenticated examples. Shotguns show greater conformity, and basic styles were identified by the Colt factory as numbers 1 and 2 for the Model 1883 Hammerless, and numbers 1, 3, 4, 6, and 7 for the Hammer Model of 1878. All of these patterns were what can best be described as a British scroll with Germanic influences. Since the Colt shipping ledgers are complete for both models of shotgun, the engraving on any piece can be identified as to exact style by an inquiry to the factory Research Department by serial number. The research will attest to whether or not a shotgun or other Colt gun marked with a specific serial number was shipped from the factory engraved. Records are virtually complete for all Colt arms beginning about 1872, though most of the first 30,000 Single Action Army revolvers are not listed.

The Colt firm had great pride in its talented artisans and regularly displayed engraved arms at expositions and sportsman's shows. An impressive array of such arms was shown at the Philadelphia Centennial Exposition of 1876. A total of 18 engraved and ivory- and pearl-gripped Single Action Army revolvers was in that display, plus about 325 other Colt handguns and long arms. Fancy Colts are also known to have been displayed at the Sportsman shows at Madison Square Garden, New York City, in 1895 and 1896. *Shooting and Fishing* magazine's issue of May 19, 1896, said this about the engraved guns in the Colt display at the 1896 show:

> *The familiar business-like Frontier models, .44 and .45 caliber, some of them elaborately and beautifully engraved and inlaid with gold* [and] *fitted with ivory and pearl handles, finished in outline carving showing heads of Texas steers* [are exhibited], *and also 2. . . old models* [percussion] *are there, both very heavy, and both finished in bright and blued steel, silver, and gold inlaid work, while figures of solid gold are embossed in relief.*

Traditionally such fancy arms have been part of Colt displays since Samuel Colt's first demonstrations of his new repeating firearms, in the 1830's. Today, engraved firearms are still present in Colt's display at sporting goods shows and at the National Rifle Association Annual Meetings and Exhibits.

After the turn of the century, with the decline in demand for engraved firearms, Cuno Helfricht is believed to have done much of the Colt work himself, with the help of at least one and probably two regular assistants. In 1910 the renowned R.J. Kornbrath came to Hartford, but he is not known to have actively engraved for the Colt firm until after

Helfricht's retirement in 1921. Besides Kornbrath, Helfricht's successors were Wilbur A. Glahn and William H. Gough. All three men are covered in detail in following chapters.

YOUNG BROTHERS, ENGRAVERS

Of Gustave Young's three sons, Alfred became a master machinist and for many years worked for Smith & Wesson. Eugene and Oscar both served apprenticeships under their father as engravers and die cutters. Eugene's initial work other than for his father was under Cuno Helfricht, during the period c. 1879-81. To quote Helfricht (Hartford, September 16, 1882): ". . . Eugene Young has been in my employ for over two years, on Gun Engraving, Stamp Cutting, etc., and I recommend him as a steady, honest young man." A notebook kept by Eugene while at Colt identifies his work as including some pistols, but most assignments were the Model 1878 Hammer shotgun. Interestingly enough, Eugene's notebook indicates an average week of six ten-hour days. And when he joined Helfricht in 1879, Eugene was only sixteen years of age.

Apparently in a quest for both good paying work and job experience, Eugene left Colt and joined the Wilcox Silver Plate Company, Meriden, Connecticut. His employer there, Foreman C. J. Heineman, found Eugene "a faithful and efficient workman. I cheerfully recommend him to any one requiring his services". In the fall of 1882 he left New England, and moved to Illinois. From 1882 through 1884 Eugene was an engraver with the Elgin Watch Company, Elgin, Illinois, and during part of 1884 and 1885 he served in the same capacity with the Aurora Watch Company, Aurora, Illinois. Both firms recommended him highly; G. F. Johnson of the Aurora company referring to him as "one of the most capable and skillful engravers that I have ever met."

Some time in 1883 the firm of Young Brothers, Engravers, was established in Chicago. Eugene and Oscar were partners in this endeavor, with Oscar apparently being on hand at the Chicago address (107 Randolph Street), and Eugene doing work after hours from Elgin and Aurora. Their advertising during this period included the legend: "Engraving on Wood and All Kinds of Metal." Probably the amount of work done on firearms during their operation in Chicago was limited.

However, in approximately 1888 Young Brothers returned to Springfield and rejoined their father at his Broad Street address. The firm was obviously quite versatile and prepared to accept virtually any type of work, including: "Gun and Pistol Engraving, Wood Cutting, Fine Steel Stamps and Dies."

In their book of testimonials the firm of Young Brothers included an endorsement from Smith & Wesson: "They are superior workmen, having acquired their trade under their father, Mr. Gustave Young, whose well-known skill in die-sinking, stamp-cutting and engraving has been transmitted to the sons in a marked degree. We unhesitatingly recommend the firm to all requiring work in their line." Other testimonials were on file from J. Stevens Arms and Tool Company ("We consider *[your die cutting and engraving]* as fine work as we have ever had, and shall continue to place our orders with you"), Colt's Patent Fire Arms Mfg. Co., Tiffany & Company (New York), plus various watch and tool makers. An interesting and informative recommendation on Smith & Wesson stationery states (August 19, 1890):

This is to certify that Young Bros. served a thorough and practical apprenticeship under me, according to European standard, in all branches of engraving, and have since assisted me at various times on difficult work for World's Fairs, etc., and have proved themselves artists in their line. Respectfully,

GUSTAVE YOUNG

Although Young Brothers continued as engravers of firearms into the twentieth century, the bulk of their work was in die and stamp cutting. In 1906, however, Oscar joined Smith & Wesson, and his capacity there was as an engraver. He died in 1912. Brother Eugene continued as an independent workman, eventually training his only son Robert to succeed him in the business. Though he had the natural ability Robert was unhappy with long periods of confined work indoors, and in the 1920's he left his father's employ to become a letter carrier for the United States Post Office. Eugene Young died in 1924, at age 61.

Thus the Young family's active years in America as arms engravers and die cutters spans the years c. 1847 through 1924. Several points of interest are apparent in reviewing the story of the Young Brothers, and their father Gustave Young. Perhaps the first and the most obvious is their Germanic lineage, a factor held in common with most other American gun engravers in that era: As examples, L. D. Nimschke, the several Ulrichs, the Glahns, Cuno Helfricht, Herman Bodenstein, Hugo Reuss, and R. J. Kornbrath. All of these gentlemen engraved in what we commonly refer to today as a Germanic style, and many of them developed from this what we refer to today as an American style.

Another factor of significance is that most of the gun engravers in the era of G. Young and Young Brothers were also general engravers and die cutters. Helfricht and the Glahns are known both as engravers and as die cutters. And the renowned Kornbrath worked for many years with Hugo Reuss, who during his active years in the twentieth century was known more as a die cutter than as an engraver. Of added interest, the die cutter heritage common to most of these men is known today with a few of our most accomplished contemporary engravers: A. A. White is an example. White's first formal training was

in die and stamp work, the trade of his father.

DATA FROM COLT LEDGERS

A study of the original Colt factory shipping ledgers for the pre-World War II Single Action Army revolvers reveals some quite interesting information on their engraved decoration. The grand total of engraved Single Action Army revolvers (excluding the Bisley Model and Flattop Target Model) from 1873 through 1940 is approximately 3,000. A number of these guns also included hand engraved inscriptions or monograms.

For the period of Cuno Helfricht (through c. 1921) the total of engraved Single Action Army revolvers was approximately 2,550; approximately 40 of these were the Sheriff's Model, engraved and/or inscribed.

As a matter of interest, the research was tabulated so that the period of 1873 through the end of 1900 was covered separate from that of 1901 through 1921. For 1873 through 1900: The total of engraved Single Action Army revolvers was approximately 1,500, of which several included hand-engraved inscriptions. This number included approximately 23 Sheriff's Models, engraved and/or inscribed. Notes also reveal a very few etched pearl grips, although pearl itself was rather common, and carved pearl was not rare; a very few guns are recorded as "etched". Another great rarity was inscribed grips. Inscriptions located on barrels were rare. Gold inlaid inscriptions and any gold inlay of any form are of extreme rarity. One gun was observed having the backstrap inscription in "German text". Monograms on stocks or on the guns themselves are also unusual. Special combinations of finishes were observed in a few instances; e.g., nickel or silver plating with gold plated trim, or full gold plating, or blue, case hardening, and gold plating. A few engraved guns had special sights, and one gun was observed without front sight *and* engraved (serial number 329243).

The earliest quantity of engraved Single Actions began in the 32000 serial range, though a few engraved pieces of this model were listed with lower numbers.

For 1901 through the end of 1921: Approximately 1,050 engraved Single Action Army revolvers were listed, of which several included hand engraved inscriptions. Of these there were about seventeen engraved Sheriff's Models (some of them also inscribed).

Two pairs of extremely interesting revolvers were numbers 229592, 226214 and 275643, 278226. The former pair was listed as presented to Pawnee Bill from Colt's factory, and so inscribed; engraved, pearl grips, blued, 7½" barrels, .45 caliber, shipped July 1902. The latter pair appeared in the records as also presented to Pawnee Bill from Colt, and so inscribed; engraved, pearl grips, nickel plated, 4¾" barrels, .45 caliber, gold plated cylinders, shipped

June 1906. These deliveries may have coincided with visits made by Pawnee Bill to Hartford, in a wild west show act.

Beginning about 1901 the factory records reveal costs for engraving, which represents a means of indicating which grade of decoration was being used.

However, these cost figures appear only on an occasional basis, later replaced with grade references by number, and still later by grade references in letters (e.g., A, B, and C). The latter indicators did not begin until c. 1929, but the number indicators continued on an occasional basis to as late as 1936.

Unusual items of interest which were noted in the records for the period 1901 through 1921 included the following: Copper inlays, listed both for pearl grips and on steel; equally unusual and of great rarity were enamel inlays on pearl, a gold piece inlaid on a stock, inscription located on an ejector tube, carved mountain sheep head pearl grips, genuine silver front sight, nameplate inlay of inscribed gold, inscription made in raised letters, and a quite historic revolver for one of the classic American Western movie stars: number 331793, silver plated, ox head pearl carved on both sides of grips, No. 2 engraving, TOM MIX inscribed on the barrel; 7½", .32-20; shipped in November of 1915. Again, as in the period 1873-1900, unusual combinations of finishes were listed, though with increased rarity.

ESTABLISHED 1883.

YOUNG BROS.

General Engravers, Stamp Cutters and Die Sinkers.

GUN AND PISTOL ENGRAVING, WOOD CUTTING,
FINE STEEL STAMPS AND DIES A SPECIALTY.

39 Broad Street.

Springfield, Mass..

YOUNG BROS.

ENGRAVERS AND STAMP CUTTERS,

MANUFACTURERS OF

SEALS, FINE DIES AND STEEL STAMPS.

Engraving on Wood and all Kinds of Metal. * Fine Steel
* Stamps A Specialty. *

107 W. RANDOLPH STREET,
CHICAGO, ILL.

Letterhead (top) and trade card from two shops of the Young Brothers. The Chicago enterprise did not prove as successful as hoped, and the boys returned to Springfield where both lived the rest of their lives. *(Johnie Bassett Collection)*

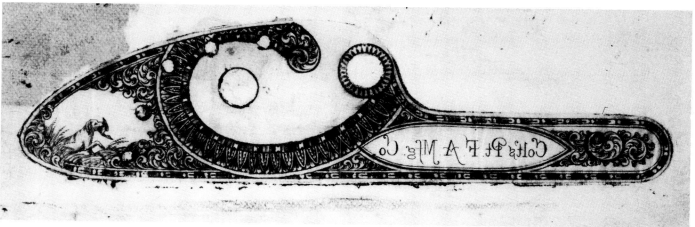

Original gunmaker's pulls from the Young family archives. Lockplate from a Model 1878 Hammer Colt shotgun; the top prints (at right the Charter Oak tree) appear to be from a Model 1855 Sidehammer Colt revolver. Top prints attributed to Gustave Young; the bottom to one of his sons — either Eugene or Oscar. *(Johnie Bassett Collection)*

Original art work by Hugo Reuss; in the period of post World War I. The emphasis is on die work. Reuss worked three years for Helfricht, and went into business for himself in 1887. Two other pieces of advertising art by Reuss, from the same period, refer to him as an engraver and die sinker, but neither mentions his gun work. After leaving Helfricht's employ, Reuss appears to have concentrated on the die cutting, and on fine jewelry work. *(Johnie Bassett Collection)*

The only known signed specimen of engraving by Cuno A. Helfricht — his commercial sign. At the lower right corner, in script: *C. Helfricht*. Enamel was applied to give contrast to the border and inscriptions, and the name C. HELFRICHT was enamelled and inlaid in German silver. Of brass, measuring 14 9/16" x 12 3/4". A unique specimen of Colt and engraving memorabilia, which also proves that Helfricht's artistry was not limited exclusively to the Colt firm. *(Private Collection)*

A business card (above) of Cuno A. Helfricht, made up for his use c. 1880. Known specimens were printed on different colored cards, some with rather modern-art like designs. *(Author's Collection)*

Colt's factory exhibit at the Philadelphia Centennial Exposition, 1876. Many of the guns were elaborately engraved; plating, ivory and pearl grips abound. Probably the most spectacular display of Colt arms ever put on by the company. Even the three gold inlaid percussion revolvers from the Colt Museum collection (now in the Connecticut State Library) were shown. *(Colt Collection of Firearms, Connecticut State Library)*

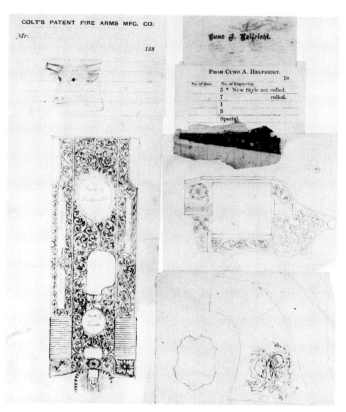

Group of drawings and other documents from the papers of Cuno A. Helfricht. At top right, an original business card; beneath it one of the forms used for the engraving of the Model 1883 shotguns. The small item underneath is an ink impression ("gunmaker's pull") taken from a fancily engraved Model 1862 Police revolver frame. Second from bottom at right is a scroll design sketch in pencil for one of the early models of double action, swingout cylinder revolvers. At bottom right the design for a relief carved wooden grip, with a three letter monogram bordered by an oak leaf and acorn design. At top left a steerhead sketch for an ivory or pearl grip. At lower left the pencil sketch for the slide of a Model 1903 or Model 1908 Hammerless automatic pistol. The name C.L.F. Robinson is that of the company president from the years 1911-16. All drawings attributed to Cuno Helfricht. *(Helfricht Family Collection)*

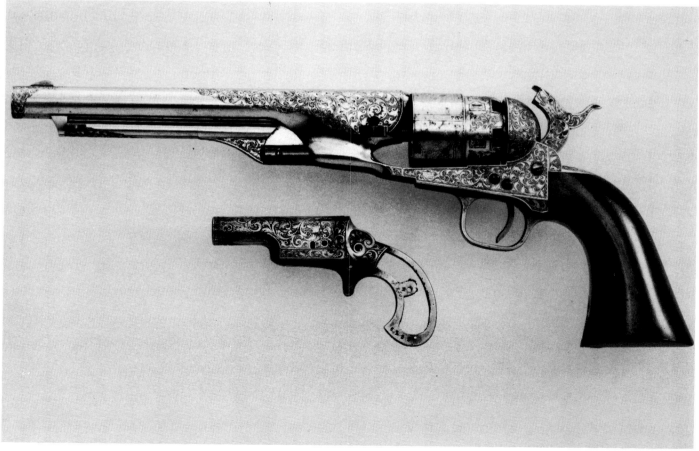

Two Colt pistols known to have been engraved by Cuno Helfricht. Extra deluxe scroll coverage on both the Model 1860 Army (top) and the Third Model Deringer. Serial numbers 167676 and 6135 respectively. Neither piece has been finished, and they were apparently kept by the engraver as samples of his work. The style on both is *ala* **Gustave Young**. *(Helfricht Family Collection)*

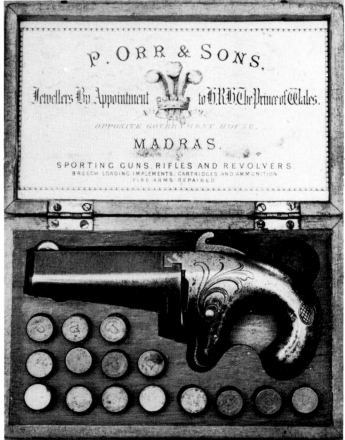

One of the latest specimens of the Gustave Young style scroll on a percussion Colt revolver; Model 1849 serial number 331334, c. 1873. Not done by Young, but attributed to Helfricht or a member of his shop. Rare lack of COLTS/PATENT marking on frame. *(William H. Myers Collection)*

Serial number 2853 of the First Model Deringer was engraved on the frame only. Finished in blue (barrel) and silver plating (frame). Bears British proofmarks. Rare casing and label. *(George S. Lewis Jr. Collection)*

First Model Colt Deringer, finished in nickel plating. Note scroll on both the frame and barrel. Serial number 977. Engraving was standard on both the First and Second Model Deringers. Rare original pasteboard carton. *(George S. Lewis Jr. Collection)*

No. 1 Model Colt Deringer number 874 is finished in nickel plating, with blued trigger and case hardened hammer. Stamped with British proofmarks. A standard pattern of engraving. *(George Taylor Collection)*

(Below) Standard coverage on First Model Colt Deringer number 4605. 2 1/2″ barrel; blued barrel, silver plated frame; British proof stampings on barrel. *(Fred Sweeney Collection)*

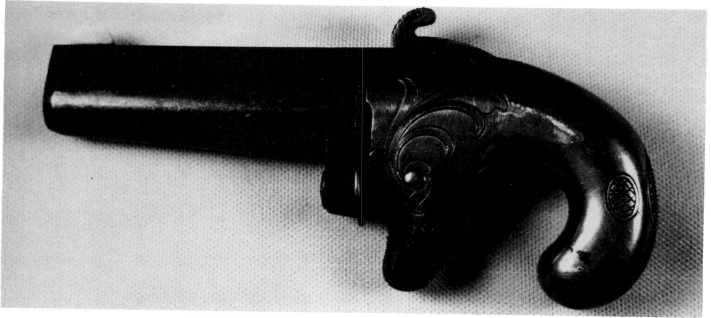

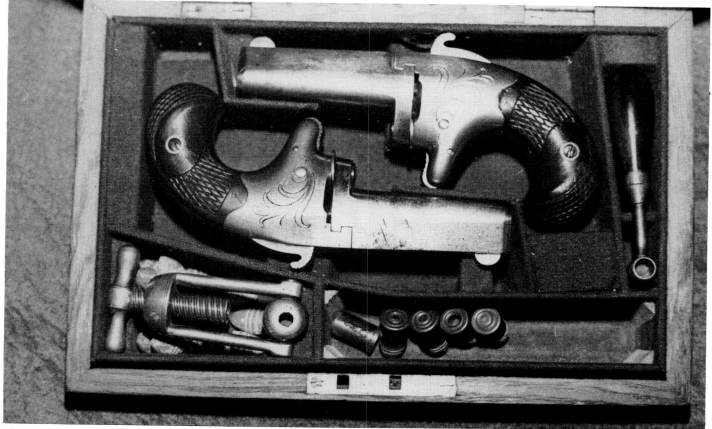

Quite rare cased pair of *centerfire* **Second Model Deringers, numbers 9014 and 8971. English oak case, lined in felt. Plated finish, with checkered walnut grips; British proof stampings.** *(Stanley I. Kellert Collection)*

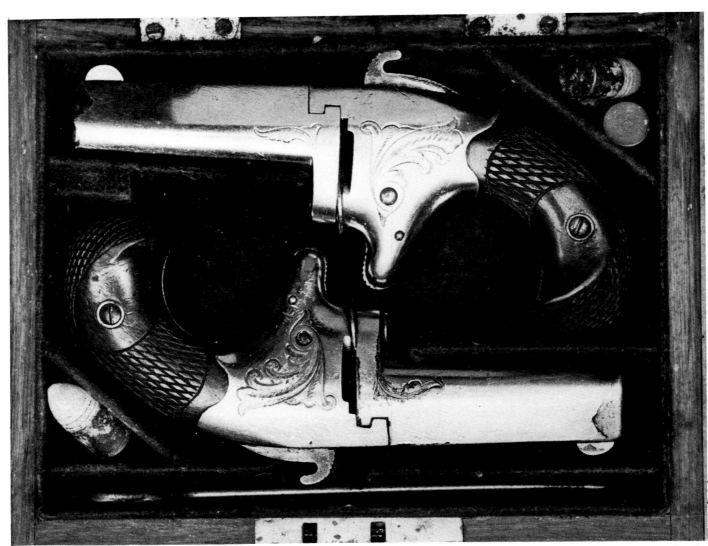

The only cased pair of brass frame Second Model Colt Deringers known to collectors. English casing of oak.
Engraved coverage on barrels and frames. Nickel plated finish; the grips of checkered and varnished walnut.
British proof stampings.   Serial numbers 2522 and 2529. Note slight variation in scrolls from number 2525
which follows, though the three pistols were no doubt engraved at the same time. The company did not dis-
courage such variance, realizing that being hand engraved, each gun would not come out exactly the same as
any other. *(George S. Lewis Jr. Collection)*

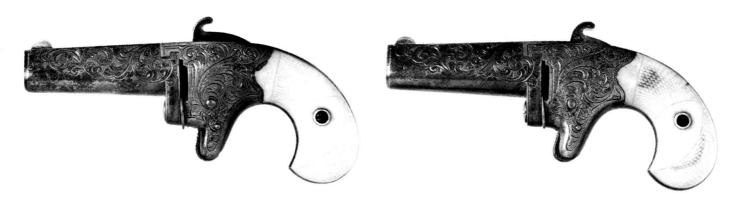

Second Model Colt Deringers, serial numbers 815 and 1312. Quite profuse scroll coverage, with checkered ivory
grips. Factory ledgers list only a handful of the First, Second and Third Model Deringers, so that providing
background data from Colt on these arms is a virtual impossibility. *(Dr. Chester P. Bonoff Collection)*

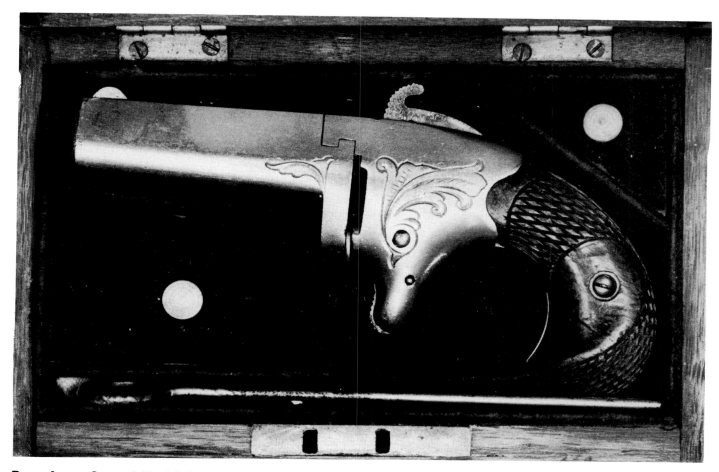

Brass frame Second Model Colt Deringer; serial number 2525. Oak casing of English manufacture. The pistol finished in nickel plating, with checkered and varnished walnut grips. British proofmarks. *(George S. Lewis Jr. Collection)*

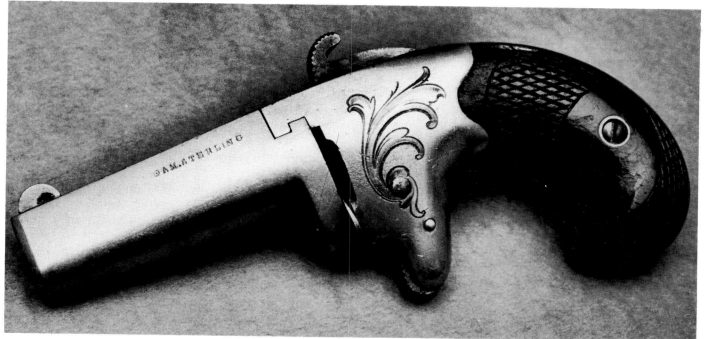

Unique solid *sterling silver* Second Model Colt Deringer, a presentation to the American Sterling company. Documented by a Colt factory ledger entry. Checkered and varnished walnut grips. Serial number 3642. The use of silver for manufacture of pistol barrel and frame is of the utmost rarity in the history of Colt firearms. An identically marked Second Model pistol, number 3847, is also known, and documented; from the collection of Mr. and Mrs. James R. Kaekel. *(George S. Lewis Jr. Collection)*

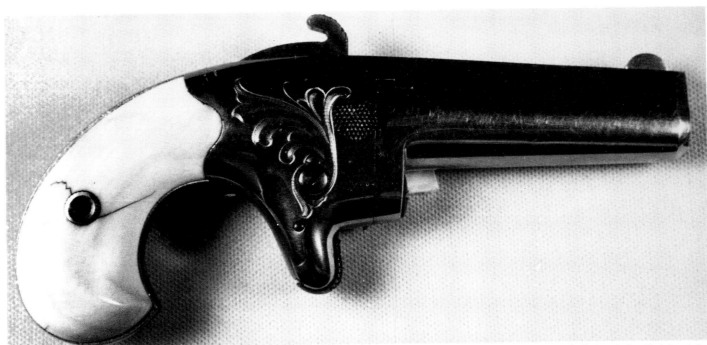

Second Model Colt Deringer, factory standard style and coverage; number 6897. 2 1/2" barrel; finished in nickel with ivory grips. *(Fred Sweeney Collection)*

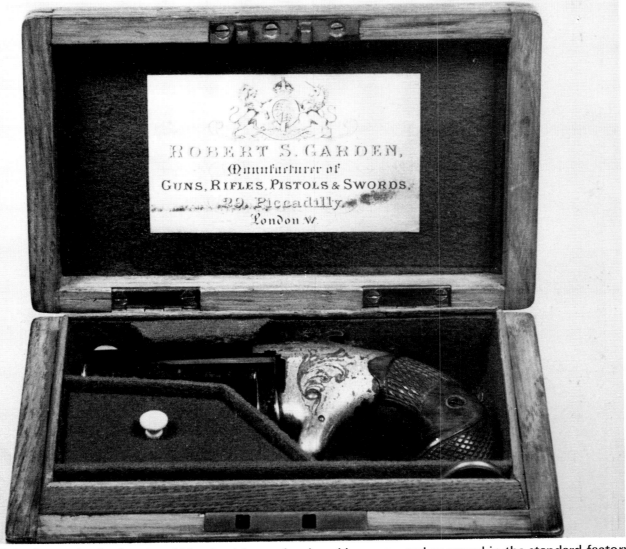

Cased No. 2 Deringer pistol, plated and blued, with case hardened hammer, and engraved in the standard factory pattern. Checkered walnut grips. Oak casing with handsome trade label. *(Collection of William Reid, Esq.)*

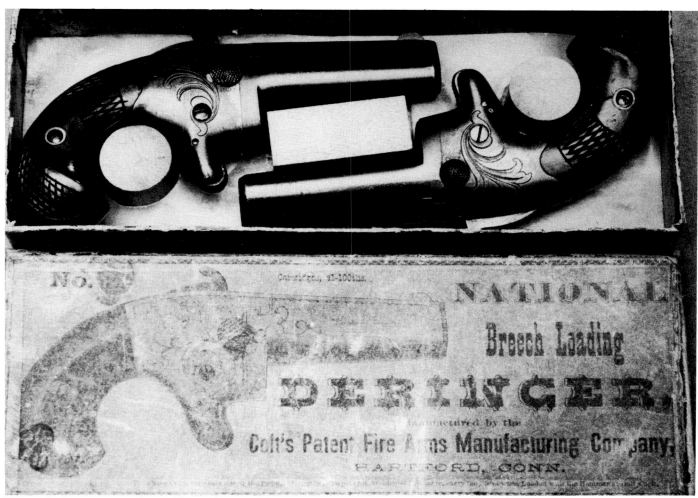

The only factory pasteboard boxed pair of Second Model Colt Deringers known to collectors. Blued barrels; silver plated frames; checkered and varnished walnut grips. Scrollwork on frames only. Serial numbers 9189 and 9387. Note use of the National tradename and picture of the National pistol on the box lid. *(George S. Lewis Jr. Collection)*

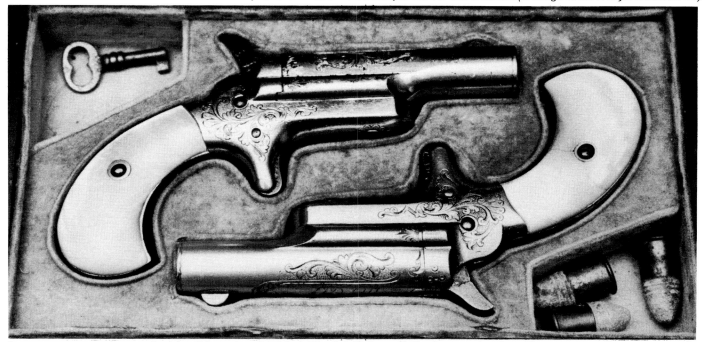

A rare rosewood case holds this pair of Third Model "Thuer" Deringer pistols. Factory scroll coverage of a scarce style. Nickel plating; with pearl grips. Case hardened hammers; blued screws and triggers. Serial numbers 13 and 19. *(George S. Lewis Jr. Collection)*

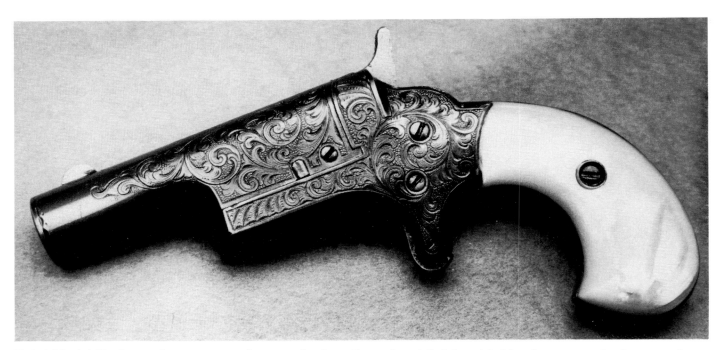

Third Model Deringer; factory engraving; pearl grips; silver plated finish, with blued screws and trigger, and case hardened hammer. Serial number 3132. The scroll is very much like that used frequently by Nimschke; an instance of the closeness in style and quality which sometimes makes attribution difficult. *(George S. Lewis Jr. Collection)*

Consecutively serial numbered pair of Third Model Deringers; numbers 26083E and 26084E. Nickel plated, with case hardened hammers and blued screws and triggers. Ivory grips. Cigar style pocket casing. Note chatter marks from the engraver's chisel; proof that the engraving was done by the hammer and chisel technique. Third Model Deringers were engraved in small quantities; unlike their First and Second Model contemporaries. *(William W. Edmunds Collection)*

Serial number 4901 Third Model Deringer includes the marking 200 on the left side of the frame. No front sight or working parts; just the barrel and frame, which have been nickel plated. It is the author's opinion that this pistol is another of the sample guns for pattern use by the Helfricht shop. *(Karl Glahn Collection)*

Sample for engraving, number 6126, also by Helfricht himself, and including the gripstrap marking 200. This could well indicate $2.00 standard of coverage, and payment of that figure to the engraver for the work. Finished in silver plating on the frame, and blue on the barrel. As with numbers 6119 and 6135, no COLT marking is on the barrel, and there are no grips present. *(John N. Pickering Collection)*

Serial number 6119 Third Model Deringer served as a sample for Helfricht's shop, and lacks a front sight or barrel roll marking, as well as finish and grips. Helfricht himself was responsible for the embellishment on this pistol, and the workmanship is excellent; c. early or mid 1970's. 150 marked on the left side of the gripstrap signifies the $1.50 grade of decoration, and is believed to represent the amount paid the engraver on a piece work basis. See also Deringer #6135, which is likewise a pattern gun, and bears on its left frame strap the marking: 250. Pattern pieces in the engraving field are of the utmost rarity. *(Private Collection)*

Serial number 8093 of the Cloverleaf House Model, .41 caliber, revolver. Nickel plated finish; grips of varnished walnut. The scroll a typical Helfricht style. Coverage on engraved House Model pistols was usually on the frame only. A few quite deluxe pieces were produced. Round cylinder House Model pistols were rarely engraved. *(L. Allan Caperton Collection)*

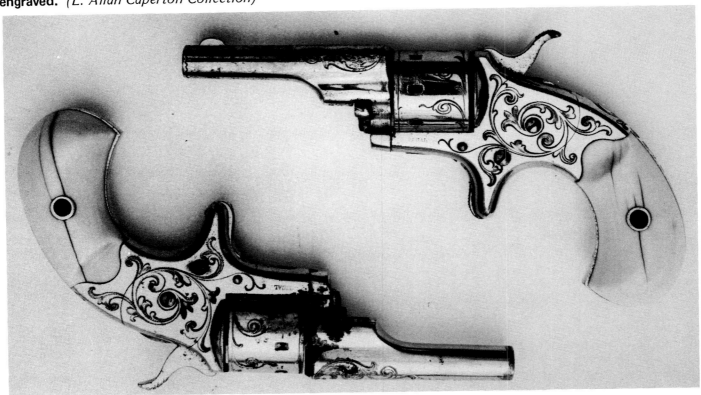

Finely decorated pair of Open Top .22 caliber revolvers, serial numbers 49302 and 49370. These nickel plated, ivory gripped pistols were shipped from Colt in February 1875, to B. Kittredge & Company, Cincinnati, Ohio. They were part of a shipment totalling 55 pistols of the same type. The pattern is identical, but two different engravers are responsible for the work, as a close comparison of quality and chisel cuts reveals. *(David S. Woloch Collection)*

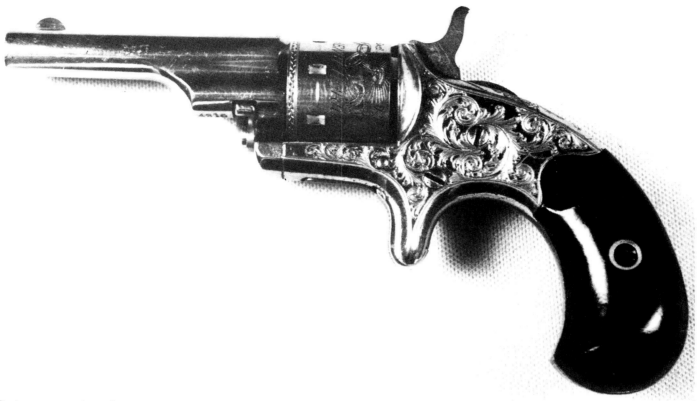

Quite unusual style and coverage on Open Top .22 number 4316; 2 3/8″ barrel, select walnut grips, nickel plated. The cylinder inscribed PRESENTED To HENRY HERRICK By E.J. DYER, and engraved with masonic emblems of an all-seeing eye, clasped hands, and three links of a chain. *(Fred Sweeney Collection)*

Third Model Deringer number 5047 is nickel plated, with high polish ebony grips. The cigar type casing of leather and velvet includes an embossed crest on the lid, documenting the set was property of a British peer. *(David S. Woloch Collection)*

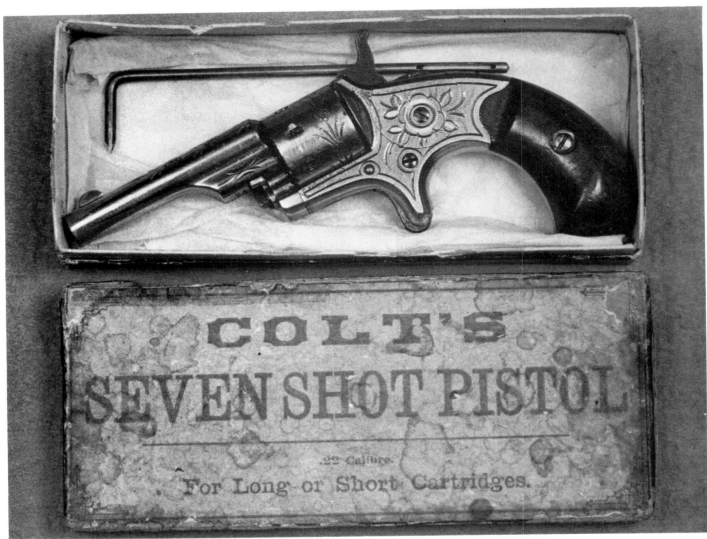

Complete with the rare factory pasteboard box, Open Top .22 number 24993 contains on the carton end documentation of its decoration and finish. Grips of walnut. Note enclosure of the screwdriver-cleaning rod. *(George S. Lewis, Jr. Collection)*

Open Top .22 number 79802 is full nickel plated, and has ivory grips. The coverage is in contrast with the variety of engravings found on most other deluxe pistols of this model. *(R.M. Scott Paul Collection)*

Shipped engraved to Schuyler, Hartley & Graham, in September 1875, Open Top .22 number 66478 is nickel plated, has pearl grips, and is rather handsomely embellished. *(R.M. Scott Paul Collection)*

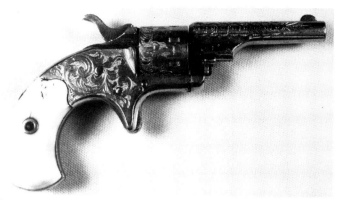

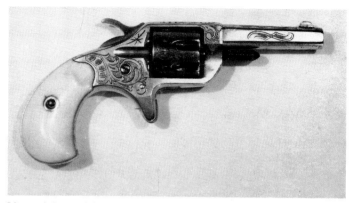

Still another variation in style of engraving on an Open Top .22; number 91825 was shipped from the factory in October 1888 to Hartley & Graham. Recorded in the ledgers as factory engraved, nickel plated, with ivory grips. 2 3/8'' barrel. Note coverage on the frame, cylinder, and barrel; particularly profuse on the frame and cylinder. *(Fred Sweeney Collection)*

New Line .22 number 16131 has ivory grips, and nickel finish. Still another pattern of coverage on these diminuitive pistols. *(R.M. Scott Paul Collection)*

New Line .22 number 20014; featuring an interesting treatment on the cylinder of the most basic scrolls, and a similar approach to the topstrap and the barrel. Frame offers a more developed coverage. Grips of pearl; finish on frame, cylinder, and barrel is nickel plating. *(Art Ressel Collection)*

Scarce ensemble of engraved New Line .22, with rubber grips, etched barrel (left side), and factory pasteboard box; shipped October of 1876, to H. & D. Folsom Arms Co., New York. Serial number 30751. Note profusion of zig-zag motifs on barrel, frame, and cylinder; scrolls in the design of the sideplate are done with a punch. *(Fred Sweeney Collection)*

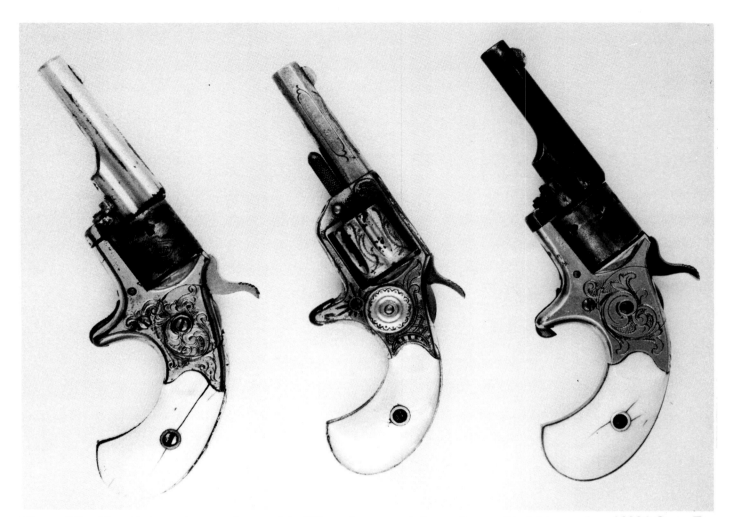

Three .22 caliber Colt pocket revolvers with different engraved decorations. At right, number 44236 Open Top (c. 1874) with the Helfricht scroll style on frame only; no coverage on barrel or cylinder; ivory grips. At left, Open Top number 79734, with a fancier version of the same scroll, plus a simple design on the cylinder; no barrel engraving; ivory grips. At center, number 18097 of the New Line .22; with scroll and border coverage on frame, barrel, and cylinder; pearl grips. Made in 1876. Serial number 78686 Open Top, in the Lewis Yearout Collection, has a frame scroll like number 44236, and barrel and cylinder work very close to that found on numbers 49302 and 49370. Noticeable variation is to be observed in engraved Open Top and New Line .22 pistols. *(John Miller Collection)*

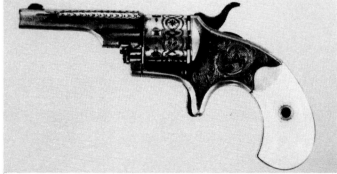

Open Top .22 number 62224; of c. 1875. Nickel plated; with grips of ivory. Scrolls on the frame; with zig-zag lines and punched and engraved motifs on the barrel and cylinder. A standard pattern. In the Open Top .22 pistols, a greater proportion of engraved pieces was produced than in most other models of Colt firearms. Coverage was customarily on the frame, cylinder, and barrel. *(R. Q. Sutherland Collection)*

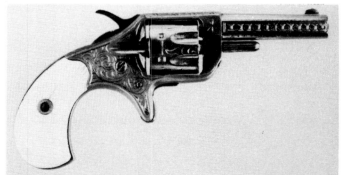

Serial number 2729 New Line .22. Still another variation in scroll and border coverage. It is likely that the engravers changed designs from time to time, simply out of boredom from repeating the patterns over and over again. Standard coverage was on the frame, cylinder and barrel; and engraving on the New Line .22 pistols is not uncommon. Ivory and pearl grips were frequently employed on engraved New Line .22 revolvers. *(R. Q. Sutherland Collection)*

Nickel and gold plated New Line features profuse engraving, ivory grips, and oak and velvet casing with cartridge block. *(Courtesy Hansen & Company)*

Extra fancy scroll coverage on a .38 caliber New Line; serial number 5275. Nickel plated finish; ivory grips. The decor is another instance where one could confuse Nimschke work with that of Helfricht's shop. Engraved .38 and .41 caliber New Lines are scarce; finished usually in nickel plating. *(L. Allan Caperton Collection)*

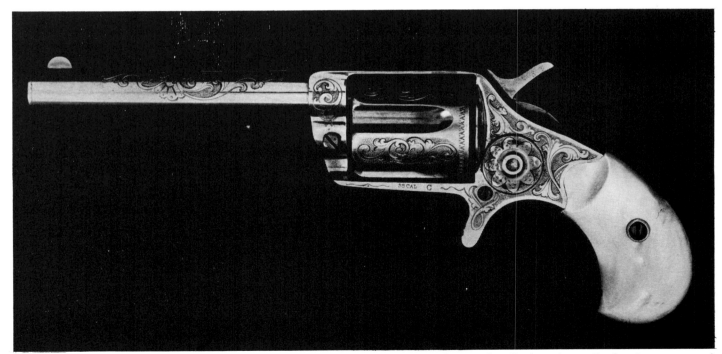

Serial number 10992; .38 caliber New Line. Nickel plated, with gold plated cylinder pin, cylinder, hammer and trigger. Pearl grips. Scarce 4" barrel. Stylistically close to the special scroll noted in Chapter IX, this pistol was probably done by Oscar Young, c. 1879. Though not present on this piece, some New Line revolvers had their model name engraved on the barrel. B. Kittredge & Company of Cincinnati is known to have done this on a number of pistols in all five New Line calibers, but these guns normally were not otherwise engraved. The New House and New Police versions of the New Line are extremely rare engraved; only a few specimens have come to the attention of collectors. Coverage on the frame, barrel, and cylinder; plated finish prevailed. *(David S. Woloch Collection)*

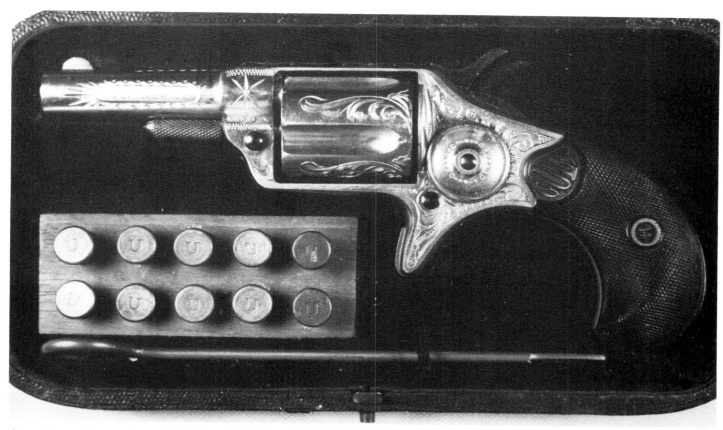

New Line .32 number 18069 has a 2 1/4'' barrel, rubber grips, nickel finish, blued hammer, screws, and cylinder pin latch; etched COLT NEW 32 barrel marking. Factory engraved; shipped to Colt's London Agency in October 1883.   Casing of cigar style, black leather with purple satin and velvet interior.   Backstrap inscribed with the dealer's name, Cogswell & Harrison, 226 Strand, London. *(Fred Sweeney Collection)*

New Line number 5275 is richly engraved, plated in nickel, and has ivory grips. 2 1/4'' barrel; 38 c.f. caliber. *(Fred Sweeney Collection)*

Cop and Thug (New Police) .38 New Line, serial 18210. 4 1/2" barrel. Backstrap inscribed *Henry E. Hastings,* *Christmas 1883.* **Nickel plated; grips of pearl. Rare model deluxe embellished; the condition as it was the day it left the Colt factory.** *(Private Collection)*

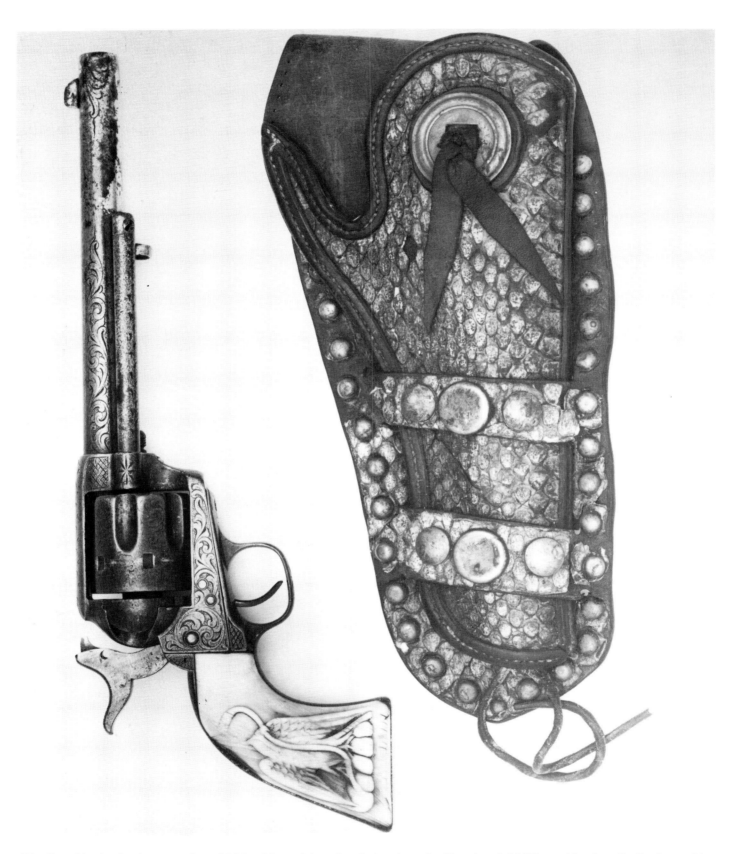

Rimfire Single Action number 1891, shipped by the Colt plant in March of 1880, to Hartley & Graham, New York; finish, barrel length, and stocks not listed.   Revolver was finished and engraved on H & G order, the grips fitted were of Mexican eagle carved ivory. Because of the occasional close duplication of engraving styles, 1891 may be from the Nimschke shop, or could have been from Helfricht's at the Colt plant. Accompanied by exotic period holster. *(Tom Seymour Collection)*

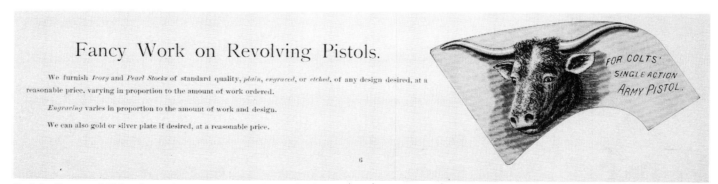

Single Action Army of William F. "Buffalo Bill" Cody; serial number 129108. .44-40 caliber; 4¾" barrel; finished in blue and case hardening; sold and shipped to John P. Lowers Sons, Denver, March of 1889. The inscription is the crisp and masterful script of Cuno A. Helfricht, and the scroll and border coverage is a more elaborate than customary job by him. *(Raymond J. Petry Collection)*

Colt's first published catalogue appeared in 1888; previously the company had issued occasional price listings in brochure or broadside form. From 1888 through c. 1903, the catalogues were published every other year. "Fancy Work" for revolvers is from Colt's catalogue of 1888. The same steerhead grip and text also were in the 1890 and 1892 catalogues, although the latter entry concentrated on grips and did not mention engraving on the guns themselves. The 1894 catalogue did not include the "Fancy Work on Revolvers" section. The last of the early large format catalogues, issued in 1905, included the mention of decorative details in the foreword, under the heading, "FINISH": "Our arms can be supplied with gold or silver plating, inlaid work or engraving; pearl and ivory stocks, plain, with monogram, or special design; — prices depending upon the amount and character of work desired."

(John Hintlian Collection)

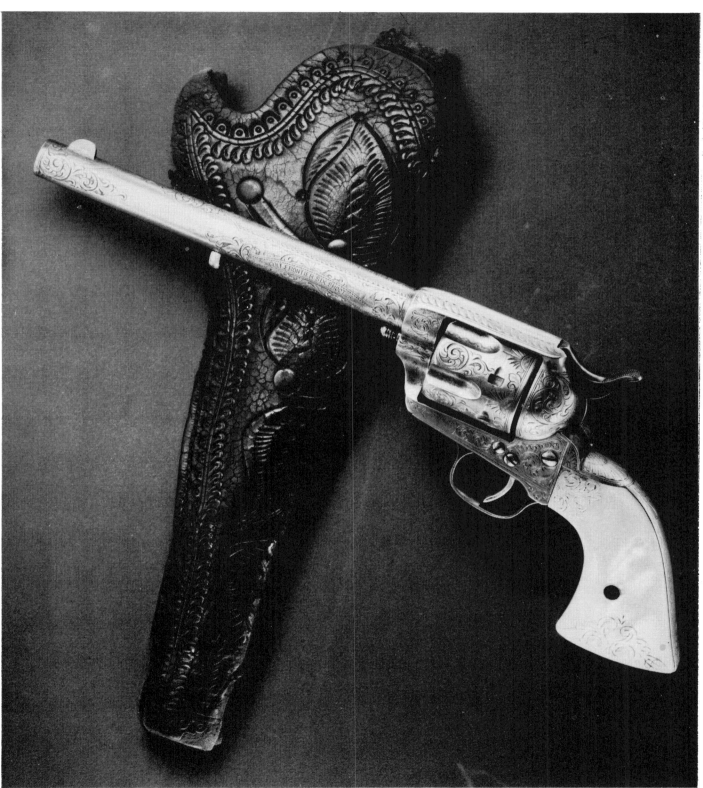

Serial number 53125 Single Action; c. 1880. A very unusual feature is the hand engraved marking on the left side of the barrel, in an arched riband. Profuse coverage of scrolls and border motifs. Plated finish and pearl grips. Colt factory serial ledgers list approximately 2,550 Single Action Army revolvers engraved in the Helfricht period, from the early 1870's to c. 1921. Some historic Americans are named as recipients or purchasers of deluxe Single Action Colts — among them W. F. "Buffalo Bill" Cody, W. B. "Bat" Masterson, Captain Jack Crawford, Marshall Bill Tilghman, Granville Stuart, and G. W. "Pawnee Bill" Lillie. Engraved pieces sold so well in the nineteenth and early twentieth centuries that they were carried by the factory as stock items. Gold inlay on the Single Action Army is of great rarity, and only a handful bore that very special feature. A few Flattop Single Actions were engraved, one of them (with gold inlay) for Buffalo Bill. *(R. Q. Sutherland Collection)*

Shipped to Hartley & Graham, January 1890, number 130753 left the factory engraved, nickel plated, rubber grips (likely changed by H & G to the present pearl), .44-40, and 4 3/4" barrel. The right side pearl grip has incised Mexican eagle and snake motif, but the enamel in the carving has gone, so this detail doesn't show. *(James E. Kattner Collection)*

Single Action 136951 appears to have been from the hand of Helfricht himself. Factory records list engraving, blue (and case hardened) finish, .41 caliber, 5 1/2" barrel, and shipped in March 1892 to E.C. Meacham Arms Co., St. Louis. *(Art Ressel Collection)*

Single Action 111471 left the factory in September 1884, and is further documented as of .45 caliber, 7 1/2″ barrel, silver plated, pearl grips, and engraved; shipped to William Nelon, and one of a pair. The grips are incised and enamelled; a buffalo head and scrollwork on the right side, and a nude woman and scrolls on the left. Coverage of scroll and other decorative devices on 111471 is rather profuse. *(Jack Slaughter Collection)*

Rare combination of Helfricht engraving (from the master's own hand), and backstrap inscription on Single Action 146838, shipped in September 1892, and recorded as .45, 7 1/2″ barrel, blue (and case hardened) finish, rubber grips, engraved, with backstrap inscription; shipped to Bandle Arms Co., Cincinnati, Ohio. *(Ridge Todd Collection)*

Single Action 165114 left the factory in June 1896, and the records reveal: .44-40 caliber, 4 3/4" barrel, silver plated with gold cylinder, pearl grips, engraved, and shipped to Olsmith Arms Company. The quite stylish decoration suggests that Helfricht himself was the engraver. Backstrap inscribed: *J. Peacock Green*. *(Mike Clark Collection)*

Inscribed *W.B. Jackson Greyhorse, I.T.*, Single Action number 183373 was built for W.B. Jackson, U.S. Marshal. His handcuffs and badge are also illustrated. .45 caliber; pearl grips; finish in nickel plating. Wear on the barrel, ejector tube, cylinder, and frame partly from Jackson's use of a leather holster, and travel of the revolver in and out. *(Jonathan M. Peck Collection)*

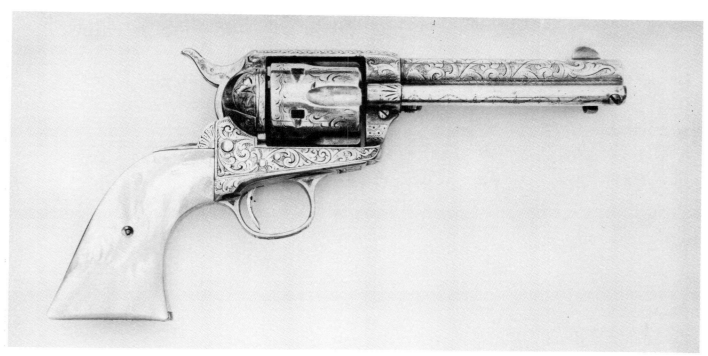

Single Action Army number 192104; in what would in later years be rated as a Grade C; except for the comparatively limited coverage on the cylinder. By contrast, scrolls on the frame and barrel are profuse. Factory ledgers state the gun was .38-40, 4¾" barrel, engraved, finished in silver plating with hammer and triggerguard gold plated; the pearl grips furnished by the dealer. Sold to Simmons Hardware Company, St. Louis, and shipped December 1899 to Armin & Lane; one gun in shipment. Single Action number 146148 (in the Lewis Yearout Collection) has a 5½" barrel, and engraved coverage nearly identical to number 192104. But a comparison of a number of engraved Single Actions from the Helfricht period indicates that the engravers did not follow patterns exactly, and were allowed certain freedoms to prevent boredom and (presumably) to add to the appeal of Colt engraving. *(David S. Woloch Collection)*

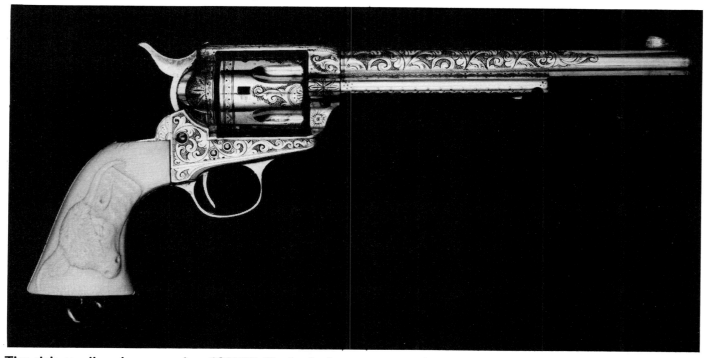

The rich scrollwork on number 193765 Single Action appears to be from the hand of Cuno Helfricht himself. Shipment was made in July 1900 to N.D. Nichols & Company, billed to Colt's San Francisco Agency. Most profuse standard pattern of engraving; .32-20 caliber; 7½" barrel; full silver plating; with steerhead ivory grips and rare butt swivel. Despite the full scroll coverage on the frame and barrel, the ejector rod housing has only zig-zag line, punched dot, and wavy line motifs. *(David S. Woloch Collection)*

In .32-20 caliber and with carved American eagle pearl grips, number 224048 Single Action left the factory in May of 1902; further details from the Colt records note: 4 3/4'' barrel, nickel plated, engraved; shipped to Farwell, Ozmun, Kirk & Co., St. Paul, Minnesota. This revolver formerly in the collection of country and western performing artist Hank Williams, Jr. *(Jack Slaughter Collection)*

Scarce and desirable factory inscription, *Jas. E. Mc.Gee.* is on the backstrap of Single Action 286836. Colt ledgers further verify the following: .45 caliber, 4 3/4'' barrel, silver plated, carved eagle pearl grips, engraved, and shipped December 1906 to A. Steinfeld & Co., Tucson, Arizona. McGee was an Arizona Ranger and also served as sheriff of Florence, Arizona. *(Erich Baumann Collection)*

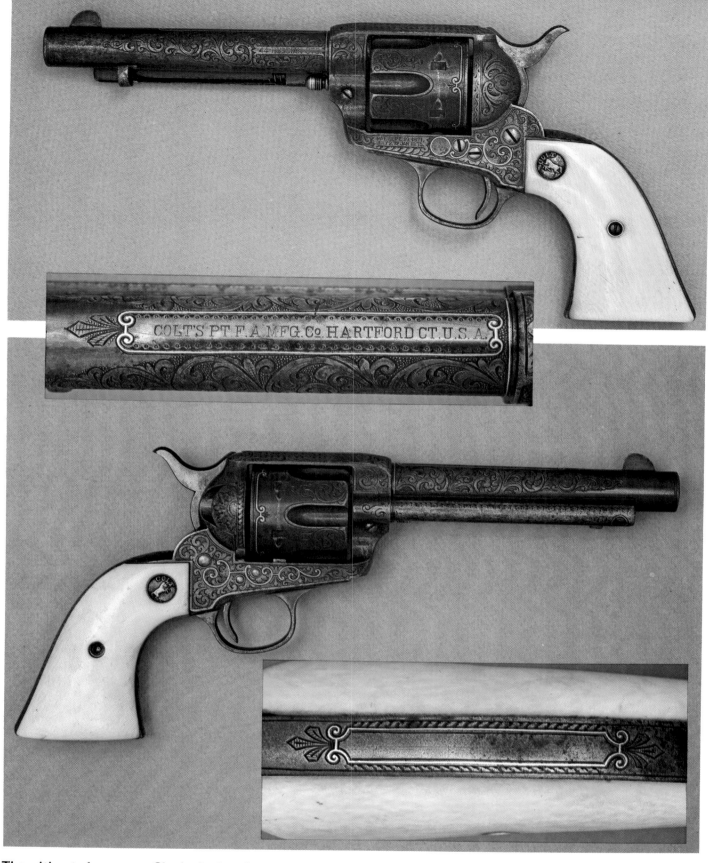

The ultimate in pre-war Single Action Army revolvers — factory gold inlay by Cuno A. Helfricht himself. Serial number 242701. The gun is listed in Colt factory ledgers as follows: .44 Russian caliber, 5½" barrel, engraved and gold inlaid, pearl grips (since shattered, and replaced by ivory as illustrated), sold and shipped to a dealer in Birmingham, Alabama, September 11, 1903; only one gun in the shipment. The flush gold inlays are as follows: Barrel band at breech, line and scroll border around the barrel marking, circle around the rampant colt frame stamping, scroll and line work on each side of the frame, line and scroll border around an escutcheon panel on the backstrap, stepped S-curve scroll on bottom of the triggerguard, and scroll and line border encircling the breech of the cylinder. Scroll and border engraving is of the ultra-deluxe grade and quality befitting a gold inlaid Single Action. Coverage is on the barrel, ejector rod tube, frame, loading gate, triggerguard, backstrap, and cylinder. Only three specimens of gold inlaid and engraved pre-war Single Action Army revolvers are known to collectors at this writing. Factory gold inlay represents the ultimate in rarity and desirability on Colt firearms. *(Wallace Beinfeld Collection)*

Carved steerhead pearl grips and silver plating are two of the details covered by the factory ledgers on Single Action Army 313299. Other facts presented include .44-40 caliber, 5 1/2'' barrel, engraved, and shipment in May 1910 to Edward Hart Company, sold to Charles Ilfeld Co., Las Vegas, New Mexico. *(Jack Slaughter Collection)*

Full silver plated (with blued screws) Single Action 318380 was engraved by Helfricht, and included some unusual decorative devices. Note the waved-wriggle line pattern on the sides of the barrel (near muzzle) and on the breech end of the cylinder. Pearl grips; .45 caliber. *(Jonathan M. Peck Collection)*

Number 319573 Single Action is blue and case hardened, and is engraved by the Helfricht shop on the barrel, ejector tube, frame, cylinder, and gripstraps.   Pictured on the dust jacket of James E. Serven's COLT FIRE-ARMS FROM 1836. *(William L. Rogowski Collection)*

Single Action Army 321405 left the Colt plant in December 1911, going to Phelps Dodge & Co., Douglas, Arizona.   Caliber .38-40, 4 3/4" barrel, nickel plated, carved ivory grips, engraved. *(William L. Rogowski Collection)*

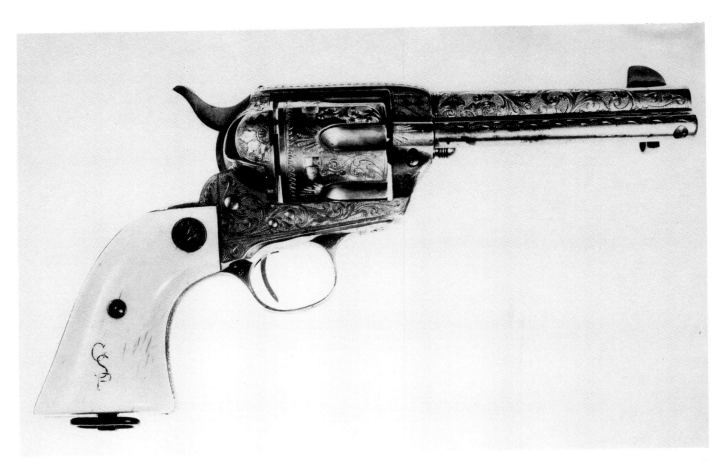

General George S. Patton's famous Single Action Army revolver; scroll engraved in factory number 2 style. Plated finish. Note the military feature of a lanyard swivel on the butt. Simple GSP monogram on the right grip. Serial number 332088; .45 caliber. *(West Point Museum)*

Single Action 314770 was shipped in October 1910 to H. & D. Folsom & Co., .45 caliber, 4 3/4" barrel, nickel plated, engraved. Documentation with the revolver indicates it served as the sidearm of Len R. McFarlane, U.S. Deputy Marshal, Harris County, Texas, c. 1910-24. *(Paul Sorrell Collection; photographed by James Parker)*

Extremely stylishly decorated Single Action 252818 belonged to a true gunfighter of the old West, Bob Meldrum (see initials on butt). The original owner was a friend of Tom Horn, and served as a peace officer. Quite a bit of intriguing history has been located on Meldrum, by collector Dick Dawson. Attributed to the hand of Helfricht himself, the Meldrum revolver is one of the most distinctively embellished Single Actions known. *(Dick Dawson Collection)*

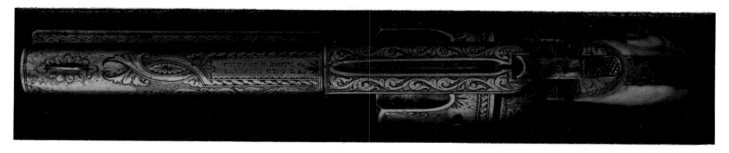

Daniel Carter Beard's deluxe Single Action Army revolver; number 222427. The decoration of a medium grade of coverage. Blue and case hardened finish; gold plated triggerguard and backstrap. Engraving, special finish, and medallion pearl grips added at a later date (c. 1912-21) when the revolver was returned to the factory for special work. Beard was a friend of Theodore Roosevelt and founder of the Boy Scouts of America. Coverage similar to number 174225; but notice alternating scroll and geometric zig-zag line decor on the chambers of the cylinder. *(David S. Woloch Collection)*

Single Action number 174225 has less scroll on the barrel than the previous group of Single Action revolvers, but about the same coverage on the frame and cylinder. Shipped from the factory June 1900; to S. Hirsfeld; sold to J. F. Schmelzer & Sons, Kansas City. Nickel plated; with gold plated cylinder; two guns in shipment. *(David S. Woloch Collection)*

Number 230218 Single Action; c. 1902. Plated finish; pearl grips. Colt ledgers list this piece as shipped blue, stocks not indicated, to M. Hartley Company, New York, July 1902. The engraving is of the period, and was done either by returning to Colt, or by an outside source working for Hartley. The coverage and style are, in any event, nearly the same as Colt factory work. *(George R. Repaire Collection)*

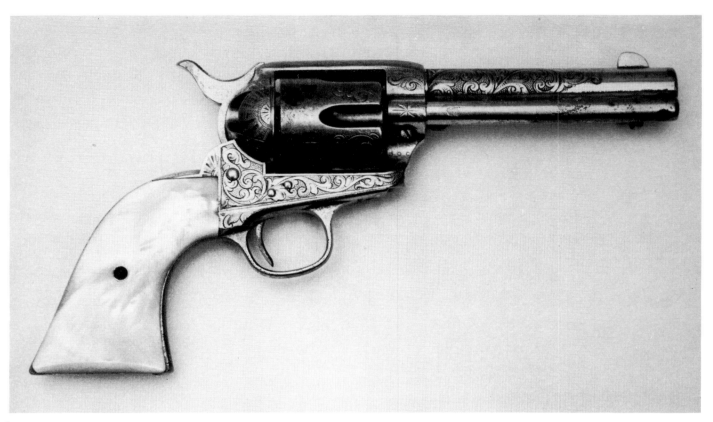

Single Action 293068; shipped to Krakauer, Zork & Moye, El Paso, Texas, in May 1907, and documented by Colt ledgers further as follows: .41 caliber, 4 3/4" barrel, nickel plated, engraved, one in shipment. A specimen of medium coverage, but this time with scrolls on each chamber of the cylinder. *(R.M. Scott Paul Collection)*

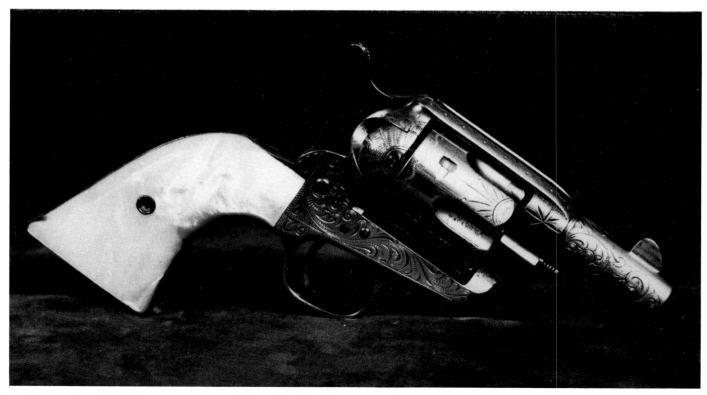

Serial number 115126; rare engraved Sheriff's Model. Colt ledgers document the pistol as follows: 2½" barrel, .44-40 caliber, nickel plated, pearl grips, shipped February 1886, to A.G. Spalding Brothers, Chicago; one gun in shipment. The Colt address marking was rolled onto the bottom of the barrel, due to the engraving; normal positioning for the 2½" barrel would have been on the left side. Engraved Sheriff's Model Single Actions are seldom encountered. Colt ledgers list approximately 40. *(Raymond H. Vanyek Collection)*

Rare Sheriff's Model Single Action, number 172730, 3 1/2" barrel, finished blue and case hardened, and shipped February 11, 1898, to Simmons Hardware Co., St. Louis, for H.L. Dyer. *(Paul Sorrell Collection)*

Sheriff's Model Single Action number 127740; listed in the Colt records as shipped December 1898 to E.J. Post & Company, Albuquerque, New Mexico. Inscribed *Marcelino Baca* **on the backstrap; nickel plated; pearl grips; .44-40; 3½" barrel; one gun in shipment. In the book** *Law and Order Ltd.,* **Baca is shown holding what appears to be this pistol, his thumb on the hammer. Inscribed or monogrammed Single Action revolvers are seldom encountered.** *(N. Brigham Pemberton Collection)*

Serial number 152484 Single Action (c. 1893), has a medium amount of coverage, with scroll and a spray of lines, dots and half circles alternating on the cylinder chambers. Full nickel plated finish, with pearl grips. Typically limited coverage on the ejector rod housing, consisting in this instance of zig-zag lines and punched dots. *(Dr. R. L. Moore Jr. Collection)*

Richly styled Single Action number 165585 has full silver plating with unusual silver mounted hard rubber grips. Backstrap inscribed: J.S.W. U.S.M., for J. Shelby Williams, U.S. Marshal, Paris, Texas. Mountings on the stocks likely done in Texas or Mexico, to add a bit of extra lustre to an already striking (and historic) revolver. *(Jonathan M. Peck Collection)*

Serial number 163504 Single Action, closely identical to number 152484. Plated finish; pearl grips. Noticeable variances are on the left and right sides of the frames (at juncture with breech), the scroll around the barrel markings, the recoil shield motifs, the central area of scroll on the right sides of the frames, and the designs on the ejector rod housings. Some of these differences are visible here. Such variants appear to have been at the engraver's discretion, within limits of style and coverage. *(Hugh E. Hayes Collection)*

Serial number 193469 Single Action; documented by Colt ledgers as shipped August 1900 to J.A. Mahoney; sold to Simmons Hardware, St. Louis. Gun left Colt engraved, silver plated, and with carved eagle pearl grips. Three identical revolvers in the shipment. The relief pearl grip design is quite unusual. Believed to be a specimen of the least grade coverage on the Single Action Army; no scroll on the cylinder, and about 3/5 scroll length on the barrel; nothing at the muzzle end. *(David S. Woloch Collection)*

Sent to Praeger Hardware Co., San Antonio, Texas, Single Action 324096 is a prime example of Helfricht scroll and border work, and the Colt records state: .38-40, 4 3/4" barrel, nickel plated, engraved, shipped in June of 1912, to the Praeger firm. *(Paul Sorrell Collection)*

Colt ledgers record number 328539 Single Action as grade 2 1/2 engraved, .45 caliber, 4 3/4" barrel, nickel plated, carved ivory grips; sold to Shelton Payne Arms Co., El Paso, Texas, in February 1914. *(William L. Rogowski Collection)*

Right side of this Single Action is profusely cut away; the left side embellished by Cuno Helfricht, c. 1915. Number 330946; 4 3/4″ barrel; nickel plated; steerhead pearl grips. *(Colt Collection of Firearms, Connecticut State Library)*

331270 Single Action is recorded in factory ledgers as .45, 4 3/4″ silver plated, Grade 2 engraved, carved steerhead pearl grips, and shipped having a long fluted cylinder to C.L. Theo Bering, Jr., January 1915. Note extremely unusual coverage on the barrel, and the distinctive quality of Cuno Helfricht. Revolver has a Texas Ranger pedigree. *(Paul Sorrell Collection; photographed by James Parker)*

Scarce combination of gold and nickel finish (the gold on hammer and trigger) appears on this Single Action Army number 331632, attributed to Helfricht himself. .45 caliber; steerhead pearl grips. Classic example of the Helfricht style scroll and other decorative motifs. *(Jonathan M. Peck Collection)*

Personal Single Action Army of Captain J.J. Sanders, Texas Rangers (Co. A), and so documented by the Colt ledgers: Number 333575, .45 caliber, 5 1/2" barrel, Grade 2 engraving, carved steerhead ivory grips, silver plated, shipped in December 1916 to Colonel J.F. Stockton and Captain J.J. Sanders. One revolver only in shipment. On the butt, the inscription: *CO·A·TEX·RANGER.* A photograph in the Texas Archives Library shows Captain Sanders astride his horse, and this revolver in a holster on the Captain's right hip. Engraving from the Helfricht shop, but not executed by the master himself. *(Paul Sorrell Collection)*

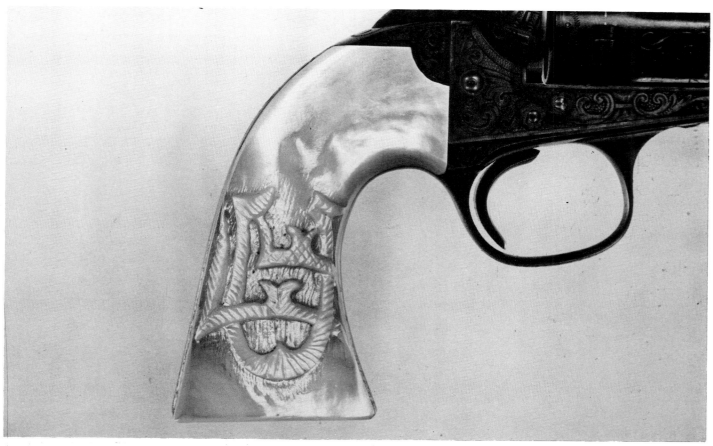

Engraved by the Helfricht shop, number 314626 Bisley is listed as .45, 4 3/4", blue (and case hardened), with F.G.F. carved pearl grips; shipped to Hibbard, Spencer Bartlett & Co., c/o J.L. Kleiman, Chicago, in September 1910. Although the factory shipping ledger did not note engraving, the company Work Order Ledger records from the period c. 1890 to 1914 note: Order #4978, 314626, Bisley Model Revolver, ordered August 19, 1910, 4 3/4" barrel 45 Colt caliber, blue finish, engraved, pearl grips carved monogram FGF, completed 9/19, 1910. Occasionally clerks failed to put in all the required data in shipping ledgers, as distinctly proven in Bisley 314626. *(George S. Lewis, Jr., Collection)*

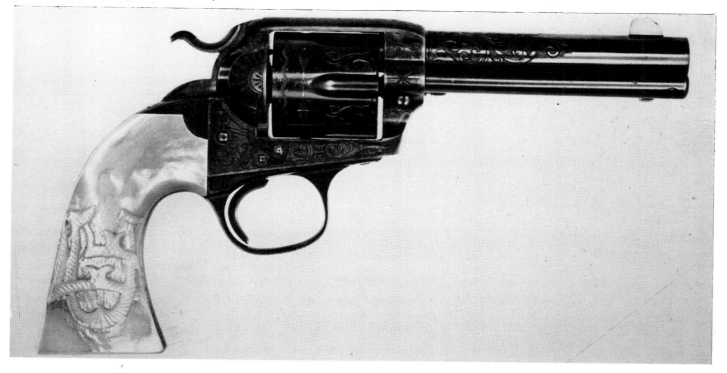

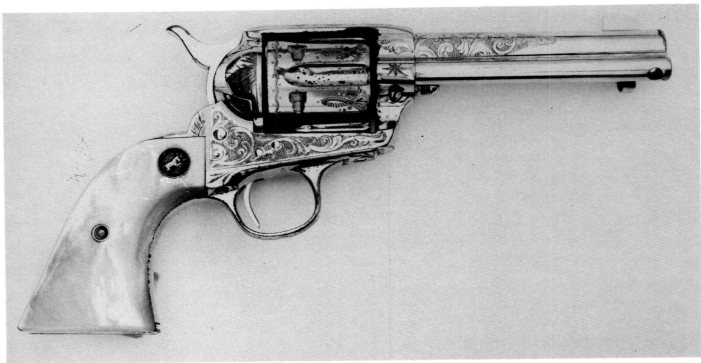

The extremely rare combination of engraving on a specimen of the long-fluted cylinder Single Action Army; the only known piece in the series. Serial number 331445; shipped May 1915, to Valley Mercantile Company; sold to Shapleigh Hardware of St. Louis. Nickel plated; pearl grips; one gun in shipment. Coverage and style of engraving nearly duplicate that on number 193469, but differences are apparent. Note rampant colt medallion inset on the grips; first appearing in 1912. *(David S. Woloch Collection)*

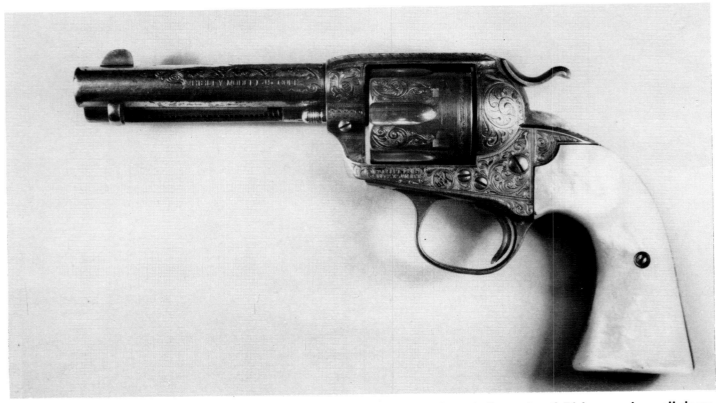

Particularly desirable is an inscribed, and engraved, and carved pearl, and silver plated Bisley revolver; all documented by the Colt ledgers for number 278932. Further listed is .45 caliber, 4 3/4" barrel, carved steer head grips, sold to G.G. Gonzales (the name inscribed on the backstrap), and shipped in June 1906 to Wyeth Hardware & Manufacturing Co. *(Jack Slaughter Collection)*

From the shop of Cuno Helfricht, serial number 53073 is recorded in factory ledgers as shipped in May 1880 to B. Kittridge & Co., engraved, nickel plated, with ivory grips, and in .44-40 caliber. Note etched barrel marking of COLT FRONTIER SIX-SHOOTER. *(Tom Odom Collection)*

Barrel detail from Single Action 105737, a .44-40 shipped in August of 1884, shows the very stylish scroll so characteristic of the Helfricht shop. *(Lewis E. Yearout Collection)*

Rubber grips were part of the specified details on Single Action number 107009. The revolver was shipped in March 1884, to Schoverling, Daly & Gales, New York, and is further documented as in .45 caliber, with 4 3/4" barrel, nickel plated, and engraved. Zig-zag lines figured prominently in the decoration, including on the backstrap and triggerguard strap, and the breech end of the cylinder. *(William A. Dascher Collection)*

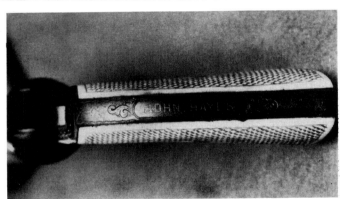

A piece of outstanding rarity in the history of Colt engraving. Combined on this Bisley Model revolver, number 177031, are such details as gold inlay (JOHN HAYES on the backstrap), combination finish, (blued, with case hardened frame, and gold plated cylinder), factory checkered ivory grips, and full grade of engraved coverage. Hayes was Chief of Police in Kansas City from 1898 to 1907. Engraving attributed to Cuno Helfricht's own hand. Not more than 60 Bisley Model revolvers are listed in Colt records as engraved; number of inscribed or monogrammed Bisleys was less than 40. Less than 10 of the Flattop model were engraved. *(George S. Lewis Jr. Collection)*

Bisley 313622 features the quite rare carved monogram pearl grip (F.G.F. on right side), and factory engraving; shipment was in March 1910 to J.I. Kleinman, sold to Hibbard Spencer Bartlett of Chicago, Illinois; .45 caliber, 4 3/4" barrel, and blue (and case-hardened) finish. *(Jack Slaughter Collection)*

Truly exceptional Bisley Flattop Target revolver, number 326568 is considered the finest of its type to have left the Colt plant. Although not complete, the factory ledgers do list this revolver as a 7 1/2" specimen, .44 S & W Special cartridge, Target model, with carved eagle pearl grips, blue (and case hardened) finish, engraved; shipped to the New York Sporting Goods Co., in October of 1914. A six pointed star on the right side of the rear bow of the triggerguard indicates that some work was done on the revolver after having been returned at a later date to the factory. The revolver has an extra cylinder, gold plated (now in the revolver), and was probably returned to have that properly fitted. *(David S. Woloch Collection)*

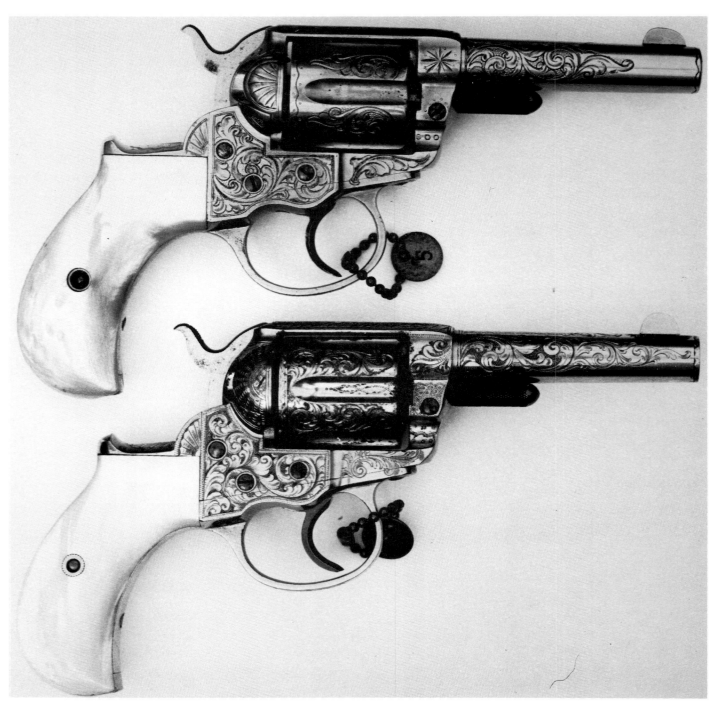

Two quite contrasting Lightning model revolvers; at top, serial number 23097. Shipped by Colt March 1880; engraved, nickel plated, with pearl grips, to Simmons Hardware Company, St. Louis. .38 caliber; 3½" barrel. Bottom, serial number 50796, left Colt April 1884, to E.F. Bodwell. .38 caliber, 3½" barrel; engraved, nickel plated, with pearl grips. Bodwell was a Colt factory employee for many years, serving as a bookkeeper and in other capacities. The coverage of the Bodwell Lightning is extra deluxe, deep chiselled and quite profuse. The work is a cut above most other engraved pistols of this model. *(David S. Woloch Collection)*

Shipped in May of 1878, to B. Kittredge & Co., Lightning 6599 is further listed in the Colt records as .41 caliber, 5″ barrel, ivory grips, nickel plated, and engraved. Rare with hammer engraved, and obviously the pattern influenced by the wolfhead treatment from the percussion period. Revolver is also significant as an early Lightning having ejector rod assembly — which may help to explain the deluxe embellishments. *(James E. Kattner Collection)*

Lightning number 34354 was shipped in April 1882 to Simmons Hardware Co., St. Louis, and recorded as engraved, with ivory grips, nickel plated, the barrel of 3 1/2″ length, and the caliber .38. Eight Lightnings of the same configuration were in this shipment. *(Art Ressel Collection)*

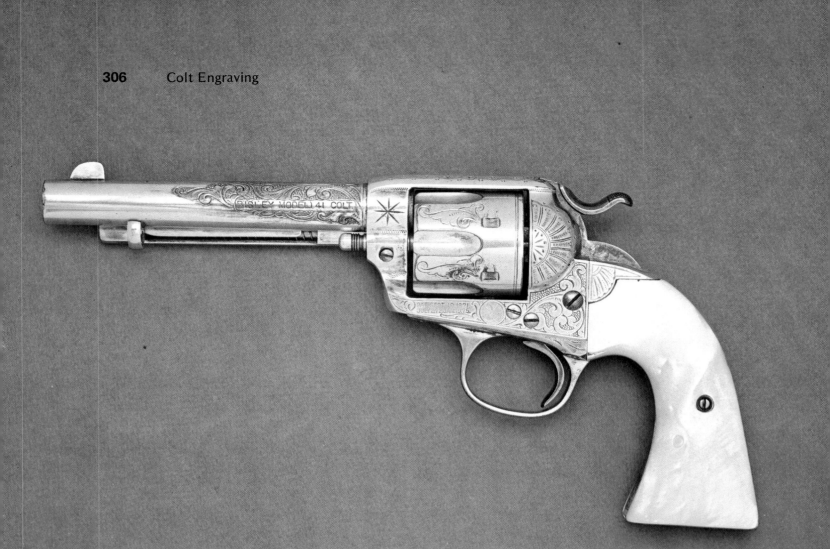

Rare silver plated and engraved Bisley from the Cuno A. Helfricht shop. The amount of coverage is equal to what the factory in later years identified as Grade B, and what for several years was rated as Grade No. 1. The Colt factory shipping ledgers list the following details for this gun, serial number 239294: .41 caliber, 5½" barrel, engraved, pearl grips, silver plated, sold to Walter Tips Company, Austin, Texas, and shipped to a J. A. Schkade (address unknown). The revolver was shipped February 28, 1903, and one gun only was in the consignment. The number of engraved and silver plated Bisley Model revolvers was extremely limited. *(Buddy Hackett Collection)*

Model 1877 Lightning, serial 42582, with scarce short barrel. Full nickel plating. *(Jack H. Meyers Photograph; John R. Woods Collection)*

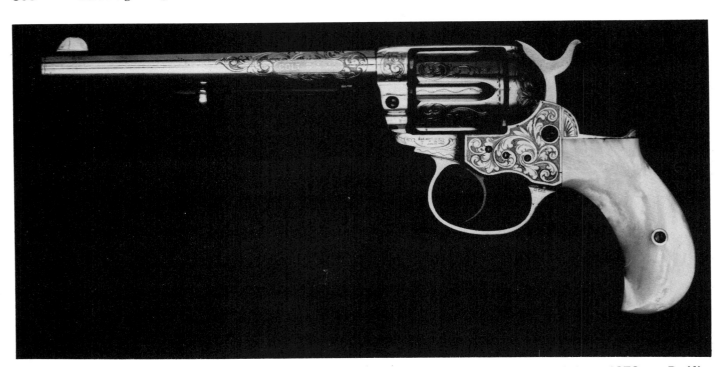

Model 1877 Lightning revolver; number 6751.   Recorded in Colt ledgers as shipped June 1878, to B. Kitt-redge & Company, Cincinnati; engraved, nickel plated, with pearl grips. 6″ barrel; .41 caliber; three identical guns in shipment.   Factory records indicate approximately 250 Lightnings engraved in .38 caliber, and approximately 475 in .41 caliber.   Their usual finish was nickel plating.   Not more than a half dozen Light-nings were gold inlaid.   Engraved coverage was generally on the following parts: Barrel, cylinder, frame, ejector rod housing (when present), and gripstraps. *(David S. Woloch Collection)*

Quite fancily decorated, number 6628 Lightning features profuse coverage, percussion type wolfhead hammer engraving, and is recorded by the factory ledgers as .41 caliber, 5″ barrel, nickel plated, engraved, shipped to Hodgkins and Haigh in May 1878. Grips not listed. *(James E. Kattner Collection)*

Lightning 54437 was shipped to Mommenge & Geisler, October 1885; further documented as .38 caliber, 3 1/2"
barrel, engraved, nickel finish, pearl grips. Note the unusual pattern on the cylinder, without scrollwork. *(Lewis
E. Yearout Collection)*

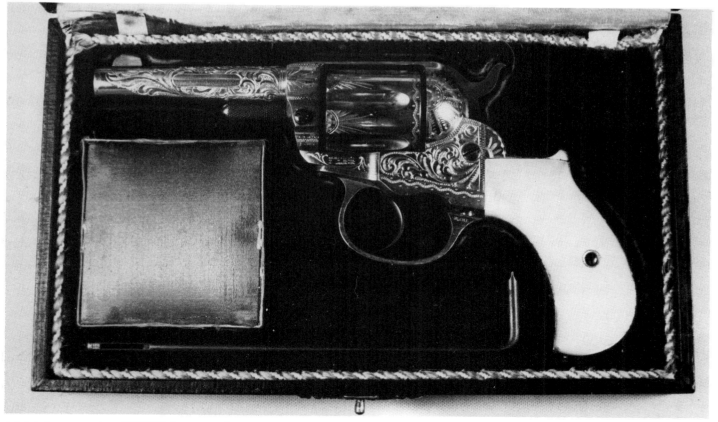

Lightning number 56937 features factory scroll and border motifs, pearl grips, nickel plating with etched barrel
marking (left side), 3 1/2" barrel, and the rare leather over wood casing, lined in velvet and satin. **Shipped from
Colt's in September of 1886.** *(Fred Sweeney Collection)*

Factory engraved and attributed to the G. Young shop, serial number 2376 (*right*) has an intriguing history, having been used by Colt's for exhibition purposes. It appears on a listing of Henry Folsom & Co., St. Louis, dated October 15th 1877, wherein a number of display revolvers were returned by that firm to the Colt plant, after having been used at an exposition in St. Louis in the fall of that year. The Folsom listing notes 2376 as follows: "[Colts D A 38] Pearl [Nickel Engraved] 25 40 [value of $25.40] ." A diploma and $10 was awarded to Folsom for their exhibit. Folsom had offices in England, New York, and St. Louis (firm name of H. & D. Folsom & Co.), and ranked among the foremost of the Allies (jobbers) for Colt's. Among the desirable features of 2376 is its relief chiselled caliber marking on the barrel, and the obviously show-gun oriented quality of its engraved decoration. Colt factory ledgers show the revolver to have been shipped to Solomon Goetz in New York City, January 22nd 1878. *At center*, number 109758, .41 caliber, nickel plated, with pearl grips; from the Cuno Helfricht shop. *At left*, also from the Helfricht shop, number 126238, .38 caliber, 5" barrel, silver plated, with pearl grips. The initials PA are carved on the right stock, and the owner's name *Pascual del Avellano* is inscribed on top of the barrel. Shipped to Hibbard, Spencer, Bartlett and Co., Chicago, for G. Rios and Co., Parral, Chihuahua, Mexico. Avellano was prominent in Mexico as a journalist, lawyer, and jurist during Pancho Villa's regime. (*Dr. Richard C. Marohn Collection*)

Lightning 66729 appears in the factory ledgers as follows: .38 caliber, 3 1/2'' barrel, nickel plated with gold cylinder, pearl grips, engraved, and shipped in August 1888 to Western Arms & Cycle Co., Salt Lake City, Utah. The casing is the scarce and desirable leather and velvet pattern and includes the roped style trim as illustrated. *(David S. Woloch Collection)*

Shipped some eight years after its manufacture, number 77561 Lightning is recorded as .41, 4 1/2'' barrel, nickel, pearl grips, engraved, sent July 1898 to E.C. Meacham Arms Co., St. Louis. The close association of style and coverage to Single Action Army factory engraving is apparent. *(James E. Kattner Collection)*

Lightning number 100981 was shipped engraved, nickel, .38, 6″ barrel, July 1895, to Hartley & Graham. Compare with 68662 Lightning, whose decoration is virtually identical. The pattern on both revolvers is one associated with Hartley & Graham and their engraving team, best known of which is L.D. Nimschke. *(James E. Kattner Collection)*

Lightning number 89034 is an extremely rare .32 caliber, and the factory documentation further notes: 6" barrel, nickel finish, ox head pearl grips, engraved, sold to W.B Belknap & Co., Louisville, Kentucky, for H.O. Ballou; shipment in September 1892. An excellent example of Helfricht engraving, with scarce carved pearl grips (seldom seen on the Lightning model), and desirable caliber. *(George S. Lewis, Jr. Collection)*

A most unusual Model 1877 Lightning, number 97436 left the factory in February of 1894, was shipped to Hartley & Graham, New York, was factory engraved, and in caliber .38, with 3 1/2" barrel, blue (and case hardened), and with wood grips. Note profuse coverage, the monogram on the top flat of the backstrap, and the combination of fine scrolls of a shotgun style with the larger scrolls most often found on engraved Lightnings. Coverage is even on the sides of the triggerguard! *(Dr. Gerald F. Sauer Collection)*

Shipped in August of 1887, to C.D. Ladd, Lightning number 61661 is further recorded in the Colt ledger books as a .38 caliber, 3 1/2" barrel, nickel plated, ivory grips, and engraved. *(Paul Sorrell Collection)*

Number 66657 was shipped to a Colt agency; .41 caliber, 4 1/2", nickel finish, pearl grips, engraved. Distinctly similar to much of the Helfricht shop's coverage and style on Single Action Army revolvers. *(James E. Kattner Collection)*

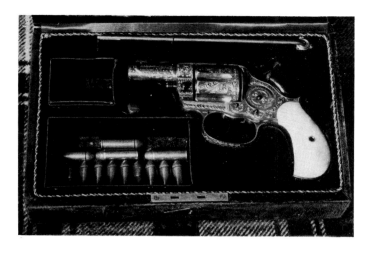

Serial number 81837 Lightning; with elaborate coverage attributed to Helfricht himself. Plenty of scroll; but the original factory shipping ledger neglected to indicate the presence of engraving. Such mistakes, though quite uncommon, did happen. Even as deluxe as is number 81837, there was no coverage on the hammer or the screws. *(David S. Woloch Collection)*

An extraordinary engraved specimen of the Model 1878 Frontier Double Action revolver. Fitted in a factory casing of leather, lined in silk and velvet, with accessories and .45 caliber ammunition. The address marking stamped on the left side of the barrel. Pearl grips; plated finish; hammerless. Profuse Helfricht scroll. *(R. E. Hable Collection)*

A distinctive scroll and other decorative devices were cut and punched on Model 1878 Sheriff's Model number 5942; shipment was to J.P. Lower Co., Denver, in May 1881, engraved, pearl grips, nickel plated, .45 caliber, 4″ barrel. Compare with Model 1878 number 4576 on page 202 of *The Colt Heritage*, a show gun sent to Australia in 1880. Colt ledgers indicate the total number of engraved Model 1878 Double Action revolvers to have been approximately 200. Coverage was usually on the barrel, frame, cylinder, triggerguard, and gripstraps; also on the ejector rod if present. Gold inlaid pieces of the Frontier Model 1878 revolver are *extremely* rare. *(Lewis E. Yearout Collection)*

Important because in some of its features the scroll and decorative treatment are suggestive of L.D. Nimschke, Lightning number 100981 is recorded as shipped July of 1895 to Hartley & Graham, nickel plated, and engraved; .38 caliber, 6'' barrel. Single tentacles come off the scrolls on the barrel and cylinder, in much the same fashion as the three tentacle clusters have been observed on known Nimschke pieces. The zig-zag border device on the side of the triggerguard and visible on the frame are also often found on Nimschke pieces, as is the sunburst-like device on the side of the upper form of the backstrap. *(James E. Kattner Collection)*

An extra-deluxe Model 1878 Sheriff's Model, number 13621 features the name **CLAY COOPER** relief chiselled in a riband on the right side of the barrel. Nickel plated finish; pearl grips. *(Woolaroc Museum; P.R. Phillips Collection)*

An elegantly embellished specimen of craftsmanship from the Helfricht shop, number 43265 Model 1878 is silver plated, and features carved Mexican eagle pattern pearl grips. On the backstrap: *General Agustin Castro/on Recuerdo. (George Taylor Collection)*

A Colt Double Action Model of 1877, serial #93260, .32 caliber, 6" barrel with ejector, blue and case hardened finish, factory engraved with 2-piece pearl grips. According to the records, it left the factory as engraved, blue. The type of grips were not listed. It now has 2-piece pearl grips. The gun was shipped as one in a shipment on April 4, 1893 to Hartley and Graham, New York, New York. This specimen is in near mint condition. *(Richard C. Marohn, M.D. Collection)*

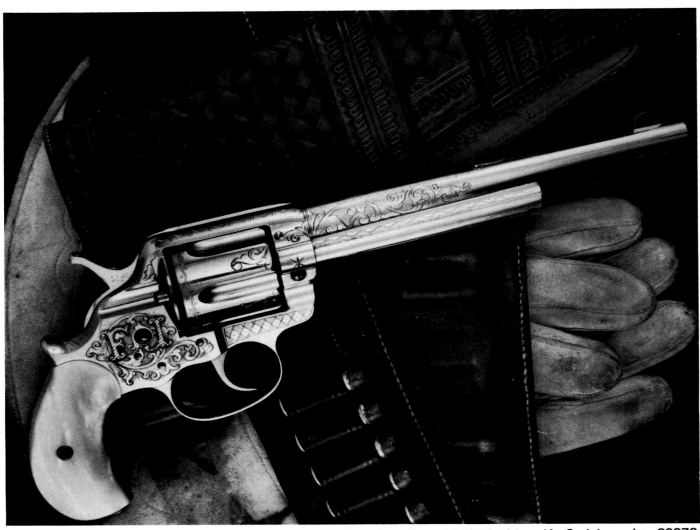

A crisply cut Model 1878 D.A. Frontier revolver attributed to Cuno Helfricht himself. Serial number 20378; Colt ledgers state nickel finish, .44-40 caliber, and 7½" barrel, but do not indicate "engraved" — an error of the factory bookkeeper. Illustrated also are the gloves of F.J. (F. Jungling, whose name is marked inside) and his holster. The monogram is of great rarity on any Colt firearm. *(David S. Woloch Collection)*

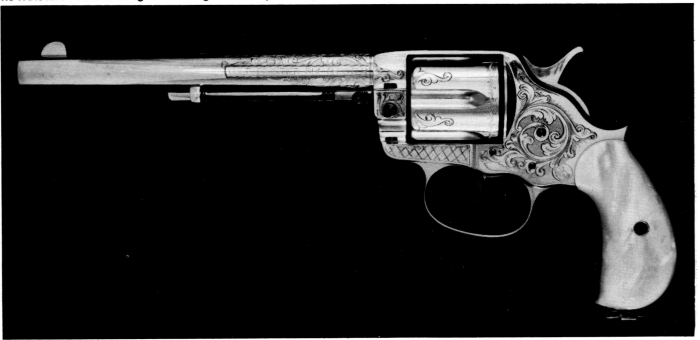

Handsomely embellished Model 1878 number 20895 from the Helfricht shop; shipped in February 1888 to Schoverling, Daly & Gales, New York. Grips of ivory; finish nickel plating; caliber .45, and the barrel length 5 1/2". *(John A. Kopec Collection)*

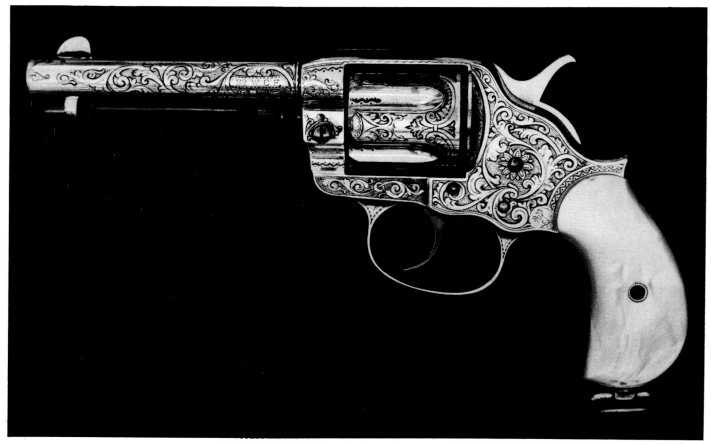

One of the most profusely embellished Model 1878 revolvers known to collectors. Number 36854; .32-20, 4¾" barrel, silver plated, engraved, pearl grips, and shipped January 1897 to Thompkins LaSalle; one gun in the shipment. Attributed to Helfricht personally; the scroll and border decor is exceptional. *(David S. Woloch Collection)*

Attributed to an assistant of Helfricht, number 32006 Model 1889 Navy bears the ampersand (&) mark on the right rear bow of the triggerguard, and has a deep scroll and border pattern of coverage. Finished in nickel and gold plating, with pearl grips. Estimated date of decoration is post-1901. *(David S. Woloch Collection)*

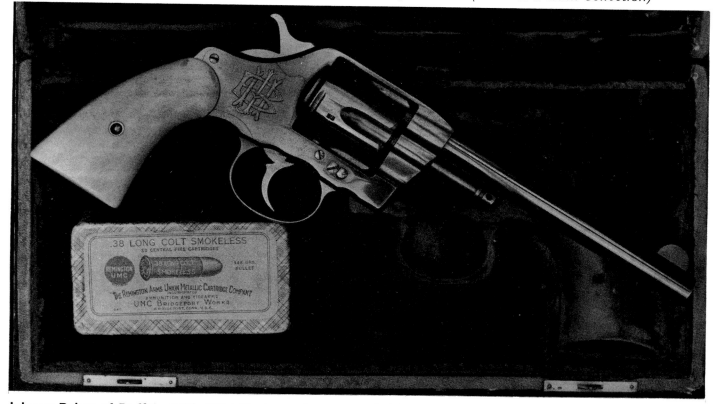

Johnny Baker of Buffalo Bill's Wild West was the owner of this elegantly gold inlaid Model 1892 Double Action revolver, number 15475. The records listed the following: .38 caliber, 6'' barrel, ivory grips, monogram J.H.B. inlaid in gold on sideplate; shipment to J.H. Mayer, Port Jefferson, New York, in April of 1895. Also in this shipment was Buffalo Bill's gold inlaid and deluxe engraved Single Action Army Target revolver, serial number 161328. The Baker revolver is finished in a rich, deep, dark blue. Baker was a highly popular cowboy star with Buffalo Bill for many years, and was treated by Cody as a son. The casing is rare, and Colt factory of the period. *(David S. Woloch Collection)*

One of the most historic and deluxe groups of Colt revolvers known to collectors. All are Model **1889** Navy configuration, and are documented by Colt factory records. At center, number **12403** a gift to Porfirio Diaz (President of Mexico on and off for over 34 years; died **1915**) on his birthday. Colt ledgers state: .41 caliber, 6'' barrel, nickel with gold plated cylinder, pearl grips, engraved. Sold and shipped to A. Combaluzier, Mexico City, May 7, 1891. Detail is from the inscribed right grip of the gun. The upper and lower revolvers, a pair, numbers **19351** and **19354**, were apparently ordered by Diaz himself at a later date. They were shipped by Colt on April 26, 1892, to A. Combaluzier, Mexico City; 6'' barrels, .41 caliber, nickel with gold plated cylinders, pearl grips with PD monogram (one on right stock, one on left), engraved. The guns were shipped as a pair. Scrollwork is of the most elaborate order on all three revolvers and the work appears to have come from the bench of Helfricht himself. *(Walter Douglas Collection, Royal Military College of Canada, Kingston, Ontario)*

Gold inlays by various recognized craftsmen. Top left, New Service 318715, by R.J. Kornbrath. To right, the famed Sears Single Action 172485 (now in the Stanley Shapiro collection), by Helfricht. Left center, Model 1911 Automatic 93183 by W.H. Gough (extremely rare with gold inlaid monogram). Right center, by Wilbur Glahn, Police Positive 363377; the silver plaque from the lid of its factory casing. Lower left, Model 1892 number 15475, with Helfricht gold monogram — this revolver belonged to Johnny Baker of Buffalo Bill's Wild West Show. Bottom right, Model 1892 number 76809, with another deluxe rarity — a gold monogram, also by Helfricht. *(David Woloch Collection, Tom Beiswenger Photograph)*

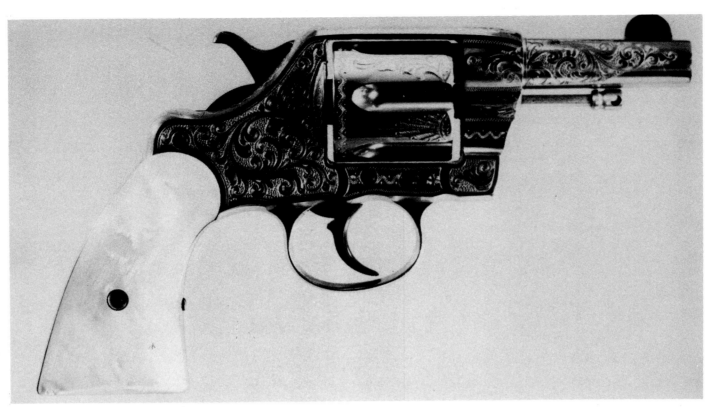

Model 1889 Navy revolver; number 12400. Scarce 3″ barrel; medium engraved coverage, with alternating scroll and sunburst-punched dot decor on the cylinder chambers. Shipped in May 1891 to the Collins Gun Company, Omaha, Nebraska. Nickel plated; pearl grips. Colt ledgers indicate approximately 80 Model 1889 revolvers were engraved; in addition, about a dozen pieces were cut only with monograms or inscriptions. *(R. Q. Sutherland Collection)*

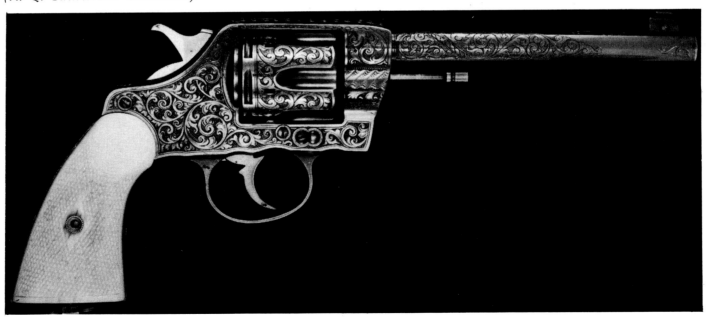

Model 1903 New Army and Navy revolver; number 201070. Colt ledgers identify this exceptional piece as shipped August 1903 "for Government competitive prize" to Captain Thompson, c/o U.S. Government; engraved, checkered ivory grips, blued finish, .38 caliber, 6″ barrel. Thompson may have been John T. Thompson, inventor of the submachine gun bearing his name; what appears to be the initials J.T.T. are scratched inside the grips. Coverage is more profuse than the Diaz guns on the cylinder, and more intricate on the frame. The barrels are about equal, considering that the Thompson revolver also has scrolls at the muzzle end, and to the rear of the front sight. Attributed to Cuno Helfricht's own hand. *(David S. Woloch Collection)*

New Army and Navy revolver done quite similarly to the Thompson piece number 201070. Less scroll on the barrel, but a similar cylinder and frame treatment. Checkered ivory grips. Serial number 219751. Colt ledgers indicate that about 90 of the various models of the New Army and Navy revolver (1892, 1894, 1895, 1896, 1901 and 1903) were engraved. Of these about 10 were also gold inlaid. Approximately 140 pieces bore inscriptions or monograms only. *(Wayne Rohlfing Collection)*

Officers Model Target revolver; number 286256. Colt ledgers document the extremely rare gold inlaid JC monogram, and the data as follows: Engraved, .38 caliber, blued, ivory grips, fine bead sights, checkered trigger, shipped October 1907 to C.C. Crossman; one gun in the shipment. The ledger by error stated the barrel at 6″ length; correct length is 7½″. Engraving and gold inlay by Helfricht. Including production through 1949 of the .32 and .38 calibers, approximately 180 Officers Model revolvers were engraved; Colt ledgers show gold inlays on six of these, and silver inlays on one. Some 95 OM revolvers of the same type and period bore inscriptions or monograms, five of these done in gold. *(David S. Woloch Collection)*

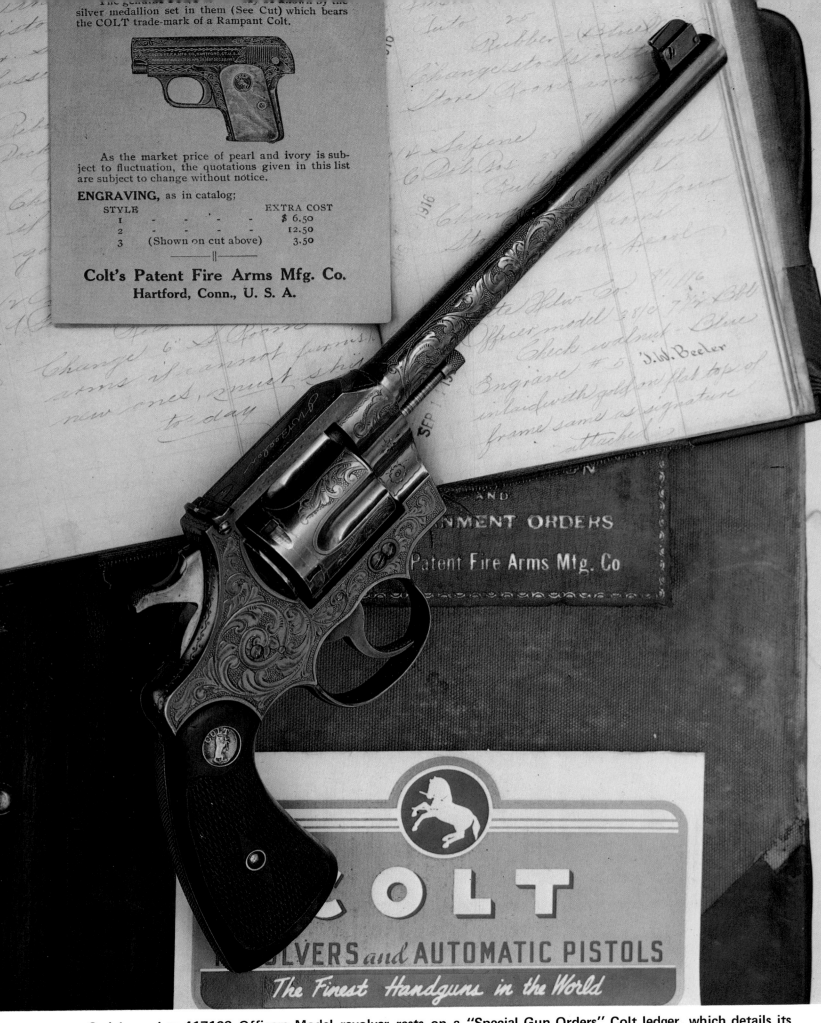

Serial number 417169 Officers Model revolver rests on a "Special Gun Orders" Colt ledger, which details its embellishments. Note signature flush gold inlaid on the topstrap (extremely *rare* detail, simulating an individual's signature). 7 1/2" barrel; .38 caliber; Helfricht style engraving. *(David S. Woloch Collection)*

Supremely rare New Army and Navy revolver documented fully in the Colt ledgers as follows: .38 caliber, 4 1/2" barrel, gold plated cylinder, carved American eagle pearl grips, engraved, with gold inlaid inscription (listed as pictured); shipment to J.F. Schmelzer Arms Co., Kansas City, Missouri, July 1898. Lamb was Police Commisioner of Kansas City, Mo., and also rose to the rank of Colonel in the Missouri National Guard. *(Ronald A. Ogan Collection)*

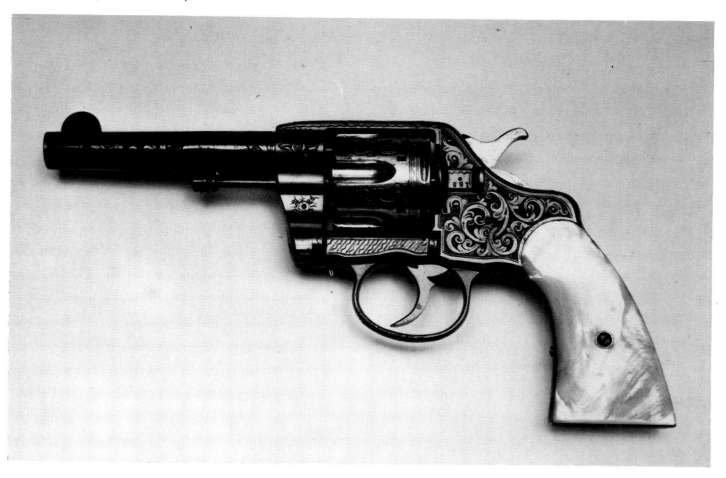

Number 76809 Model 1892 Double Action is superbly gold inlaid with an S.C.W. monogram. Like the Johnny Baker inlay, the flush gold is finely hatched for added detail and emphasis. A six pointed star motif on the triggerguard indicates the revolver had been returned to the factory, likely to allow for the monogram's inlay. *(David S. Woloch Collection)*

Factory inscribed Model 1892 number 147457, on the sideplate and the backstrap. On the backstrap: *G.B. Regar 2nd Troop P.C.C. N.G.P.* The mate to this revolver, shipped at the same time, bore serial number 147429, and its backstrap was inscribed: *R.S. Hart, Jr. 2nd Troop P.C.C. N.G.P.* Shipment was to Thomas J. Stewart (or First Lt. J.P. Wood), in November 1900. The P.C.C. abbreviates Philadelphia City Cavalry, and the N.G.P, National Guard of Pennsylvania. Further information in the March 1976 *Arms Gazette* magazine. *(James E. Kattner Collection)*

Army Special number 23661 is Helfricht engraved on the left side, and profusely cut away on the right. Built as a showgun by the Colt plant; finished in blue; grips of checkered walnut. *(Colt Collection of Firearms, Museum of Connecticut History, Connecticut State Library)*

As an aid for photography, chalk was rubbed into the scrollwork of Army Special number 324917, a revolver which is documented as having left the Colt plant in July of 1912, caliber .41, 4 1/2" barrel, blue finish, and engraved; shipped to Norwell-Shapleigh Hardware, St. Louis, Missouri. *(R.M. Scott Paul Collection)*

Rarely encountered are factory engraved Officer's Model Target revolvers; number 362169 is listed in Colt's ledgers as: .38 caliber, 7 1/2" barrel, pearl grips, nickel plated, engraved, and shipped in June 1914 to Abercrombie & Fitch, New York. The plated finish is also a rarity for a target revolver. *(Albert E. Brichaux Collection)*

Number 313120 of the Officers Model Target was used by Colt as a showpiece. Factory records show the gun to have been shipped on loan account July 1909 to William R. Burkhard, St. Paul, Minnesota; it was returned a month later. Number 313120 was then shipped in February 1910 to Hibbard, Spencer, Bartlett Company, Chicago, and was returned in April. Coverage is medium, and the craftsman again appears to have been Helfricht, rather than a member of his shop. .38 caliber; 7½" barrel; blued, engraved, and fitted with pearl grips. Coverage would be rated at a medium amount. *(David S. Woloch Collection)*

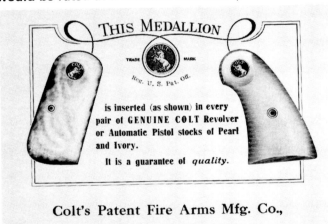

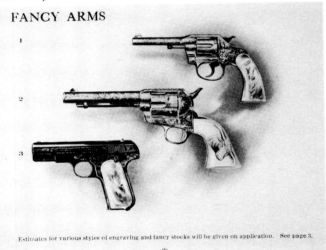

(Left) In the pocket size catalogue of 1911-2, Colt first published this grip medallion illustration. Serving to promote the company's ivory and pearl stocks, grips of this kind had been in the line since the 1850's. However, freshly featured was the die struck rampant colt stock medallion, first appearing c. 1911. The crisp deepset style remained standard through 1929, when it was replaced by the low relief, less detailed type, still in use today. The medallion plate was last used in the 1923 pocket size catalogue. *(John Hintlian Collection)*

(Right) Except for the year 1903, handgun decoration in Colt's series of pocket size catalogues (issued 1903 through 1923; generally published annually and sometimes with greater frequency) carried a note under "FINISH" advising the customer: "Our arms can be supplied with gold or silver plating, inlaid work and engraving, pearl and ivory stocks, plain with monogram, or special design,—prices depending upon the amount and character of work desired." Beginning in 1909 an illustrated page on engraving (shown here) was a regular feature, and was in addition to the statements under "FINISH", which beginning the same year carried an added sentence referring the reader to: "On page. . . will be found illustrations of three popular models with fancy stocks in pearl and ivory, and with style and amount of engraving ranging from $2.50 to $20.00." The scroll pictured is that of Helfricht. Illogically, the fanciest grade was 2, the least fancy 1, and the medium grade 3. Tracing the listings through to 1923 an occasional price increase was noted. The same illustration of Helfricht guns was used in Colt catalogues (a medium size format began c. 1923) until replaced in the 1929 edition by pictures of Wilbur A. Glahn's work. That Helfricht died in 1927 undoubtedly was a factor in the continued use of obsolete engraving illustrations several years following his retirement in 1921. *(John Hintlian Collection)*

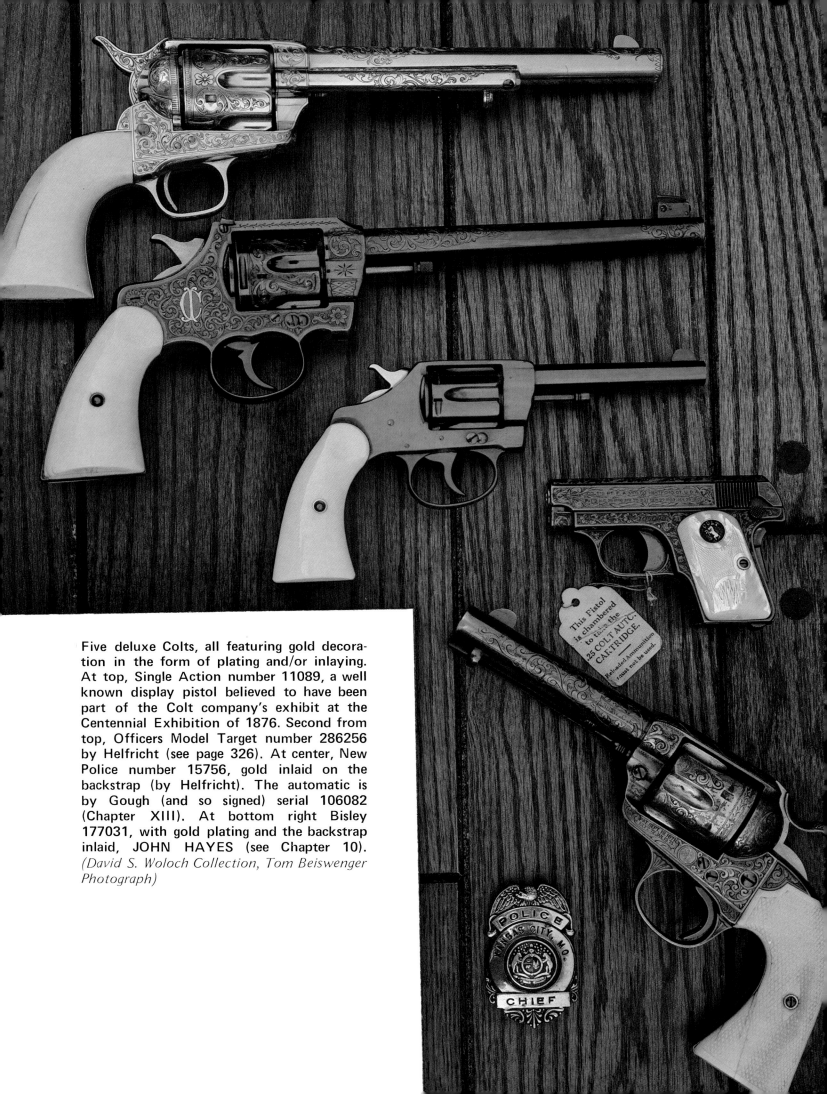

Five deluxe Colts, all featuring gold decoration in the form of plating and/or inlaying. At top, Single Action number 11089, a well known display pistol believed to have been part of the Colt company's exhibit at the Centennial Exhibition of 1876. Second from top, Officers Model Target number 286256 by Helfricht (see page 326). At center, New Police number 15756, gold inlaid on the backstrap (by Helfricht). The automatic is by Gough (and so signed) serial 106082 (Chapter XIII). At bottom right Bisley 177031, with gold plating and the backstrap inlaid, JOHN HAYES (see Chapter 10). *(David S. Woloch Collection, Tom Beiswenger Photograph)*

Army Special number 336435 was shipped by Colt in July, 1912, to Norwell Shapleigh Hardware Company, St. Louis. Factory ledgers document the engraving, and indicate .38 caliber, 6" barrel, and pearl grips. Minimal scroll and border coverage, perhaps a special degree for the large orders then being placed by Norwell Shapleigh for engraved guns. The Army Specials were made from 1908 through 1927, and factory records list about 475 as engraved, plus another 65 or so with inscriptions or monograms only. Of the above, about 15 Army Specials were inlaid with gold or silver. Norwell Shapleigh acquired over 375 engraved Army Specials, c. 1912; one of the largest engraving orders in the history of the Colt firearms company. *(R. Q. Sutherland Collection)*

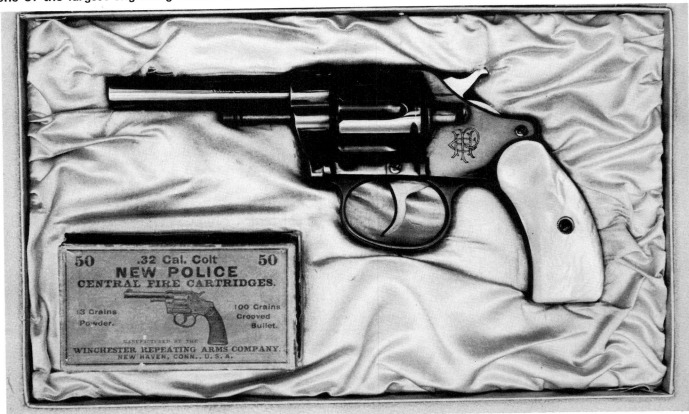

The flush gold inlaid CHP monogram is the major special feature of this New Pocket revolver, number 10384. Delivery from Colt was to company official F.E. Belden, in October 1897. Finish blue, pearl grips, 3½" barrel, .32 caliber. Note the quite scarce and desirable deluxe case. Less than fifteen of the New Pocket Model were engraved, and less than ten were gold inlaid. Approximately half of the latter were in the form of monograms or inscriptions only. Less than fifteen New Pocket revolvers were inscribed. *(David S. Woloch Collection)*

PRICE LIST OF
Colt Revolvers and Automatic Pistols.

REVOLVERS:

New Service,		$16.75
New Service Target,		27.00
Colt Army Special,		15.50
Officers' Model Target,		18.50
Police Positive Special,		14.00
Police Positive, Cal. .32 and .38		14.00
Police Positive Target, Cal. .22 and .32,		15.00
Pocket Positive,		13.00
Single Action Army,		15.50
Single Action, Bisley Model,		15.50
Bisley Model Target,		26.50

AUTOMATIC PISTOLS:

Government Model,	Cal. .45	22.00
Military Model,	Cal. .38	21.00
Pocket Model,	Cal. .38	20.00
Pocket Model, Hammerless,	Cal. .380	17.50
Pocket Model, Hammerless,	Cal. .32	15.00
Pocket Model, Hammerless,	Cal. .25	12.00

PRICE LIST
Showing Extra Cost of
Wood, Pearl and Ivory Stocks.

WOOD		IVORY		PEARL	
Plain	Checked	Plain	Eagle or Ox-Head	Plain	Eagle or Ox Head
$ .90	$2.75	$7.50	$10.50	$9.00	$12.00
.90	2.75	7.50	10.50	9.00	12.00
.90	1.75	6.00	9.50	5.00	9.00
.90	1.75	6.00	9.50	5.00	9.00
.90	1.75	5.00	8.50	4.50	8.00
.90	1.75	5.00	8.50	4.50	8.00
.90	1.75	5.00	8.50	4.50	8.00
.90	1.75	3.25		2.75	
.90	2.75	8.00	11.50	8.50	11.00
.90	2.75	11.50	14.50	11.50	15.50
.90	2.75	11.50	14.50	11.50	15.50
.90	2.00				
.90	2.75	4.00		4.50	
.90	2.75	4.00		4.50	
.90	2.75	3.25		3.50	
.90	2.75	3.25		3.50	
	2.25			2.50	

1913 list for pearl and ivory grips. Listings on plain and carved ivory and pearl grips first were published early in the twentieth century. Sometimes grip prices were included in Colt's lists of guns and accessories, but from c. 1913 to 1941, pearl and ivory stocks most often were run on their own sheet. *(John Hintlian Collection)*

FANCY STOCKS.

We use only the highest grade of pearl and ivory stocks on our Arms.

The genuine COLT stocks may be known by the silver medallion set in them (See Cut) which bears the COLT trade-mark of a Rampant Colt.

As the market price of pearl and ivory is subject to fluctuation, the quotations given in this list are subject to change without notice.

ENGRAVING, as in catalog;

STYLE		EXTRA COST
1		$ 6.50
2		12.50
3	(Shown on cut above)	3.50

Colt's Patent Fire Arms Mfg. Co.
Hartford, Conn., U. S. A.

C.W. Kieft Oct. 1912
(A 23)

PRICE LIST
OF

COLT Revolvers Automatic Pistols and Fancy Stocks

Cecil Wm Kieft
Middletown Conn.

Fully guaranteed for use with SMOKELESS and other powders in standard factory-loaded ammunition.

Cut of 1912

(M-52)
February 1913.
(Destroy all previous lists)

My First Colt Catg. 1913

New Service number 8928 (*top*) features profuse scroll and border coverage by Helfricht, blue finish, with rare gold plated cylinder, pearl grips, and a pedigree traced directly to the estate of former Colt president William C. Skinner. 5 1/2'', .45 caliber. At *bottom*, New Pocket number 909 was Helfricht-engraved, and bears an intriguing backstrap inscription (see inset). 3 1/2'' barrel, .32 caliber. A contemporary flap type leather holster accompanies this stylishly decorated revolver. Rare bulldog head engraved on right side of the frame. Grips of ivory. *(Bob Bostwick Collection, photographs by Esquire Photographers Inc.)*

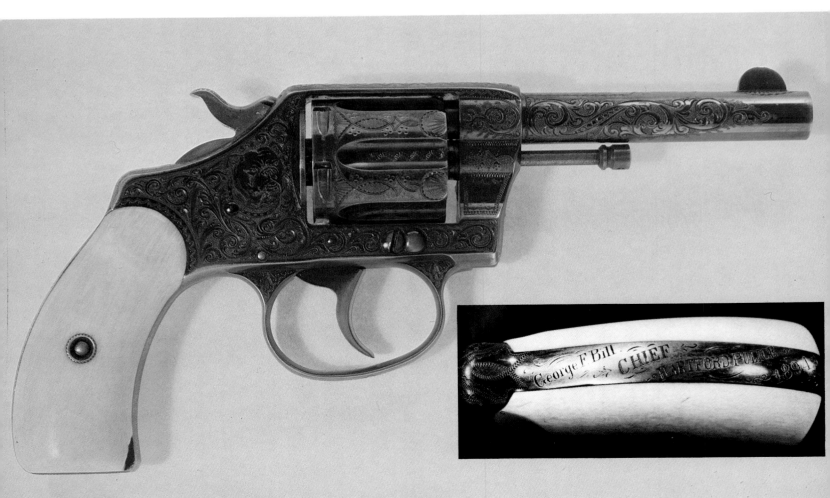

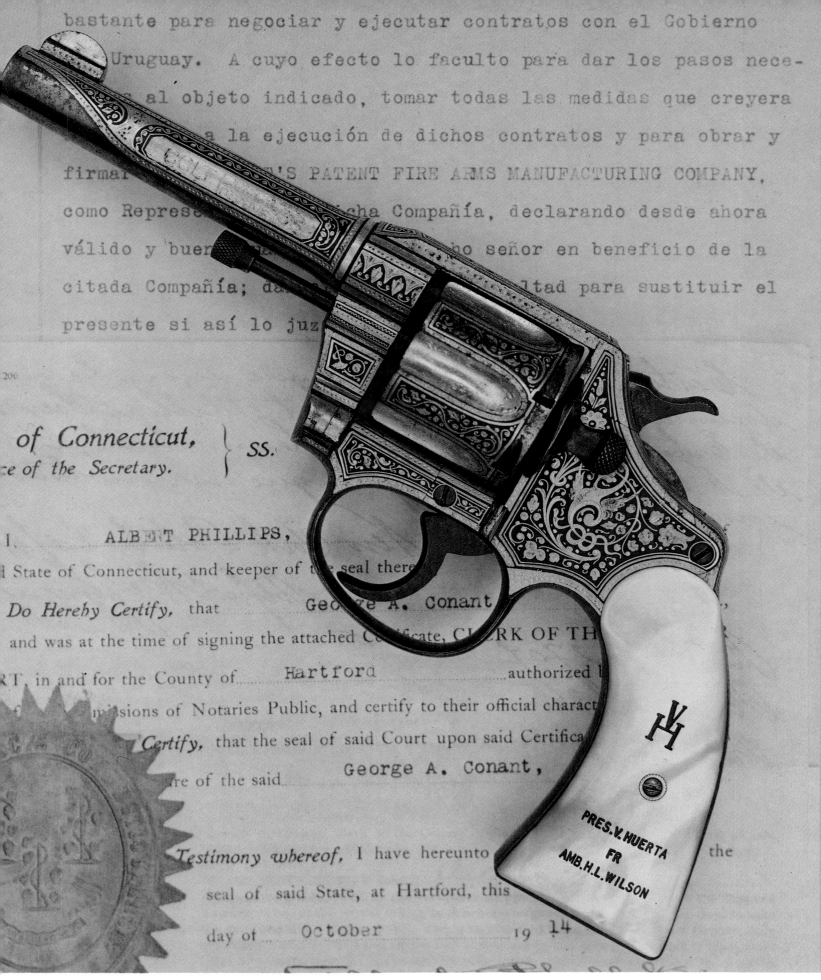

Contemporary gold damascening and plating on Police Positive number 52393, executed in Spain, likely at Toledo. This type decoration is well known on swords and knives. V. Huerta was a prominent Mexican political leader who was a successor to Porfirio Diaz. Details on Ambassador Wilson remain unknown at this writing. Unusual decor and rarely found on Colt arms as applied of the period of manufacture. *(David S. Woloch Collection)*

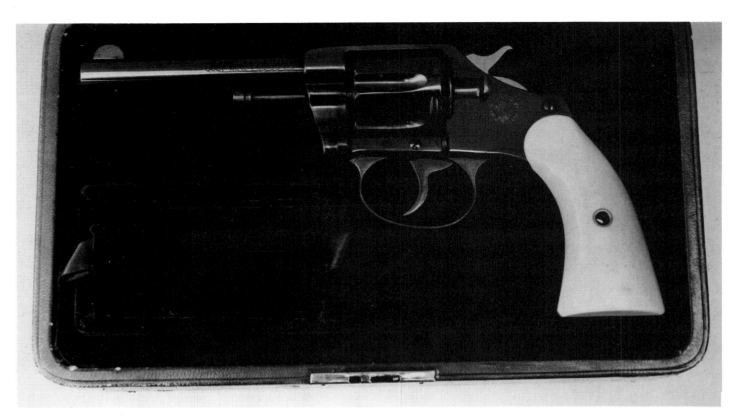

HAROLD D. COREY is gold inlaid on the backstrap of New Police number 15756. Colt records further that this revolver was shipped to Frank A. Schirmer, in July 1902; .32 caliber, 4" barrel, blue finish, with ivory grips. Factory casing of velvet and leather. *(David S. Woloch Collection)*

Chalk has been rubbed into the engraving on New Police .32 revolver number 41419, documented as factory engraved, .32 caliber, 4" barrel, finished in blue, and shipped in January of 1916 to Von Lingerke and Detmold, 349 Madison Avenue, New York. Distinctively Helfricht in scroll style, neatness of punched background, and effectiveness of design. *(James F. Howard Collection)*

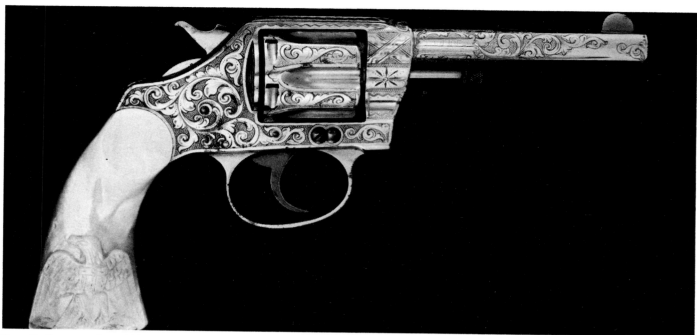

New Police number 41038. One of a pair shipped January 1906 to Von Lengerke and Detmold, New York City; .32 P.C., 4" barrel, nickel plated, with relief carved eagle motif on the right grip. The engraving including a GH monogram on the left sideplate. Special feature: Roll marking (of caliber) left off the barrel. Eagle design is an unusual one; and the engraved coverage is of the greatest amount in the standard grades. Police Positive .32 number 66672 (not illustrated; has a New Police barrel; is a transition piece from one model to the next) from the Lewis Yearout Collection, is similar to gun number 41038, but has reduced amounts of scrollwork on the cylinder and barrel; it also has the rare feature of an intertwined BC monogram on the left side of the frame. The initials are those of a Bess Carlson. The gun is also finished in nickel plating with pearl grips. New Police number 15756 (not illustrated) is one of the few Colt revolvers bearing gold inlay. Factory records state the following: .32 P.C., 4" barrel, blue finish, ivory grips, the backstrap gold inlaid: HAROLD D. COREY. Shipped to Frank A. Schirmer, July 1902; one gun only. About 25 New Police revolvers (c. 1896-1907) were engraved. A New York City Police Commissioner ordered number 480, finely engraved, inlaid with gold, gold plated and blued, and fitted with ivory grips. In the New Police Target Model, about six pieces were factory inscribed. *(David S. Woloch Collection)*

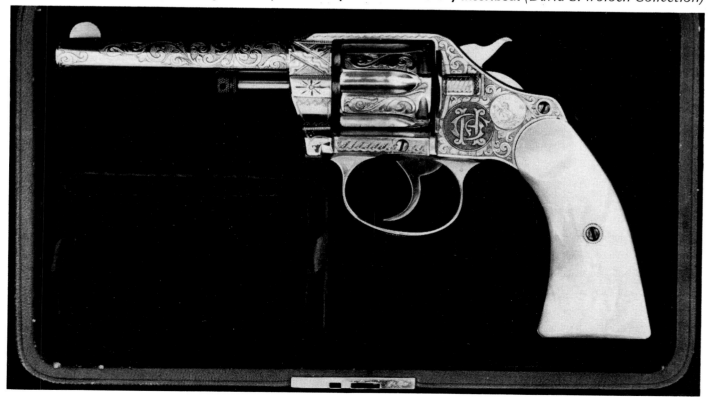

Police Positive (a transition piece also marked New Police) number 66672 left the factory in October 1908; recorded as 4″ barrel, .32 caliber, nickel plated, pearl grips, BC monogram and engraved; shipped to J.L. Baird Mercantile Co., and sold to Wyeth Hardware and Manufacturing Co., St. Joseph, Missouri. *(Lewis E. Yearout Collection)*

A late specimen of decoration from the Helfricht shop, Police Positive number 140544 was made for Sheriff O.A. Fladby, and was shipped in March 1917 to Hibbard, Spencer, Bartlett Co., Chicago. Ledgers note: .32 caliber, 2 1/2″ barrel, nickel plated, pearl grips, and factory engraved. *(Al Brichaux Collection)*

Serial number 30691 Police Positive Special was manufactured c. 1910. Full plated finish, with relief carved American eagle and flag pearl grips. A standard scroll pattern, apparently medium in coverage (compare with number 64976 which follows). Colt factory shipping records list about 325 Police Positive Special revolvers as engraved and about 215 inscribed (period c. 1908-1948). Of the former less than 20 were gold inlaid, of the latter approximately a dozen were gold inlaid. *(Hugh E. Hayes Collection)*

Serial number 64976 Police Positive Special left Colt's factory in September of 1912; shipment was to Douglas Hardware; billed to Hibbard, Spencer, Bartlett & Company, Chicago. Listed in Colt records as blued, .32-20, 4″, engraved, with pearl grips. Note use of rampant colt grip medallion. Cylinder chambers alternated scroll and intertwined zig-zag line-sunburst-punched dot motif. Crisply cut engraving attributed to Cuno Helfricht. *(David S. Woloch Collection)*

.25 Automatic from the Cuno Helfricht shop; number 16834. Shipped on loan account July 1909, and again in February 1910. Grips of ivory. *(Gerald Keogh Collection)*

Shipped in November 1912 to Lee, Glass, Andersen, of Omaha, Nebraska, number 76586 Pocket Automatic is further listed in the Colt records as .25 caliber, nickel plated, with pearl grips, and engraved. *(Paul Sorrell Collection)*

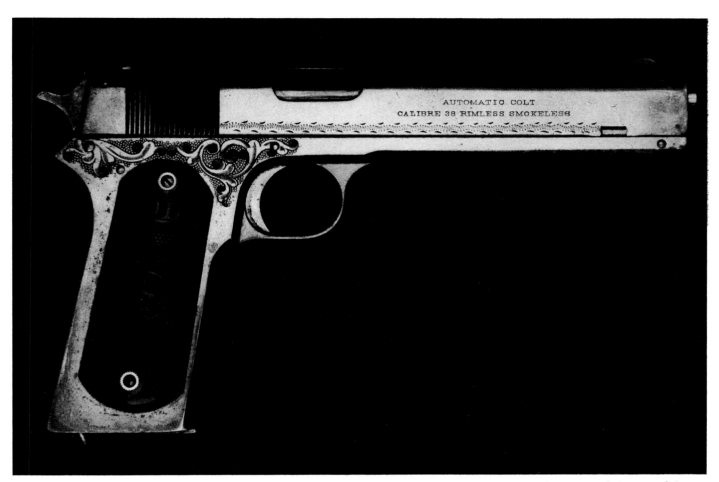

Model 1902 Military Automatic; number 34737. One of a shipment of nine engraved pistols of this model sent in July 1912 to Norwell Shapleigh Hardware Company, St. Louis. Colt ledgers list: .38 caliber, 6" barrel, blue, engraved. A simple design, this would be the least degree of coverage available in the line, and was probably a special low coverage design for the large quantity orders from Norwell Shapleigh at that period. Some twenty Model 1902 Military pistols were factory engraved, about the same number bore presentation inscriptions. Serial number 14940 was gold inlaid: *COL. WM. F. CODY.* The Model 1902 Sporting had only one specimen engraved (number 4304) and about five inscribed. The Model 1900 Automatic had only one gun engraved (number 885) and approximately 10 bore inscriptions or monograms, including one gold inlaid. *(David S. Woloch Collection)*

Number 118735 Model 1903 .32 caliber Hammerless Pocket Automatic. Shipped July 1912 to Norwell Shapleigh Hardware; blued, engraved, part of a shipment of 16. Colt ledgers list about 600 engraved .32 caliber Model 1903 pistols; two of these were also gold inlaid. Inscriptions or monograms were hand engraved on about 75 additional pieces, at least five of which were gold inlaid. These figures include Helfricht and the Glahn and Kornbrath periods (through into the 1940's, with most of them done before the 1930's). Gun number 89776 was personally engraved and gold inlaid by Helfricht, and was delivered to Colt's President C.L.F. Robinson, in May of 1910. Its decor featured portraits of Washington, Lincoln and Grant, the Colt coat of arms, a fox head, and the gold monogram MFP. *(David S. Woloch Collection)*

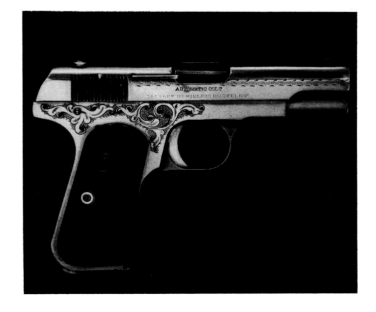

Style No. 3 engraving on .32 caliber Model 1903 Hammerless Pocket automatic pistol number 206532. Shipped from Colt in 1916, via hand delivery by company salesman G.R. Porter (later a Colt officer) to Martin J. Isaacs. Isaacs is reputed to have been a bookkeeper for the notorious Al Capone! Factory ledgers also record the finish, blue, and the presence of engraving and the inscription: *Martin J. Isaacs.* The gun was charged to presentation account, indicating the factory gave the piece to Isaacs. *(David S. Woloch Collection)*

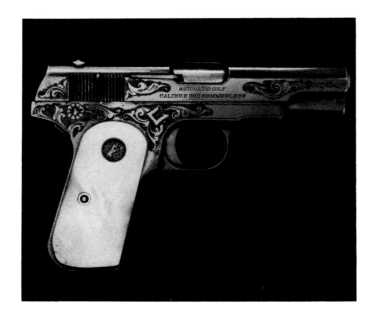

Model 1908 Automatic pistol; .380 caliber. Factory ledgers identify the engraved coverage as style number 3. Pearl grips; blued finish; shipped to R.N. Shearer, December 1914. Number 13778. In the .380 caliber Pocket Hammerless, about 235 specimens were engraved, five of them known to have been gold inlaid. Inscribed or monogrammed pistols number under 45, two known with gold inlay. Most of these guns predated the 1930's, but some were decorated in the 1940's. *(David S. Woloch Collection)*

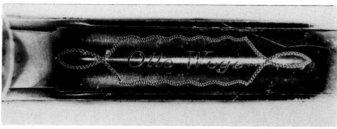

.380 Pocket Automatic number 8428 bears the inscription Otto Woge, and was shipped in March 1912 to Woge Brothers. Ivory grips. *(Lewis E. Yearout Collection)*

As befits a production run of only about 6,100 guns, the number of Model 1905 pistols with engraved decoration was quite limited. Colt ledgers list only six pistols engraved, and one of these — the gun shown here — included a gold inlaid monogram. A total of seven pistols bore inscriptions only. Serial number 3382 was shipped in July 1908, to Arkell & Douglas, New York, New York. Blued finish, wood grips, engraved, with initials P.H.M. in gold on the backstrap. *(David S. Woloch Collection)*

Tex Rickard's Helfricht-engraved Model 1911 Automatic Pistol; number C3926. A well known showman, sportsman, and entrepreneur, Rickard had in this pistol a momento reflecting his inimitable personality. Colt ledgers identify the engraving as grade no. 2; billed to W.C. Skinner (then Colt's President) and shipped to a W.S. Trumbull. For this special piece the standard slide markings were all rolled onto the right side. Ivory grips. In Model 1911 and M1911A1 pistols predating World War II, about 140 were engraved; seven of them are known to have been inlaid with gold. Inscribed or monogrammed pieces totalled about 160; four of them are recorded as having been gold inlaid. Among the pistols of special interest: Number 7542, inscribed to Coronel Caripe from Theodore Roosevelt; Number 7847, inscribed to Coronel Candido Rondon, also from Roosevelt; Number 8037, inscribed to Pedrinho Craveiro, from Roosevelt; Number 101444, a presentation, and so inscribed, from John M. and M.S. Browning; Number 144175, for Connecticut Governor John H. Trumbull, engraved and gold inlaid. *(David S. Woloch Collection)*

Model 1878 Hammer Shotgun number 19333 left the Colt plant in May of 1885, and was shipped to William Beck & Sons, Portland, Oregon. The ledgers note 12 gauge, 30″ barrels, 9 pound weight, blue finish, wood stocks, and ER engraved. Note the brief marking on the lock of *COLT'S*, the English style scrollwork, and the stylized hunting dog, all undoubtedly copied from a standard pattern. *(Al Brichaux Collection)*

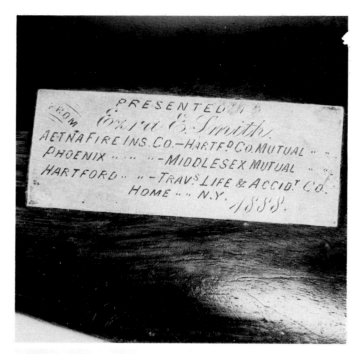

Unusual sterling silver presentation plaque on the buttstock of number 21924 Model 1878 shotgun. Shipped in April 1888. A few presentations were engraved by the factory in the Model 1878 series; among them — number 701, a special prize for the Brooklyn Gun Club; and numbers 6121, 13674, and 16188, presentation account. For a Mr. Richards, number 36 was gold inlaid and engraved. A number of grades for the Model 1878 Hammer shotguns were listed in the 1888 and 1890 Colt catalogues: Eight for the 12 gauge and six for the 10 gauge. All of the latter were engraved, but in varying degrees. Of the 12 gauge, the first two grades were not engraved. Line engraving appeared on the grades 3 through 6 of the 12 gauge, with "Engraved" listed for the top two grades. For the 10 gauge, line engraving appeared on the first four grades, and "Engraved" on the last two. "Engraved" indicated the presence of scrollwork, and was fancier than the line work. Further text on the Model 1878 indicated: "Any grade of ornamentation of the metal work will be finished". *(R.Q. Sutherland Collection)*

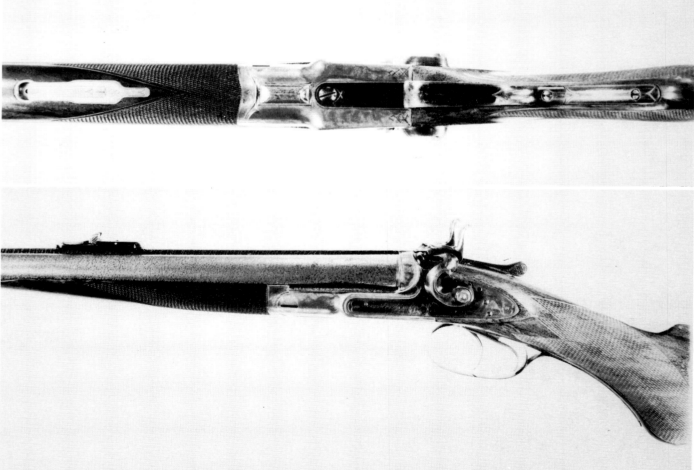

Serial number 18 of the Colt Double Rifle; .45-70 caliber, 28" barrels. Standard engraving, virtually identical to the basic engraved coverage found on the majority of Model 1878 Hammer shotguns. Coverage of simple border work on the barrels, hammers, frame, triggerguard, lower tang, barrel release lever, forend mounts, and buttplate. To date only one of the approximately 40 Double Rifles which were produced is known with extra fancy decoration (number 33). Barrel and markings customarily hand engraved; lockplate markings hand engraved or stamped. *(R. Q. Sutherland Collection)*

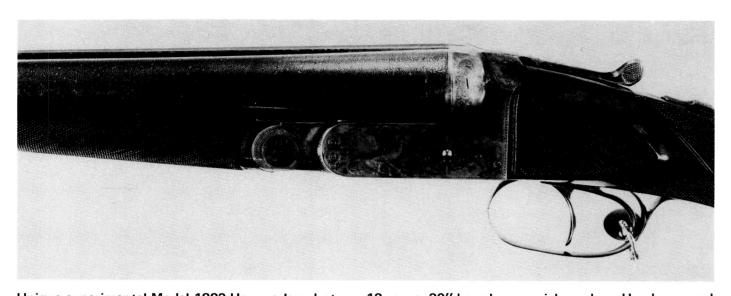

Unique experimental Model 1883 Hammerless shotgun, 12 gauge, 30" barrels, no serial number. Hand engraved barrel and breech markings. Rich damascus barrel finish. Finely engraved in British scrollwork on the frame, for-end mounts, lever, triggerguard, upper and lower tangs, and safety thumbpiece. Extra deluxe French walnut stocks.

Catalogue information regarding engraving on the Model 1883 Hammerless shotguns was listed in the 1888 issue, indicating that a special grade gun was available at $125 (the standard grade was $80): "Finest Damascus Barrels, Finest English Walnut Stock, Handsomely Engraved, 10 or 12 gauge". In the 1890 catalogue Colt added to the Hammerless listing: "Special, to order. . . . price, $150.00 to 300.00". The special guns would invariably include deluxe engraving.

The 1892 catalogue added to the line a $100 grade, with "Plain Engraving." The 1894 issue continued the 1892 listing. *(R. Q. Sutherland Collection)*

Double Rifle number 33; elaborately engraved and flush silver and gold inlaid, a gold escutcheon inlaid on the stock wrist. The barrel marking hand engraved. It is likely that number 33 was manufactured with two sets of barrels, one 28 gauge smoothbore (as illustrated) and one in rifle caliber. *(R.Q. Sutherland Collection)*

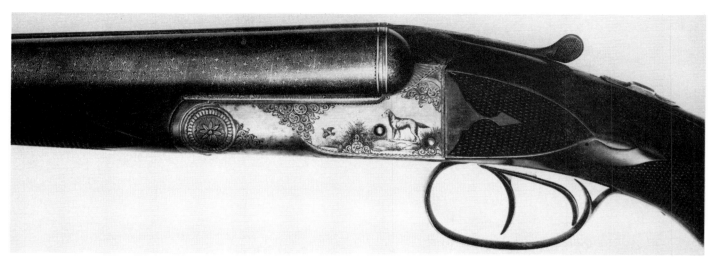

Hammerless Model 1883 shotgun, number 7654. Shipped from the factory October 1894, and recorded as 12 gauge, 30″ barrel, with extra set of 28″ barrels; grade no. 2; *H.S. Kearny*, gold inlaid. Extra degree of scroll engraving; hand cut patent markings on bottom of the frame; hand cut lower tang. Any scroll engraving or inlay on Colt shotgun barrels is of extreme rarity. *(John Miller Collection)*

President Grover Cleveland's custom made Model 1883 shotgun; 8 gauge; the triggerguard flush inlaid. Listed in Colt's ledgers as $100 grade, 34″ barrels, 12-3/16 pounds total weight! *(Richard P. Mellon Collection)*

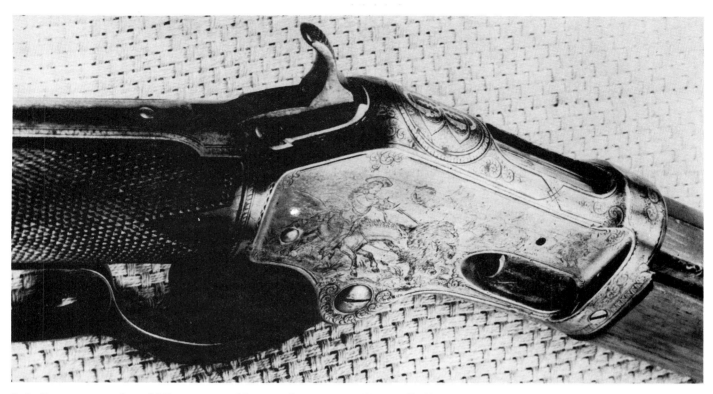

Colt Burgess number 285, presented by the factory to William F. "Buffalo Bill" Cody. On the right side of the frame, Cody is depicted hunting buffalo from horseback, with a Colt Burgess rifle. A richly engraved and inlaid monogram is on the top of the frame. British style scroll. Only two other engraved Colt Burgess rifles were made by the factory; one of these is engraved and inlaid, and was a show piece. That rifle is now on exhibition in the Colt Collection of Firearms, Connecticut State Library. A limited number of the model were engraved outside of the factory; the L. D. Nimschke record book pictures number 6365, inscribed A. LAFON. *(Anonymous Collection)*

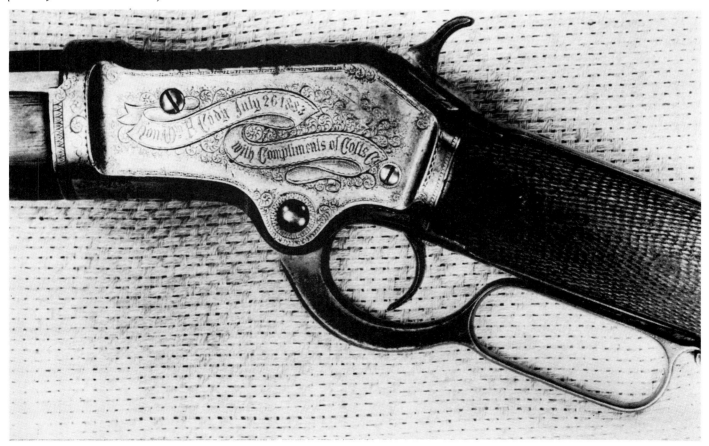

Colt Burgess carbine number 757 is engraved on the frame and barrel, with plated finish, and checkered, select walnut stocks. *(Woolaroc Museum; P.R. Phillips Collection)*

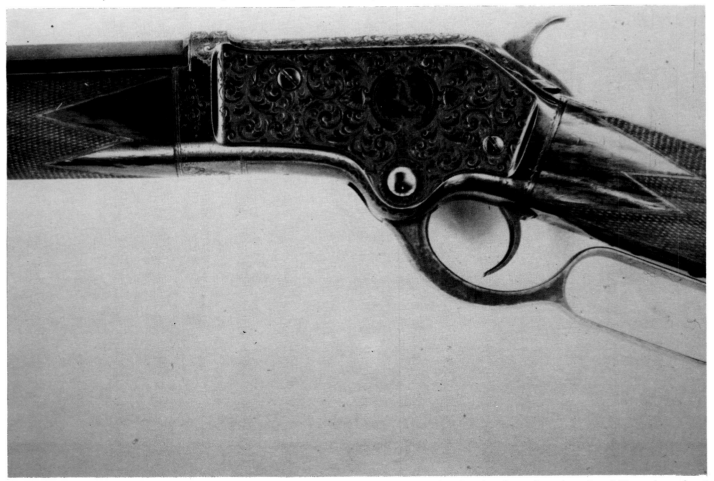

Colt Burgess number 6013 bears profuse factory engraving, and has finely checkered and grained French walnut stocks. High gloss blue finish on the frame; note how the rampant colt device has been encircled by scrolls and borders. *(Woolaroc Museum; P.R. Phillips Collection)*

Number 17375 medium frame Lightning rifle; shipped August 1886 to Semple & Mills; gold plated frame, triggerguard, and buttplate; engraved; set trigger, fancy pistol grip stock, and octagonal barrel. .32-20 caliber. The scroll style is the same as the Gustave Young type from the percussion Colt period, c. 1852-69, and is smaller in size than normally used on Helfricht-engraved large-size guns. Elk and hunter motif on the left side of the frame. One of the finest known Lightning rifles. *(R. Q. Sutherland Collection)*

Number 81114 medium frame Lightning; one of a group of rifles done together c. 1897. Others in the series bore numbers 80937, 80939, 80942, 80943, 80987, 81104, 81105, 81107, 81108, 81109, 81112, 81115, 81116, 81158, 81159, and 81160. Number 81116 is in the Lewis Yearout Collection, and has the same style and coverage of decoration as number 81114, but with variations in pattern. Note unusual vine and leaf scroll motif; buttstock is pistol grip, checkered, and of select walnut; barrel of half round- half octagonal configuration; half magazine; rich blue finish. *(Charles B. Layson Collection)*

Colt Burgess lever action rifle number 3711 was used by the company as a display piece for many years. Barrel and frame are gold inlaid, and the latter features buffalo and bear hunting motifs. Stocks of richly grained, checkered and finished French walnut. Scrollwork is along the same lines as the engraving designed by Helfricht for the Colt double barrel shotguns. *(Colt Collection of Firearms, Connecticut State Library)*

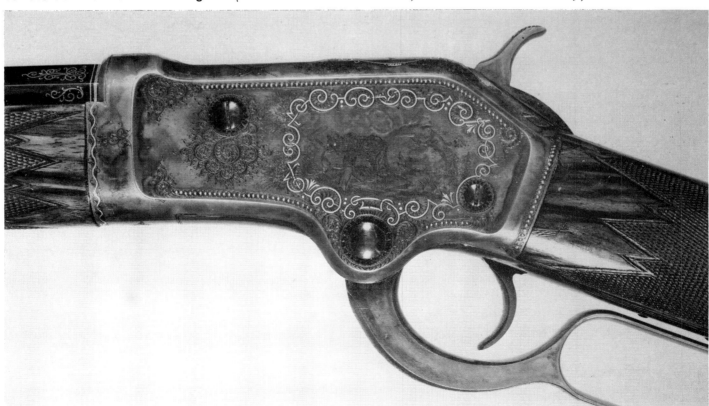

.44-40 Lightning carbine number 6165 is plated in gold and nickel, has checkered select walnut stocks, and features the rampant colt within a shield-shaped cartouche. *(Woolaroc Museum; P.R. Phillips Collection)*

.44 Lightning rifle number 81116 went to A.G. Spalding & Bros., Chicago, in April of 1897. The vine and leaf scroll seems to be the prevalent engraving type on the Lightning medium frame rifles. Scarce Lightning also in the Yearout Collection has a bear motif on the right side of the frame, and engraved rampant colt on the left side, and vine and leaf scrollwork as shown on 81116. *(Lewis E. Yearout Collection)*

Medium frame Lightning short rifle; number 6491; nickel plated frame, triggerguard, and buttplate. The scroll style on most of those few Lightning rifles known engraved is of the same American pattern used by Helfricht's shop on the majority of Colt handguns. The number of Lightning medium frame rifles and carbines factory engraved was less than 40 (about three of this number were carbines); about 20 pieces bore monograms or inscriptions. Number 73229 was the fanciest of all medium frame Lightnings; Colt ledgers list: Engraved and gold inlaid, gold plated trim, monogram on frame, fancy polished stock, with case. Hartley and Graham received about 25 medium frame Lightnings in a soft state, for engraving. The L. D. Nimschke record book pictures prints from three of these (pages 49, 52, and 56). *(Eldon Owens Collection)*

In the series of large format Colt catalogues of c. 1888-1905, decorative possibilities for the Lightning magazine rifles appeared in issues from 1888 through into the 1890's, but the 1902 and 1905 copies listed possibilities for the Lightning rifles only in the .22 caliber. Available in the various catalogues was: EXTRA FOR LIGHTNING MAGAZINE RIFLES "Engraving, $5.00 to $100.00, varying in proportion to the amount of work ordered." Decorative data listed included full nickel plating, nickel plated trimmings, silver plated trimmings, gold plated trimmings, fancy stock, fancy stock checkered, fancy stock checkered pistol grip, Swiss butt plates (except on the .22 rifles), cheekpiece on fancy stocks, case hardening, and extra finished stocks.

Decoration for the Lightning .22 caliber rifles continued in the pocket size series of factory catalogues, first published c. 1903. However, the listing was only in the 1903 issue and was discontinued thereafter; information was the same as appeared with little variation in the large format catalogues of 1888 through 1902.

Extreme rarity of gold inlaid longarms. From left, and embellished from the period in England, serial number 2497 .22 Lightning rifle. At center, 12 gauge Hammerless Model 1883 number 7654, with extra set of barrels (see page 266). At right, Double Rifle 33 with shotgun barrels (see page 347). Center and right guns from the Helfricht shop. *(David Woloch Collection, Tom Beiswenger Photograph)*

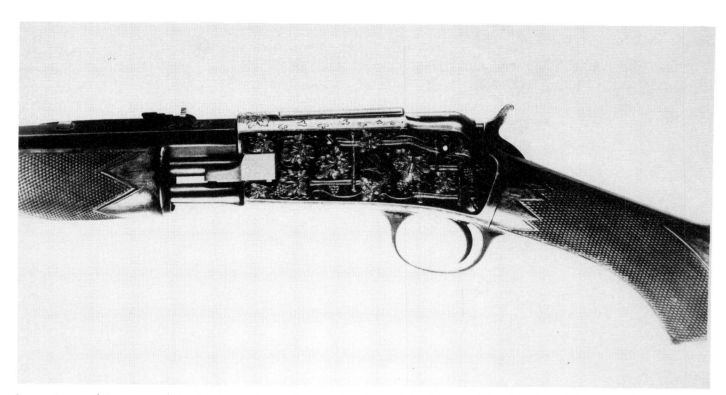

Small frame (.22 caliber) Lightning rifle; serial number 26369 (c. 1897). Blued finish; deluxe stocks. The vine and leaf scroll design is in a quite similar style and amount of coverage to that on the .22 number 36389 which follows and on the medium frame rifle number 80942. However, again there are basic variations in pattern, so that each gun was not exactly like another. The style on numbers 26369 and 36389 should be compared to architectural details pictured in the book *In Memoriam*, published 1898 by Mrs. Colt as a memorial to her late husband Samuel Colt, and her late son Caldwell. About 20 of the .22 caliber Lightning rifles were engraved; about 18 were inscribed. The fanciest of the lot was number 10570; Colt ledgers list the following: Half nickel plated finish, octagon barrel, engraved frame, inscribed on frame: *Kickapoo Medicine Camp*; barrel engraved at muzzle and breech; inscribed plaque on side of stock, *Presented to Dr. B. F. Longstreet by His Friends*; monogram *BFL*; checkered, fancy pistol grip stock; special sights — Lyman hunting at front, sporting style rear; the frame cover, hammer and tube gold plated. *(A. I. McCroskie Collection)*

Lightning rifle in .22 caliber, showing one of the most unusual engraved patterns on any Colt firearm. Blued finish. *(Jackson Arms Collection)*

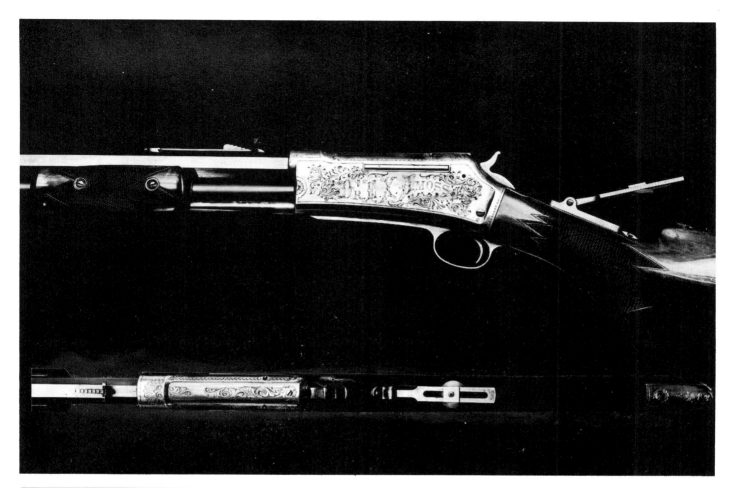

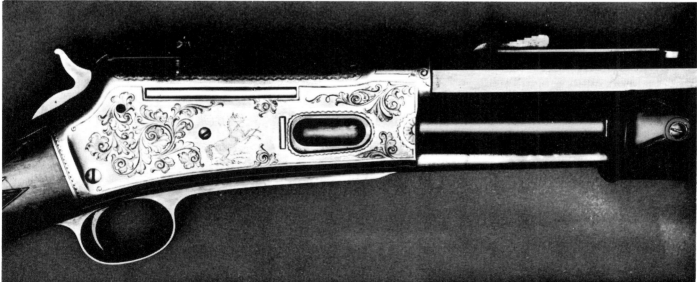

Colt ledgers list number 894 of the express caliber (large frame) Lightning rifles as: .40-60, 1/2 octagon 1/2 round barrel, blue and case hardened finish, fancy pistol grip with nickel plated butt, engraved. Shipped in November of 1887 to Strong Hackett Hardware Company, St. Paul, Minnesota. Extremely unusual elaborate inscription on the frame; finely engraved rampant colt. Engraved express Lightnings are among the great rarities in Colt collecting. Of the total production of 6,496 guns, only about 4,000 are listed in Colt ledgers; from that group, only four engraved pieces were located. It is doubtful that more than ten large frame Lightnings were engraved, and probably not more than five were inscribed. The fanciest listed was number 5963: .45-85, engraved, full pistol grip stock with cheekpiece and Swiss buttplate, case hardened frame, special sights, shipped October 1892 to E. E. Denel, Red Lodge, Montana. The two other engraved pieces listed bore numbers 5567 and 6408, the latter with 22" barrel. *(David S. Woloch Collection)*

In the Gustave Young style, top left revolver is Single Action number 11088, a display piece of the Colt factory, finished in gold and silver plating. The Bisley is number 326568, featuring gold plating and relief carved pearl grips (revolver also has an extra cylinder); by Cuno Helfricht. The New Service was stylishly embellished by R.J. Kornbrath; serial number 321691. At bottom, Porfirio Diaz's Model 1889 revolver number 12403 (see previous Chapter). The backdrop is composed of rare Colt factory ledger books. *(David Woloch Collection, Tom Beiswenger Photograph)*

Chapter XI
RUDOLPH J. KORNBRATH
MASTER ENGRAVER

Rudolph J. Kornbrath is one of the best known of all arms engravers who have lived and worked in the United States. His active career began in Ferlach, Austria, c. 1904, and he emigrated to America in 1910. Settling first in Cleveland, then in Hartford, it was only a matter of time until he was discovered by Colt and other manufacturers and by private enthusiasts of the decorated, first-quality firearm. Kornbrath remained active through 1937, when a disabling stroke ended his career. He died February 23, 1946.

Some years later the major share of Kornbrath's archive of drawings, animal pictures, pattern books, lettering guides, and other records was sold to private collector John H. Hintlian. In about 1971, the balance of the Kornbrath collection, made up of more items of the above, plus tools, specimens of engraving, a large safe, and some personal memorabilia, was purchased from the family by the author. All this material is now in the collection of Johnie Bassett.

Found in this mass of data was a profile of the master, published in *The Hartford Daily Courant*, July 2, 1933. Other than obituaries, it was (prior to c. 1955) quite out of the ordinary for an arms engraver to be the subject of a feature article in any publication. The Kornbrath story was so well done that it would be a mistake not to quote it here, especially since several passages are in his own words:

An inconspicuous little office on the fourth floor of the Hartford National Bank & Trust Company Building is the headquarters of a man who, although he is internationally famous as a master of his art, is virtually unknown in his own city.

It is not so much that Rudolph J. Kornbrath, world renowned gun engraver, is a prophet without honor in his own country as that the patrons of his esoteric art are scattered over the face of the earth. Not more than two or three of them are to be found residing in any one locality....

Every day scores of letters and packages bearing American and foreign postmarks are deposited at his office by the postman. Much of his mail comes from emperors, kings, internationally known sportsmen and other widely publicized notables.

Mr. Kornbrath, an Austrian by birth, has been engaged in his fascinating profession of gun engraving in Hartford since 1910. Few of the many hundreds of persons who daily pass the bank building at 36 Pearl Street realize that up on the fourth floor in a studio overlooking the street a master craftsman is at work improvising minutely exquisite designs on firearms of every conceivable description....

When a Courant *reporter interviewed Mr. Kornbrath he was seated at his long workshop bench, deftly engraving a design on a repeating shotgun.... His only tools were an engraving block, a small, pointed chisel, a graver, and a hammer.*

With amazing skill and rapidity he caused intricate scrolls and symmetrical designs to appear on the dull metal surface of the gun, magically converting what had previously been a smooth expanse of steel into a delicate, lace-like tracery.

Beneath every move of the chisel, guided by expert fingers, unbelievably perfect figures blossomed. Long flowing lines, gracefully intertwined intricate spirals, fragile flowers, and many reversing scrolls followed in the wake of the master's stroke.

'But don't you first trace in the design before you begin engraving?' Mr. Kornbrath was asked.

'Amateurs work that way,' he replied tolerantly. 'Sometimes, if I am doing an exceptionally intricate design I use penciled tracings. Usually I just work freehanded.'

'And your designs — are they original?'
'No two guns that I engrave are ever

decorated alike,' he replied, 'unless they constitute a pair. Of course, if someone brings in a picture of the design he wants engraved on his gun, I reproduce it for him. Otherwise, all designs are my own.'

Mr. Kornbrath, who was born in Ferlach, province of Corinthia, Austria, received his early instruction under the famous engraver Rudolph. He began his studies at a trade school in his native city when he was 13 years old.

Since that time he has earned the reputation of being the finest gun engraver in this country and his craft compares favorably with that of many of the greatest masters of Europe.

When asked how he happened to choose gun engraving as a profession, Mr. Kornbrath replied, 'It is an old art, and a beautiful one. Man's passion for decoration has come down through the ages unchanged.'

'Have you ever seen a collection of the tools of the chase?' he asked. 'To see them is a marvel. The beautifully worked blades of swords and daggers, the carving on old crossbows, the engravings on ancient muskets, are irresistibly beautiful. It is the same with engravings on guns when they are executed by a competent craftsman. The work is fascinating.'

In the February, 1932, edition of The American Rifleman, Charles L. Monson, speaking in praise of Mr. Kornbrath, says, 'We in this country have been in the habit of looking to Europe for the production of really fine hand-engraved guns. Many do not seem to realize that we have expert engravers and craftsmen among us. An example of highclass work done in this country is the engraving on a pair of .45 caliber automatic pistols done by R. J. Kornbrath, of Hartford. These pistols are probably the most beautiful pieces of hand ordnance ever seen.'

The work to which Mr. Monson refers is the engraving on a pair of pistols owned by a Texas ranchman. On the right side the figures represent a cowboy on horseback in the act of pulling taut his lariat with which he has succeeded in roping a steer by the horns. The steer is resisting the tug of the rope with all his brute force. [See .45 automatic pictured in the Kornbrath brochure and on page 274.]

The three figures on the opposite side of the weapon are unusually lifelike and fraught with the illusion of action. The first depicts a cowboy, hat in midair,

grasping the horns of a steer with which he is battling. The central figure is that of an Indian, stealthily creeping on hands and knees through the grass. The third portrays a cowboy riding a bucking steer.

On the forward portion of the slide, on top of the gun, is a gushing oil well. This figure is in harmony with the others, Mr. Kornbrath explains, since most people associate oil wells with the West. Back toward the hammer is the head of a steer, made of platinum inlay and surrounded with a gold inlaid wreath. The stocks are of ivory, carved with a steer's head. The steer's nose-ring and horns are of gold, while diamonds simulate eyes.

The main figure on the underside is a harmonious design comprised of crossed rifles, a cartridge belt, a 10 gallon hat, a holster and a rope....

Mr. Kornbrath is extremely proud of this specimen of his work, which he believes to be his best.

'I worked for many weeks engraving that pair of guns,' he said, 'and when they were finished I felt as if I had achieved something extraordinarily beautiful.'

The pistols, with their engraving and their ivory stocks, are valued at $1000 each, he says....

But a glance through the photographed collection of his works revealed many hundreds of other startling compositions. One, particularly unique and original is a decoration intended for a gun belonging to Tom Mix, noted motion picture star. The figures, surrounded by a maze of fretwork and intricate tracery, are those of a band of pioneers pushing along through the wilderness on horseback toward the setting sun. The central figure is that of a covered wagon drawn by a team of horses. At the left a band of Indian warriors on horseback are racing to attack the pioneers. The picture is vivid and lifelike....

There is nothing static or mechanical about Mr. Kornbrath's work. Although accurate in every detail, it glows with the creative genius of the true artist.

And this Austrian-born citizen of Hartford is an artist in every sense of the word. His unerring instinct for line and symmetry, his genius of composition, and his ability to imbue his figures with life and action unquestionably entitle him to that classification. He is an artist whose medium is metal.

Engraving, because of its inflexibility,

is an art which does not readily lend itself to fluency. And yet, despite this fact, Mr. Kornbrath's work has the ease, the grace and the charm of a well-executed drawing or painting. This master engraver has completely surmounted the difficulties of depicting in steel what he has once envisioned, or perhaps sketched on paper....

The work, however, is painfully tedious. The engraver must have an absolutely steady hand and an unerring sense of design. One slip of the chisel and the piece is ruined. And yet, in all the years of his work, Mr. Kornbrath says he has never yet spoiled a gun entrusted to his care.

'One learns by practice and instinct to do things right the first time,' he explains. 'First, I plan what my design is to be, and then I execute it. It's simple enough.'

Persons of every conceivable type and nationality constitute his clientele. Not long ago he engraved a gun for the Chinese minister of war, T.V. Soong.

'He wanted his name engraved in Chinese letters,' Mr. Kornbrath said with a smile. 'I did it, all right. A Chinese student in Springfield drew the letters on paper for me, and I copied them on the gun in gold inlay.'

Most of his clients, he says, are sportsmen and owners of valuable gun collections. His record book shows that he has done work for men and women in every state in the country, as well as in many countries in Europe, South America and India....

During the course of a recent interview, Mr. Kornbrath stopped in the midst of his work and asked, 'How does a partridge look in flight?'

His assistant dragged out a pile of magazines and started thumbing through them.

'Here's one,' he said after a long search.

Mr. Kornbrath studied it for a few moments, then said disappointedly, 'But it's facing in the wrong direction and I want to copy it!'

'That's the only partridge we have,' the assistant replied. 'There are plenty of ducks, pigeons, and swallows. Will any of those do?'

'No,' the engraver said. 'I want a partridge. Are you sure you haven't a partridge that faces East?'

The assistant shook his head. 'All the partridges here face West,' he said.

'I have it!' Mr. Kornbrath exclaimed, after a moment's frowning thought. Seizing

the magazine, he propped it up in front of a mirror, and presto, he had a partridge facing East!

'There's always a way of getting around everything,' he chuckled as he settled down to work again....

His office is a tiny room facing the street. His workbench, which is lined with chisels of varying sizes and shapes, stands directly beneath a low casement window so as to facilitate the lighting problem.

From eight o'clock in the morning until six o'clock at night he can be found seated at his workbench, carefully and skillfully plying his craft — beautifying firearms for persons in all corners of the world....

Behind the workbench is a long counter lined with books and magazines of many descriptions, which Mr. Kornbrath uses for reference purposes.

'You'd be surprised,' he said, 'what a wide range of knowledge a person in my trade must possess to comply with the demands of his clients. I doubt if there is an animal in existence whose likeness I have not, at some time or other, engraved on a gun. To be able to do this I must know all about their anatomies, how they move, how they look in action, and what postures they assume when at rest.'

'What designs do men usually want on their guns?' he was asked.

'There's no answer to that question.' he replied. 'Everyone wants a different design. Huntsmen usually ask for engravings of animals they have killed. The country gentleman prefers unadorned inscriptions or plain initials on the stock of his gun. Others demand elaborate decorations in Arabesque. There is no predicting what a man will want.

'Often the owner of a fine gun desires his pet dog, or an especially good specimen of game he has bagged, or a particular hunting scene he recalls, depicted on his weapon,' he explained.

'After all,' he continued, 'artistic engravure enhances a gun's value in the same degree that proper landscaping adds to the attractiveness of a home, or that beautiful settings increase the loveliness of fine gems.'

Although there is a businesslike atmosphere in Mr. Kornbrath's office, there never seems to be a time when he is too busy to chat with those who drop in to watch him work.

'Isn't it disconcerting to work while people are peering over your shoulder?'

he was asked.

'No, I don't mind,' he replied, 'I'm sure of what I'm doing.'

The only piece of furniture in the office, other than the workbench, is a chair. The only decorations on the walls are pictures of animals which Mr. Kornbrath has sketched....

For approximately 23 years he has plied his trade in Hartford. After spending a year in Cleveland he came to this city in 1910 and established an office at 26 State Street. Later he moved to 721 Main Street, and now he is located in the bank building at 36 Pearl Street.

He resides at 37 Manchester Street with his wife, Johanna [whom he married in 1916], and two sons, John, age 14; and Raymond, age three....

One of the fascinating features of Mr. Kornbrath's work is its unerring accuracy. In many cases he has engraved the same designs on both sides of a gun, and invariably the two are so nearly identical that it is impossible to detect a single point of difference between them....

One new phase of gun decorating which Mr. Kornbrath himself discovered and recently perfected is multi-colored engraving, in natural colors. He used a special type of enamel which holds on steel.

In his collection he has a pair of hammerless pump guns adorned in accordance with this technique. The guns contain likenesses of ring-neck pheasants and mallard ducks in full natural colors, including the many different shades of the brilliantly-hued wing feathers.

Ducks of other varieties, pointer dogs and numerous birds and animals associated with field shooting and wild-fowling have been reproduced in the same striking manner.

The colored part of the decoration is set down below the main surface. The result, he says, gives added protection and durability.

This new type of gun engraving recently won international recognition, and gun fanciers all over the world are writing to question Mr. Kornbrath about it [though showing promise, the technique did not prove commercially successful]....

Multi-colored engraving is, however, a type of work which requires an infinite amount of patience, accuracy and time. In the reproduction of a single bird, less than an inch in length, hundreds of separate pieces of enamel must be fitted carefully together, so that the brilliant colors blend smoothly and realistically, giving the effect of an actual, living bird.

Some of the bits of enamel used are infinitesimal in size, and must be handled with delicate instruments when they are fitted into place. No piece is more than one sixteenth of an inch square, since the graduation of color in the inlay must be achieved through the use of numerous and slowly changing color variations [this complexity was a major reason the technique did not prove a success]....

Guns, Rudolph Kornbrath explains, have always been an avocation as well as a vocation with him.

'When I was a little fellow,' he says, 'I often sat up until all hours of the night, watching my father at work. He was one of the finest gun engravers in Europe. Even in those days my fingers itched to hold those beautifully ornamented guns and to try my hand at decorating surfaces.

'When I was 13 years old I went to school and started learning the trade. Two years later my father died and I established a business of my own in Ferlach. Since then at one time or another I have had and worked on guns, pistols, revolvers and rifles of every imaginable age, style, size and make.

'I've had priceless collections in my possession. I have done work on jewelled, studded weapons owned by royalty. I have added the skills of my craft to firearms that date back many centuries [it appears that Kornbrath also did some restoration work on antique firearms, though it is not believed that he was expert in the antiques field; he had the ability to match most engraving and gold work found on collectors' guns]....

He explains that some of the finest examples of engraving are to be found on gold chalices... in the cathedrals of the thirteenth century. The goldsmiths of that day he regards as masters unequalled in any other age [the point would be debated by many authorities in the field of European decorative arts]....

When Kornbrath is not active in his studio, he is likely to be out either fishing or hunting. These sports are his pet summer and fall hobbies. He recently returned from a hunting and fishing trip to Canada.

Although gun engraving is the major phase of his work, he also decorates jewelry. He has. . . booklets filled with original sketches and designs he has made for concerns and for individuals.

Most of his gun engraving is done for individuals, although he says he has been engaged in prominent weapons for nearly every manufacturer of firearms in the United States, at one time or another.

'If you do good work,' he says, 'people will tell each other about you.'

This homely philosophy seems to have held good in Mr. Kornbrath's case, since there are many indications of 'beaten paths to his door' from the four corners of the earth.

On February 24, 1946, *The Hartford Daily Courant* published another article on Kornbrath — his obituary:

Well Known Engraver of Arms Dies
R. J. Kornbrath Was Fisherman, Sportsman
And Gun Designer

Rudolph J. Kornbrath, 64, of 37 Manchester Street, a widely known firearms engraver and designer, fisherman and sportsman, died Saturday at a local hospital after a long illness.

He was the uncle of Elsie Knox, former Hartford girl now in the movies [later married to football star Tom Harmon]. *She is the daughter of his brother, Fred Kornbrath, of Marlborough. Rudolph Kornbrath was born in Ferlach, Austria, a son of the late Ferdinand and Mary Jagoutz Kornbrath, and he lived in Hart-*

ford 36 years. He was retired at the time of his death.

In 1934, Kornbrath engraved a shotgun that was given by the Pratt and Whitney Aircraft Company in February of that year to Wiley Post, globe-girdling aviator. The engravings on the gun's mountings required more than 100 hours of painstaking work by the local expert, who then had quarters at 36 Pearl Street, and the finished product, which included delicate engravings on the barrel, required approximately another 100 hours.

Using only hand tools, Kornbrath chiselled free-hand studies of wild game and bird life in the dull metal of guns, surrounding the studies with intricate scrolls. His models were taken largely from drawings and photographs, and his clients included kings, statesmen and famous sportsmen in all parts of the world....

A detailed grouping of work by Kornbrath appears in the E.C. Prudhomme book, *Gun Engraving Review*. The makes represented encompass Colt and Winchester, and various other makers and manufacturers. Still another valuable reference is volume two of James V. Howe's *The Modern Gunsmith*, Chapter XXVI, "The Art of Gun Engraving". Enough material on Kornbrath has survived to make possible the publication of a mammoth illustrated book devoted solely to his accomplishments as a master engraver.

Smith & Wesson revolver done in an oak leaf pattern. The relief chiselled scene on the frame is copied from Albert Bierstadt's *The Last of the Buffalo.* **Note Kornbrath's signature on border above the trigger.** *(Photograph, Johnie Bassett Collection)*

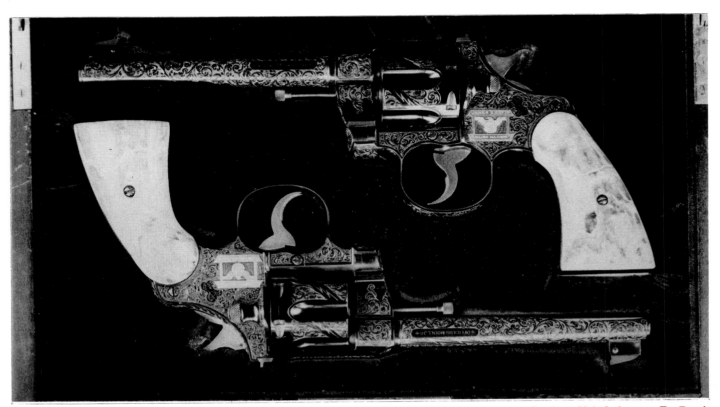

Pair of Officers Model .38 revolvers, gold inlaid and engraved for Los Angeles Police Chief James E. Davis, famed in his day for the radio show "Calling All Cars". Blued finish; casing of velvet lined wood. *(Woolaroc Museum; P.R. Phillips Collection)*

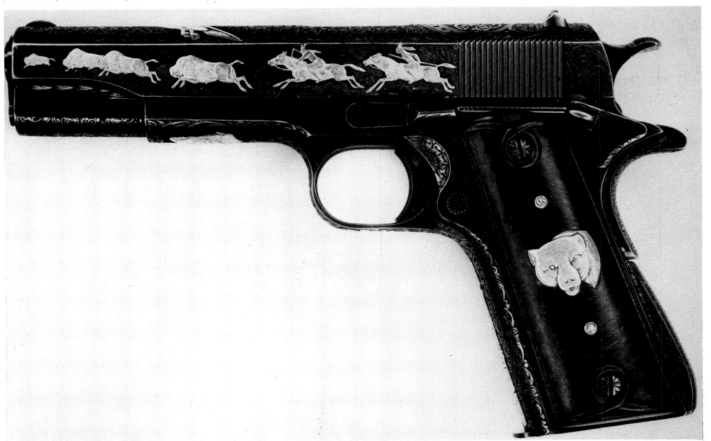

Finely engraved and gold inlaid, this Colt .45 Automatic is one of the best known of all Colts by R.J. Kornbrath. The briarwood grips are inlaid with diamonds and relief chiselled gold motifs, and the slide includes a relief gold inlaid eagle on the top, as well as a monogram. Coverage is so profuse that it even incorporates the trigger, hammer, grip safety, mainspring housing, slide stop, and slide stop safety. Blued finish. *(Private Collection)*

Official Police with American eagle and flag relief carved ivory grips; liberty bell motif on the right side of the frame. The notation in German was by Kornbrath, beginning a description of the other side. *(Photograph, Johnie Bassett Collection)*

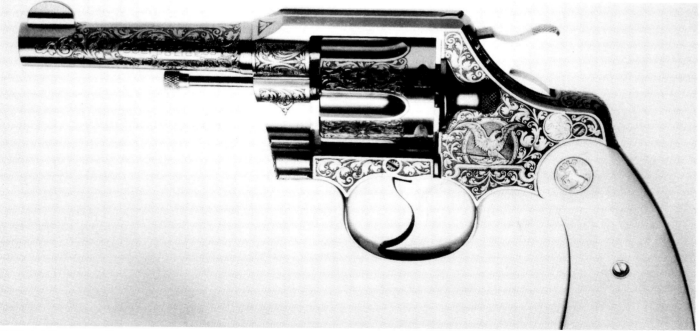

Official Police, 4", .38 caliber, with ivory grips and an American eagle and flag detail on the sideplate. Signed ENGRAVING BY "KORNBRATH" in tiny letters on the left side of the frame. Kornbrath signed most of his work, and was a quite able promoter of himself. Most deluxe Kornbrath engraving was signed in block or italic capital letters; on an extra-fancy piece, the signature might also bear the date by year, and the address, HART-FORD, CONN. However, the signing of engraving done directly for factories was at the discretion of the company. For custom order guns a factory would generally prefer to have the item signed, particularly because of the engraver's widely known name and reputation. *(Photograph, Johnie Bassett Collection)*

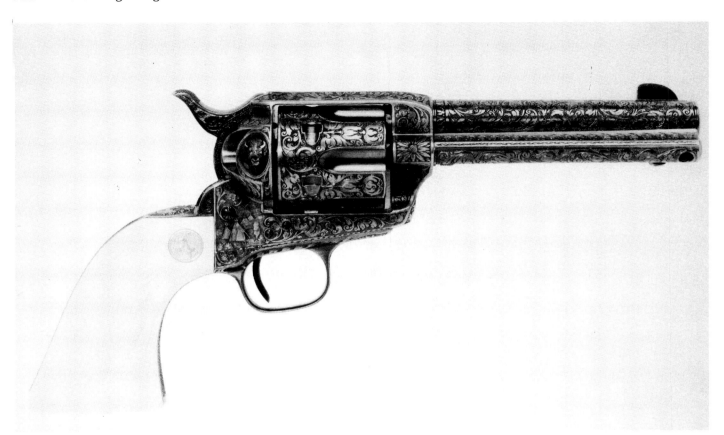

Single Action Army in a profuse pattern of coverage; Germanic scrollwork, with American Indian and animal motifs chiselled in relief. Picture of the revolver's left side is stamped within the triggerguard: R. J. KORN-BRATH/GUN ENGRAVER/HARTFORD, CONN. Photographs he sent out for client reference or for magazine illustrations were sometimes struck with the stamp for identification purposes. The original metal stamp is now in the Johnie Bassett collection of engravers' records and tools. *(Photographs, Johnie Bassett Collection)*

Featuring gold inlaid borders on the cylinder and barrel (including around the barrel address), number 318715 New Service is listed in the factory records as: .44 caliber, 7-1/2" barrel, blue finish, ivory grips, engraved, shipped in May of 1923 to Sr. Don Alfredo Gottling, Buenos Aires, Argentina. The distinctive scroll work is attributed to R.J. Kornbrath. *(David S. Woloch Collection)*

One of several mounted cards on which are glued game scenes and other pictures which were part of Korn-brath's extensive pictorial file. Most significant is the design for a Colt Dragoon at the upper right hand corner. The date of the picture (which had been published) is during the late percussion period. Unusual intertwined cylinder motif was likely to have been done in flush gold inlay. *(Johnie Bassett Collection)*

Comparison of this New Service, number 321691, should be made with the revolver number 318715. The scrolls are finer, smaller, and more intricate and developed overall, but the craftmanship is still attributed to the same hand — R.J. Kornbrath. Colt ledgers document 321691 as follows: Work order number 9772-2, .44 S & W caliber, 5-1/2" barrel, finished in the green state, shipped to Kern Supply Co., in April of 1925. Note engraved hammer, and presence of gold inlays on the cylinder, frame, and barrel. *(David S. Woloch Collection)*

Attributed to Kornbrath, Single Action Army number 355162 is finished in full nickel plating, and includes scarce decor on the screws. Carved pearl grips, by A. A. White. Full coverage on the cylinder; the frame design runs over onto the backstrap and the triggerguard strap. Colt ledgers list the following additional details: .45, 4¾" barrel, sold and shipped to Wolf and Klar, Fort Worth, Texas, April 4, 1935. One gun in shipment. *(Jonathan M. Peck Collection)*

Detective Special for an Emilio Portes, whose name is gold inlaid on the riband on sideplate.   The right side of the frame neatly cut with a tiny Mexican eagle and snake seal.   Photograph was taken prior to refinishing. *(Photograph, Johnie Bassett Collection)*

Attributed to Kornbrath, Colt ledgers list this revolver as follows: Police Positive, number 199154, .32 Police Long caliber, 4″ barrel, blue, engraved and gold inlaid, shipped to Sr. Don Alfredo Gottling, Buenos Aires, Argentina, February 24, 1924; one gun in shipment. The grips were not listed in the record, but are original steerhead ivory with Colt medallion inlays. *(Jack D. Funderburgh Collection)*

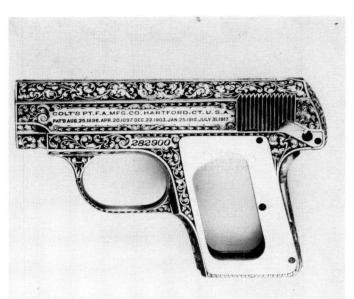

Gold inlaid and delicately engraved .25 caliber Model 1908 automatic pistol; serial number 282900. Gold inlaid name on the right side of the frame: P.B. BEKEART. Coverage is on every conceivable area, and quite stylishly accomplished. *(Photograph, Johnie Bassett Collection)*

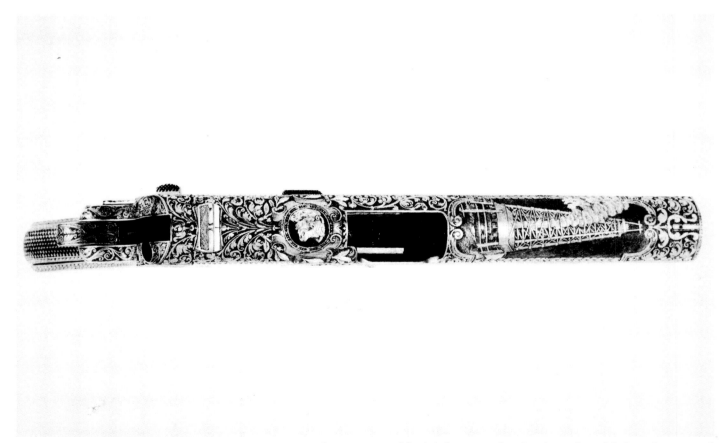

The best known of all work by Kornbrath; the Government Model Automatic pistol used on his brochure, and frequently reproduced in a variety of magazines over the years. Done for a Texas rancher and oilman, whose brand was three D's, arranged in triangular form, but reversed. The brand appears on the right side of the frame, to left of the upper area of the grip. Most of the special design details (e.g., steer's head, cowboy scenes, and monogram) were relief gold inlaid. Gold inlaid on bottom of the forward section of the receiver was a Western coat of arms design, composed of crossed rifles, holster, lariat, ten gallon hat, and a decorative riband. Same pistol was the cover illustration for Kornbrath's brochures. See also pages 274, 276 and 280. *(Photograph, Johnie Bassett Collection)*

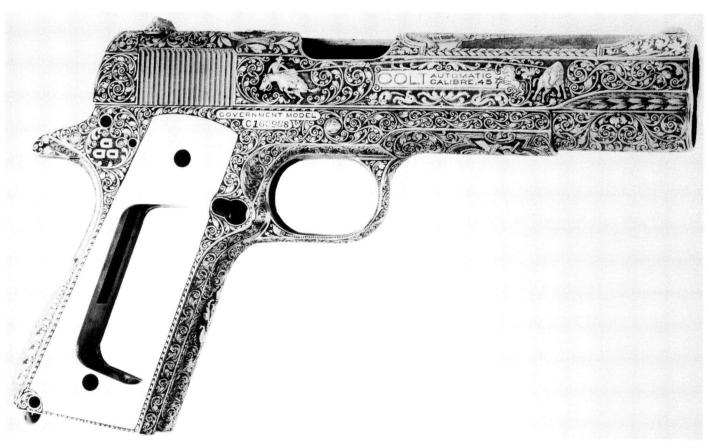

Kornbrath's masterpiece in Colt firearms was this Government Model Automatic pistol, number C160986. *(Photographs, Johnie Bassett Collection)*

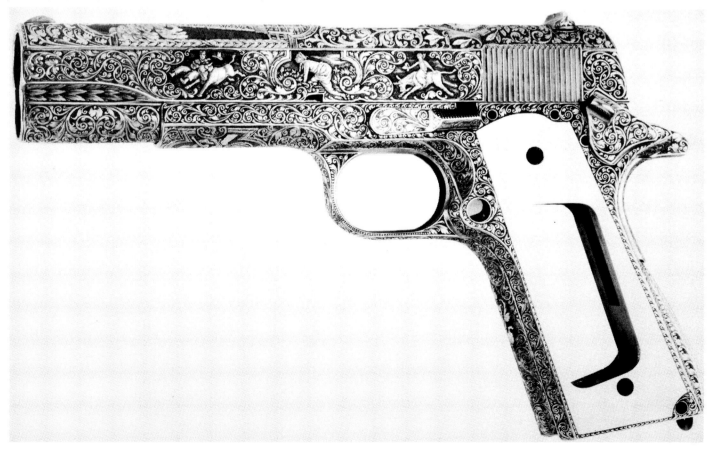

Three examples of the engraving and gold inlay of Wilbur A. Glahn. At top, serial number 575888 Official Police, engraved (grade C), N. R. Webster inscription gold inlaid, checkered frame straps, shipped to William Hoegee Company, Los Angeles, California, February 16, 1931.

At center, Officers Model Target revolver number 515559; inscribed on the backstrap: E. A. BRININSTOOL; gold and silver plated, ivory grips with steerhead motif relief carved on each side; shipped October 6, 1924 to *Hunter, Trader, and Trapper* magazine.

Bottom, Police Positive Special number 363377; engraved in grade 2½; shipped to Norman Stevens April 4, 1928. The gun is cased, and on the lid is a large silver plaque indicating presentation to Imperial Potentate Clarence M. Dunbar from his friends. *(David S. Woloch Collection/Photograph, Thomas Beiswenger)*

Chapter XII
WILBUR A. GLAHN
c. 1919 — c. 1950

Of the several families who excelled in firearms engraving in America, one of the largest was the Glahns. Their geneology is rather complex, but a number of basic facts have been determined through family records. The first engraving Glahn came to America from the Black Forest area of Germany, in 1828. The emigrant craftsman was George Glahn, and he became an employee of the American Bank Note Company. Family sources suggest that he was also a gun engraver.

Various of George's sons, grandsons, and great grandsons became engravers. Among them was another George, who is believed to have been chief engraver at the Syracuse Arms Company factory; little is known of his career, unfortunately.

Jacob Glahn, who died in 1902, first worked for the American Bank Note Company, and at later dates engraved for several other firms, including Colt's. Background data on his career was located in a letter now in the Colt Collection of the Connecticut State Library. Jacob was writing to Colt's factory about work for them; spelling, punctuation, and capitalization are his:

Syracuse Sept 27 1878

Gentlemen
Dear Sir,
Yours of the 20th came duly to hand, and am happy to see you pleased with my work. Part of contents of your letter I laid before our Superintendent for my endorsement. He said that he would write to you as soon as time permitted. In my twenty five years experience in my Buseness, this is the first time that my respectibility is questioned. This seems rather strange. But Gentlemen, I will submit cheerfully such names of Firms in your vicinity, and I hope you will Thoroughly Investigate regarding to my "respectibility". I will name the New Britain Bank Lock Co., American Sterling Co. of Naubuc. Sharps Rifle Co. and Winchester Repeating arms Co. I also wish you would write to Mr Elexander Bergen, President of the Defunct

National Arms Co. of Brooklyn, N.Y. I had the Engraving contract under this firm for Six years. It pains me and I don't suppose it is your request to produce pedegree, but am proud to say that to prove respectibility that my Ancesters were of the Oldest of Dutch Nobility (Von Glahns) who were all Honorable and Brave Solders. Who Fought under the Hugonot King untill his Disasterous End. My Relations in New York City are well to do Merchants, and those in South Carolina, all Independent planters. should you find me trustworthy I would be happy to receive your Guns, and I think I can satisfy you, or the most critical Judge of this kind of work.

I remain yours, very Respect
Jacob Glahn
26 Kenneday St
Syracuse N.Y.

At the same time a letter of recommendation was sent Colt by Joseph W. Livingston of the Nichols & Lefever gun company, Syracuse; the unedited note follows:

Gentlemen
Mr Jacob Glahn, at present employed in the factory of Messrs Nichols & Lefever, he having charge of the engraving department informs me that you desire vouches for his personal integrity, and he requests me to furnish you any testimony I may. I will here say that I have known Mr Glahn many years, and for the past Several years have seen him almost daily, he having been like myself connected with Parker Bros. Gun Works, West Meriden Conn. for the past year he has been Connected with the factory as far as my personal knowledge, he acted honorably and left them. So, if you desire to furnish him Sample guns to engrave, you can rest assured that Mr. Glahn will return them Safe, and I doubt not Satisfactory, for I consider him one of the most Compleet

artizens that is to be found to day, on his Speciality, Gun Engraving. Reasons over which I have no Controll warrents Mr. Glahn to look out for further Employment that is to say, he is rather fearful that I cannot give him Constant employment. Should you desire, and engage Mr. Glahn you will find him a very desirable hand. I doubt not Mr. Glahn Can furnish you with other Testimonials. As he has furnished Samples of his handy work to most of the gun houses of this County. I dont know that I can say more then personally I would trust Mr. Glahn with any work I had to do. . . .

A page in one of the Colt factory ledgers lists a group of shotgun parts shipped to Jacob in Syracuse, in 1879. The company obviously decided to send him work, finally accepting his "respectibility". Serial numbers of these pieces, all from Model 1878 Hammer shotguns, included: 250, 255, 256, 279, 280, 282, 284, 302, 309, 349, 385, and 394. In getting the Model 1878 shotgun program underway, Colt was in need of all the engraving help it could muster.

Still another reference to Jacob is on page 95 of *L. D. Nimschke Firearms Engraver;* the illustrated piece is a Moore revolver. Theodore Glahn (born c. 1857; died c. 1937) was an engraver for Parker Brothers, Fulton Arms, and Syracuse Arms. While at Syracuse he was assigned the decoration of a deluxe gun for Theodore Roosevelt.

Gus Glahn died prior to World War II; he is known to have engraved for the Buffalo Arms Company and for Syracuse Arms.

The member of the family of greatest interest in the present volume is Wilbur A. Glahn, born March 4, 1888; married 1906, died February 6, 1951. He learned the trade from his father, George, and was a general engraver, specializing in firearms. He is known to have worked for the Fulton Arms Company, for Remington Arms (c. 1905-19), and for Colt. Wilbur also had a number of private clients, and occasionally took in projects for other arms companies, among them High Standard. Besides metal engraving, he did carving, enameling, and inlaying on pearl and ivory grips.

Wilbur came to Hartford in 1919 and was hired by Colt's factory. He worked at the plant through 1923; leaving in that year and taking up engraving at his home workshop, but continuing to do the bulk of Colt's work. In November of 1923 Wilbur set up a shop at 11 Central Row, Hartford, and worked there through c. 1926. He shared the studio with E. R. Houghton, a jewelry engraver; the company was known as Houghton & Glahn.

Wilbur's next move was to 71 Asylum Avenue, Hartford, c. 1926. He adopted the name of the Aetna Stamp and Engraving Company (a firm which

had been established c. 1890). Besides general engraving, he worked in pearl and ivory, and sometimes handled this type assignment from R. J. Kornbrath. Wilbur was not a die cutter, but could work in that field if need be.

From his arrival in Hartford in 1919, Wilbur continued to do the bulk of the Colt company's engraving through the spring of 1950. He became ill at that time, and entered the hospital; passing away February 6, 1951.

Until c. 1933, 90% of his work was on firearms. He then entered into industrial engraving. Before long, guns settled into the background and the firm's largest customer was the Pratt & Whitney company. During this period he turned down work from the Remington and Ithaca companies but occasionally took on gun jobs from individual clients or from High Standard. Remington and Ithaca had been asking him to help with their engraving requirements ever since Wilbur first came to Hartford, in 1919.

The bulk of his assignments from Colt was on grade A, B, and C handguns. Nevertheless, the list of special guns done for the firm is impressive. Some of these custom arms, and a few for other companies, were:

A Thompson submachine gun for Obergon of Mexico, including profuse gold inlays, the Mexican seal, Obergon's name, and elaborate engraved coverage. This was a presentation from Colt's factory, producers of the Thompson, c. 1921.

A pair of deluxe handguns for the King and Queen of Siam (Thailand), prior to World War II.

A handgun for the Prince of Wales.

Several guns for show business personalities, among them Tom Mix and stripper Sally Rand. Several Texas Rangers and other law enforcement officials bought or were presented arms engraved by Wilbur.

He engraved a pair of .45 Automatic pistols for Douglas MacArthur, and said that the general held up the invasion of the Philippines until he had received these guns!

Serial number 135631 of the Model 1908 Hammerless .380 Automatic pistol was profusely engraved and gold inlaid for General George C. Marshall. The general's signature was gold inlaid on the left side of the slide.

Serial number 471890 of the Model 1903 Hammerless .32 Automatic pistol was elaborately engraved for presentation to Connecticut Governor John Trumbull, in May of 1926, by Colt's factory; the ivory grips bear a gold inlaid and engraved facsimile of the state's coat of arms.

For Auto Ordnance, Wilbur engraved and

inlaid a Thompson submachine gun intended for presentation to Joseph Stalin, the Russian dictator.

For High Standard he gold inlaid and engraved two .22 caliber automatic pistols presented to baseball star Ted Williams; each bore gold inlaid facsimiles of the slugger's signature (c. 1947). High Standard's Vice President and General Manager from the mid 1940's through c. 1954 was Wilbur's brother-in-law, George Wilson.

For the Syracuse Arms Company Wilbur engraved a fancy shotgun for the King of Greece (early in the twentieth century); another deluxe Syracuse shotgun by Wilbur was made for Theodore Roosevelt.

Wilbur's sons Karl and Wilbur continued their father's Aetna Stamp and Engraving firm, presently a company specializing in marking devices. Their office and manufacturing facility is located in Rocky Hill, Connecticut.

The author has located two sets of photostats of several models of engraved Colt firearms, by Glahn. One set was used by Colt's factory for reference in filling orders. The other set was in Glahn's shop, for his own use in cutting the standard styles as ordered by the factory. The photostats usually show both sides of a sample engraved piece, and include captions, such as: "Model P. 45/c style C. Engr." or "Model E 38. . . style A Engr." Rather than have on hand a full array of sample guns, the photostats were used. In a few instances additions were made on these pictures, to indicate variants from the standard styles; most of these changes were pencil or ink lines showing inlays ordered to complement the scroll engraving.

Besides A, B, and C work, other style identifications in use included Number 1¼, number 2½ (on Single Action Army number 347208), and number 5 (on Single Action Army number 347651). Further sample guns whose serial numbers appear in the photostats are:

Style A on Government Model Automatic
  pistol number C156705
Style B on Government Model Automatic
  pistol number C156706
Style A on Model 1903 Hammerless Pocket
  Automatic pistol number 494813
Style C on Model 1903 Hammerless Pocket
  Automatic pistol number 494771
Style A on Model 1908 Hammerless Pocket
  Automatic pistol 25ACP number 377733.
Style C on Model 1908 Hammerless Pocket
  Automatic pistol 25ACP number 377719.

The photostat series dates from c. 1928 and 1929, and all the engraving was by Wilbur Glahn. The pictures document what coverage and style the company and Glahn had agreed upon for each of the various types of engraving. However, judging from guns examined in making the present study, the engraver did not usually follow the design of each style religiously, but varied these somewhat to add to the individuality of each gun, and to avoid boredom on his own part. A quotation from Colt's catalogue of 1928 suggests such variation:

On page 23 will be found illustrations of three popular models fitted with fancy stocks in pearl and ivory. The designs marked 1, 2 and 3 are not followed exactly but vary with different models and are shown to indicate something of the style and amount of engraving that may be had ranging in price from $10.00 and upwards.

The death of Wilbur A. Glahn in 1951 marked the end of America's family dynasties of gun engravers. The Ulrichs, Youngs, and Helfrichts had faded from the picture as early as the 1920's (Youngs, Helfrichts), and as late as the 1940's (the Ulrichs). Of all four families only the Ulrichs can claim any of the current crop of engravers as their proteges — these are the Kusmit brothers, master engravers at the Winchester factory.

However, the Germanic influence of the family dynasties, and of such contemporaries as Nimschke, Bodenstein, and Kornbrath, left a permanent imprint on the stylistic preferences of America's clientele for engraved firearms. The high standards of quality, design, and style set by these exceptional craftsmen will forever serve as a major gauge by which gun engravers of the present and future will be measured. It is a valuable legacy, and an undisputable reason for the appreciation of quality antique arms by collectors whose specialties would otherwise be limited only to the modern gun.

Advertisement from the third edition for 1875 of *Fur, Fin and Feather* **magazine. Generally firearms engravers operated under their own names; using a title like "The American Gun Engraving Company" was quite out of the ordinary.**

A Sharps Borchardt Rifle by one of the Glahn family; believed to have been an early piece by Jacob. *(Photographs, Ralph E. Glahn Collection)*

Pencil sketches by Theodore Glahn; the Pontiac drawing as a suggested design for an advertisement by that automaker. The game scene was for the "three-in-one" gun lubricating oil. Theodore did a shotgun for a Congressman, in which a cow was coming out of a trap instead of a live pigeon! The client wanted something different from any other! *(Ralph E. Glahn Collection)*

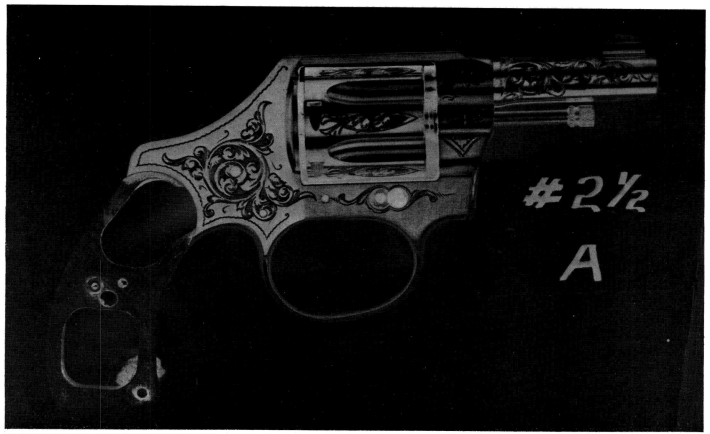

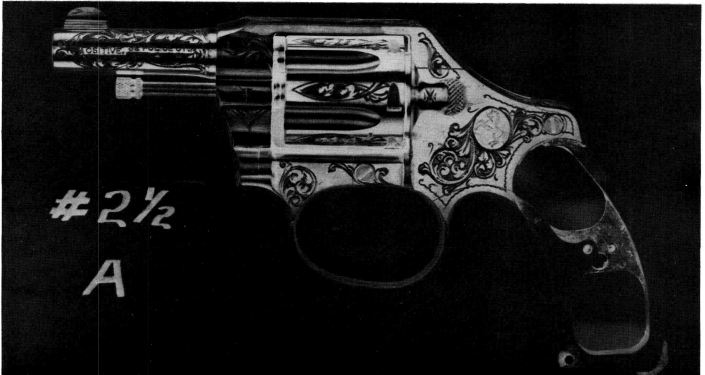

Specimen from a series of folders made up from photostatic copies taken directly from engraved revolvers of various degrees of coverage. The copies were then used as reference between the Colt factory marketing and sales force and the engraver. Revolver is a Police Positive .32, in number 2-1/2 engraving. Compare with the illustrated quotations and breakdown by model and coverage, dated 4/14/32. Other models represented in the folders are .25 Automatics (numbers 354789, 354792, and 354718, in 1-1/4, 2-1/2 and 5 grades respectively), Model 1911 .45 Automatic (number C144048, style 5), .380 Pocket Automatic (number 82360, style 1-1/4), Police Positive .38 (style 2-1/2, serial number not known), Army Special .38 (style 2-1/2, number unknown), Police Positive Special .38 (style 2-1/2, serial number unknown), and New Service .45 (serial number unknown, style 5). *(Author's Collection)*

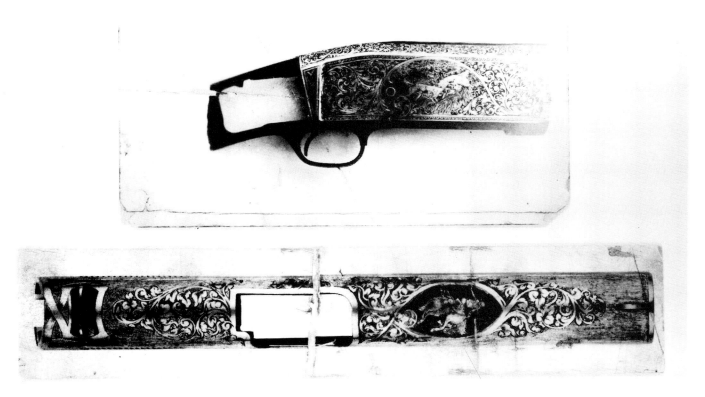

The Remington shotgun at top was by Wilbur Glahn, though the style is in marked contrast to the floral, leaf and vine scroll on the Colt Automatic pistol slide at bottom. The slide's scroll is characteristic of most of Wilbur's engraving for Colt's factory. *(Glahn Family Collection)*

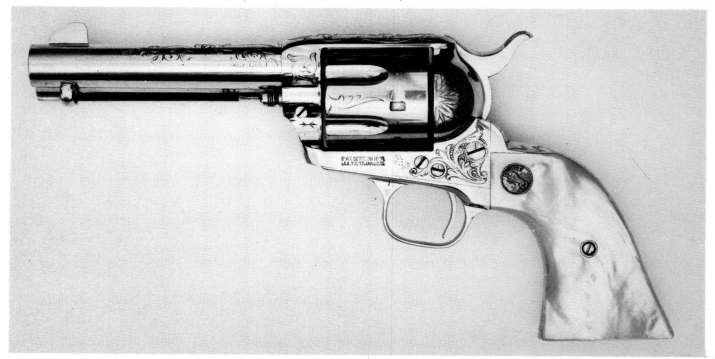

Light scroll on Single Action Army number 341201. The work is transitional, from the Helfricht style to the style which would soon be established by Wilbur Glahn. Transition pieces date from c. 1919 through c. 1921 and are quite scarce. Factory ledgers record the following data: .45, 4¾", nickel, pearl, engraved, sold to Stauffer Eshleman and Company, New Orleans, and shipped to A. J. Anderson Company, Fort Worth, Texas, November 1920. Six identical guns in the shipment. For the period 1922 through 1940, the total of engraved Single Action Army revolvers (as listed in factory records) was approximately 450; several of these included inscriptions. A few of these were gold inlaid; other specials listed were black enamel inlay on pearl, ivory stocks relief carved with the rampant colt, and a fair proportion of carved stocks in pearl and ivory. *(David S. Woloch Collection)*

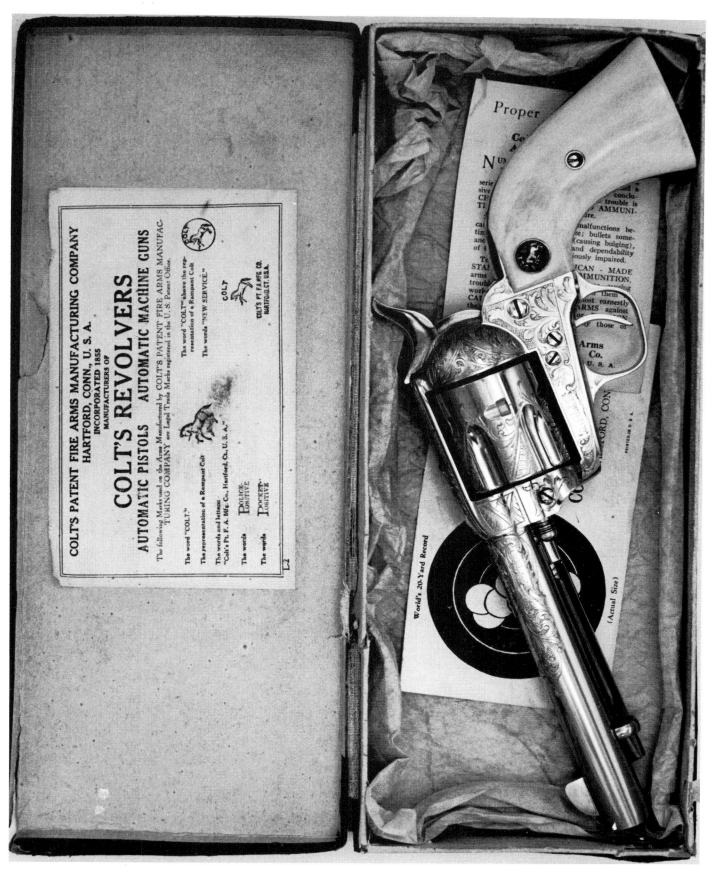

A transitional Single Action revolver by Glahn, again showing the influence of the Helfricht style; note punched dot background and the emphasis on scroll rather than a leaf, vine, and floral treatment. Factory ledgers list the revolver, number 341711, as: .45, 5½", nickel, ivory, engraved in style No. 2, sold and shipped to Lult Kemeyen Company, Cleveland, April 1921. *(David S. Woloch Collection)*

A scarce caliber engraved, .44 Russian and S & W Special number 339901 is documented in the Colt ledgers as 5-1/2" barrel, nickel plated, ivory grips, engraved and shipped in June 1920 to Ellery Arms Co. The caliber is listed as .44 S & W, but that simply represents an abbreviation of the full calibration, as clearly marked on the left side of the barrel. Important also as an early example of Wilbur A. Glahn engraving. *(William A. Dascher Collection)*

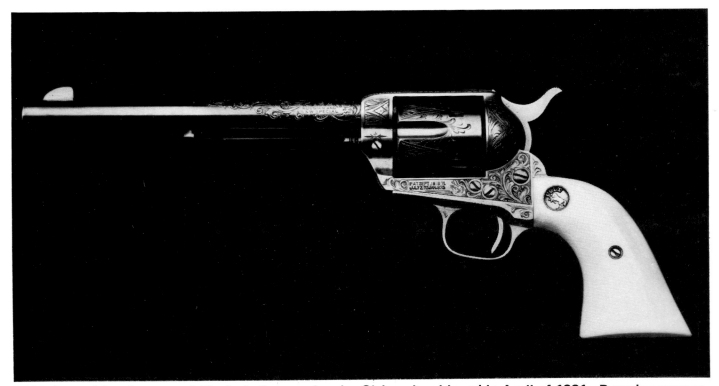

A third transitional engraved Single Action revolver by Glahn, also shipped in April of 1921. B grade coverage. Colt records list: .44 Russian and S & W Special, 7½", blue (and case hardened), ivory, engraved, shipped to Chief J. D. O'Meara. Coverage (as on the previous two transition guns) on the barrel, ejector rod housing, cylinder, frame and gripstraps. Serial number 341715. *(David S. Woloch Collection)*

Historic personal Single Action Army of film mogul and a founder of Paramount Studios, Jesse L. Lasky. Factory ledgers note: .44 Russian (and S. & W. Special), 5-1/2" barrel, blue (and case hardened), carved steerhead pearl grips, engraved, sold to B.H. Dyas Co., Los Angeles, and shipped to Jesse L. Lasky, September 21, 1921; one gun only in shipment. Quite out of the ordinary pattern of decoration by Wilbur Glahn. Among Lasky's friends, colleagues, and sometimes employees were Western film stars, directors, and producers. Research with family members suggests a likely primary reason for his purchase of the revolver was for Lasky to own a cowboy style Colt six-shooter. Serial number 343237. *(Wallace Beinfeld Collection)*

Single Action 340573 was shipped July 1920 to Corporal James Burns; the Colt records further noting: .44-40 caliber, 5-1/2'' barrel, engraved, nickel plated. An early specimen of Glahn work, while still under the influence of Helfricht's style. *(Paul Sorrell Collection)*

One of the earliest of Glahn engraved revolvers, Single Action 341201 was shipped in November 1920 to A.J. Anderson Co., Fort Worth, Texas, and was sold to Stauffer Eshleman & Co., New Orleans; .45 caliber, 4-3/4'' barrel, nickel plated, pearl grips, and engraved. Surprisingly, six revolvers of this description were sent out in that shipment. The influence of Helfricht on 341201 is particularly evident on the frame, loading gate, and barrel. *(William A. Dascher Collection)*

Interesting early example of Glahn engraving, showing the Helfricht influence, Single Action 341710 left the factory in February 1921, shipped to Blish, Mize & Silliman Hardware Co., Atchison, Kansas; .45 caliber, 5-1/2" barrel, blue (and case hardened) finish, engraved, and with pearl grips. *(William L. Rogoski Collection)*

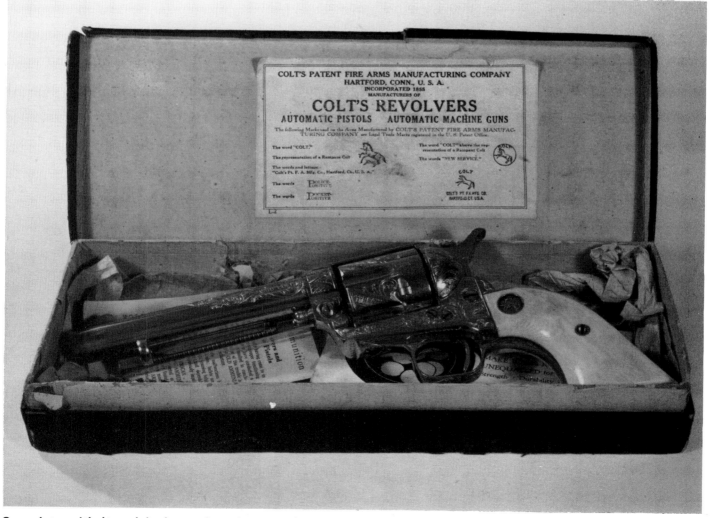

Complete with its original pasteboard carton (the label at end marked ENGRAVED), Single Action 341711 is listed by Colt's as .45 caliber, 5-1/2" barrel, nickel plated, ivory grips, engraved grade 2, and shipped in April of 1921 to Luetkemeyer Co., Cleveland, Ohio. *(William L. Rogoski Collection)*

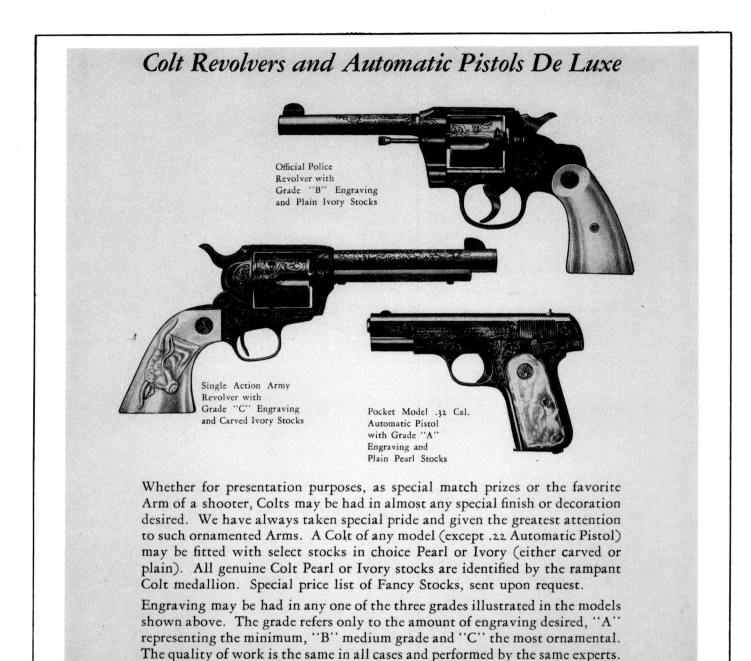

Colt Revolvers and Automatic Pistols De Luxe

Official Police
Revolver with
Grade "B" Engraving
and Plain Ivory Stocks

Single Action Army
Revolver with
Grade "C" Engraving
and Carved Ivory Stocks

Pocket Model .32 Cal.
Automatic Pistol
with Grade "A"
Engraving and
Plain Pearl Stocks

Whether for presentation purposes, as special match prizes or the favorite Arm of a shooter, Colts may be had in almost any special finish or decoration desired. We have always taken special pride and given the greatest attention to such ornamented Arms. A Colt of any model (except .22 Automatic Pistol) may be fitted with select stocks in choice Pearl or Ivory (either carved or plain). All genuine Colt Pearl or Ivory stocks are identified by the rampant Colt medallion. Special price list of Fancy Stocks, sent upon request.

Engraving may be had in any one of the three grades illustrated in the models shown above. The grade refers only to the amount of engraving desired, "A" representing the minimum, "B" medium grade and "C" the most ornamental. The quality of work is the same in all cases and performed by the same experts.

Also we can furnish Colt Arms with any special designs desired, with full gold or silver plating or inlaid State or National seals, etc., also Pearl or Ivory Stocks with inlaid enamel initials or emblems in colors. The work in this department is performed by highly skilled craftsmen only, who have had years of experience in this painstaking and beautiful designing. Estimates for all work of this character are furnished in advance.

Colt's engraving service, as pictured and described in the company's 1932 catalogue. The scroll style is that of Wilbur Glahn. A, B, and C grades featured, as were carved ivory and pearl stocks, special plating, gold or silver inlaying, and enameling on pearl and ivory. Note the company's statement: "We have always taken special pride and given the greatest attention to such ornamented Arms." Page 8 of the catalogue stated: "Silver and gold mountings, inlays, engravings and etching of special designs that delight fastidious sportsmen are done in a separate department by skilled artisans whose work recalls the celebrated armorers of old." Wilbur Glahn's work did not appear pictured in a Colt catalogue until the issue of 1929, some ten years after he joined the company. This engraving page from the 1932 catalogue is virtually identical to the illustration and text in the 1929 issue. Colt's catalogues of 1929 through 1941 show no significant variation in presenting material on engraving, and are basically as pictured and quoted above. Elsewhere in these issues were references to the availability of nickel, silver or gold plating, done by the factory, in "a very heavy smooth plate". *(John Hintlian Collection)*

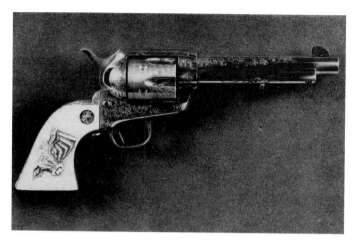

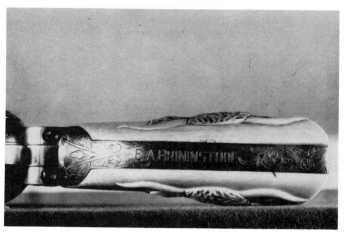

An early specimen of Glahn's own style; Single Action number 343242 dates from c. 1922. Coverage is the B grade, and the finish is silver plating, with the cylinder in gold. Factory steerhead ivory grips, also attributed to Wilbur Glahn, and quite rare with the carved design on both sides. Brininstool was a newspaperman and a prolific writer on the American West, one of the first authorities on General George Armstrong Custer. See also matching Officers Model Target revolver, serial number 515559, later in this chapter. *(Collection of the late Murray G. Peterson)*

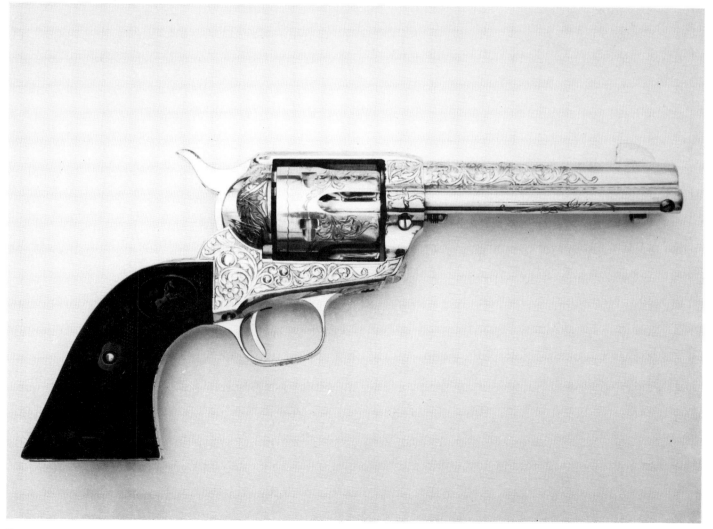

Grade B coverage on Single Action Army number 347911. Listed in Colt's shipping records: .38-40, 4¾", nickel, rubber grips, engraved, shipped to Albert Steinfeld & Company, Tucson, Arizona, October 1925. The style of Wilbur Glahn is distinctly in contrast to that of his predecessor, Cuno Helfricht, and this is especially obvious in gun number **347911**. *(David S. Woloch Collection)*

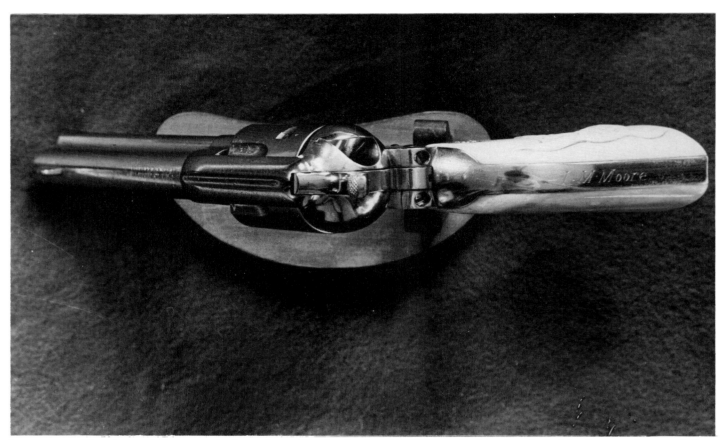

A rare combination of features is found on Single Action 347679: Gold plated finish, ivory grips, and the backstrap inscribed *L·M·Moore,* Colt ledgers further note .45 caliber, 4-3/4'' barrel, and shipment in June 1925 to Belknap Hardware & Manufacturing Co., Louisville, Kentucky. *(William A. Dascher Collection)*

A most distinctive feature of number 348094 Single Action is the carved monogrammed and engraved ivory grip (as shown), and the right grip of carved steerhead design. Other features documented by Colt records include .45 caliber, 5-1/2'' barrel, blue (and case hardened) finish, engraved, shipped in October 1925 to Ben Ziesman, and sold to Montana Hardware Co., of Butte. *(Albert E. Brichaux Collection)*

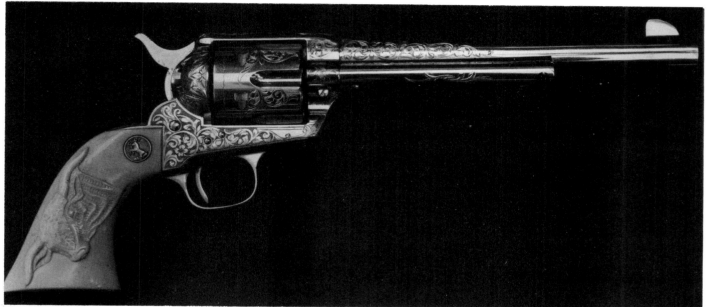

With its gold overlaid backstrap inscription and full nickel plating, Single Action 347103 ranks high in rarity for embellished Colt firearms. The factory records note: .45 caliber, 7-1/2'' barrel, nickel plated, steerhead carved ivory grips, engraved, R.A.LAMKIN on backstrap, sold to A.J. Anderson of Fort Worth, Texas, and shipped to R.A. Lamkin, July 1925. *(David S. Woloch Collection)*

Colt records state Single Action number 350673 to have been shipped in March of 1929, to Frank T. Budge Co., Miami, Florida; .45 caliber, 5-1/2'' barrel, finished in blue (and case hardening), with carved steerhead ivory grips, and grade 2 engraving. *(Albert E. Brichaux Collection)*

A quite distinctive decorative variation appears on Single Action number 348726, shipped from Colt in January of 1926. The monogram inlaid on the pearl grips and engraved on the right side of the frame is listed as an R.H. The left side of the frame features a rare engraved rampant colt, to the *left* of the patent markings. Recorded by Colt as: .45, 5½'', blue (and case hardened), pearl (relief carved steerhead on the right grip), engraved in style No. 2 with R.H. on side, sold to Von Lengerke and Antoine, Chicago, and shipped in January 1926 to F.A. Mudgett. The owner carried the revolver in a hand tooled leather holster which also bore the R.H. monogram. *(Raymond H. Vanyek Collection)*

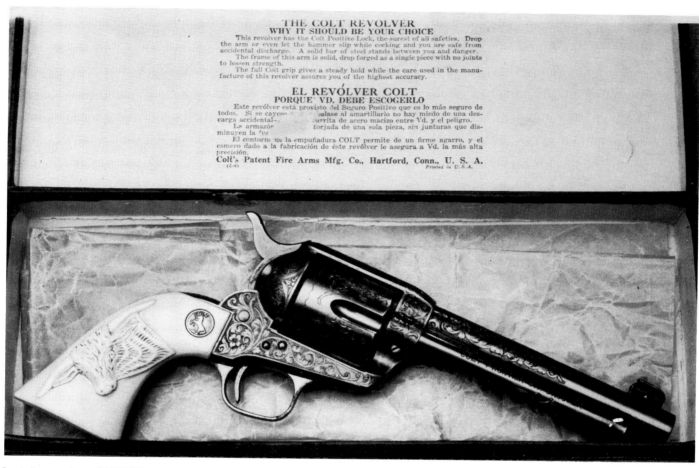

Serial number 350327 grade B Single Action in original shipping carton, and with the rarity of a monogram on the butt (H·O·M·) and the hand inscribed marking on the ejector tube. Colt ledgers document the above, and also list: .45, 5½", blue (and case hardened), ivory grips in steerhead pattern, and *(rare)* target front sight. H.O.M. was H.O. Marietta of Des Plaines, Illinois. *(George S. Lewis Jr. Collection)*

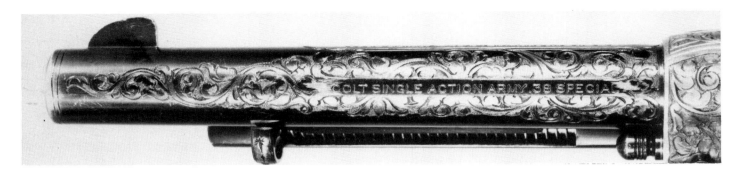

Number 352778 Single Action features the supreme rarity of a 6" barrel, as well as .38 Special caliber (scarce few engraved), a butt swivel, and what appears to be grade C *(plus)* **engraved coverage. The ejector rod head is engraved (customary on grade C coverage), and the grips are Colt medallion ivory. A leaf design runs down the backstrap.** *(William L. Rogoski Collection)*

Single Action 351872 is in .45 caliber, with 4-3/4" barrel, engraved, has carved steerhead ivory grips, and is blue and case hardened. *(William L. Rogoski Collection)*

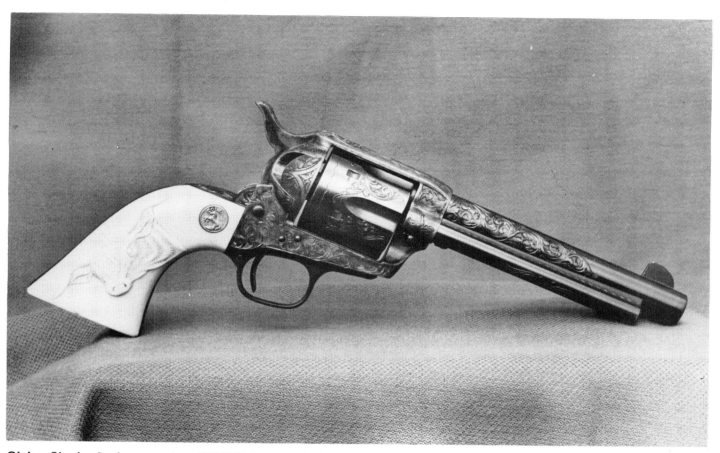

Glahn Single Action number 350673 is recorded by the factory books as Grade 2 engraved, with steerhead carved ivory grips, blue (and case hardened) finish, 5-1/2" barrel, .45 caliber, shipped in March 1929 to Frank T. Budge Co., Miami, Florida, under factory order 12369/1. *(Dr. Johnny Spellman Collection)*

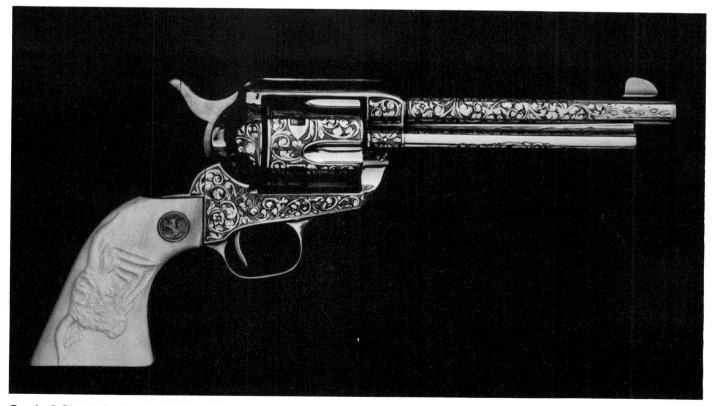

Grade C Single Action by Wilbur Glahn; recorded by Colt as: .38-40, 5½", silver plated, ivory, engraved; shipped in October 1935 to Shapleigh Hardware Company, St. Louis, Missouri. Comparison with No. 2 and B grade revolvers shows the extensive degree of coverage on a C revolver of the period. *(David S. Woloch Collection)*

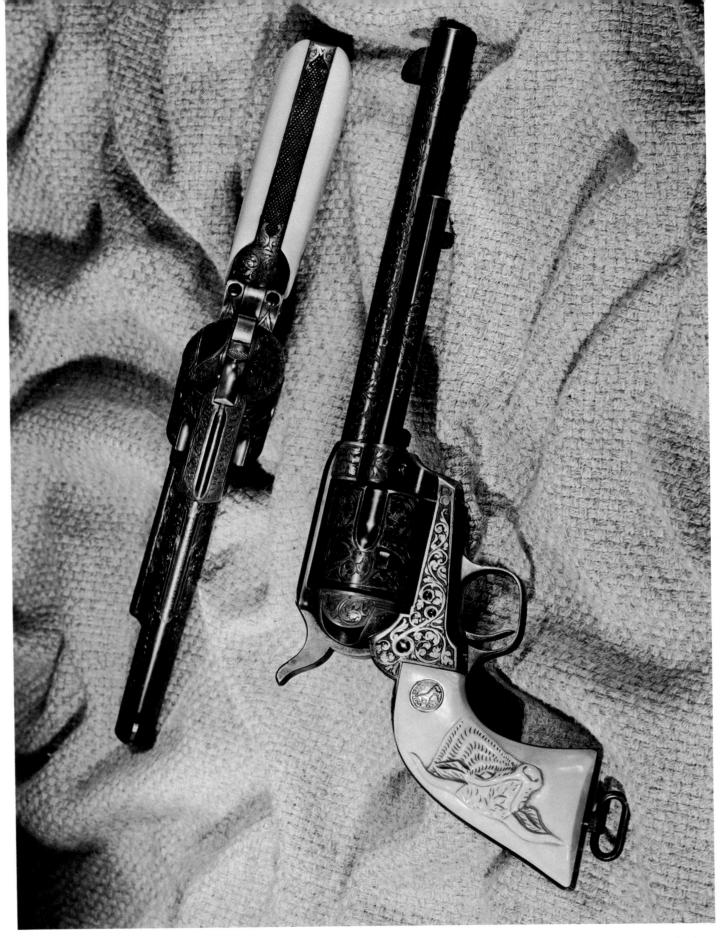

Single Action Army revolvers, serial numbers 354042 (bottom) and 354497 (top). Both by Wilbur A. Glahn, and engraved within a matter of months of each other. Number 354042 is listed in Colt ledgers as .45 caliber, 7½'' barrel, blue, with carved ivory steerhead grips, engraved; shipped to Indianapolis, Indiana October 9, 1931, and only one gun in the shipment. Number 354497, a .38 Special, is recorded as 7½'' barrel, blue, ivory grips, engraved, and inscribed on the butt (done in matching style to the engraving). Note checkered backstrap, Shipped to Detroit, Michigan, April 23, 1932; one gun in the shipment. The revolvers make a striking pair of Single Actions by Glahn. *(Jonathan M. Peck Collection/Photograph, Meyers Studio)*

Built on factory order 14679/1, Single Action 351933 was shipped in May 1928, to Ruckman Store Co., and sold to Belknap Hardware Mfg. Co., Louisville, Kentucky. Colt records also note .45 caliber, 4-3/4" barrel, blue (and case hardened) finish, carved steerhead ivory grips, and engraved. *(Jack Slaughter Collection)*

Shipped in September of 1929 to Abercrombie & Fitch Co., New York, number 352803 Single Action is further recorded in factory ledgers as .45 caliber, with 5-1/2" barrel, blued (and case hardened) finish, with ivory grips, and engraved grade C. *(Albert E. Brichaux Collection)*

Single Action 353113 appears in the Colt ledgers as follows: .45 caliber, 5-1/2'' barrel, nickel plated, steerhead carved ivory grips, grade C engraving, and shipped in August 1930 to W.H. Hoegee Co., Los Angeles, California. *(Albert E. Brichaux Collection)*

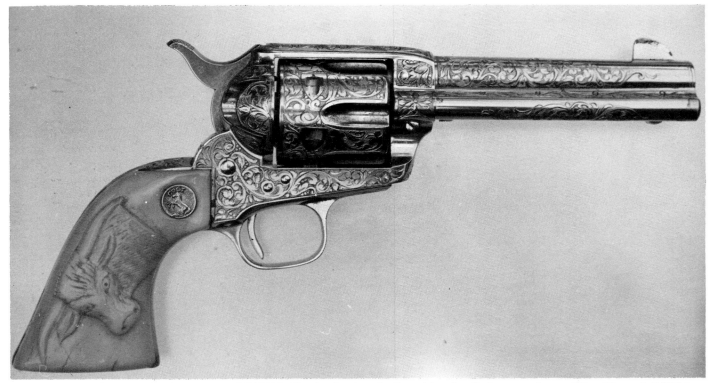

Rather profusely engraved, number 354056 Single Action is listed in the Colt records as .45 caliber, 4-3/4'' barrel, nickel plated, ivory grips, engraved; on the backstrap, A.G. Lemos. Shipment was to Neucis Hardware & Implement; in November 1930. Research has documented the revolver as later the personal sidearm of Harold Slack, Co. A, Texas Rangers; Slack also served the U.S. government as a customs agent. *(Paul Sorrell Collection)*

Single Action Army made in the early 1900's, and later returned to the factory (approximately late 1934) for engraving. The & mark appears on the right side of the rear bow of the triggerguard; nickel finish; pearl grips. Floyd Randolph was sheriff of Ardmore, Oklahoma c. 1935-40. Revolver presented to him by Texas oil man V.S. Joiner on the occasion of Randolph's election to office. Present owner purchased the revolver from the sheriff's daughter. *(Paul Sorrell Collection)*

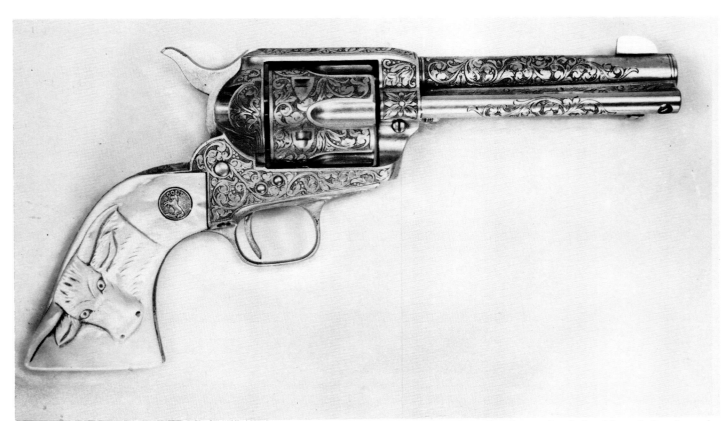

Rare fully gold plated Single Action number 354396, presentation inscribed on the left side of the barrel: *To Arthur/from a Grateful County.* Gift was made in Tiffin, Ohio, 1931, to Sheriff A.L. Stuckert, on his retirement. .38-40 caliber; note relief carved steerhead grips, and the special ALS monogram on the left stock, done in enamel. *(Jonathan M. Peck Collection)*

An extremely rare feature of Single Action number 354541 is the shrine emblem inlaid (quoting the factory ledgers) on the carved ivory grips. The records further note: .45 caliber, 5-1/2" barrel, blue (and case hardened) finish, engraved, and shipped to Spetnagel Hardware Co., Chillicothe, Ohio. The factory order number was 19921/1. *(Paul Sorrell Collection)*

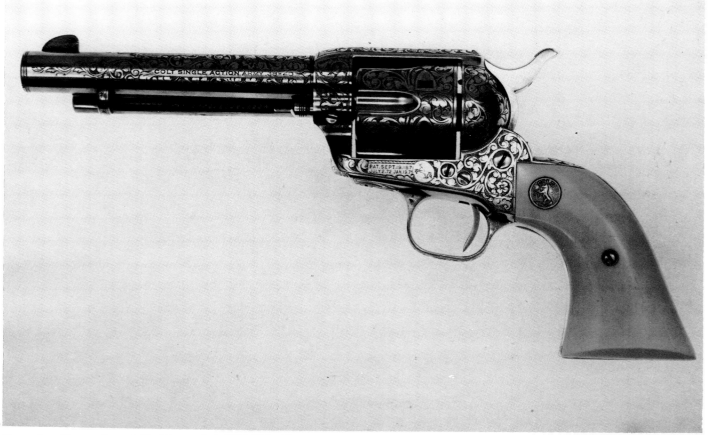

Rare in silver plated finish, serial 355459 Single Action is further covered by Colt records as .38-40 caliber, 5-1/2" barrel, carved steerhead ivory grips, engraved, and shipped in October 1935 to Shapleigh Hardware Co., St. Louis, Missouri. Compare with Single Action 353113 for minor differences in executing the scroll designs. *(Albert E. Brichaux Collection)*

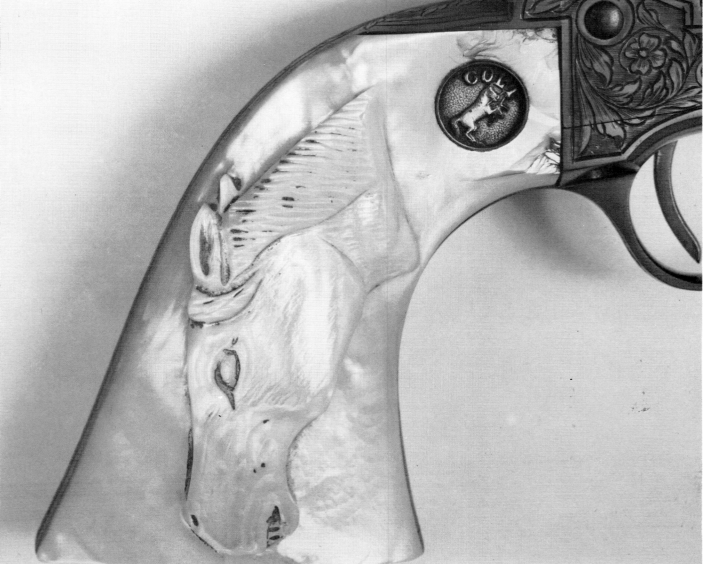

Quite rare horsehead carved pearl grips grace Single Action finished in blue and case hardening, with 5-1/2'' barrel, and in .45 caliber. *(Private Collection)*

Serial number 350804 Single Action; listed as grade No. 2 engraving. Comparing the pattern with number 348726 and with other specimens shows that Glahn often varied details from one job to the next, to avoid repetition and boredom. Colt ledgers list: .45, 5½", blue (and case hardened), ivory with carved steerhead, engraved grade No. 2, sold and shipped to Powell & Clement Company, Cincinatti, Ohio, January 1929. Though not illustrated, the gun is complete with the original factory carton. Note the new type rampant colt grip medallions, no longer the deep set style with crisp detail and sharp relief. *(David S. Woloch Collection)*

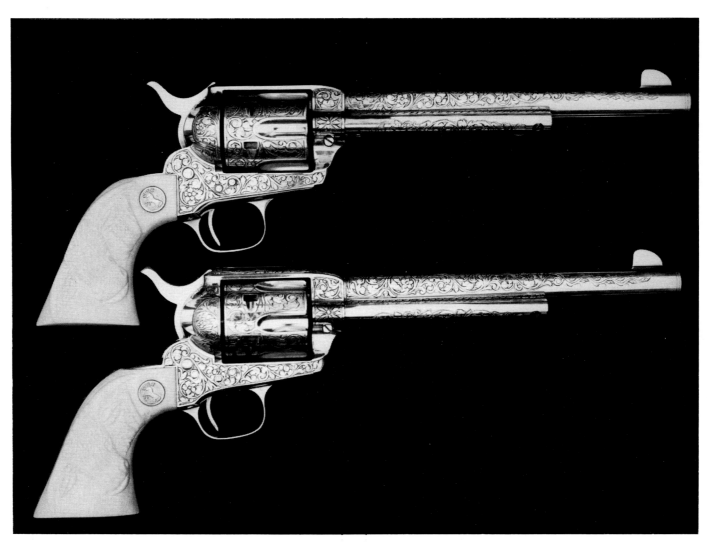

Matched pair of Single Action revolvers; numbers 356118 and 356293. C engraved in the distinctive Wilbur Glahn style. Colt records list: .45, 7½″, silver plated, sold and shipped to Hoffman Hardware Company, January 1938. By error the engraving and ivory grips were not included in the factory listing. Matched pairs of engraved Single Action Army revolvers — from any period — are of considerable rarity. *(David S. Woloch Collection)*

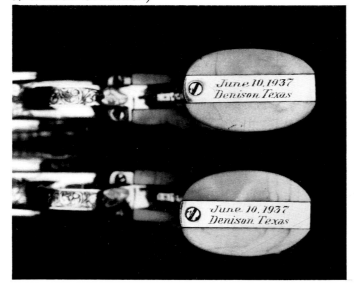

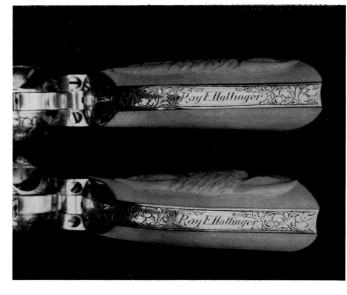

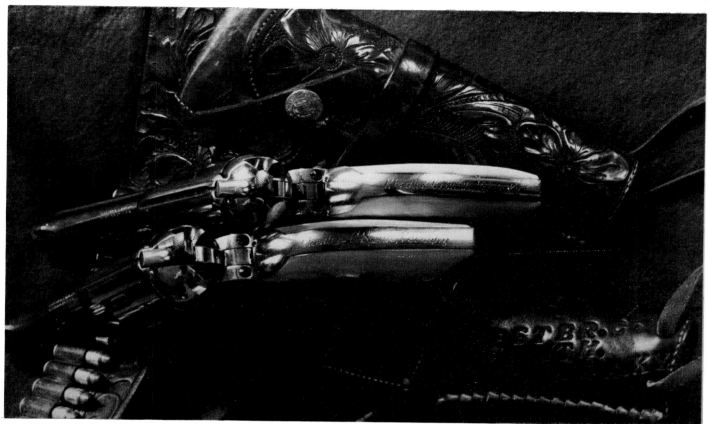

Built for an agent of the F.B.I., Single Actions 357434 and 357435 are documented by the Colt factory as .357 Magnum caliber, 4-3/4" barrels, nickel plated, with backstrap roll marking, shipped in October 1940 to The Sutcliffe Company, Louisville, Kentucky. The revolvers were processed on factory order 9370 and have a 3-1/2 pound trigger pull. Information received with the revolvers identifies agent Smith as from Verda, Harlan County, Kentucky, and indicates he occasionally worked for the F.B.I. in an undercover capacity. Among other distinctions, Smith served approximately 15 consecutive years as the Grand Marshal of the Kentucky Mountain Laurel Festival, Pineville, Kentucky. These revolvers were carried as service pieces (note holster markings) and also for big game hunting in the North and Northwest. A charging bear was killed by Smith with one of the revolvers. *(William A. Dascher Collection)*

At the tail end of prewar Colt Single Actions, number 357500 was shipped in September of 1940, to Shapleigh Hardware Co., St. Louis, Missouri, and is further listed in the Colt ledgers as: .38 Special, 5-1/2" barrel, blue (and case hardened) finish, and engraved grade C. The grips are carved pearl steerhead. *(George S. Lewis, Jr. Collection)*

The highest serial numbered, latest shipped, nickel plated, engraved, .45 Colt Single Action Army from the prewar production known to collectors, number 357554 is documented in the Colt ledgers as follows: shipped January 30th 1941, to Von Lengerke & Antoine, Chicago, engraved grade C, with carved pearl steerhead grips, 7-1/2" barrel, nickel plated, .45 caliber. Certainly a milestone in the history of engraved Colt Single Actions. *(Johnny Spellman, D.V.M., Collection)*

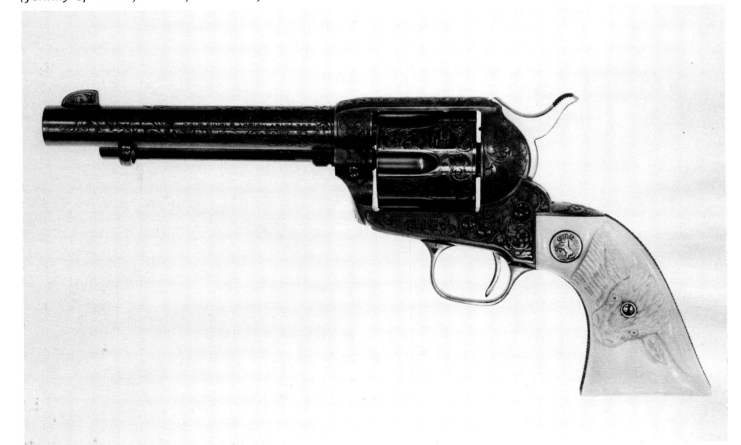

One of the more elaborate specimens of Glahn work, number 357593 is in .357 Magnum caliber, is blue and case hardened, and the ledger notes carved steerhead ivory, 3 lb. trigger pull, grade C engraved, shipped in January 1941 to H. & D. Folsom Arms Co., New York. Note presence of engraving even on the front sight, and the fact that both backstrap and triggerguard strap (as well as trigger) are checkered. The steerhead ivory grips are carved both sides. *(Dr. Johnny Spellman Collection)*

Rare Bisley engraved by Glahn, this revolver, number 282422, in .44 Russian and S & W Special, was shipped in October 1906 to Schoverling, Daly and Gales. Sometime after c. 1920, the revolver was returned to the factory, and Glahn engraved. Blue and case hardened finish; gripstraps and the trigger hand checkered. *(William L. Rogoski Collection)*

A set of Bisley and Single Action revolvers engraved by Glahn to match, late in the 1930's. Bisley number 263480 was first shipped from the factory in 1905; Single Action number 344554 left c. 1923. Blued and case hardened finishes; factory refinish marks, * and &, on triggerguards. These pistols form the only set of an engraved Bisley and Single Action known from the Glahn period. Formerly in the William M. Locke Collection. *(David S. Woloch Collection)*

Processed on Colt factory order 7318/1. New Service number 318984 was shipped to Wolf & Klar, Ft. Worth, Texas, in April of 1923. Factory records note the following additional information: .45 caliber; 5-1/2" barrel; nickel plated, engraved. The scrolls are of a smaller size than normally found on Glahn engraved pieces, while the coverage is still rather profuse. New Service Shooting Masters were made c. 1932 — c. 1941; less than ten were engraved; about five were inscribed. *(Paul Sorrell Collection)*

Serial number 314785 of the Police Positive .32 on a .38 frame. Grade A coverage; the revolver recorded in the factory ledgers: .32, 4'', nickel, pearl grips, engraved, sold and shipped to Abercrombie & Fitch Company, New York, September 1930. Note contrast in pattern from other A grade revolvers illustrated. Considering as a group the Police Positive .38 revolvers (produced from 1905 through 1943; Number 1 through 177000 range; number 329000 through 406725): About 170 specimens were engraved; about seven of them with gold inlay (one including *rare* barrel bands in silver). About half of the total number of engraved guns went to Norwell Shapleigh of St. Louis, c. 1912. About 88 pieces are recorded as specially inscribed or monogrammed, about three of these *gold* inlaid. *J.B. CLEMENT* was gold inlaid on the backstrap of serial number 1. *(David S. Woloch Collection)*

Police Positive Special number 327712 was processed on Colt factory order 16653/6. Ledgers state it was shipped to the town of Arlington, Massachusetts, for Thomas Urquhart, Chief of Police; .38 caliber, 4'' barrel, blue finish, engraved; shipment in June of 1929. *(Paul Sorrell Collection)*

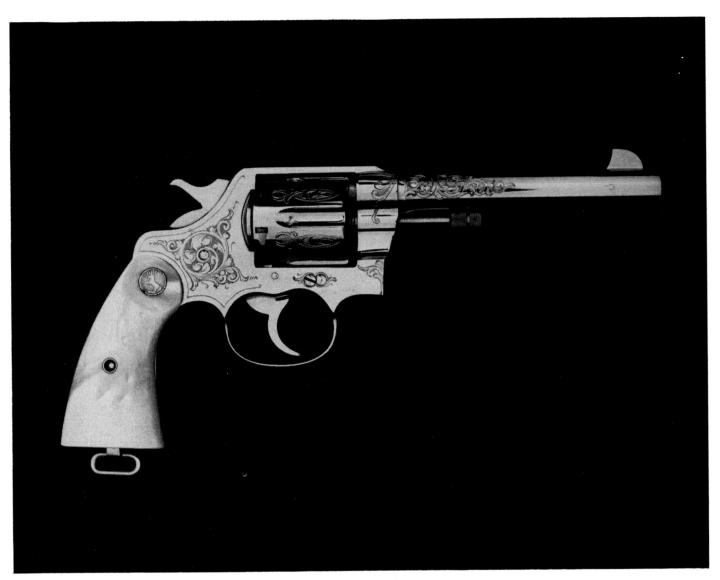

Specimen of Glahn's A grade coverage on a New Service revolver, number 329829. Colt records state: .45, 5½″, nickel, pearl, engraved, sold to Simmons Hardware Company, St. Louis, Missouri, and shipped to Bowens & Son, July 1928. The backstrap inscription is illustrated. Compare with number 314785 Police Positive .32; the engraving is identical. The New Service Model was produced from 1898 through 1944. Colt ledgers show less than 75 engraved, and less than 100 bearing engraved inscriptions or monograms. A small proportion were gold inlaid, mainly on inscriptions. *(David S. Woloch Collection)*

Production records of the Colt factory show Army Special number 335818 to have been engraved, under the date entry January 6th 1922. Glahn scroll in the style of Cuno Helfricht. *(Paul Sorrell Collection)*

Officers Model Target number 5577 has the rare combination of engraved and an inscribed frame. Colt ledgers note: .22 caliber, 6″ barrel, blue finish, engraved, inscribed on frame, and shipped in July 1931 to Howard J. Knutson; processed on factory order 11984/1. *(Albert E. Brichaux Collection)*

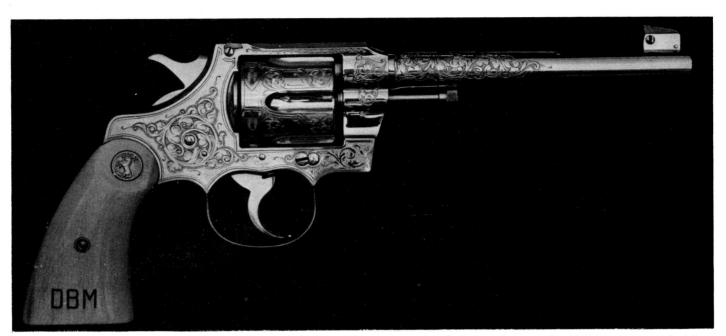

Officers Model Target number 585683 listed by Colt as nickel plated, ivory grips, DBM on stock in blue, engraved, shipped in 1934 to D.B. Mannoni, a police officer at State Highway Patrol Post. Coverage is a B grade, and the monogram ivory grips are rare. *(David S. Woloch Collection)*

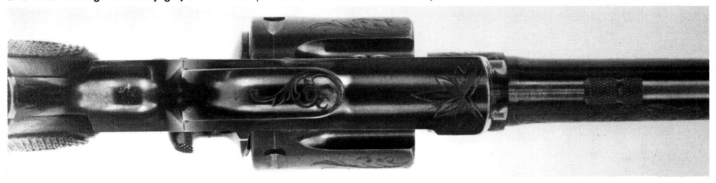

A truly exotic Colt deluxe is Officers Model Target number 8477; its triggerguard cutaway. Factory ledgers listed the following features: .22 caliber, 6" barrel, blue finish, grade A engraved, shipped in March 1934 to Lawlor Sporting Goods Co., Lincoln, Nebraska. The scroll is rather unusual Glahn style, since it lacks any background shading. Records do not indicate the cutaway guard, but that detail is attributed to Colt work. *(Albert E. Brichaux Collection)*

B engraved Shooting Master number 348289. Shipped from Colt in April 1940; .38, 6'', blue, pearl, engraved — grade B, sold and shipped to F.W. Robinson Ltd., Kentville, Nova Scotia. Note the *Col. F.W.R.* monogram. Heavy leatherette covered Colt carton (maroon color), with SHOOTING MASTER imprinted on the top of the lid in gold leaf; also marked inside lid as illustrated. *(David S. Woloch Collection)*

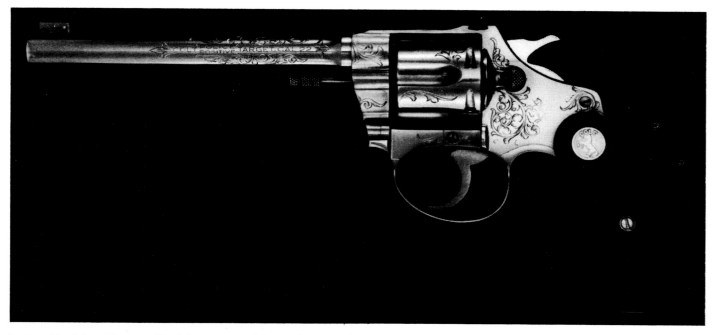

Police Positive Target Model number 41512 (c. 1935). .22 caliber, 6'' barrel. Grade A scroll coverage, blued finish. Checkered walnut grips; retains original carton. Target pistols are seldom found engraved. Of the model G Police Positive .22 Target revolvers (made from 1910 through 1925), approximately ten were engraved; one of that number was gold inlaid. Seven Model G revolvers bore inscriptions, one of them having a silver plaque on the grip. Colt executive C.L.F. Robinson, in April 1910, received a deluxe specimen gold inlaid on steel and on the pearl grips. The top strap of that gun bore a C.L.F.R. crest. Of the Model C (produced 1925-1941), three specimens were engraved; about 13 were inscribed. *(David S. Woloch Collection)*

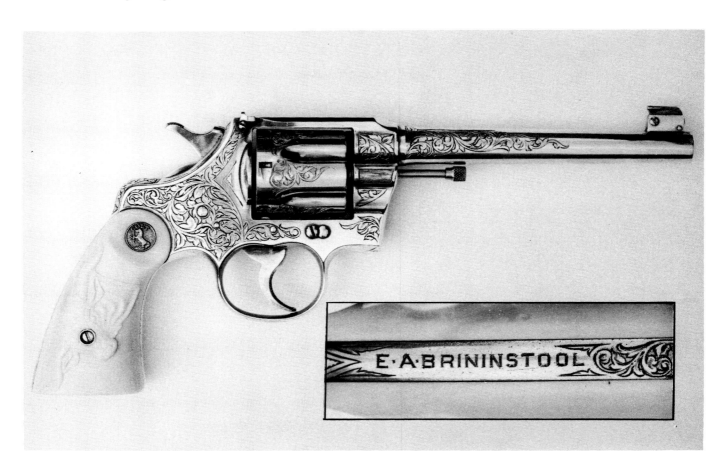

E. A. Brininstool's Officers Model Target number 515559. Grade B engraving with backstrap inscription. Recorded by Colt as: .38, 6" silver plated with gold plated cylinder, ivory grips with carved oxhead on both sides, engraved, E. A. Brininstool on the backstrap, sold to *Hunter-Trader-Trapper* magazine, shipped to Brininstool, October 1924. A mate to the Single Action Army number 343242, pictured earlier in this chapter, also by Glahn, and with matching finish and carved ivory grips. Pictured in color on page 290. *(David S. Woloch Collection)*

Shipped in August 1929 to P. Von Frantzius (inventor of "Franzite" grips), Officer's Model number 560150 is further recorded in the Colt ledgers as .38 caliber, 7-1/2" barrel, 1/8 inch sights, blued finish, and engraved. The revolver was built on factory order 16946/1, and the grips are ivory. *(Albert E. Brichaux Collection)*

Officers Model Target number 538042; grade B engraving. Colt's records show: .38, 4" with gold bead front sight, blue, engraved, sold and shipped to H. & D. Folsom Arms Company, New York, April 1928. Includes the original Colt carton. Note: Rare in this model engraved with the 4" barrel length. American eagle and shield carved pearl grips. Compare scroll pattern with the Grade B Brininstool Officers Model number 515559. *(David S. Woloch Collection)*

Official Police number 554637, grade B engraved. Colt's records state: .38, 5", blue, pearl grips, engraved, sold and shipped to Von Lengerke & Antoine, Chicago, February 1931. Comparison with Official Police number 548601, c. 1929, shows an identical pattern of B grade coverage. With Wilbur Glahn it appears there was less variation between guns of the same engraved grades of coverage than in the case of Helfricht and his shop. Gun number 548601, also in the Woloch Collection, is not illustrated. The approximate total of Official Police revolvers engraved from c. 1927 to date is less than 350. Under 100 in that period bore hand engraved inscriptions or monograms (this number does not include several hundreds with shooting competition inscriptions). None of the Official Police .22 caliber revolvers was engraved; ten bore factory engraved inscriptions. *(David S. Woloch Collection)*

An intriguing grade B revolver, Official Police number 587963. Colt records list the following: .38, 5'', blue, pearl, engraved, sold and shipped to the Town of New Castle, Chappaqua, New York, in August of 1933. The recipient of this presentation is alleged to have been a madame in a New Castle bordello. *(David S. Woloch Collection)*

As rare as is gold inlaying on Colt firearms, the use of silver is far more rare. Number 583469 Official Police left the Colt plant silver inlaid, engraved, with ivory grips, .38 caliber, 4'' barrel, January of 1934, shipped to Abercrombie & Fitch Co., New York City. The backstrap also bears an inscription: W. DALRYMPLE — T.P.P.D. The silver scrolls are on the frame, cylinder, and barrel. *(David S. Woloch Collection)*

Extreme rarity of an Official Police presentation from J.H. Fitz-Gerald of Colt's to Dr. S.M. Martin, documented in the Colt ledgers as follows: .38 caliber, 6" barrel (1/10" front sight), blued finish, engraved, 3-1/2 pound trigger pull, shipped to J.H. Fitz-Gerald of Colt Patent Firearms, Hartford, in December of 1929. Fitz was the well known ballistics expert, showman, and public relations figure who served with the Colt firm for many years. Martin authored a chapter in the Fitz-Gerald book, SHOOTING, and was Dr. Schuler McCuller Martin (M.D.), of Troy, New York. *(Ronald N. Swanson Collection)*

Both monogrammed and engraved, Model 1908 .25 Automatic number 394759 is listed in the Colt records as: .25 caliber, 2" barrel, blue finish, pearl grips, grade A engraved, sold to T.P. Calkin, and shipped in November 1931 to Harold Newcombe. The F.W.R. monogram on the right side of the frame was for F.W. Robinson, Kentville, Nova Scotia, and comparison should be made with the Shooting Master on page 310. *(George S. Lewis, Jr. Collection)*

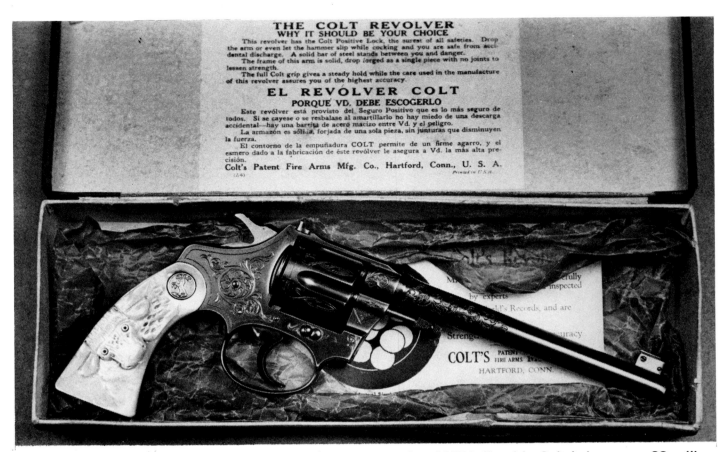

Extremely rare C frame Police Positive Target/revolver, number 31651, listed in Colt ledgers as: .22 caliber, 6" barrel, blue, engraved, carved steerhead pearl grips, shipped in April 1926 to John Pritzlaff & Co., Milwaukee, Wisconsin. Complete with its original pasteboard box. *(George S. Lewis, Jr. Collection)*

Shipped to the original Abercrombie & Fitch Co., New York, in July 1939, number 457447 Detective Special was engraved grade B, and is further recorded as having pearl grips, finished in blue, .38 caliber, and having a 2″ barrel. The factory order was number 8519. *(Albert E. Brichaux Collection)*

Documented as engraved grade A, number 131108 .380 Pocket Automatic was shipped in December 1938, to L.J. Eppinger, Inc., Detroit, Michigan; nickel plated, with pearl grips. It left with another pistol of identical configuration, a matched pair. *(Albert E. Brichaux Collection)*

Featuring carved pearl grips and scroll engraving, number 356629 .25 Automatic is nickel plated, and was shipped September 6, 1925 to Quinn & Co., Providence, Rhode Island. The factory records state gold plating as the original finish, but this is considered a clerk's error, since pistol shows no signs of any other finish but nickel. *(Paul Sorrell Collection)*

Grade A coverage on Model 1911A1 pistol number C147731 (c. 1926). .45 caliber, blue, ivory and engraved. Typical Glahn style. Of the first model National Match Automatic (c. 1933 – c. 1941) about 25 pistols were engraved, three of them gold inlaid (one of the latter made without a triggerguard). Some 20 pistols bore hand engraved inscriptions. The Ace .22 Automatic pistol: Colt records indicate that of the production run from 1931-41, and in 1947, a total of about 22 was engraved, five of them gold inlaid. About ten Ace pistols were hand inscribed. The Service Model Ace Automatic (c. 1935-42; 1945): Eight were engraved; three were inscribed (two of them in gold). The .22-.45 Conversion Kit (c. 1938-43; 1946): Four were engraved. The .45-.22 Conversion Unit (c. 1938-40): numbers U4, U5, and U6 were engraved. The Super .38 Automatic (c. 1929 to date): About 32 were engraved pre-World War II; about 17 inscribed in the same period. About six postwar pistols were engraved, a few more than that number hand inscribed. The Super Match .38 Automatic (c. 1935 – c. 1941): 36 specimens engraved, one pistol inscribed. *(David S. Woloch Collection)*

Serial number 408907 of the Model 1908 .25 caliber Automatic pistol. Shipped in October 1940 to Peden Iron and Steel Company, Houston, Texas; blue, ivory, grade A engraved. The coverage appears to be more than grade A, but the pistol's diminutive size squeezes the same A work from a larger gun onto a much smaller area. Manufactured from 1908-41, the Model 1908 pistol includes the work of Helfricht, Kornbrath, Glahn, and W. H. Gough. About 375 are recorded engraved, about eight having gold inlay. Less than 75 bore engraved inscriptions or monograms, about three done in gold. Tom Mix had pistol number 291619 (c. 1921), inscribed on the frame with his name, finished in silver plating, and fitted with pearl grips. *(William H. Hays Collection)*

Grade A coverage on Woodsman number 61262. Shipped to Murta Appleton and Company, Philadelphia, in March 1930; .22, 6½", blue, engraved style No. 1. Typical Wilbur Glahn scroll style quite clear on the flat surfaces. Approximately 115 Woodsman Target model pistols (1915-43) were engraved, one of them inlaid with gold. About 50 were inscribed. Data includes the Sport and Target model pistols of the period. Of the First Model Match Target Woodsman (1938-44), about eight were engraved, about six inscribed (one of these gold inlaid). *(David S. Woloch Collection)*

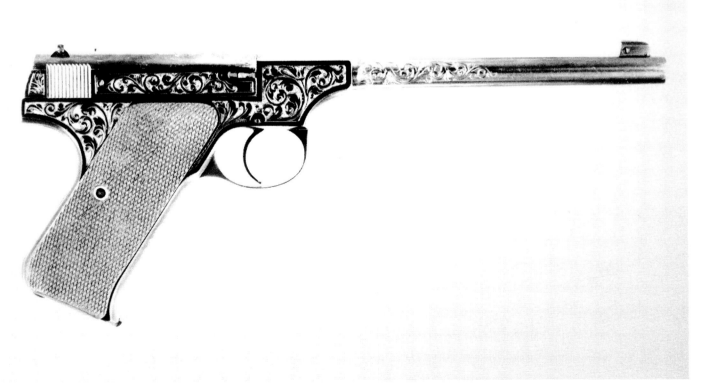

Grade B coverage on Woodsman number 59084. Shipped to Wolf & Klar, Fort Worth, Texas, in January of 1929. 6½", blue, checkered walnut grips. *(R. Q. Sutherland Collection)*

Colt ledgers record the following on Woodsman number 130772: Shipped in March of 1938, .22 caliber, 6-1/2″ barrel, blue finish, wood grips, style A engraved, sold to Morley-Murphy Co., Green Bay, Wisconsin, and shipped March 1938 to Neal Hoh, Marshfield, Wisconsin. *(George S. Lewis, Jr. Collection)*

Of great rarity, and at this writing still in the possession of the original purchaser, this nickel plated pair of Super Match .38 Automatic pistols was shipped in July of 1940, to Cullum & Boren Co., Dallas, Texas. Barrels of 5″ length, carved eagle ivory grips, grade C engraved; serial numbers 34973 and 34985. Note the presence of *J.F.B.* monograms on the side of number 34973 (bottom; its carved eagle design on the left stock); on 34985 the *J.F.B.* is engraved on the left side of the frame. *(John F. Bickley Collection)*

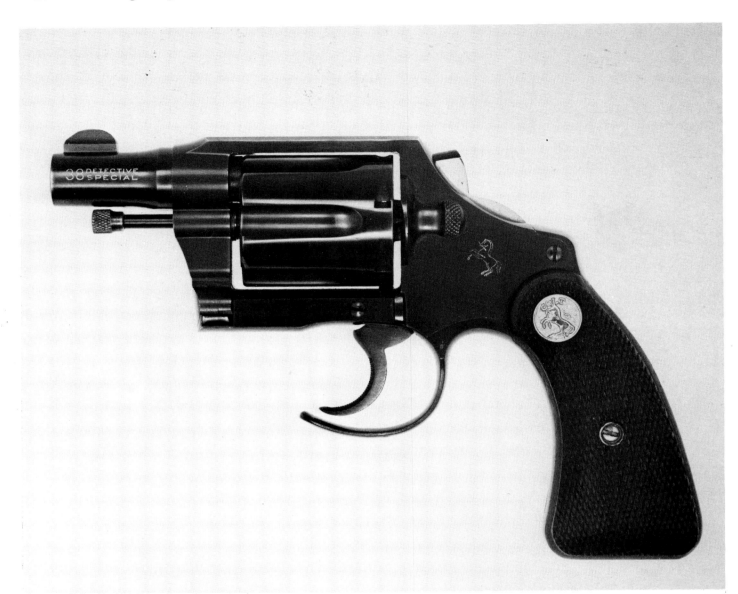

Though not engraved, Detective Special 418162 is worthy of attention due to its custom gun work, and original ownership by Colonel Charles Lindbergh. The factory documentation notes: .38 caliber, 2″ barrel, blue, special cut away model with cut off hammer spur and cut away triggerguard; shipment to Colt's New York office, attention, Albert Foster, Jr., for Colonel Lindbergh. The Colonel's interests included the outdoors, hunting, and shooting, and he is known to have been on safari with the renowned East African firm of Ker, Downey & Selby, Ltd., headquartered in Nairobi, Kenya. On a visit to Hartford in July 1927, "Lucky Lindy" was presented a Colt .45 Automatic pistol by Connecticut Governor Trumbull, on behalf of the Colt firm. The Lindbergh cutaway "Fitz-Gerald Model" Detective Special number 418162 was undoubtedly another factory presentation. *(Albert E. Brichaux Collection)*

Surely one of the most historic of Glahn-engraved Colts, number **471890** was a presentation to Governor John H. Trumbull of Connecticut, and features profuse scroll engraving, and ivory grips gold inlaid with a JHT monogram and the coat of arms and motto of the State of Connecticut. *(Colt Collection of Firearms, Connecticut State Library)*

Graham H. Anthony, Colt company executive from 1944 into the 1950's, examining engraved revolver presented with an engraved Government Model Automatic pistol to President Harry S. Truman. The cased set is now displayed at the Harry S. Truman Library, Independence, Missouri. Engraving may be by Glahn, or by Bill McGraw of the Ithaca Gun Company. The author did not have the opportunity to examine these weapons to enable an attribution. *(Colt's Firearms Division)*

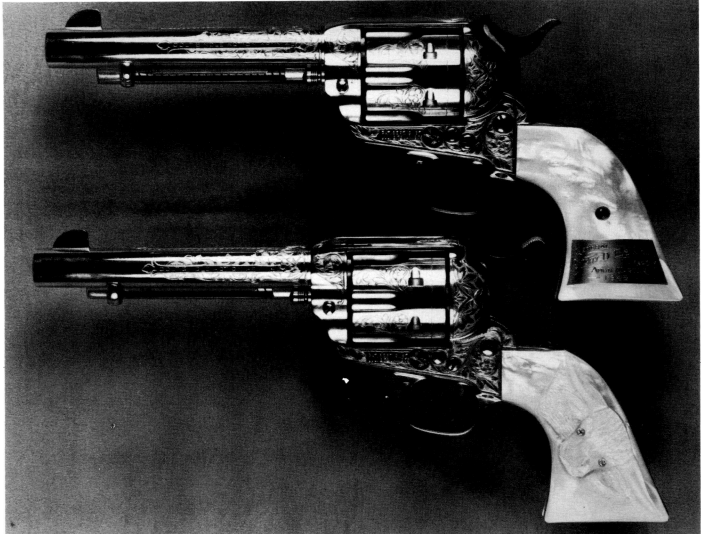

Single Action Army revolvers presented to General Dwight D. Eisenhower by his friend Amon Carter, in 1945. Serial numbers 357562 and 357564. The grips have gold plaque inlays on one side, and relief carved steerhead motif (with jeweled eyes) on the other. Since the set was made with the grip positioning on the revolvers reversed, they could be worn in double holsters, either having the plaques on the outside (left and right), or the steerhead motifs. Though the coverage is only about grade B, the revolvers are of prime historical interest. *(Courtesy Dwight D. Eisenhower Library)*

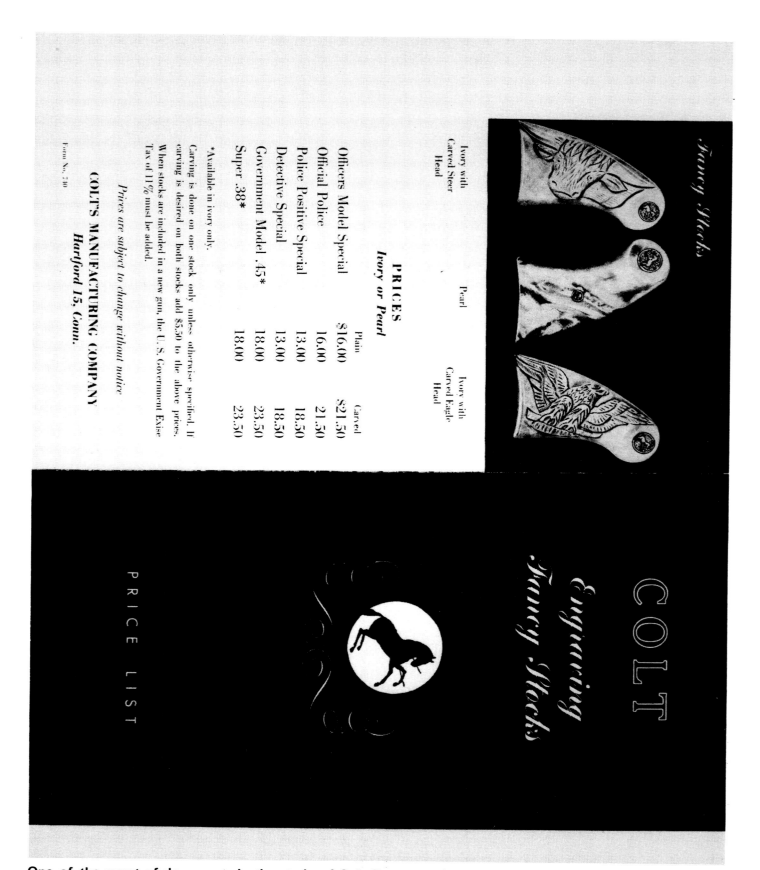

One of the rarest of documents in the study of Colt firearms, a brochure published specifically on engraving and special grips. Dating from c. 1947-48, the scroll appears to be Glahn's, but is distorted by the printer's use of an air brush for reproduction contrast on the three revolvers. Note prices; in 1941, A had been at $15, B at $25, and C at $45. *(John Hintlian Collection)*

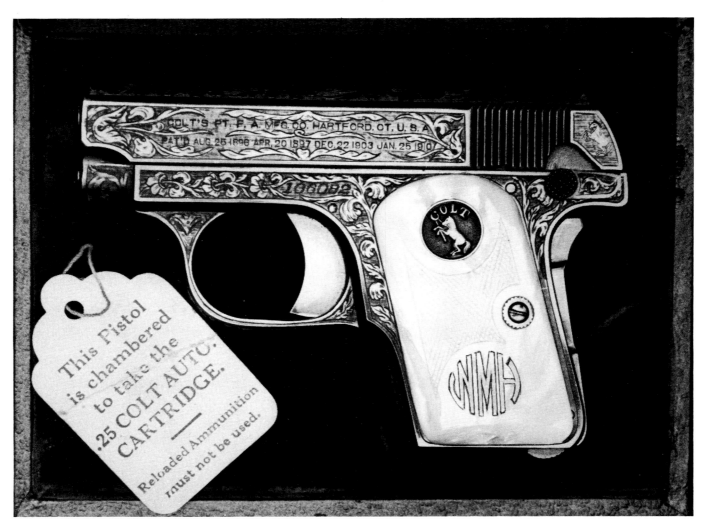

An early example of William H. Gough's decorative work on a Colt firearm, shipped in January 1914. Model 1908 .25 Automatic number 106082 is inscribed in an arc on the frame, beneath the pearl grip: DES & ENG BY W. H. GOUGH. A rare and quite early example of a factory engraved firearm bearing the craftsman's signature (interpreting "factory engraved" to mean work done for the firm directly, whether in or outside of the factory buildings). Colt ledgers reveal the following: .25, 2", soft, stocks not listed, engraved, shipped to William H. Gough, Utica, New York [for engraving], sold to Murta Appleton & Company, Philadelphia, Pennsylvania. Rare gold inlaid, checkered pearl grips; attributed to Gough. Gun cased in a standard factory leatherette box with silk and velvet lining. Note lined background to the engraving (in contrast to the punched dot standard on Helfricht work of the period) and the distinctive floral and vine scroll style. *(David S. Woloch Collection)*

Chapter XIII
WILLIAM H. GOUGH
c. 1910 — c. 1940

Although not known to have worked at Colt's factory, William H. Gough appears in the firm's records on enough occasions to indicate that he was something of a backup craftsman behind Glahn and Kornbrath. Working as early as the first part of the twentieth century on Winchesters, his name appears on several original photographs of firearms of that make, from the archives of the Ulrichs. Gough's work for Winchester appears in some detail in *The Book of Winchester Engraving*, so it will not be explored here.

Oliver M. Knode, retired Vice President of Savage Arms, knew Gough personally. In a letter to the writer, Knode advised:

> Bill Gough was the factory contract engraver at Savage in Utica before and going into WWII. He had a small office and work area (enclosed) inside the factory and had a few women trained to do the standard, simpler jobs such as the "K" 99's and the lower grade Fox doubles like the Sterlingworths and SP (or SPE's) etc.

> When I knew him in 1939-40 he was elderly and I never thought much of his work as produced at that time. He did a gold-inlaid (U.S. Seal etc.) Thompson Submachine gun which the U.S. Govt. was or did present to King Farouk. . . .

> I don't believe he did any engraving after the war was over, if indeed he was still living.

Gough's style was in considerable contrast to the Germanic scrolls with punched dot backgrounds standard with most of his contemporaries. However, one engraver with whom he had a marked similarity in style was Wilbur A. Glahn. It is at times difficult to tell one man's work from the other's.

An interesting source of data on Gough appeared in an as yet unidentified newspaper published Sunday, May 28, 1939. The article was headlined: "Utica Gunsmiths Produce President's Wedding Gift to Prince of Iran". Pictured were details of a Model 99 Savage rifle made on order of President Roosevelt. Gough's distinctive leaf and vine scrolls were clearly depicted, bordering the Presidential eagle and the crest of Iranian royalty, and a presentation inscription which read:

> To
> His Imperial Highness
> Shahpur Mohammed Reza Pahlavi
> From
> Franklin D. Roosevelt
> President
> of the United States of America

Guns engraved by Gough for Colt are usually so listed in the company shipping ledgers. Some of the pieces illustrated here are documented as having gone to Gough in Utica; then returned to Hartford for finishing. Although not a craftsman with the skills of a Helfricht, Gough's work is highly prized by collectors due to its rarity in comparison with most other Colt engravers. His career is also of interest because he is the first Colt engraver known to have signed work that he did for the factory.

An article published in a Utica newspaper, August 29, 1954, is the best published source on Gough. It is quoted here *verbatim:*

CRESTS OF EASTERN KINGS ETCHED IN STEEL BY UTICAN

> When King Farouk of Egypt had a special kind of gun turned out for him by the Savage Arms Corp., (that was quite a spell before his subjects concluded they had had enough of him), the job of engraving the gun fittingly with Egypt's royal crest was delegated to a comparatively obscure Utican, William H. Gough, master of his art.

> And when Franklin Delano Roosevelt, then President, wanted to present the Shah of Persia with a rifle (this also was made at the Savage Arms plant), it was Bill Gough who had the job of combining the Persian royal coat of arms with that of the U.S., in an elegant steel and gold

engraving for the Shah's gun.

These are just two of the scores of famous folk for whom during his 60 years as one of the country's specialists in gun engraving, Gough has furnished top work, by way of assignments from various gun manufacturing establishments. He has been employed by every one of the large arms concerns in the country and right now is engaged on a Remington Arms assignment which has taken up much of his summer.

So far as he knows Gough is the only special gun engraver in Central New York. Eighty next March, an inspiring person, young at heart and with a captivating sense of humor, he looks a particularly youthful 68 or 70, and is as lithe and active as most men half his age. His work requires the closest attention to details, but he wears glasses only for driving his car.

An Englishman by birth, his father 90 years ago was a gun engraver, one of the best, in a Birmingham arms plant. 'Naturally,' the Utican says, 'being a British boy, I followed in my father's footsteps, when it came to decide on a profession. His work was typical of English engravers, as delicate and beautiful as the watercolor paintings in which English artists excelled

in his day. English hand-engraving then, and today, for that matter, contrasted notably with that of the German and Belgian engravers, outstanding in their field. Their carving is deeper, heavier.' [He served an apprenticeship in Birmingham, and later would advance his studies in Meriden, Connecticut and Philadelphia.]

Gough was living in Meriden, Conn., to which he came as a youth, when he began his life's occupation. He studied engraving ornamentation with Frank Sporrns, then head designer for the International Silver Co., in Meriden. In that city, as a young fellow, Gough worked for the Parker gun manufacturing plant for the Colt revolver concern in Hartford, Conn.; went on to Philadelphia where he was employed as an engraver for the Fox Gun Co.

In the latter city he established a shop, in conjunction with his work for the Fox plant, and took commissions in special engraving jobs from many parts of the country. There he worked on engravings for Aubrey guns, then manufactured by Sears Roebuck Co.; for guns turned out by the Norwich Arms Corp. and Hollenbeck guns, manufactured in Virginia.

Gough was in his late 40s when he came

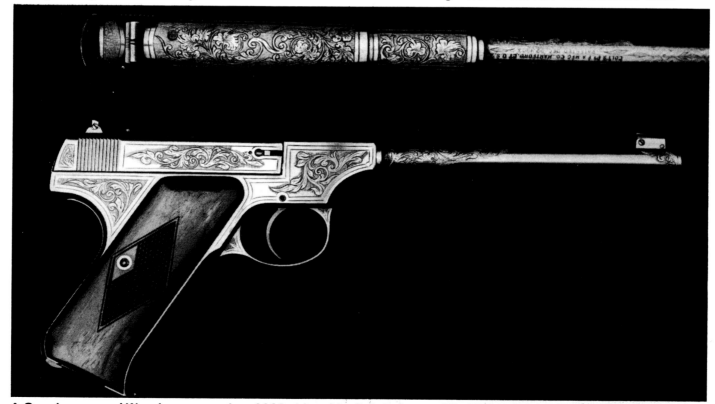

A Gough engraved Woodsman; number 4446. Listed in Colt ledgers: .22, 6½'', soft, checkered walnut, engraved, shipped to William H. Gough, Utica, New York [for engraving], sold to Murta Appleton & Company, Philadelphia, November 1916. Three guns of this description were in the shipment. A combination of scroll and leaf motifs. Note the lined backgrounds preferred by Gough. He apparently wanted to break with the traditional patterns of scroll in use by the majority of his contemporaries in the firearms field. *(David S. Woloch Collection)*

to Utica to work for the Savage Arms Corp. as a special engraver. He was with that plant for 20 years, the last two as a tool maker. Along with his responsibilities at the plant he opened a shop of his own shortly after coming to Utica, more recently, for 15 years, located in the Gardner block and now for the past two years in the McLoughlin Building, Genesee St.

This mid-town headquarters for his speciality is a study in disorder, with tables, chairs and stools littered with the work at hand and the instruments for doing it.

He does a good bit of jewelry and watch repairing too, but that sort of thing is just an accomodation. Gun engraving is his first love.

He'll tell you, if you stop to visit with him, of the job he did on a Colts revolver for Gen. Huerto, president of Mexico. And of the time he engraved a gun for Ty Cobb, presented him by Philadelphia fans. The great baseball hitter, introduced by the almost equally famous 'Stony' McGlynn, then head of the Philadelphia Ledger's sports department, used to come to the engraver's shop regularly to visit with him.

The proprietor of the famous Texas 101 Ranch and many of the cowboys in the 101 Ranch show, which toured the country annually for years, all carried pistols engraved by the Utican.

Men who order engravings for their guns are very particular about the designs, Gough explains. They call for birds, heads of hunting dogs, bear, moose and deer, combined with the dates of hunting achievements, family crests and other ornamentations. Gough makes the free hand drawings, on the steel plates with a pen or brush, carries out the final work with a gold inlay.

At his Walker Rd. home the engraver 'lets off steam,' he says, in producing one of the finest vegetable gardens in that locality where he raises everything from potatoes to Hubbard squash.

Gough has four children. They are Irving, Hollywood, Fla., realtor; Charles, Philadelphia, an ice-cream manufacturer; Alfred, Brewster, Mass., proprietor of a typewriter concern, and Phyllis, who lives at home and attends Whitesboro Central School. The Goughs, including Phyllis, are active members of the Church of the Reconciliation.

John B. Deveans of Utica, a friend and engraving student of Gough, located the August 1954 news story, and provided some comments and added material: "Just before the war he had an engraving business employing about 20 craftsmen. After the war broke out he lost several assistants and replaced them with women. As time and the war went on the women replaced most of the engravers. He stated in his talks with me that the women were very good at the engraving trade. He was doing engraving work for Remington Arms when we met — picking up the work and doing it at home. Mr. Gough made all of his own engraving chisels of Sanderson steel."

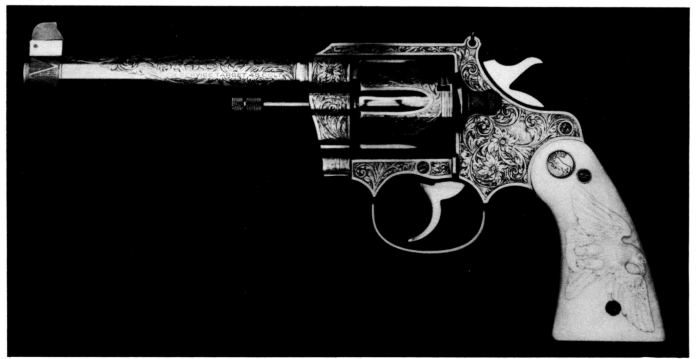

Gough engraving on a customized New Service Target revolver; number 328252 (c. 1928). Colt serial ledgers indicate the revolver was shipped "soft". Profuse coverage; distinctive scroll, leaf and floral style. *(Richard Elrad Collection)*

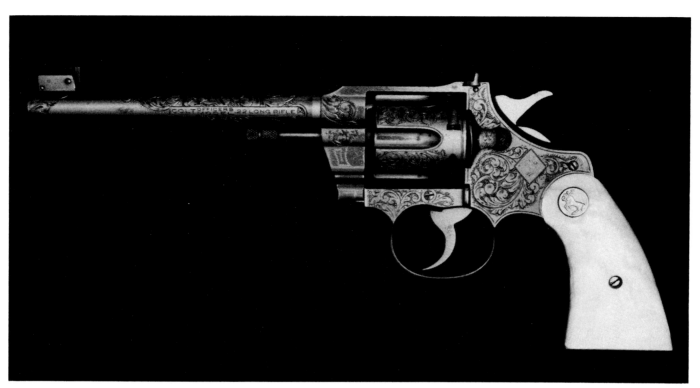

Officers Model Target number 20246; .22 caliber, 6″ barrel, blued finish, pearl grips. The embellishment repeats the style on the Woodsman number 99627 and the Police Positive Special number 460823. *(David S. Woloch Collection)*

National Match automatic pistol, serial number 197390; listed in the Colt shipping records as: blued, pearl grips, engraved in grade B, shipped November 16, 1938 on loan account, to a New York City address. The matching Conversion Unit .22-.45 bears serial number U 107 and is listed in the ledgers as blued, engraved in grade B, and shipped on loan account to the same address and on the same date as the National Match pistol. Rare velvet lined wooden factory casing for the set. *(David S. Woloch Collection)*

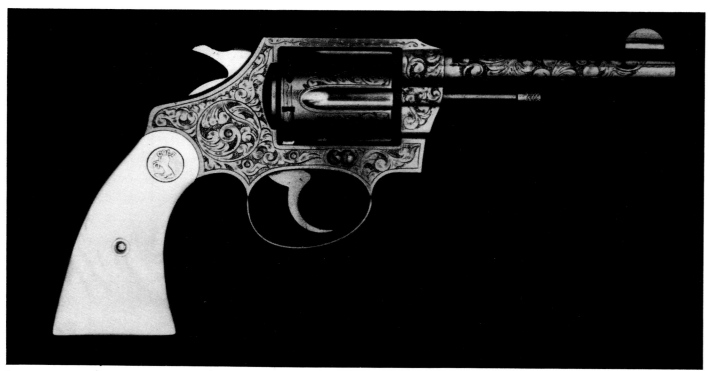

Police Positive Special number 460823 (c. 1938). Blued finish; pearl grips. More of the same distinct scroll, the coverage profuse. *(David S. Woloch Collection)*

Extremely rare combination of gold inlaying (monogram on top of the frame) and Gough engraving, on .45 Automatic number C93183. Documented in the factory records as shipped to J.P. Shannon, Philadelphia, at request of Murta Appelton & Co., Philadelphia, March 1917. FHC monogram in gold on top of the frame, profuse Gough engraving, rare checkered walnut grips. This pistol also pictured elsewhere in color in the present edition. *(Private Collection)*

Attributed to W.H. Gough, number 354900 is documented by the factory ledgers as .45, 4 3/4" barrel, blue (and case hardened) finish, ivory grips, engraved, and shipped in July 1936 to Wolf & Klar, Fort Worth, Texas. Engraving is deep, and the coverage rather profuse. *(Dr. Johnny Spellman Collection)*

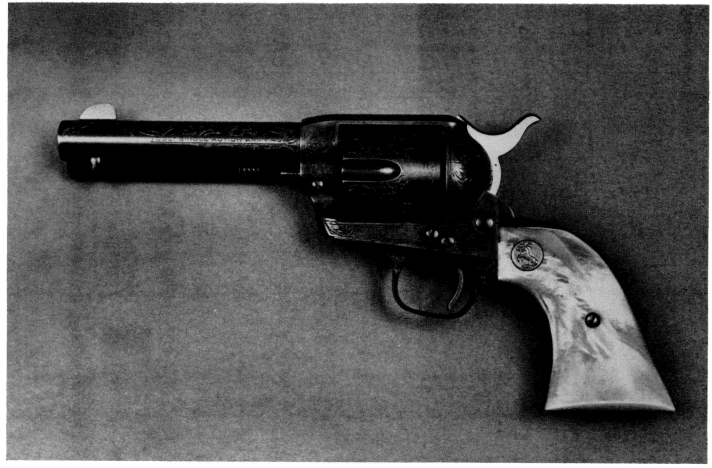

A late specimen of Gough engraving, Single Action 356856 was shipped in June of 1939: .45 caliber, 4 3/4" barrel, blue (and case hardened) finish, pearl grips, class B engraved, and sent to Emmons Hawkins Hardware Co., Huntington, West Virginia. *(George S. Lewis, Jr. Collection)*

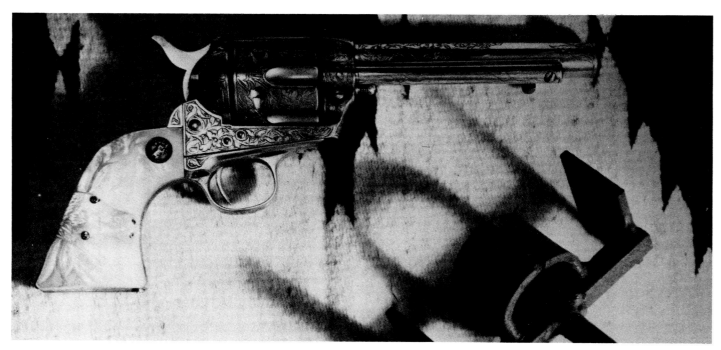

By W.H. Gough, number 328849 Single Action Army is finished in full silver plating, grips of relief carved pearl with ruby and diamond inlays, caliber .45, 5 1/2" barrel, with an interesting background. Joe C. Miller of the 101 Ranch Wild West Show purchased revolver June 26th 1914 as a gift for his brother Zack. The Show was then about to leave for England on a tour. *(Wayne Hill Collection)*

See following pages for information on this scroll style believed by Gough. Colt ledgers record quite a bit of information on Single Action 354898: .45 caliber, 4 3/4" barrel, blue (and case hardened) finish, carved steer-head ivory grips, grade B engraved, and shipped in May 1933 to Abercrombie & Fitch Co., New York City. The records also indicate this revolver was returned to the factory in January 1935 and then shipped in April to Harry W. Lidstone of Colt's Marketing Department. Lidstone took the revolver to Dallas, Texas (apparently for display), and returned it to the factory inventory in May. The revolver was shipped again to the Camp Perry national shooting matches in August 1935. The revolver went out again on loan account to Abercrombie & Fitch in November 1935, and came back to Colt's January 23, 1936. The last record of shipment from the factory was again to A & F, New York, January 28, 1936. Sample pieces like 354898 have a special fascination to the collector, since they played important roles in helping to promote Colt products. *(William A. Dascher Collection)*

Super .38, serial number 103, engraved by Gough. Listed in Colt records: Charged to arms selling expense. Shipped to Albert Foster Jr., New York, January 1932. Work order number 53-399. The engraving has a different appearance, due to cutting deeper than usual. The shading background lines are engraved over the serial number. Generally craftsmen used a scroll decor to emphasize or to border the serial. On profuse coverage assignments, Gough frequently ran his backgrounds through numbers or other markings. Rare buffalo motif pearl grips. *(David S. Woloch Collection)*

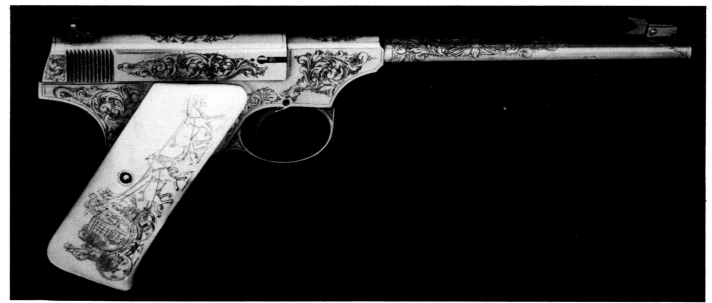

Identity of the engraver of Woodsman .22 number 99627 is unknown. The factory lists: .22, 6½″, blue, engraved grade B, sold and shipped to Von Lengerke & Antoine, Chicago, December 1936. Stocks not listed. The scroll may have been late work by Gough, well up in years at the time; if so, the quality indicates he would have been wise to have stayed with his quite distinctive scroll, leaf and vine style. Punched dot background, the shaded lines on scrolls, and the rather billowy scroll shapes do not represent work of a high order. But the scarcity of specimens of Colt firearms with this distinctive style makes the variation of rarity and importance to the collector. *(David S. Woloch Collection)*

Model 1903 Pocket Automatic pistol, number 324219 (c. 1919); another specimen of Gough's distinctive style. Colt ledgers record blue, engraved, and pearl grips. Lined background cuts are made right through the slide markings. *(David S. Woloch Collection)*

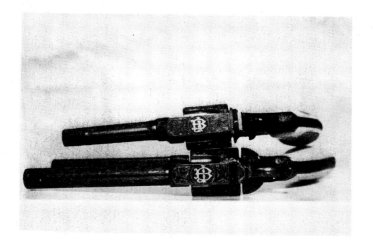 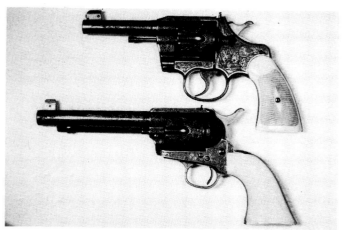

Matched set of Officers Model Target and Single Action Army Flattop revolvers; the work of Gough, c. 1917. Engraved and gold inlaid on order of Albert Foster Jr., for his attorney James Bowen. The Flattop Single Action number 162882 was sent to Foster in November of 1909. The gun was subsequently altered by the factory by fitting a 5½" barrel, a new hammer, and checkered ivory grips. It was then engraved by Gough. Number 420470 O.M. Target was shipped by Colt in April of 1917. Note the matching checkered ivory grips, blued finish, engraving, and the low relief gold monogram. Matched sets made up of different model guns are of utmost rarity in the field of decorated Colt firearms. *(R. Q. Sutherland Collection)*

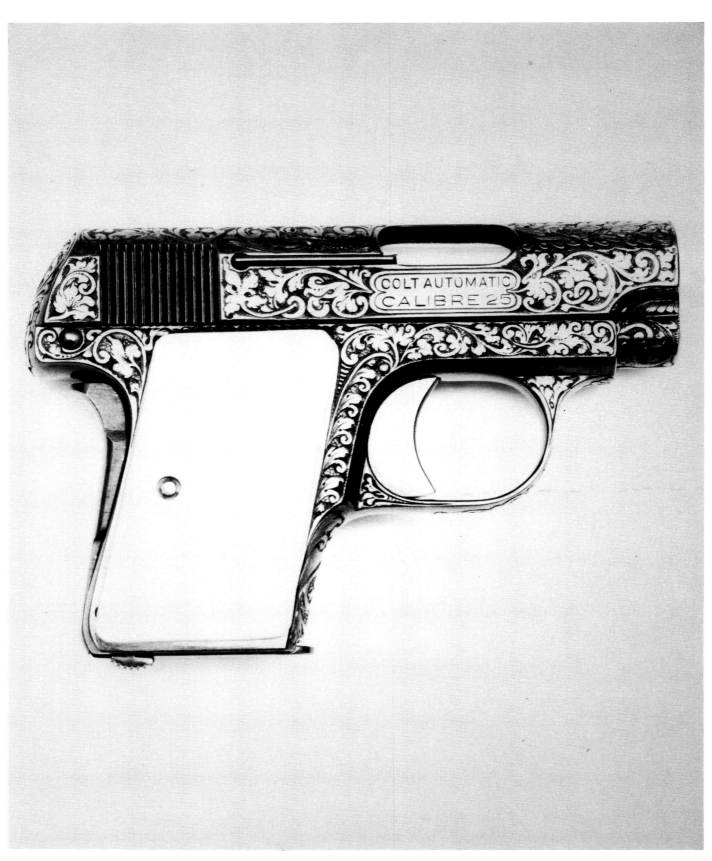

Full scroll by Herbert on .25 caliber Model 1908 Automatic serial number 344765. Finished in blue, with pearl grips. Engraved in 1959. The scroll is in a Germanic style, as he preferred to use for most of his work.
(Al DeJohn Collection)

Chapter XIV
ALVIN F. HERBERT
c. 1954 — 1969

Al Herbert's career with Colt spanned only about fifteen years, but in that time he turned out more than most engravers could in a twenty five year period. Working a full week for Colt, he also maintained an outside shop where he took in jewelry engraving, presentation inscriptions, and — on occasion — guns from private parties and from other gunmakers. For many years he was one of the sources of lettering for A. A. White Engravers, Inc. The author spent many an hour on Saturdays in Al Herbert's upstairs shop on State Street in downtown Hartford.

Herbert was very modest about his abilities, but when he spoke one could see the quiet pride he took in always doing his best, and conscientiously trying to please. Initially trained at jewelry engraving, he was especially talented at lettering and monograms. He admired the work of Kornbrath, and his favorite scroll style was based on one of the master's best Germanic patterns.

Ebony and *Guns* magazines published feature articles on Herbert and his work. Thousands of gun enthusiasts and the general public saw him demonstrate gun engraving at the New England States' Expositions, at various sportsman's shows, and on television. He enjoyed giving interviews, and posed for photographers without pretention. Herbert was a credit to the trade.

His life was summed up in brief by an obituary published by one of the Springfield newspapers, September 5, 1969:

FAMED GUN ENGRAVER DIES

Alvin F. Herbert, 68, of 190 Northampton Ave., who achieved international fame as a gun engraver, decorating weapons for the late President Dwight D. Eisenhower and Gen. Charles De Gaulle, among others, died Thursday in Wesson Memorial Hospital.

He was born in Saint Vincent, West Indies, Jan. 3, 1901 and had been a resident of this city for 41 years, moving to Springfield from Cambridge. He was the operator of Herbert's Sales & Service Radio Store on Hancock and Main Streets for many years.

He was employed as a gun engraver at Smith & Wesson, later worked at Colt's Patent Firearms as a master engraver, not only for guns, but delicate work on jewelry and trophies. His masterpiece was an embossed Colt revolver which commemorated the Colt firm's 125th anniversary. He also engraved guns for Sammy Davis, Jr., former chief of police of Springfield, Raymond P. Gallagher, Mayor LaGuardia of New York, ex-Cuban President Fulgencio Batista and many movie stars.

His work was featured in several national publications, among them Ebony *magazine and* Guns *magazine. . . .*

Some further statistics on Colt factory engraved guns during the Alvin F. Herbert period; note that his years of c. 1954-69 overlap with the White era from 1961 to date. Factory records do not generally identify engravers of specific guns, so the methods of detection are by examining pieces for signatures and scroll and inlay style.

Single Action Army revolvers: *Estimated less than 50 engraved, the majority in Grades A and C. A few New Frontiers and Buntline Specials included in the above figure.*

Frontier Scout revolvers: *Extremely rare engraved. A machine roll scroll design was standard on Scout buttstraps after c. 1962.*

Fourth Model (.22 short rimfire) Deringer: *Extremely rare engraved.*

Detective Special: *Estimated at less than 25; the most spectacular number 805129, relief gold inlaid in a floral and vine motif, with the grips gold inlaid and mounted on the right stock with a diamond; by Alvin A. White.*

Cobra revolver: *Approximately 10 engraved.*

Diamondback revolver: *Less than 10 engraved; the first one by Alvin A. White and ordered by Richard N. Kennedy, Jr.*

of Georgia.

Trooper revolver: *Approximately 10 engraved.*

.357 Magnum revolver: *Less than 10 engraved.*

Python revolver: *Estimated at approximately 30, the major proportion in grade A and C style. The Python has been the most popular of double action Colt revolvers for engraving since 1955. One inscribed specimen was presented by the factory to Ian Fleming, author of the James Bond "007" novels.*

Junior Colt .25/.22 Automatic pistol: *About two engraved.*

Government Model .45 Automatic pistol: *About 25 or less engraved; the fanciest piece by Herbert was number 300000-C for W. H. Goldbach.*

Super .38 Automatic pistol: *Approximately a half dozen engraved.*

Gold Cup National Match Automatic pistol: *About 15 or less engraved.*

Commander Automatic pistol: *About 15 or less engraved.*

Woodsman Target and Sport .22 Automatic pistols: *Two on record engraved post WWII. None of the Targetsman was engraved.*

Second and Third Model Match Target Woodsman Automatic pistols: *About a half dozen engraved post WWII.*

Rifles: *The Colt '57' and Coltsman Bolt Action rifles made prior to 1963 were not engraved. The Custom grade Coltsman rifles of 1963-65 had an etched motif on the triggerguard-floorplate area. The work was done in Finland by the Sako arms factory. A few of the Colt '57' and Coltsman rifles were inscribed and presented by the factory.*

Semi-Automatic shotgun: *Made for Colt by Luigi Franchi, Brescia, Italy, the custom model included hand engraving on the receiver as standard. Game scenes comprised the relatively simple decor. Made from 1962-66.*

Alvin F. Herbert with a Single Action Army in his ball-vise, at work in Colt's engraving shop. When using the hammer and chisel he peered through a large magnifier (with neon light fixture), as visible here. Herbert's powerful arms and shoulders were an asset when cutting modern steels.

A Herbert masterpiece — gold inlaid and engraved for presentation by Colt to President Eisenhower (1957). The revolver and its deluxe case are now displayed in the Eisenhower Museum, Abilene, Kansas. Graham Anthony, Chairman of the Board, Colt's Manufacturing Company, personally presented the President with another gift from the company, an engraved pair of Official Police revolvers. Writing to Anthony, August 6, 1953 (on White House stationery), Eisenhower said: *I want to take this opportunity to express once again my grateful thanks for the beautiful pistols you brought to me this afternoon. Please convey my appreciation also to your associates in the Colt Company whose expert workmanship went into the making of these fine weapons — they are truly handsome. The personally engraved case, too, is very attractive — my deepest gratitude for this wonderful gift.*

French President Charles De Gaulle was the recipient of a cased Colt Single Action revolver. The gift was from Colt's factory, on the occasion of De Gaulle's visit to the United States in the spring of 1960. Shown holding the gun is Dr. Marcel M. Thau, leader of Hartford's French community, who made the presentation to De Gaulle. The backstrap and the case plaque were inscribed by Herbert.

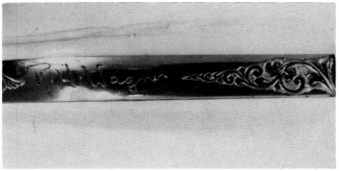

Deluxe scrollwork covers much of this nickel plated Single Action Army, done on order of Colt Historian R.H. Wagner by Alvin Herbert, from the late 1950s to c. 1963. Note signature on the backstrap, and the low-relief carved wooden casing. Serial number 145128; steerhead carved ivory grips; .45 caliber, 5 1/2" barrel. An especially interesting and important Single Action, considering the many years of service of Ron Wagner with Colt's (totalling over 53), and his position first as historian, and currently as Historian Emeritus. *(R.H. Wagner Collection)*

By Alvin F. Herbert c. 1958, number 11992SA is a .45, 7 1/2" barrel, with full blue finish, and recorded as "deluxe" engraved. Shipment was to Colt salesman A.B. Shorb, of Milan, Michigan, in March 1958. At the time Shorb was District Sales Manager. Note engraving even on the stock screw. *(Dr. Johnny Spellman Collection)*

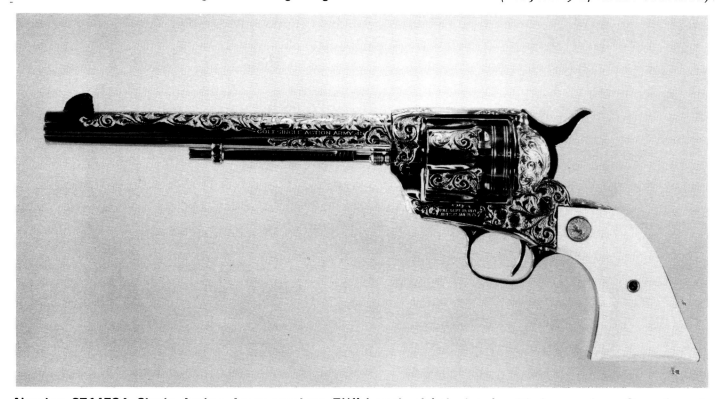

Number 27145SA Single Action Army revolver; 7½" barrel, nickel plated, with ivory grips. One of a pair engraved c. 1959 by Herbert for presentation to R. Kent Sutherland by his father. Grade C coverage in the engraver's favorite scroll style. *(R. Kent Sutherland Collection)*

Used by the Colt firm as a sample of engraving, number 18954SA is recorded as sent to A.B. Shorb of the company's marketing department for use at the N.S.G.A. Show, Chicago, in January 1961. The revolver had been specially embellished on factory order 9237, of March 5th 1958. .45 caliber, 4 3/4" barrel, and *full blue* finish. Compare with 18957SA, on the same factory order. *(Albert E. Brichaux Collection)*

Colt ledgers list number 9083Q Frontier Scout as .22 caliber, 4 3/4" barrel, blue, black plastic grips, shipped in February 1958 to Perley E. Armstrong of New Hartford, Connecticut. Apparently Armstrong, a Colt employee, brought this revolver to Al Herbert, who subsequently engraved it. Coverage is on the frame, gripstraps, cylinder, ejector rod housing, and barrel. Chalk has been rubbed into the frame and gripstrap cuts to reveal the detail for the camera. *(Art Ressel Collection)*

The 125th Anniversary Model show gun, engraved and inlaid by Herbert for Colt's use during and after the 1961 anniversary year. Featured in gold were the Colt factory dome, the *Monitor* and the *Merrimac,* American eagle, big game, Indian, and covered wagon motifs, scenes from World Wars I and II, a portrait bust of Samuel Colt, and a picture of Colt as a boy carving the first model of his revolver. The backstrap was gold inscribed: COMMEMORATING 125th/ANNIVERSARY 1836-1961. Valued at $12,500, the company has been offered that figure several times for the gun, but to date has not accepted. The scroll was cut in Herbert's preferred style, featuring Germanic scrolls with leaf finials. *(Colt's Firearms Division)*

14999SA was shipped for the National Rifle Association display of the Colt factory, in 1961. Factory ledgers further record .45, 7 1/2" barrel, factory order 9105, and sent to the attention of A.B. Shorb, Sales Manager, Colt's. The revolver was accompanied by another Single Action of like configuration; apparently the two constituting a pair. *(Albert E. Brichaux Collection)*

Number 17923SA Single Action Army left the factory in July of 1958, and was shipped to Warshal's Sporting Goods Co., Seattle, Washington. The ledgers further note: .38 caliber, 7 1/2" barrel, "De Luxe" engraved, wood grips, blue (and case hardened) finish. Note how Herbert ran the scroll upwards from the triggerguard onto the frame, and then over onto the backstrap; also note the double line bands at the breech of the cylinder. The June 1966 *Guns* magazine has a detailed article on Herbert, and provides material in addition to that presented herein. *(Albert E. Brichaux Collection)*

Attributed to Al Herbert, number 18957SA is in .44 Special, has a 7 1/2" barrel, full blue finish, and is listed in the Colt records with the reference "special handling" and factory order 9237. The original pasteboard box accompanying the revolver is marked with the serial number and the word "standard". The latter reference could suggest that 18957SA was to serve as a pattern gun for engraved style and coverage. *(Albert E. Brichaux Collection)*

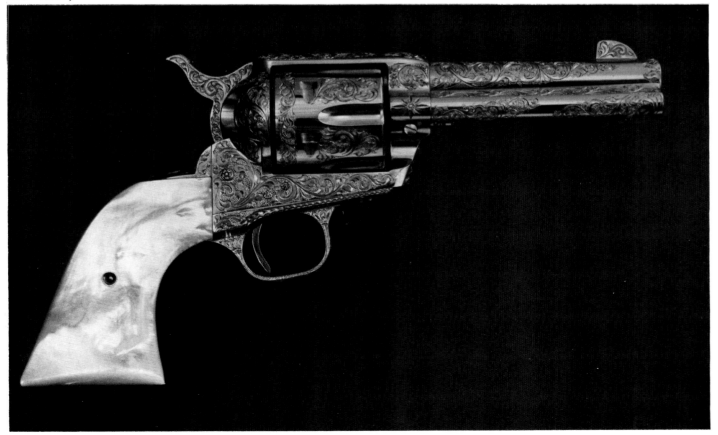

Serial number 38531SA Single Action Army, cutaway on one side, and fully engraved on the other. Special features include 4" barrel, nickel finish, pearl grips, and Grade C scroll coverage. Made for the author while employed by the Colt company as Assistant Manager, Public Relations. Shipped in September of 1964. The scroll style was patterned after that used by Alvin White for Grade A, B, and C engraving. *(W.C. Ford Collection)*

Thoroughly documented Single Action Army, presented by the Colt factory to big game hunter and all-around arms writer Warren Page. Serial number 38225SA, 7 1/2" barrel, .45 caliber. P.A. Benke was President of the Colt Firearms Co. at the time. Twentieth Century Colt factory presentation arms are *supreme* rarities. *(Private Collection)*

Frontier Scout 8965Q was done by A.F. Herbert and then presented as a gift to his friend Walter Thuer, grandson of F. Alexander Thuer. Aluminum alloy frame was left in the white, as was the gripframe. Factory deluxe Frontier Scout revolvers are *extremely* rare, and only a handful were hand engraved. *(Dr. Johnny Spellman Collection)*

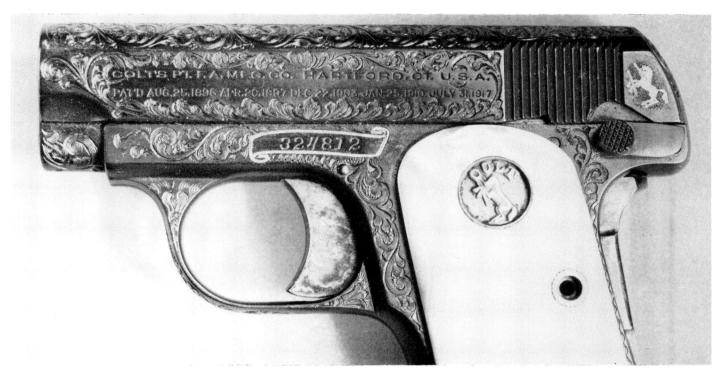

By Al Herbert for Walter Thuer, .25 Automatic number 324812 includes gold inlaid rampant colt and gold bordering around the serial. The author remembers seeing Herbert engaged, over a period of a few years, in carefully embellishing this pistol. Grips of pearl; finish full blue, by the Colt factory. *(W.F. McLaughlin Collection, photograph courtesy Norm Flayderman)*

The last deluxe firearm made by Herbert prior to his death. Serial number 300000-C Government Model .45 Automatic, done at the order of former Colt President William H. Goldbach, c. 1968. On loan exhibition for several years in the Colt Collection of Firearms, Connecticut State Library, the descriptive brochure published by the library states: *. . . . the theme is World War I. Relief gold motifs include portraits of General Pershing and President Woodrow Wilson, a World War I artillery battery, an infantry charge, the rampant colt, the serial number, slide markings, and various scrolls and borders. The relief carved ivory grips include a WHG script monogram* [the grips were made in Southeast Asia]. *(William H. Goldbach Collection)*

Serial number RPM No. 1 Single Action Army, with extra cylinders. Flush and relief gold inlay, with 18k gold buttcap, on which is engraved the Mellon family coat of arms. The casing of leather, lined in felt; made in England and partitioned and fitted in the British style. A separate American walnut casing was also made for the revolver and cylinders. One of the most exquisite of firearms done by White in his entire career. *(Richard P. Mellon Collection/Photograph, S. P. Stevens)*

Chapter XV
A. A. WHITE

A strong demand for the best quality engraving exists in the contemporary market. But in the twentieth century the number of qualified artisans who can satisfy this demand has been gradually decreasing. There are many gun engravers active today, but only a handful who have the skill and creative flair to meet the requirements of the most discriminating buyer.

Thus it was that A. A. White Engravers was created in 1961, to satisfy a need just then being attended to by the Colt's Patent Fire Arms Manufacturing Company. Their requirement was for volume engraving and gold inlay of deluxe firearms, and their intent was a vigorous promotion of such items.

Since 1961, when the new engraving operation was manned by a single manager and engraver Alvin White, A. A. White Engravers expanded to a staff of several qualified master engravers, each of them specialists in various aspects of arms decoration. The author was appointed Vice President and Managing Director of the firm in January 1966, and served in that capacity through c. 1975. In 1976 A. A. White Engravers, Inc. was disbanded, after having become the largest company in America devoted exclusively to hand engraving.

Contracts and work orders for the White Corporation came from Colt and a half dozen other prominent gunmaking firms. The balance of orders were from private clients. Projects included presentation pistols for J. Edgar Hoover, Presidents Nixon, Ford, Johnson, and Kennedy, Premier Leonid I. Brezhnev, Chuck Connors, members of the Ford and Mellon families, and Prince Abdol Reza of Iran. Gun writers Elmer Keith, Jack O'Connor, Warren Page, John T. Amber, and the late Pete Kuhlhoff all received presentation pieces made by White. Other personalities with guns decorated by White or by the company include William B. Ruger, Larry Sheerin, T. E. Bass, *Arms Gazette* publisher Wallace Beinfeld, John Mecom, Blake Edwards, Hank Williams, Jr., and a number of Congressmen, Senators, Governors, and prominent businessmen. Among large orders for White Engravers, Inc. from Colt were several models of engraved commemoratives, grades A, B, and C scrollwork, and over 500 sets of bullet traps and triggerguards for the Sharps Single Shot Rifle program.

White's own work has appeared in color on more than two dozen magazine covers — a record in the arms field — and he has been featured in articles appearing in *Guns, Guns & Ammo, Shooting Times, Guns & Ammo Annual, Gun Digest, Sports Afield,* and the *American Rifleman.* Awards for engraved weapons were given by A. A. White Engravers, Inc., in White's name at the Hartford Antique Gun Shows and at certain of the Sahara Antique Gun Shows in Las Vegas. The company has exhibited at National Rifle Association meetings and at selected arms shows in the United States. In print was a color illustrated catalogue and a mailing brochure, with information on the work of Alvin White and his associates.

A brief but cogent portrait of White appeared in the *American Rifleman* magazine, January 1967, in the column "America's Leading Gunsmiths". Excerpts are published here through permission of the National Rifle Association:

A worker in precious metals, fine woods, ivory, and pearl is a rather rare breed of firearms craftsman today. Yet Alvin A. White of Sandwich, Mass., has been a professional firearms engraver for [30] years, his active interest in this precise skill extending back to his boyhood.

Today White is a master engraver for Colt [on exclusive contract to the firm of A. A. White Engravers, Inc.]. White's ornamentation has included gold and silver inlaid handguns, the Samuel Colt Sesquicentennial guns in both deluxe and custom models, and Colt's 3 standard grades of engraving.

During World War II, White served 4 years in the Air Corps, in Canada, Africa, and the Pacific.

'On return from duty, I was asked by friends to do gun work for them and this blossomed into a career. That I was doing this type of work apparently spread by word of mouth,' White explains.

White got his first professional training in his home city of Attleboro during the depression when a jewelry trade school was opened.

'I had worked as a die cutter previously and, as a hobby, had done a great deal of hand work,' White says.

'Although the school did not give us formal training, it provided tools and materials and we were allowed to make whatever we wanted. This arrangement was ideal for my training. I attended the school for about 6 months and was the first of its students to get a job,' White points out.

'I also took courses at the Rhode Island School of Design at Providence in design and in shaping or modeling.'

White and his wife, Violet, have two daughters, Nancy, 12, and Moira, 10.

Asked if he would recommend a youngster to follow the profession, White says he would, 'assuming the youth had the ability and the interest in guns. I would recommend an apprenticeship with someone who could teach and at the same time encourage the individuality of the student.'

When asked if he thought the financial rewards for firearms engraving and ornamentation to be adequate, White has a brief and unequivocal 'Yes'.

On the matter of doing specialty work rather than general gunsmithing, White says: 'I would recommend what might be termed general specialty work. That would be mastery of work in the several materials which can be used to produce a decorated firearm. I feel this places greater demands on the ingenuity and creativity of the artisan'.

Now in his early 50's, White has been interested in guns since boyhood — an interest probably sparked by his father, an active hunter who particularly enjoyed fox hunts.

Besides collecting firearms and armor of colonial times, White occasionally restores antique firearms and edged weapons. He also has an interest in antique furniture, wood decoys, glass, and Japanese art.

Alvin White's style of scrollwork is influenced by British taste of the late flintlock period, and in most instances does not include punched dot backgrounds. His standard scroll is of a medium size, and is finely shaded, often with lined background cuts. Gold inlaid subjects are invariably done in 18 karat, which he feels allows for extra detail and greater wear and durability in comparison to soft gold, e.g., 22k. The author has seen this point demonstrated by watching White beat a relief inlaid 18k gold elk with a solid hunk of walnut — the gold

remained undamaged. A collector of Oriental art, White is an ardent admirer of Japanese metal work ("they were the best" he states), the influence of which can be seen in the style of his finely chiselled and engraved birds and animals.

Signatures appear on nearly all work done personally by White. His most distinctive markings are gold inlaid rectangles, relief stamped from dies of his own manufacture. The two major variations are "AA WHITE/ENG." and "Colt's A.A. White ENG." The same stamps are also used for marking silver and gold buckles, and appear on other non-firearm items made by White personally. On some occasions his signature is engraved. In a few instances two or more signatures have appeared on extra-fancy commissions. The usual location of his signature is on the left side of the triggerguard strap or receiver, beneath the grips. White's quality and style are distinctive, and, like the work of any expert craftsman, cannot be duplicated exactly.

Inspector stamps were sometimes used by the A. A. White Engravers company, and these were AW or WE, in tiny letters. The AW and WE markings did not often appear on work done by White personally, but usually represented engraving by other members of the firm.

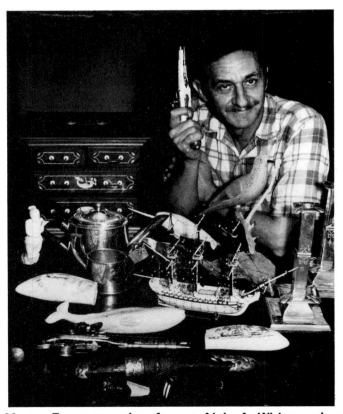

Master Engraver and craftsman Alvin A. White, maker of every item in the photograph. The pieces required the skills of a silversmith, jeweler, ivory carver, engraver, model maker, scrimshander, gunmaker, decoy carver, and knifemaker.

CUSTOM ENGRAVING SERVICE

TYPE "A" ENGRAVING...

Provides coverage of approximately one third the barrel, portions of the cylinder, frame and sideplate.

Retail Price $150.00

TYPE "B" ENGRAVING...

Provides coverage of approximately two thirds of the barrel, portions of the cylinder and partial coverage of the frame and sideplate.

Retail Price $225.00

TYPE "C" ENGRAVING...

Provides coverage of approximately the entire weapon, including the sides, the backstrap down to the stock, the butt, and the trigger guard.

Retail Price $300.00

CUSTOM ENGRAVING...

Custom Engraving is often desired when a Colt handgun is to be used for presentation purposes or as a special match prize. Any special design can be furnished, such as State or National seals, scenes of hunting or other occasions, gold or silver inlay or plating, enameled initials, emblems, etc. Submit special specifications to Colt's Arms Sales Department. A request for an estimate will be given prompt attention.

The terms "A", "B" and "C" refer only to the degree of coverage of the Colt handgun of your choice. All three types of work are done by the same engraver whose painstaking artistry is obvious in all degrees.

11

Colt's custom engraving service, pictured in the company's large-format catalogues of c. 1964 through c. 1970. The grade A and B guns and the gold inlaid Detective Special are all by Alvin White. Automatic pistol was the work of the late Alvin F. Herbert. Variations of this page appeared in brochures published by Colt in the same period, and in smaller-format catalogues of c. 1968-72. NOTE: The prices quoted are no longer in effect. *(John Hintlian Collection)*

The ''Charter Oak Commemorative'' pair of unique New Frontier Sheriffs Model Single Action Army revolvers, serial numbers 1ACP and 2ACP. Gold inlaid and engraved by Alvin A. White, who also made the gold mounted Charter Oak grips and screwdriver. Further details on these arms are provided elsewhere in the Alvin White chapter. *(John Snodgrass Collection/Photograph, Thomas Beiswenger)*

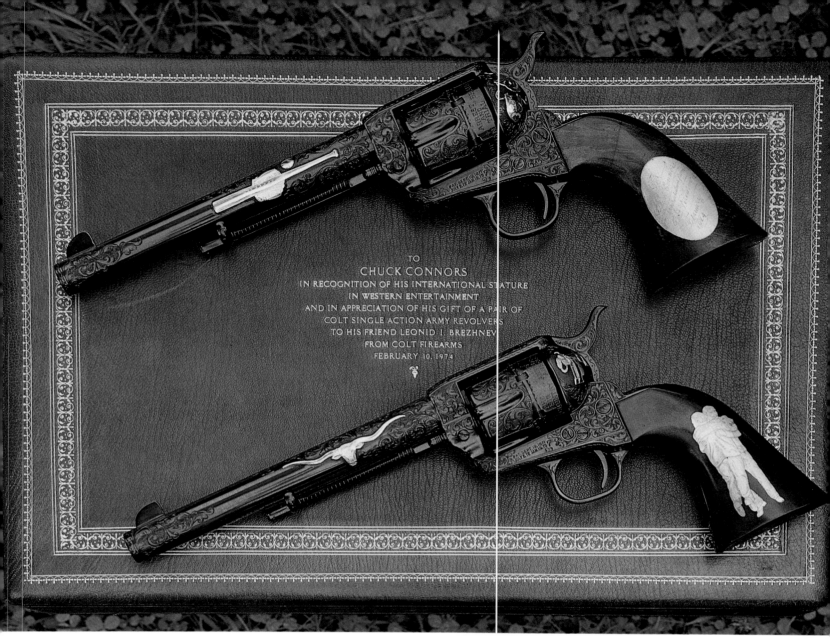

TO
CHUCK CONNORS
IN RECOGNITION OF HIS INTERNATIONAL STATURE
IN WESTERN ENTERTAINMENT
AND IN APPRECIATION OF HIS GIFT OF A PAIR OF
COLT SINGLE ACTION ARMY REVOLVERS
TO HIS FRIEND LEONID I. BREZHNEV
FROM COLT FIREARMS
FEBRUARY 10, 1974

Unique and historic, this pair of custom built presentation Single Action Army revolvers figure prominently in attempts to develop relations between the United States and the Soviet Union. Serial numbers CC-1 and CC-2, gold inlaid. Grips feature plaques in sterling silver, showing presentation of a pair of Single Actions by Connors to Leonid Brezhnev at San Clemente, which in turn prompted the Colt firm to give the present pair to the famed actor and professional athlete. The bear-hug picture appeared in a great many newspapers and magazines around the world, and followed Brezhnev's acceptance of Connors' own gift Colts. The writer was later advised that Connors' gift pistols (also a pair of Single Actions) were subsequently used by Brezhnev while boar hunting back in his native Russia. Besides the deluxe embellishments, the extra-long grips and gripstraps and the stock inlays were by A. A. White, on order of the Colt firm. Casing by Arno Werner, in gold embossed leather, lined in gold velvet. *(Private Collection, G. Allan Brown photograph)*

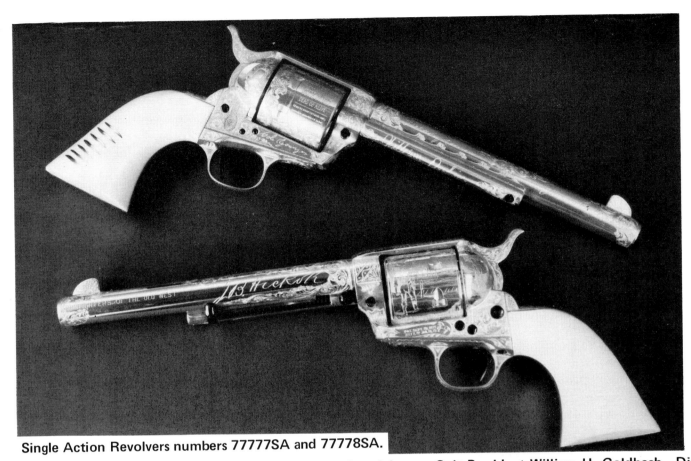

Single Action Revolvers numbers 77777SA and 77778SA.

Set of five deluxe Colt firearms done by White on order of former Colt President William H. Goldbach. Displayed for several years in the Connecticut State Library Museum, Hartford. Featured in the April 1973 *Guns & Ammo* magazine, in the Winter 1971 issue of *The Commemorative Collector,* and in various other publications. The first piece made by White for Goldbach was Government Model Automatic serial number WWII S-2, silver and gold inlaid and deluxe engraved. The World War II theme features a design based on Goldbach's service in the Navy and Army air forces during that conflict. The left side of the pistol commemorates Navy air experience; the right side incorporates Army air corps service. The overall title for the gun is the "20th Air Force Commemorative". Inscription of Goldbach's name and title are gold inlaid on the grip frame. Grips are of flush gold inlaid rosewood. This was the second produced in a custom series of extra-deluxe commemorative World War II model pistols, only four of which were completed out of the planned run of 25. The pair of silver plated Single Actions are numbered 77777SA and 77778SA. Number 77777SA is embellished with the theme "Gunfighters of the Old West", and has signatures of Hickok, Garrett, Earp and others of that ilk engraved in facsimile, a Frederic Remington gunfight motif on the cylinder and recoil shield, and various motifs associated with gunfighters. The matching revolver, number 77778SA, is inscribed "Outlaws of the Wild West", and is engraved with signatures of Jesse and Frank James, Cole Younger, and other contemporaries. A Frederic Remington print, "Hands Up", is on the cylinder and recoil shield, and a Jesse James wanted poster is on the opposite side of the cylinder. Several pictorial outlaw motifs are cut on various parts. Both revolvers were scroll engraved in Helfricht style and feature ivory grips with notches inlaid in 18k gold. Backstraps of both revolvers bear inscriptions of Goldbach's name and title. The Single Action with extra cylinder is number 66666SA, "The Colonel Samuel Colt Special". The right side features the evolution of the Colt theme, in gold; and the left side highlights the life of Colonel Colt. The extra cylinder is flush and relief gold inlaid with key Colt trademarks from 1836 through the present. Backstrap inscription composed of Goldbach's name and title at Colt. The Single Action with gold plated cast sterling silver grips is the prototype, serial number 1, of the Centennial Model commemorative. The grip is inscribed similarly to the backstraps of the three Single Actions described above; left side features an engraved portrait of Theodore Roosevelt, the right side a portrait of General George Patton—both men carrying Single Action Army revolvers. Colt historical inscriptions, markings, and motifs abound, covering the Single Action Model's one hundred years of popularity and use. Note 14k gold front sight blade notch and the "Tex and Patches" relief gold cylinder motif. All Goldbach revolvers are in .45 caliber, with 7½" barrels. This unique "Set of Five" represents the most deluxe series of Colt arms made by White to date for any one client. Their background of ownership by a Colt officer is quite unusual. Surprisingly, only a few officers of the company are known to have collected Colt firearms. *(William H. Goldbach Collection)*

Government Model number WWII S-2.

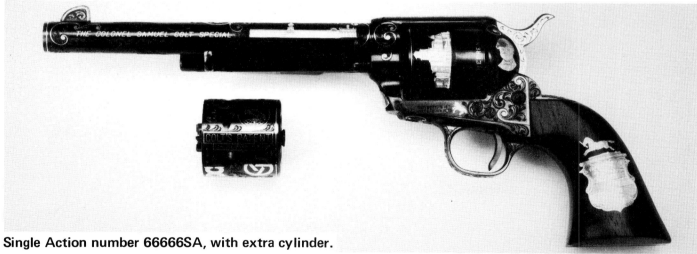

Single Action number 66666SA, with extra cylinder.

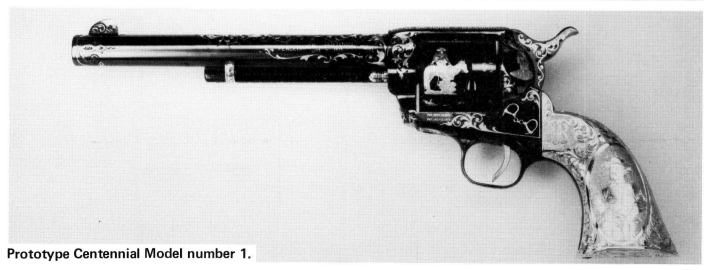

Prototype Centennial Model number 1.

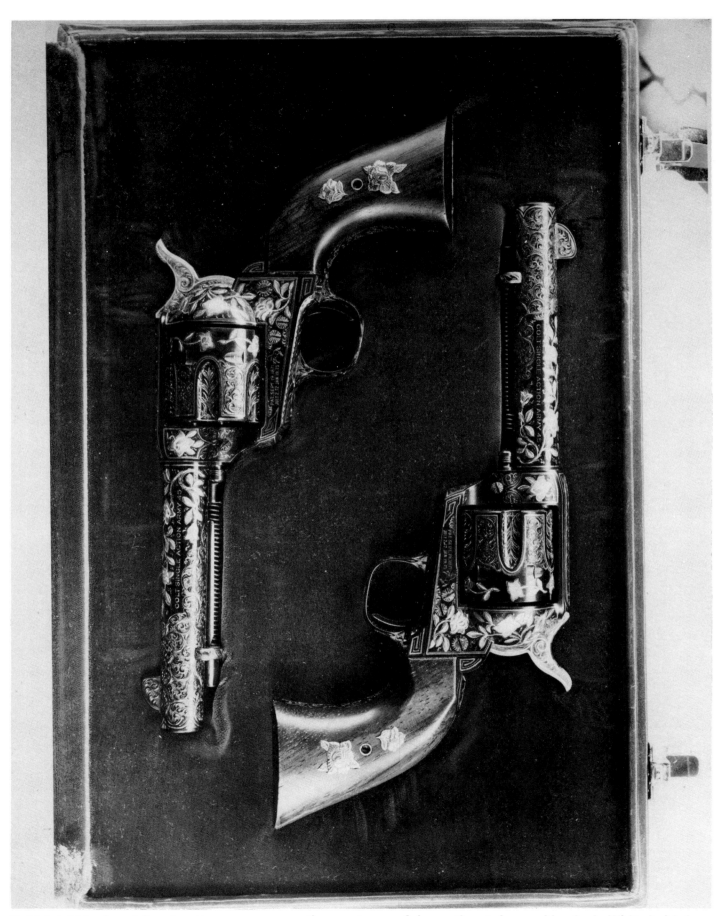

Gold inlaid leaf and floral patterns are among the most rare of decorative styles used by A. A. White in his long career. This pair of 5 1/2″ Single Action revolvers also features select walnut grips inlaid with relief chiselled flowers. *(P. R. Phillips Collection; on display at the Woolaroc Museum)*

Serial Number 8213 modern Model 1851 Colt Navy; gold and silver plated, with the address gold inlaid within a blued rectangle on top of the barrel. One of the few modern Colt Navies engraved by White personally. *(Paul Skogstad Collection)*

Serial number 6163 of the modern Colt Navy revolvers by A. A. White Engravers, Inc. Coverage is in the early vine style scroll of c. 1848-51, and is on the barrel, loading lever, frame, hammer (wolf head), and gripstraps. Approximately fifty specimens of the new Navy have been engraved by the White company to date, all finished in blue and case hardening except for six in full silver plating. A second group of special order round triggerguard new Navies was ordered by White Engravers from Colt; these bore serial numbers 8201 through 8215. A few from this group were done in a Gustave Young style scroll, and the balance were embellished by various craftsmen in other styles. Some squareback triggerguard modern Navies have been scroll engraved in the patterns of number 6163, and jestfully presentation inscribed "From the Inventor" or "Presented by Col. Colt", etc., specifically for a few arms collectors. Such pieces are obviously of modern manufacture (note that the original squareback Navy serial numbers stop at about 4200, at which range Colt began their modern series). One such piece, number 4658, bears the backstrap inscription: *Presented by Col. COLT/To R.L. Hamilton.* All the new Colt Navies are distinctively modern, and are not to be confused with genuine antique arms of the period c. 1850-51. The reader should note that Colt purposely produced these arms with a great many differences from the nineteenth century originals, to prevent widespread faking and confusion between their old and new models. *(Private Collection)*

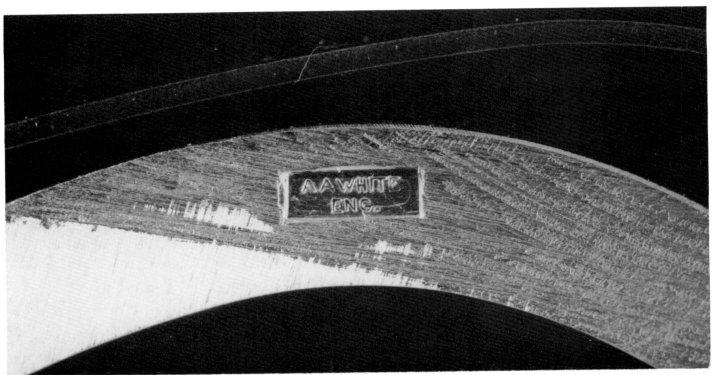

A specimen of gold inlaid cartouche signature of A. A. White. Generally the marking will have been punched onto the triggerguard strap, as here shown on Single Action number 62296SA. Extremely difficult detail photo by James Allen Logue. Revolver profusely scroll engraved and features a relief chiselled portrait of Wyatt Earp and engraved buffalo and marshal's badge motifs. *(Edward G. Wozniak, D. O., Collection)*

Modern Colt Model 1851 Navy by White; done in an antique style of scroll, with the Colt coat of arms on the left side of the barrel lug, and a sailing ship motif on the right side. One piece ivory grips; the gun finished in blue and case hardening, with silver plated gripstraps. Serial number 7143. *(William H. Myers Collection)*

Number **44447SA** Single Action appears in the Colt ledgers as by A.A. White, type C engraving, blue (and case hardened) finish, 4 3/4" barrel, .45, under factory order 11480; shipped to Kerr's Sport Shop Inc., Beverly Hills, California, in January 1968. *(Albert E. Brichaux Collection)*

Frame detail from the "Gunfighter" Single Action made by A. A. White on special order of quick draw specialist Bob Arganbright. Nickel plated finish, .45 caliber. Motifs include quick draw rig engraved on the recoil shield, Buntline Special on barrel, names of gunfighters inscribed on the cylinder, and Helfricht type scrollwork on major parts. *(Bob Arganbright Collection)*

Serial number **16444**, U.S. marked and inspected, is the lowest serial numbered gun in the group. An authentic and early Single Action engraved by Alvin White of A.A. White engravers, Inc. features a carved bust of Sitting Bull on the recoil shield. Engraved tomahawk, teepee, peace pipe, bow and arrow and other Indian motifs engraved on the cylinder. The right side of the frame is gold inlaid with an Indian village scene. The finish is blue, with grips of one-piece ivory. America's Western Indian tribes offered a last — and often a most stubborn — resistance to settlement of what evolved into the United States of America. The Indians were the first in America, and thus this revolver was the first in a group of guns especially engraved; see also Chapter XVII. *(Buddy Hackett Collection)*

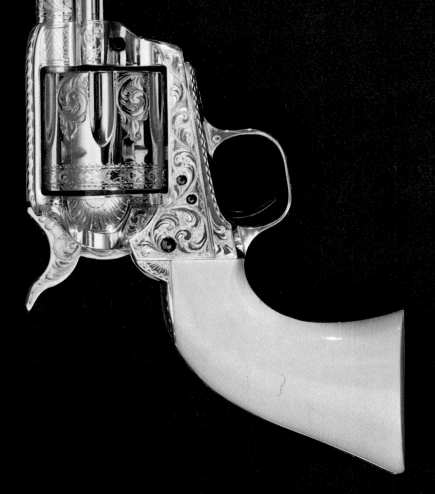

Custom ordered Single Action Army, built by the Custom Gun Shop, and engraved in the Cuno Helfricht style, by A.A. White, for Barry Gray. Gold and silver plating by Fountain Plating, Inc., West Springfield, Mass. Signed A.A. WHITE on bottom of the frame, and AAW in script on the triggerguard strap, beneath the ivory grips. Barry Gray, for over 30 years with WMCA, Straus Communications, New York City, originated the talk show format. He has been on New York (and for a while Miami Beach) radio since the mid 1940's, and has held over 40,000 interviews with celebrities from a wide variety of fields — especially show business, the world of finance, politics, and publishing. An avid student of the American West, Barry Gray is well aware of the unequalled position of firearms in the last five hundred years of world history, and particularly in the American experience. *(Barry Gray Collection; photographed by G. Allan Brown)*

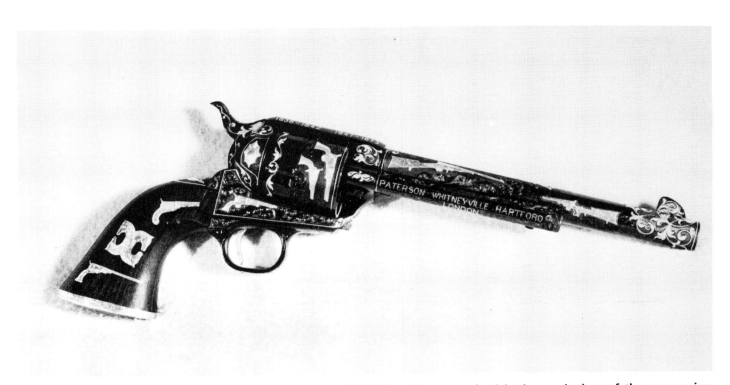

Serial number WBF No. 3 Single Action Army, gold inlaid and engraved with the evolution of the percussion Colt on the right side and the history of Samuel Colt and the factory on the left. The 18k gold butt cap is engraved with a motif simulating the cylinder roll engraved cartouche decor on the Dragoon model revolver, within which is cut the WBF No. III serial marking. Detail shows left side of the barrel and the opposite side of the cylinder; motifs in gold are the Colt factory and Colonel Colt's mansion *Armsmear*. Latter picture taken prior to bluing. Three guns of this general design were made by White, each in contrasting variations of elaborate and profuse coverage. Number 66666SA appears earlier in the present chapter, number JRF-1 (not illustrated) was made for an advanced collector of Colt firearms. *(Walter B. Ford III Collection)*

Cylinder scenes in gold inlay and engraving by Alvin White for a deluxe Single Action revolver number RPM No. 1. The bird and deer scenes and the scrolls were executed in flush gold inlay. The complete revolver features an engraved 18k gold buttcap, flush and relief gold inlaid motifs on all major parts, and profuse scroll coverage. This revolver and RKM No. 1 (done for presentation to Richard King Mellon) represent two of the most exquisitely embellished Colt revolvers done to date by White. *(Richard P. Mellon Collection)*

Two of the presidential revolvers gold inlaid and engraved by White for presentation by Colt's Firearms Company. At top, Single Action Army for President Lyndon Baines Johnson (No. LBJ-1); at bottom, the John F. Kennedy New Frontier, No. PT 109. Detail shows the PT 109 serial number and portion of the gold presidential seal. Kennedy's revolver was never fully completed, due to his assassination. The Richard M. Nixon presentation revolver bore serial No. GOP 1, and was the most exquisite of presidential revolvers done by White to date. *(Courtesy Colt's Firearms Division)*

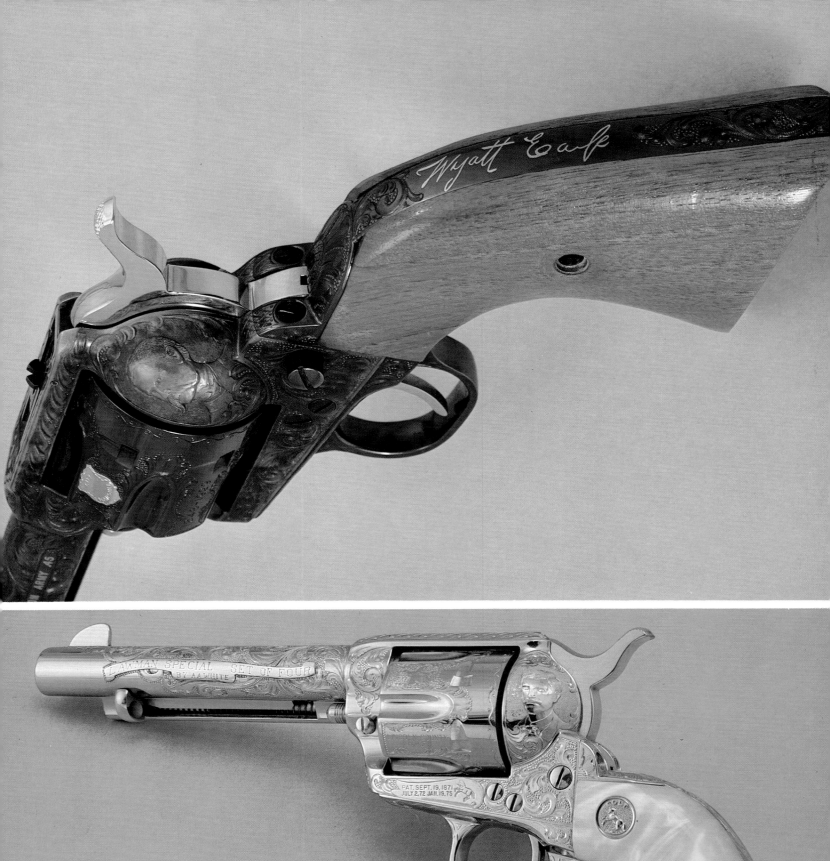

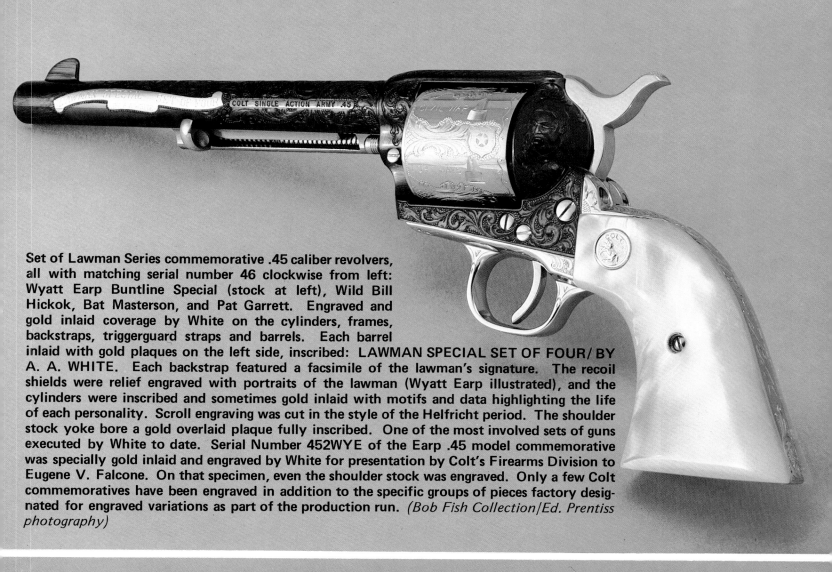

Set of Lawman Series commemorative .45 caliber revolvers, all with matching serial number 46 clockwise from left: Wyatt Earp Buntline Special (stock at left), Wild Bill Hickok, Bat Masterson, and Pat Garrett. Engraved and gold inlaid coverage by White on the cylinders, frames, backstraps, triggerguard straps and barrels. Each barrel inlaid with gold plaques on the left side, inscribed: LAWMAN SPECIAL SET OF FOUR/ BY A. A. WHITE. Each backstrap featured a facsimile of the lawman's signature. The recoil shields were relief engraved with portraits of the lawman (Wyatt Earp illustrated), and the cylinders were inscribed and sometimes gold inlaid with motifs and data highlighting the life of each personality. Scroll engraving was cut in the style of the Helfricht period. The shoulder stock yoke bore a gold overlaid plaque fully inscribed. One of the most involved sets of guns executed by White to date. Serial Number 452WYE of the Earp .45 model commemorative was specially gold inlaid and engraved by White for presentation by Colt's Firearms Division to Eugene V. Falcone. On that specimen, even the shoulder stock was engraved. Only a few Colt commemoratives have been engraved in addition to the specific groups of pieces factory designated for engraved variations as part of the production run. *(Bob Fish Collection/Ed. Prentiss photography)*

Prepared by A. A. White for the Colt factory, c. 1961, these two revolvers have been reproduced frequently in periodicals over the years, and rank among the best known of White's creations. Blued finishes, flush and relief gold inlays. Grips on the Buntline are relief carved ivory, the right grip with 18k gold horns. The 4 3/4'' revolver has African Kingwood grips, mounted on the right side with a relief chiselled steer skull motif. *(Art Kiely photograph for Colt Firearms Division)*

A.A. White executed but two pairs of grips on the can-can girl motif; this set is now on display at the Woolaroc Museum, Bartlesville, Oklahoma, and was done on order of P.R. Phillips. Revolver gold inlaid and deluxe engraved. An extraordinary detail of the grips is the fact they are carved from a single piece of ivory, rather than from two slabs glued together with a center block.

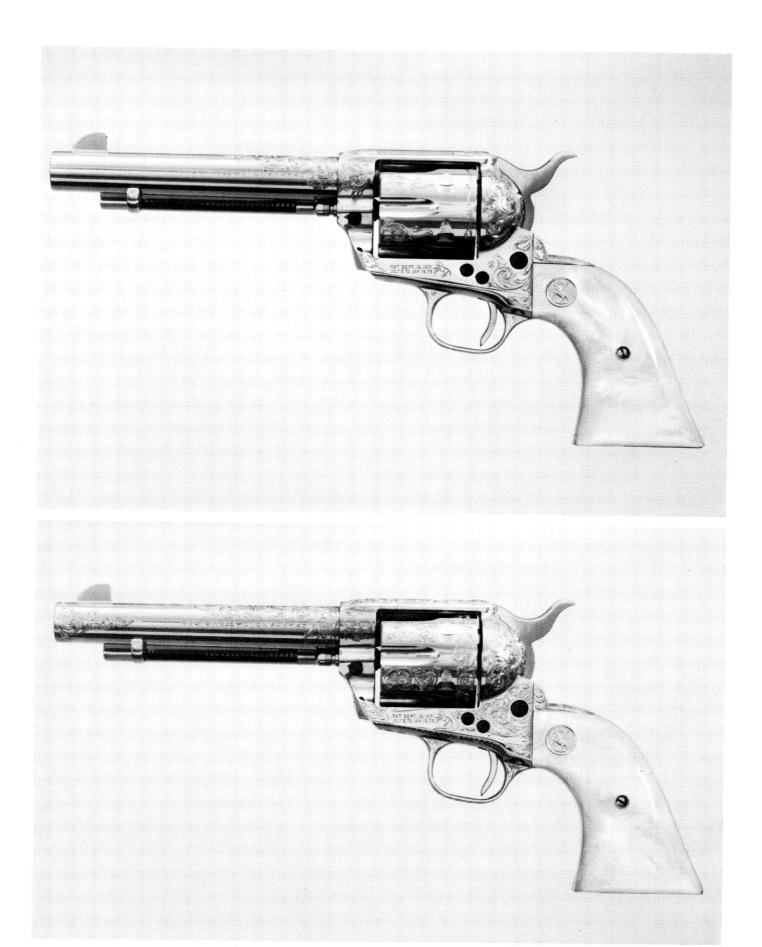

Style A (top) and C scroll by White on Single Actions 37806SA and 37808SA. *(Colt's Firearms Division)*

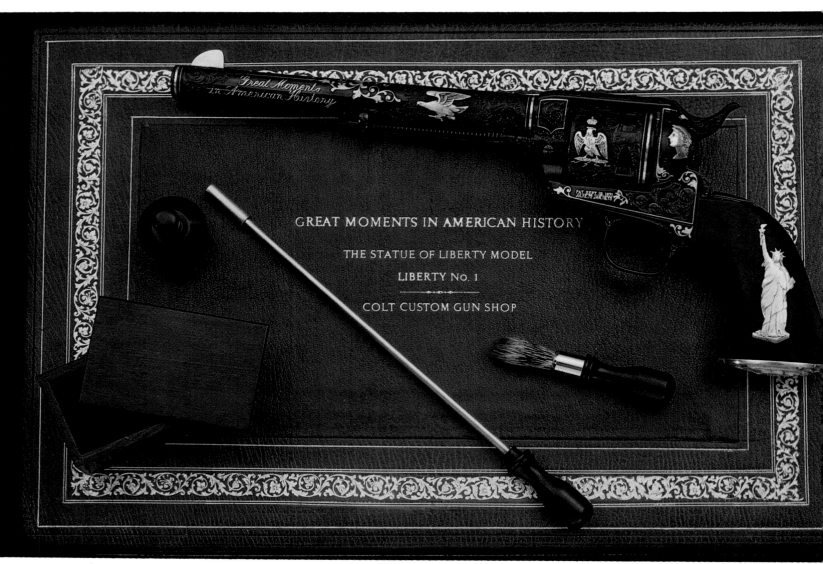

LIBERTY No. 1, Single Action Army deluxe, was commissioned by the Colt firm from A.A. White, and is part of a limited number of super-deluxe Single Actions in the "Great Moments in American History" series. Standard with each revolver will be the inscription on left side of the barrel, a relief gold buttcap of an American eagle, gold inlaid Colt barrel and frame markings, 18 karat gold front sight, 8" barrel, .45 caliber, gold scrolls and borders, gold barrel bands, profuse scroll coverage, special serial number distinct to each model, the backstrap gold inlaid with the model designation (illustrated piece bears script gold inlay: *Statue of Liberty Model*), and various flush and relief gold inlays pertaining to the specific theme. Deluxe leather casing with scroll embossed gold leaf decor, lined in velvet, by Arno Werner, chief bookbinder for Harvard University's Houghton Library (rare book collection). *(Courtesy Colt Firearms Division)*

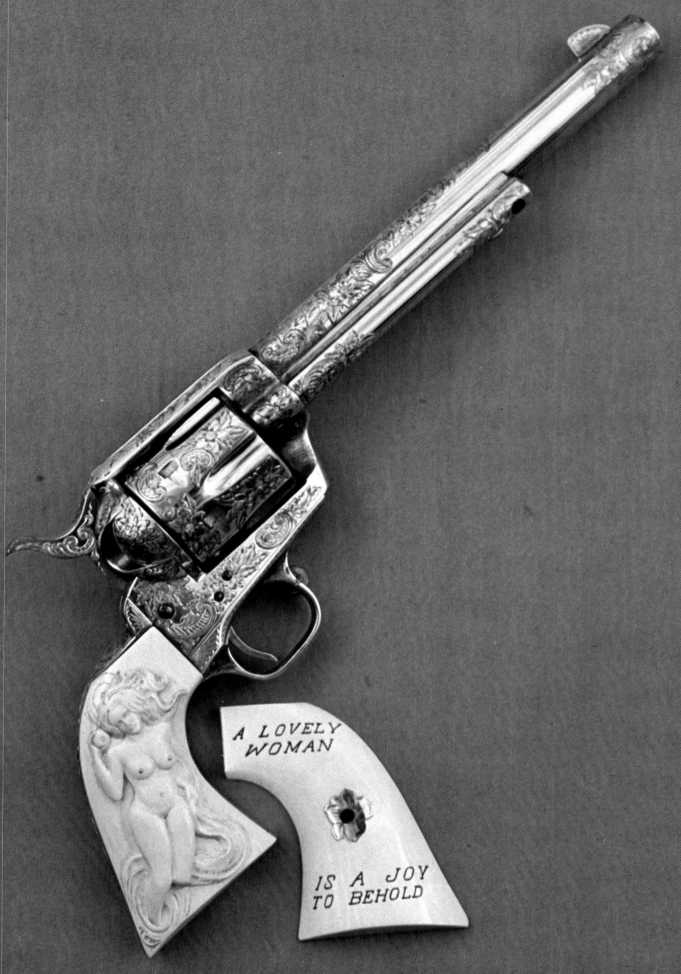

Gold and silver plated Single Action Army, with relief carved and inscribed ivory grips. The barroom nude motif, the age-old poem, the scroll style, and the combination gold and silver plating show the influence of deluxe Single Actions from the 1880's and 1890's. *(Richard P. Mellon Collection/Photograph, Bruce Pendleton, from Merrill K. Lindsay's* Great American Collections*)*

Text inscribed on grip: A LOVELY WOMAN IS A JOY TO BEHOLD

Serial number 250 M2 of the $500 grade World War I commemorative series. The $500 or Custom model pistols, totalling 300 guns, were done by the A. A. White Engravers, Inc., staff. The frames featured gold inlaid serial numbers, and frames and slides had a medium amount of scroll coverage; slide scenes and banner inscriptions were hand cut over pre-rolled designs. The $1,000 grade pistols (Deluxe model) totalled 100 pieces, and were contracted for engraving and gold inlay exclusively by Alvin A. White. All bear his gold inlaid signature cartouche on the receiver, beneath the grips. Design featured profuse scrollwork, gold inlaid borders on the slide, gold inlaid serial numbers, and finely engraved slide scenes and banner inscriptions. Serial numbering as follows: Chateau Thierry model, Deluxe grade — numbers 1CT to 25CT; Custom grade — numbers 26CT to 100CT. Belleau Wood model, Deluxe grade — numbers 101BW to 125BW; Custom grade — numbers 126BW to 200BW. 2nd Battle of the Marne model, Deluxe grade — numbers 201M2 to 225M2; Custom grade — numbers 226M2 to 300M2. Meuse Argonne Model, Deluxe grade — numbers 301MA to 325MA; Custom grade— numbers 326MA to 400MA. Prototype guns for the Custom grade were numbers WWI-1 through WWI-4, and for the Deluxe grade, number WWI-5. *(W. Gene Moser Collection)*

Slide scene detail from the Chateau Thierry Custom grade World War I pistol. This specimen served as the inspection standard for the 75 other pistols in that group. *(Colt's Firearms Division)*

Deluxe gold inlaid rosewood grips and a graceful scroll style without punched background were selected for Combat Commander 70BS34082, made on special order as a birthday gift for a prominent Middle Eastern ruler. Finished in blue, including sandblast finish on top and bottom areas of slide and on lower and back areas of frame. *(Private Collection)*

Nickel plated and class C engraved, Government Model number 299586-C is signed by A.A. White (initials A.A.W.), and was shipped in August 1966 to Thompson Sporting Goods, Long Beach, California. Processed on Factory Order 11364. Since pearl grips were not at that time available from the factory, these were located after shipment. *(Albert E. Brichaux Collection)*

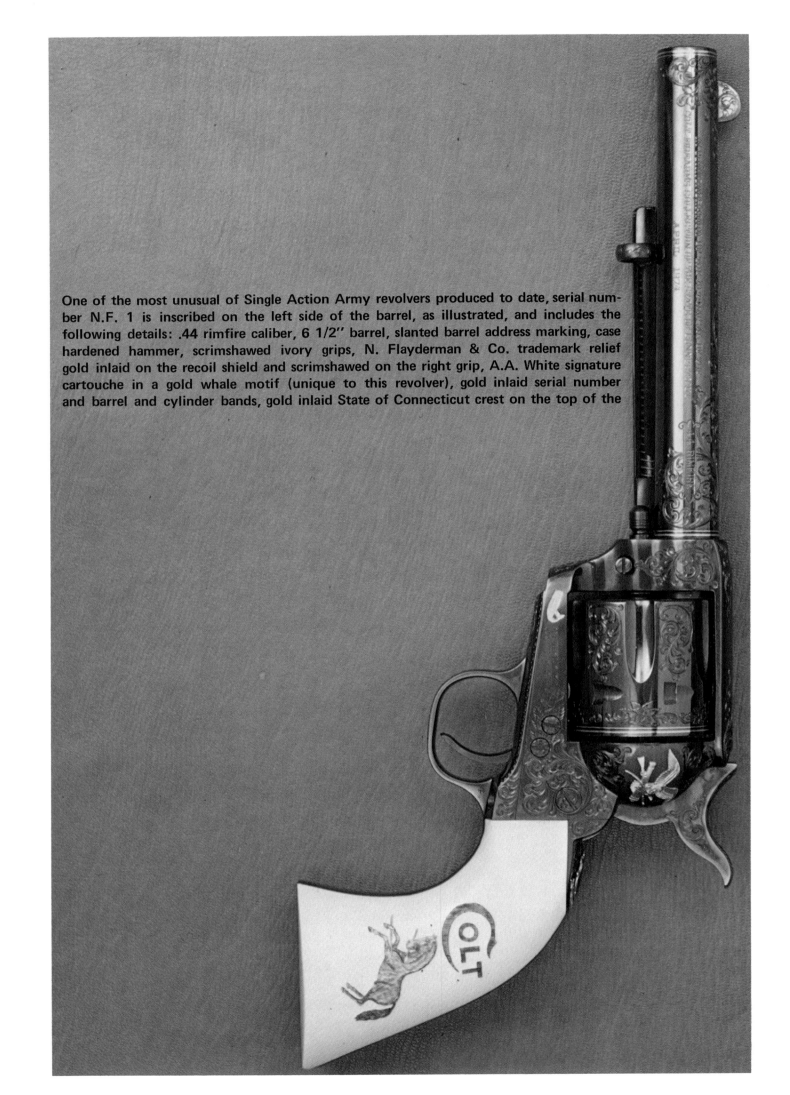

One of the most unusual of Single Action Army revolvers produced to date, serial number N.F. 1 is inscribed on the left side of the barrel, as illustrated, and includes the following details: .44 rimfire caliber, 6 1/2'' barrel, slanted barrel address marking, case hardened hammer, scrimshawed ivory grips, N. Flayderman & Co. trademark relief gold inlaid on the recoil shield and scrimshawed on the right grip, A.A. White signature cartouche in a gold whale motif (unique to this revolver), gold inlaid serial number and barrel and cylinder bands, gold inlaid State of Connecticut crest on the top of the

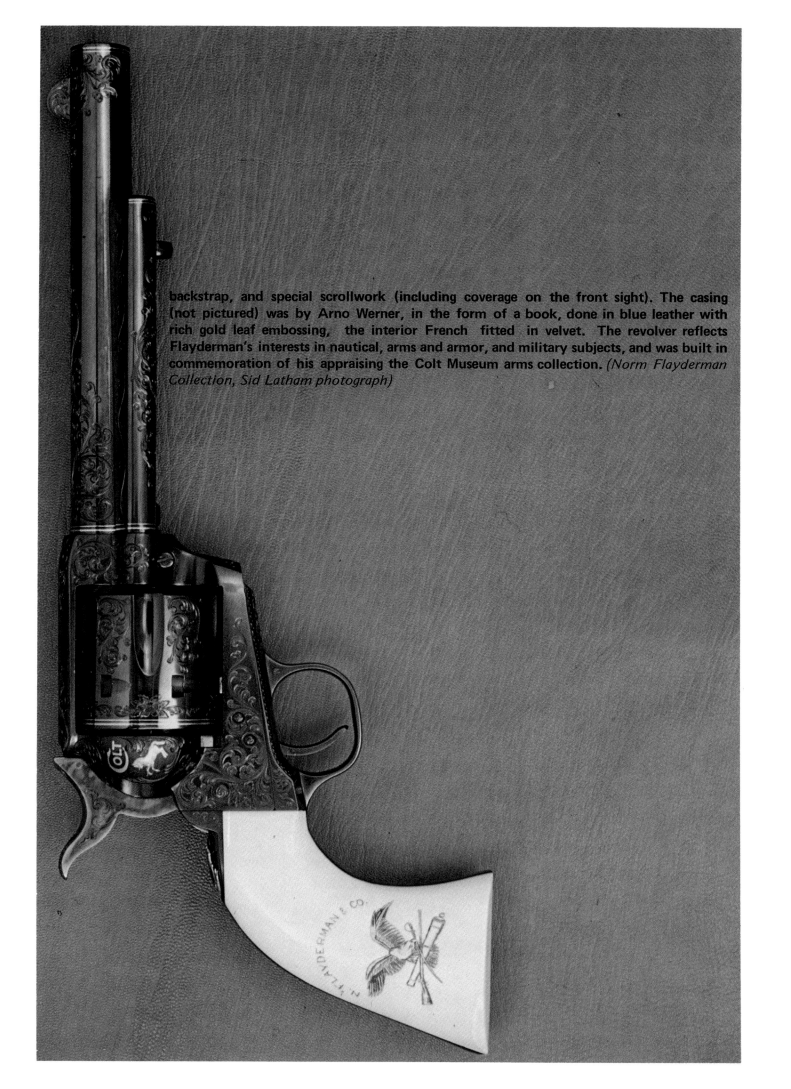

backstrap, and special scrollwork (including coverage on the front sight). The casing (not pictured) was by Arno Werner, in the form of a book, done in blue leather with rich gold leaf embossing, the interior French fitted in velvet. The revolver reflects Flayderman's interests in nautical, arms and armor, and military subjects, and was built in commemoration of his appraising the Colt Museum arms collection. *(Norm Flayderman Collection, Sid Latham photograph)*

Displayed next to an American eagle pattern flask for the Baby Dragoon and early Model 1849 Pocket revolvers, the miniature flask at right was engraved by A. A. White to accompany a miniature of the Second Model Dragoon built by John Corliss. Miniatures made or worked on by White are supremely rare. *(Ronald N. Swanson Collection)*

Relief gold inlaid Python, with gold mounted rosewood grips, decorated on order of P. R. Phillips, and now on display at the Woolaroc Museum, Bartlesville, Oklahoma. A most out-of-the-ordinary decor, which requires much gold and substantial relief chiselling after the metal has been inlaid. Various colors of gold were used, to accentuate the contrast against the blued steel.

Serial number 70G17348 Government Model .45 Automatic pistol. High relief gold inlays on the slide and receiver; WBF III flush gold script monogram on the grip safety. The front sight of 18k gold; the ivory grips inlaid with relief chiselled 18k gold longhorn steer motif. Top of the slide inlaid with a high relief gold American eagle, a favorite design motif of Alvin White. Signature on this piece appears in a gold cartouche on the receiver (beneath the grip). *(Walter B. Ford III Collection)*

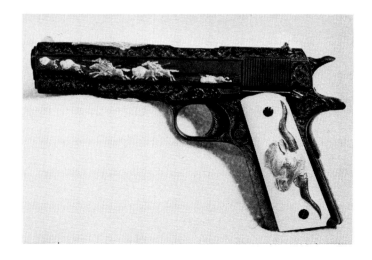

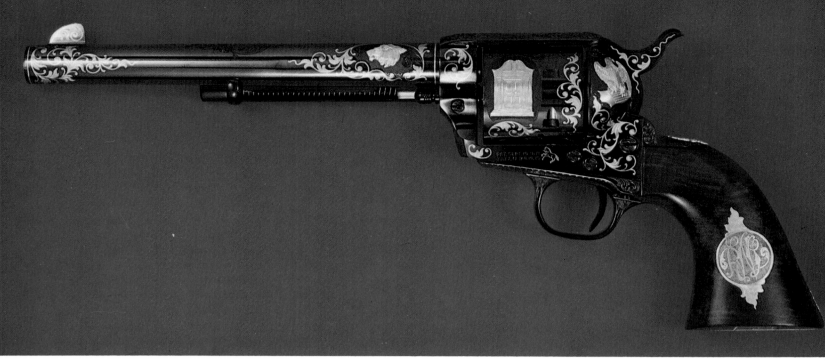

The right side of this A. A. White Single Action (RLW-1) is pictured elsewhere in black and white. Decorative devices on this arm represent personal enthusiasms of the client, including architectural device on the cylinder (owner's front door), patriotic American eagle on recoil shield, African lion on barrel, acanthus leaf and Camp Fire Club of America logo on the backstrap (in relief gold), the spine of a book in relief gold on the buttstrap, Ferrari and Mercedes emblems on butt of the select walnut grips in engraved flush gold, the serial number inlaid on the frame, owner's name in flush gold script inlaid on the backstrap, and a profusion of scroll engraved and gold inlaid devices. Revolver also cased in a deluxe wood, leather, and velvet box, accompanied by cartridges, and an inlaid cleaning rod and oil bottle embellished by former Colt factory engraver Daniel Goodwin. One of the most exotic and unusual of all deluxe Alvin White firearms. *(Private Collection, Sid Latham photograph)*

Custom built on order of the Colt Firearms Company, c. 1961, Python number 20998 has served for much of the period since then as a factory sample piece. It has been published more often than any other Python revolver including in *Guns & Ammo, Shooting Times, The Colt Heritage*, A.A. White Engravers Inc. catalogue, and on a 28″ x 36″ color poster promoting *The Colt Heritage* book. The right side of the revolver features a relief gold inlaid bear and cubs (one of them scurrying up a tree), a gold escutcheon on the ivory grip, and profuse scrolls and borders in gold and engraving. The muzzle is also engraved as are (quite rare) the trigger and hammer, front sight, barrel rib, and the front end of the rib beneath the barrel (has a squirrel motif). One of the finest examples of arms engraving by A.A. White. *(Private Collection, Sid Latham photograph)*

The Rampant Colt, by Alvin White, a limited edition bronze authorized by Colt's Firearms Division. 50 cast in bronze, two in sterling silver; all numbered and signed. 10½" height; 1" thick cherry base. One of various pieces of sculpture done by White in his multi-faceted career as a craftsman and arms engraver. *(Paul Skogstad Collection)*

The Philadelphia Bicentennial Single Actions, designed by Paul Frank and Carl Braden, and ordered by them both. Relief gold work by A.A. White, the scrollwork and the bulk of the gold borders and flush inlays by Robert Burt and Leonard Francolini. The grips of relief carved ivory, mounted in 24 karat gold rampant colts and *fleu de lis* devices, with buttcaps of 18 and 24 karat, featuring American eagle decor. Casing by Arno Werner of leather and velvet, with gold and silver Bicentennial Logo lid plaque by A.A. White.

This exquisite pair of revolvers took nearly four years from the concept stage to final delivery. They have been featured in Colt factory publications, in *The Colt Heritage*, and elsewhere, and have received considerable publicity and have been on display on several occasions.

Serial numbers PBC-1 and PBC-2. .45 caliber; 7-1/2" barrels. Portrait busts in relief 18 karat on top flats of the backstraps are of John Hancock and George Washington, their signatures in flush gold on the right side of each barrel. Paul Revere's ride, Molly Pitcher on the battlefield, the Spirit of '76, American eagle barrel motifs, the Constitution frigate, a moon and Liberty Bell and American flag device, Independence Hall, and a PF (for Paul Frank) monogram are among the carefully thought out and executed design details. *(Paul Frank, Jr., and Carl A. Braden Collection)*

Chapter XVI
The Colt Custom
Gun Shop

In conjunction with expanding and revitalizing its engraving program, by the end of 1975 Colt's employed four full time engravers; George B. Spring having joined the then staff of R.B. Burt, Leonard Francolini, and Daniel Goodwin. Burt had been at Colt since 1970, as Master Engraver; Francolini was hired in 1972, and Goodwin in 1974.

The Colt engraving studio was enlarged and rebuilt, with ample space for a staff of six, and for the variety of tools which a full force requires. The shop is part of the complex known as the Custom Gun Shop, managed by Jan Mladek, with long-time employee Al DeJohn as superintendent. With six full-time craftsmen, Colt would be able to boast the largest staff of qualified engravers of any gunmaker in America. That is also the largest group of in-house engravers employed by the company since the days of Cuno Helfricht.

As part of the expanded decorative facility at the factory, an unprecedented fourth grade of scrollwork has been added to the line. Known as class D, the coverage for this profuse scroll is full, even including the screws. Further available: Engraving or inlaying of any type or design. Delivery is relatively prompt, and prices are quoted based on the customer's design requirements. The writer suggests it is usually best for the reduction of correspondence time for the client to indicate how much one is willing to spend and then to see what can be done for that amount.

Still another aspect of the new factory approach to engraving is the vigorous promotion of arms decoration at shows such as those of the National Sporting Goods and the National Rifle Associations. At the N.S.G.A.'s 1974 showing in Chicago, Master Engraver Burt was on hand, and the featured Colt display piece was the "One-of-a-Kind" Python which he had made specifically for sealed bid sale. The elaborately engraved, inlaid, stocked, and cased revolver brought a record $7,600. Successful bidder was Colt dealer Arthur L. Toll, president of Nationwide Sports Distributors. The favorable response to the "one-of-a-kind" concept suggests the possibility of further uniquely embellished models at future showings.

While Alvin F. Herbert was still employed by Colt, Earl Bieu was hired as a student engraver, in July of 1966. Bieu's style is illustrated in the excerpt from Colt's catalogues of c. 1968-72. Remaining with the company nearly four years, his output was not large, and guns done by Bieu are not common. His nephew, Dennis Kies, worked for Colt during most of the period c. 1968-72, and learned engraving from Herbert and from Bieu. His style was the same as that of his uncle. Specimens of Colt guns by Kies and Bieu are scarce and are sought after by collectors.

Robert B. Burt began gun engraving in August of 1968, learning the trade under Master Engraver R. J. Smith, at the Smith & Wesson factory, Springfield, Massachusetts. After two years at S & W, Burt succeeded Herbert and Bieu at Colt. At the time, 1970, he was 26 years old — the youngest craftsman in the twentieth century to be appointed Master Engraver at Colt's factory

Besides his vocation of gun engraving and inlaying, Burt draws, paints, and carves. His interest in engraving was inspired while a student at the School of Practical Art of Boston (now known as the Boston Institute of Art). In 1973 he was featured at Montreal's "Man and His World" exposition, demonstrating firearms decoration at the arms pavilion. *The Hartford Times* ran an illustrated, detailed article on his work in their issue of July 16, 1972.

A list of prominent personalities who own deluxe guns engraved and/or gold inlaid by Burt includes Dale Robertson, Sammy Davis Jr., Senator Barry Goldwater, Congressman Robert L. F. Sikes, singer Hank Williams Jr., former Secretary of the Treasury John B. Connally, Mel Torme, President N. Ceausescu of Roumania, President Park of Korea, and Premier Leonid I. Brezhnev of the Soviet Union.

Leonard Francolini, assistant engraver to Burt, was taught die cutting while employed by Preston Engraving, Windsor, Connecticut, and joined Colt's factory in 1972. He learned gun engraving from R. B. Burt, beginning even before being hired by Colt. As Burt's assistant, Francolini has already executed some presentation pieces for the Prime Minister and Defense Minister of Korea, and for President Suharto of Indonesia.

In his years with Colt Francolini has learned the hammer and chisel technique, the inlaying of soft metals on steel, design and layout methods, and every other aspect of gun engraving. As a hobby, he does wood carving and makes miniature ships and a variety of other models in bottles.

To order contemporary factory engraving on Colt firearms, it is best to contact a Colt dealer or to write the company's Customer Service Department, stating in as much detail as possible all decorative requirements. As noted earlier in the present chapter, the client may even wish to indicate the amount of money he intends to invest. One of the features of factory work is that the finished piece is accompanied by a documenting letter from the engraver himself. Collectors are realizing that the engraved gun is the most desirable category of production variation to own in a modern Colt firearm. Colt is fully aware of this, and thus makes every effort to satisfy the demands of discriminating collectors, shooters, and hunters.

As of 1981 the Colt Custom Gun Shop engraving staff consists of Bryson Gwinnell (joined the factory in 1977), Steve Kamyk (came to Colt's from Smith & Wesson in 1976), Howard Dove (1978), and Van-Gwinnell (1980). A couple of additional craftsmen are expected to be hired shortly, to help accommodate the substantial work load. The demand for quality craftsmanship on firearms is tremendous, and the Custom Shop has developed its capacity and skills to a point which rivals Colt's position in the heyday of Cuno Helfricht. To quote from the author's introduction to "The Personal Touch" catalogue (available· from Colt at $5):

> Unquestionably the "blue chips of gun collecting," finely decorated and otherwise customized Colt arms have great investment value and are consistently in demand ... Samuel Colt himself launched the custom and decorative tradition of his products, hiring the leading engravers and

ordering for himself, the general public and for the giants of finance, industry, the military and royalty, what are recognized as the finest handguns made in 19th Century America. The unique tradition of custom and deluxe firearms was a highlight of Samuel Colt's unparalleled contribution to gunmaking.

From the period following Colt's death (1862) into modern times, the firm he founded has added to its impressive list of achievements in the field of custom firearms ... Colt's Custom Gun Shop opens up an entire world for the firearms enthusiast where the deluxe and the special are again available as in the heyday of fine quality special order arms of the 19th Century. It offers the services of the most complete and qualified department of its kind in the American firearms field.

Benefiting from 140 years of experience and comprised of an expert team of management, marketing, engineering, production, engraving and gunsmithing personnel, the Custom Gun Shop is uniquely qualified to handle client requirements. No firm can match Colt's experience and expertise in the challenging combination of art, history, elegance, beauty and collectibility which the quality gun offers. The Colt Custom Gun Shop is unmatched in offering those ingredients necessary to create first-rate heirlooms of intrinsic value.

Today, very few manufactured products of true quality remain on the market. Considering the degree of intricacy and custom hand fitting, few products can rival the best grade firearm. Colt Firearms is offering a quality service unequaled in modern America and one in which Samuel Colt — inventor, founder, pioneer manufacturer (and connoisseur of the custom gun) — would himself take deep and justifiable pride.

The Colt Bicentennial Third Model Dragoon, sold in February 1976 at auction for $55,000, and purchased by Arthur L. Toll, President of Nationwide Sports Distributors, Southampton, Pennsylvania. From the proceeds, Colt presented $3,752 to the U.S. Olympic Committee, "to assist and support the American shooting teams in the 1976 Olympics". The exquisitely embellished revolver featured gold inlaid bicentennial motifs, gold scrolls and borders, gold inscriptions, and deluxe walnut stocks with a fancy inscribed and gold inlaid plaque. The special serial number was 1776-1976. To quote the company's news release issued at the time of sale, "Not since the days of Colonel Colt has such an ambitious project in firearms embellishment been undertaken by a major U.S. gun maker. The inspiration for the Bicentennial Dragoon were the pistols of the same model, gold inlaid, engraved, and cased, presented by Col. Colt to Czar Nicholas I of Russia and the Sultan of Turkey c. 1854."

Engraving and inlaying was by Robert Burt, Leonard Francolini, and Daniel Goodwin. The deluxe casing was in French walnut, and accessories were an engraved and serial numbered flask, bullet mold, and screwdriver-nipple wrench. A leather bound book documenting the revolver's manufacture and sale accompanied the outfit, and was made specifically for Colt by Arno Werner, Master Bookbinder. *(Carl Ross Collection)*

Number 62357SA 12" Buntline was shipped in December 1974 to M & N Distributors, Torrance, California. Engraved by Leonard Francolini, in C coverage, and finished in blue and case hardening. *(Albert E. Brichaux Collection)*

Colt's 1979 European Show Model, built specifically for display at the Paris and Nuremburg shows in that year, and displayed by the firm at various other important shows since then. To quote from the news release published at the time of initial exhibition, in Paris, March 4th: "The European Show Model follows in the footsteps of the famous guns that Colonel Colt brought to Europe, exhibited, sold and presented to heads of state beginning in the 1850's. The 1979 show gun is a rightful complement to the famous Colt series of NSGA Show guns which are considered by many as the ultimate rarities in arms collecting." Serial number PARIS No. 1; among special details, a portrait bust of Samuel Colt in relief on the recoil shield, rampant colt on left side of the frame in gold, Arc de Triomphe in relief gold on the left side of the cylinder, and the Eiffel Tower in relief gold on the right side, *fleur de lis* on the top flat of the backstrap, various inscriptions in flush gold (including the date of Colt's French patent filing, 16 Nov. 1835 and Samuel Colt's signature), the symbol of the City of Paris in relief gold on the loading gate, the serial number 1 Colt prototype revolver in relief gold on the barrel, various gold scroll and border details, and ivory grips. The front sight is notched in gold, and the backstrap is inscribed in script: *Colt's European Show Model 1979 by Colt's Custom Gun Shop Hartford Connecticut.* Arno Werner built the casing for the set in elegant leather, gold tooled to match the backstrap inscription, and lined in leather and velvet. Gold inlaid and engraved by A.A. White and so signed.

Scroll engraving and border work was done in the fashion of Cuno Helfricht, and the finish was executed in the finest Colt Royal Blue. *(Courtesy Colt Firearms Division)*

Single Actions 73045SA and 73046SA illustrate class D scroll and border work by Steve Kamyk. Full silver plated finish, 45 caliber, 4-3/4" barrels. Original shipment was to J.W. Murchison, Inc., Wilmington, North Carolina, in February 1978. The pair was built for Henry H. Burgwyn, whose initials are on each backstrap; a double presentation casing was also supplied by the factory for this most unusual pair. *(Dr. Johnny Spellman Collection)*

.357 caliber Single Actions are rarely observed engraved. Number 62313SA left the factory in April 1974, and was shipped to Berns Wholesale Hardware, Denver. Ledgers record the engraver as Robert Burt, on factory order 12331; and further note, .357 Magnum caliber, 7-1/2" barrel, blue (and case hardened) finish, wood grips, C engraving. The scrollwork a richly cut pattern *ala* Cuno Helfricht and A.A. White. *(Gianfranco Spellman, D.V.M., Collection)*

The Colt "One of a Kind" Python, serial number E45753, made for sealed bid sale as the featured attraction of the company's 1974 NSGA Show exhibit. The Colt news release on the gun, dated February 10, 1974, stated: *The Python has flush gold inlaid scrollwork on the barrel and on the frame, side plate, cylinder, trigger guard and backstrap. On the left side of the barrel are a raised gold inlaid motif of a coiled python and the inscription 'Python .357' in flush gold inlaid lettering. The left side of the frame carries a raised gold inlaid motif of the Rampant Colt. Stocks are American walnut carved in Germanic style of scrollwork and have gold plated Colt Firearms medallions on both sides. The case is oil finished walnut, fitted inside with red velvet. Key, lock and piano hinge are all brass. A presentation plaque is fitted to the outside of the lid. Colt Firearms will engrave it with an inscription and the name of the ultimate purchaser. The purchaser will receive a letter signed by Colt Firearms president David C. Eaton and Mr. Burt detailing the background of the gun.* A followup news release announced the name of the buyer, Arthur L. Toll, and the top bid price of $7,600. *(Arthur L. Toll Collection)*

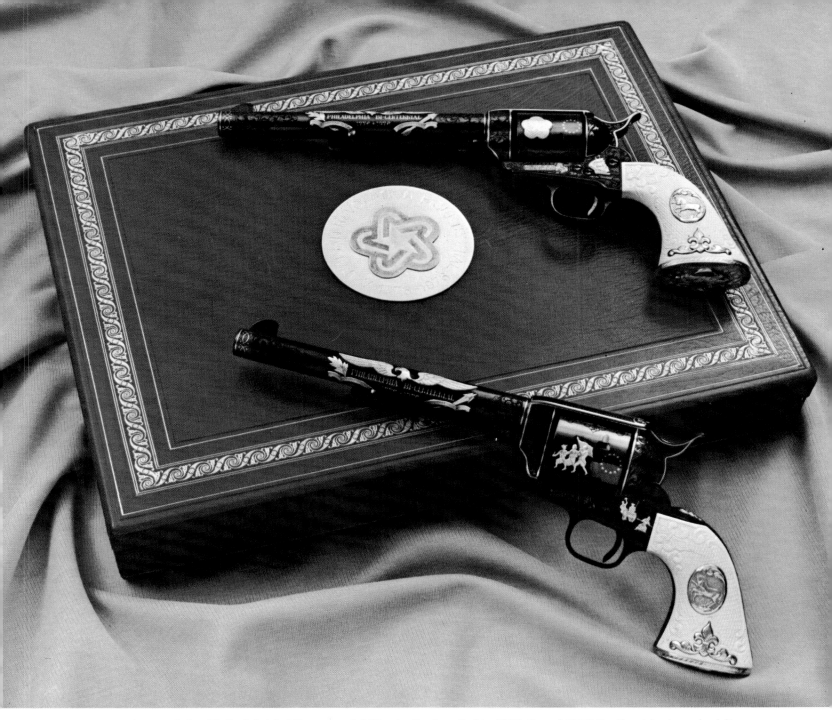

Complete cased set of the Philadelphia Bicentennial Single Action Colts, PBC-1 and PBC-2. See black and white pictures for details. By Robert Burt, Leonard Francolini and A.A. White. *(Paul Frank, Jr. and Carl A. Braden Collection)*

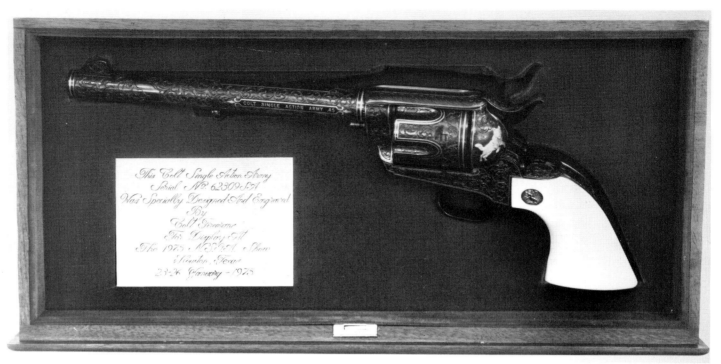

Number 62309SA was Colt's 1975 N.S.G.A. show revolver, and was shipped in January of that year to Terence Bond of Grand Island, New York. The factory ledgers note the caliber as .45 and the barrel length 7-1/2''; full blue finish; grips of Colt medallion ivory. Engraved coverage of class D, by Leonard Francolini. 24 karat gold inlaid in relief on the left side of the recoil shield was a timber wolf; relief inlaid in gold on the loading gate was an American eagle. Flush inlaid barrel markings and gold borders encircle those markings; gold bands on the breech and muzzle end of the barrel, the cylinder (note double line border following the flute contours), frame, and the ejector tube. Red velvet lined walnut casing; note brass plaque inscribed with details on the set. *(Albert E. Brichaux Collection)*

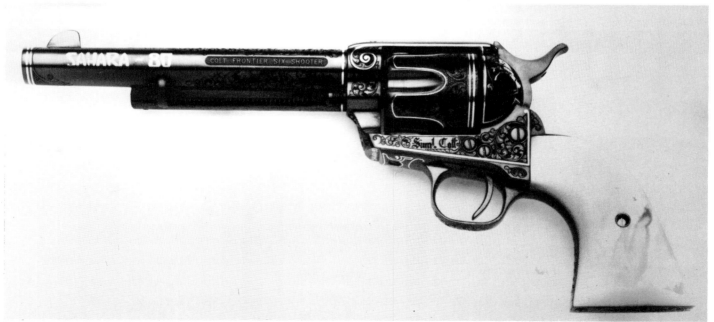

Gold inlaid and engraved Single Action .44-40 by Bob Burt for auction sale at the 1980 Las Vegas Antique Arms Show, which was held at the Hotel Sahara. Serial number SAHARA-80. Specially built 6-1/2'' barrel; among other deluxe features are the etched COLT FRONTIER SIX-SHOOTER barrel marking, the *Saml. Colt* in old English on the left side of the frame (instead of patent date markings), relief gold rampant colt on the left recoil shield, a mountain lion on the right side of the frame, gold border and scroll work, gold barrel and cylinder bands, and all blue finish. The grips are the quite rare mother of pearl. Sale was accompanied by a considerable degree of fanfare and publicity, a distinct advantage of pieces from Colt's Custom Gun Shop.

Matched pair numbers 62298SA and 62299SA were processed on Colt factory order 12560, were grade C embellished by Leonard Francolini, and are further documented by the plant as follows: .45 caliber, 7-1/2" barrels, blue (and case hardened) finishes, wood grips, shipped to Mitchell Powers, Bristol, Tennessee, and sold to Wiseman's, Johnson City, Tennessee, October 1975. Both revolvers are signed on the backstrap under the grips, by Francolini. *(Gianfranco Spellman, D.V.M., Collection)*

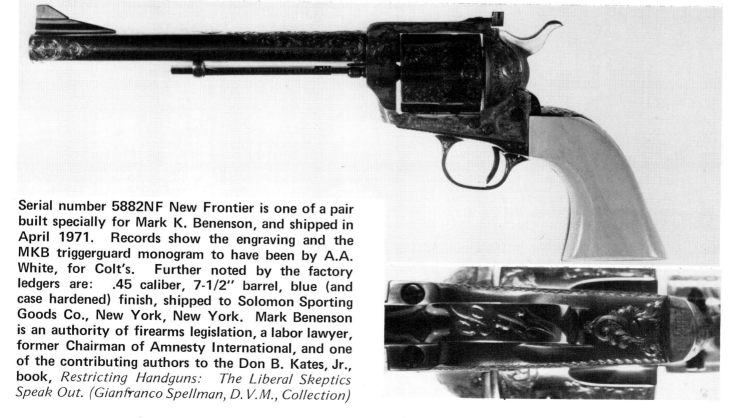

Serial number 5882NF New Frontier is one of a pair built specially for Mark K. Benenson, and shipped in April 1971. Records show the engraving and the MKB triggerguard monogram to have been by A.A. White, for Colt's. Further noted by the factory ledgers are: .45 caliber, 7-1/2" barrel, blue (and case hardened) finish, shipped to Solomon Sporting Goods Co., New York, New York. Mark Benenson is an authority of firearms legislation, a labor lawyer, former Chairman of Amnesty International, and one of the contributing authors to the Don B. Kates, Jr., book, *Restricting Handguns: The Liberal Skeptics Speak Out. (Gianfranco Spellman, D.V.M., Collection)*

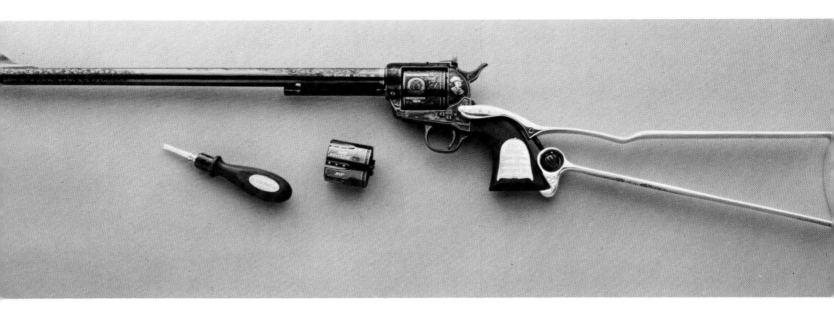

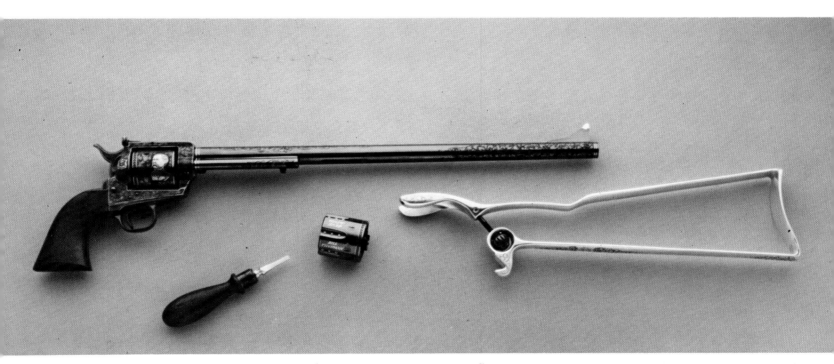

Colt New Frontier Buntline Special number BUNTLINE NO. 1, gold inlaid and deluxe engraved for the 1977 National Sporting Goods Association Show, with $1000 of the proceeds donated to the U.S. Olympic shooting teams. The decoration, to quote from the company news release, was a salute to "the much storied presentation of five of the long barreled Colts to Dodge City lawmen Wyatt Earp, Bat Masterson, Charlie Bassett, Bill Tilghman and Neal Brown by Ned Buntline, the dime novel author and promoter of western lore. Whether the controversy over Buntline's presentation is fanciful or not, [the] Show Gun is a genuine salute to the rugged marshals of the Old West and the traditions of law and order they fought to uphold."

Note the shoulder stock, of bronze, silver plated, and superbly scroll engraved. The extra cylinder is of .45 ACP, with gold inlaid inscriptions of the above noted half dozen names, associated with the story of the Buntline Special; relief inlaid gold stars are in the cylinder flutes. Casing was of oak, lined in velvet.

Decoration by Robert Burt, Leonard Francolini, Daniel Goodwin, and George Spring, with the front sight notch in gold by A.A. White. *(Albert and Paula Brichaux Collection)*

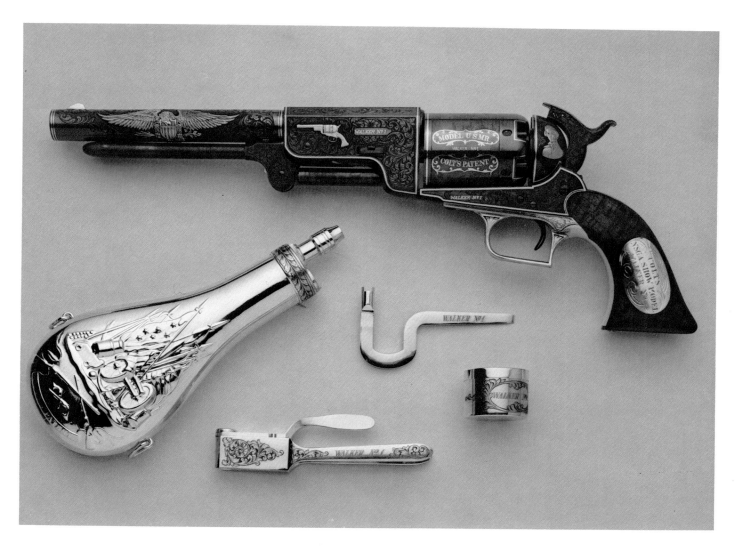

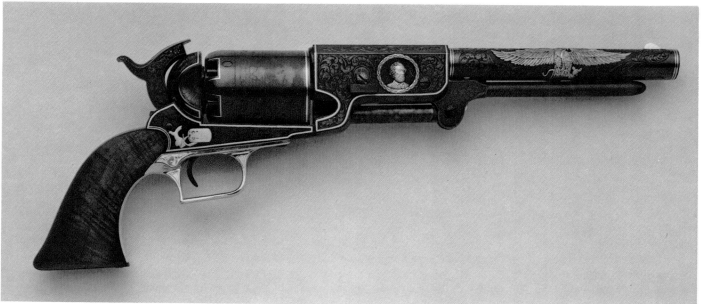

The Colt N.S.G.A. Show Model for 1979 was Walker Colt serial number WALKER No. 1. Engravers were Robert Burt, Leonard Francolini, Daniel Goodwin, Bryson Gwinnell, and Steve Kamyk. Profusely gold inlaid with motifs which detail the history of the Walker model, including American and Mexican eagles, the prototype Walker, the special serial number, portrait busts of Captain Walker and Samuel Colt, the Walker's mechanism as depicted in original Colt advertising, and scroll and inscriptions from the roll engraved cylinder scene. Note also the gold borders and barrel and cylinder bands, and the engraved and inscribed oval gold grip plaque. Accessories numbered to match the revolver, and casing was of magnificent oak, lined in gold tooled leather and velvet by Arno Werner. On the lid was a breathtaking gold plaque, pierced and inscribed, by Leonard Francolini.

Purchased at auction by Sam Pancotto, who had previously acquired the Tiffany Grip Special set, the 1978 N.S.G.A. Show Gun. *(Carl Ross Collection)*

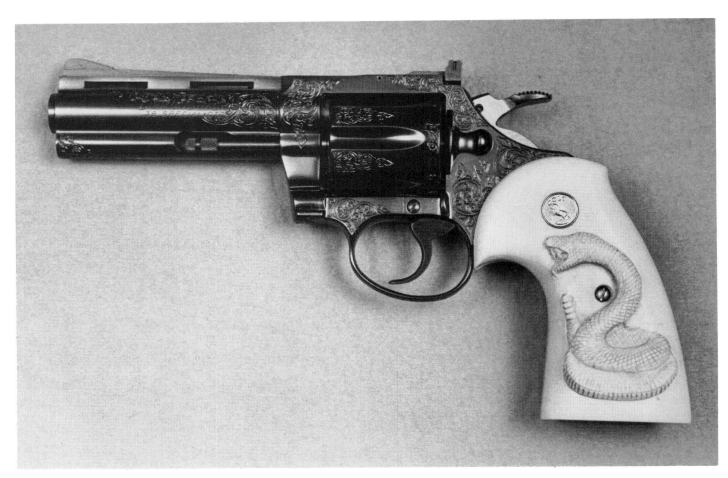

Custom engraved and fitted with carved ivory grips on order of the present owner, Diamondback number D6226 features scrollwork on the barrel, frame, cylinder, and crane, and relief carved ivory grips with rattlesnake and American eagle motifs. Shipped in January 1968 to Simmons Gun Specialty, Olathe, Kansas, on order of George S. Lewis, Jr. 4″ barrel; .38 caliber; blue finish. *(George S. Lewis, Jr. Collection)*

Number 22SPL of the Custom Edition series totalling 50 Single Action Army revolvers in .44 Special caliber. Quoting from the Colt factory letter on the above revolver: "Inscription on left side of barrel 'Custom Edition' inlaid in 24K gold. Serial numbers inlaid in 24K gold. Custom walnut French-fitted case with gold velvet lining. It is interesting to note the engraving scrollwork is an adaptation of the style used on most engraved Colt Single Action revolvers of the period of c. 1873-1921. This firearm is one of the first custom group of its kind made in strictly limited number and coincides with the launching of the Colt Custom Gun Shop." Finished in blue and case hardening; type C+ scroll engraving; shipped to Kamloops Distributing Company in March 1977. *(Albert E. Brichaux Collection)*

Colt Pony automatic pistol, number CPA-001094. An experimental lot of nearly 50 specimens of this model had been manufactured, but were never placed on the market. Specimen illustrated is the only one to have been factory embellished, and it features gold inlaying by Leonard Francolini; shipment was in May of 1974, and purchase was by a Colt employee. A fancy French fitted walnut presentation case was also included in this special order. Blued finish; .380 caliber; 3-1/8" barrel; ivory grips made by Colt. *(Albert E. Brichaux Collection)*

Colt's 1979 Show Gun, the Tiffany Grip Special, serial number SAA1. An utterly magnificent masterwork of gold inlaying, engraving, combination finishes, gold and sterling silver Tiffany grip, and sterling silver and *vermeil* casing. The design of SAA1 documents the Tiffany grips made for Colt revolvers during the Civil War era (see Chapter VII). The freshly designed Tiffany grip was created especially for this revolver by A.A, White. Finishes include silver plating, and bluing on the barrel, bluing on the cylinder, case hardening on the frame, and gold plating of the hammer and trigger, ejector rod housing, ejector rod head, cylinder pin and screws.

The spectacular casing was made on special order for Colt by Tiffany & Co., who also authorized the name "Tiffany Grip Special" for this unique revolver outfit. Unfortunately the casing was not finished at the time of auction sale, otherwise the set would surely have brought substantially more than it did, $49,500. The buyer was Sam Pancotto, Chicago contractor and big game hunter.

Revolver appeared on the cover of Colt's 1979 product catalogue, using the picture reproduced above. Signatures of the engravers were inscribed on the right side of the frame: Robert Burt, Leonard Francolini, Steve Kamyk, Daniel Goodwin, and A.A. White. Case lining, in blue velvet, French style, was by Arno Werner. Revolver also included an extra cylinder, gold inlaid, blued, and silver plated, chambered for .45 ACP cartridges. *(Albert and Paula Brichaux Collection)*

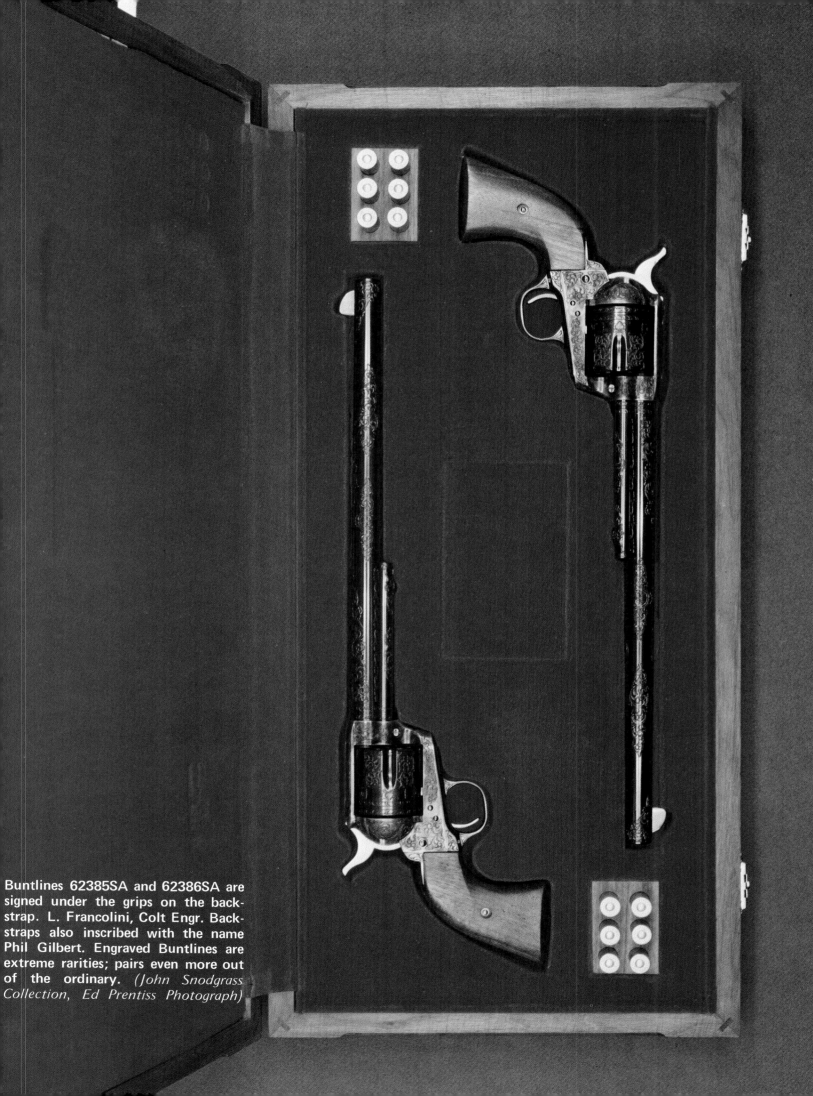

Buntlines 62385SA and 62386SA are signed under the grips on the back-strap. L. Francolini, Colt Engr. Back-straps also inscribed with the name Phil Gilbert. Engraved Buntlines are extreme rarities; pairs even more out of the ordinary. *(John Snodgrass Collection, Ed Prentiss Photograph)*

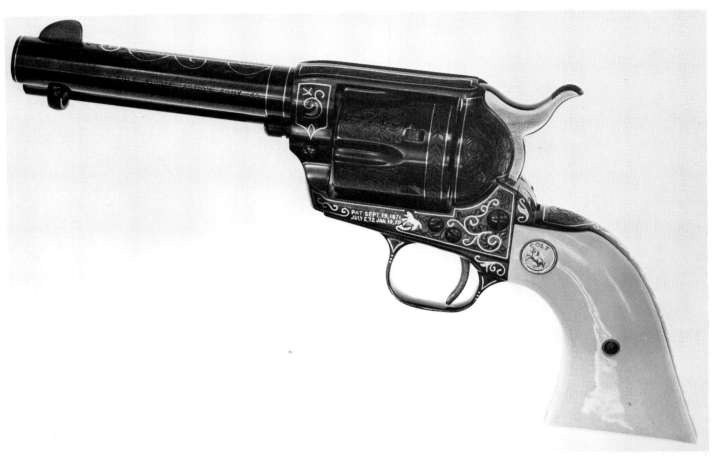

The only custom deluxe engraved and inlaid revolver done by Earl Bieu while at Colt, number 40967SA is a .45, 4-3/4" barrel, blue (entirely), with ivory grips, and shipped in June of 1971. Bieu Colts are quite rare, due to the short period of time he was employed by the firm. *(Albert E. Brichaux Collection)*

Earl Bieu was the engraver of Single Action 38186SA; the factory further records the following: .45 caliber, 5-1/2" barrel, nickel plated, pearl grips, full coverage, backstrap inscribed, and shipment in May of 1968. Note that even the front sight, the screws, and hammer were embellished. *(Albert E. Brichaux Collection)*

Python 31381, 2-1/2", blue, with carved walnut stocks, was executed in full coverage scrollwork by Earl Bieu. Colt factory ledgers also indicate modification to FitzGerald cutaway configuration (triggerguard partially cut away at front and the hammer spur machined off). Shipped February 1964. *(Albert E. Brichaux Collection)*

Single Actions numbers 61699SA and 61700SA (matched pair) were engraved in grade C coverage by William T. Mains, on Colt factory order 12297; the ledgers state further: .45 caliber, 4-3/4″ barrels, nickel plated, wood grips; shipment in October 1972 to T.J. Antiques & Sporting Goods, Columbus, Georgia. *(Albert E. Brichaux Collection)*

By Leonard Francolini, Single Actions SA04058 and SA04059 were engraved in special B coverage, plus flush gold borders, barrel and cylinder bands, American eagle, bison, coyote-moon and rampant colt motifs in relief gold, and grips of ivory. Built on Colt factory order number 10942, the pair are numbers four and five of the last 10 jobs done by Francolini while still in Colt's full time employ. .45 caliber; 7-1/2″ barrels. Note Royal Blue finish, including the frames, and the elegant contrast of the gold against the rich blue and classic ivory. *(Private Collection)*

By Leonard Francolini, Single Action Army number HG IV features special C coverage scrollwork, plus paratrooper wings on the topflat of the backstrap, script inscribed backstrap, gold serial number on the triggerguard, cylinder and frame, blue and case hardened finish, ivory and walnut grips, and velvet lined wooden factory casing. The casing is quite unusual, including bullet block and special compartment for the extra set of grips. A most distinctive design overall, and done with a special personal touch. *(Horace Greeley IV Collection, Photograph by G. Allan Brown)*

Shipment of number 57792SA Single Action .45 was in December of 1970; .45 caliber, 7-1/2" barrel, nickel plated, rubber grips, type C engraving, by Daniel Cullity. *(Albert E. Brichaux Collection)*

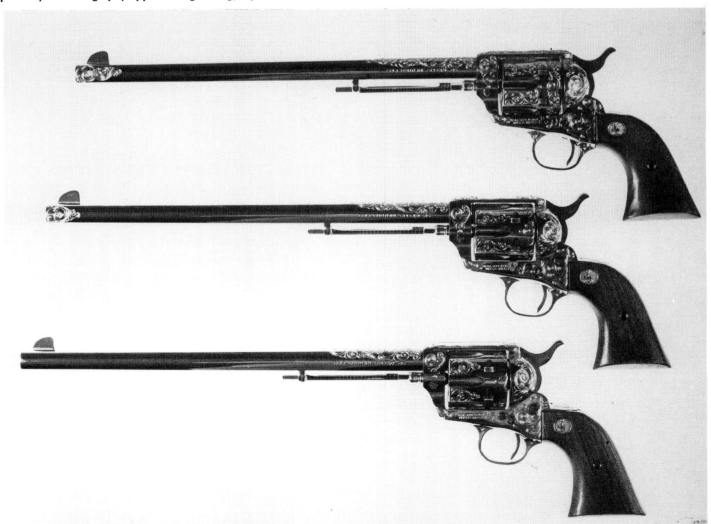

A quite exotic custom order, this grouping of Buntline Specials was engraved on order of Swanson Custom Firearms, Denver, Colorado, and is recorded in the factory ledgers as: Numbers 61205SA, 61206SA, 61207SA, engraved in A, B, and C scroll coverage respectively. Further information records .45 Colt caliber, 12" barrels, nickel plated finishes, wood grips, and shipment in November 1971. Engraving by W.D. Cullity. *(Gianfranco Spellman, D.V.M., Collection)*

numbers are: *USA-1* and *USA-2*, *PBC-1* and *PBC-2*, *NF-1*, *GAS-1*. This service is only available on custom order guns.

Styles of Engraving

Colt offers five basic styles of hand engraved scroll work, each style unique to itself, thus offering that extra bit of "Personal Touch" to the individual desiring a custom engraved handgun. Scrolls will vary in size, depending on the size, shape and contour of the firearm.

German-Style Scroll

The Germanic style features detailed, intertwined scrolls, with floral devices, and finely punched or shaded (hatched) backgrounds. R. J. Kornbrath was a specialist in this pattern. German craftsmen emigrating to America in the mid-19th century created the American style scroll from these patterns.

American-Style Scroll

A style developed by arms engravers active in the U.S. from the mid 19th century.

Primarily smoothly flowing foliate scrollwork, with or without a punched dot background. The most popular engraving style on American arms since the 1850's.

English-Style Scroll

The English gunmakers developed this pattern in the 18th and 19th centuries, and it continues as a major scroll in modern times. The style features tight, close, delicate scrolls, with fine line work and shading, and, for contrast, some areas left without any embellishment.

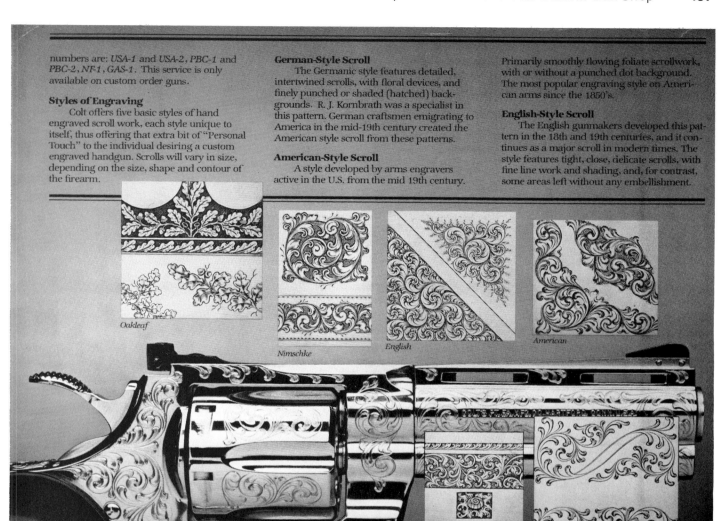

Variety of scroll styles available on order from the Custom Gun Shop, as published in the 1979 edition of "The Personal Touch" catalogue. Original set of sample plates were steel, and are in the Colt company's sales collection. The historical sources of these styles are evident.

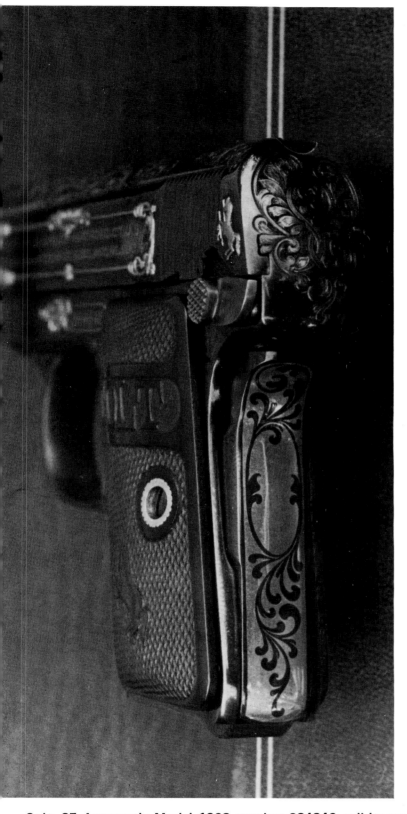

Colt .25 Automatic Model 1908 number 284846 exibits some of the most inspired gold inlaying and engraving by Leonard Francolini. The combination of flush and relief gold inlays, the intricacy of the border and scroll gold devices, the unusual degree of detail to all motifs, and the overall design are of such elegance and so superbly executed that despite the diminutive size of the pistol, one can study the decoration for hours and still find fresh nuances. Considered by the engraver as one of his proudest achievements in arms decoration. The grip safety is masterfully inlaid in gold, with the scroll devices of steel, brilliantly contrasted by their blued finish against the rich 24 karat color. On the muzzle end of the slide, a relief chiselled eagle, its wing tips extending upwards to encircle the barrel. Signature LEONARD FRANCOLINI is gold inlaid on the tip of the assembly rod which protrudes through the chest of the eagle. *(Author's Collection, G. Allan Brown Photographs)*

Single Action Army 62783SA and .45 Automatic 2420389 which were presented as a cased set to Ferdinand Marcos, marking the thirtieth anniversary of his service as President of the Philippines and the U.S. Bicentennial. By Lynton McKenzie; pistols were polished prior to engraving by Dick Hodgson, who also built the casing (not pictured). Note precise scrollwork, ivory grips, gold inlays, and the deluxe screw heads and grip screw bolsters.

Chapter XVII
FREELANCE ENGRAVERS
Post World War II

More so now than at any time in the past, Colt firearms are embellished in quantity by non-factory, freelance, engravers. Most of the work is done in America, but a significant number of Colts are given deluxe decor in Europe, in the Orient, Canada and Mexico. It is impossible to illustrate examples by all contemporary non-factory craftsmen, but a cross section appears on the pages which follow. Names and addresses of active arms engravers are published annually in the *Gun Digest*, as are illustrated samples of modern work.

The *Gun Digest*, its editor John T. Amber, and its long-time engraving consultant E. C. Prudhomme, are due a great deal of credit for arousing public interest in arms engravers, and in promoting and encouraging the craft. With retirement of Amber, his successor, Ken Warner, continues the tradition of support for the engraver in the *Gun Digest*. An important new work on contemporary engraving has been written by Roger Bleile, and published 1980 by Wallace Beinfeld. Entitled the American Engraver, the book is an indispensable source for any lover of fine firearms.

The individual who has a fondness for engraved Colt firearms is today in his element. Never before has such a variety of engravers been available to do the work; counting Americans, Europeans, and Japanese, the number exceeds 300 at this writing. Gun collector's shows, National Rifle Association and sportsman's shows, gun and non-gun periodicals and newspapers frequently show finely decorated firearms. Museums are realizing the drawing power of fancy guns as featured exhibits. Increasingly publishers find illustrations of deluxe weapons as an aid in selling adventure books or otherwise rather plain gun volumes.

When all is said and done, every gun enthusiast, as a matter of pride, owes it to himself to own at least one specimen of firearm engraved to his own order — thus carrying on a tradition continued in style by Samuel Colt and the Colt firearms company, and begun originally by the titled and wealthy over 400 years ago. Such is a noble and enduring tradition, as strong now as ever before, and potentially ever stronger in the future.

By Cole Agee for Wild Bill Elliott, well known Western movie star, Single Action number 350594 features Agee's famed cattle brand approach. Note the letter to Elliott accompanying the revolver, in which the engraver quotes prices for his work. *(Photograph courtesy of George E. Virgines)*

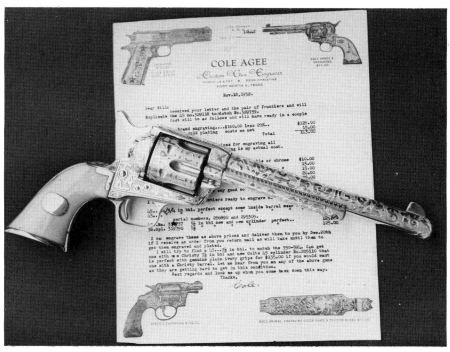

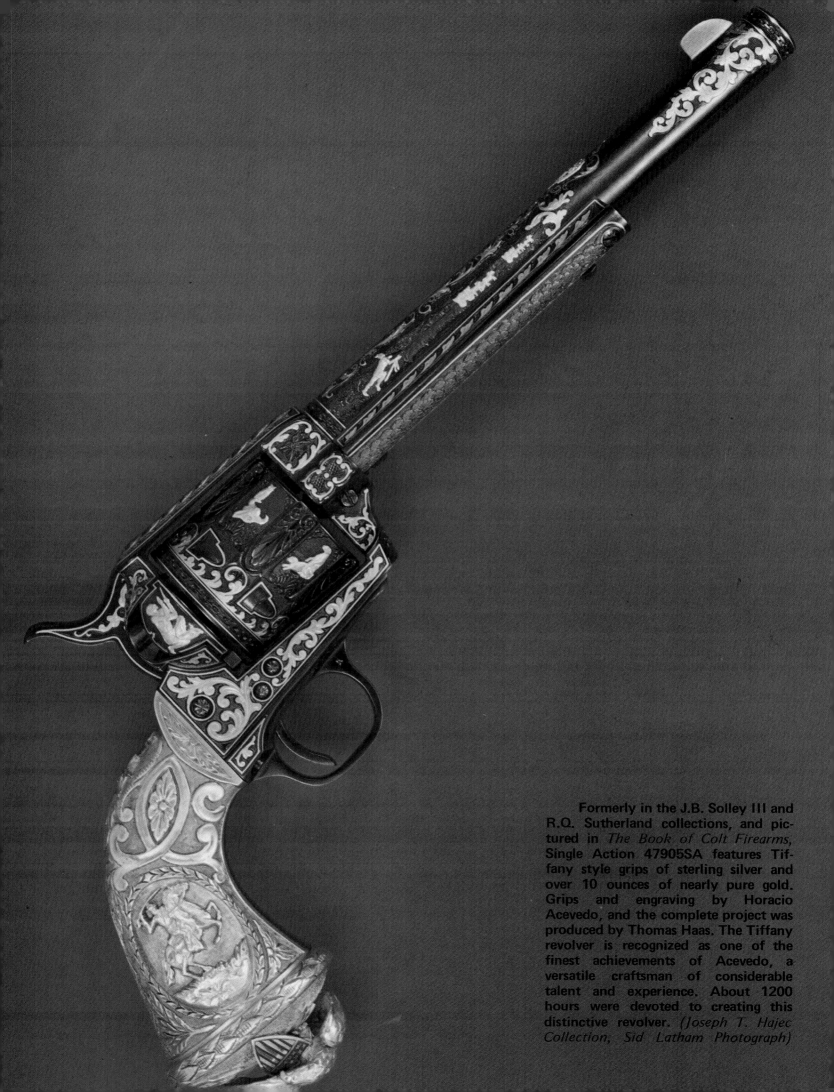

Formerly in the J.B. Solley III and R.Q. Sutherland collections, and pictured in *The Book of Colt Firearms*, Single Action 47905SA features Tiffany style grips of sterling silver and over 10 ounces of nearly pure gold. Grips and engraving by Horacio Acevedo, and the complete project was produced by Thomas Haas, The Tiffany revolver is recognized as one of the finest achievements of Acevedo, a versatile craftsman of considerable talent and experience. About 1200 hours were devoted to creating this distinctive revolver. *(Joseph T. Hajec Collection, Sid Latham Photograph)*

Remarkable pair of Single Action revolvers, numbers R.H./294556 and L.H./294556. A creative masterpiece by Thomas Haas, Guns Unlimited, scroll engraved in the Cuno Helfricht style, finished in nickel plating, and fitted with relief carved ivory grips mounted in gold and diamonds. The one revolver is the absolute mirror image of the other, and to the writer's knowledge, no other set of Colt arms like this pair has ever been produced. *(Buddy Hackett Collection)*

Cattlebrand engraved by the late Cole Agee of Ft. Worth, Texas, serial number 355817 Single Action is one of a limited number so embellished by Agee. This was a style of embellishment which he innovated in the WWI period. Revolver had originally been shipped to the Phil B. Bekeart Co., San Francisco, .38 Special, blue (and case hardened). Agee had the revolver plated in nickel after engraving, and fitted the pearl grips. *(William A. Dascher Collection)*

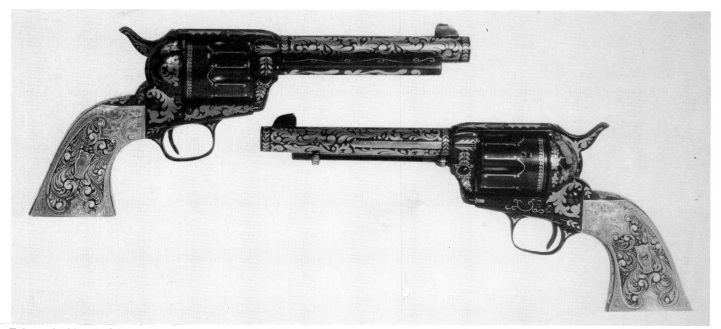

Edward H. Bohlin of Hollywood, California, is a name particularly well known for saddles, holsters, and guns made for Western film stars. This pair of Single Action Army revolvers features profuse gold-work and grips of gold and sterling silver. *(Photograph courtesy of George E. Virgines)*

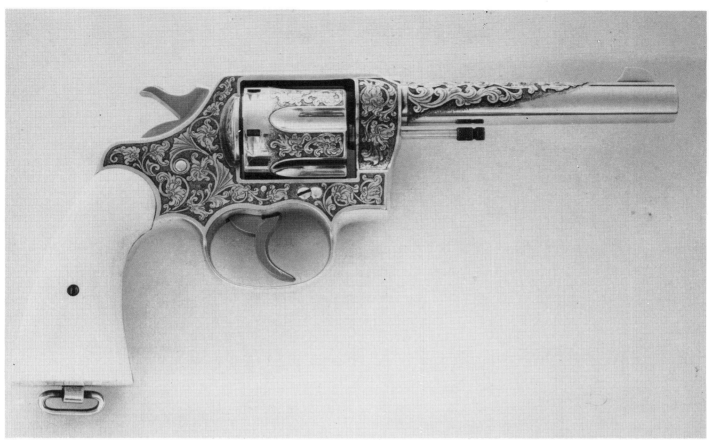

New Service number 112477 was engraved and relief chiselled by Carl Bleile, of American Creative Engravers, Cincinnati. Finish is silver plating, with gold hammer and trigger; grips of ivory. Backstrap inscription: DO RIGHT FEAR NOT. The brothers Carl and Roger Bleile work together in the field of arms embellishment, although this pistol is by Carl. *(Private Collection)*

Single Action Army by Bernie's Engraving, of El Paso, Texas. Scrolls a faithful interpretation of the Cuno Helfricht style. Note stylish lettering of COLT FRONTIER SIX SHOOTER legend within a riband on the left side of the barrel. *(Courtesy Bernie's Engraving)*

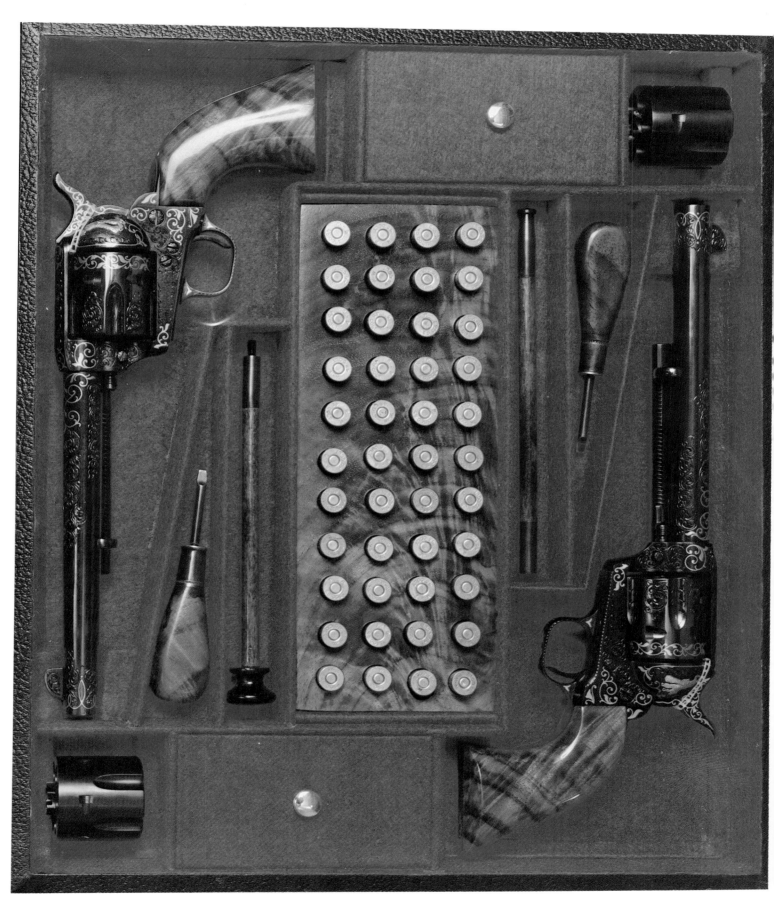

Single Actions numbers 3698SA and 3699SA, a matched pair profusely engraved and gold inlaid by Joe Condon. The relief inlays (note recoil shields) were based on bronzes by Michael Garman. Custom casing by Dr. R.W. Carroll. Grips and cartridge block of richly grained and finished select walnut. *(Dr. R.W. Carroll Collection)*

Serial number 112222 honors the lawmen of the west. It represents the work of Horacio Acevedo, of Thomas Haas' Guns Unlimited. Featuring a gold inlaid bust of Wild Bill Hickok carved in relief on the recoil shield. To administer the law, and protect the citizen, the lawman was a key civilizing agent in the winning of the west. Considered by many as the greatest of the western peace officers, Wild Bill Hickok is commemorated by engraved and inlaid scenes of his days as a stagecoach driver, Union Army Civil War Scout, his famous gunfights and his days as a wild west showman. The ejector gate housing is inlaid with a famous poster of Wild Bill's showman days. *(Buddy Hackett Collection)*

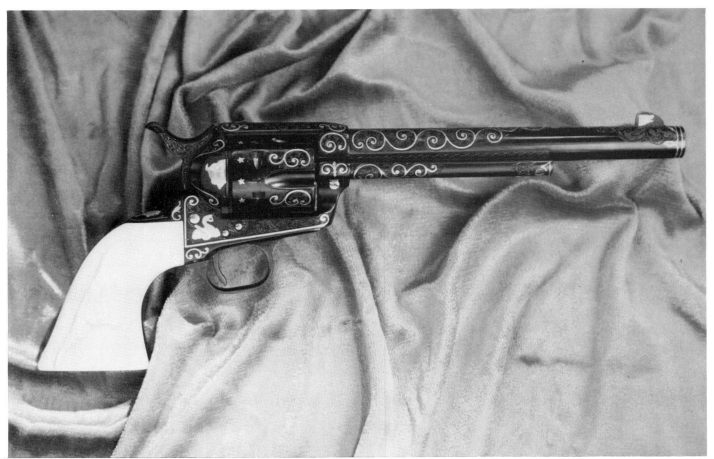

The Single Action Army shown here was made on special order for Sammy Davis, Jr., and features gold scrollwork, an American Indian bust on the recoil shield (in gold), and bison and snake devices, as well as American stars and other game details (including on the front sight, in gold). The carved ivory grips have a relief longhorn steer on the right side. *(Sammy Davis, Jr. Collection)*

By Joe Condon for Elvis Presley, the gold inlaid sideplate motif, TCB, is an abbreviation for "Take Care of Business." Right side of the revolver features an American eagle motif, in gold. *(Private Collection)*

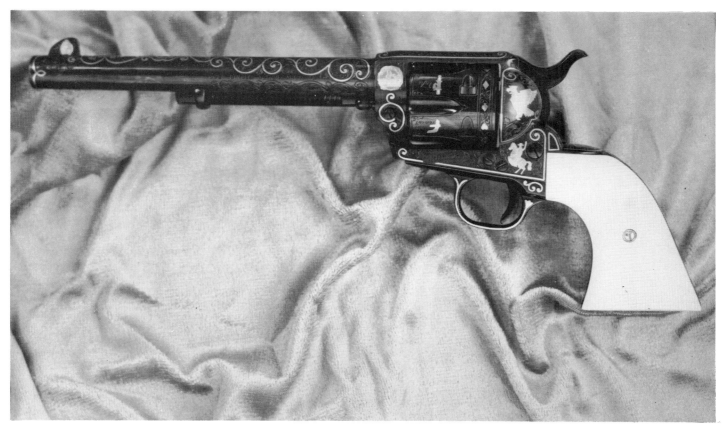

It was Buddy Hackett who conceived the idea of a Las Vegas Commemorative, all executed by Condon, and consisting of 50 Grade I gold inlaid presentation pieces, and 150 Grade II silver models. Pictured here is Buddy Hackett's Grade I revolver, on which the major Las Vegas hotels and casinos are represented, a Las Vegas sheriff's badge on the ivory grips (right side), and other motifs of the client's choice. *(Buddy Hackett Collection)*

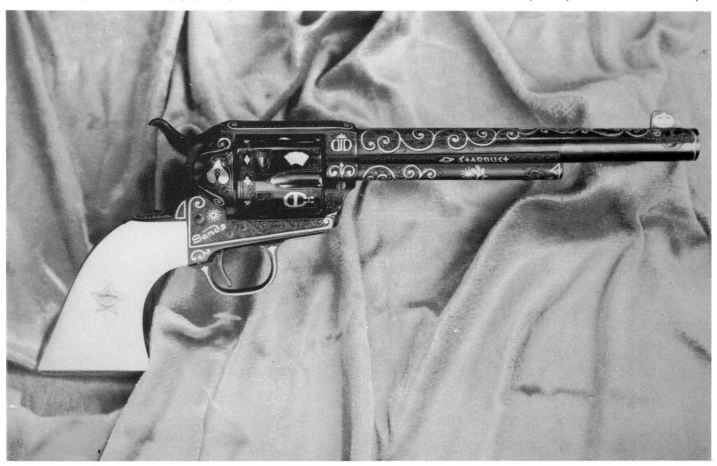

Joe Condon's "Dirty Harry Special," on which the Las Vegas "Engraver to the Stars" lavished over **400** hours and **4** ounces of 24 karat gold. Clint Eastwood and his celebrated film detective of the San Francisco Police Department are presented in relief and flush gold inlays, among which are Alcatraz, the S & W .44 Magnum, a minutely detailed S.F.P.D. Inspector's Badge (bearing the same number as used by Eastwood in the film), the names of the three Dirty Harry pictures ("Magnum Force", "Dirty Harry", and "The Enforcer"), and the star wielding his mighty .44 Magnum Revolver. Grips of carved, engraved ivory. Revolver is cased in oak and leather, with ivory handled screwdriver, cleaning rod, and other utensils.

(Opposite) Sheriff's Model .44-40, gold inlaid, engraved, and fitted with ivory grips by Joe Condon.

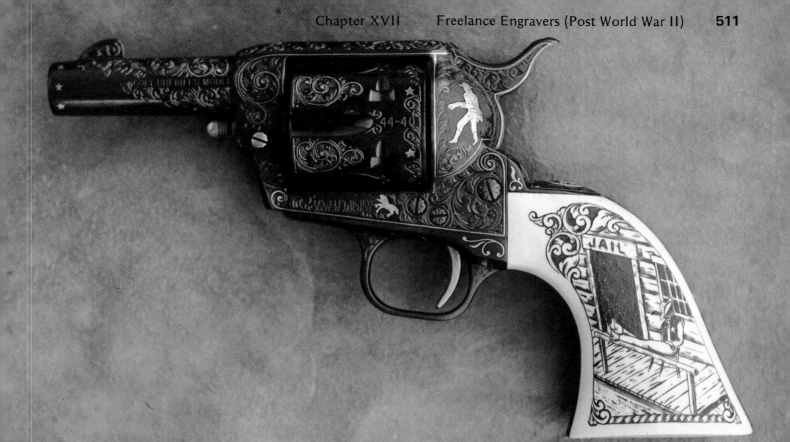

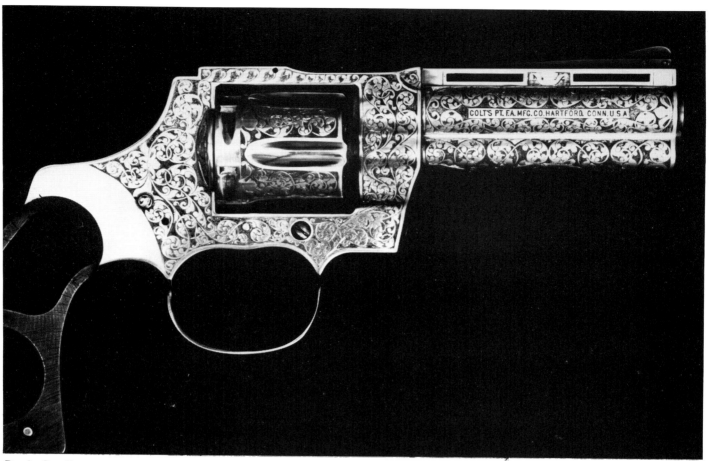

Paul S. Deveney, a gunsmith-engraver, retired Navy chief petty officer, and former stockbroker, prefers the German style, and executed this Python revolver accordingly. He also has undertaken training of apprentices in his hometown of Newton, North Carolina. *(Private Collection)*

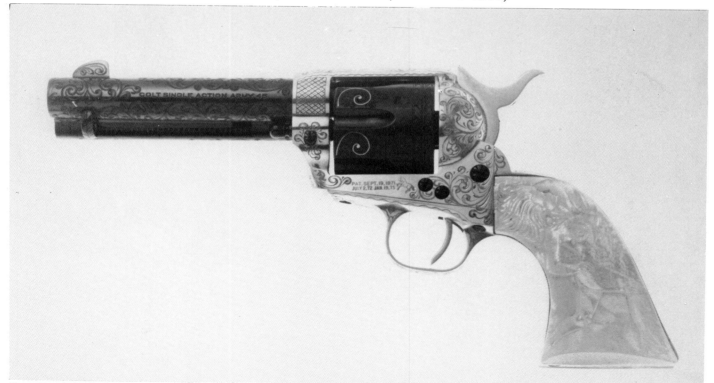

By Daniel Cullity, Single Action Army number 19168SA features silver plating on the frame, triggerguard, and backstrap, bluing on the barrel and cylinder, and gold inlaying on the cylinder. The grips are by A.A. White, and feature a relief carved nude woman; the medium is mother of pearl. Coverage includes even the screw heads and the front sight. *(Steve Mammano Collection)*

One of the last major Colt handguns completed by Joe Fugger, serial number 73580 Super .38 Automatic exhibits intricate leaf and scroll devices and various American West motifs. Finished in grey on all parts, with the hammer engine turned, as is the barrel breech. Fugger worked for Griffin & Howe for many years (a subsidiary of Abercrombie & Fitch), and when coming to America early in the 20th century, spent his first working period in Hartford with Kornbrath. *(Woolaroc Museum, Philip R. Phillips Collection)*

Matched pair of Single Actions, 49010SA and 49011SA, by Ken Eyster Heritage Gunsmiths of Centerburg, Ohio. The inspiration for the design and finish came from the Bianchi Holster Company deluxe set of Colt Single Actions, as pictured in the March 1974 issue of *Guns & Ammo* magazine, and elsewhere. .45 caliber; 5-1/2" barrels; silver plated finish; relief carved ivory grips. *(Fred O. Koester Collection)*

Single Action number 34982 U.S. marked, honors the U.S. Army in the West; it is by Frank E. Hendricks, Jr. of F.E. Hendricks Master Engravers. The Indian tribes stubbornly resisted the great American westward migration, and it was military strength which, over a period of approximately 50 years, conquered the Wild West. General George Crook, chief of the Army's Indian fighters, is commemorated in gold on the revolver's recoil shield. His hat, saber, gloves, and other memorabilia are also gold inlaid. A classic cavalry charge is dramatically gold encrusted on the side of the frame. *(Buddy Hackett Collection)*

Serial number 59149SA was engraved by K.C. Hunt as part of the "Winning of the West" series. Jesse James' portrait was engraved in gold on the recoil shield. Gold motifs signify gamblers, prostitutes, convicts, inebriates, gunslingers, and other low life of the pioneer West. On the backstrap was depicted the ultimate judgment for many an outlaw — the gallows. Only 24 karat gold was used, applied and engraved in Hunt's distinctive style. Despite their innumerable evil deeds, the outlaw element has given the American West much of its aura of color and adventure. *(Buddy Hackett Collection)*

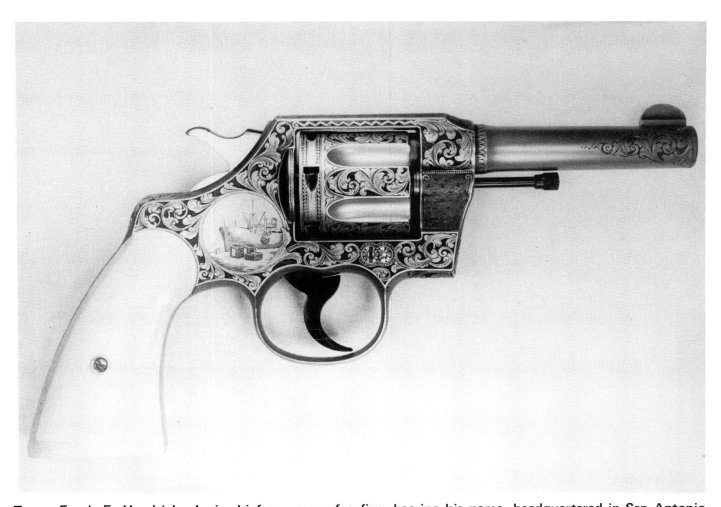

Texan Frank E. Hendricks Jr. is chief engraver of a firm bearing his name, headquartered in San Antonio. He is ranked as one of the foremost contemporary Americans in the field of arms decoration, and is well known for creating quite original designs, and working in a variety of styles and mediums. Official Police engraved by Frank E. Hendricks for C. W. Pratt, commemorating the success of his grandfather, a cotton broker, who exported raw material by the shipload from Houston, Texas. Ivory grips also by Hendricks, and have the San Jacinto Monument carved in relief on the left side. The special frost finish brings out detail much better than blue, and is a specialty of the Hendricks Master Engravers shop. *(C. W. Pratt Collection)*

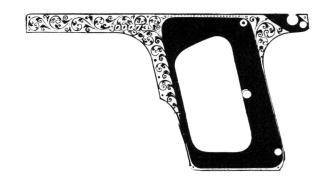

Minutely detailed Germanic style scrollwork by Frank E. Hendricks on a Model 1908 Hammerless Automatic pistol; serial number 200073. The black and white print, made in ink on paper from the pistol itself, shows better detail than a photograph. Print reversed for reproduction. *(F. E. Hendricks Master Engravers, Inc.)*

Model 1851 Navy executed in the Gustave Young style by K.C. Hunt, from the new series of Colt production brought out in the early 1970s. Finished in blue, with gold plated gripstraps, and case hardened loading lever and hammer. Illustrated in color, the *The Colt Heritage*, in which the deluxe leather and velvet casing by Arno Werner is also detailed. *(Private Collection)*

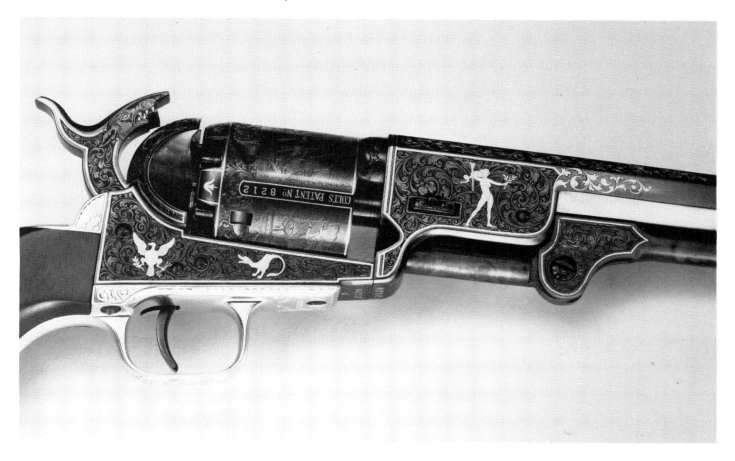

Ben Lane Jr. decorated the "Lucky Ladies" set of Single Actions, 68082 and 97567 as an expression of respect for the Cuno Helfricht scroll style. Carved ivory grips also by Lane, depicting a nude Eve with the apple, a favorite barroom art work of the Old West. Lane has made a speciality of working in the styles of the renowned German masters active in the U.S. from the 1850s up to post WWI. *(Ben Lane Jr. Collection, Roy Laing Photograph)*

An exact copy of the famous "Sultan of Turkey" Colt. The original and duplicate are among the most beautiful and graceful of all American firearms. Designed by Mr. Haas, the gun was engraved by Mr. Acevedo. *(Collection of Buddy Hackett)*

The personal engraved Colt Single Action of George E. Virgines, author of *Saga of the Colt Six-Shooter*, number 57327SA was embellished by Bill Johns in the scroll style reminiscent of the Single Actions of Cuno Helfricht and his shop. .45 caliber; 4-3/4" barrel; nickel plated; grips of Mexican silver. Virgines is well known not only for his writings on Colt Single Actions, but as a quick draw specialist and exhibition shooter and an active member of The Westeners' Chicago Corral. *(George E. Virgines Collection)*

Engraving and gold inlaying by Tommy Kaye, Beaumont, Texas. .357 Magnum caliber; blue and case hardened finish. James Bowie theme, with his portrait on the left recoil shield, and an early Bowie knife on the loading gate. *(Paul Sorrell Collection)*

By Jim Kelso of Iron Age Craftworks, Single Action Army number SA02169 has a gold and silver inlaid recoil shield motif of King Arthur's sword Excalibur, the sword in the stone. Borders gold inlaid; scroll engraving with Nimschke and A.A. White influences. Grips of ivory with a carved scroll cartouche. Blued, with case hardened frame; finished by George McVey, of Dem-Bart checkering tool renown. *(Dr. Lester Mittlestaedt Collection)*

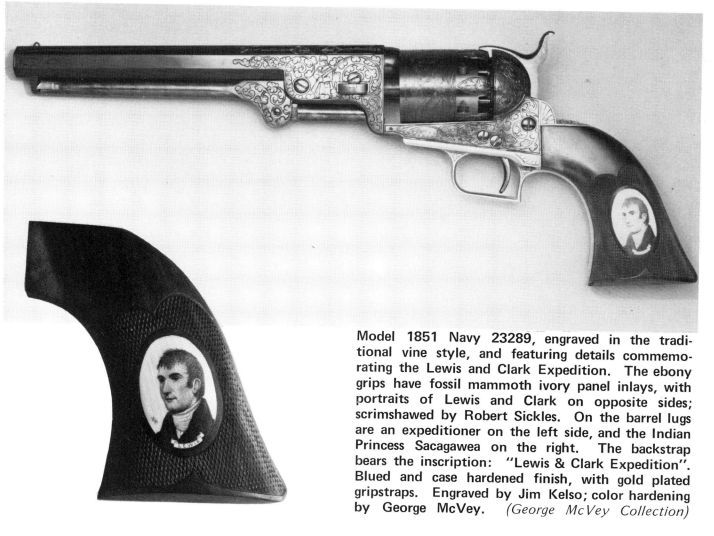

Model 1851 Navy 23289, engraved in the traditional vine style, and featuring details commemorating the Lewis and Clark Expedition. The ebony grips have fossil mammoth ivory panel inlays, with portraits of Lewis and Clark on opposite sides; scrimshawed by Robert Sickles. On the barrel lugs are an expeditioner on the left side, and the Indian Princess Sacagawea on the right. The backstrap bears the inscription: "Lewis & Clark Expedition". Blued and case hardened finish, with gold plated gripstraps. Engraved by Jim Kelso; color hardening by George McVey. *(George McVey Collection)*

"The Settlers" was engraved by Lynton S.M. McKenzie, of the New Orleans Arms Company. The recoil shield contains a motif of farm implements symbolically arranged, overlaid with a representation of the Bible. Engraved also are scenes of the great Utah desert, the first Mormon fort, and the great Tabernacle in Salt Lake City. A pioneer pulling a cart, inlaid in gold, symbolizes the settlers' primitive move to the western wilderness. The Victorian scroll style dominant in McKenzie's engraving is strongly evident. Each of the five master craftsmen worked in their own preferred style of engraving and gold inlay; Serial number 38964 *(Buddy Hackett Collection)*

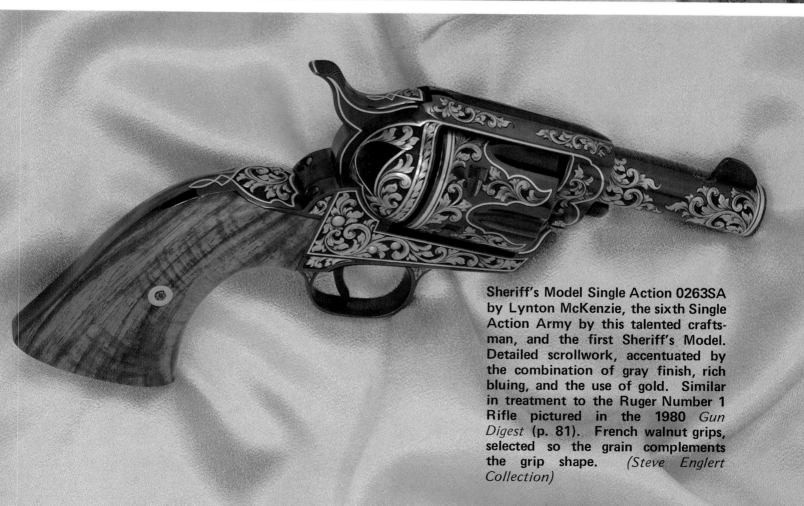

PAT. SEPT. 19. 1871
JULY 2. 72 JAN. 19. 75

Sheriff's Model Single Action 0263SA by Lynton McKenzie, the sixth Single Action Army by this talented craftsman, and the first Sheriff's Model. Detailed scrollwork, accentuated by the combination of gray finish, rich bluing, and the use of gold. Similar in treatment to the Ruger Number 1 Rifle pictured in the 1980 *Gun Digest* (p. 81). French walnut grips, selected so the grain complements the grip shape. *(Steve Englert Collection)*

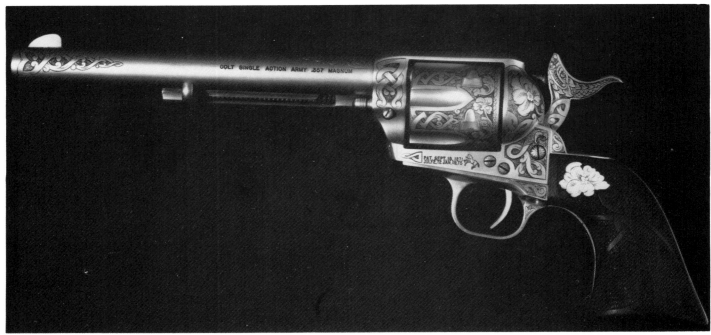

Single Action Army 94097SA, by Jim Kelso, presents an unusual Celtic knotwork scroll style, wolfshead hammer, and engraved mother of pearl rose inlaid on carved and checkered ebony grips. Frost nickel finish on the frame, cylinder, and barrel, with the hammer, backstrap, triggerguard, and ejector tube gold plated. *(Dr. L.W. Mittlestaedt Collection)*

Honoring the Nez Perce tribe's brilliant leader, Chief Joseph, Colt Bisley number 166095 by Jim Kelso features a bust of the chief on the recoil shield, engraved and chiselled, and a tepee village on the loading gate. Gold borders are on the lower frame, cylinder, and barrel, and arrows are on the top of the frame. Grips of ivory with relief carved tomahawk on the left side and a peace pipe on the right. The backstrap is inscribed: "I will fight no more forever". Finished in blue, with grayed frame and backstrap, and case hardened hammer and trigger. All finishing by George McVey. *(Dr. L.W. Mittlestaedt Collection)*

Serial number 355121 Single Action was engraved and gold and silver inlaid by O.C. Kuhl, San Francisco, for Gene Autry. The Western film star's name is inscribed on the backstrap, and the engraver's signature marking is cut on the forward section of the triggerguard strap. Finished in gold plating. .44 caliber; 4-3/4'' barrel; carved ivory grips. *(Cowboy Hall of Fame, Oklahoma City, Gift of Gene Autry)*

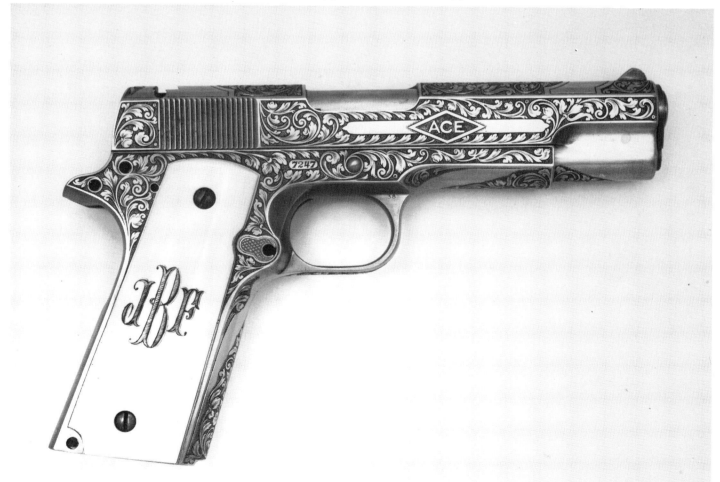

Prewar Ace richly scroll engraved by Ben Lane, Jr. for John F. Bickley. Grips of ivory with engraved monogram. Photographed in the white, prior to finishing. *(John F. Bickley Collection)*

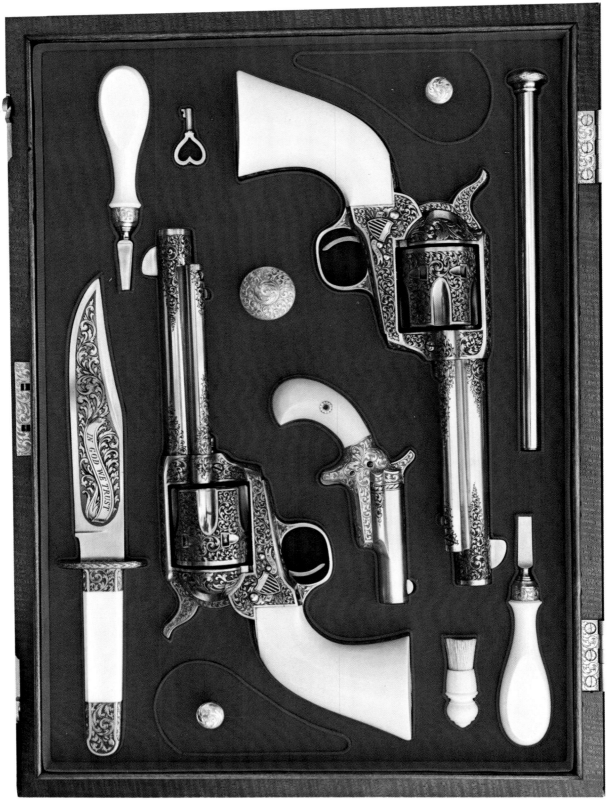

Exhibition set of Single Action Army revolvers, by Lynton McKenzie, New Orleans Arms Company. Serial numbers 53495SA and 53496SA. One of the most intricate and deluxe of modern cased American arms. Single Actions include the numbers 1 and 2 gold inlaid, in the style of a pair of best quality British guns or duelling pistols. Used as a display set by New Orleans Arms, this was their first major project, designed to dramatize the abilities of engraver-gunsmith McKenzie, formerly employed in Britain by Purdey's, Holland & Holland, Rigby, etc. Revolvers, accessories and knife mounts are now finished in blue or color hardening. Heavy gold plating was used in finishing the oil bottle, screwdriver ferrules, compartment knobs, and case furniture. Scroll style is the best British large scroll of the Victorian era, with fine line background shading. Patriotic motifs on the revolvers (including on top of backstraps and bottoms of each grip) are relief chiselled 24 karat gold. Breeches relief carved like a best quality Purdey shotgun. The richly embellished knife features a running leaf border on the crossguard, and a leaf and ribbon pattern on the edges of the grip mounts — all in raised, sculptured gold. Blade was engraved, and the background etched. The set was made to mark McKenzie's entry into arms decoration in the United States, and was planned to the last detail for a year before he came over. *(Courtesy of New Orleans Arms Company)*

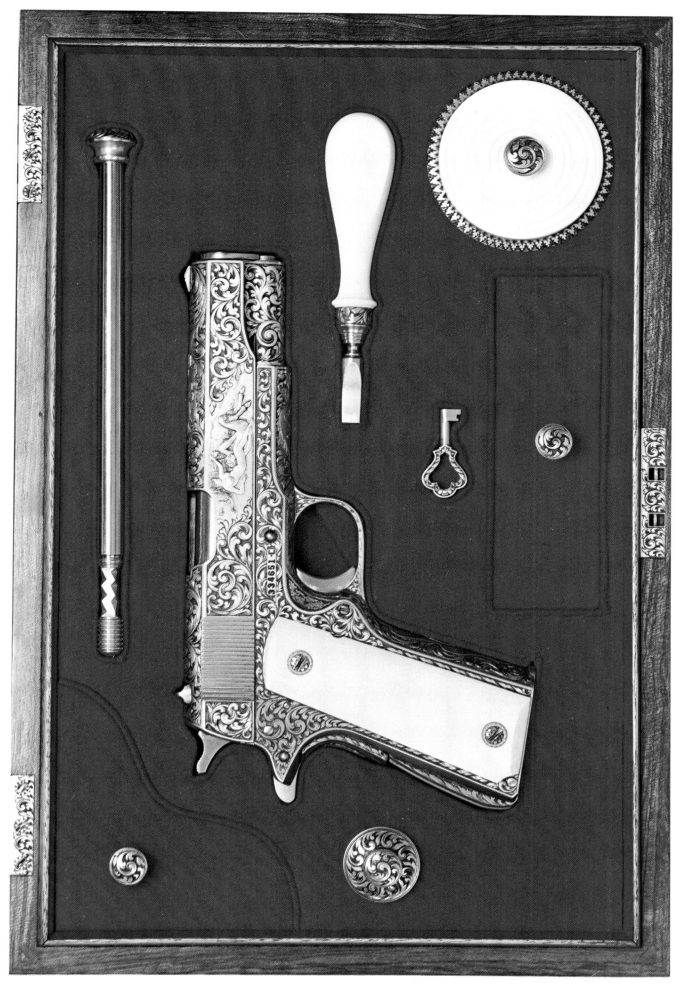

Deluxe Government Model Automatic pistol number 334651-C with engraved and gold inlaid erotic motifs; full French style casing with ivory mounted and engraved accessories. By Lynton McKenzie, and executed in his finest Victorian scroll. The delicate maiden motif appears on the front of the gripstrap, beneath the trigger-guard. Satyr and nymph are richly relief gold inlaid on top and on both sides of the slide.

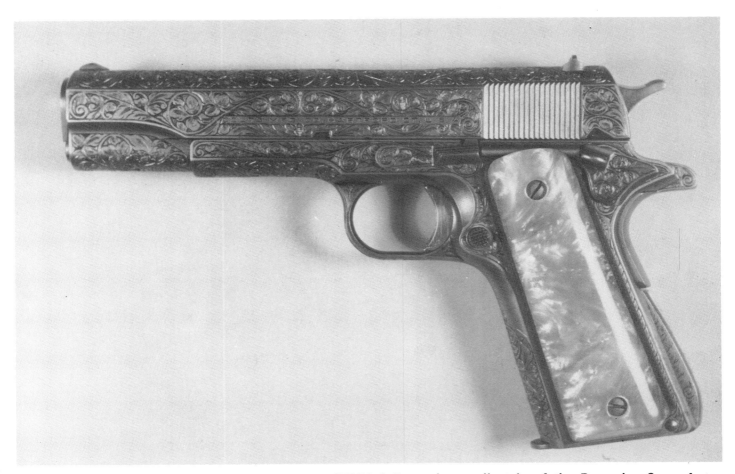

Jay Modloff's scrollwork on Super .38 number 65671 follows the scroll style of the Browning 9mm Automatic's Renaissance grade. See also the revised edition of *The Book of Winchester Engraving* (now in preparation) for further work of this craftsman, a resident of Sycamore, Illinois. *(Private Collection)*

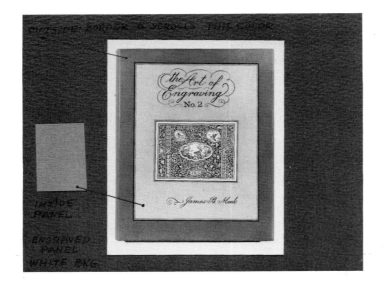

Preliminary design work by James B. Meek, for the second volume of his widely heralded *The Art of Engraving* book. This new work promises to add even more information and advice and significant samples of craftsmanship to the corpus of material Meek first presented in his first book. Brownell's of Montezuma, Iowa, prominent supplier to the firearms trade of engravers' and gunsmiths' tools, books, and related materials, published the first work, and is doing the second as well. *(Author's Collection)*

The late Tom Overbey engraved Single Action Army number 41283SA in a combination of fine scrolls, with a monogram on the loading gate. Relief carved American eagle grips were by the owner. Overbey was an experienced jewelry engraver, who became increasingly intrigued by arms decoration. His lettering on firearms was superb, and he was becoming more and more confident on gun work at the time of his death, in 1976. His employer for many years was the renowned Richmond jewelry house of Schwartzchild. *(K.W. McNeer Collection)*

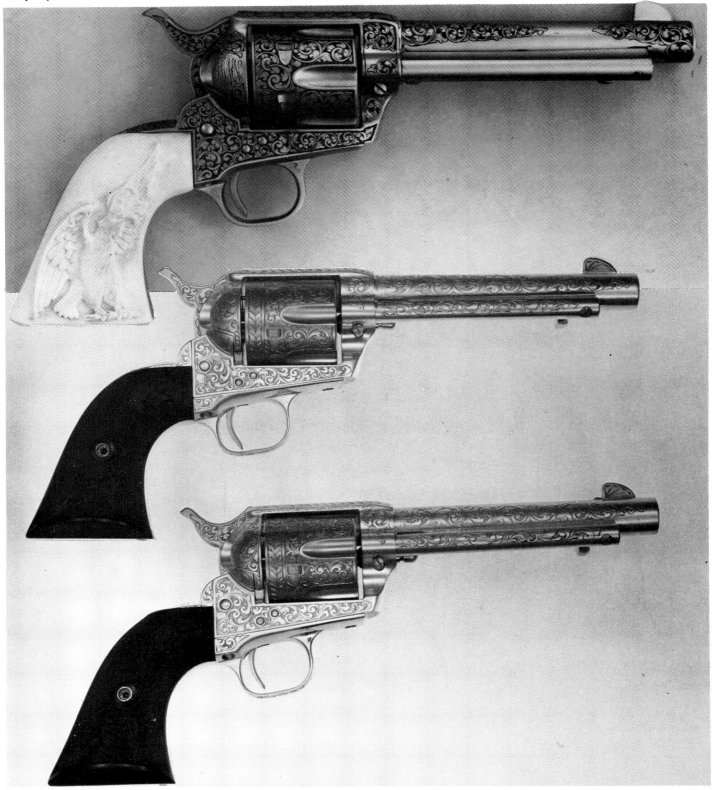

Matched pair of 5-1/2'' barrelled Single Actions by Bob Valade for quick draw artist and Hollywood veteran Arvo Ojala. Finished in gold and silver plating. Valade is a firearms engraver first and foremost, but also is frequently in demand for knife work; his major client in that regard is Gerber, makers of the ''legendary blades''. *(Arvo Ojala Collection)*

Extraordinary pair of .45 Single Action Army revolvers, elaborately and finely engraved and gold and silver inlaid by Rene Delcour and Phil Grifnee. Some of the inspiration for this involved project was Western art; Albert Bierstadt's Last of the Buffalo and Frederic Remington's Lightning Stampede are two of the paintings miniaturized in gold (on the cylinders). Cattle brands, longhorn steer motifs, Indian symbols, rampant colts, barrel markings, patent markings, serial numbers, barrel bands, borders and decorative scrolls are also executed profusely in 24K gold. Note extra cylinders, fluted, also engraved and gold inlaid, and the matching ivory mounted accessories. The casing by Paul Skogstad, done in leather and lined in suede. Numbers 62314SA and 62315SA. (Private Collection, G. Allan Brown Photograph)

Model 1877 Lightning, engraved by E.C. Prudhomme on the barrel, ejector tube, cylinder, backstrap and triggerguard. On the top flat of the backstrap a monogram, FGR (F.G. Refner), was gold inlaid. Case hardening on the frame was left untouched, but the engraved parts required professional rebluing. *(V.C. Knight Collection, Sid Latham Photograph)*

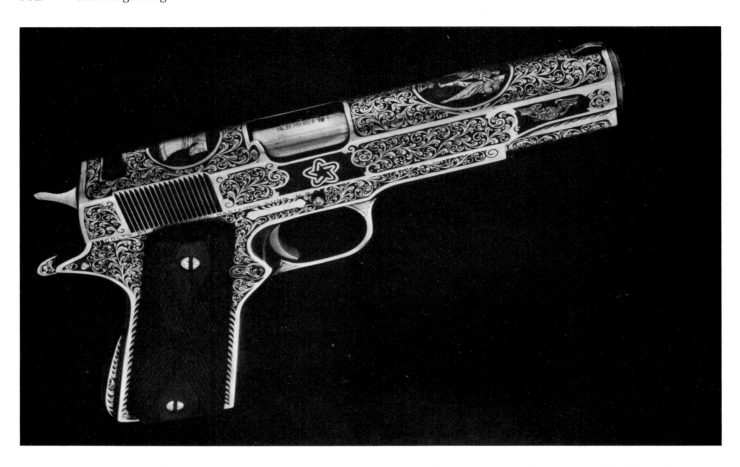

As a tribute to the U.S. Bicentennial, Ray Viramontez gold inlaid and engraved Colt MK IV/Series '70 Government Model .45 number 70G35378 with patriotic motifs, his special and minutely detailed scroll style, and gold borders. Among the patriotic details in relief gold are the "Spirit of '76", the Liberty Bell, the Bicentennial logo, a portrait bust of George Washington, the American eagle, and the segmented snake flag design. Photos show pistol before bluing, and the final set of grips were elephant ivory. *(Private Collection)*

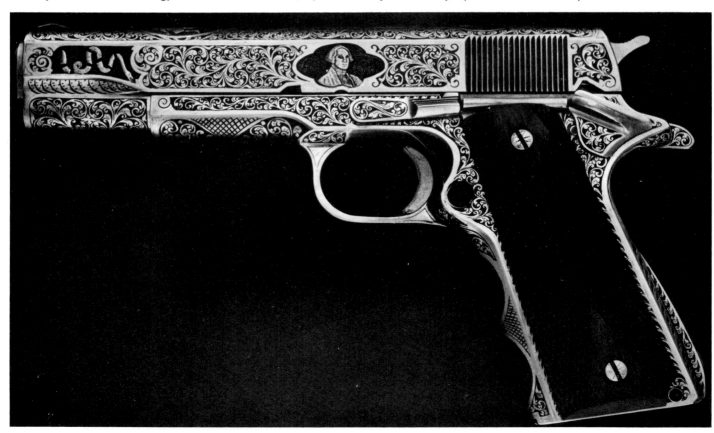

Government Model Automatic engraved by John Rohner in 1971. This intricately decorated pistol was done entirely by using the Gravermeister, rather than the customary manual tools. Every engraver or student in the field must investigate the possibility of adding the Gravermeister to their array of tools. Further details on this revolutionary new device appears in *The Book of Winchester Engraving. (John Rohner Collection)*

Sample plate by Russell J. Smith; illustrating a variety of styles, lettering, animal, leaf, and bird motifs. The eagle at center is high relief inlaid in a combination of several soft metals. An unusual and distinctive means of demonstrating an engraver's versatility and skill. *(R. J. Smith Collection)*

Set A Number 3 of 20 from the Freedom Colt series by Dwain Wright, The Muffin House, Bend, Oregon. Revolver dedicated to Abraham Lincoln, and is on permanent display at the Secret Service Building, Charlotte, North Carolina. Coverage is about 80% of the metal surfaces, and includes Presidential seals signed by former President Ford. Semi-relief scrollwork, with full relief portrait of Lincoln on the recoil shield; ivory grips carved in motifs popular in the Civil War period; silver plated; rosewood casing, French fitted, a glass cover fits over the lower half. The Freedom Colt series was inspired by the U.S. Bicentennial, and totalled 20 Colt Single Actions in Set A, 20 in Set B, five in Set C, and one only in Set D and Set E. Of the latter two sets, D was made up of serial numbers 1 of Sets A, B, and C, and E was structured from deluxe Colt Buntline, 7-1/2'' Single Action, and an 1851 Colt Navy and .41 deringer. *(Amado Hernandez Collection)*

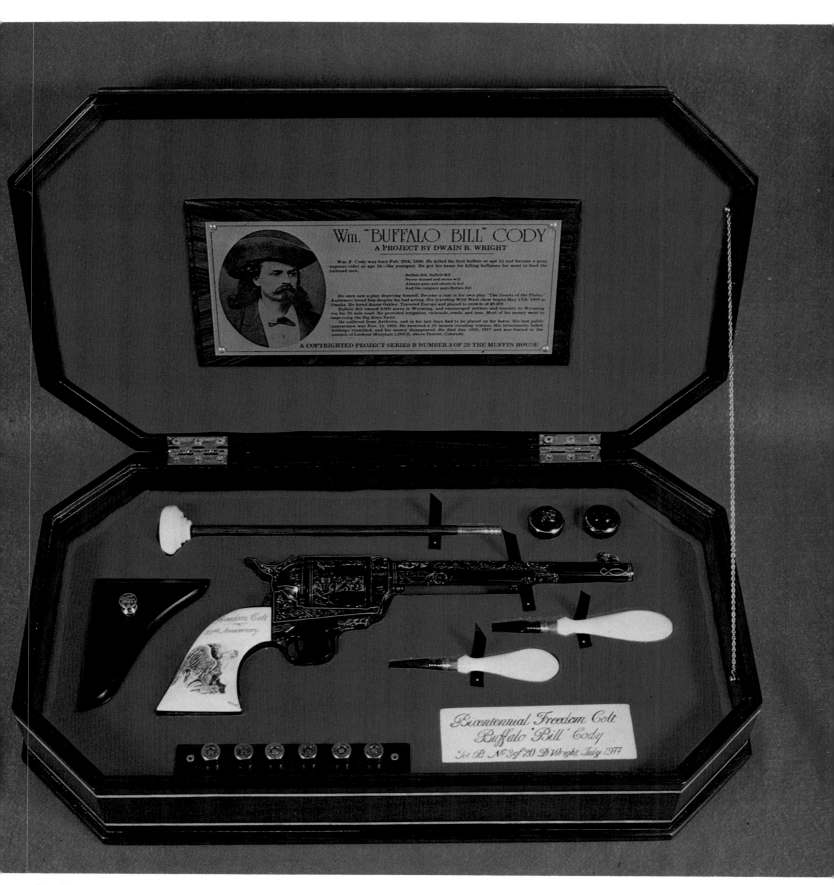

Set B number 3 of 20 from the Freedom Colt series by Dwain Wright, The Muffin House. The dedication of Number 3 is to W.F. "Buffalo Bill" Cody. Inlays in 24 karat gold, that of Buffalo Bill weighing one ounce (recoil shield). The grips of carved ivory, in ultra high relief. Mineral dies colored the eagle and shield device. Casing of pearl-inlaid Indian rosewood, accessories with ivory handles. Oil bottles gold inlaid and engraved. Interior plaque of ivory, engraved; inside the lid a photo-engraved plaque done from Wright's own artwork. Approximately 490 hours were required to complete this involved outfit. *(Fred Fiet Collection)*

Scrollwork in the Germanic style by Ray Viramontez. Government Model Automatic with about three fourths coverage, leaving the upper and lower portions of the slide, and the bottom of the frame and front of the grip blank for contrast. Nickel plated finish. Photography by Viramontez, using a special technique developed by himself for engraved firearms. *(Private Collection)*

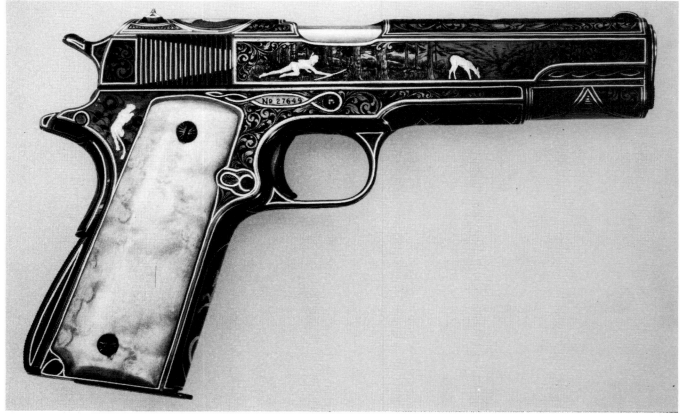

Elaborately inlaid and engraved Government Model .45 Automatic, by Floyd E. Warren. Serial number 27649. Finished in blue, with birds eye maple grips. The line border work, in flush 24karat gold, is extensive and crisply executed. *(Private Collection)*

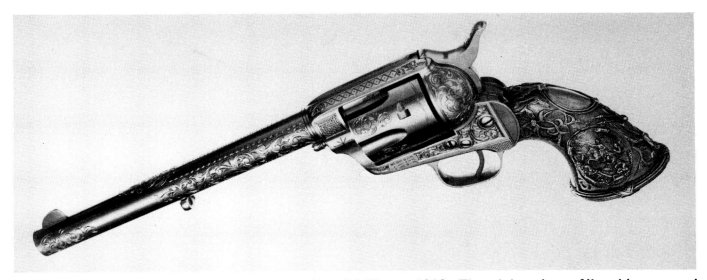

Modern scroll with a cast Tiffany style grip, by Hans Pfeiffer; c. 1969. Though based on a Nimschke approach of the 1870's, Pfeiffer has revised the pattern to his own decorative preferences. Plated finish. *(Private Collection)*

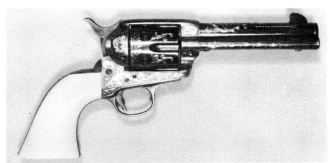

By Paul Showalter for James E. Serven, distinguished historian and arms expert. Engraving and silver overlays were added after the revolver was blued, creating a silvery effect. Grips of one piece ivory. Serial number 316702. *(James E. Serven Collection)*

Leaf and vine scroll coverage on a customized Single Action Army; engraved by John Rohner, 1962. Rohner, with Don Glaser, also an able arms engraver, invented and developed the revolutionary Gravermeister.

Freedom Colt Set A number 2, dedicated by engraver Dwain Wright to Walt Whitman. Steel portrait of Whitman (on the left recoil shield) is relief chiselled in 7/32″ depth. Full engraving, with gold plated finish; ivory grips, checkered. Charcoal blue screws and trigger. This revolver served as the prototype for the Freedom Colt A series, and was the first piece done in the Freedom Colt project. Black walnut casing, although Indian rosewood was the standard wood for the Freedom Colts. *(Dwain Wright Collection)*

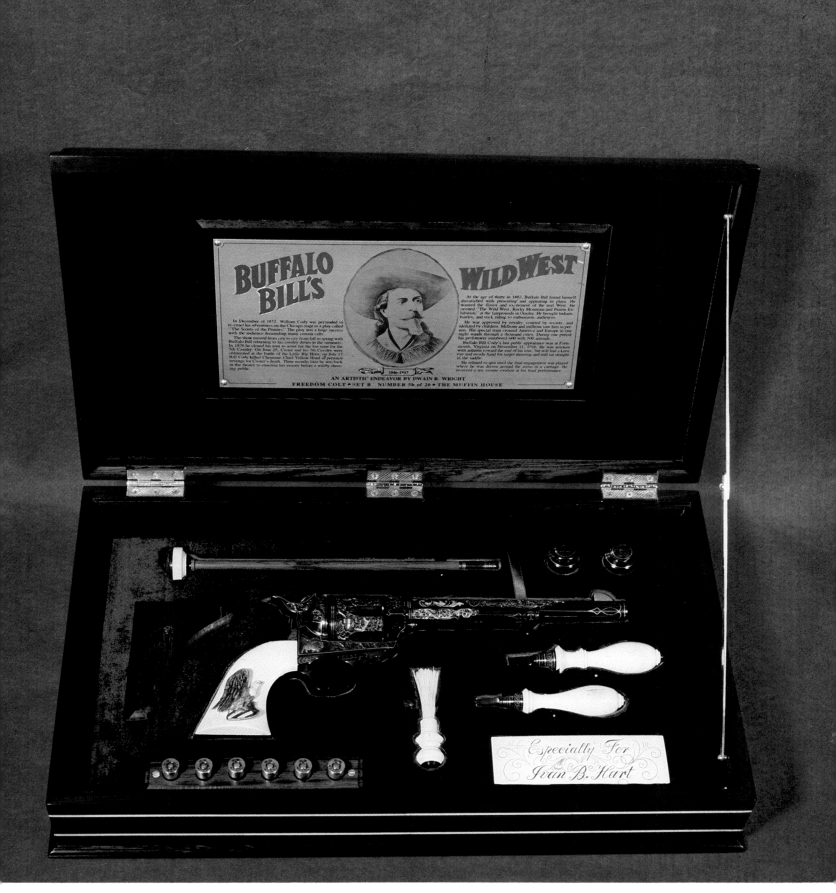

From Dwain Wright's Freedom Colt series, set number 5 of group B, this deluxe outfit was dedicated to Buffalo Bill Cody. Note combination of gold and scroll decoration, plus the colorful and unusual ivory grips. *(Ivan B. Hart Collection)*

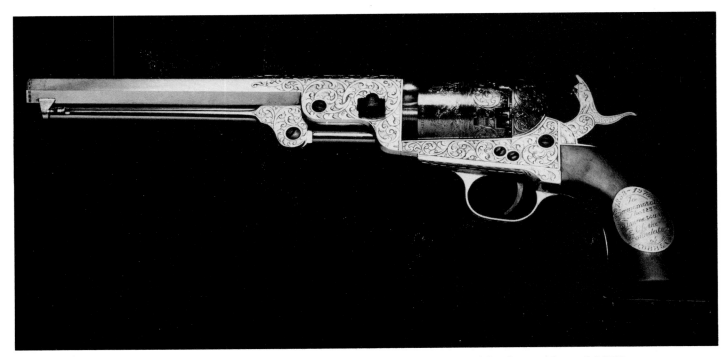

By P. Vinnicombe of Australia, Colt Navy number 85293 was completed in September of 1978, to commemorate the 125th anniversary of the foundation of Cobb & Co. Vinnicombe works in a variety of styles, and is also a talented gunsmith. *(Cobb & Co. Collection)*

Mel Wood first took up engraving in 1971, as a diversion from the quite demanding field of missile instrumentation management work at Vandenberg Air Force Base. He was the subject of "The Engraved Guns of Mel Wood", in the Petersen Publishing Co. *Custom Handguns* book, the article authored by Jim Woods, and picturing several examples of engraving and gunsmithing. Colt. 45 is an example of Wood's distinctive scroll style. *(Private Collection)*

Scroll engraved in Germany on order of Colonel Thomas E. Bass of Colt Industries' Washington, D.C. office. The revolvers are from the Colt 125th Anniversary Model commemorative, and bear serial numbers 945AM and 1630AM. Engraving by Carl Bock, Frankfurt, the design concept by the late Howard C. Gibson. Grips are of engraved and colored elephant ivory. On the bottom of each triggerguard was inscribed: *"Be not afraid of any man/No matter what his size./When danger threatens call on me/And I will equalize!"* Revolvers were presented by Bass to his friend Dale Robertson, and are now displayed at the Texas Ranger Museum, Waco. *(Dale Robertson Collection)*

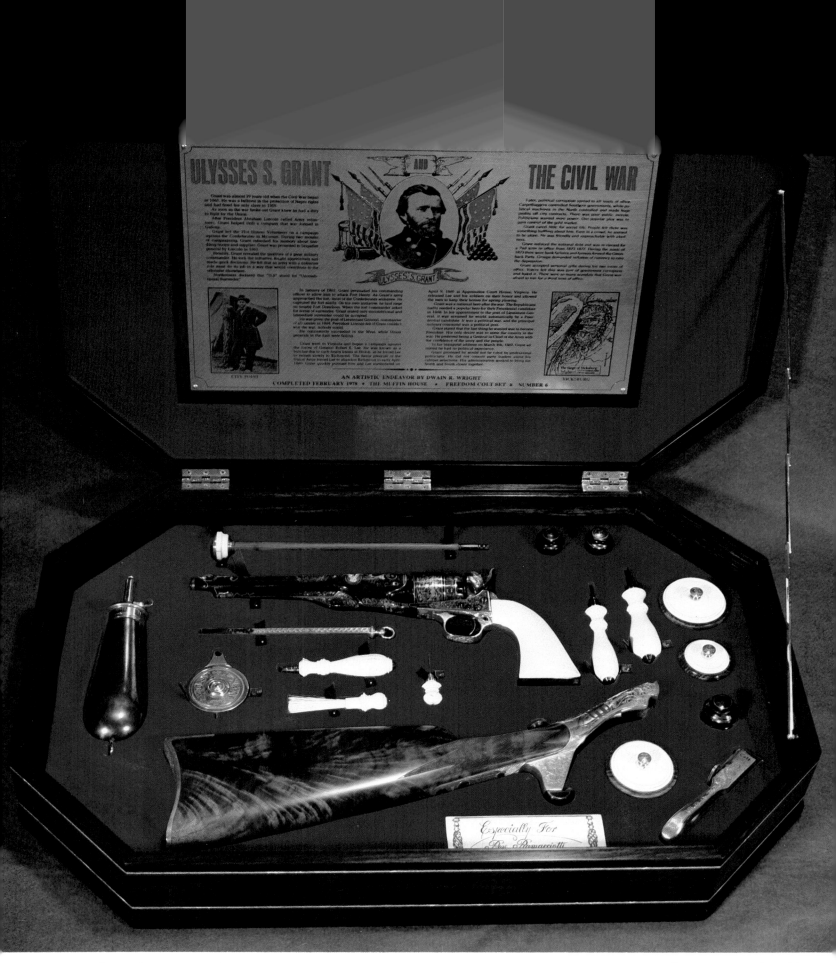

One of the more elaborate of the Freedom Colt arms, Set B number 6 is an 1860 Army Colt, engraved, gold inlaid, charcoal blued and gold plated, with shoulder stock in deluxe flame grain walnut. Among Wright's credentials are a masters degree in graphic design from UCLA, and a bachelors degree in commercial art and illustration from Woodbury University. His interests include wildlife painting, hunting, fishing, flying, and arms collecting; as a source for some of his work he draws upon a reference library (primarily art-oriented) of some 2500 volumes. *(Ray Ramaciotti Collection)*

Gold Country Freedom Colt set B, number 9 of 20. The casing a special Carpathian elm verneer over walnut. Pearl grips; gold inlaid and engraved decoration. This revolver the only of all the Freedom Colts built from a pre-WWII Colt revolver, and the only one having a 4 3/4'' barrel. Completed in February, 1980. *(Claude Le Brun Collection)*

General Titles

Abbiatico, Mario. *Modern Firearms Engraving.* Gardone, Valtrompia, Italy, Edizioni Artistiche Italiane, 1980. English text; superb craftsmanship.

Abbiatico, Mario, Gianoberto Lupi, and Franco Vaccari. *Grandi Incisioni su Armi d'Oggi.* Florence, Italy, Editoriale Olimpia, 1977. Profusely illustrated presentation of the master engravers of Italy; Italian text.

Amber, John T. *Gun Digest.* Chicago, The Gun Digest Company, various editions feature gun engraving (the annual first appeared in 1947). Several of the volumes carry articles by E.C. Prudhomme on engraving. Amber was succeeded c. 1979 by Ken Warner.

Bergling, J.M. *Art Monograms and Lettering.* Coral Gables, Florida, V.C. Bergling, Twentieth Edition, 1964. Valuable reference for engravers, widely used in the jewelry trade.

and A. Tuston Hay. *Heraldic Designs and Engravings.* Coral Gables, Florida, V.C. Bergling, 1966. Another useful volume for the jewelry and arms engraver.

Blackmore, Howard L. *Royal Sporting Guns at Windsor.* London, Her Majesty's Stationery Office, 1968.

Bleile, C. Roger. *American Engravers.* North Hollywood, Beinfeld Publishing Co., 1980. Study of contemporary American arms engravers.

Carpenter, Charles H., Jr., with Mary Grace Carpenter. *Tiffany Silver.* New York, Dodd, Mead & Co., 1978. Presents an intriguing and informative chapter of firearms and swords.

Garton, George. *Colt's SAA Post War Models.* North Hollywood, Beinfeld Publishing Co., 1979. Special chapter devoted to engraving; a volume of importance, which has added to the enthusiasm of growing numbers of collectors who actively pursue the postwar Colt firearms. Profusely illustrated.

Graham, Ron, John A. Kopec, and C. Kenneth Moore. *A Study of the Colt Single Army Revolver.* La Puente, California, published by the authors, 1976; revised edition, 1979. Includes chapter detailing engraving, profusely illustrated. An important work and the standard book of reference on the prewar Single Action Army.

Goldschmidt, Friedrich. *Kunstlerische Waffengravuren Ferlacher Meister.* Schwabisch Hall, Journal-Verlag, 1978. Published in German, this book is the last word on the work of the Ferlach master engravers.

Grancsay, Stephen V. *Master French Gunsmith's Designs of the Mid-Seventeenth Century.* Facsimile reproduction, preface and notes by S.V. Grancsay, New York, New York, Greenberg, 1950.

Master French Gunsmiths' Designs. New York, New York, Winchester Press, 1970. Rich collection of French pattern books used by gun decorators from the seventeenth to the nineteenth centuries; with commentary, profuse illustration of pertinent firearms, and exhaustive bibliography and references.

Gusler, Wallace B., and James D. Lavin. *Decorated Firearms 1540-1870.* Williamsburg, the Colonial Williamsburg Foundation, 1977. Valuable source of arms embellishment, based on the renowned collection of Clay P. Bedford.

Hable, R.E., and R.L. Wilson. *Colt Pistols.* Dallas, Jackson Arms, 1976. Lavish presentation of the Hable Collection of Colt firearms, from Patersons on up to the modern period of production, with emphasis on historical and engraved specimens.

Hawkins, Peter, Christopher Brunker, and R.L. Wilson. *Colt/Christie's Rare and Historic Firearms.* New York, Christie, Manson & Woods International Inc., 1981.

Hayward, John F. *The Art of the Gunmaker.* London, Barrie & Rockliff, 1962-63. Two volumes, later editions (revised) also published.

Howe, James Virgil. *The Modern Gunsmith.* New York, New York, Funk & Wagnalls Company, 1934-41. Volume 2 and Supplement. Includes an important chapter on gun engraving, with emphasis on Kornbrath.

Lenk, Torsten. *The Flintlock: Its Origin and Development.* London, Holland Press, 1965. Translation by G.A. Urquhart; edited by J.F. Hayward.

Lindsay, Merrill. *One Hundred Great Guns.* New York, New York, Walker & Company, 1967. With detailed color illustrations by Bruce Pendleton.

Madis, George. *The Winchester Book.* Lancaster, Texas, Art and Reference House, 1961. Various editions since that date. A few of the engravers represented in the book are known to have also done Colt firearms.

Meek, James B. *The Art of Engraving.* Montezuma, Iowa, Brownell's Inc., 1974. The only detailed text currently available on how to engrave firearms. A key volume in engraving literature.

Phillips, P.R., and R.L. Wilson. *Paterson Colt Pistol Variations.* Dallas, Jackson Arms, 1979. Only detailed publication on the first and most prized of Colt handguns and longarms. Information on deluxe arms and presentations complements material in *The Book of Colt Engraving.*

Prudhomme, E.C. *Gun Engraving Review.* Shreveport, Louisiana, published by the author, 1961. An important volume in promoting interest in arms engraving and engravers. Profusely illustrated.

Rosa, Joseph G. *Colonel Colt London.* London, Arms and Armour Press, 1976. Exhaustive and profusely illustrated source; several engraved specimens pictured.

Tarassuk, Leonid. *Antique European and American Firearms at the Hermitage Museum.* Leningrad, U.S.S.R., Iskusstvo Publishing House, 1971. Features elaborately decorated royal firearms of European and American production. Color and black and white illustrations of the presentation Colt revolvers given to Czars Nicholas I and Alexander II, and the Grand Dukes Michael and Constantine, and Nikolay.

Wilkerson, Don. *The Post-War Colt Single-Action Revolver.* Apple Valley, Minnesota, published by the author, 1978. Includes special chapter on engraving, authored by John Spellman, D.V.M. An important work which has contributed to the tremendous demand for contemporary Colt craftsmanship. Profusely illustrated. Revised and updated edition, 1980; with expanded engraving chapter by Albert Brichaux.

Wilson, R.L. (Editor). *Antique Arms Annual.* San Antonio, Texas, S.P. Stevens and Leo Bradshaw and the Texas Gun Collectors Association, 1971. Profusely illustrated in color and black and white with a large assortment of decorated Colts, Winchesters, and other makes of firearms.

Wilson, R.L. *The Book of Winchester Engraving.* Studio City, California, Wallace Beinfeld Publications, 1974. Companion volume to *The Book of Colt Engraving* and to the new *Colt Engraving.*

    Colt Handguns. Tokyo, World Photo Press, 1979. First Japanese Colt book; profusely illustrated.

    The Colt Heritage. New York, New York, Simon & Schuster, 1979. Published simultaneously in London by MacDonald & Janes. Foreword by George A. Strichman, Chairman of the Board, Colt Industries. The official history of Colt firearms, the subject lavishly presented with emphasis on the artistic and historical qualities of Colt arms.

    L.D. Nimschke Firearms Engraver. Teaneck, New Jersey, John J. Malloy, 1965. Preface by John J. McKendry, Metropolitan Museum of Art, New York. The personal work record of one of nineteenth century America's foremost engravers, with detailed text, photographs of deluxe-engraved arms, and indexes.

    Samuel Colt Presents. Hartford, Connecticut, Wadsworth Atheneum, 1961. Covering cased, engraved, and presentation Colt arms of the period 1836-73; all models of Colt percussion firearms are represented, most of them engraved and/or inscribed, and many of them cased.

Periodicals and Monographs

Dow, Richard Alan, and R.L. Wilson. "The Czar's Colts", *Nineteenth Century*, Winter 1980.

Elisofon, Eliot. "Sam Colt's Pistols", *Life*, March 2, 1962. Nine page article (seven pages in color) of historic and deluxe Colt percussion firearms, based on the "Samuel Colt Presents" exhibition, 1961.

McKenzie, L.S.M. "Old New Orleans Presents", catalogue of engravings offered by the New Orleans Arms Company, 20 pages, 1972. Features the engraving and inlay work of Lynton McKenzie, and other services of the firm.

Ogan, Ronald A., and Ben Lane, Jr. "Colt Factory Single Action Engraving Techniques", *The Gun Report*, March 1978. Interesting illustrated article on prewar Single Action scroll and border decoration.

Parsons, John E. "New Light on Old Colts", Harrison, New York, published by the author, 1955. Originally published in the Texas Gun Collector magazine. Includes detailed references to serial number data from Colt ledgers of the Civil War period.

Ross, Andrew G. "Gun Engravers Turn Fine Sporting Arms into Works of Art", *Outdoor Life,* December 1950. 20 illustrations.

The R.W. Norton Art Gallery. "Artistry in Arms", catalogue of engraving and gunsmithing display at the Norton Art Gallery, May 16 – June 27, 1971, 42 pages. Features the engraving and inlay work of E.C. Prudhomme. Shreveport, Louisiana, 1971.

The R.W. Norton Art Gallery. "E.C. Prudhomme Master Gun Engraver", catalogue of work of Prudhomme, on display at the Norton Art Gallery, April 1 – May 13, 1973, 32 pages. Foreword by John T. Amber. Shreveport, Louisiana, 1973.

Ryan, Bill. "Our Most Excellent Rifles", *The American Sportsman,* Fall 1968. Complemented with color photographs by Arie deZanger; featuring the work of Joseph Fugger.

Wilson, R.L. and Roy G. Jinks. "Tiffany' Stocked Firearms", *Antique Arms Annual,* 1971.

Wilson, R.L. "Colt's Army .45", *Gun Report,* June 1968.

"Is There Proof That Joseph Wolf Engraved Firearms", *Gun Report,* October 1967.

"Some Nimschke-Engraved Colt Pistols", *Gun Report,* March 1969.

"Gold Inlaid Colt Revolvers", *Arms Fair '69 Guide,* 1969.

"Pocket Guide to Good and Bad Firearms Engraving", brochure published privately by A.A. White Engravers Inc., 1969.

"A.A. White Engravers, Inc.", catalogue of engravings offered by the firm, 20 pages, 1969.

"A.A. White Engravers Inc.", brochure of engravings offered by the firm, 1974.

"Gun Engraving", *Guns & Ammo Annual 1969,* 20 page article with 66 illustrations, Petersen Publishing Company.

"Engrave Your Favorite Gun", *Guns & Ammo Annual 1970,* Petersen Publishing Company.

"Masterpieces of the Gun Engraver's Art", *Guns & Ammo Annual 1971,* Petersen Publishing Company.

"The History of Gun Engraving In America", *Guns & Ammo Annual 1972,* Petersen Publishing Company.

"Fine Engraving is Still Taught", *Guns & Ammo Annual 1974,* Petersen Publishing Company.

"Gun Engraving [in Europe] ", *Guns of the World,* Petersen Publishing Company, 1973.

"Engraving Secrets", *Basic Gun Repair,* Petersen Publishing Company, 1973.

"Firearms Engraving in Nineteenth Century America", *The Bulletin of the American Society of Arms Collectors,* Fall, 1973.

"Gunmetal Mastery", *Sports Afield,* August 1971.

"L.D. Nimschke Firearms Engraver", *American Rifleman,* January 1966.

"The Youngs: Standouts in the Gun Engraver's Heyday", *American Rifleman,* May 1968.

"50 Years of Gun Engraving at Colt's", *American Rifleman,* October 1969.

"Enterprising Sam Colt's Profitable Presentations", *American Rifleman,* July 1969.

"A Most Select Collection of Colts", *Guns & Ammo,* April 1973.

"The New Collecting Breeds", *Man at Arms,* July/August 1979. Discusses the Colt Custom Gun Shop and the active satisfying of collector requirements by contemporary Colt production.

"The Van Syckel Dragoons", *Man at Arms,* March/April 1980.

"A Return to Tradition The Paris Show Gun", *Man at Arms,* July/August 1980.

"A.A. White Prince of Craftsmen", *Man at Arms,* September/October, November/December 1980.

"The Colt Custom Gun Shop", *Colt American Handgunning Annual 1978.* Commentary on the unique success story of Colt's department of custom delights.

Dr. Leonid Tarassuk. *The 'Russian' Colts.* North Hollywood, Beinfeld Publishing Co., 1979. Detailed monograph on gold inlaid percussion Colts, the material featuring the presentations from Colonel Colt to Czars Nicholas I and Alexander II, and to the Grand Dukes Michael and Constantine, and Nikolay.

BIBLIOGRAPHY

Published materials on the decoration of American firearms are limited in number. The field is a highly specialized one, and remains unexplored in many areas. The present book is based nearly entirely on original research in unpublished sources. But the items listed in the following selected bibliography will be of further interest to the reader. An exhaustive bibliography on arms decoration, with the emphasis on European sources, appears in Stephen V. Grancsay's Master *French Gunsmiths' Designs*, published in 1970. The reader should consult that volume for information beyond the scope of *Colt Engraving*.

Miscellaneous Unpublished Sources:

Archives and memorabilia of the following engravers: R. J. Kornbrath, Wilbur A. Glahn, Cuno A. Helfricht, A. F. Herbert, and Gustave, Eugene, and Oscar Young. Most of the above material from the engraving collection of Johnie Bassett. Several descendants of the above engravers were interviewed for data.

Shipping and inventory ledgers of the Colt's Firearms Division, 1861 through 1974, at Colt's Hartford office.

Colt company ledgers, correspondence, catalogues, photographs, firearms, and various memorabilia in the Colt Collection of Firearms, Connecticut State Library, Hartford. The Collection presented to the State of Connecticut, 1957, by the Colt's Patent Fire Arms Manufacturing Company, Inc.

Samuel Colt papers in the Connecticut Historical Society, Hartford. Documents covering the years c. 1830 through 1862, primarily correspondence to and from Samuel Colt.

Approximately fifty letters in the Colt Collection, Wadsworth Atheneum Hartford, bequest of Mrs. Samuel Colt (1905). Many of the letters are addressed to Colonel Colt, expressing appreciation for gifts of firearms. See *Samuel Colt Presents*, page 291, for a listing of several of these documents.

John Hintlian Library, containing a complete collection of Colt firearms company catalogues and price lists, from c. 1851 through 1974, with some listings of earlier periods.

The Hartford Courant and *Hartford Times* newspapers, various issues from c. 1847 through 1865.

Hartford city directories, c. 1847 — c. 1925.

Four original gun engravers' pattern books from the L. D. Nimschke archive, John J. Malloy collection. See *L. D. Nimschke Firearms Engraver*, pages xvi, xvii, and xxv, for details.

INDEX OF ENGRAVERS